ADVANCES IN
BEHAVIORAL FINANCE

ADVANCES IN BEHAVIORAL FINANCE

RICHARD H. THALER
EDITOR

Russell Sage Foundation

New York

The Russell Sage Foundation

The Russell Sage Foundation, one of the oldest of America's general purpose foundations, was established in 1907 by Mrs. Margaret Olivia Sage for "the improvement of social and living conditions in the United States." The Foundation seeks to fulfill this mandate by fostering the development and dissemination of knowledge about the country's political, social, and economic problems. While the Foundation endeavors to assure the accuracy and objectivity of each book it publishes, the conclusions and interpretations in Russell Sage Foundation publications are those of the authors and not of the Foundation, its Trustees, or its staff. Publication by Russell Sage, therefore, does not imply Foundation endorsement.

Library of Congress Cataloging-in-Publication Data

Advances in behavioral finance / Richard H. Thaler, editor.
    p.   cm.
    Includes bibliographical references and index.
    ISBN 10: 0-87154-845-3—ISBN 10: 0-87154-844-5 (pbk)
    ISBN 13: 978-0-87154- 845-0—ISBN 13: 978-0-87154-844-3 (pbk)
    1. Investments—Psychological aspects. I. Thaler, Richard H.,
1945–
HG4515.15.A38   1993
332.6'01'9—dc20   93-12149
                                           CIP

RUSSELL SAGE FOUNDATION
112 East 64th Street, New York, New York 10021

To my parents.

Contributors

Lawrence M. Ausubel, University of Maryland

Victor L. Bernard, University of Michigan

Fischer Black, Goldman, Sachs & Co.

Navin Chopra, Temple University

David M. Cutler, Harvard University

Werner F.M. De Bondt, University of Wisconsin

J. Bradford De Long, Harvard University

Jeffrey A. Frankel, University of California-Berkeley

Kenneth R. French, University of Chicago

Kenneth A. Froot, Harvard University

Josef Lakonishok, University of Illinois

Charles M.C. Lee, University of Michigan

James M. Poterba, Massachusetts Institute of Technology

Jay R. Ritter, University of Illinois

Richard Roll, University of California-Los Angeles

Hersh M. Shefrin, Santa Clara University

Robert J. Shiller, Yale University

Andrei Shleifer, Harvard University

Meir Statman, Santa Clara University

Jeremy Stein, Massachusetts Institute of Technology

Lawrence H. Summers, Department of Treasury

Richard H. Thaler, Cornell University

Robert W. Vishny, University of Chicago

Robert J. Waldmann, European University Institute

Acknowledgments

I would like to thank the Russell Sage Foundation and its president, Eric Wanner, for funding the behavioral finance working group where many of these papers were first presented. The foundation's continued support, as evidenced by the publication of this book, is greatly appreciated. The preparation of the book was made considerably easier and more fun because of Lisa Nachtigall's help. I would also like to thank the National Bureau of Economic Research, which has hosted these meetings in recent years. Special thanks go to Benjamin Friedman for originally inviting us to be a part of his research program, and to Bob Shiller, for co-organizing these meetings. Thanks is also due to all the authors for cooperating with the production of this book, and especially to Vic Bernard who wrote a special chapter. Finally, my biggest debt is to my friend, colleague, and former student, Werner De Bondt, who organized our first working group meetings at Russell Sage and has taught me much of what I know about finance.

Contents

PART VI
INDIVIDUAL BEHAVIOR

Introduction

There is an interesting contrast between the academic discipline of financial economics and the coverage the field receives on the nightly newscast. Whenever financial markets make it on the news the story is always accompanied by pictures of people engaged in wild activity, either shouting bids and asks on the trading floor, or talking on three phones simultaneously in a trading room away from the floor. The image one gets from the news is that financial markets are dominated by *people*. In contrast, a reading of a standard finance textbook, such as the excellent one by Brealey and Myers, can create the impression that financial markets are nearly devoid of human activity. There is great attention to methods of computing important numbers such as present values and rates of return, an analysis of risk and how it is priced, much discussion of how much a firm should borrow and how much it should pay out in dividends (answer: it doesn't matter), and even a primer on how to price options. But virtually no people. Very little in the text would be changed if all the people in both the corporate sector and the financial sector were replaced by automatons.

This observation leads to a question. Since we know that there are indeed humans involved in financial markets, are the markets any different because of their presence? Would the financial world be materially different if investors, traders, managers, and workers were all replaced by computer programs? The chapters in this book suggest that the answer is yes. People make a difference.

Why has financial economics largely ignored the people in preference to the prices? There are several reasons. A glib response (at least partly true) is that there are better data on prices than people. Thanks to the people at CRSP and COMPUSTAT, financial economists have had data that are the envy of other social scientists. Seventy years of stock price data on computer tape are hard to resist. In contrast, there are very few data available on the behavior of individual agents. Even if one wanted to study what the people are doing it would be hard.

However, while lack of data has certainly been an issue, most financial economists have not really felt deprived. Until recently, it was possible to hold the view that there was no reason to study the behavior of people when the prices were behaving so nicely. The financial world as described in Eugene Fama's 1970 efficient markets survey was one that had no urgent need for people. Markets were efficient, prices were unpredictable, and financial economists did not know how to spell the word *anomaly*.

Of course, times have changed. As Fama says in his 1991 sequel, the issues have gotten "thornier," and he devotes a long section to evidence on return predictability. Indeed, the findings of the last two decades have been startling. Small firms, firms with low price-earnings ratios or low ratios of market price to book value of assets, and losing firms all appear to earn higher returns than we would expect. There are also surprising calendar effects, most notably in January. Finally, there is growing evidence that the capital asset pricing model β has no predictive power. That is, after controlling for size or price to book value, stocks with high β's earn no more than stocks with low β's. These research findings, and the experience of the 1987 stock market crash, have made financial economists more cautious. If β does not matter, and stock prices can fall 20 percent in a day without any news, can we really be sure that people are irrelevant?

Theory provided additional excuses for ignoring the people in financial markets. Although most financial economists freely admitted that many participants in financial markets were far from rational (e.g., brokers, chartists, and portfolio managers) this was not thought to matter. One smart trader with enough money was said to be sufficient to keep markets in line. If all prices are set by the rational arbitrageurs, then financial markets with a mixture of rational and irrational traders are identical to a textbook market with only rational traders.

This simple view is no longer tenable. A series of papers has investigated the theory of markets with mixtures of agents. The conclusions that emerge are complex, but it is fair to say that the conditions for irrational agents to be rendered irrelevant are quite special. Most of the time, the behavior of both rational and less than fully rational agents matters. This means that it is no longer possible to have complete confidence in the usual approach (which is to characterize optimal behavior and then assume this behavior is universal). We need to be concerned with how real investors actually behave, that is, behavioral finance.

What is behavioral finance? The best way to define a field is by example, and at this time the papers in this book represent the best of what I would call behavioral finance. The common thread in these papers is the combination of a concern with real world problems and a willingness to consider all explanations in the search for understanding. I think of behavioral finance as simply "open-minded finance". Sometimes, in order to find the solution to an empirical puzzle, it is necessary to entertain the possibility that some of the agents in the economy behave less than fully rationally some of the time. Any financial economist willing to consider this possibility seriously is ready to take a try at behavioral finance.

Naturally, as in any book of this kind, there were difficult choices to be made in selecting the set of papers to be included. In this case, the process of selection was partially a democratic one. The members of the Russell Sage/National Bureau of Economic Research working group on behavioral finance reviewed a tentative table of contents and helped cut the volume down to a feasible size. If your favorite paper does not appear here, please be assured that I wanted to include it but was outvoted.

I have organized the chapters into six sections. Section 1 has chapters about "Noise," the term popularized by Fischer Black's presidential address with that title. Black discusses the role of noise in financial markets. He uses the term in many ways, but perhaps one way to think about noise is that it is the opposite of news. Rational traders make decisions on the basis of news (facts, forecasts, etc.). Noise traders make decisions based on anything else. The chapter by Bradford De Long, Lawrence Summers, Andrei Shleifer, and Robert Waldmann uses Black's noise concept in a theoretical model. They investigate a world populated by rational traders and noise traders, the latter displaying time-varying shifts in sentiment. These shifts in sentiment are shown to create a new kind of risk. Assets that are held widely by noise traders bear the risk that the noise traders will become less optimistic about the future, causing the price of the assets to fall. Rational investors then demand a premium to be willing to bear this risk. An interesting special case of this noise trader model applies in the case of closed-end funds. Closed-end funds have long been a puzzle to efficient market theorists, since the shares in such a fund often sell for prices that differ considerably from the value of the assets the fund owns. These financial curiosities are investigated in the chapter by Charles Lee, Shleifer, and myself. We show that closed-end funds are held primarily by individual investors, and that the discounts on closed-end funds are correlated with the prices of other securities held by individual investors (e.g., small firms).

The second section is devoted to the topic of volatility. It begins with the classic paper by Robert Shiller that asks a provocative question. Since the (detrended) present value of dividends has been essentially constant for the last century, and stock prices are supposed to be a forecast of the present value of future dividend payments, why have stock prices varied so much? This paper has created a major controversy in the financial economics community.[1] Suffice it to say that when all the econometric smoke clears, the week of October 19th, 1987 makes Shiller's conclusions look very good. This point is reinforced by David Cutler, James Poterba, and Lawrence Summers—who ask, what moves stock prices? They show that many big price moves occur in the absence of important news, and conversely, economic news cannot explain a large portion of stock price changes. Of course, the question of excessive volatility is directly related to the issue of whether stock prices are equal to their "true" or fundamental value.[2] The chapter in this section by Lawrence Summers makes it clear how difficult it can be to test this proposition. Robert Shiller's second chapter in this section introduces the idea that fashions and fads may influence financial markets. It is an interesting commentary on the state of economics that Shiller finds it necessary to justify the idea that fashions are important determinants of behavior in other domains. Though economists themselves are not known to be particularly fashion oriented, one might have thought that they would have noticed that other people's behavior seems to change over time: hemlines go up and down, ties and lapels get wider and narrower, disco music comes and (thankfully) goes. Shiller argues forcefully that fashions also influence financial markets. (This chapter also contains the most provocative sentence in the book—look for it.) The final chapter of this section, by Kenneth French and Richard Roll, is concerned with the question of whether stock markets might create their own volatility. They find that, not surprisingly, stock prices vary much more (per hour) during periods when the markets are open than when they are closed. Of course, this result might be explained by the fact that the markets are open during normal business hours when other news is being generated, so French and Roll use a controlled experiment inadvertently conducted by the New York Stock Exchange in 1968. In the second half of that year, the exchange was having trouble keeping up with the volume of trading and decided to close the markets for a series of Wednesdays. Since these Wednesdays were normal business days, French and Roll could examine whether the change in price from Tuesday's close to Thursday's opening

1. For an update, see Stephen LeRoy, "Efficient Capital Markets and Martingales," *Journal of Economic Literature*, 27, December 1989,1583–1621, as well as Shiller's book, *Market Volatility* (MIT Press, 1989).

2. This issue is also addressed in Lee, Shleifer, and Thaler's chapter on closed-end funds.

was less volatile when markets were closed. It was, suggesting, at least to this reader, that traders react to each other as well as to news.

Section 3 is devoted to the topic of overreaction and underreaction. The first chapter, by Werner De Bondt and myself, was the result of an attempt to predict a stock market anomaly from the psychology of decision making. De Bondt and I were familiar with the work of Daniel Kahneman and Amos Tversky which showed that people have a tendency to make predictions that are not sufficiently regressive. That is, rather than being proper Bayesian decision makers, people tend to overweight recent information and underweight long-term tendencies (prior odds). We made the prediction, at the time outlandish, that stocks with extreme performance over some extended time period would display mean reversion. Indeed, we found that extreme losers outperformed the market, and extreme winners underperformed the market, though less so. Like Shiller's paper, this paper has proven to be controversial, with critics claiming that the results are explained by one of two factors: the small size of the losing firms, or their high degree of risk. These issues are taken up by Navin Chopra, Josef Lakonishok, and Jay Ritter in the next chapter. They find that even after controlling carefully for risk and size, losing firms earn excess returns, especially in the smaller deciles. In Victor Bernard's chapter, a seemingly contrary set of results is discussed, that is, the apparent underreaction of stock prices to earnings announcements. The phenomenon, labeled post-earnings-announcement drift, is that when a firm makes an earnings announcement that is surprisingly good or bad the stock price tends to go up or down in the days following the next three quarterly earnings announcements. Bernard tries to make sense of these two surprising sets of results. In the final chapter in this section, Jeremy Stein takes the overreaction idea to another domain: options markets. He observes that stock price volatility is strongly mean reverting. This implies that the prices of short-term options should behave differently than the prices of long-term options. Specifically, when volatility increases, short-term option prices should increase more than their long-term counterparts. The evidence Stein presents is inconsistent with this implication of rationality. He finds that long-term options "overreact".

Section 4 contains a pair of papers that share an international perspective. The first, by Kenneth Froot and Jeffrey Frankel, addresses a well-known anomaly in currency markets called the forward-discount bias. There is a simple proposition about exchange rates that implies that the difference between the spot rate and the forward rate is a prediction about the future movement of currency rates. The forward-discount bias refers to the fact that this prediction fails to hold, and, surprisingly, currencies seem to move in the opposite direction from that predicted by the theory. In this chapter, Froot and Frankel investigate whether the bias can be attributed to risk. They make a convincing argument that it cannot, and suggest that the bias lies in expectations. In the other chapter, Kenneth French and James Poterba discuss a less-well-known anomaly that might be called the "invest-at-home bias". Basic diversification theory implies that investors can decrease risk while holding returns constant by investing in assets that are not highly correlated with their existing portfolio. One way to do so is to invest abroad. The anomaly is that even in small countries people tend to invest very heavily in their own country. A plausible behavioral interpretation is that investors are more confident about investing domestically, even if both foreign and domestic markets are efficient and investors are no better at picking winning stocks at home than abroad.

Section 5 is devoted to corporate finance. The first chapter, by Hersh Shefrin and Meir Statman, is concerned with the major puzzle in the field: why do firms pay dividends? We know that in a world without taxes dividend policy would be irrelevant, but when dividends are taxed at a higher rate than capital gains, stockholders should complain if a firm pays cash dividends. Instead, stockholders seem to do just the opposite—they complain when dividends are cut. Shefrin and Statman offer a behavioral explanation using the concepts of mental accounting and self-control. In their theory, firms pay dividends because stockholders like them! Andrei Shleifer and Robert Vishny take up the important topic of short-term thinking in corporations. Do financial markets, and especially arbitrageurs, help or hurt? Shleifer and Vishny show that rational behavior of arbitrageurs may contribute to the problem, rather than solve it, because arbitrage is more costly for long-term assets than for short-term assets. Richard Roll's chapter is concerned with explaining the puzzling phenomenon of corporate takeovers. The puzzle is that while the target firm stockholders do very well when their firm is purchased, stockholders in the acquiring firm do not appear to make any money. Why do firms make takeovers if they cannot expect to make a profit? Roll offers the "hubris" hypothesis as an answer. Put simply, managers of acquiring firms, flush with cash from recent successes (perhaps due to luck), are convinced that they are "good managers" and will be able to run the target firm better than the current managers. This is consistent with a massive literature in psychology showing that individuals tend to be overconfident.[3] The

3. See, for example, Sarah Lichtenstein, Baruch Fischhoff, and Lawrence Phillips, "Calibration of Probabilities: The State of the Art to 1980," in Daniel Kahneman, Paul Slovic, and Amos Tversky, eds., *Judgment Under Uncertainty: Heuristics and Biases* (Cambridge University Press, 1982).

final chapter in this section, by Jay Ritter, concerns the curious case of the pricing of initial public offerings, also called new issues. IPOs are interesting because they seem to come in waves and are initially underpriced. Ritter finds that over longer periods IPOs are actually overpriced, and offers an explanation in which investors are periodically overoptimistic about the future of young companies, a bias that firms exploit.

The final section of the book is about individual behavior, and begins with Robert Shiller's chapter on popular models. Although the behavior of people has been an important theme in the papers in this book, people remain in the background most of the time. In this chapter, Shiller takes the direct approach of asking real investors what they think. While economists may prefer to study actual behavior rather than responses to survey questions, surely we can learn something from asking actual market participants some simple questions. Shiller reports here three sets of surveys on three interesting topics: the crash of 1987, the real estate boom in California in the late 1980s, and the hot IPO market mentioned above. Shiller tries in these surveys to discover what models of price dynamics actual investors seem to have. One of his conclusions is that participants think that "investor psychology" is important, particularly in the stock market. Shefrin and Statman's chapter is concerned with the relation between price and volume. In many markets, including stock markets and especially real estate markets, when prices fall volume seems to go down. In stock markets this is particularly surprising, since there are tax advantages to selling losers. Shefrin and Statman offer a mental accounting explanation of the phenomenon that is based on the premise that investors do not like to close a mental account with a loss. The last chapter of the book, by Lawrence Ausubel, describes the fascinating market for credit cards. Although there are over 4,000 banks that issue credit cards in the U.S., the market appears to be strangely noncompetitive. In particular, the interest rate that a bank charges does not seem sensitive to the bank's cost of funds. Ausubel offers an explanation based, in part, on individuals selecting a credit card as if they would never fail to repay their balance on time, though their objective chance of incurring interest charges is actually quite high.

What are the main conclusions to be drawn from this collection? I would suggest two. First, it is possible to do good economic research even if the assumption of universal rationality is relaxed. Second, we can understand much more about the behavior of markets, even financial markets, if we learn more about the behavior of the people who operate in these markets.

PART

I

NOISE

1

Noise

FISCHER BLACK

I use the word "noise" in several senses in this paper.

In my basic model of financial markets, noise is contrasted with information. People sometimes trade on information in the usual way. They are correct in expecting to make profits from these trades. On the other hand, people sometimes trade on noise as if it were information. If they expect to make profits from noise trading, they are incorrect. However, noise trading is essential to the existence of liquid markets.

In my model of the way we observe the world, noise is what makes our observations imperfect. It keeps us from knowing the expected return on a stock or portfolio. It keeps us from knowing whether monetary policy affects inflation or unemployment. It keeps us from knowing what, if anything, we can do to make things better.

In my model of inflation, noise is the arbitrary element in expectations that leads to an arbitrary rate of inflation consistent with expectations. In my model of business cycles and unemployment, noise is information that hasn't arrived yet. It is simply uncertainty about future demand and supply conditions within and across sectors. When the information does arrive, the number of sectors where there is a good match between tastes and technology is an index of economic activity. In my model of the international economy, changing relative prices become noise that makes it difficult to see that demand and supply conditions are largely independent of price levels and exchange rates. Without these relative price changes, we would see that a version of purchasing power parity holds most of the time.

I think of these models as equilibrium models. Not rational equilibrium models, because of the role of noise and because of the unconven-

From: *The Journal of Finance*, vol. XLI, No. 3, pp. 529–543, July 1986. Reprinted by permission of the American Finance Association.

3

tional things I allow an individual's utility to depend on, but equilibrium models nonetheless. They were all derived originally as part of a broad effort to apply the logic behind the capital asset pricing model to markets other than the stock market and to behavior that does not fit conventional notions of optimization.

These models are in very different fields: finance, econometrics, and macro-economics. Do they have anything in common other than the use of the word "noise" in describing them? The common element, I think, is the emphasis on a diversified array of unrelated causal elements to explain what happens in the world. There is no single factor that causes stock prices to stray from theoretical values, nor even a small number of factors. There is no single variable whose neglect causes econometric studies to go astray. And there is no simple single or multiple factor explanation of domestic or international business fluctuations.

While I have made extensive use of the work of others, I recognize that most researchers in these fields will regard many of my conclusions as wrong, or untestable, or unsupported by existing evidence. I have not been able to think of any conventional empirical tests that would distinguish between my views and the views of others. In the end, my response to the skepticism of others is to make a prediction: someday, these conclusions will be widely accepted. The influence of noise traders will become apparent. Conventional monetary and fiscal policies will be seen as ineffective. Changes in exchange rates will come to provoke no more comment than changes in the real price of an airline ticket.

Perhaps most important, research will be seen as a process leading to reliable and relevant conclusions only very rarely, because of the noise that creeps in at every step.

If my conclusions are not accepted, I will blame it on noise.

1. Finance

Noise makes financial markets possible, but also makes them imperfect.[1]

If there is no noise trading, there will be very little trading in individual assets.[2] People will hold individual assets, directly or indirectly, but

1. The concept of noise trading and its role in financial markets that I develop in this paper was developed through conversations with James Stone.

2. Jaffe and Winkler (1976) have a model where the traders who make speculative markets stable are those who trade to adjust their risk level or who misperceive their forecasting ability or who trade for reasons other than maximizing expected return for a given level of risk. Figlewski (1978) has a model where there are two types of traders who differ in forecasting ability. Since neither kind of trader explicitly takes into account the information the other kind of trader has, each is to some degree trading on noise.

they will rarely trade them. People trading to change their exposure to broad market risks will trade in mutual funds, or portfolios, or index futures, or index options. They will have little reason to trade in the shares of an individual firm.[3] People who want cash to spend or who want to invest cash they have received will increase or decrease their positions in short term securities, or money market accounts, or money market mutual funds, or loans backed by real estate or other assets.

A person with information or insights about individual firms will want to trade, but will realize that only another person with information or insights will take the other side of the trade. Taking the other side's information into account, is it still worth trading? From the point of view of someone who knows what both the traders know, one side or the other must be making a mistake.[4] If the one who is making a mistake declines to trade, there will be no trading on information.

In other words, I do not believe it makes sense to create a model with information trading but no noise trading where traders have different beliefs and one trader's beliefs are as good as any other trader's beliefs. Differences in beliefs must derive ultimately from differences in information.[5] A trader with a special piece of information will know that other traders have their own special pieces of information, and will therefore not automatically rush out to trade.

But if there is little or no trading in individual shares, there can be no trading in mutual funds or portfolios or index futures or index options, because there will be no practical way to price them. The whole structure of financial markets depends on relatively liquid markets in the shares of individual firms.

Noise trading provides the essential missing ingredient. Noise trading

3. Rubinstein (1975), Milgrom and Stokey (1982), and Hakansson, Kunkel, and Ohlson (1982) show in a state preference world that differences in information may affect prices without causing people to trade. Grossman and Stiglitz (1980) show that there may be no equilibrium when rational investors trade in the market portfolio. Grossman (1978) shows the same thing for a world with trading in individual assets. Diamond and Verrecchia (1981) redefine a rational expectations equilibrium in the presence of noise and show the conditions under which their equilibrium exists. In Tirole's model (1982), "speculation" relies on inconsistent plans, and thus is ruled out by rational expectations. Kyle (1984), (1985), (1985a) and Grinblatt and Ross (1985) look at quite different models of equilibrium where traders have market power. Kyle specifically examines the effects of changing the number of noise traders in both kinds of equilibrium.

4. This assumes that the traders start with well diversified portfolios. In Admati (1985), the traders start with suboptimal portfolios of assets.

5. Varian (1985) distinguishes between "opinions" and "information." He says that only differences in opinions will generate trading. In the kind of model he is working with, I think the differences of opinion will not exist.

is trading on noise as if it were information. People who trade on noise are willing to trade even though from an objective point of view they would be better off not trading. Perhaps they think the noise they are trading on is information. Or perhaps they just like to trade.[6]

With a lot of noise traders in the market, it now pays for those with information to trade. It even pays for people to seek out costly information which they will then trade on. Most of the time, the noise traders as a group will lose money by trading, while the information traders as a group will make money.

The more noise trading there is, the more liquid the markets will be, in the sense of having frequent trades that allow us to observe prices. But noise trading actually puts noise into the prices. The price of a stock reflects both the information that information traders trade on and the noise that noise traders trade on.

As the amount of noise trading increases, it will become more profitable for people to trade on information, but only because the prices have more noise in them. The increase in the amount of information trading does not mean that prices are more efficient. Not only will more information traders come in, but existing information traders will take bigger positions and will spend more on information. Yet prices will be less efficient.[7] What's needed for a liquid market causes prices to be less efficient.

The information traders will not take large enough positions to eliminate the noise. For one thing, their information gives them an edge, but does not guarantee a profit. Taking a larger position means taking more risk. So there is a limit to how large a position a trader will take. For another thing, the information traders can never be sure that they are trading on information rather than noise. What if the information they have has already been reflected in prices? Trading on that kind of information will be just like trading on noise.[8] Because the actual return on a portfolio is a very noisy estimate of expected return, even after adjusting

6. In Laffont (1985), traders gather costly information because it has direct utility for reasons other than trading. Once they have it, they trade on it. If people start with efficient portfolios, though, even the arrival of free information may not make them want to trade. We may need to introduce direct utility of trading to explain the existence of speculative markets.

7. This result is specific to a model where noise traders trade on noise as if it were information. In Kyle's (1984), (1985), (1985a) model, having more noise traders can make markets more efficient.

8. Arrow (1982) says that excessive reaction to current information characterizes all the securities and futures markets. If this is true, it could be caused by trading on information that has already been discounted.

for returns on the market and other factors, it will be difficult to show that information traders have an edge. For the same reason, it will be difficult to show that noise traders are losing by trading. There will always be a lot of ambiguity about who is an information trader and who is a noise trader.

The noise that noise traders put into stock prices will be cumulative, in the same sense that a drunk tends to wander farther and farther from his starting point. Offsetting this, though, will be the research and actions taken by the information traders. The farther the price of a stock gets from its value, the more aggressive the information traders will become. More of them will come in, and they will take larger positions. They may even initiate mergers, leveraged buyouts, and other restructurings.

Thus the price of a stock will tend to move back toward its value over time.[9] The move will often be so gradual that it is imperceptible. If it is fast, technical traders will perceive it and speed it up. If it is slow enough, technical traders will not be able to see it, or will be so unsure of what they see that they will not take large positions.[10]

Still, the farther the price of a stock moves away from value, the faster it will tend to move back. This limits the degree to which it is likely to move away from value. All estimates of value are noisy, so we can never know how far away price is from value.

However, we might define an efficient market as one in which price is within a factor of 2 of value, i.e., the price is more than half of value and less than twice value.[11] The factor of 2 is arbitrary, of course. Intuitively, though, it seems reasonable to me, in the light of sources of uncertainty about value and the strength of the forces tending to cause price to return to value. By this definition, I think almost all markets are efficient almost all of the time. "Almost all" means at least 90%.

Because value is not observable, it is possible for events that have no information content to affect price. For example, the addition of a stock to the Standard & Poors 500 index will cause some investors to buy it. Their buying will force the price up for a time. Information trading will force it back, but only gradually.[12]

9. Merton (1971) describes a model where long run prices are efficient but short run prices need not be.

10. Summers (1986) emphasizes the difficulty in telling whether markets are efficient or not. This difficulty affects market participants and researchers alike.

11. I think this puts me between Merton (1985) and Shiller (1981), (1984). Deviations from efficiency seem more significant in my world than in Merton's, but much less significant in my world than in Shiller's.

12. This effect was discovered independently by Shleifer (1986) and Gurel and Harris (1985).

Similarly, when a firm with two classes of common stock issues more of one class, the price of the class of stock issued will decline relative to the price of the class of stock not issued.[13]

Both price and value will look roughly like geometric random walk processes with non-zero means. The means of percentage change in price and value will change over time. The mean of the value process will change because tastes and technology and wealth change. It may well decline when value rises, and rise when value declines. The mean of the price process will change because the relation between price and value changes (and because the mean of the value process changes). Price will tend to move toward value.

The short term volatility of price will be greater than the short term volatility of value. Since noise is independent of information in this context, when the variance of the percentage price moves caused by noise is equal to the variance of the percentage price moves caused by information, the variance of percentage price moves from day to day will be roughly twice the variance of percentage value moves from day to day. Over longer intervals, though, the variances will converge. Because price tends to return to value, the variance of price several years from now will be much less than twice the variance of value several years from now.

Volatilities will change over time. The volatility of the value of a firm is affected by things like the rate of arrival of information about the firm and the firm's leverage. All the factors affecting the volatility of a firm's value will change. The volatility of price will change for all these reasons and for other reasons as well. Anything that changes the amount or character of noise trading will change the volatility of price.

Noise traders must trade to have their influence. Because information traders trade with noise traders more than with other information traders, cutting back on noise trading also cuts back on information trading. Thus prices will not move as much when the market is closed as they move when the market is open.[14] The relevant market here is the market on which most of the noise traders trade.

Noise traders may prefer low-priced stocks to high-priced stocks. If they do, then splits will increase both the liquidity of a stock and its

13. Loderer and Zimmermann (1985) discovered this effect in connection with offerings in Switzerland, where multiple classes of stock are common.

14. French and Roll (1985) find that the volatilities of stock returns are much lower across periods when markets are closed than across periods when markets are open.

day-to-day volatility. Low-priced stocks will be less efficiently priced than high-priced stocks.[15]

The price of a stock will be a noisy estimate of its value. The earnings of a firm (multiplied by a suitable price-earnings ratio) will give another estimate of the value of the firm's stock.[16] This estimate will be noisy too. So long as noise traders do not always look at earnings in deciding how to trade, the estimate from earnings will give information that is not already in the estimate from price.[17]

Because an estimate of value based on earnings will have so much noise, there will be no easy way to use price-earnings ratios in managing portfolios. Even if stocks with low price-earnings ratios have higher expected returns than other stocks, there will be periods, possibly lasting for years, when stocks with low price-earnings ratios have lower returns than other comparable stocks.

In other words, noise creates the opportunity to trade profitably, but at the same time makes it difficult to trade profitably.

2. Econometrics

Why do people trade on noise?

One reason is that they like to do it. Another is that there is so much noise around that they don't know they are trading on noise. They think they are trading on information.[18]

Neither of these reasons fits into a world where people do things only to maximize expected utility of wealth, and where people always make the best use of available information. Once we let trading enter the utility

---

15. Ohlson and Penman (1985) find that when stocks split, their return volatilities go up on the ex-split date by an average of about 30%. This may be due to a higher proportion of noise traders, though they also find no increase in trading volume on the ex-split date. Amihud (1985) feels that another possible explanation for this result is the increase in the bid-asked spread following a stock split.

16. For a discussion of the relation between earnings and stock price, see Black (1980).

17. Basu (1983) summarizes the evidence that stocks with high earnings-price ratios have higher expected returns than stocks with low earnings-price ratios, even after controlling for size of firm and risk. De Bondt and Thaler (1985) give more evidence on the existence of temporary dislocations in price, and on the psychological factors that may influence the noise traders who create these opportunities.

18. Kahneman and Tversky (1979) have a more sophisticated model of why people make decisions for what are seemingly non-rational reasons. Their theory may help describe the motivation of noise traders. For applications of their theory to economics and finance, see Russell and Thaler (1985).

function directly (as a way of saying that people like to trade), it's hard to know where to stop. If anything can be in the utility function, the notion that people act to maximize expected utility is in danger of losing much of its content.

So we want to be careful about letting things into the utility function. We want to do it only when the evidence is compelling. I believe that this is such a case.

Another such case is dividend payments by firms. Given our tax laws, it seems clear that share repurchase in a non-systematic way is better than payment of dividends. If people want to maximize only expected utility of after-tax wealth, there will be no reason for firms to pay regular dividends. And when they do pay dividends, they will apologize to the stockholders (at least to individual stockholders) for causing them the discomfort of extra taxes.[19]

The idea that dividends convey information beyond that conveyed by the firm's financial statements and public announcements stretches the imagination.[20] It is especially odd that some firms pay dividends while making periodic offerings of common stock that raise more money than the firms are paying in dividends. For such firms, we cannot say that dividends force the firm to go through the rigors of a public offering of stock. Even if they pay no dividends, they will still be issuing common stock.[21]

I think we must assume that investors care about dividends directly. We must put dividends into the utility function.

Perhaps we should be happy that we can continue to think in terms of expected utility at all. There is considerable evidence now that people do not obey the axioms of expected utility. Of special concern is the finding that people will take certain gambles to avoid losses, but will refuse the same gambles when they involve prospective gains. Can this be consistent with risk aversion?[22]

I think that noise is a major reason for the use of decision rules that seem to violate the normal axioms of expected utility. Because there is

19. In Black (1976), I described the dividend puzzle. The solution to the puzzle, I now believe, is that we must put dividends directly into the utility function. For one way of putting dividends into the utility function, see Shefrin and Statman (1985). For another way of resolving the dividend puzzle, and of relating it to the capital structure puzzle, see Myers (1984).

20. For a statement of the case that dividends do convey information, see Miller (1985).

21. Kalay and Shimrat (1985) observe, however, that firms issuing common stock do tend to reduce their dividends.

22. This phenomenon is discussed extensively by Tversky and Kahneman (1981).

so much noise in the world, people adopt rules of thumb. They share their rules of thumb with each other, and very few people have enough experience with interpreting noisy evidence to see that the rules are too simple. Over time, I expect that the transmission through the media and through the schools of scientific ways of interpreting evidence will gradually make the rules of thumb more sophisticated, and will thus make the expected utility model more valid.

Even highly trained people, though, seem to make certain kinds of errors consistently. For example, there is a strong tendency in looking at data to assume that when two events frequently happen together, one causes the other. There is an even stronger tendency to assume that the one that occurs first causes the one that occurs second. These tendencies are easy to resist in the simplest cases. But they seem to creep back in when econometric studies become more complex. Sometimes I wonder if we can draw any conclusions at all from the results of regression studies.

Because there is so much noise in the world, certain things are essentially unobservable.

For example, we cannot know what the expected return on the market is. There is every reason to believe that it changes over time, and no particular reason to believe that the changes occur smoothly. We can use the average past return as an estimate of the expected return, but it is a very noisy estimate.[23]

Similarly, the slopes of demand and supply curves are so hard to estimate that they are essentially unobservable. Introspection seems as good a method as any in trying to estimate them. One major problem is that no matter how many variables we include in an econometric analysis, there always seem to be potentially important variables that we have omitted, possibly because they too are unobservable.[24]

For example, wealth is often a key variable in estimating any demand curve. But wealth is itself unobservable. It's not even clear how to define it. The market value of traded assets is part of it, but the value of non-traded assets and especially of human capital is a bigger part for most individuals. There is no way to observe the value of human capital for an individual, and it is not clear how we might go about adding up the values of human capital for individuals to obtain a value of human capital for a whole economy.

I suspect that if it were possible to observe the value of human capital, we would find it fluctuating in much the same way that the level of the

23. Merton (1980) shows how difficult it is to estimate the expected return on the market.

24. Leamer (1983) and Black (1982) discuss the profound difficulties with conventional econometric analyses.

stock market fluctuates. In fact, I think we would find fluctuations in the value of human capital to be highly correlated with fluctuations in the level of the stock market, though the magnitude of the fluctuations in the value of human capital is probably less than the magnitude of the fluctuations in the level of the stock market.[25]

It's actually easier to list observables than unobservables, since so many things are unobservable. The interest rate is observable. If there were enough trading in CPI futures, the real interest rate would be observable. So far, though, there are not enough noise traders in CPI futures to make it a viable market.

Stock prices and stock returns are observable. The past volatility of a stock's returns is observable, and by using daily returns we can come close to observing the current volatility of a stock's returns. We can also come close to observing the correlations among the returns on different stocks.

Economic variables seem generally less observable than financial variables. The prices of goods and services are hard to observe, because they are specific to location and terms of trade much more than financial variables. Quantities are hard to observe, because what is traded differs from place to place and through time.

Thus econometric studies involving economic variables are hard to interpret for two reasons: first, the coefficients of regressions tell us little about causal relations even when the variables are observable; and second, the variables are subject to lots of measurement error, and the measurement errors are probably related to the true values of the variables.

Perhaps the easiest economic variable to observe is the money stock, once we agree on a definition for it. I think that accounts for some of the fascination it holds for economic theorists. In my view, though, this easiest to observe of economic variables has no important role in the workings of the economy. Money is important, but the money stock is not.

Still, the money stock is correlated with every measure of economic activity, because the amount of money used in trade is related to the volume of trade. This correlation implies neither that the government can control the money stock nor that changes in the money stock influence economic activity.[26]

Empirical studies in finance are easier to do than empirical studies in

25. Fama and Schwert (1977) study the relation between human capital and the stock market. They do not find a close relation.

26. King and Plosser (1984) look at the possibility that economic activity influences the money stock rather than the other way around.

economics, because data on security prices are of generally higher quality than the available data in economics. But there are major pitfalls in trying to interpret even the results of studies of security prices.

For example, many recent empirical studies in finance have taken the form of "event studies," which look at stock price reactions to announcements that affect a firm.[27] If there were no noise in stock prices, this would be a very reliable way to find out how certain events affect firms. In fact, though, the stock price reaction tells us only how investors think the events will affect firms, and investors' thoughts include both noise and information.

Moreover, if investors care directly about certain attributes of a firm (such as its dividend yield) independently of how those attributes affect its value, event studies will pick up these preferences along with the effects of the events on value. When a firm increases its dividend, its price may go up because investors like dividends, even though the present value of its future dividends in a world where the marginal investor is taxed may have gone down.

Is there any solution to these problems? No single, simple solution, I believe. Correlations among economic and financial variables do give us some information of value. Experimental studies in economics and finance have value. Analysis of "stylized facts" is often useful. Unusual events can provide special insight. In the end, a theory is accepted not because it is confirmed by conventional empirical tests, but because researchers persuade one another that the theory is correct and relevant.[28]

3. Macroeconomics

If business cycles were caused by unanticipated shifts in the general price level or in the level of government spending, we might not call that kind of uncertainty noise. It's too simple. Because it is so simple, I don't think this kind of uncertainty can play a major role in business cycles. I have not seen any models with all the kinds of markets we have in the economy where shifts in the general price level or in the level of government spending are large enough or powerful enough or unanticipated enough to cause significant business cycles.[29]

27. For a typical event study, together with discussion of a factor that may make event studies hard to interpret properly, see Kalay and Loewenstein (1985).

28. This point of view is taken in part from McCloskey (1983).

29. For a review of research in business cycle theory, see Zarnowitz (1985). For an attempt to explain large business cycles with seemingly innocent changes in the price level, see Mankiw (1985).

On the other hand, if business cycles are caused by unanticipated shifts in the entire pattern of tastes and technologies across sectors, we might call that uncertainty noise. I believe that these shifts are significant for the economy as a whole because they do not cancel in any meaningful sense. The number of sectors in which there is a match between tastes and technology varies a lot over time. When it is high, we have an expansion. When it is low, we have a recession.[30]

One reason the shifts do not cancel is that they are not independent across sectors. When the costs of producing goods and services that require oil are high, they will be high across many related sectors. When demand for vacation homes is high, it will be high for many kinds of related services at the same time. The more we divide sectors into subsectors, the more related the subsectors will be to one another.

It is not clear whether the increasing diversity and specialization that go along with the transition from a simple economy to a complex modern economy will be associated with larger or smaller business cycles. On the one hand, the diversity in a more complex economy means that a single crop failure or demand shock cannot have such a devastating effect; but on the other hand, the specialization in a more complex economy means that when there is a mismatch between tastes and technology, it is costly to move skills and machines between sectors to correct the mismatch.

Money and prices play no role in this explanation. Everything is real.[31] For a small sample of the kind of thing I have in mind, suppose I gear up to produce dolls, while you gear up to produce art books. If it turns out that you want dolls and I want art books, we will have a boom. We will both work hard, and will exchange our outputs and will have high consumption of both dolls and art books. But if it turns out that you want action toys and I want science books, we will have a bust. The relative price of toys and books may be the same as before, but neither of us will work so hard because we will not value highly that which we can exchange our outputs for.

This is just one kind of example. The variations can occur in use of machines as well as in use of people, and the underlying uncertainty can concern what we can make as well as what we want.

Unanticipated shifts in tastes and technology within and across sectors

30. For a more extensive discussion of this point of view, see Black (1981), (1982).

31. The most closely related work in the more conventional business cycle literature is Long and Plosser (1983) and Lilien (1982). Bernanke (1983) has an entirely real explanation for swings in the production of durable goods: it is sectoral in the sense that specific investments are irreversible. Topel and Weiss (1985) use uncertainty about employment conditions in different sectors to help explain unemployment; their methods can also be applied, I think, to explaining cyclical fluctuations in unemployment.

are what we call information in discussing financial markets. In economic markets, it seems more appropriate to call these shifts noise, to contrast them with shifts in the aggregates that conventional macroeconomic models focus on. In other words, the cause of business cycles is not a few large things that can be measured and controlled, but many small things that are difficult to measure and essentially impossible to control.

Noise or uncertainty has its effects in economic markets because there are costs in shifting physical and human resources within and between sectors. If skills and capital can be shifted without cost after tastes and technology become known, mismatches between what we can do and what we want to do will not occur.

The costs of shifting real resources are clearly large, so it is plausible that these costs might play a role in business cycles. The costs of putting inflation adjustments in contracts or of publicizing changes in the money stock or the price level seem low, so it is not plausible that these costs play a significant role in business cycles.

Presumably the government does not have better information about the details of future supply and demand conditions within and between sectors than the people working in those sectors. Thus there is little the government can do to help the economy avoid recessions. These unknown future details are noise to the workers and managers involved, and they are noise twice over to government employees, even those who collect statistics on individual industries.

I cannot think of any conventional econometric tests that would shed light on the question of whether my business cycle theory is correct or not. One of its predictions, though, is that real wages will fluctuate with other measures of economic activity. When there is a match between tastes and technology in many sectors, income will be high, wages will be high, output will be high, and unemployment will be low. Thus real wages will be procyclical. This is obviously true over long periods, as from the Twenties to the Thirties and from the Thirties to the Forties, but is also seems true over shorter periods, especially when overtime and layoffs are taken into account.[32]

How do inflation and money fit into this picture?

I believe that monetary policy is almost completely passive in a country like the U.S.[33] Money goes up when prices go up or when income goes up because demand for money goes up at those times. I have been unable to construct an equilibrium model in which changes in money cause changes in prices or income, but I have had no trouble constructing

32. Bils (1985) reviews previous work in this area, and gives evidence that real wages are indeed procyclical.

33. My views are explained more fully in Black (1970), (1972), (1974).

an equilibrium model in which changes in prices or income cause changes in money.[34]

Changes in money often precede changes in income, but this is not surprising, since demand for money can depend on expected income as well as current income. Changes in wealth (measured at market value) also precede changes in income.

In the conventional story, open market operations change perceived wealth, which leads to a change in demand for existing assets, and thus to a change in the price level. But open market operations have no effect on wealth when wealth is measured at market value. They merely substitute one form of wealth for another. Some say that open market operations cause a change in interest rates, which then have further effects on the economy. But this cannot happen in an equilibrium model. There is no temporary equilibrium, with the price level and rate of inflation unchanged, where a different interest rate will be equal to the certain component of the marginal product of capital. If we allow the price level and rate of inflation to change, then there are many equilibria, but there are no rules to tell us how one is chosen over another. There is no logical story explaining how the change in money will cause a shift from one equilibrium to another.

If monetary policy doesn't cause changes in inflation, what does?

I think that the price level and rate of inflation are literally indeterminate. They are whatever people think they will be. They are determined by expectations, but expectations follow no rational rules. If people believe that certain changes in the money stock will cause changes in the rate of inflation, that may well happen, because their expectations will be built into their long term contracts.

Another way to make the same point is this. Within a sector, the prices of inputs and outputs are largely taken as given. Decisions on what and how much to produce are made taking these prices as given. Thus each sector assumes that the rates of inflation of its input and output prices are given. In my models, this includes the government sector in its role as supplier of money. If we are in an equilibrium with one expected rate of inflation (assuming neither gold prices nor exchange rates are fixed), and everyone shifts to a lower expected rate of inflation, we will have (with only minor modifications) a new equilibrium.

One way to describe this view is to say that noise causes changes in the rate of inflation.

If we have a gold standard, where the price of gold is adjusted over

---

34. For an analysis of possible explanations for some of the correlations between money and other variables, see Cornell (1983).

time to make the general price level follow a desired path, and where the government stands ready to buy or sell gold at the temporarily fixed price without allowing its inventory to fluctuate much, then inflation will be controlled rather than random.[35] But it seems unlikely that we will adopt a gold standard of this kind or of any other kind anytime soon.

Similarly, if a small country adopts a policy of varying its exchange rate with a large country to make its price level follow a desired path, where its government stands ready to buy or sell foreign exchange at the temporarily fixed rate without allowing its foreign exchange inventory to fluctuate much, then its inflation rate will be controlled rather than random. This is possible for any country that has wealth and stable taxing power, because the country can always sell assets for foreign exchange, and can then buy the assets back (almost) with the foreign currency it obtains.

However, it is not clear what is gained by controlling the price level. If business cycles are caused by real factors rather than by things that are affected by the rate of inflation, then many of the reasons for controlling inflation vanish.

In my view, then, there is a real international equilibrium that is largely unaffected by price levels or monetary policies, except in countries with unstable financial markets or national debt that is large compared with taxable wealth. This real equilibrium involves a world business cycle and national business cycles driven by the degree to which there is a match between tastes and technology.

The real equilibrium also involves changing relative prices for all kinds of goods and services, including relative prices for the "same" goods and services in different locations. Different locations can be around the corner or around the world. Since information and transportation are so costly (especially information), there is no form of arbitrage that will force the prices of similar goods and services in different locations to be similar.

Moreover, the real equilibrium involves constantly changing trade flows for various pairs of countries. There is no reason for trade to be balanced between any pair of countries either in the short run or in the long run. And an imbalance in trade has no particular welfare implications.[36]

---

35. For an old version of this argument, see Fisher (1920). For a new version, together with discussion of the possibility of keeping gold inventories roughly fixed while controlling the price of gold and the price level, see Black (1981).

36. This is a common result in international economics. For my treatment of it, see Black (1978).

Since the real equilibrium is fixed at a point in time, though it is continually changing through time, a higher domestic currency price for an item at one point in time will mean a higher domestic currency price for all items at that same point in time. There will be some lags in making price changes, and many lags in posting or reporting price changes, but these will not affect the equilibrium significantly.

If we were able to observe the economy at a given point in time with two different domestic price levels, we would see that the real equilibrium is largely independent of price levels and exchange rates, and we might call this situation "purchasing power parity." Since we must actually observe the economy as it evolves over time, we cannot see that purchasing power parity holds. We see relative price changes occurring, and fluctuations in the level of economic activity, while exchange rates and money stocks are changing. We think that exchange rates and money are causing relative price changes and business fluctuations.[37]

But that is only because the noise in the data is clouding our vision.

Goldman, Sachs & Co. I am grateful for comments on earlier drafts by Peter Bernstein, Robert Merton, James Poterba, Richard Roll, Hersh Shefrin, Meir Statman, Lawrence Summers, and Laurence Weiss.

References

ADMATI, ANAT R. "A Noisy Rational Expectations Equilibrium for Multi-Asset Securities Markets." *Econometrica* 53 (May 1985), 629–657.

AIZENMAN, JOSHUA. "Testing Deviations from Purchasing Power Parity (PPP)." National Bureau of Economic Research Working Paper No. 1475, October, 1984.

AMIHUD, YAKOV. "Biases in Computed Return Variance: An Application to Volatility Increases Subsequent to Stock Splits." Unpublished manuscript, December, 1985.

ARROW, KENNETH J. "Risk Perception in Psychology and Economics." *Economic Inquiry* 20 (January 1982), 1–9.

37. Davutyan and Pippenger (1985) suggest some ways in which standard tests of purchasing power parity may be flawed. Moreover, our tests of purchasing power parity are inadequate unless we consider transport costs, as Aizenman (1984) notes. Transport costs can be very large for services and some goods.

BASU, SANJOY. "The Relationship between Earnings' Yield, Market Value and Return for NYSE Common Stocks: Further Evidence." *Journal of Financial Economics* 12 (June 1983), 129–156.

BERNANKE, BEN S. "Irreversibility, Uncertainty, and Cyclical Investment." *Quarterly Journal of Economics* (February 1983), 85–106.

BILS, MARK J. "Real Wages over the Business Cycle: Evidence from Panel Data." *Journal of Political Economy* 93 (August 1985), 666–689.

BLACK, FISCHER. "Banking and Interest Rates in a World Without Money: The Effects of Uncontrolled Banking." *Journal of Bank Research* 1 (Autumn 1970), 8–20.

———. "Active and Passive Monetary Policy in a Neoclassical Model." *Journal of Finance* 27 (September 1972), 801–814.

———. "Uniqueness of the Price Level in Monetary Growth Models with Rational Expectations." *Journal of Economic Theory* 7 (January 1974), 53–65.

———. "The Dividend Puzzle." *Journal of Portfolio Management* 2 (Winter 1976), 5–8.

———. "The Ins and Outs of Foreign Investment." *Financial Analysts Journal* 34 (May/June 1978), 25–32.

———. "The Magic in Earnings: Economic Earnings Versus Accounting Earnings." *Financial Analysts Journal* 36 (November/December 1980), 19–24.

———. "A Gold Standard with Double Feedback and Near Zero Reserves." Unpublished manuscript, 1981.

———. "The ABCs of Business Cycles." *Financial Analysts Journal* 37 (November/December 1981), 75–80.

———. "The Trouble with Econometric Models." *Financial Analysts Journal* 38 (March/April 1982), 29–37.

———. "General Equilibrium and Business Cycles." National Bureau of Economic Research Working Paper No. 950, August, 1982.

CORNELL, BRADFORD. "The Money Supply Announcements Puzzle: Review and Interpretation." *American Economic Review* 73 (September 1983), 644–657.

DAVUTYAN, NURHAN, and JOHN PIPPENGER. "Purchasing Power Parity Did Not Collapse During the 1970's." *American Economic Review* 75 (December 1985), 1151–1158.

DE BONDT, WERNER F. M., and RICHARD THALER. "Does the Stock Market Overreact?" *Journal of Finance* 40 (July 1985), 793–805.

DIAMOND, DOUGLAS W., and ROBERT E. VERRECCHIA. "Information Aggregation in Noisy Rational Expectations Economy." *Journal of Financial Economics* 9 (September 1981), 221–235.

FAMA, EUGENE F., and G. WILLIAM SCHWERT. "Human Capital and Capital Market Equilibrium." *Journal of Financial Economics* 4 (January 1977), 95–125.

FIGLEWSKI, STEPHEN. "Market 'Efficiency' in a Market with Heterogeneous Information." *Journal of Political Economy* 86 (August 1978), 581–597.

FISHER, IRVING. *Stabilizing the Dollar.* New York: Macmillan, 1920.

FRENCH, KENNETH R., and RICHARD ROLL. "Stock Return Variances: The Arrival of Information and the Reaction of Traders." Graduate School of Management, UCLA Working Paper, July, 1985.

GRINBLATT, MARK S., and STEPHEN A. ROSS. "Market Power in a Securities Market with Endogenous Information." *Quarterly Journal of Economics* 100 (November 1985), 1143–1167.

GROSSMAN, SANFORD. "Further Results on the Informational Efficiency of Competitive Stock Markets." *Journal of Economic Theory* 18 (June 1978), 81–101.

————, and JOSEPH E. STIGLITZ. "On the Impossibility of Informationally Efficient Markets." *American Economic Review* 70 (June 1980), 393–408.

GUREL, EITAN, and LAWRENCE HARRIS. "Price and Volume Effects Associated with Changes in the S&P 500 List: New Evidence for the Existence of Price Pressures." Unpublished manuscript, April, 1985.

HAKANSSON, NILS, J. GREGORY KUNKEL, and JAMES OHLSON. "Sufficient and Necessary Conditions for Information to have Social Value in Pure Exchange." *Journal of Finance* 37 (December 1982), 1169–1181.

JAFFE, JEFFREY F., and ROBERT L. WINKLER. "Optimal Speculation Against an Efficient Market." *Journal of Finance* 31 (March 1976), 49–61.

KAHNEMAN, DANIEL, and AMOS TVERSKY. "Prospect Theory: An Analysis of Decision Under Risk." *Econometrica* 47 (March 1979), 263–291.

KALAY, AVNER, and ADAM SHIMRAT. "On the Payment of Equity Financed Dividends." Unpublished manuscript, December, 1985.

KALAY, AVNER, and URI LOEWENSTEIN. "Predictable Events and Excess Returns: The Case of Dividend Announcements." *Journal of Financial Economics* 14 (September 1985), 423–449.

KING, ROBERT G., and CHARLES I. PLOSSER. "Money, Credit, and Prices in a Real Business Cycle." *American Economic Review* 74 (June 1984), 360–380.

KYLE, ALBERT S. "Market Structure, Information, Futures Markets, and Price Formation." In GARY G. STOREY, ANDREW SCHMITZ, and ALEXANDER H. SARRIS, eds. *International Agricultural Trade* (Boulder and London: Westview Press, 1984), pp. 45–63.

————. "Continuous Auctions and Insider Trading." *Econometrica* 53 (November 1985), 1315–1335.

————. "Informed Speculation with Imperfect Competition." Unpublished manuscript, December 1985a.

LAFFONT, JEAN-JACQUES. "On the Welfare Analysis of Rational Expectations Equilibria with Asymmetric Information." *Econometrica* 53 (January 1985), 1–29.

LEAMER, EDWARD E. "Let's Take the Con Out of Econometrics." *American Economic Review* 73 (March 1983), 31–43.

LILIEN, DAVID M. "Sectoral Shifts and Cyclical Unemployment." *Journal of Political Economy* 90 (July/August 1982), 777–793.

————. "A Sectoral Model of the Business Cycle." USC Modelling Research Group Working Paper #8231, December, 1982.

LODERER, CLAUDIO, and HEINZ ZIMMERMANN. "Rights Issues in Switzerland: Some Findings to Consider in the Debate over Financing Decisions." Unpublished manuscript, July, 1985.

LONG, JOHN B., and CHARLES I. PLOSSER. "Real Business Cycles." *Journal of Political Economy* 91 (February 1983), 39–69.

MANKIW, N. GREGORY. "Small Menu Costs and Large Business Cycles." *Quarterly Journal of Economics* 100 (May 1985), 529–538.

MCCLOSKEY, DONALD N. The "Rhetoric of Economics." *Journal of Economic Literature* 21 (June 1983), 481–517.

MERTON, ROBERT C. "Optimum Consumption and Portfolio Rules in a Continuous-Time Model." *Journal of Economic Theory* 3 (December 1971), 373–413.

————. "On Estimating the Expected Return on the Market: An Exploratory Investigation." *Journal of Financial Economics* 8 (December 1980), 323–361.

————. "On the Current State of the Stock Market Rationality Hypothesis." Sloan School of Management Working Paper #1717-85, October, 1985.

MILGROM, PAUL, and NANCY STOKEY. "Information, Trade and Common Knowledge." *Journal of Economic Theory* 26 (January 1982), 17–27.

MILLER, MERTON H. "The Information Content of Dividends." Unpublished manuscript, July, 1985.

MYERS, STEWART C. "The Capital Structure Puzzle." *Journal of Finance* 39 (July 1984), 575–592.

OHLSON, JAMES A., and STEPHEN H. PENMAN. "Volatility Increases Subsequent to Stock Splits: An Empirical Aberration." *Journal of Financial Economics* 14 (June 1985), 251–266.

RUBINSTEIN, MARK. "Security Market Efficiency in an Arrow-Debreu Economy." *American Economic Review* 65 (December 1975), 812–824.

RUSSELL, THOMAS, and RICHARD THALER. "The Relevance of Quasi Rationality in Competitive Markets." *American Economic Review* 75 (December 1985), 1071–1082.

SHEFRIN, HERSH, and MEIR STATMAN. "Comparing Two Theories of Dividend Function." Unpublished manuscript, April, 1985.

SHILLER, ROBERT J. "Do Stock Prices Move Too Much to be Justified by Subsequent Changes in Dividends?" *American Economic Review* 71 (June 1981), 421–436.

————. "Stock Prices and Social Dynamics." *Brookings Papers on Economic Activity* 2 (December 1984), 457–498.

SHLEIFER, ANDREI. "Do Demand Curves for Stocks Slope Down?" *Journal of Finance* 41 (July 1986), 579–590.

SUMMERS, LAWRENCE H. "Do We Really Know That Financial Markets are Efficient?" *Journal of Finance* 41 (July 1986), 591–602.

TIROLE, JEAN. "On the Possibility of Speculation under Rational Expectations." *Econometrica* 50 (September 1982), 1163–1181.

TOPEL, ROBERT, and LAURENCE WEISS. "Sectoral Uncertainty and Unemployment." University of California at San Diego Economics Department Discussion Paper 85-27, September, 1985.

TVERSKY, AMOS, and DANIEL KAHNEMAN. "The Framing of Decisions and the Psychology of Choice." *Science* 211 (30 January 1981), 453–458.

VARIAN, HAL R. "Differences of Opinion and the Volume of Trade." University of Michigan Department of Economics Discussion Paper C-67, June, 1985.

ZARNOWITZ, VICTOR. "Recent Work on Business Cycles in Historical Perspective: A Review of Theories and Evidence." *Journal of Economic Literature* 23 (June 1985), 523–580.

2

Noise Trader Risk in Financial Markets

J. BRADFORD DE LONG,
ANDREI SHLEIFER, LAWRENCE H. SUMMERS,
and ROBERT J. WALDMANN

There is considerable evidence that many investors do not follow economists' advice to buy and hold the market portfolio. Individual investors typically fail to diversify, holding instead a single stock or a small number of stocks (Lewellen, Schlarbaum, and Lease 1974). They often pick stocks through their own research or on the advice of the likes of Joe Granville or "Wall Street Week." When investors do diversify, they entrust their money to stock-picking mutual funds that charge them high fees while failing to beat the market (Jensen 1968). Black (1986) believes that such investors, with no access to inside information, irrationally act on noise as if it were information that would give them an edge. Following Kyle (1985), Black calls such investors "noise traders."

Despite the recognition of the abundance of noise traders in the market, economists feel safe ignoring them in most discussions of asset price formation. The argument against the importance of noise traders for price formation has been forcefully made by Friedman (1953) and Fama (1965). Both authors point out that irrational investors are met in the market by rational arbitrageurs who trade against them and in the process drive prices close to fundamental values. Moreover, in the course of such trading, those whose judgments of asset values are sufficiently mistaken to affect prices lose money to arbitrageurs and so eventually disappear from

From: *Journal of Political Economy*, 1990, vol. 98, no. 4, pp. 703–738. © 1990 by The University of Chicago. All rights reserved. 0022-3808/90/9804-0004$01.50. Reprinted by permission of The University of Chicago Press.

23

the market. The argument "that speculation is . . . destabilizing . . . is largely equivalent to saying that speculators lose money, since speculation can be destabilizing in general only if speculators on . . . average sell . . . low . . . and buy . . . high" (Friedman 1953, p. 175). Noise traders thus cannot affect prices too much and, even if they can, will not do so for long.

In this paper we examine these arguments by focusing explicitly on the limits of arbitrage dedicated to exploiting noise traders' misperceptions. We recognize that arbitrageurs are likely to be risk averse and to have reasonably short horizons. As a result, their willingness to take positions against noise traders is limited. One source of risk that limits the power of arbitrage—fundamental risk—is well understood. Figlewski (1979) shows that it might take a very long time for noise traders to lose most of their money if arbitrageurs must bear fundamental risk in betting against them and so take limited positions. Shiller (1984) and Campbell and Kyle (1987) focus on arbitrageurs' aversion to fundamental risk in discussing the effect of noise traders on stock market prices. Their results show that aversion to fundamental risk can by itself severely limit arbitrage, even when arbitrageurs have infinite horizons.

But there is another important source of risk borne by short-horizon investors engaged in arbitrage against noise traders: the risk that noise traders' beliefs will not revert to their mean for a long time and might in the meantime become even more extreme. If noise traders today are pessimistic about an asset and have driven down its price, an arbitrageur buying this asset must recognize that in the near future noise traders might become even more pessimistic and drive the price down even further. If the arbitrageur has to liquidate before the price recovers, he suffers a loss. Fear of this loss should limit his original arbitrage position.

Conversely, an arbitrageur selling an asset short when bullish noise traders have driven its price up must remember that noise traders might become even more bullish tomorrow, and so must take a position that accounts for the risk of a further price rise when he has to buy back the stock. This risk of a further change of noise traders' opinion away from its mean—which we refer to as "noise trader risk"—must be borne by any arbitrageur with a short time horizon and must limit his willingness to bet against noise traders.

Because the unpredictability of noise traders' future opinions deters arbitrage, prices can diverge significantly from fundamental values even when there is no fundamental risk. Noise traders thus create their own space. All the main results of our paper come from the observation that arbitrage does not eliminate the effects of noise because noise itself creates risk.[1]

The risk resulting from stochastic changes in noise traders' opinions raises the possibility that noise traders who are on average bullish earn a higher expected return than rational, sophisticated investors engaged in arbitrage against noise trading. This result obtains because noise trader risk makes assets less attractive to risk-averse arbitrageurs and so drives down prices. If noise traders on average overestimate returns or underestimate risk, they invest more in the risky asset on average than sophisticated investors and may earn higher average returns. This result is more interesting than the point that if noise traders bear more fundamental risk they earn higher returns: our point is that noise traders can earn higher expected returns solely by bearing more of the risk that they themselves create. Noise traders can earn higher expected returns from their own destabilizing influence, not because they perform the useful social function of bearing fundamental risk.

Our model also has several implications for asset price behavior. Because noise trader risk limits the effectiveness of arbitrage, prices in our model are excessively volatile. If noise traders' opinions follow a stationary process, there is a mean-reverting component in stock returns. Our model also shows how assets subject to noise trader risk can be underpriced relative to fundamental values. We apply this idea to explain the underpricing of closed-end mutual funds, as well as the long-run underpricing of stocks known as the Mehra-Prescott (1985) puzzle. Finally, our model has several implications for the optimal investment strategy of sophisticated investors and for the possible role of long-term investors in stabilizing asset prices.

We develop our two main arguments—that bearing noise trader risk raises noise traders' returns and that noise trader risk can explain several financial anomalies—in five sections. Section I presents a model of noise trader risk and shows how prices can diverge significantly from fundamental values. Section II calculates the relative expected returns of noise traders and of sophisticated investors. Section III analyzes the persistence of noise traders in an extended model in which successful investors are imitated (as in Denton [1985]). Section IV presents qualitative implications of the model for the behavior of asset prices and market participants. Section V presents conclusions.

---

1. Our paper is related to other examinations of Friedman's arguments, including Hart and Kreps (1986), Ingram (1987), and Stein (1987). Also relevant are Haltiwanger and Waldman (1985) and Russell and Thaler (1985). We discuss these papers after presenting our model.

1. Noise Trading as a Source of Risk

The model contains noise traders and sophisticated investors. Noise traders falsely believe that they have special information about the future price of the risky asset. They may get their pseudosignals from technical analysts, stockbrokers, or economic consultants irrationally believe that these signals carry information. Or in formulating their investment strategies, they may exhibit the fallacy of excessive subjective certainty that has been repeatedly demonstrated in experimental contexts since Alpert and Raiffa (1982). Noise traders select their portfolios on the basis of such incorrect beliefs. In response to noise traders' actions, it is optimal for sophisticated investors to exploit noise traders' irrational misperceptions. Sophisticated traders buy when noise traders depress prices and sell when noise traders push prices up. Such active contrarian investment strategies push prices toward fundamentals, but not all the way.

1.1 The Model

Our basic model is a stripped-down overlapping generations model with two-period-lived agents (Samuelson 1958). For simplicity, there is no first-period consumption, no labor supply decision, and no bequest. As a result, the resources agents have to invest are exogenous. The only decision agents make is to choose a portfolio when young.

The economy contains two assets that pay identical dividends. One of the assets, the safe asset s, pays a fixed real dividend r. Asset s is in perfectly elastic supply: a unit of it can be created out of, and a unit of it turned back into, a unit of the consumption good in any period. With consumption each period taken as numeraire, the price of the safe asset is always fixed at one. The dividend r paid on asset s is thus the riskless rate. The other asset, the unsafe asset u, always pays the same fixed real dividend r as asset s. But u is not in elastic supply: it is in fixed and unchangeable quantity, normalized at one unit. The price of u in period t is denoted p_t. If the price of each asset were equal to the net present value of its future dividends, then assets u and s would be perfect substitutes and would sell for the same price of one in all periods. But this is not how the price of u is determined in the presence of noise traders.

We usually interpret s as a riskless short-term bond and u as aggregate equities. It is important for the analysis below that noise trader risk be marketwide rather than idiosyncratic. If noise traders' misperceptions of the returns to individual assets are uncorrelated and if each asset is small relative to the market, arbitrageurs would eliminate any possible mispricing for the same reasons that idiosyncratic risk is not priced in the standard capital asset pricing model.

There are two types of agents: sophisticated investors (denoted i) who have rational expectations and noise traders (denoted n). We assume that noise traders are present in the model in measure μ, that sophisticated investors are present in measure $1 - \mu$, and that all agents of a given type are identical. Both types of agents choose their portfolios when young to maximize perceived expected utility given their own beliefs about the ex ante mean of the distribution of the price of u at $t + 1$. The representative sophisticated investor young in period t accurately perceives the distribution of returns from holding the risky asset, and so maximizes expected utility given that distribution. The representative noise trader young in period t misperceives the expected price of the risky asset by an independent and identically distributed normal random variable ρ_t:

$$\rho_t \sim N(\rho^*, \sigma_\rho^2). \tag{1}$$

The mean misperception ρ^* is a measure of the average "bullishness" of the noise traders, and σ_ρ^2 is the variance of noise traders' misperceptions of the expected return per unit of the risky asset.[2] Noise traders thus maximize their own expectation of utility given the next-period dividend, the one-period variance of p_{t+1}, and their false belief that the distribution of the price of u next period has mean ρ_t above its true value.

Each agent's utility is a constant absolute risk aversion function of wealth when old:

$$U = -e^{-(2\gamma)w}, \tag{2}$$

where γ is the coefficient of absolute risk aversion. With normally distributed returns to holding a unit of the risky asset, maximizing the expected value of (2) is equivalent to maximizing

$$\bar{w} - \gamma\sigma_w^2, \tag{3}$$

where w is the expected final wealth, and σ_w^2 is the one-period-ahead variance of wealth. The sophisticated investor chooses the amount λ_t^i of the risky asset u held to maximize

$$
\begin{aligned}
E(U) &= \bar{w} - \gamma\sigma_w^2 \\
&= c_0 + \lambda_t^i[r + {}_tp_{t+1} - p_t(1 + r)] - \gamma(\lambda_t^i)^2({}_t\sigma_{p_{t+1}}^2),
\end{aligned}
\tag{4}
$$

2. The assumption that noise traders misperceive the expected price hides the fact that the expected price is itself a function of the parameters ρ^* and σ_ρ^2. Thus we are implicitly assuming that noise traders know how to factor the effect of future price volatility into their calculations of values. This assumption is made for simplicity. We have also solved a more complicated model that parameterizes noise traders' beliefs by their expectations of future prices, not by their misperceptions of future returns. The thrust of the results is the same.

where c_0 is a function of first-period labor income, an anterior subscript denotes the time at which an expectation is taken, and we define

$$_t\sigma^2_{p_{t+1}} = E_t\{[p_{t+1} - E_t(p_{t+1})]^2\} \tag{5}$$

to be the one-period variance of p_{t+1}. The representative noise trader maximizes

$$\begin{aligned} E(U) &= \bar{w} - \gamma\sigma^2_w \\ &= c_0 + \lambda^n_t[r + {}_tp_{t+1} - p_t(1 + r)] - \gamma(\lambda^n_t)^2({}_t\sigma^2_{p_{t+1}}) + \lambda^n_t(\rho_t). \end{aligned} \tag{6}$$

The only difference between (4) and (6) is the last term in (6), which captures the noise traders' misperception of the expected return from holding λ^n_t units of the risky asset.

Given their beliefs, all young agents divide their portfolios between u and s. The quantities λ^n_t and λ^i_t of the risky asset purchased are functions of its price p_t, of the one-period-ahead distribution of the price of u, and (in the case of noise traders) of their misperception ρ_t of the expected price of the risky asset. When old, agents convert their holdings of s to the consumption good, sell their holdings of u for price p_{t+1} to the new young, and consume all their wealth.

One can think of alternative ways of specifying noise trader demands.[3] There are well-defined mappings between misperceptions of returns ρ_t and (a) noise traders' fixing a price p_t at which they will buy and sell, (b) noise traders' purchasing a fixed quantity λ^n_t of the risky asset, or (c) noise traders' mistaking the variance of returns (taking them to be σ^{2*} instead of σ^2). The equilibrium in which noise traders matter found in our basic model exists regardless of which primitive specification of noise traders' behavior is assumed.

Solving (4) and (6) yields expressions for agents' holdings of u:

$$\lambda^i_t = \frac{r + {}_tp_{t+1} - (1 + r)p_t}{2\gamma({}_t\sigma^2_{p_{t+1}})}, \tag{7}$$

3. Let noise traders set

$$p_t = 1 - \frac{2\gamma}{r}\sigma^2 + \frac{\mu\rho^*}{r} + \frac{\mu(\rho_t - \rho^*)}{1 + r},$$

where σ^2 is the total variance—the sum of "fundamental" dividend variance, noise trader–generated price variance, and any covariance terms—associated with holding the risky asset u for one period. Alternatively, let noise traders set the quantity of the risky asset that they buy—whatever its price—as $\lambda^n_t = 1 + [\rho_t/(2\gamma)\sigma^2]$ or let the noise traders misperceive the variance of returns on the risky asset, taking as the variance

$$\sigma^{2*} = \sigma^2\left(\frac{\gamma\sigma^2 - \rho_t}{\gamma\sigma^2 + \rho_t}\right).$$

$$\lambda_t^n = \frac{r + {}_tp_{t+1} - (1 + r)p_t}{2\gamma({}_t\sigma^2_{p_{t+1}})} + \frac{\rho_t}{2\gamma({}_t\sigma^2_{p_{t+1}})}. \tag{8}$$

We allow noise traders' and sophisticated investors' demands to be negative; they can take short positions at will. Even if investors hold only
positive amounts of both assets, the fact that returns are unbounded gives
each investor a chance of having negative final wealth. We use a standard
specification of returns at the cost of allowing consumption to be negative
with positive probability.[4]

Under our assumptions on preferences and the distribution of returns,
the demands for the risky asset are proportional to its perceived excess
return and inversely proportional to its perceived variance. The additional term in the demand function of noise traders comes from their
misperception of the expected return. When noise traders overestimate
expected returns, they demand more of the risky asset than sophisticated
investors do; when they underestimate the expected return, they demand
less. Sophisticated investors exert a stabilizing influence in this model
since they offset the volatile positions of the noise traders.

The variance of prices appearing in the denominators of the demand
functions is derived solely from noise trader risk. Both noise traders and
sophisticated investors limit their demand for asset u because the price
at which they can sell it when old depends on the uncertain beliefs of
next period's young noise traders. This uncertainty about the price for
which asset u can be sold afflicts all investors, no matter what their beliefs
about expected returns, and so limits the extent to which they are willing
to bet against each other. If the price next period were certain, then
noise traders and sophisticated investors would hold with certainty different beliefs about expected returns; they would therefore try to take infinite bets against each other. An equilibrium would not exist. Noise trader
risk limits all investors' positions and in particular keeps arbitrageurs
from driving prices all the way to fundamental values.

1.2 The Pricing Function

To calculate equilibrium prices, observe that the old sell their holdings,
and so the demands of the young must sum to one in equilibrium. Equations (7) and (8) imply that

$$p_t = \frac{1}{1 + r}[r + {}_tp_{t+1} - 2\gamma({}_t\sigma^2_{p_{t+1}}) + \mu\rho_t]. \tag{9}$$

---

4. An appendix of our working paper (De Long et al. 1987) presents an example in which
asset prices and consumption are always positive.

Equation (9) expresses the risky asset's price in period t as a function of period t's misperception by noise traders (ρ_t), of the technological (r) and behavioral (γ) parameters of the model, and of the moments of the one-period-ahead distribution of p_{t+1}. We consider only steady-state equilibria by imposing the requirement that the unconditional distribution of p_{t+1} be identical to the distribution of p_t. The endogenous one-period-ahead distribution of the price of asset u can then be eliminated from (9) by solving recursively:[5]

$$p_t = 1 + \frac{\mu(\rho_t - \rho^*)}{1 + r} + \frac{\mu\rho^*}{r} - \frac{2\gamma}{r}({}_t\sigma^2_{p_{t+1}}). \tag{10}$$

Inspection of (10) reveals that only the second term is variable, for γ, ρ^*, and r are all constants, and the one-step-ahead variance of p_t is a simple unchanging function of the constant variance of a generation of noise traders' misperception ρ_t:

$$_t\sigma^2_{p_{t+1}} = \sigma^2_{p_{t+1}} = \frac{\mu^2\sigma^2_\rho}{(1 + r)^2}. \tag{11}$$

The final form of the pricing rule for u, in which the price depends only on exogenous parameters of the model and on public information about present and future misperception by noise traders, is

$$p_t = 1 + \frac{\mu(\rho_t - \rho^*)}{1 + r} + \frac{\mu\rho^*}{r} - \frac{(2\gamma)\mu^2\sigma^2_\rho}{r(1 + r)^2}. \tag{12}$$

1.3 Interpretation

The last three terms that appear in (12) and (10) show the impact of noise traders on the price of asset u. As the distribution of ρ_t converges to a point mass at zero, the equilibrium pricing function (12) converges to its fundamental value of one.

The second term in (12) captures the fluctuations in the price of the risky asset u due to the variation of noise traders' misperceptions. Even though asset u is not subject to any fundamental uncertainty and is so

---

5. The model cannot have stationary bubble equilibria, for the safe asset is formally equivalent to a storage technology that pays a rate of return r greater than the growth rate of the economy. The number of stationary equilibria in the model does, however, depend on the primitive specification of noise traders' behavior. For example, if noise traders randomly pick each period the price p_t at which they will buy and sell unlimited quantities of the risky asset, then (trivially) there is only one equilibrium. If the noise traders randomly pick the quantity λ^i_t that they purchase, then the fundamental solution in which p_t is always equal to one is an equilibrium in addition to the equilibrium in which noise traders matter.

known by a large class of investors, its price varies substantially as noise traders' opinions shift. When a generation of noise traders is more bullish than the average generation, they bid up the price of u. When they are more bearish than average, they bid down the price. When they hold their average misperception—when $\rho_t = \rho^*$—the term is zero. As one would expect, the more numerous noise traders are relative to sophisticated investors, the more volatile asset prices are.

The third term in (12) captures the deviations of p_t from its fundamental value due to the fact that the average misperception by noise traders is not zero. If noise traders are bullish on average, this "price pressure" effect makes the price of the risky asset higher than it would otherwise be. Optimistic noise traders bear a greater than average share of price risk. Since sophisticated investors bear a smaller share or price risk the higher ρ^* is, they require a lower expected excess return and so are willing to pay a higher price for asset u.

The final term in (12) is the heart of the model. Sophisticated investors would not hold the risky asset unless compensated for bearing the risk that noise traders will become bearish and the price of the risky asset will fall. Both noise traders and sophisticated investors present in period t believe that asset u is mispriced, but because p_{t+1} is uncertain, neither group is willing to bet too much on this mispricing. At the margin, the return from enlarging one's position in an asset that everyone agrees is mispriced (but different types think is mispriced in different directions) is offset by the additional price risk that must be run. Noise traders thus "create their own space": the uncertainty over what next period's noise traders will believe makes the otherwise riskless asset u risky and drives its price down and its return up. This is so despite the fact that both sophisticated investors and noise traders always hold portfolios that possess the same amount of fundamental risk: zero. Any intuition to the effect that investors in the risky asset "ought" to receive higher expected returns because they perform the valuable social function of risk bearing neglects to consider that noise traders' speculation is the only source of risk. For the economy as a whole, there is no risk to be borne.

The reader might suspect that our results are critically dependent on the overlapping generations structure of the model, but this is not quite accurate. Equilibrium exists as long as the returns to holding the risky asset are always uncertain. In the overlapping generations structure, this is assured by the absence of a last period. For if there is a last period in which the risky asset pays a nonstochastic dividend and is liquidated, then both noise traders and sophisticated investors will seek to exploit what they see as riskless arbitrage. If, say, the liquidation value of the risky asset is $1 + r$, previous-period sophisticated investors will try to trade arbitrarily large amounts of asset u at any price other than one, and noise traders will try to trade arbitrarily large amounts at any price other than

$$p_t = 1 + \frac{\rho_t}{1 + r}. \qquad (13)$$

The excess demand function for the risky asset will be undefined and the model will have no equilibrium. But in a model with fundamental dividend risk the assumption that there is no last period and, hence, the overlapping generations structure are not necessary. With fundamental dividend risk, no agent is ever subjectively certain what the return on the risky asset will be, and so the qualitative properties of equilibrium in our model are preserved even with a known terminal date. The overlapping generations structure is therefore not needed when fundamental dividend risk is present.

The infinitely extended overlapping generations structure of the basic model does play another function. It assures that each agent's horizon is short. No agent has any opportunity to wait until the price of the risky asset recovers before selling. Such an overlapping generations structure may be a fruitful way of modeling the effects on prices of a number of institutional features, such as frequent evaluations of money managers' performance, that may lead rational, long-lived market participants to care about short-term rather than long-term performance. In our model, the horizon of the typical investor is important. If sophisticated investors' horizons are long relative to the duration of noisy traders' optimism or pessimism toward risky assets, then they can buy low, confident that they will be able to sell high when prices revert to the mean. As we show below, as the horizon of agents becomes longer, arbitrage becomes less risky and prices approach fundamental values. Noise trader risk is an important deterrent to arbitrage only when the duration of noise traders' misperceptions is of the same order of magnitude as or longer than the horizon of sophisticated investors.

2. Relative Returns of Noise Traders and Sophisticated Investors

We have demonstrated that noise traders can affect prices even though there is no uncertainty about fundamentals. Friedman (1953) argues that noise traders who affect prices earn lower returns than the sophisticated investors they trade with, and so economic selection works to weed them out. In our model, it need not be the case that noise traders earn lower returns. Noise traders' collective shifts of opinion increase the riskiness of returns to assets. If noise traders' portfolios are concentrated in assets subject to noise trader risk, noise traders can earn a higher average rate of return on their portfolios than sophisticated investors.

2.1 Relative Expected Returns

The conditions under which noise traders earn higher expected returns than sophisticated investors are easily laid out. All agents earn a certain net return of r on their investments in asset s. The difference between noise traders' and sophisticated investors' total returns given equal initial wealth is the product of the difference in their holdings of the risky asset u and the excess return paid by a unit of the risky asset u. Call this differe ce in returns to the two types of agents ΔR_{n-i}:

$$\Delta R_{n-i} = (\lambda_t^n - \lambda_t^i)[r + p_{t+1} - p_t(1 + r)]. \tag{14}$$

The d ference between noise traders' and sophisticated investors' demands or asset u is

$$\lambda_t^n - \lambda_t^i = \frac{\rho_t}{(2\gamma)_t \sigma_{p_{t+1}}^2} = \frac{(1 + r)^2 \rho_t}{(2\gamma)\mu^2 \sigma_\rho^2}. \tag{15}$$

Note that as μ becomes small, (15) becomes large: noise traders and sophisticated investors take enormous positions of opposite signs because the small amount of noise trader risk makes each group think that it has an almost riskless arbitrage opportunity. In the limit in which $\mu = 0$, equilibrium no longer exists (in the absence of fundamental risk) because the two groups try to place infinite bets against each other.

The expected value of the excess return on the risky asset u as of time t is

$$_t[r + p_{t+1} - p_t(1 + r)] = (2\gamma)_t \sigma_{p_{t+1}}^2 - \mu\rho_t = \frac{(2\gamma)\mu^2 \sigma_\rho^2}{(1 + r)^2} - \mu\rho_t. \tag{16}$$

And so

$$_t(\Delta R_{n-t}) = \rho_t - \frac{(1 + r)^2 (\rho_t)^2}{(2\gamma)\mu\sigma_\rho^2}. \tag{17}$$

The expected excess total return of noise traders is positive only if both noise traders are optimistic (ρ_t is positive, which makes [15] positive) and the risky asset is priced below its fundamental value (which makes [16] positive).

Taking the global unconditional expectation of (17) yields

$$E(\Delta R_{n-i}) = \rho^* - \frac{(1 + r)^2(\rho^*)^2 + (1 + r)^2\sigma_\rho^2}{(2\gamma)\mu\sigma_\rho^2}. \tag{18}$$

Equation (18) makes obvious the requirement that for noise traders to earn higher expected returns, the mean misperception ρ^* of returns on the risky asset must be positive. The first ρ^* on the right-hand side of (18) increases noise traders' expected returns through what might be called the "hold more" effect. Noise traders' expected returns relative to those of sophisticated investors are increased when noise traders on average hold more of the risky asset and earn a larger share of the rewards to risk bearing. When ρ^* is negative, noise traders' changing misperceptions still make the fundamentally riskless asset u risky and still push up the expected return on asset u, but the rewards to risk bearing accrue disproportionately to sophisticated investors, who on average hold more of the risky asset than the noise traders do.

The first term in the numerator in (18) incorporates the "price pressure" effect. As noise traders become more bullish, they demand more of the risky asset on average and drive up its price. They thus reduce the return to risk bearing and, hence, the differential between their returns and those of sophisticated investors.

The second term in the numerator incorporates the buy high–sell low or "Friedman" effect. Because noise traders' misperceptions are stochastic, they have the worst possible market timing. They buy the most of the risky asset u just when other noise traders are buying it, which is when they are most likely to suffer a capital loss. The more variable noise traders' beliefs are, the more damage their poor market timing does to their returns.

The denominator incorporates the "create space" effect central to this model. As the variability of noise traders' beliefs increases, the price risk increases. To take advantage of noise traders' misperceptions, sophisticated investors must bear this greater risk. Since sophisticated investors are risk averse, they reduce the extent to which they bet against noise traders in response to this increased risk. If the create space effect is large, then the price pressure and buy high–sell low effects inflict less damage on noise traders' average returns relative to sophisticated investors' returns.

Two effects—hold more and create space—tend to raise noise traders' relative expected returns. Two effects—the Friedman and price pressure effects—tend to lower noise traders' relative expected returns. Neither pair clearly dominates. Noise traders cannot earn higher average returns if they are on average bearish, for if ρ^* does not exceed zero, there is no hold more effect and (18) must be negative. Nor can noise traders earn higher average returns if they are too bullish, for as ρ^* gets large the price pressure effect, which increases with $(\rho^*)^2$, dominates. For intermediate degrees of average bullishness, noise traders earn higher expected returns. And it is clear from (18) that the larger γ is, that is, the more risk averse agents are, the larger is the range of ρ^* over which noise traders earn higher average returns.

2.2 Relative Utility Levels

The higher expected returns of the noise traders come at the cost of holding portfolios with sufficiently higher variance to give noise traders lower expected utility (computed using the true distribution of wealth when old). Since sophisticated investors maximize true expected utility, any trading strategy alternative to theirs that earns a higher mean return must have a variance sufficiently higher to make it unattractive. The average amount of asset s that must be given to old noise traders to give them the ex ante expected utility of sophisticated investors can be shown to be

$$\frac{(1 + r)^2}{(4\gamma)\mu^2}\left(1 + \frac{\rho^{*2}}{\sigma_\rho^2}\right). \tag{19}$$

This amount is decreasing in the variance and increasing in the square of the mean of noise traders' misperceptions. The size of their mistakes grows with ρ^*, but the risk penalty for attempting to exploit noise traders' mistakes grows with σ_ρ^2. Noise traders receive the same average realized utility when $\rho^* = x$ as when $\rho^* = -x$, but when $\rho^* > 0$, they may receive higher average returns. When $\rho^* < 0$, noise traders receive both lower realized utility levels and lower average returns.

Sophisticated investors are necessarily better off when noise traders are present in this model. In the absence of noise traders, sophisticated investors' opportunities are limited to investing at the riskless rate r. The presence of noise traders gives sophisticated investors a larger opportunity set, in that they can still invest all they want at the riskless rate r, but they can also trade in the unsafe asset. Access to a larger opportunity set clearly raises sophisticated investors' expected utility.[6]

6. If the stock of the risky asset is endogenous—if there is a nontrivial capital supply decision—sophisticated investors can be worse off with noise traders present. If noise traders make capital riskier and reduce the price of risk, they reduce the opportunity set of sophisticated investors and their welfare (De Long et al. 1989).

Noise traders receive higher average consumption than sophisticated investors, and sophisticated investors receive higher average consumption than in fundamental equilibrium. Yet the productive resources available to society—its labor income per period, its ability to create the productive asset s, and the unit amount of asset u yielding its dividend r per period—are unchanged by the presence of noise trading. The source of extra returns is made clear by the following thought experiment. Imagine that before some date τ there are no noise traders. Up until time τ, both assets sell at a price of one. At τ it is unexpectedly announced that in the next generation noise traders will appear. The price p_τ of the asset u drops; those who hold asset u in period τ suffer a capital loss. This capital loss is the source of the excess returns and of the higher consumption in the equilibrium with noise. The period τ young have more to invest in s because they pay less to the old for the stock of asset u. If at time ω it became known that noise traders had permanently withdrawn, then those who held u at time ω would capture the present value of what would otherwise have been future excess returns as p_ω jumped to one. The same super-normal return would also be received by a generation that suddenly acquired the opportunity to "bust up" the risky asset by turning it into an equivalent quantity of the safe asset. The fact that the generation that suffers from the arrival of noise traders is pushed off to negative infinity in the model creates the appearance of a free lunch.[7]

2.3 A Comparison with Other Work

The fact that bullish noise traders can earn higher returns in the market than sophisticated traders implies that Friedman's simple "market selection" argument is incomplete.[8] Since noise traders' wealth can increase faster than sophisticated investors', it is not possible to make any blanket statement that noise traders lose money and eventually become unimportant. One should not overinterpret our result. The greater variance of noise traders' returns might give them in the long run a high probability of having low wealth and a low probability of having very high wealth. Market selection might work against such traders even if their expected value of wealth is high since they would be poor virtually for certain. A

7. In practice, the cost of future noise trader risk in a security will be paid for by whoever sells it to the public. In the case of a stock, the cost will be paid by the entrepreneur.

8. The key difference from Friedman's (1953) model is that here the demand curve of sophisticated investors shifts in response to the addition of noise traders and the resulting increase in risk. Because of this shift, sophisticated investors' expected returns may fall even though their expected utility rises.

more appropriate selection criterion would take this into account, but we have not found a tractable way to implement such a selection criterion in a model in which noise traders affect prices.[9]

At this point we can compare our results with recent discussions of Friedman's argument that destabilizing speculation is unprofitable, and so profitable speculation must be stabilizing. Hart and Kreps (1986) point out that an injection of rational investors able to perform profitable intertemporal trade could destabilize prices. In our model, rational speculation is always stabilizing, but average returns earned by rational speculators need not be as high as those earned by noise traders. In Stein (1987), speculators' access to private information allows for profitable destabilizing speculation. In our model, arbitrageurs know exactly the way in which noise traders are confused today, and noise traders have no private information. The uncertainty that affects noise traders and sophisticated investors equally concerns the behavior of noise traders tomorrow. Haltiwanger and Waldman (1985) and Russell and Thaler (1985) study the effects of irrational behavior on prices in the presence of externalities and of restrictions on trade, respectively. Our model is related to Russell and Thaler's, in that the short horizon of arbitrageurs can be interpreted as a form of restriction on trade.

3. Imitation of Beliefs

We have already observed that noise traders earn higher expected returns than sophisticated investors. This at least raises the possibility that their importance does not diminish over time. Our two-period model does not permit us to examine the accumulation of wealth by noise traders. As an alternative approach, we consider two rules describing the emulative behavior of new generations of traders. While it is possible to think of the succession of generations of investors in our model as families, a more relevant image of a new investor entering the market is that of a pension fund searching for a new money manager. Our new investors collect information about the performance of the past generation and decide which strategy to follow. The first approach is to postulate that new investors respond only to recent returns achieved by different investment strategies and are not able to accurately assess the ex ante risks undertaken. For this case, we show that noise traders' effects on prices do not inevitably diminish over time. In our second approach, new investors select their investment strategies on the basis of recent utility

---

9. De Long et al. (1988) consider the evolution of the wealth distribution in a model in which noise traders have no effect on prices.

levels realized by these strategies. For this case, we show that noise traders' influence necessarily diminishes over time. We stress, however, that even readers preferring the second imitation rule should consider the *empirical* implications of our model. Under the P. T. Barnum rule that a noise trader is born every minute, a steady supply of new noise traders enters the market every period (as in our basic model) even if their strategies are not imitated.

3.1 A Model of Imitation Based on Realized Returns without Fundamental Risk

Each generation of investors earns exogenous labor income when young and consumes all its wealth when old. Each generation has the same number of investors following noise trader and sophisticated investor strategies as the previous one, except a few investors in each generation change type on the basis of the past relative performance of the two strategies. If noise traders earn a higher return in any period, a fraction of the young who would otherwise have been sophisticated investors become noise traders, and vice versa if noise traders earn a lower return. Moreover, the higher the difference in realized returns in any period, the more people switch. Letting μ_t be the share of the population that are noise traders and R_t^n and R_t^s be the realized returns of noise traders and sophisticated investors, we assume that

$$\mu_{t+1} = \max\{0, \min[1, \mu_t + \zeta(R_n - R_i)]\}, \qquad (20)$$

where ζ is the rate at which additional new investors become noise traders per unit difference in realized returns.[10]

Equation (20) says that success breeds imitation: investment strategies that made their followers richer win converts. Underlying this imitation rule is the idea that new money entering the market is not completely sure which investment strategy to pursue. If sophisticated investors have earned a high return recently, new investors try to allocate their wealth mimicking sophisticated investors, or perhaps even entrusting their wealth to sophisticated money managers. If noise trader strategies have earned a higher return recently, new investors imitate those strategies to a greater extent. One way to interpret this imitation rule is that *some* new investors use what Black (1986) calls pseudosignals, such as the past return, to decide which strategy to follow.

10. An alternative learning rule, studied by Bray (1982), would make the conversion parameter ζ a function of time: $\zeta_t = \zeta_0/t$. Under this alternative conversion rule, the noise trader share would converge to an element of the set $\{0, 1\}$ in the model without fundamental risk and to an element of the set $\{\mu_L, 1\}$ in the model with fundamental risk studied in the following subsection.

This model can be easily solved only if ζ is very close to zero. If ζ is significantly different from zero at the scale of any one generation, then those investing in period t have to calculate the effect of the realization of returns on the division of those young in period $t + 1$ between noise traders and sophisticated investors. If ζ is sufficiently small, then returns can be calculated under the approximation that the noise trader share will be unchanged.

Equation (12), the pricing rule with a constant number of noise traders, with μ changed to μ_t, gives the limit as ζ converges to zero of the pricing rule for the model with imitation:

$$p_t = 1 + \frac{\mu_t(\rho_t - \rho^*)}{1 + r} + \frac{\mu_t\rho^*}{r} - \frac{(2\gamma)\mu_t^2\sigma_\rho^2}{r(1 + r)^2}. \tag{21}$$

The expected return gap between noise traders and sophisticated investors is equation (17) when the proportion of noise traders is fixed at μ. With the proportion μ_t variable, the limit of the expected return gap as ζ converges to zero is given by

$$E_t(\Delta R_{n-i}) = \rho_t - \frac{(1 + r)^2(\rho_t)^2}{(2\gamma)\mu_t\sigma_\rho^2}. \tag{22}$$

Over time, μ_t tends to grow or shrink as (22) is greater or less than zero. It is then clear that although there is a value for μ_t at which $E_t(\mu_{t+1}) = \mu_t$, this value is unstable. As the share of noise traders declines, sophisticated investors' willingness to bet against them rises. Sophisticated investors then earn more money from their exploitation of noise traders' misperceptions, and the gap between the expected returns earned by noise traders and those earned by sophisticated investors becomes negative. If the noise trader share μ_t is below

$$\mu^* = \frac{(\rho^{*2} + \sigma_\rho^2)(1 + r)^2}{2\rho^*(\gamma\sigma_\rho^2)}, \tag{23}$$

then μ_t tends to shrink. If μ_t is greater than μ^*, noise traders create so much price risk as to make sophisticated investors very reluctant to speculate against them. Noise traders then earn higher average returns than sophisticated investors and grow in number. In the long run, noise traders dominate the market or effectively disappear, as shown in figure 1.

3.2 An Extension with Fundamental Risk

This subsection extends our model of imitation to the case of fundamentally risky returns on the unsafe asset. We show that the long-run distribution of the share of noise traders is very different from the case without

Figure 1   Dynamics of the noise trader share with no fundamental risk

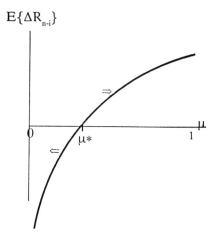

fundamental risk. Specifically, for sufficiently small values of ζ, the expected noise trader share for the steady-state distribution of μ_t is always bounded away from zero.

Let asset u pay not a certain dividend r but an uncertain dividend

$$r + \epsilon_t, \tag{24}$$

where ϵ_t is serially independent, normally distributed with zero mean and constant variance, and, for simplicity, uncorrelated with noise traders' opinions ρ_t. Asset demands then become

$$\lambda_t^i = \frac{r + E_t p_{t+1} - (1 + r) p_t}{2\gamma(\sigma_{p_{t+1}}^2 + \sigma_\epsilon^2)} \tag{25}$$

and

$$\lambda_t^n = \frac{r + E_t p_{t+1} - (1 + r) p_t}{2\gamma(\sigma_{p_{t+1}}^2 + \sigma_\epsilon^2)} + \frac{\rho_t}{2\gamma(\sigma_{p_{t+1}}^2 + \sigma_\epsilon^2)} \tag{26}$$

instead of (7) and (8). The only change is the appearance in the denominators of the asset demand functions of the total risk involved from asset u—the sum of noise trader price risk and fundamental dividend risk—instead of simply noise trader–generated price risk.

The pricing function if there is fundamental risk is transformed from (21) into

$$p_t = 1 + \frac{\mu_t \rho^*}{r} - \frac{2\gamma}{r}\left[\sigma_\epsilon^2 + \frac{\mu^2 \sigma_\rho^2}{(1 + r)^2}\right] + \frac{\mu_t(\rho_t - \rho^*)}{1 + r} \qquad (27)$$

in the limit as ζ converges to zero. The noise trader risk term is replaced by the total risk associated with holding u. The difference between expected returns of noise traders and those of sophisticated investors becomes

$$E[\Delta R_{n-i}(\mu)] = \rho^* - \frac{\rho^{*2} + \sigma_\rho^2}{2\gamma\left[\dfrac{\sigma_\rho^2 \mu}{(1 + r)^2} + \dfrac{\sigma_\epsilon^2}{\mu}\right)} \qquad (28)$$

if μ is greater than zero and

$$E[\Delta R_{n-i}(0)] = \rho^*. \qquad (29)$$

While the hold more, average price pressure, and Friedman effects are not changed by the addition of fundamental risk, the create space effect—the denominator of the second term on the right-hand side of (28)—is increased. Since holding asset u is now more risky, sophisticated investors are less willing to trade in order to exploit noise traders' mistakes. We continue to assume that $\zeta = 0$ in the calculation of prices, so that (27) is the pricing rule for this model and (28) is the difference in expected returns.

Equation (12) shows that, in the absence of fundamental risk, a sequence of economies in which μ approaches zero also has $E(\Delta R_{n-i})$ approach negative infinity. By contrast, equation (28) shows that, with fundamental risk present, $E(\Delta R_{n-i})$ approaches ρ^* as μ approaches zero. There is an intuitive explanation for the substantially different dynamics for $\sigma_\epsilon^2 = 0$ and $\sigma_\epsilon^2 > 0$. If $\sigma_\epsilon^2 > 0$, then noise traders' and sophisticated investors' demands remain bounded as μ approaches zero. For a sufficiently small noise trader share, therefore, sophisticated investors must have positive holdings of the risky asset—the very small number of noise traders cannot hold it all— and so the risky asset must offer an expected return higher than the safe rate in equilibrium. If $\sigma_\epsilon^2 = 0$, then noise traders' and sophisticated investors' demands become unbounded as μ approaches zero and the unsafe asset loses its risk. Noise traders' positions then lose them arbitrarily large amounts each period.

For parameter values that satisfy both $\rho^* > 0$ and

$$\sigma_\epsilon^2 > \frac{(1 + r)^2 (\rho^* + \sigma_\rho^2)^2}{16\gamma^2 \rho^{*2} \sigma_\rho^2}, \qquad (30)$$

equation (28) has no real roots and noise traders always earn higher expected returns. In this case, for sufficiently small values for ζ the expected long-run noise trader share is close to one.

For parameter values such that (30) fails, (28) has two positive real roots. If the lower root $\mu_L < 1$, noise traders do not always earn higher expected returns and the expected long-run noise trader share is not in general close to one. For this case, we have proved the following proposition.

PROPOSITION. Let the pricing rule be given by (27) and the imitation rule by (20). Suppose that the equation $E[\Delta R(\mu)] = 0$ has at least one real root for $\mu \in [0, 1]$. Consider a sequence of economies indexed by n, differing only in their values of the imitation parameter ζ_n, such that $\zeta_n \to 0$ as $n \to \infty$. Then there is a $\delta > 0$ such that $E(\mu_t) \to \mu \geq \delta$ as $n \to \infty$, where the expectation is taken over the steady-state distribution of μ_t.

An appendix containing a proof is available from the authors on request.

When imitation is based on realized returns, for some parameter values the expected noise trader share of the population approaches one as ζ approaches zero. The proposition above shows, and figure 2 illustrates, that if asset u is fundamentally risky, there are no parameter values for which the expected noise trader share of the population approaches zero as ζ becomes small. This result suggests that at least one plausible form of dynamics ensures that noise traders matter and affect prices in the long run.

3.3 Imitation Based on Utility

The imitation rule (20) is based on the assumption that the rate of conversion depends on the difference in realized *returns* and not on the difference in realized *utilities*. It implicitly assumes that converts do not take account of the greater risk that noise traders bear to earn higher returns. This form of imitation requires investors to use past investors' realized returns as a proxy for success even though their own objective is to maximize not wealth but utility.

An alternative imitation rule is to make the number of new noise traders depend on the difference in *utilities* realized last period from sophisticated investor and noise trader strategies. This rule is different from (20): with concave utility, there is more switching away from a strategy in response to past low returns than switching toward a strategy in response to past high returns. Under this imitation rule, the share of noise traders in the economy in fact converges to zero as ζ approaches

Figure 2   Dynamics of the noise trader share with fundamental risk

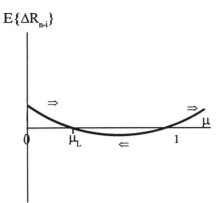

zero, in contrast to our result under (20). Since sophisticated investors maximize true expected utility, on average the realized utility of a sophisticated investor is higher than the realized utility of a noise trader. That is, under this imitation rule the higher variance of noise traders' returns costs them in terms of winning converts because it costs them in terms of average utility. For each initial state of the system, the noise trader share tends to fall under a utility difference–based imitation rule until it reaches the neighborhood of the reflecting barrier at $\mu = 0$. The expected noise trader share for the steady-state distribution of μ is no longer bounded away from zero as ζ approaches zero.

This alternative rule has considerable appeal in that imitation is based on the realization of agents' true objectives. Nonetheless, there are two reasons to prefer the wealth-based imitation rule (20). First, we find it plausible that many investors attribute the higher return of an investment strategy to the market timing skills of its practitioners and not to its greater risk. This consideration may be particularly important when we ask whether individuals change their own investment strategies that have just earned them a high return. When people imitate investment strategies, they appear to focus on standard metrics such as returns relative to market averages and do not correct for ex ante risk. As long as enough investors use the pseudosignal of realized returns to choose their own investment strategy, noise traders will persist. The second reason to focus on returns-based imitation is that Friedman (1953) argued that noise traders must earn lower average *returns* and so become unimportant. He did not argue that money-making noise traders would fail to attract imitators because potential imitators would attribute their success to luck rather than to skill. Our focus on an imitation rule in which higher wealth wins converts is closer to Friedman's argument.

4. Noise Trading and Asset Market Behavior

This section describes some implications of our model for financial markets (see also Black 1986). We show that in the presence of noise trader risk, asset returns exhibit the mean reversion documented by a great deal of empirical work, asset prices diverge on average from fundamental values as suggested by Mehra and Prescott (1985) and by the comparison of the portfolio and market values of closed-end mutual funds, and long-term investors stabilize prices. Finally, we discuss the effects of noise trader risk on corporate finance.

4.1 Volatility and Mean Reversion in Asset Prices

In our model with noise traders absent—with both ρ^* and σ_ρ^2 set equal to zero—the price of u is always equal to its fundamental value of one. When noise traders are present, the price of u—identical to s in all fundamental respects—is excessively volatile in the sense that it moves more than can be explained on the basis of changes in fundamental values. None of the variance in the price of u can be justified by changes in fundamentals: there are no changes in expected future dividends in our model or in any fundamental determinant of required returns.

Accumulating evidence suggests that it is difficult to account for all the volatility of asset prices in terms of news. Although Shiller's (1981) claim that the stock market wildly violated variance bounds imposed by the requirement that prices be discounted present values relied on controversial statistical procedures (Kleidon 1986), other evidence that asset price movements do not reflect changes in fundamental values is more clear-cut. Roll (1984) considers the orange juice futures market, where the principal source of relevant news is weather. He demonstrates that a substantial share of the movement in prices cannot be attributed to news about the weather that bears on fundamental values. Campbell and Kyle (1987) conclude that a large fraction of market movements cannot be attributed to news about future dividends and discount rates.

Such excess volatility becomes even easier to explain if we relax our assumption that all market participants are either noise traders or sophisticated investors who bet against them. A more reasonable assumption is that many traders pursue passive strategies, neither responding to noise nor betting against noise traders. If a large fraction of investors allocate a constant share of their wealth to stocks, then even a small measure of noise traders can have a large impact on prices. When noise traders try to sell, only a few sophisticated investors are willing to hold extra stock, and consequently prices must fall considerably for them to do so. The fewer sophisticated investors there are relative to the noise traders, the larger is the impact of noise.[11]

If asset prices respond to noise and if the errors of noise traders are temporary, then asset prices revert to the mean. For example, if noise traders' misperceptions follow an AR(1) process, then the serial correlation in returns decays geometrically as in the "fads" example of Summers (1986), who stresses that even with long time series it is difficult to detect slowly decaying transitory components in asset prices. Since the same problems of identification that plague econometricians affect speculators, actual market forces are likely to be less effective in limiting the effects of noise trading than in our model, where rational investors fully understand the process governing the behavior of noise traders.

Moreover, even if sophisticated investors accurately diagnose the process describing the behavior of noise traders, if misperceptions are serially correlated, they will not be willing to bet nearly as heavily against noise traders: the risk of a capital loss remains and is balanced by a smaller expected return since the next-period price is not expected to move all the way back to its fundamental value. A high unconditional variance of prices can coexist with only a small opportunity to exploit noise traders.

For an example of how rapidly unconditional price variance grows as misperceptions become persistent, assume that misperceptions follow an AR(1) process with innovation η_t and autoregressive parameter ϕ. In this case the unconditional variance of the price of u is[12]

$$\sigma_p^2 = \frac{\mu^2\sigma_\rho^2}{[r + (1 - \phi)]^2} = \frac{\mu^2\sigma_\eta^2}{[r + (1 - \phi)]^2(1 - \phi^2)}. \tag{31}$$

11. A simple example may help to make our point. Suppose that all investors are convinced that the market is efficient. They will hold the market portfolio. Now suppose that one investor decides to commit his wealth disproportionately to a single security. Its price will be driven to infinity.

12. Demand for assets depends not on the unconditional price variances but on the conditional one-step-ahead price risk. The variance of the price of u about its one-step-ahead anticipated value is

$$_t\sigma_{p_{t+1}}^2 = \frac{\mu^2\sigma_\eta^2}{[r + (1 - \phi)]^2}$$

in the case of serially correlated misperceptions.

Noise traders who earn higher expected returns than sophisticated inves-tors can thus cause larger deviations of prices from fundamental values if misperceptions are serially correlated. The difference in expected returns is given by

$$E(\Delta R_{n-t}) = \rho^* - \frac{[r + (1 - \phi)]^2(\rho^*)^2}{(2\gamma)\mu\sigma_\eta^2} - \frac{[r + (1 - \phi)]^2}{(2\gamma)\mu(1 - \phi^2)}. \tag{32}$$

Highly persistent transitory components in asset prices can be very large and still consistent with noise traders' earning higher returns than sophis-ticated investors.

There is significant evidence that stock prices indeed exhibit mean-reverting behavior. Fama and French (1988b) and Poterba and Summers (1988) demonstrate that long-horizon stock returns exhibit negative serial correlation. The fact that prices revert to the mean also implies that measures of scale have predictive power for asset returns: when prices are above p^*—that is, are high relative to their historical average multiple of dividends—prices are likely to fall in our model. In fact, Campbell and Shiller (1987), Fama and French (1988a), and other studies find that dividend/price and earnings/price ratios appear to contain substantial power for detecting transitory components in stock prices.

Many studies including Mankiw and Summers (1984) and Mankiw (1986) note that anomalies exactly paralleling the dividend/price ratio anomaly are present in the bond market. Long rates have predictive power for future short rates, but it is nonetheless the case that when long rates exceed short rates, they tend to fall and not to rise as predicted by the expectations hypothesis. While convincing stories about changing risk factors are yet to be provided, this behavior is exactly what one would expect if noise trading distorted long bond yields. Specifically, if we think of the short-term bond as asset s and the long-term bond as asset u, then the price of u exhibits the mean-reverting behavior observed in the data on long-term bonds.

In a world with mean-reverting noise traders' misperceptions, the optimal investment strategy is very different from the buy and hold strat-egy of the standard investment model. The optimal strategy for sophisti-cated investors is a *market timing* strategy that calls for increased expo-sure to stocks after they have fallen and decreased exposure to stocks after they have risen in price. The strategy of betting against noise traders is a contrarian investment strategy: it requires investment in the market at times when noise traders are bearish, in anticipation that their senti-ment will recover. The fundamentalist investment strategies of Graham and Dodd (1934) seem to be based on largely the same idea, although they are typically described in terms of individual stocks. The evidence on mean reversion in stock returns suggests that, over the long run, such contrarian strategies pay off.

As our model shows, successful pursuit of such contrarian investment strategies can require a long time horizon, and such strategies are by no means safe because of the noise trader risk that must be run. In fact, our model shows precisely why apparent anomalies such as the high dollar of the mid 1980s and the extraordinary price/earnings ratios on Japanese stocks in 1987–89 can persist for so long even when many investors recognize these anomalies. Betting against such perceived mispricing requires bearing a lot of risk. Even if the price is too high now, it can always go higher in the short run, leading to the demise of an arbitrageur with limited resources or a short time horizon.

Contrarian investment strategies work because arbitrageurs can take advantage of mean reversion in noise traders' beliefs. An alternative rational investment strategy would be to gather information about future noise trader demand shifts and to trade in anticipation of such shifts. Such information can come from examining trading volume, price patterns, buy/sell ratios, and other "chartist" indicators. Trading based on forecasting the behavior of others is not modeled here, but we consider it elsewhere (De Long et al. 1990). With short horizons, it may well be more attractive for smart money to pursue these anticipatory strategies than to wait for the reversion of noise traders' beliefs to their mean (Shleifer and Vishny 1990). In this case, we anticipate that many sophisticated investors will try to "guess better than the crowd how the crowd will behave" rather than pursue contrarian long-term arbitrage.

4.2 Asset Prices and Fundamental Values: Closed-End Mutual Funds

The efficient markets hypothesis states that assets ought to sell for their fundamental values. In most cases, fundamental value is difficult to measure, and so this prediction cannot be directly tested. But the fundamental value of a closed-end fund is easily assessed: the fund pays dividends equal to the sum of the dividends paid by the stocks in its portfolio and so should sell for the market price of its portfolio. Yet closed-end funds sell and have sold at large and substantially fluctuating discounts (Malkiel 1977; Herzfeld 1980), which have been relatively small during the bull markets of the late 1960s and the 1980s and large during the bear markets of the 1970s.

Available explanations of discounts on closed-end funds are not completely satisfactory. Two of the most prominent explanations rely on the agency costs of fund management and on the miscalculation of net asset value because of a failure to deduct the fund's capital gains tax liability. The agency theory for discounts, however, cannot explain how closed-end funds are ever rationally formed since the original investors throw away the present value of future agency costs without earning higher returns. The agency explanation is also inconsistent with the evidence that funds with higher transaction costs and stock turnover do not sell at higher discounts (Malkiel 1977) and with the correlated variability of discounts across funds (Herzfeld 1980). With respect to tax-based theories, Brauer (1984) and Brickley and Schallheim (1985) find that prices of closed-end funds rise on the announcement of open-ending or of liquidation. This result is difficult to interpret if the closed-end fund's discount reflects its unrealized capital gain tax liability since, if anything, discounts should *widen* when the fund is open-ended and tax payments can no longer be deferred. Nor can the capital gains story explain how funds trade at a premium when they get started.

The concept of noise trader risk can explain both the persistent and variable discounts on closed-end funds and the creation of such funds.[13] Think of the safe asset *s* in our model as the stocks in the closed-end fund and of the unsafe asset *u* as the fund itself. As in our model, the two securities are perfect substitutes as far as dividends are concerned and so should sell at the same price in equilibrium without noise traders. Note that it does not matter for our purposes if there is noise trading in the stocks themselves and therefore a mispricing of *s* as well. All we need is additional noise trader misperception of returns on the closed-end fund *u* that is separate from this misperception of returns on the underlying stocks. Finally, we need to assume that noise traders' misperceptions of returns on closed-end funds are correlated with other (possibly irrational) sources of systematic risk since idiosyncratic noise trader risk is not priced in our model.

Under these assumptions, the results from our basic model can be directly applied to closed-end funds. Noise traders' misperceptions about the returns on the funds become a source of risk for any short-horizon investor trying to arbitrage the difference between the fund and its underlying assets. Thus when an investor buys the fund *u* and sells short the underlying stocks *s*, he bears the risk that at the time he wants to liquidate his position the discount will be wider. Just as in our model, noise traders can become more bearish on the fund in the future than they are today, and so an arbitrageur will suffer a loss. Such risk of

---

13. It does not explain why such funds are not broken up immediately once a discount appears.

changes in noise traders' opinions of closed-end funds leads to the market's discounting of their price on average relative to the net asset value even if noise traders themselves are neither bullish nor bearish on average, that is, $\rho^* = 0$. The discount arises solely because holding the fund entails additional noise trader risk: we do not assume that noise traders are on average bearish about closed-end funds.[14]

This theory of discounts on closed-end funds makes several accurate predictions. First, it explains how the funds can get started even when on average they will be underpriced. Closed-end funds get started when noise traders are unusually optimistic about the returns on closed-end funds, that is, when ρ_t *for the funds* is unusually high. In such a case, it would pay entrepreneurs to buy stocks (asset *s*), repackage them as closed-end funds (asset *u*), and sell the closed-end funds to optimistic noise traders at a premium. This result has the implication, which has not yet been tested, that new closed-end funds are formed in clusters at the times when other closed-end funds sell at a premium.

The fluctuations in noise trader opinion of the expected return on the funds also explain why the discounts fluctuate, widening at some times and turning into premiums at others (when the funds get started). Fluctuations in discounts are in fact the reason that there is an average discount. No other theory of discounts predicts that closed-end funds sometimes sell at a premium, that changes in discounts are correlated across funds, or that new funds are started when old closed-end funds sell at a premium.

Two key assumptions must be made for this theory of closed-end fund discounts to be coherent. First, noise trader risk on the funds should

---

14. One can see how the fact that closed-end fund shares are subject not only to fundamental risk (risk affecting the value of the fund's portfolio) but also to noise trader risk (risk that the closed-end fund discount might change) affects investment decisions in the investment advice given by Malkiel (1973, 1975, 1985, 1989). He confidently recommended in 1973 that investors purchase then heavily discounted (20–30 percent) closed-end fund shares: such an investor would do better than by picking stocks or investing in an open-end fund unless "the discount widened in the future." The confidence of Malkiel's recommendation stemmed from his belief that "this . . . risk is minimized . . . [since] discounts [now] . . . are about as large as they have ever been historically" (1975, p. 263). And the obverse is his belief that the holder of a closed-end fund should be prepared to sell if the discount narrowed, not only if the discount disappeared, but also if the discount narrowed. The 4th ed. of *A Random Walk down Wall Street* does not recommend the purchase of closed-end fund shares in spite of the fact that many closed-end funds still sell at discounts. The noise trader risk that discounts may widen again in the future is a disadvantage that apparently weighs heavily against the relatively small advantages given by the small then-current discount. The 5th ed. once again recommends the purchase of closed-end funds now that the discount has widened.

be systematic and not idiosyncratic. Consistent with this assumption, discounts on different closed-end funds do seem to fluctuate together (Herzfeld 1980). Second, investors in the economy must have horizons that are with some probability shorter than the time to liquidation of the fund. If some investors on the contrary have very long horizons, they can buy the closed-end fund and sell short the underlying securities, wait until the fund is liquidated, and so lock in a capital gain without bearing any risk. Consistent with this observation, discounts become much narrower on the announcement of the open-ending of a closed-end fund (Brauer 1984). The application of our model to closed-end funds illustrates the essential role played by the finite horizon of investors.

4.3 Asset Prices and Fundamental Values: The Mehra-Prescott Puzzle

In our model, if noise traders earn higher expected returns than sophisticated investors, then the average price of u must be below its fundamental value. The expected value of p_t is

$$E(p) = p^* = 1 - \frac{2\gamma\mu\sigma_\rho^2}{r(1 + r)^2} + \frac{\mu\rho^*}{r}. \tag{33}$$

Since noise traders hold more of the risky asset and earn negative capital gains on average, they can earn higher expected returns than sophisticated investors only if the dividend on the unsafe asset amounts to a higher rate of return on average than the same dividend on the safe asset. For this to hold, the unsafe asset must sell at an average price below its fundamental value of one.

The result that noise traders earn a higher expected return whenever the unsafe asset is priced below its fundamental value may shed some light on the well-known Mehra-Prescott puzzle. Mehra and Prescott (1985) show that the realized average return on U.S. equities over the last 60 years has been around 8 percent, and the realized real return on safe bonds only around zero. Such a risk premium seems to be inconsistent with the standard representative consumer model applied to U.S. data unless that consumer has an implausibly large coefficient of risk aversion.

If we interpret asset u in our model as the aggregate stock market and asset s as short-term bonds, our model can shed light on the Mehra-Prescott puzzle. Since noise trader risk drives down the price of u, equities yield a higher return in our model than the riskless asset does. Moreover, this difference in yields obtains despite the fact that aggregate consumption does not vary too much with the expected return on equities. The reason is that the consumption of sophisticated investors satisfies the Euler equation with respect to the true distribution of expected returns exactly, but the consumption of noise traders does not. In fact, the share of wealth invested (and thus not consumed) by noise traders is low when the true expected return is high, and high when the true expected return is low. The presence of noise traders thus makes aggregate consumption less sensitive to the variation of true expected returns than it should be. A large equity premium can thus coexist with a low covariance of returns on equities with aggregate consumption. Although the mechanics of our model are very different from the model in Ingram (1987), this particular implication works similarly to her explanation of the equity premium, which relies on the insensitivity of the consumption of a group of rule-of-thumb agents to expected returns.

It is important to stress that our model sheds light on the Mehra-Prescott puzzle only if equities are underpriced, which is itself a necessary condition for noise traders to earn higher expected returns. In other words, the fact that the Mehra-Prescott equity premium obtains in an economy is evidence for the proposition that the expected returns of noise traders are likely to be higher than those of sophisticated investors. In the context of our model, the existence of an equity premium in the U.S. economy suggests that American noise traders are on average bullish on the assets that they disturb and may earn higher average returns than American arbitrageurs.

4.4 Long Horizons

Noise trader risk makes coherent a widely held view of the relative social merits of "speculation" and "investment" that has found little academic sympathy. Many participants in financial markets have argued that the presence of traders who are looking for only short-term profits is socially destructive. The standard economist's refutation of this argument relies on recursion: If one seeks to buy a stock now to sell in an hour, one must calculate its price in an hour. But its price in an hour depends on what those who will purchase it thinks its price will be a further hour down the road. Anyone who buys an asset, no matter how short the holding period, must perform the same present value calculation as someone who intends to hold the asset for 50 years. Since a linked chain of short-term "traders" performs the same assessment of values as a single "investor," the claim that trading is bad and investing good cannot be correct. Prices will be unaffected by the horizon of the agent as long as the rate of discount and willingness to bear risk are unchanged.

In our model this analysis does not apply. The horizon of agents matters. If agents live for more than two periods, the equilibrium is closer to the "fundamental" equilibrium than if agents live for two periods. As an example, consider an infinitesimal measure of infinitely lived but risk-averse sophisticated traders. Suppose that p_t is less than one. An infinitely lived agent can sell short a unit of s and buy a unit of u. He collects a gain of $1 - p_t$, and he has incurred no liability in any state of the world. The dividend on u will always offset the dividend owed on s. The fact that an infinitely lived agent can arbitrage assets s and u without ever facing a settlement date implies that any infinitely lived sophisticated investor could push the price of u to its fundamental value of one.

Although arbitrage is not riskless for long but finite-lived agents, their asset demands are more responsive to price movements than those of two-period-lived agents. There are two reasons for this. First, even if an $n > 2$ period-lived sophisticated investor can liquidate his position in asset u only in the last period of his life, he bears the same amount of resale price risk as his two-period-lived counterpart but gets some insurance from dividends. If, for example, he buys an undervalued asset u, he receives a high dividend yield for several periods before he sells. Because as the horizon expands so does the share of dividends in expected returns, agents with longer horizons buy more at the start. Second, a long-lived sophisticated investor has in fact many periods to liquidate his position. Since he makes money on arbitrage if the price reverts to the mean at any time before his death, having several opportunities to liquidate reduces his risk. For these two reasons, raising sophisticated investors' horizons makes them more aggressive and brings the price of u closer to fundamentals.

The embedding of the financial market in an overlapping generations model in which agents die after two periods is a device to give rational utility maximizers short horizons. This device may adequately model institutional features of asset markets—triennial performance evaluations of pension fund money managers, for example—that may lead even fully rational agents to have short horizons. Realistically, even an agent with a horizon long in terms of time may have a horizon "short" in the context of this model. If dividend risk is great enough and if noise trader misperceptions are persistent, then agents might well find it unattractive to buy stocks and hold them for a long time hoping that the market someday recognizes their value. For in the meantime, during which the assets might have to be sold, market prices may deviate even further from fundamental values. The claim that short horizons are bad for the economy is both coherent and true in our model.

4.5 Observations on Corporate Finance

Throughout this paper, we have focused on the implications of marketwide noise trader risk. The reason is that in our model, just as in a standard asset valuation model, idiosyncratic risk is unpriced. A number of implications of noise trading, however, including those stressed by Black (1986), rely on misperceptions of firm-specific returns. To allow such idiosyncratic misperceptions to matter, the model must include transactions costs that limit the universe of stocks that each sophisticated investor holds (Mayshar 1983). Although such a model is beyond the scope of this paper, we mention a few issues that idiosyncratic risk raises in the context of corporate finance.

In a model with noise traders the Modigliani-Miller theorem does not necessarily apply. To see this, consider the standard homemade leverage proof of the theorem. This proof demonstrates that a rational investor can undo any effects of firm leverage and maintain the same real position regardless of a firm's payout policy. It does not suggest that less than rational traders will do so. Given that noise traders in general affect prices, it follows that unless they happen to trade so as to undo the effects of changes in leverage, the Modigliani-Miller theorem will not hold.

It is plausible to think that noise traders do not get confused about the value of assets that have a certain and immediate liquidation value. Noise traders are more likely to become confused about assets that offer fundamentally risky payouts in the distant future. Assets of long duration that promise fundamentally uncertain as opposed to immediate and certain cash payouts may thus be subject to an especially great amount of noise trader risk. In this case, a firm might choose to pay dividends rather than reinvest even if there are tax costs to dividends. If dividends make equity look more like a safe short-term bond to noise traders, then paying dividends can reduce the total amount of noise trader risk borne by a firm's securities. Paying dividends might raise the value of equity if the reduction in the discount entailed by noise trader risk exceeds additional shareholder tax liability. Moreover, dividends are not equivalent to share repurchases unless *noise traders* perceive the two to be complete substitutes. If investors believe that future stock repurchases are of uncertain value because noise traders disturb the price of equity, then the equity of a firm repurchasing shares can be subject to greater undervaluation than that of a firm paying dividends. A bird in the hand is truly better than one in the bush.

Jensen (1986) summarizes evidence showing that the more constrained the allocation of the firm's cash flows, the higher its valuation by the market. For example, share prices rise when a firm raises dividends, swaps debt for equity, or buys back shares. In contrast, share prices fall when a firm cuts dividends or issues new shares. These results are consistent with our model if making the returns to equity more determinate reduces the noise trader risk that it bears. Increases in dividends that make equity look safer to noise traders may reduce noise trader risk and raise share prices. Swaps of debt for equity have the same effect, as do share buybacks. As long as a change in capital structure convinces noise traders that a firm's total capital is more like asset s and less like asset u than they had previously thought, changes in capital structure raise value.

The discussion above suggests that noise trader risk is a cost that an issuer of a security that will be publicly traded must bear. Both traded equity and traded long-term debt will be underpriced relative to fundamentals if their prices are subject to the whims of noise traders' opinions. Why then are securities traded publicly? Put differently, why don't all firms go private to avoid noise trader risk? Presumably firms have publicly traded securities if the benefits, such as a broader base from which to draw capital, a larger pool to use to diversify systematic risk, and liquidity, exceed the costs of the noise trader–generated undervaluation. Assets for which these benefits of public ownership are the highest relative to the costs of noise trader risk are the assets that will be issued into markets with public trading. While the issuers of these securities will try to minimize the costs of noise trader risk by "packaging" the securities appropriately, they will not be able to eliminate such risk entirely.

5. Conclusion

We have shown that risk created by the unpredictability of unsophisticated investors' opinions significantly reduces the attractiveness of arbitrage. As long as arbitrageurs have short horizons and so must worry about liquidating their investment in a mispriced asset, their aggressiveness will be limited even in the absence of fundamental risk. In this case noise trading can lead to a large divergence between market prices and fundamental values. Moreover, noise traders may be compensated for bearing the risk that they themselves create and so earn higher returns than sophisticated investors even though they distort prices. As we discuss in the paper, this result at the least calls for a closer scrutiny of the standard argument that destabilizing speculation must be unprofitable and so noise traders will not persist in the market.

This paper has also argued that a number of financial market anomalies can be explained by the idea of noise trader risk. These anomalies include the excess volatility of and mean reversion in stock market prices, the failure of the expectations hypothesis of the term structure, the Mehra-Prescott equity premium, the undervaluation of closed-end mutual funds, and several others. The essential assumption we use is that the opinions of noise traders are unpredictable and arbitrage requires bearing the risk that their misperceptions become even more extreme tomorrow than they are today. Since "unpredictability" seems to be a general property of the behavior of irrational investors, we believe that our conclusions are not simply a consequence of a particular parameterization of noise trader actions.

Our model suggests that much of the behavior of professional arbitrageurs can be seen as a response to noise trading rather than as trading on fundamentals. Many professional arbitrageurs spend their resources examining and predicting the pseudosignals noise traders follow in order to bet against them more successfully. These pseudosignals include volume and price patterns, sentiment indices, and the forecasts of Wall Street gurus. Just as it pays entrepreneurs to build casinos to exploit gamblers, it pays rational investors to spend considerable resources to exploit noise traders. In both cases, private returns to the activity probably exceed social returns.

Our focus on irrationality in financial markets departs from that of earlier studies of rational but heterogeneously informed investors (Grossman and Stiglitz 1980; Townsend 1983; Varian 1986; Stein 1987). Many of the results in this paper could perhaps be derived using a fully rational model with differentially informed investors, provided that one gets away from the "no-trade" theorems (Milgrom and Stokey 1982).

Apart from the question of tractability, we have focused on models of irrationality for three reasons. First, in the context of fluctuations in the aggregate market, we find the idea of privately informed investors somewhat implausible. While one can always think of a person's opinion as private information, this seems like playing with words. Speaking of the private information of a market timer like Joe Granville—who himself insists that he has a "system" rather than an informational advantage—makes little sense to us. Second, given the traditional argument that the stock market price aggregates information and opinions, it is important to examine the extent to which there is a tendency of prices to reflect "good" rather than "bad" opinions. Even more than Figlewski's (1979) result that "bad" opinions can influence market prices for a long time, our paper suggests skepticism about the long-run irrelevance of "bad" opinions. Third, our analysis illustrates the point that studying irrational behavior does not always require specifying its content. We have shown that something can be learned about financial markets simply by looking at the effect of *unpredictability* of irrational behavior on the opportunities of rational investors. The idea of noise trader risk is much more general than our particular examples. In future research, it would be valuable to consider asset markets with more primitive descriptions of irrationality. One advantage of such an approach would be to generate more restrictive predictions that are easier to reject.

We would like to thank the National Science, Russell Sage, and Alfred P. Sloan foundations for financial support. We have benefited from comments from Robert Barsky, Fischer Black, John Campbell, Andrew Caplin, Peter Diamond, Miles Kimball, Bruce Lehmann, Charles Perry, Robert Vishny, Michael Woodford, and especially from Kevin M. Murphy and Barry Nalebuff.

References

ALPERT, MARC, and RAIFFA, HOWARD. "A Progress Report on the Training of Probability Assessors." In *Judgment under Uncertainty: Heuristics and Biases,* edited by DANIEL KAHNEMAN, PAUL SLOVIC, and AMOS TVERSKY. Cambridge: Cambridge Univ. Press, 1982.

BLACK, FISCHER. "Noise." *J. Finance* 41 (July 1986): 529–43.

BRAUER, GREGORY A. "'Open-ending' Closed-End Funds." *J. Financial Econ.* 13 (December 1984): 491–507.

BRAY, MARGARET M. "Learning, Estimation, and the Stability of Rational Expectations." *J. Econ. Theory* 26 (April 1982): 318–39.

BRICKLEY, JAMES A., and SCHALLHEIM, JAMES S. "Lifting the Lid on Closed-End Investment Companies: A Case of Abnormal Returns." *J. Financial and Quantitative Analysis* 20 (March 1985): 107–17.

CAMPBELL, JOHN Y., and KYLE, ALBERT. "Smart Money, Noise Trading, and Stock Price Behavior." Manuscript. Princeton, N.J.: Princeton Univ., 1987.

CAMPBELL, JOHN Y., and SHILLER, ROBERT J. "Cointegration and Tests of Present Value Models." *J.P.E.* 95 (October 1987): 1062–88.

DE LONG, J. BRADFORD; SHLEIFER, ANDREI; SUMMERS, LAWRENCE H.; and WALDMANN, ROBERT J. "Noise Trader Risk in Financial Markets." Working Paper no. 2395. Cambridge, Mass.: NBER, October 1987.

———. "The Survival of Noise Traders in Financial Markets." Working Paper no. 2715. Cambridge, Mass.: NBER, September 1988.

———. "The Size and Incidence of the Losses from Noise Trading." *J. Finance* 44 (July 1989): 681–96.

———. "Positive Feedback Investment Strategies and Destabilizing Rational Speculation." *J. Finance* 45 (June 1990).

DENTON, FRANK T. "The Effect of Professional Advice on the Stability of a Speculative Market." *J.P.E.* 93 (October 1985): 977–93.

FAMA, EUGENE F. "The Behavior of Stock Market Prices." *J. Bus.* 38 (January 1965): 34–105.

FAMA, EUGENE F., and FRENCH, KENNETH R. "Dividend Yields and Expected Stock Returns." *J. Financial Econ.* 22 (October 1988): 3–25. (*a*)

———. "Permanent and Temporary Components of Stock Prices." *J.P.E.* 96 (April 1988): 246–73. (*b*)

FIGLEWSKI, STEPHEN. "Subjective Information and Market Efficiency in a Betting Market." *J.P.E.* 87 (February 1979): 75–88.

FRIEDMAN, MILTON. "The Case for Flexible Exchange Rates." In *Essays in Positive Economics.* Chicago: Univ. Chicago Press, 1953.

GRAHAM, BENJAMIN, and DODD, DAVID L. *Security Analysis.* New York: McGraw-Hill, 1934.

GROSSMAN, SANFORD J., and STIGLITZ, JOSEPH E. "On the Impossibility of Informationally Efficient Markets." *A.E.R.* 70 (June 1980): 393–408.

HALTIWANGER, JOHN C., and WALDMANN, MICHAEL. "Rational Expectations and the Limits of Rationality: An Analysis of Heterogeneity." *A.E.R.* 75 (June 1985): 326–40.

HART, OLIVER D., and KREPS, DAVID M. "Price Destabilizing Speculation." *J.P.E.* 94 (October 1986): 927–52.

HERZFELD, THOMAS J. *The Investor's Guide to Closed-End Funds: The Herzfeld Edge.* New York: McGraw-Hill, 1980.

INGRAM, BETH FISHER. "Equilibrium Modelling of Asset Prices: Rationality v. Rules of Thumb." Manuscript. Ithaca, N.Y.: Cornell Univ., 1987.

JENSEN, MICHAEL C. The Performance of Mutual Funds in the Period 1945–1964." *J. Finance* 23 (May 1968): 389–416.

———. "Agency Costs of Free Cash Flow, Corporate Finance, and Take-overs." *A.E.R. Papers and Proc.* 76 (May 1986): 323–29.

KEYNES, JOHN MAYNARD. *The General Theory of Employment, Interest and Money.* London: Macmillan, 1936.

KLEIDON, ALLAN W. "Anomalies in Financial Economics: Blueprint for Change?" *J. Bus.* 59, no. 4, pt. 2 (October 1986): S469–S499.

KYLE, ALBERT S. "Continuous Auctions and Insider Trading." *Econometrica* 53 (November 1985): 1315–35.

LEWELLEN, WILBUR G.; SCHLARBAUM, GARY E.; and LEASE, RONALD C. "The Individual Investor: Attributes and Attitudes." *J. Finance* 29 (May 1974): 413–33.

MALKIEL, BURTON G. *A Random Walk down Wall Street.* New York: Norton, 1973; 2d ed., 1975; 4th ed., 1985; 5th ed., 1989.

———. "The Valuation of Closed-End Investment-Company Shares." *J. Finance* 32 (July 1977): 847–59.

MANKIW, N. GREGORY. "The Term Structure of Interest Rates Revisited." *Brookings Papers Econ. Activity,* no. 1 (1986), pp. 61–110.

MANKIW, N. GREGORY, and SUMMERS, LAWRENCE H. "Do Long-Term Interest Rates Overreact to Short-Tem Interest Rates?" *Brookings Papers Econ. Activity,* no. 1 (1984), pp. 223–42.

MAYSHAR, JORAM. "On Divergence of Opinion and Imperfections in Capital Markets." *A.E.R.* 73 (March 1983): 114–28.

MEHRA, RAJNISH, and PRESCOTT, EDWARD C. "The Equity Premium: A Puzzle." *J. Monetary Econ.* 15 (March 1985): 145–61.

MILGROM, PAUL, and STOKEY, NANCY. "Information, Trade and Common Knowledge." *J. Econ. Theory* 26 (February 1982): 17–27.

POTERBA, JAMES M., and SUMMERS, LAWRENCE H. "Mean Reversion in Stock Prices: Evidence and Implications." *J. Financial Econ.* 22 (October 1988): 27–59.

ROLL, RICHARD. "Orange Juice and Weather." *A.E.R.* 74 (December 1984): 861–80.

RUSSELL, THOMAS, and THALER, RICHARD H. "The Relevance of Quasi Rationality in Competitive Markets." *A.E.R.* 75 (December 1985): 1071–82.

SAMUELSON, PAUL A. "An Exact Consumption-Loan Model of Interest with or without the Social Contrivance of Money." *J.P.E.* 66 (December 1958): 467–82.

SHILLER, ROBERT J. "Do Stock Prices Move Too Much to Be Justified by Subsequent Changes in Dividends?" *A.E.R.* 71 (June 1981): 421–36.

———. "Stock Prices and Social Dynamics." *Brookings Papers Econ. Activity,* no. 2 (1984), pp. 457–98.

SHLEIFER, ANDREI, and VISHNY, ROBERT. "Equilibrium Short Horizons of Investors and Firms." *A.E.R. Papers and Proc.* 80 (May 1990).

STEIN, JEREMY C. "Informational Externalities and Welfare-reducing Speculation." *J.P.E.* 95 (December 1987): 1123–45.

SUMMERS, LAWRENCE H. "Does the Stock Market Rationally Reflect Fundamental Values?" *J. Finance* 41 (July 1986): 591–601.

TOWNSEND, ROBERT M. "Forecasting the Forecasts of Others." *J.P.E.* 91 (August 1983): 546–88.

VARIAN, HAL. "Differences of Opinion and the Volume of Trade." Manuscript. Ann Arbor: Univ. Michigan, 1986.

3

Investor Sentiment and the Closed-End Fund Puzzle

CHARLES M. C. LEE, ANDREI SHLEIFER, and RICHARD H. THALER

Few problems in finance are as perplexing as the closed-end fund puzzle. A closed-end fund, like the more popular open-end fund, is a mutual fund which typically holds other publicly traded securities. Unlike an open-end fund, however, a closed-end fund issues a fixed number of shares that are traded on the stock market. To liquidate a holding in a fund, investors must sell their shares to other investors rather than redeem them with the fund itself for the net asset value (NAV) per share as they would with an open-end fund. The closed-end fund puzzle is the empirical finding that closed-end fund shares typically sell at prices not equal to the per share market value of assets the fund holds. Although funds sometimes sell at premia to their net asset values, in recent years discounts of 10 to 20 percent have been the norm.

Several past studies have attempted to solve the puzzle by pointing out that the methods used to value the securities in the portfolio might overstate the true value of the assets. Three factors are often cited as potential explanations: agency costs, tax liabilities, and illiquidity of assets. The agency costs theory states that management expenses incurred in running the fund are too high and/or the potential for subpar managerial performance reduces asset value. The tax explanation argues that capital gains tax liabilities on unrealized appreciations (at the fund level) are not captured by the standard calculation of NAV. Finally, be-

From: *The Journal of Finance*, vol. XLVI, No. 1, pp. 75–109, March 1991. Reprinted by permission.

cause some funds hold restricted or letter securities which have trading restrictions, the argument has been made that such assets are overvalued in the calculation of NAV. While each of these explanations is logical and may explain some portion of the observed discounts, we show below that even collectively these factors fail to account for much of the existing evidence.

Our primary purpose is to evaluate empirically an alternative explanation for the closed-end fund puzzle presented by Zweig (1973) and Delong, Shleifer, Summers, and Waldmann (1990) (DSSW). Zweig (1973) suggests that discounts on closed-end funds reflect expectations of individual investors. DSSW develop a model in which rational investors interact in financial markets with noise traders who are less than fully rational. An important feature of their model is the existence of unpredictable fluctuations in "noise trader sentiment," defined as the component of expectations about asset returns not warranted by fundamentals. Investor sentiment can represent trading on noise rather than news (Black (1986)) or trading on popular models (Shiller (1984)). In the case of closed-end funds, fluctuations in investor sentiment can lead to fluctuations in demand for closed-end fund shares which are reflected in changes in discounts. In addition to Zweig's early idea that fund discounts reflect investor sentiment, the DSSW model explains why funds can sell at discounts even if investors are not, on average, pessimistic. Our paper reviews and extends the implications of this model, and then presents empirical evidence largely consistent with these implications.

Before the various explanations of closed-end fund pricing can be evaluated, it is important to provide a more complete description of the facts. There are four important pieces to the puzzle which together characterize the life cycle of a closed-end fund:

1) Closed-end funds start out at a premium of almost 10 percent, when organizers raise money from new investors and use it to purchase securities (Weiss (1989) and Peavy (1990)). Most of this premium is a natural derivative of the underwriting and start-up costs which are removed from the proceeds, thus reducing the NAV relative to the stock price. The reason that investors pay a premium for new funds when existing funds trade at a discount is the first part of the puzzle to be explained.

2) Although they start at a premium, closed-end funds move to an average discount of over 10 percent within 120 days from the beginning of trading (Weiss (1989)).[1] Thereafter, discounts are the norm. For illus-

---

1. The sample in the Weiss study is closed-end funds started during 1985–87. The average discount figure cited relates to stock funds investing in U.S. companies.

Figure 1   Percentage discount or premium of Tricontinental Corporation at the end of each year during 1960–1986.

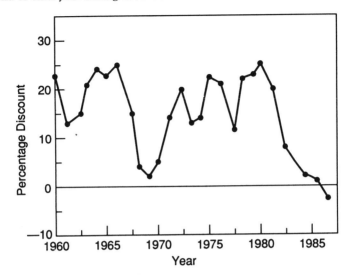

The percentage discount is computed as $100 \times (NAV - SP)$; where NAV is the per share net asset value and SP is the share price of the fund. The mean (median) of the percentage discount or premium is 14.43 (15.0). The maximum (minimum) value is 25.0 (-2.5) and the standard deviation is 8.56.

trative purposes, Figure 1 shows the year-end discounts on the Tricontinental Corporation (TRICON) fund during 1960–1986. Tricontinental is the largest closed-end stock fund trading on U.S. exchanges, with net assets of over \$1.3 billion as of December, 1986. Although there are some periods where the fund sells at a premium relative to the NAV, most of the time it sells at a discount, which frequently hovers around 20 percent.[2]

3) As Figure 1 illustrates for TRICON, discounts on closed-end funds are subject to wide fluctuations over time. During 1960–1986, year-end discounts for TRICON ranged from 25 percent to a premium of 2.5 percent. It is by no means the case that the discount is a constant fraction of net asset value (or a constant dollar amount). The fluctuations in the discounts appear to be mean reverting (Sharpe and Sosin (1975)). Thompson (1978), Richards, Fraser, and Groth (1980), Herzfeld (1980), Ander-

2. Throughout this paper, discounts are expressed in terms of percentage of NAV. Positive discounts reflect stock prices which are below NAV.

son (1986), and Brauer (1988) all document significant positive abnormal returns from assuming long positions on funds with large discounts.

4) When closed-end funds are terminated through either a liquidation or an open-ending, share prices rise and discounts shrink (Brauer (1984), Brickley and Schalheim (1985)). Most of the positive returns to shareholders accrue when discounts narrow around the announcement of termination. A small discount persists, however, until final termination or open-ending.

Our purpose is to understand this four-piece puzzle. In Section I we argue that standard explanations of the puzzle cannot, separately or together, explain all four pieces of the puzzle. We review the DSSW explanation of the puzzle in Section II and discuss some implications of this explanation. Section III covers data and variables description. Section IV presents our tests of the new implications, and Section V deals with some objections. Section VI presents supplementary evidence bearing on this explanation of closed-end fund discounts, and Section VII concludes.

1. Standard Explanations of the Closed-End Fund Puzzle

Agency costs, illiquidity of assets, and tax liabilities have all been proposed as potential explanations of closed-end fund discounts. However, these arguments, even when considered together, do not explain all four pieces of the closed-end fund puzzle. This section reviews these arguments.

1.1 Agency Costs

Agency costs could create discounts for closed-end funds if management fees are too high or if future portfolio management is expected to be subpar (Boudreaux (1973)). There are several problems with agency costs as a theory of closed-end fund pricing. First, neither current nor future agency costs can account for the wide fluctuations in the discounts. Management fees are typically a fixed percentage of NAV and certainly do not fluctuate as much as do discounts. The present value of future management fees can in principle fluctuate with interest rates. However, as we show later (Table IX), changes in discounts are not significantly correlated with interest rate changes. Second, agency costs cannot explain why rational investors buy into closed-end funds *initially* at a premium, since they should expect the funds to sell at a discount eventually. For that matter, agency and trading costs cannot explain why new and seasoned funds ever sell at premia. Third, agency costs do not seem to explain much of the cross-sectional variation in discounts. Malkiel (1977) did not find a significant relationship between management fees and/or fund performance and discount levels. By grouping funds into two groups, based on their discounts, Roenfeld and Tuttle (1973) did find, in a very small sample, marginal support for a contemporaneous relationship between fund performance and discounts. However, assuming rational expectations, a more appropriate test is to check for a relation between discounts and *future* NAV performance of funds, not past or current performance. Lee, Shleifer, and Thaler (1991) show that there is, if anything, a positive correlation between discount levels and future NAV performance; funds with large discounts tend to have higher subsequent NAV performance than those with low discounts. This result is the opposite of what might be expected from rational discounting of agency costs.

1.2 Illiquidity of Assets

Two other theories posit that the NAV published by the funds exaggerates the true asset value. The first theory, the *restricted stock hypothesis*, says that funds hold substantial amounts of letter stock, the market value of which is lower than its unrestricted counterpart, and that such holdings are overvalued in the calculation of NAV.[3] This idea can be ruled out immediately as a general explanation of discounts since many of the largest funds that trade at discounts hold only liquid publicly traded securities. For example, TRICON does not have any significant restricted holdings. An examination of the annual financial statements of TRICON reveals that for the years during the period studied, the assets which either required Board of Directors' valuation or were marked as "unidentified" common stocks are always less than 0.5 percent of the total NAV of the fund.

The effect of holding restricted stocks is also mitigated by regulation, which requires the funds to discount such securities in computing NAV to an amount which their Boards of Directors have determined (and publicly attest) is a fair market value equivalent. Nevertheless, there is a small but significant relationship in the cross section between the level of restricted holdings and the level of discounts (see for example Malkiel (1977) and Lee, Shleifer, and Thaler (1991)). Apparently, the market does not believe the funds have adequately discounted these securities. Restricted stock holdings can thus explain a portion of the discount on

---

3. Letter, or restricted, stock refers to securities of a corporation which may not be publicly traded without registration under the Securities Act of 1933, because they have not been previously registered. A fund acquires these securities through private placement and agrees to a "letter" contract restricting their resale to the public within a specified time period. These securities can be resold privately with the letter attached.

certain specialized funds, but it offers no explanation for the substantial discounts of large, diversified funds.

Another version of the illiquidity argument, the *block discount hypothesis*, is based on the observation that reported NAV's are computed using the trading price of a marginal share. Since closed-end funds sometimes hold substantial blocks of individual securities, the realizable proceeds from a liquidation would be much lower than the reported NAV. Like the restricted stock hypothesis, this argument runs counter to the evidence that large abnormal positive returns are realized when closed-end funds are open-ended (Brauer (1984), Brickley and Schallheim (1985)). Also, neither theory makes any contribution to explaining the other parts of the puzzle.

1.3 Capital Gains Tax Liabilities

The NAV of a closed-end fund does not reflect the capital gains tax that must be paid by the fund if the assets in the fund are sold.[4] The tax liability associated with assets which have appreciated in value would reduce the liquidation value of the fund's assets. This theory runs into a serious problem with the evidence in Brauer (1984) and Brickley and Schallheim (1985). These papers show that on open ending, closed-end fund prices move up to net asset values rather than the net asset values falling down to the fund share prices, as would be the case if the measured net asset values were too high.[5] Moreover, Malkiel (1977) demonstrates that under fairly generous assumptions, the tax liabilities can account for a discount of no more than 6 percent.[6] Also, the tax theory suggests that discounts should widen when the market rises (since unreal-

---

4. The fund has a choice of retaining or distributing its net realized capital gains. If the fund distributes these gains, owners of the fund's shares must pay tax on the distributions according to their own personal tax status. If the fund retains a portion of its net realized capital gains, it is required to pay taxes in accordance with the highest marginal personal tax rate. A tax receipt is then issued to the shareholders which is deductible from personal income taxes.

5. As pointed out to us by Jeffrey Pontiff, the evidence from open-ended funds is subject to selection bias. Another possibility, which is difficult to test, is that the NAV is properly measured only for the funds that open-end.

6. The key assumptions in this calculation are the percentage of unrealized appreciation in the assets, the period of time before the asset is sold by the fund, and the holding period of the investor after the sale. Malkiel assumed the unrealized appreciation was 25 percent of the fund's assets and, in the worst case, the asset was sold immediately by the fund and the shares were sold immediately thereafter by the investor (which would maximize his tax liability) to arrive at the 6 percent amount. A more probable estimate, given the 25 percent unrealized appreciation, would be around 2 percent.

ized appreciation tends to increase in a bull market), contrary to the evidence we present below.

To summarize, standard explanations have been marginally successful (for some funds) in explaining Part 2 of our 4-part puzzle, i.e., the existence of discounts. However, the existing theories do not provide satisfactory explanations for the other parts of the puzzle: why funds get started, why the discounts fluctuate over time, and why large positive abnormal returns are realized when the fund is open-ended. Perhaps most important, each of these explanations deals with the puzzle of closed-end funds selling at discounts and fails to explain why sometimes funds sell at premia, particularly when they are started. Even taken collectively, these explanations cannot account for all the evidence. In the next section, we present an alternative explanation that not only accommodates these apparent anomalies, but also yields further testable hypotheses.

2. Investor Sentiment

2.1 Noise Trader Risk

DSSW (1990) present a model of asset pricing based on the idea that the unpredictability of the opinions of not-fully-rational investors (or noise traders) impounds resale price risk on the assets they trade. In this model, there are two types of investors: rational investors and noise traders. Rational investors form rational expectations about asset returns. In contrast, noise traders' expectations about asset returns are subject to the influence of sentiment: they overestimate the expected returns (relative to the rational expectation) in some periods and underestimate them in others. Each period, rational investors and noise traders trade the assets based on their respective beliefs. Because assets are risky and all investors are risk averse, the equilibrium price reflects the opinions of both the rational investors and the noise traders.

DSSW then make two crucial assumptions. First, they assume that rational investors' horizons are short, so that they care about the interim resale prices of the assets they hold, not just the present values of dividends. This assumption is realistic. Portfolio managers are subject to frequent, periodic evaluations which shorten their horizons while individuals often have liquidity needs for selling. Also, the longer a rational investor keeps his trade open the higher are the cumulative transaction costs if either cash or assets have to be borrowed for that trade. Short sales, in particular, are difficult and costly over any long horizon. These costs of arbitrage tend to shorten investors' horizons and make them concerned with interim resale prices (Shleifer and Vishny (1990)).

Second, DSSW assume that noise traders' sentiment is stochastic and cannot be perfectly forecasted by rational investors. In particular, a rational investor cannot perfectly forecast how optimistic or pessimistic noise traders will be at the time he wants to sell the asset. Because rational investors care about the resale prices of assets, the unpredictability of noise trader sentiment impounds an additional risk on the assets they trade. The extra risk is that at the time a rational investor wants to sell an asset, noise traders might be bearish about it, causing its price to be low. As long as a rational investor might want to sell the asset in finite time, the risk of an adverse sentiment shift is every bit as real as fundamental risk of low dividends. This noise trader risk is borne by both rational investors and noise traders.

If different noise traders traded randomly across assets, the risk their sentiment would create would be diversifiable, just as idiosyncratic fundamental risk is diversifiable in conventional pricing models. However, if fluctuations in the same noise trader sentiment affect many assets and are correlated across noise traders, then the risk that these fluctuations create cannot be diversified. Like fundamental risk, noise trader risk arising from the stochastic investor sentiment will be priced in equilibrium. As a result, assets subject to noise trader risk will earn a higher expected return than assets not subject to such risk. Relative to their fundamental values, these assets will be underpriced.

DSSW discuss closed-end funds as an interesting application of their model. Suppose that noise traders' expectation about future returns is subject to unpredictable changes. Some of the time noise traders are optimistic about returns on these securities and drive up their prices relative to fundamental values. For securities where fundamental values are hard to observe, the effects of this optimism will be hard to identify. But in the case of closed-end funds, investor optimism will result in their selling at premia or at smaller discounts. Other times, noise traders are pessimistic about returns on these securities, drive down their prices, and so closed-end funds sell at larger discounts. In this way, stochastic changes in demand for closed-end funds by investors with unpredictably changing expectations of returns cause stochastic fluctuations in the discounts.

In this model, the risk from holding a closed-end fund (and any other security subject to the same stochastic sentiment) consists of two parts: the risk of holding the fund's portfolio and the risk that noise trader sentiment about the funds changes. In particular, any investor holding a closed-end fund bears the risk that the discount widens in the future if noise traders become relatively more pessimistic about closed-end funds. As long as this risk from the unpredictability of future investor sentiment is systematic, i.e., if investor sentiment affects many assets at the same time, this risk will be priced in equilibrium. When investor sentiment risk is systematic, it will affect a wide range of securities which includes, but is not limited to, closed-end funds. Investor sentiment in the DSSW model, therefore, reflects expectations which are market-wide rather than closed-end fund specific.

2.2 Individual Investor Sentiment

One additional element is needed in applying the DSSW model to closed-end funds—differential clienteles. Specifically, it is necessary to assume that noise traders are more likely to hold and trade closed-end funds than the underlying assets in the funds' portfolios. If the same investors are investing in both the underlying securities and in the fund shares, then any change in investor sentiment will affect both the NAV and the share price, resulting in no change in the discount. Changes in the discount reflect not the aggregate effect of investor sentiment changes but the differential effect of the sentiment of the closed-end fund investing clientele relative to the investing clientele of the underlying assets. In this paper, we speculate that the discount movements reflect the differential sentiment of individual investors since these investors hold and trade a preponderance of closed-end fund shares but are not as important an ownership group in the assets of the funds' investment portfolio.

There is ample evidence that closed-end funds are owned and traded primarily by individual investors. For example, Weiss (1989) found that three calendar quarters after the initial offering of new closed-end funds, institutions held less than 5 percent of the shares, in comparison to 23 percent of the shares of a control sample of IPO's for operating companies. Similarly, we found the average institutional ownership in the closed-end funds in our sample (Appendix I) at the beginning of 1988 to be just 6.6 percent (median 6.2 percent). For the sake of comparison, average institutional ownership for a random sample of the smallest 10 percent of NYSE stocks is 26.5 percent (median 23.9 percent), and 52.1 percent (median 54.0 percent) for the largest 10 percent of NYSE stocks. Using intraday trading data, we have also found that in 1987, 64 percent of the trades in closed-end funds were smaller than \$10,000. This number is 79 percent for the smallest 10 percent of NYSE stocks and only 28 percent for the largest 10 percent of NYSE stocks.[7] Collectively, the

7. Decile membership is based on total market capitalization at the beginning of each year. Firms are sorted by CUSIP, and every third firm is selected to form the random sample. Inclusion in the final sample is subject to availability of data. There were 44–48 firms in each decile portfolio of the final sample. Percentage institutional ownership is based on the

evidence strongly indicates that closed-end funds are both held and traded primarily by individual investors.

This evidence leads us to conjecture that the sentiment that affects closed-end fund discounts should also affect other securities that are held and traded predominantly by individual investors. As the evidence cited above shows, one set of such securities is small firms. If smaller capitalization stocks are subject to the same individual investor sentiment as closed-end funds, then fluctuations in the discounts on closed-end funds should be correlated with the returns on smaller stocks. When enough stocks in addition to closed-end funds are affected by the same investor sentiment, risk from this sentiment cannot be diversified and is therefore priced.

2.3 Arbitrage

The notion that holding a closed-end fund is riskier than holding its portfolio runs into an obvious objection. Why can't a rational arbitrageur buy the fund selling at a discount and sell short its portfolio? Since the fund costs less than its underlying assets, there is wealth left over after this perfectly hedged transaction, and the dividends that the fund distributes will cover the dividends on the investor's short position. In practice, however, there are several problems with this strategy.

First, if the fund changes its portfolio, the arbitrageur must similarly change the portfolio that is sold short. This may be difficult to accomplish in a timely manner. Second, investors do not get the full proceeds of a short sale: the hedge is not costless.[8] Third, even if these practical problems could be solved, the hedge would not be a pure arbitrage opportunity unless the arbitrageurs have an infinite time horizon and are never forced to liquidate their positions.[9] If, in contrast, an arbitrageur might need to liquidate at some finite time, then he faces the risk that the discount has widened since the time the arbitrage trade was put on. If the discount widens, the arbitrage trade obviously results in a loss. Arbitrageurs would never need to liquidate their positions if they re-

---

first issue of the *Standard and Poor's Stock Report* in each year after adjusting for known closely-held shares and block holdings. That is, the values reported are percentages of institutional holdings, divided by (100 − percent of closely-held or block shares). The intraday trading data is from the Institute for the Study of Security Markets (ISSM) based at Memphis State University.

8. See Herzfeld (1980) for a similar strategy that can be implemented using call options.

9. For an analysis of the conditions necessary for arbitrage to eliminate irrationality, see Russell and Thaler (1985).

ceived the full proceeds from the initial short sales, since the initial investment would have been negative, and all future cash flows would be zero. But, since arbitrageurs do not get full proceeds, they might need to liquidate to obtain funds. In such cases, bearing noise trader risk is unavoidable. As long as arbitrageurs do not have infinite horizons, arbitrage against noise traders is not riskless because the discount can widen. Because of this risk, arbitrageurs take only limited positions, and mispricing can persist.

A possible alternative to the "buy and hold" arbitrage is a takeover of a closed-end fund, followed by a sell-off of its assets to realize the net asset value. The theoretical impediment to such takeovers has been identified by Grossman and Hart (1980) who show that free-riding fund shareholders would not tender their shares to the bidder unless they receive full net asset value. Because making a bid is costly, the bidder who pays full NAV cannot himself profit from the bid, and so no bids will take place. In practice, managerial resistance and regulatory restrictions represent formidable hurdles for the would-be bidder. For example, by 1980 the Tricontential and Lehman funds had each defeated four attempts at reorganization (Herzfield (1980)). More recently, in 1989 the Securities and Exchange Commission helped block the takeover of the Cypress fund. If acquires' profits from closed-end fund takeovers are meager after transaction costs, then it is not surprising that such takeovers have not been more common.

2.4 Investor Sentiment and the Four Part Puzzle

Changing investor sentiment has a number of empirical implications for the pricing of closed-end funds. Most importantly, because holding the fund is riskier than holding its portfolio directly, and because this risk is systematic, the required rate of return on assets held as fund shares must, on average, be higher than the required return on the same assets purchased directly. This means that the fund must, on average, sell at a discount to its NAV to induce investors to hold the fund's shares. Note that to get this result we do not need to assume that noise traders are, on average, pessimistic about funds: the average underpricing of closed-end funds comes solely from the fact that holding the fund is riskier than holding its portfolio. This theory is therefore consistent with the main puzzle about closed-end funds: they sell at a discount.

The theory is also consistent with the other three pieces of the puzzle. First, it implies that when noise traders are particularly optimistic about closed-end funds (and other assets subject to the same movements in investor sentiment), entrepreneurs can profit by putting assets together into closed-end funds and selling them to the noise traders. In this model, rational investors do not buy closed-end funds at the beginning. On the contrary, if they could borrow the shares they would sell the funds short.[10] It seems necessary to introduce some type of irrational investor to be able to explain why anyone buys the fund shares at the start when the expected return over the next few months is negative. Noise traders, who are sometimes far too optimistic about the true expected return on the fund shares, serve that purpose in the model. In this theory, then, there is no "efficiency" reason for the existence of closed-end funds. Like casinos and snake oil, closed-end funds are a device by which smart entrepreneurs take advantage of a less sophisticated public.

Second, the theory implies that discounts on closed-end funds fluctuate with changes in investor sentiment about future returns (on closed-end funds and other securities). In fact, this theory *requires* that discounts vary stochastically since it is precisely the fluctuations in the discounts that make holding the fund risky and therefore account for average underpricing. If the discounts were constant, then the arbitrage trade of buying the fund and selling short its portfolio would be riskless even for a short horizon investor, and discounts would disappear.

Third, the theory explains why funds' share prices rise on the announcement of open-ending and why discounts are reduced and then eliminated at the time open-ending or liquidation actually occurs. When it is known that a fund will be open-ended or liquidated (or, as Brauer (1988) points out, even when the probability of open-ending increases appreciably), noise trader risk is eliminated (or reduced), and so is the discount. Notice that this risk is largely eliminated when open-ending or liquidation is announced, since at that time any investor can buy the fund and sell short its portfolio knowing that upon open-ending his arbitrage position can be profitably closed for sure. The risk of having to sell when the discount is even wider no longer exists. The small discount that remains after the announcement of open-ending or liquidation can only be explained by the actual transactions costs of arbitrage (the inability to receive short-sale proceeds or the unobservability of the fund's portfolio) or the effect of some of the standard explanations mentioned earlier. The investor sentiment theory thus predicts that the discounts which remain after the announcement of open-ending or liquidation should become small or disappear eventually.

---

10. Peavy (1990) shows that underwriters of closed-end funds buy shares in the aftermarket of support the price. Discussions we had with a professional trader of closed-end funds indicate that short selling of closed-end fund IPO's is extremely difficult.

2.5 Additional Implications

The investor sentiment explanation of discounts on closed-end funds appears to perform better than alternative theories in explaining the key stylized facts. More interestingly, it has a number of additional implications which have not been derived or tested in the context of other theories of discounts. As with the implications discussed above, the new implications are derived from the idea that discounts on closed-end funds reflect widespread changes in investor sentiment rather than idiosyncratic changes in each fund's management or operations.

The first implication is that levels of and changes in discounts should be highly correlated across funds. Since the same sentiment drives discounts on all funds as well as on other securities, changes in this sentiment should determine changes in discounts.

Second, the observation that funds can get started when noise traders are optimistic about their returns can be taken further. Specifically, to the extent closed-end funds are substitutes, the model predicts that new funds should get started when investors favor seasoned funds as well, i.e., when old funds sell at a premium or at a small discount. This effect might be obscured by short-selling constraints on new funds, and the fact that new funds are not perceived as perfect substitutes for seasoned funds. Nevertheless, we test this implication by examining the behavior of the discounts on seasoned funds when new funds are started.

The third implication of the theory is perhaps the most interesting and surprising. The theory requires that for investor sentiment to affect closed-end fund prices, despite the workings of arbitrage, the risk created by changes in investor sentiment must be systematic. The same investor sentiment that affects discounts on closed-end funds must affect other assets as well which have nothing to do with closed-end funds. For example, returns on some portfolios of stocks might be correlated with changes in the average discount on closed-end funds, controlling for market returns. Portfolios affected by the same sentiment as closed-end funds should do well when discounts narrow and poorly when discounts widen. The theory itself does not specify which securities will be influenced by the same sentiment as closed-end funds. However, as we argued above, smaller capitalization stocks are good candidates since individual investors specialize in holding both smaller stocks and closed-end funds.

Other models of closed-end fund discounts are either silent about these predictions, or else they yield opposite results. The evidence we present below, then, is either orthogonal to alternative theories, or else enables us to differentiate between them and the investor sentiment explanation of discounts.

3. Data and Variable Description for the Basic Analysis

Our closed-end fund data were collected from two main sources. Information on annual discounts and net asset values, as well as background information on each fund, was obtained from the 1960 to 1987 editions of Wiesenberger's *Investment Companies Services* annual survey of mutual funds. We were also able to obtain the year that each fund started from these sources.[11] A total of 87 funds were initially identified through this source, of which 68 were selected for monthly analysis because they were known to have CUSIP identifiers.[12] For these funds, we collected the weekly net asset value per share, stock price, and discount per share as reported by the *Wall Street Journal* (WSJ) between July, 1956 and December, 1985 (inclusive). Each week, generally on Monday, the WSJ reports Friday closing prices, NAV, and discounts. To convert the data into a monthly series, the Friday which was closest to each month end was taken, so each observation is within 3 days of the last day of the month.[13] The NAV per share information from the WSJ was then combined with the number of shares outstanding at the end of each month (obtained from the monthly master tape of the Center for Research of Security Prices (CRSP)) to arrive at the total net asset value for each fund.

For several of the tests which follow we constructed a value-weighted index of discounts (VWD) both at the annual and monthly levels as follows:

$$\text{VWD}_t = \sum_{i=1}^{n_t} W_i \, \text{DISC}_{it},$$

11. More detailed information, such as the composition of the TRICON portfolio, were obtained by examining the financial statements of the fund. Also, to ensure that funds which were open-ended during our period of study were included in the count of fund starts, we checked funds reported in Wiesenberger against the list of funds in Brickley and Schallheim (1985) as well as Brauer (1984).

12. We are indebted to Greg Brauer for providing us with this list of funds.

13. The use of a monthly interval allows for comparison with other macroeconomic variables. Various validity checks were employed both during the data collection and later analysis to ensure the integrity of this data. The inputting of a NAV and stock price, for example, generated an automatic discount calculation on the input screen which was checked against the figure reported in the WSJ. After input, univariate statistics were computed on all large funds to check for outliers, and unusual observations were traced back to the WSJ. Occasional inaccuracies in the WSJ figures were corrected through appeal to numbers reported in adjacent weeks. There were two weeks for which the WSJ did not appear to have reported this data. In constructing the monthly series the next closest Friday's close was used.

where

$$W_i = \frac{NAV_{it}}{\sum\limits_{i=1}^{n_t} NAV_{it}},$$

NAV_{it} = net asset value of fund i at end of period t,

$$DISC_{it} = \frac{NAV_{it} - SP_{it}}{NAV_{it}} \times 100,$$

SP_{it} = stock price of fund i at end of period t,

n_t = the number of funds with available $DISC_{it}$ and NAV_{it} data at the end of period t.

We also computed changes in the value-weighted index of discounts (ΔVWD). For this measure, we computed VWD in a similar fashion, except we required that each fund included in the index must have the DISC and NAV data available for months t and t − 1, so that monthly changes in the index are computed over the same asset base. In other words, we require common membership in adjacent months. We then defined ΔVWD to be:

$$\Delta VSD_t = VWD_t - VWD_{t-1}$$

The change in the value-weighted index of discounts (ΔVWD) was computed both annually and with monthly data. For the monthly series, we computed this variable several ways. In the first case we excluded funds which specialize in foreign securities, specifically the ASA Fund and the Japan Fund. In the second case we excluded bond funds (funds which invest primarily in debt securities). The results were similar irrespective of the ΔVWD measure used. The reported findings were based on ΔVWD computed using both foreign and domestic stock funds (i.e., excluding bond funds but including both the ASA Fund and the Japan Fund). This time-series spanned 246 months (7/65 to 12/85).

Of the original sample of 68 funds, 18 were either missing data from the WSJ or did not have shares information available on CRSP and 30 others were bond funds. This left a total of 20 stock funds which participated in the monthly ΔVWD series (see Appendix I for listing). Of these remaining funds, some had relatively short life spans, others may occasionally have missing data points, so the actual number of funds included in computing VWD and ΔVWD varied from month to month. The stock fund ΔVWD series had monthly memberships ranging from 7 funds to 18 funds. In the vast majority of months, at least 10 funds were in the index. We show later that the key findings in this paper are relatively insensitive to the choice of funds which are included in the value-weighted index.

4. Evidence

4.1 Co-movements in Discounts of Different Funds

The investor sentiment model predicts that the discounts on closed-end funds will be correlated. Figure 2 shows the levels of discounts for all closed-end stock funds at the end of each year during 1960–1986. The clear impression is that discounts on individual funds are highly correlated. In fact, the average pairwise correlation of *year-end discounts* for domestic funds is 0.497 (0.607 for diversified domestic funds). Individual pairwise correlations range from insignificant with specialized funds to above 0.8 for some diversified domestic funds. The average pairwise correlation of *annual changes* in discounts among domestic stock funds is 0.389.

Figure 2   Percentage discount or premium at the end of the year for all closed-end stock funds during 1960–1986.

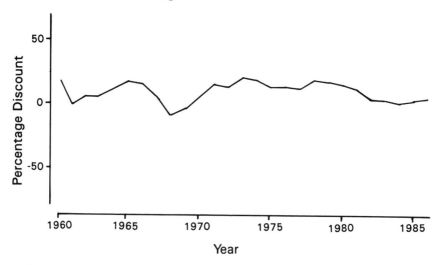

The percentage discount is computed as $100 \times (NAV - SP)$; where NAV is the per share net asset value and SP is the share price of the fund. The sample includes all 46 stock funds reported in the *Wiesenberger Investment Companies Services* Annual survey during this period. The discount on a value-weighted portfolio of these funds is represented by the solid line.

The same conclusion emerges from an examination of monthly pairwise correlations. Tables I and II present the monthly correlations of both levels and changes in discounts for several major funds. The ten funds in these tables have the highest number of available observations over the study period. With the notable exception of American South African (ASA) Fund and the Japan Funds (two foreign funds), and perhaps Petroleum Resources (a fund specializing in oil and gas stocks), the levels of discounts on different funds show a high level of correlation.[14] The average pairwise correlation of month-end discounts for domestic funds is 0.530 (0.643 for diversified domestic funds). The average pairwise correlation of monthly changes in discounts among domestic stock funds is 0.248 (0.267 for diversified domestic funds). That this comovement is captured by the VWD variable is seen in the strong correlation of this variable to the discounts of each individual fund. This is true even for the two foreign funds.

It seems clear from Tables I and II that discounts of different domestic funds tend to move together. In fact, these high correlations between discounts justify the construction of the value-weighted discount. The positive correlations are consistent with the hypothesis that discounts on different funds are driven by the same investor sentiment. Tables I and II also illustrate the point that neither the levels nor the changes in discounts on closed-end funds are related very strongly to levels of stock prices or stock returns. The correlation between the returns on the value-weighted market index (VWNY) and the changes in the value-weighted discount index (ΔVWD) is not significantly different from zero. A similar result was obtained by Sharpe and Sosin (1975). Thus, if discounts are driven by movements in investor sentiment, this sentiment is not strongly correlated with the aggregate stock market returns. As we argued above, these movements reflect the differential sentiment of individual investors.

4.2 When Do Funds Get Started?

The investor sentiment approach to the pricing of closed-end funds predicts that new funds get started when old funds sell at premiums or at small discounts. Testing this hypothesis presents several problems. First, over most of the period we examine, very few funds get started. Although

---

14. The reasons for the low correlations of discounts of foreign and domestic funds may have to do with special influences on foreign funds, such as exchange and trading controls, and possibly with different investor sentiments about foreign funds. ASA also has unique risks in that it specializes in South African gold stocks.

Table 1   Correlation of Monthly Discounts of Individual Funds

Correlation between *levels of discounts at month end* for nine individual funds, the discount on a value-weighted portfolio of all closed-end stock funds (VWD) and the total value of all New York Stock Exchange firms, NYVAL (7/65 to 12/85). The pairwise Pearson product-moment correlation and *p*-value for a two-tailed test of the null hypothesis of zero correlation are shown, as is the number of observations.

	AdExp	ASA	CentSec	GenAm	Japan	Lehman	Niag	Petr	TriCon	VWD
AdExp	—									
ASA	0.266 0.0001 225	—								
CentSec	0.654 0.0001 159	−0.286 0.0003 155	—							
GenAm	0.737 0.0001 242	0.065 0.3279 227	0.596 0.0001 159	—						
Japan	0.430 0.0001 239	0.235 0.0004 225	0.512 0.0001 158	0.395 0.0001 241	—					

	C1	C2	C3	C4	C5	C6	C7	C8	C9	C10
Lehman	0.830 / 0.0001 / 240	0.303 / 0.0001 / 225	0.693 / 0.0001 / 159	0.785 / 0.0001 / 242	0.643 / 0.0001 / 239	—				
Niag	0.596 / 0.0001 / 242	0.106 / 0.1104 / 227	0.266 / 0.0007 / 158	0.633 / 0.0001 / 244	0.533 / 0.0001 / 241	0.753 / 0.0001 / 242	—			
Petr	0.378 / 0.0001 / 243	0.165 / 0.0129 / 226	0.159 / 0.0447 / 159	0.254 / 0.0001 / 243	−0.084 / 0.1947 / 240	0.230 / 0.0002 / 241	0.198 / 0.0019 / 243	—		
TriCon	0.651 / 0.0001 / 241	0.075 / 0.2630 / 226	0.651 / 0.0001 / 157	0.459 / 0.0001 / 243	0.533 / 0.0001 / 240	0.666 / 0.0001 / 241	0.671 / 0.0001 / 243	0.279 / 0.0001 / 242	—	
VWD	0.810 / 0.0001 / 243	0.427 / 0.0001 / 228	0.539 / 0.0001 / 159	0.711 / 0.0001 / 245	0.651 / 0.0001 / 242	0.893 / 0.0001 / 243	0.767 / 0.0001 / 245	0.281 / 0.0001 / 244	0.805 / 0.0001 / 244	—
NYVAL	−0.019 / 0.7721 / 243	0.477 / 0.0001 / 228	−0.860 / 0.0001 / 159	−0.254 / 0.0001 / 245	−0.053 / 0.4130 / 242	−0.046 / 0.4714 / 243	−0.084 / 0.1891 / 245	−0.016 / 0.7976 / 244	−0.316 / 0.0001 / 244	−0.056 / 0.2787 / 246

Table II Correlation of Changes in the Monthly Discounts of Individual Funds

Correlation of *changes in the monthly discounts* between nine individual funds, a value-weighted portfolio of all closed-end stock funds (ΔVWD) and the monthly return on a value-weighted portfolio of all New York Stock Exchange firms, VWNY (7/65 to 12/85). The pairwise Pearson product-moment correlation and *p*-value for a two-tailed test of the null hypothesis of zero correlation are shown, as is the number of observations.

	AdExp	ASA	CentSec	GenAm	Japan	Lehman	Niag	Petr	TriCon	ΔVWD
AdExp	—									
ASA	−0.054 0.3687 207	—								
CentSec	0.424 0.0001 155	0.037 0.6530 149	—							
GenAm	0.301 0.0068 237	−0.622 0.3687 211	0.063 0.4374 155	—						
Japan	−0.028 0.6732 232	0.0189 0.7870 208	−0.0311 0.7030 153	0.0181 0.7831 235	—					

Lehman	0.304 0.0001 235	0.061 0.3808 210	0.339 0.0001 155	0.406 0.0001 238	0.037 0.6700 233	—				
Niag	0.173 0.0075 237	0.082 0.236 211	0.178 0.028 153	0.188 0.0034 241	0.118 0.0719 235	0.263 0.0001 238	—			
Petr	0.269 0.0001 239	0.051 0.4650 209	0.056 0.4884 155	0.247 0.0001 239	0.173 0.0081 234	0.173 0.0077 236	0.249 0.0001 239	—		
TriCon	0.358 0.0001 235	-0.171 0.0133 209	0.238 0.0033 151	0.242 0.0002 239	0.053 0.4187 233	0.309 0.0011 236	0.247 0.0001 239	0.201 0.0018 237	—	
ΔVWD	0.419 0.0001 239	0.384 0.0001 213	0.300 0.0001 155	0.435 0.0001 243	0.165 0.0109 237	0.629 0.0001 240	0.413 0.0001 243	0.381 0.0001 241	0.561 0.0001 241	—
VWNY	0.159 0.0138 239	-0.143 0.037 213	0.199 0.0131 155	0.059 0.3638 243	-0.241 0.0002 237	0.1061 0.3229 240	0.225 0.0004 243	-0.027 0.6760 241	0.120 0.0629 241	0.013 0.8446 245

this fact makes sense given that funds almost always trade at a discount during this period, it makes testing more difficult. Second, it takes time to organize and register a fund, which means that funds can start trading much later than the time they are conceived. These delays also raise the possibility that fund offerings are withdrawn when market conditions change, creating a bias in the time series of fund starts. Third, new funds tend to be brought to market with features which distinguish them from existing funds. In the early 1970's the funds which got started were primarily bond funds and funds specializing in restricted securities, types that had not previously existed. In the bull market of 1985–87, numerous foreign funds and so called "celebrity funds" (funds managed by well-known money managers) came to market. The former offered easy access to markets in specific foreign countries, and the latter offered an opportunity to cash in on the expertise of famous managers. To the extent seasoned funds and existing funds are not seen as perfect substitutes, new funds could get started even when seasoned funds sell at discounts.

In this paper, we do not delve deeply into fund organization and marketing issues but rather present some simple statistics. Figure 3 plots

Figure 3   The number of closed-end stock funds started and the discount on stock funds at the beginning of the year.

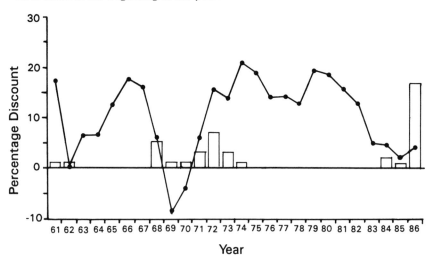

This graph shows the number of closed-end stock funds started during the year and the percentage discount on a value-weighted portfolio of closed-end stock funds at the beginning of each year during 1961 to 1986. The line graph represents the percentage discount at the beginning of the year. The bar graph represents the number of stock funds started during the year.

the number of stock funds started each year against the VWD at the beginning of the year. Note that fund starts tend to be clustered through time. Periods when many funds start roughly coincide with periods when discounts are relatively low. Table III compares the value-weighted discounts on seasoned funds in years when one or more new stock funds begin trading and in years where no stock funds begin trading. Between 1961 and 1986, there are 12 years in which one or more stock funds get started and 14 years in which no stock funds start. The average beginning-of-year discount in the former years is 6.40 percent, and the average beginning-of-year discount in the latter years is 13.64 percent. The difference between the average discounts in the two subsamples of years is

Table III   Statistical Comparison of the Value-Weighted Discount at the Beginning of the Year for Years with Fund Starts and Years without Fund Starts

Statistical comparison of the value-weighted discount at the beginning of the year for years in which *one or more closed-end stock funds* were started versus the years in which no stock funds started.**

	Years in which one or More Stock Funds Started	Years in which No Stock Funds Started
Mean value-weighted discount at the beginning of the year	6.40	13.64
Number of years	12	14
t-statistic for a test of a difference in means between two random samples assuming unequal variance	−2.51**	
t-statistic for a test of a difference in means between two random samples assuming equal variance	−2.63**	
z-statistic for the Wilcoxon rank sum test of a difference in means between two random samples	−2.24**	

**Significant at the 1% level in one-tailed tests (5% in two-tailed tests).

significant at the 1 percent level. This result lends some support to the argument that new funds get started when discounts on old funds are lower, though the discounts are nontrivial even in the years with new start-ups. Given the caveats discussed above, the evidence on start up of new funds appears at least consistent with the investor sentiment hypothesis.

4.3 Discount Movements and Returns on Portfolios of Stocks

In this subsection, we present evidence on perhaps the least obvious prediction of the theory, namely that changes in the discounts on closed-end funds should be correlated with returns on baskets of stocks that may have nothing to do with the funds themselves. In particular, we look at portfolios of firms with different capitalizations, under the theory that the individual investors are significant holders and traders of smaller stocks, and so changes in their sentiment should affect both closed-end funds and smaller stocks. Since we have established that discounts on different funds move together, we use the change in the value-weighted discount (ΔVWD) as a proxy for discount changes. Our measure of market returns are returns on the value-weighted index of NYSE stocks. Finally, the portfolios of stocks we consider are ten size-ranked portfolios. The first portfolio (Decile 1) are the 10 percent of all stocks that have the smallest equity value on NYSE, and the tenth portfolio (Decile 10) are the 10 percent with the largest equity value. The portfolio rebalancing algorithm used to compute decile portfolio returns follows Chen, Roll and Ross (1986). Membership of each decile was determined at the beginning of each year and kept constant for the rest of the year. The returns of each firm in the decile were weighted by its beginning-of-month market capitalization. In case of missing returns, a firm was excluded from the portfolio for the current and following month.[15]

Table IV presents the results of time series regressions of returns of decile portfolios on market returns and on changes in VWD. As in previous studies, we find that all portfolios have market betas in the neighborhood of 1, with the smallest firms having a beta of 1.3 and largest firms having a beta of 0.93. Beta estimates are almost identical when these

---

15. Since discounts are reported as of each Friday's close, the use of full monthly returns introduces a potential timing problem. We correct for this by computing the monthly market returns and the returns of the decile portfolios using the exact dates on which the discounts are computed. Slightly weaker results than those of Table IV would obtain if full monthly returns are used, although the coefficient on ΔVWD would still be significant in all deciles at the one percent level (two-tailed), except for Decile 9, which is significant at the two percent level. Special thanks to Raymond Kan for suggesting this improvement.

Table IV   The Time-Series Relationship between Returns on Size-Decile Portfolios, the Market Return, and Changes in Closed-End Fund Discounts

The time-series relationship (7/65 to 12/85) between monthly returns on decile portfolios (dependent variables), changes in the monthly discount on a value-weighted portfolio of closed-end stock funds (ΔVWD), and the monthly return on a value-weighted portfolio of New York Stock Exchange firms (VWNY). Decile 10 contains the largest firms, Decile 1 the smallest. Membership in each decile is determined at the beginning of year and kept constant for the rest of the year. Returns of each firm are weighted by the beginning-of-month market capitalization. In case of missing returns, a firm is excluded from the portfolio for the current and following month. The dependent variable in the last row is the excess return of small firms over large firms, computed by subtracting Decile 10 returns from Decile 1 returns. The number of observations is 245. t-statistics are shown in parentheses.

Return on the Decile Portfolio	Intercept	ΔVWD	VWNY	Adjusted R^2
1 (smallest)	0.0062	−0.0067 (−4.94)	1.238 (18.06)	58.7
2	0.0042	−0.0049 (−4.83)	1.217 (23.66)	70.3
3	0.0036	−0.0039 (−4.20)	1.202 (26.09)	74.0
4	0.0033	−0.0038 (−5.07)	1.163 (30.64)	79.7
5	0.0027	−0.0029 (−4.12)	1.148 (32.90)	81.8
6	0.0024	−0.0028 (−4.65)	1.124 (37.08)	85.1
7	0.0013	−0.0015 (−3.03)	1.134 (45.30)	89.4
8	0.0015	−0.0015 (−3.45)	1.088 (51.32)	91.5
9	0.0003	−0.0010 (−3.14)	1.057 (66.93)	94.8
10 (largest)	−0.0005	0.0010 (3.84)	0.919 (71.34)	95.4
1–10	0.0067	−0.0077 (−4.93)	0.319 (4.05)	13.5

regressions are run without the VWD variable. For all portfolios, we also find evidence of a correlation between returns and changes in the VWD holding market returns constant. For Decile 10, the largest firms, we find that stock prices do poorly when discounts narrow. For the other nine portfolios, stocks do well when discounts shrink.[16] The signs of the effects are as expected. When individual investors become optimistic about closed-end funds and smaller stocks, these stocks do well and discounts narrow. When individual investors become pessimistic about closed-end funds and smaller stocks, smaller stocks do badly and discounts widen.[17]

For Decile 1, a drop of one percent in the monthly value weighted discount index is accompanied by an extra return of 0.67 percent per month. Since the median absolute change in the monthly discount index over our study period is 1.40, this means in a typical month the discount factor is associated with a monthly fluctuation of 0.94 percent in the Decile 1 returns. The median monthly absolute return for Decile 1 firms over this period is 3.912 percent. Thus, in a typical month, approximately 24 percent of the monthly small firm returns is accountable by discount changes, even after controlling for general market movements. For Deciles 2 through 9, the effect is in the same direction but weaker. The effect on the returns of Decile 10 firms, while statistically significant, is of a different sign and much smaller; in a typical month, about five percent of the total return is accountable by discount changes.[18]

The coefficients on the change in VWD are monotonic in portfolio size. For the smallest stocks, which typically have the highest individual ownership, the comovement with closed-end funds is the greatest. For larger capitalization stocks, which have lower individual ownership, this comovement is weaker. Finally, the largest stocks, which by the end of this period had over 50 percent institutional ownership, seem to move in the opposite direction from the discounts. We have replicated these

16. In Table IV, the American South-Africa (ASA) Fund is included in the calculation of the VWD. The results do not materially change if this fund is excluded.

17. The evidence presented thus far is inconsistent with the unmeasured capital gains tax liability hypothesis of discounts. This theory predicts that when stocks do well, closed-end funds should accrue unrealized capital gains, and discounts should in general widen, holding the turnover rates on fund assets constant. However, Table II shows that the correlation between returns on the market and changes in discounts is about zero (the statistically insignificant correlation is negative which goes against the tax theory). Table IV also indicates that discounts narrow when small stocks do well which is also inconsistent with the tax explanation.

18. Based on $(1.40 \times 0.10)/2.534$, where 2.534 is the median absolute return on the Decile 10 portfolio.

findings using equal-weighted rather than value-weighted market returns and found the same monotonicity of coefficients. When an equal-weighted market index is used, however, the five portfolios of largest firms all show negative comovement with the value-weighted discount, while the five smaller portfolios all have positive coefficients. These results are consistent with the view that what is relevant about size in our regressions is individual ownership. Firms which are smaller (larger) than "average" comove positively (negatively) with discounts on closed-end funds because they have a higher (lower) concentration of individual investors than the "average" firm in the market index.

A final piece of evidence germane to this analysis comes from the seasonal pattern of discounts. Brauer and Chang (1990) present the striking result that prices of closed-end funds exhibit a January effect even though prices of the funds' portfolios do not. We confirmed this result in our data: the mean January ΔVWD is significantly negative, meaning discounts shrink in January. Interestingly, Ritter (1988) documents that 40 percent of the year-to-year variation in the turn-of-the-year effect is explained by the buy-sell activities of individual investors. These findings, of course, accord well with the notion that closed-end fund prices are affected by individual investor trading, some of which occurs at the end of the year, and not just by fundamentals. However, to ensure that Table IV results are not restricted to the turn-of-the-year, we performed the same regressions with January and December observations removed. The coefficients on ΔVWD remained significant for all ten deciles at the 1 percent level and the monotonicity is preserved.

To summarize, the evidence suggests that discounts on closed-end funds narrow when smaller stocks do well. This correlation is stronger, the smaller the stocks. These results are consistent with the hypothesis that individual investor sentiment is particularly important for the prices of smaller stocks and of closed-end funds. In the next section, we test the robustness of this finding.

5. Further Evidence on Size Portfolios

5.1 Do Closed-End Funds Hold Small Stocks?

Our finding that smaller stocks do well when discounts on closed-end funds narrow runs into an objection. Suppose that closed-end funds holdings are concentrated in smaller stocks which are thinly traded. Then prices used in the calculation of net asset value are often stale, whereas closed-end fund prices are relatively fresh. This means that when smaller stocks do well, closed-end funds that hold these stocks appreciate, but the net asset value does not rise by as much as it should because some of the smaller stock prices used to compute the NAV are stale. Reported NAV's could also be stale if closed-end funds report changes in NAV sluggishly. The effect would be the same as if assets were infrequently traded. In their case, the discount narrows (i.e., the stock price of the fund moves up relative to its NAV) precisely when smaller stocks do well. The key finding of the previous section could then result from the mismeasurement of the net asset value.

This objection relies on the critical assumption that closed-end funds invest in smaller stocks (so their stock prices move together with the prices of smaller firms). This assumption is suspect in light of Brauer and Chang's (1990) finding that the portfolio holdings of closed-end funds do not exhibit a January effect. To evaluate this assumption more directly, we examine the portfolio of TRICON. Table V describes TRICON's hold-ings, distributed by decile, every 5 years starting in 1965. It is clear from this table that TRICON's holdings are concentrated in stocks in the largest two deciles, which, together with short-term holdings and cash equivalents, represent about 80 percent of the fund's holdings. Short-term holdings and stocks in the top 5 deciles typically represent over 90 percent of the fund's earning assets. In contrast, the fund typically holds less than 4 percent of its assets in stocks from the bottom five deciles. Since the stocks in the top two deciles are virtually never mispriced because of nontrading, and since the stocks in the top five deciles are rarely mispriced, it is hard to believe that TRICON's portfolio is subject to large mistakes in the calculation of net asset value because of nontrad-ing or sluggish reporting.

In Table VI we again regress decile returns on VWNY and changes in discounts as in Table IV, but this time changes in TRICON's discount are used instead of the changes in the value-weighted discount (ΔVWD). The results are very similar to those in Table IV although parameter estimates are closer to zero, presumably because of a larger idiosyncratic component to TRICON's discounts. Nonetheless, it remains the case that smaller stocks do well when TRICON's discount narrows even though TRICON is holding virtually no small stocks. This finding is inconsistent with the hypothesis that our results can be explained by nontrading or delayed reporting.[19] Incidentally, TRICON itself is a Decile 8 stock, and its comovement with small stocks cannot be explained by the size of its own market capitalization.

---

19. We also regressed the difference between the small and large firm returns (Decile 1 returns minus Decile 10 returns) against market movements and the change in discounts for each of ten major funds. For all ten funds, the coefficient on the discount variable was negative, significantly so for eight of the funds. Thus the relationship between small firm

Table V Composition of the Tricontinental Corporation Investment Portfolio

Composition of the investment portfolio of Tricontinental Corporation (Tricon) at the end of the year, distributed by the total market capitalization of the individual investments. To construct this table, each holding in the Tricon portfolio for each of the years listed was identified from the financial statements of the fund. For the majority of holdings, market capitalization was obtained through the CRSP tapes; market capitalization for the remainder were traced to Moody's Security Manuals and manually checked against Decile cutoffs for each year. Values are shown in thousands of dollars. Decile cutoffs for each year are the same as those used on earlier regressions and are obtained from CRSP. Cash and short-term holdings include government T-bills and corporate debt instruments, net of short-term liabilities of the fund. Other holdings represent equity securities for which the market capitalization was not readily obtainable.

	1985		1980		1975		1970		1965	
Decile 1	0.0	0.0	0.0	0.0	2902.4	0.5	3644.7	0.6	8486.8	1.5
Decile 2	0.0	0.0	3316.5	0.4	548.5	0.1	7514.0	1.2	5856.0	1.0
Decile 3	2793.8	0.2	0.0	0.0	3507.9	0.6	125.8	0.0	0.0	0.0
Decile 4	0.0	0.0	7000.0	0.8	2051.2	0.4	1575.0	0.3	0.0	0.0
Decile 5	2477.9	0.2	19125.0	2.2	9840.5	1.7	9715.5	1.6	8016.2	1.4
Decile 6	4575.0	0.4	38519.2	4.4	5903.5	1.0	14304.3	2.4	0.0	0.0
Decile 7	63575.5	5.3	58238.9	6.6	28283.5	5.0	21934.8	3.7	23832.0	4.3
Decile 8	118981.2	10.0	88204.4	10.1	53320.2	9.4	51241.0	8.5	76452.2	13.7
Decile 9	306874.7	25.7	181298.3	20.7	69407.0	12.2	49787.5	8.3	82263.8	14.7
Decile 10	558993.8	46.8	391753.9	44.7	344500.4	60.7	371398.4	61.7	336612.2	60.2
Short-term holdings & cash equivalents	128745.1	10.8	67978.2	7.8	41905.7	7.4	60690.5	10.1	17940.0	3.2
Other holdings	8143.2	0.7	20890.9	2.3	5474.4	1.0	9702.1	1.6	0.0	0.0
Total value of portfolio	1195160.3	100.0%	876325.3	100.0%	567645.2	100.0%	601633.6	100.0%	559459.2	100.0%

Table VI   The Time-Series Relationship between Returns on Size-Decile Portfolios, the Market Return, and Changes in the Discount of Tri-Continental Corporation.

The time-series relationship (7/65 to 12/85) between monthly returns on decile portfolios (dependent variables), changes in the monthly discount of Tri-Continental (TriCon) and the monthly return on a value-weighted portfolio of New York Stock Exchange firms (VWNY). Decile 10 contains the largest firms, Decile 1 the smallest. Membership in each decile is determined at the beginning of year and kept constant for the rest of the year. Returns of each firm is weighted by the beginning-of-month market capitalization. In case of missing returns, a firm is excluded from the portfolio for the current and following month. The dependent variable in the last row is the excess return of small firms over large firms, computed by subtracting Decile 10 returns from Decile 1 returns. The number of observations is 241. t-statistics are shown in parentheses.

Return on the Decile Portfolio	Intercept	TriCon	VWNY	Adjusted R^2
1 (smallest)	0.0062	−0.0026 (−2.74)	1.263 (17.52)	56.0
2	0.0044	−0.0021 (−2.98)	1.236 (23.11)	68.9
3	0.0039	−0.0017 (−2.70)	1.214 (25.46)	72.9
4	0.0036	−0.0013 (−2.41)	1.174 (29.39)	78.3
5	0.0030	−0.0011 (−2.40)	1.156 (31.96)	81.0
6	0.0025	−0.0014 (−3.41)	1.135 (36.28)	84.6
7	0.0014	−0.0009 (−2.76)	1.142 (44.99)	89.4
8	0.0016	−0.0010 (−3.54)	1.097 (51.41)	91.7
9	0.0004	−0.0007 (−3.21)	1.062 (66.21)	94.8
10 (largest)	−0.0006	0.0005 (2.94)	0.916 (69.80)	95.4
1−10	0.0069	−0.0031 (−2.85)	0.347 (4.20)	8.1

5.2 The Stability of Results over Time

A further concern about our analysis is whether the results are stable over time. In Table VII we reproduce the results from Table IV except we split the sample in the middle (September 1975). For the earlier subsample, the results are stronger than in Table IV, with both the significance and the monotonicity of coefficients reemerging. For the second half, the results are significantly weaker. Although the coefficients on the change in the value-weighted discounts are negative for the first nine decile portfolios and positive for the tenth, their magnitude and statistical significance are much smaller than in the first half of the sample.

What can cause this instability of coefficients over time? One possibility is that the variation in the VWD was smaller in the later subperiod, yielding less explanatory power. Indeed, the standard deviation of ΔVWD falls from 2.40 to 1.95 from the first subperiod to the second. However, there is a more basic economic reason why the second period results might be different—the steady increase in institutional ownership of small firms. As we mentioned earlier, 26.5 percent of the shares of the smallest decile firms were held by institutions by 1988. An examination of a random sample of the smallest decile firms in 1980 revealed that institutions held only 8.5 percent of the shares. In just 8 years, institutions have more than tripled their holdings in first decile firms. At the same time, institutions have continued to avoid closed-end funds, presumably because money managers are reluctant to delegate money management. One possible interpretation of the evidence, then, is that in the second half of our sample, individual investors became relatively less important in determining stock prices, particularly for the stocks of smaller firms. As a result, individual investor sentiment, which continues to be reflected in the discounts on closed-end funds, is no longer as strongly reflected in the pricing of smaller stocks.

To test this conjecture, we formed a portfolio consisting of all NYSE firms, other than closed-end funds, which had less than 10 percent institutional ownership in 1985.[20] We look at these firms in 1985 because over time institutional holdings have increased, and so firms that have less than 10 percent institutional ownership in 1985 are likely to have even

---

excess returns and discount changes is relatively insensitive to the choice of the fund. However, the t-statistics on $\Delta DISC_i$ for individual‑funds are lower than the t-statistic on ΔVWD in Table IV, suggesting the portfolio approach was successful in removing idiosyncratic variations in the individual fund discounts.

20. More precisely, we required that the total of institutional and closely-held shares, as reported by the January issue of the *Standard and Poor's Stock Report*, be less than 10 percent of a firm's outstanding common shares.

Table VII Stability of the Time-Series Relationship between Returns on Size-Decile Portfolios, the Market Return, and Changes in Closed-End Fund Discounts

Analysis of the stability of the time-series relationship between monthly returns on decile portfolios (dependent variables), changes in the monthly discount on a value-weighted portfolio of closed-end stock funds (ΔVWD) and the monthly return on a value-weighted portfolio of New York Exchange firms (VWNY). Decile 10 contains the largest firms, Decile 1, the smallest. Membership in each decile is determined at the beginning of year and kept constant for the rest of the year. Returns of each firm is weighted by the beginning-of-month market capitalization. In case of missing returns, a firm is excluded from the portfolio for the current and following month. The dependent variable in the last row is the excess return of small firms over large firms, computed by subtracting Decile 10 returns from Decile 1 returns. The number of observations for the first period is 122, the second period is 123. t-statistics are shown in parentheses.

Return on the Decile Portfolio	First 123 months (7/65 to 9/75)				Second 123 months (10/75 to 12/85)			
	Intercept	ΔVWD	VWNY	Adj. R^2	Intercept	ΔVWD	VWNY	Adj. R^2
1 (smallest)	0.0054	−0.0101 (−5.50)	1.355 (13.83)	63.2	0.0079	−0.0022 (−1.08)	1.140 (12.08)	54.9
2	0.0015	−0.0070 (−4.89)	1.303 (16.97)	71.1	0.0078	−0.0022 (−1.52)	1.129 (16.79)	70.3

3	0.0016	-0.0057 (-4.60)	1.269 (19.18)	75.6	0.0064	-0.0014 (-1.00)	1.137 (17.80)	72.5
4	0.0022	-0.0050 (-4.88)	1.206 (21.99)	80.2	0.0048	-0.0022 (-1.98)	1.123 (21.16)	79.1
5	0.0010	-0.0042 (-4.59)	1.193 (24.27)	83.1	0.0050	-0.0010 (-0.95)	1.104 (22.29)	80.5
6	0.0014	-0.0038 (-4.58)	1.184 (26.79)	85.6	0.0041	-0.0016 (-1.81)	1.060 (25.71)	84.7
7	0.0006	-0.0021 (-2.90)	1.184 (31.04)	88.8	0.0025	-0.0009 (-1.31)	1.080 (33.44)	90.3
8	0.0016	-0.0018 (-2.98)	1.123 (35.67)	91.3	0.0017	-0.0012 (-1.89)	1.053 (36.56)	91.8
9	0.0000	-0.0013 (-2.82)	1.084 (44.58)	94.3	0.0009	-0.0007 (-1.52)	1.027 (50.93)	95.6
10 (largest)	-0.0002	0.0014 (4.16)	0.902 (50.18)	95.5	-0.0010	0.0004 (1.11)	0.937 (50.12)	95.4
1–10	0.0056	-0.0115 (-5.47)	0.4530 (4.04)	25.2	0.0089	-0.0027 (-1.12)	0.2038 (1.87)	2.5

lower institutional ownership before 1985. In other words, the ownership structure of these firms is similar to that of closed-end funds. In 1985, there were only 56 such firms on NYSE, of which we found CUSIP numbers for 52. Interestingly, 37 (71 percent) of these stocks are public utilities which are not fundamentally related to closed-end funds in any obvious way. It is also of interest that only 8 (15 percent) of these firms are in the smallest size decile and 26 firms (50 percent) are in Deciles 5 and higher, so this is not a portfolio of small firms. Given our conjecture that individual ownership, rather than size per se, causes comovement with closed-end fund discounts, we expect a positive correlation between the returns of these stocks held largely by individuals and the changes in discounts on closed-end funds.

Table VIII presents the regression of the portfolio returns of individual-owned firms on market returns and the change in the value-weighted discount. For the whole period, and for both of the two subperiods, the coefficients on ΔVWD are significant, even after controlling for market movements. Firms held primarily by individuals do well, controlling for

Table VIII   The Time-Series Relationship Between Returns of Firms with Low Institutional Ownership, the Market Return, and Changes in Closed-End Fund Discounts

The time-series relationship between the monthly returns on a portfolio of firms with low institutional ownership (the dependent variable), changes in the monthly discount on a value-weighted portfolio of closed-end stock funds (ΔVWD), and the monthly return on a value-weighted portfolio of New York Stock Exchange firms (VWNY). The dependent variable is the equally-weighted mean monthly return on a portfolio of firms whose total institutional ownership of common stocks outstanding is 10% or less. Membership in the portfolio is based on the total shares held by institutions and insiders as reported in the January, 1985 edition of the *S&P Stock Report*. A total of 52 firms is in the portfolio. Number of observations is 245, 122, and 123, respectively, for the three time periods. *t*-statistics are shown in parentheses.

Time Period	Intercept	ΔVWD	VWNY	Adjusted R^2
All months	0.0012	−0.0035	0.744	59.8
(7/65–12/85)		(−4.30)	(18.67)	
First 123 months	−0.0020	−0.0042	0.790	60.9
(7/65–9/75)		(−3.74)	(13.50)	
Second 123 months	0.0051	−0.0025	0.677	57.5
(10/75–12/85)		(−2.17)	(12.60)	

the market, when discounts on closed-end funds narrow. This finding corroborates our explanation of the weaker correlation between changes in discounts and returns on smaller stocks in the second subperiod. Specifically, individual investors, whose sentiment closed-end fund discounts capture, became less important in holding and trading small firms. Thus, the weaker results in Table VII for the second subsample, as well as Table VIII results for individual-owned firms, both support the individual investor sentiment interpretation of the evidence.

6. Are Discounts a Sentiment Index?

We have interpreted the discount on closed-end funds as an individual investor sentiment index. This section presents further evidence to substantiate this interpretation. First, we examine the relationship between this index and the risk factors identified by Chen, Roll, and Ross (1986). If the discounts are highly correlated with measures of fundamental risk, then our interpretation may be suspect. Second, we check whether the discounts are related to the net withdrawals from open-end funds and to the volume of initial public offerings of stocks other than closed-end funds. The latter tests are comparisons of discounts with other indices of investor sentiment.

6.1 Relationship of Discount Changes to Other Macroeconomic Factors

One question raised by our empirical evidence is whether the sentiment factor that we identify with the VWD is a new factor or whether it just proxies for macroeconomic factors previously identified in the literature. Chen, Roll and Ross (1986) present a number of macroeconomic variables that affect stock returns in time-series regressions and expected returns in cross-section regressions. They interpret the variables to be risk factors. The variables include "innovations" in: industrial production, risk premia on bonds, the term structure of interest rates, and expected inflation. Table IX presents the monthly correlations of changes in these factors with changes in the value-weighted discount (ΔVWD).

The main pattern that emerges from this table is that changes in discounts are not highly correlated with changes in "fundamental" factors. The correlations with "hard" macroeconomic variables such as production are very small. There is some correlation (0.157) between the changes in the discount and changes in the expected inflation rate (DEI). When expected inflation rises, so does the discount. We know of no fundamental explanation for this finding. Notice that changes in discounts are not correlated with the unanticipated change in the term structure (UTS).

Table IX Correlation between Changes in the Value-Weighted Discount and Innovations in Various Macroeconomic Variables

Correlation between the monthly change in discount on a value-weighted porfolio of closed-end stock funds, innovations in various macroeconomic variables, and the excess return earned by small (Decile 1) firms over large (Decile 10) firms for the period 7/65 to 12/85. The pairwise Pearson product-moment correlation and p-value for two-tailed test of the null hypothesis of zero correlation are shown. The number of observations is either 245 or 246. The macroeconomic variables are obtained from Chen, Roll, and Ross (1986) and are briefly described here. ΔVWD is the monthly change in the discount on a value-weighted portfolio of closed-end stock funds. DECSIZ is the monthly return on the smallest decile firms (Decile 1) minus the monthly return on the largest decile firms (Decile 10). EWNY and VWNY are the returns on equal-weighted and value-weighted portfolios of NYSE firms, respectively. MP(t + 1) is the seasonally unadjusted the monthly change in industrial production, as measured by $\log(IP(t + 1)) - \log(IP(t))$, where IP($t$) is the seasonally unadjusted production at month t. YP(t + 12) is the yearly change in industrial production as measured by $\log(IP(t + 12)) - \log(IP(t))$. UPR($t$) is the unanticipated change in risk premia at month t, measured by UBAA $-$ LGB where UBAA is the return of under Baa bonds at month t, and LGB is the return on long term government bonds at month t. UTS(t) is the unanticipated change in term structure at month t, as measured by LGB $-$ TB where LGB is the return on long term government bonds at month t and TB is the Treasury-Bill return of month t as observed at the end of month t $-$ 1. DEI(t) is the change in expected inflation measured by EI(t + 1) $-$ EI(t) where EI is the expected inflation for month t as at month t $-$ 1 computed by subtracting expected real interest of month t (Fama-Gibbons (1984)) from the T-Bill return of month t. UI(t) is unanticipated inflation measured by I(t) $-$ EI(t) where I(t) is the realized inflation for month t (CRSP SBBI), and EI(t) is the expected inflation for month t as at month t $-$ 1.

	DECSIZ	EWNY	VWNY	MP	YP	UPR	UTS	DEI	UI
ΔVWD	-0.268	-0.093	-0.0126	-0.003	-0.006	-0.053	-0.052	0.157	0.057
	0.0001	0.1489	0.8446	0.9571	0.9303	0.4099	0.4207	0.0137	0.3721

This result is counter to the agency cost argument which predicts that when long rates fall the present value of future management fees rise, so discounts should increase.

Another way to see whether the discount is an independent factor is to add this variable to an equation explaining returns using the other risk factors. Table X presents results of regressions of the monthly difference in returns between smallest and largest deciles of firms on changes in various factors. The results show that, even when changes in Chen, Roll, and Ross's "fundamental" factors are controlled for, changes in the VWD still have a pronounced and significant effect on the difference in returns between small and large firms. In fact, in Model 7, which includes the value-weighted NYSE index, the Chen, Roll, and Ross factors, and the change in the value-weighted discount, the discount variable has the highest t-statistic. The value-weighted discount seems to be a factor with an independent influence on returns. Even if changes in investor sentiment are (weakly) correlated with changes in "fundamental" factors, they still have a large influence of their own.

6.2 Evidence from Open-End Funds Redemptions

Malkiel (1977) found that discounts on closed-end funds narrow when purchases of open-end funds outstrip redemptions. His interpretation of this finding is similar to our own—similar market forces drive the demand for both open- and closed-end funds.

To examine this issue more closely, we have extended Malkiel's sample through the entire 246 months of our study period (7/65 to 12/85), and performed a similar analysis. After February 1982, there is an enormous increase in net purchases of open-end funds. Since this appears to be a regime change relative to the previous experience, we have estimated our regressions separately for two periods: 1965–1981 and 1965–1985. The results are presented in Table XI.

The results in Table XI confirm Malkiel's finding that discounts increase with net redemptions from open-end funds. The ratio of redemptions to sales is significant in both time periods, and the difference in redemptions and sales is significant if the last 3 years of the sample are excluded. Although the overall explanatory power of these regressions is low, these results lend further credence to the view that changes in closed-end fund discounts reflect changes in individual investor sentiment. In this case, the evidence suggests that the investors whose sentiment changes are also investors in open-end funds. These tend to be individual rather than institutional investors.

Table X   The Relationship between Small Firm Excess Returns, Macroeconomic Innovations, and Changes in the Value-Weighted Discount

The time-series relationship (7/65 to 12/85) between the excess return earned by small (Decile 1) firms over large (Decile 10) firms, innovations in various macroeconomic variables and the monthly change in discount on a value-weighted portfolio of closed-end stock funds shown as ΔVWD. The number of observations is 245 and t-statistics are shown in parentheses. The macroeconomic variables are obtained from Chen, Roll, and Ross (1986) and are briefly described here. The dependent variable is the monthly return on the smallest decile firms (Decile 1) minus the monthly return on the largest decile firms (Decile 10). EWNY and VWNY are the returns on equal-weighted and value-weighted portfolios of NYSE firms, respectively. $MP(t + 1)$ is the monthly change in industrial production, as measured by $\log(IP(t + 1)) - \log(IP(t))$, where $IP(t)$ is the seasonally unadjusted production at month t. $YP(t + 12)$ is the yearly change in industrial production as measured by $\log(IP(t + 12)) - \log(IP(t))$. $UPR(t)$ is the unanticipated change in risk premia at month t measured by UBAA minus LGB where UBAA is the return of under Baa bonds at month t, and LGB is the return on long term government bonds at month t. $UTS(t)$ is the unanticipated change in term structure at month t as measured by $LGB - TB$ where LGB is the return on long term government bonds at month t and TB is the Treasury-Bill return of month t as observed at the end of month $t - 1$. $DEI(t)$ is the change in expected inflation measured by $EI(t + 1) - EI(t)$ where EI is the expected inflation for month t as at month $t - 1$ computed by subtracting expected real interest of month t (Fama-Gibbons (1984)) from the T-Bill return of month t. $UI(t)$ is unanticipated inflation, measured by $I(t) - EI(t)$ where $I(t)$ is the realized inflation for month t (CRSP SBBI), and $EI(t)$ is the expected inflation for month t as at month $t - 1$.

Model	Intercept	VWNY	EWNY	YP	MP	DEI	UI	UPR	UTS	ΔVWD	Adj. R^2
1	0.0086	—	—	0.0150 (0.23)	0.4212 (3.07)	0.768 (0.16)	-3.793 (-1.98)	0.789 (4.26)	0.480 (2.84)	—	12.1
2	0.0090	—	—	—	0.4256 (3.14)	0.851 (0.18)	-3.774 (-1.98)	0.799 (4.44)	0.489 (2.99)	—	12.5
3	-0.0002	—	0.7400 (11.61)	—	0.3572 (3.28)	-6.210 (-1.64)	-0.391 (-0.25)	-0.129 (-0.78)	-0.464 (-3.00)	—	43.8
4	0.0064	0.2973 (2.92)	—	—	0.4439 (3.32)	-2.004 (-0.43)	-2.989 (-1.57)	0.518 (2.57)	0.166 (0.85)	—	15.2
5	0.0084	—	—	—	0.4332 (3.28)	3.347 (0.73)	-3.643 (-1.97)	0.731 (4.16)	0.463 (2.91)	-.0068 (-4.08)	17.9
6	-0.0005	—	0.7264 (11.82)	—	0.3670 (3.49)	-3.907 (-1.06)	-0.344 (-0.23)	-0.173 (-1.09)	-0.471 (-3.16)	-.0060 (-4.53)	48.1
7	0.0055	0.3294 (3.34)	—	—	0.4546 (3.51)	0.317 (0.07)	-2.77 (-1.51)	0.415 (2.12)	0.103 (0.54)	-.0072 (-4.40)	21.2

Table XI   The Relationship Between Net Redemption on Open-End Funds, the Market Return, and Changes in the Value-Weighted Discount

The time-series relationship between net redemption on open-end funds (dependent variable), the monthly return on a value-weighted portfolio of New York Stock Exchange firms (VWNY), and changes in the monthly discount on a value-weighted portfolio of closed-end stock funds (ΔVWD). The net redemption on open-end funds is measured two ways: by the monthly ratio of net redemptions to sales on open-end funds (R/S) and by the monthly net redemption on open-end funds expressed as a percentage of total funds assets at the beginning of the month (NRED). R/S is computed as redemptions/sales. NRED is computed as (redemptions-sales)/total fund assets. Monthly redemptions, sales, and fund assets data are obtained from the Investment Companies Institute and represent all open-end funds with long-term investment objectives (i.e., exclude money market and short-term municipal bond funds). t-statistics are shown in parentheses.

PANEL A—7/65 to 12/85

Model	Dep. Var.	Intercept	VWNY	ΔVWD	Adj. R^2	No. of Obs.
1	R/S	0.855	−1.864	0.029	4.9	245
			(−3.03)	(2.35)		
2	NRED	−0.005	−0.044	0.0001	3.0	245
			(−3.05)	(0.38)		

PANEL B—7/65 to 2/82

Model	Dep. Var.	Intercept	VWNY	ΔVWD	Adj. R^2	No. of Obs.
1	R/S	0.949	−1.417	0.034	4.5	199
			(−2.18)	(2.53)		
2	NRED	−0.001	−0.009	0.0003	3.6	199
			(−1.73)	(2.50)		

6.3 Evidence from Initial Public Offerings

Another domain in which individual investors are important is the initial public offerings of corporations other than closed-end funds (IPO's). The investor sentiment hypothesis suggests that these IPO's should be more prevalent in times when individual investors are optimistic, so the stocks will fetch high prices relative to their fundamental values. While institutional investors are more important buyers of IPO's than they are of closed-end funds (Weiss (1989) estimates that, on average, 23 percent of

Table XII   The Relationship between Number of IPO's, the Dividend-to-Price Ratio on S&P500, and the Value-Weighted Discount at the Beginning of the Year

The time-series relationship between the annual number of Initial Public Offerings (dependent variable), the dividend to price ratio of S&P500 stocks at the beginning of the year expressed as a percentage (Div/Price), and the level of the value-weighted discount on a portfolio of closed-end funds at the beginning of the year (VWD_{t-1}). The computation of the dividend to price ratio on the S&P500 index follows Fama and French (1988). The number of observations is 20. t-statistics are shown in parentheses.

Intercept	VWD_{t-1}	Div/Price	Adjusted R^2
456.9	−19.3	—	40.9
	(−3.76)		
230.1	−21.8	61.8	41.5
	(−3.90)	(1.09)	

IPO stocks are held by institutions three quarters after the offering). Individuals still account for over 75 percent of buying of IPO's, and we expect their sentiment to affect the timing of these offerings.

To measure the intensity of IPO activity we use the annual number of IPO's from Ibbotson, Sindelar, and Ritter (1988). We regress this measure of IPO volume on the beginning of the year value-weighted discount. Of course, IPO activity might be responsive to fundamentals as well. For example, firms might go public to raise capital when the future looks particularly bright. To control for this factor, we also include the dividend price ratio of the S&P 500, a measure of the expected growth rate of dividends. The regressions are run on an annual rather than a monthly basis to alleviate the strong serial correlation in monthly IPO's, although monthly results are similar. The results are displayed in Table XII and Figure 4.

The first regression shows that in fact IPO volume is highly correlated with the VWD. The coefficient is significant at the 1 percent level, and the adjusted R-square of the regression is 41 percent. The significance of this relationship is also apparent from Figure 4. When the value-weighted discount shrinks from 15 percent to zero, the number of IPO's in the subsequent year rises by approximately 300 which is roughly one standard deviation. The second regression shows, to our surprise, that the

Figure 4   The number of IPO's and the discount at the beginning of the year.

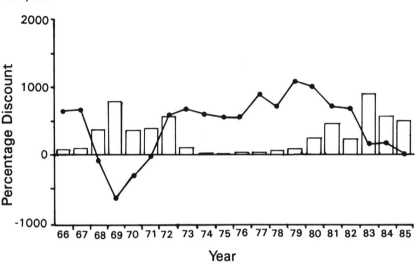

This graph shows the number of Initial Public Offerings (IPO's) during the year and the percentage discount on a value-weighted portfolio of closed-end funds at the beginning of the year during 1966 to 1985. The line graph represents the value-weighted discount at the beginning of the year × 50. The bar graph represents the number of IPO's during the year (Source for IPO data: Ibbotson, Sindelar and Ritter (1988)).

dividend price ratio on the S&P 500 index does not affect the pace of the IPO activity. The regressions seem to suggest that individual investor sentiment is important in determining when companies go public, but the expected growth rate is not. The IPO evidence is consistent with our interpretation of discounts on closed end funds as a measure of individual investor sentiment.

7. Conclusions and Implications

In this paper, we tested the theory that the changing sentiment of individual investors toward closed-end funds and other securities explains the fluctuations of prices and discounts on closed-end funds. In this theory, discounts are high when investors are pessimistic about future returns and low when investors are optimistic. Average discounts exist because the unpredictability of investor sentiment impounds a risk to holding a closed-end fund in addition to the risk inherent in the fund's portfolio. The theory appears to be consistent with the published evidence on closed-end fund prices, and several new predictions of the theory have been confirmed. The evidence suggests that discounts on closed-end funds are indeed a proxy for changes in individual investor sentiment and that the same sentiment affects returns on smaller capitalization stocks and other stocks held and traded by individual investors.

The basic conclusion of this paper is that closed-end fund discounts are a measure of the sentiment of individual investors. That sentiment is sufficiently widespread to affect the prices of smaller stocks in the same way that it influences the prices of closed-end funds. Changing investor sentiment makes funds riskier than the portfolios they hold and so causes average underpricing of funds relative to fundamentals. Since the same investor sentiment affects smaller stocks and so makes them riskier, *smaller stocks must also be underpriced relative to their fundamentals.* The result that small firms appear to earn excess returns is, of course, well known in finance as the small firm effect. Thus, if our theory is correct, the small firm effect may be, in part, clientele related. Interestingly, the theory also predicts that the portion of the small firm effect due to noise trader risk will diminish as individual investors become less significant traders in small firm shares. The fact that the small firm effect has diminished in recent years lends intriguing support to this idea.

While our findings do not imply risk-free arbitrage opportunities, they do point to the existence of nonfundamental risks within the market. The fact that such risks are priced yields two important implications:

1. Securities subject to such risks will trade, on average, at discounts from their fundamentals.
2. Movements in security prices (i.e., stock returns) may be attributable to movements in investor sentiment.

The noise trader model of DSSW does not limit underpricing to smaller firms or firms held primarily by individuals since all firms subject to sentiment fluctuations should trade at discounts relative to their fundamentals. However, the clientele of closed-end funds is such that our empirical results pertain only to such firms. There may, of course, be other sentiment measures (institutional investor sentiment?) that affect security prices. Changes in such sentiments would influence returns on the segments of security markets favored by the investors in question and so lead to systematic mispricing.

Appendix I

List of the twenty closed-end stock funds used in constructing the monthly changes in the value-weighted index of discounts (earlier name in parentheses)

ASA Ltd. (American South African)

Abacus Fund, Inc.

Adams Express Co.

Advance Investors Corp.

American International Corp.

Carriers and General Corp.

Dominick Fund, Inc.

Eurofund International, Inc. (Eurofund, Inc.)

General American Investors, Inc.

MA Hanna Co.

International Holdings Corp.

Japan Fund, Inc.

Lehman Corp.

Madison Resources, Inc. (Madison Fund, Inc.)

Niagara Shares Corp.

Petroleum and Resources Corp. (Petroleum Corp. of America)

Surveyor Fund, Inc. (General Public Service Corp.)

Tricontinental Corp.

United Corp.

United States and Foreign Securities Corp.

We would like to acknowledge helpful comments from Greg Brauer, Eugene Fama, Ken French, Raymond Kan, Merton H. Miller, Sam Peltzman, Mark Ready, Sy Smidt, René Stulz, Lawrence Summers, Robert Vishny, Robert Waldmann, and an anonymous referee, and financial support from Russell Sage Foundation and Social Sciences and Humanities Research Council of Canada. Thanks also to Greg Brauer, Nai-Fu Chen, Thomas Herzfeld, and Jay Ritter for providing data, and Sheldon Gao and Erik Herzfeld for research assistance.

References

ANDERSON, SETH C. 1986. Closed-end funds versus market efficiency, *Journal of Portfolio Management* Fall, 63–67.

BLACK, FISCHER. 1986. Presidential address: Noise, *Journal of Finance* 41, 529–543.

BOUDREAUX, K. J. 1973. Discounts and premiums on closed-end mutual funds: A study in valuation, *Journal of Finance* 28, 515–522.

BRAUER, GREGORY A. 1984. Open-ending closed-end funds, *Journal of Financial Economics* 13, 491–507.

———. 1988. Closed-end fund shares' abnormal returns and the information content of discounts and premiums, *Journal of Finance* 43, 113–128.

——— and ERIC CHANG. 1990. Return seasonality in stocks and their underlying assets: Tax loss selling versus information explanations, *Review of Financial Studies* 3, 257–280.

BRICKLEY, JAMES A. and JAMES S. SCHALLHEIM. 1985. Lifting the lid on closed-end investment companies: A case of abnormal returns, *Journal of Financial and Quantitative Analysis* 20, 107–118.

CHEN, NAI-FU, RICHARD ROLL, AND STEPHEN ROSS. 1986. Economic forces and the stock market, *Journal of Business* 59, 383–403.

DE LONG, J. B., A. SHLEIFER, L. H. SUMMERS, and R. J. WALDMANN. 1990. Noise trader risk in financial markets, *Journal of Political Economy* 98, 703–738.

FAMA, EUGENE F. and MICHAEL GIBBON. 1984. A comparison of inflation forecasts, *Journal of Monetary Economics* 13, 327–348.

——— and KENNETH R. FRENCH. 1988. Dividend yields and expected stock returns, *Journal of Financial Economics* 22, 3–26.

GROSSMAN, SANFORD J. and OLIVER D. HART. 1980. Takeover bids, the free-rider problem, and the theory of the corporation, *Bell Journal of Economics and Management Science* Spring, 42–64.

HERZFELD, THOMAS J. 1980. *The Investor's Guide to Closed-end Funds* (McGraw-Hill, New York, NY).

IBBOTSON, ROGER G., JODY L. SINDELAR, and JAY R. RITTER. 1988. Initial public offerings, *Journal of Applied Corporate Finance* 1, 37–45.

LEE, CHARLES M. C., ANDREI SHLEIFER, and RICHARD H. THALER. 1991. Explaining closed-end fund discounts, Unpublished manuscript, University of Michigan, Harvard University, and Cornell University.

MALKIEL, BURTON G. 1977. The valuation of closed-end investment company shares, *Journal of Finance* 32, 847–859.

———. 1985. *A Random Walk Down Wall Street*, 4th ed. (Norton Press, New York, NY).

PEAVY, JOHN W. 1990. Returns on initial public offerings of closed-end funds, *Review of Financial Studies* 3, 695–708.

RICHARDS, R. M., D. R. FRASER, and J. C. GROTH. 1980. Winning strategies for closed-end funds, *Journal of Portfolio Management* Fall, 50–55.

RITTER, JAY R. 1988. The buying and selling behavior of individual investors at the turn of the year, *Journal of Finance* 43, 701–717.

ROENFELDT, RODNEY L. and DONALD L. TUTTLE. 1973. An examination of the discounts and premiums of closed-end investment companies, *Journal of Business Research* Fall, 129–140.

RUSSELL, THOMAS and RICHARD H. THALER. 1985. The relevance of quasi rationality in competitive markets, *American Economic Review* 75, 1071–1082.

SHARPE, WILLIAM F. and HOWARD B. SOSIN. 1975. Closed-end investment companies in the United States: Risk and return, in B. JACQUILLAT, ed.: *European Finance Association 1974 Proceedings* (North Holland, Amsterdam), 37–63.

SHILLER, ROBERT J. 1984. Stock prices and social dynamics, *Brookings Papers on Economic Activity* 2, 457–498.

SHLEIFER, ANDREI and ROBERT W. VISHNY. 1990. Equilibrium short horizons of investors and firms, *American Economic Review Papers and Proceedings* 80, 148–153.

THOMPSON, REX. 1978. The information content of discounts and premiums on closed-end fund shares, *Journal of Financial Economics* 6, 151–186.

WEISS, KATHLEEN. 1989. The post-offering price performance of closed-end funds, *Financial Management* Autumn, 57–67.

WIESENBERGER, A. 1960–1986. *Investment Companies Services*, annual surveys (Warren, Gorham, and Lamont, New York, NY).

ZWEIG, MARTIN E. 1973. An investor expectations stock price predictive model using closed-end fund premiums, *Journal of Finance* 28, 67–87.

PART
II
VOLATILITY

4

Do Stock Prices Move Too Much to be Justified by Subsequent Changes in Dividends?

ROBERT J. SHILLER

A simple model that is commonly used to interpret movements in corporate common stock price indexes asserts that real stock prices equal the present value of rationally expected or optimally forecasted future real dividends discounted by a constant real discount rate. This valuation model (or variations on it in which the real discount rate is not constant but fairly stable) is often used by economists and market analysts alike as a plausible model to describe the behavior of aggregate market indexes and is viewed as providing a reasonable story to tell when people ask what accounts for a sudden movement in stock price indexes. Such movements are then attributed to "new information" about future dividends. I will refer to this model as the "efficient markets model" although it should be recognized that this name has also been applied to other models.

It has often been claimed in popular discussions that stock price indexes seem too "volatile," that is, that the movements in stock price indexes could not realistically be attributed to any objective new information, since movements in the price indexes seem to be "too big" relative to actual subsequent events. Recently, the notion that financial asset prices are too volatile to accord with efficient markets has received some

From: *American Economic Review,* vol. 71, No. 3, pp. 421–436, June 1981. Reprinted by permission of the American Economic Association.

econometric support in papers by Stephen LeRoy and Richard Porter on the stock market, and by myself on the bond market.

To illustrate graphically why it seems that stock prices are too volatile, I have plotted in Figure 1 a stock price index p_t with its *ex post* rational counterpart p_t^* (data set 1).[1] The stock price index p_t is the real Standard and Poor's Composite Stock Price Index (detrended by dividing by a factor proportional to the long-run exponential growth path) and p_t^* is the present discounted value of the actual subsequent real dividends (also as a proportion of the same long-run growth factor).[2] The analogous series for a modified Dow Jones Industrial Average appear in Figure 2 (data set 2). One is struck by the smoothness and stability of the *ex post* rational price series p_t^* when compared with the actual price series. This behavior of p^* is due to the fact that the present value relation relates p^* to a long-weighted moving average of dividends (with weights corresponding to discount factors) and moving averages tend to smooth the series averaged. Moreover, while real dividends did vary over this sample period, they did not vary long enough or far enough to cause major movements in p^*. For example, while one normally thinks of the Great Depression as a time when business was bad, real dividends were substantially below their long-run exponential growth path (i.e., 10–25 percent below the growth path for the Standard and Poor's series, 16–38 percent below the growth path for the Dow Series) only for a few depression years: 1933, 1934, 1935, and 1938. The moving average which determines p^* will smooth out such short-run fluctuations. Clearly the stock market decline beginning in 1929 and ending in 1932 could not be rationalized in terms of subsequent dividends! Nor could it be rationalized in terms of subsequent earnings, since earnings are relevant in this model only as indicators of later dividends. Of course, the efficient markets model does not say $p = p^*$. Might one still suppose that this kind of stock market crash was a rational mistake, a forecast error that rational people might make? This paper will explore here the notion that the very volatility of p (i.e., the tendency of big movements in p to occur again and again) implies that the answer is no.

1. The stock price index may look unfamiliar because it is deflated by a price index, expressed as a proportion of the long-run growth path and only January figures are shown. One might note, for example, that the stock market decline of 1929–32 looks smaller than the recent decline. In real terms, it was. The January figures also miss both the 1929 peak and 1932 trough.

2. The price and dividend series as a proportion of the long-run growth path are defined below at the beginning of Section I. Assumptions about public knowledge or lack of knowledge of the long-run growth path are important, as shall be discussed below. The series p^* is computed subject to an assumption about dividends after 1978. See text and Figure 3 below.

Figure 1

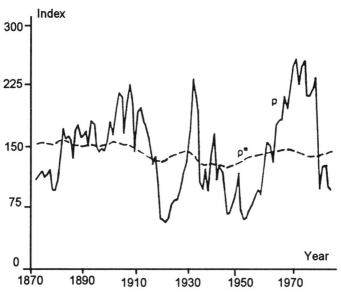

Note: Real Standard and Poor's Composite Stock Price Index (solid line p) and *ex post* rational price (dotted line p^*), 1871–1979, both detrended by dividing a long-run exponential growth factor. The variable p^* is the present value of actual subsequent real detrended dividends, subject to an assumption about the present value in 1979 of dividends thereafter. Data are from Data Set 1, Appendix.

To give an idea of the kind of volatility comparisons that will be made here, let us consider at this point the simplest inequality which puts limits on one measure of volatility: the standard deviation of p. The efficient markets model can be described as asserting that $p_t = E_t(p_t^*)$, i.e., p_t is the mathematical expectation conditional on all information available at time t of p_t^*. In other words, p_t is the optimal forecast of p_t^*. One can define the forecast error as $u_t = p_t^* - p_t$. A fundamental principle of optimal forecasts is that the forecast error u_t must be uncorrelated with the forecast; that is, the covariance between p_t and u_t must be zero. If a forecast error showed a consistent correlation with the forecast itself, then that would in itself imply that the forecast could be improved. Mathematically, it can be shown from the theory of conditional expectations that u_t must be uncorrelated with p_t.

If one uses the principle from elementary statistics that the variance of the sum of two uncorrelated variables is the sum of their variances, one then has var(p^*) = var(u) + var(p). Since variances cannot be nega-

Figure 2

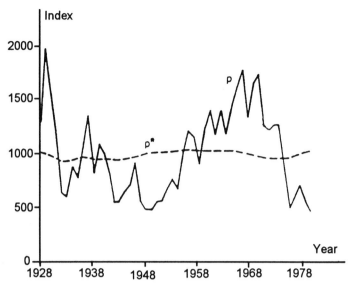

Note: Real modified Dow Jones Industrial Average (solid line p) and *ex post* rational price (dotted line p^*), 1928–1979, both detrended by dividing by a long-run exponential growth factor. The variable p^* is the present value of actual subsequent real detrended dividends, subject to an assumption about the present value in 1979 of dividends thereafter. Data are from Data Set 2, Appendix.

tive, this means $var(p) \leq var(p^*)$ or, converting to more easily interpreted standard deviations,

$$\sigma(p) \leq \sigma(p^*). \tag{1}$$

This inequality (employed before in the papers by LeRoy and Porter and myself) is violated dramatically by the data in Figures 1 and 2 as is immediately obvious in looking at the figures.[3]

---

3. Some people will object to this derivation of (1) and say that one might as well have said that $E_t(p_t) = p_t^*$, i.e., that forecasts are correct "on average," which would lead to a reversal of the inequality (1). This objection stems, however, from a misinterpretation of conditional expectations. The subscript t on the expectations operator E means "taking as given (i.e., nonrandom) all variables known at time t." Clearly, p_t is known at time t and p_t^* is not. In practical terms, if a forecaster gives as his forecast anything other than $E_t(p_t^*)$, then his forecast is not optimal in the sense of expected squared forecast error. If he gives a forecast which equals $E_t(p_t^*)$ only on average, then he is adding random noise to the optimal forecast. The amount of noise apparent in Figures 1 and 2 is extraordinary. Imagine what we would think of our local weather forecaster if, say, actual local temperatures followed the dotted line and his forecasts followed the solid line!

This paper will develop the efficient markets model in Section I to clarify some theoretical questions that may arise in connection with the inequality (1) and some similar inequalities will be derived that put limits on the standard deviation of the innovation in price and the standard deviation of the change in price. The model is restated in innovation form which allows better understanding of the limits on stock price volatility imposed by the model. In particular, this will enable us to see (Section II) that the standard deviation of Δp is highest when information about dividends is revealed smoothly and that if information is revealed in big lumps occasionally the price series may have higher kurtosis (fatter tails) but will have *lower* variance. The notion expressed by some that earnings rather than dividend data should be used is discussed in Section III, and a way of assessing the importance of time variation in real discount rates is shown in Section IV. The inequalities are compared with the data in Section V.

This paper takes as its starting point the approach I used earlier (1979) which showed evidence suggesting that long-term bond yields are too volatile to accord with simple expectations models of the term structure of interest rates.[4] In that paper, it was shown how restrictions implied by efficient markets on the cross-covariance function of short-term and long-term interest rates imply inequality restrictions on the spectra of the long-term interest rate series which characterize the smoothness that the long rate should display. In this paper, analogous implications are derived for the volatility of stock prices, although here a simpler and more intuitively appealing discussion of the model in terms of its innovation representation is used. This paper also has benefited from the earlier discussion of LeRoy and Porter which independently derived some restrictions on security price volatility implied by the efficient markets model and concluded that common stock prices are too volatile to accord with the model. They applied a methodology in some ways similar to that used here to study a stock price index and individual stocks in a sample period starting after World War II.

It is somewhat inaccurate to say that this paper attempts to contradict the extensive literature of efficient markets (as, for example, Paul Cootner's volume on the random character of stock prices, or Eugene Fama's survey).[5] Most of this literature really examines different proper-

---

4. This analysis was extended to yields on preferred stocks by Christine Amsler.

5. It should not be inferred that the literature on efficient markets uniformly supports the notion of efficiency put forth there, for example, that no assets are dominated or that no trading rule dominates a buy and hold strategy (for recent papers see S. Basu; Franco Modigliani and Richard Cohn; William Brainard, John Shoven and Lawrence Weiss; and the papers in the symposium on market efficiency edited by Michael Jensen).

ties of security prices. Very little of the efficient markets literature bears directly on the characteristic feature of the model considered here: that expected *real* returns for the aggregate stock market are constant through time (or approximately so). Much of the literature on efficient markets concerns the investigation of nominal "profit opportunities" (variously defined) and whether transactions costs prohibit their exploitation. Of course, if real stock prices are "too volatile" as it is defined here, then there may well be a sort of real profit opportunity. Time variation in expected real interest rates does not itself imply that any trading rule dominates a buy and hold strategy, but really large variations in expected returns might seem to suggest that such a trading rule exists. This paper does not investigate this, or whether transactions costs prohibit its exploitation. This paper is concerned, however, instead with a more interesting (from an economic standpoint) question: what accounts for movements in real stock prices and can they be explained by new information about subsequent real dividends? If the model fails due to excessive volatility, then we will have seen a new characterization of how the simple model fails. The characterization is not equivalent to other characterizations of its failure, such as that one-period holding returns are forecastable, or that stocks have not been good inflation hedges recently.

The volatility comparisons that will be made here have the advantage that they are insensitive to misalignment of price and dividend series, as may happen with earlier data when collection procedures were not ideal. The tests are also not affected by the practice, in the construction of stock price and dividend indexes, of dropping certain stocks from the sample occasionally and replacing them with other stocks, so long as the volatility of the series is not misstated. These comparisons are thus well suited to existing long-term data in stock price averages. The robustness that the volatility comparisons have, coupled with their simplicity, may account for their popularity in casual discourse.

1. The Simple Efficient Markets Model

According to the simple efficient markets model, the real price P_t of a share at the beginning of the time period t is given by

$$P_t = \sum_{k=0}^{\infty} \gamma^{k+1} E_t D_{t+k} \qquad 0 < \gamma < 1 \tag{2}$$

where D_t is the real dividend paid at (let us say, the end of) time t, E_t denotes mathematical expectation conditional on information available at time t, and γ is the constant real discount factor. I define the constant real interest rate r so that $\gamma = 1/(1 + r)$. Information at time t includes

P_t and D_t and their lagged values, and will generally include other variables as well.

The one-period holding return $H_t \equiv (\Delta P_{t+1} + D_t)/P_t$ is the return from buying the stock at time t and selling it at time $t + 1$. The first term in the numerator is the capital gain, the second term is the dividend received at the end of time t. They are divided by P_t to provide a rate of return. The model (2) has the property that $E_t(H_t) = r$.

The model (2) can be restated in terms of series as a proportion of the long-run growth factor: $p_t = P_t/\lambda^{t-T}$, $d_t = D_t/\lambda^{t+1-T}$ where the growth factor is $\lambda^{t-T} = (1 + g)^{t-T}$, g is the rate of growth, and T is the base year. Dividing (2) by λ^{t-T} and substituting one finds[6]

$$
\begin{aligned}
p_t &= \sum_{k=0}^{\infty} (\lambda\gamma)^{k+1} E_t d_{t+k} \\
&= \sum_{k=0}^{\infty} \bar{\gamma}^{k+1} E_t d_{t+k}.
\end{aligned}
\tag{3}
$$

The growth rate g must be less than the discount rate r if (2) is to give a finite price, and hence $\bar{\gamma} \equiv \lambda\gamma < 1$, and defining $\bar{r}$ by $\bar{\gamma} \equiv 1/(1 + \bar{r})$, the discount rate appropriate for the p_t and d_t series is $\bar{r} > 0$. This discount rate $\bar{r}$ is, it turns out, just the mean dividend divided by the mean price, i.e., $\bar{r} = E(d)/E(p)$.[7]

We may also write the model as noted above in terms of the *ex post* rational price series p_t^* (analogous to the *ex post* rational interest rate series that Jeremy Siegel and I used to study the Fisher effect, or that I used to study the expectations theory of the term structure). That is, p_t^* is the present value of actual subsequent dividends:

$$
p_t = E_t(p_t^*)
\tag{4}
$$

---

6. No assumptions are introduced in going from (2) to (3), since (3) is just an algebraic transformation of (2). I shall, however, introduce the assumption that d_t is jointly stationary with information, which means that the (unconditional) covariance between d_t and z_{t-k}, where z_t is any information variable (which might be d_t itself or p_t), depends only on k, not t. It follows that we can write expressions like var(p) without a time subscript. In contrast, a realization of the random variable the *conditional* expectation $E_t(d_{t+k})$ is a function of time since it depends on information at time t. Some stationarity assumption is necessary if we are to proceed with any statistical analysis.

7. Taking unconditional expectations on both sides of (3) we find

$$
E(p) = \frac{\bar{\gamma}}{1 - \bar{\gamma}} E(d)
$$

using $\bar{\gamma} = 1/1 + \bar{r}$ and solving we find $\bar{r} = E(d)/E(p)$.

where

$$p_t^* = \sum_{k=0}^{\infty} \bar{\gamma}^{k+1} d_{t+k}.$$

Since the summation extends to infinity, we never observe p_t^* without some error. However, with a long enough dividend series we may observe and approximate p_t^*. If we choose an arbitrary value for the terminal value of p_t^* (in Figures 1 and 2, p^* for 1979 was set at the average detrended real price over the sample) then we may determine p_t^* recursively by $p_t^* = \bar{\gamma}(p_{t+1}^* + d_t)$ working backward from the terminal date. As we move back from the terminal date, the importance of the terminal value chosen declines. In data set (1) as shown in Figure 1, $\bar{\gamma}$ is .954 and $\bar{\gamma}^{108} = .0063$ so that at the beginning of the sample the terminal value chosen has a negligible weight in the determination of p_t^*. If we had chosen a different terminal condition, the result would be to add or subtract an exponential trend from the p^* shown in Figure 1. This is

Table 1   Definitions of Principal Symbols

γ = real discount factor for series before detrending; $\gamma = 1/(1 + r)$

$\bar{\gamma}$ = real discount factor for detrended series; $\bar{\gamma} \equiv \lambda\gamma$

D_t = real dividend accruing to stock index (before detrending)

d_t = real detrended dividend; $d_t \equiv D_t/\lambda^{t+1-T}$

Δ = first difference operator $\Delta x_t \equiv x_t - x_{t-1}$

δ_t = innovation operator; $\delta_t x_{t+k} \equiv E_t x_{t+k} - E_{t-1} x_{t+k}$; $\delta x \equiv \delta_t x_t$

E = unconditional mathematical expectations operator. $E(x)$ is the true (population) mean of x

E_t = mathematical expectations operator conditional on information at time t; $E_t x_t \equiv E(x_t|I_t)$ where I_t is the vector of information variables known at time t

λ = trend factor for price and dividend series; $\lambda \equiv 1 + g$ where g is the long-run growth rate of price and dividends

P_t = real stock price index (before detrending)

p_t = real detrended stock price index; $p_t \equiv P_t/\lambda^{t-T}$

p_t^* = ex post rational stock price index (expression 4)

r = one-period real discount rate for series before detrending

$\bar{r}$ = real discount rate for detrended series; $\bar{r} = (1 - \bar{\gamma})/\bar{\gamma}$

$\bar{r}_2$ = two-period real discount rate for detrended series; $\bar{r}_2 = (1 + \bar{r})^2 - 1$

t = time (year)

T = base year for detrending and for wholesale price index; $p_T = P_T$ = nominal stock price index at time T

shown graphically in Figure 3, in which p^* is shown computed from alternative terminal values. Since the only thing we need know to compute p^* about dividends after 1978 is p^* for 1979, it does not matter whether dividends are "smooth" or not after 1978. Thus, Figure 3 represents our uncertainty about p^*.

There is yet another way to write the model, which will be useful in the analysis which follows. For this purpose, it is convenient to adopt notation for the innovation in a variable. Let us define the innovation operator $\delta_t \equiv E_t - E_{t-1}$ where E_t is the conditional expectations operator. Then for any variable X_t the term $\delta_t X_{t+k}$ equals $E_t X_{t+k} - E_{t-1} X_{t+k}$ which is the change in the conditional expectation of X_{t+k} that is made in response to new information arriving between $t-1$ and t. The time subscript t may be dropped so that δX_k denotes $\delta_t X_{t+k}$ and δX denotes δX_0 or $\delta_t X_t$. Since conditional expectations operators satisfy $E_j E_k = E_{\min(j,k)}$ it follows that $E_{t-m} \delta_t X_{t+k} = E_{t-m} (E_t X_{t+k} - E_{t-1} X_{t+k}) = E_{t-m} X_{t+k} - E_{t-m} X_{t+k} = 0$, $m \geq 0$. This means that $\delta_t X_{t+k}$ must be uncorrelated for all k with all information known at time $t-1$ and must,

Figure 3

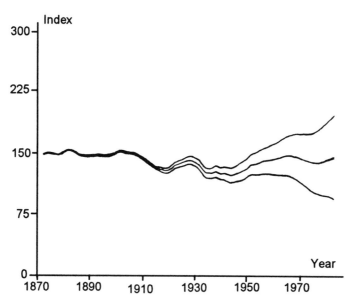

Note: Alternative measures of the *ex post* rational price p^*, obtained by alternative assumptions about the present value in 1979 of dividends thereafter. The middle curve is the p^* series plotted in Figure 1. The series are computed recursively from terminal conditions using dividend series d of Data Set 1.

since lagged innovations are information at time t, be uncorrelated with $\delta_{t'} X_{t+j}$, $t' < t$, all j, i.e., innovations in variables are serially uncorrelated.

The model implies that the innovation in price $\delta_t p_t$ is observable. Since (3) can be written $p_t = \bar{\gamma}(d_t + E_t p_{t+1})$, we know, solving, that $E_t p_{t+1} = p_t / \bar{\gamma} - d_t$. Hence $\delta_t p_t \equiv E_t p_t - E_{t-1} p_t = p_t + d_{t-1} - p_{t-1}/\bar{\gamma} = \Delta p_t + d_{t-1} - \bar{r} p_{t-1}$. The variable which we call $\delta_t p_t$ (or just δp) is the variable which Clive Granger and Paul Samuelson emphasized should, in contrast to $\Delta p_t \equiv p_t - p_{t-1}$, by efficient markets, be unforecastable. In practice, with our data, $\delta_t p_t$ so measured will approximately equal Δp_t.

The model also implies that the innovation in price is related to the innovations in dividends by

$$\delta_t p_t = \sum_{k=0}^{\infty} \bar{\gamma}^{k+1} \delta_t d_{t+k}. \tag{5}$$

This expression is identical to (3) except that δ_t replaces E_t. Unfortunately, while $\delta_t p_t$ is observable in this model, the $\delta_t d_{t+k}$ terms are not directly observable, that is, we do not know when the public gets information about a particular dividend. Thus, in deriving inequalities below, one is obliged to assume the "worst possible" pattern of information accrual.

Expressions (2)–(5) constitute four different representations of the same efficient markets model. Expressions (4) and (5) are particularly useful for deriving our inequalities on measures of volatility. We have already used (4) to derive the limit (1) on the standard deviation of p given the standard deviation of p^*, and we will use (5) to derive a limit on the standard deviation of δp given the standard deviation of d.

One issue that relates to the derivation of (1) can now be clarified. The inequality (1) was derived using the assumption that the forecast error $u_t = p_t^* - p_t$ is uncorrelated with p_t. However, the forecast error u_t is not serially uncorrelated. It is uncorrelated with all information known at time t, but the lagged forecast error u_{t-1} is not known at time t since p_{t-1}^* is not discovered at time t. In fact, $u_t = \sum_{k=1}^{\infty} \bar{\gamma}^k \delta_{t+k} p_{t+k}$, as can be seen by substituting the expressions for p_t and p_t^* from (3) and (4) into $u_t = p_t^* - p_t$, and rearranging. Since the series $\delta_t p_t$ is serially uncorrelated, u_t has first-order autoregressive serial correlation.[8] For this reason, it is

8. It follows that var(u) = var$(\delta p)/(1 - \bar{\gamma}^2)$ as LeRoy and Porter noted. They base their volatility tests on our inequality (1) (which they call theorem 2) and an equality restriction $\sigma^2(p) + \sigma^2(\delta p)/(1 - \bar{\gamma}^2) = \sigma^2(p^*)$ (their theorem 3). They found that, with postwar Standard and Poor earnings data, both relations were violated by sample statistics.

inappropriate to test the model by regressing $p_t^* - p_t$ on variables known at time t and using the ordinary t-statistics of the coefficients of these variables. However, a generalized least squares transformation of the variables would yield an appropriate regression test. We might thus regress the transformed variable $u_t - \bar{\gamma}u_{t+1}$ on variables known at time t. Since $u_t - \bar{\gamma}u_{t+1} = \bar{\gamma}\delta_{t+1}p_{t+1}$, this amounts to testing whether the innovation in price can be forecasted. I will perform and discuss such regression tests in Section V below.

To find a limit on the standard deviation of δp for a given standard deviation of d_t, first note that d_t equals its unconditional expectation plus the sum of its innovations:

$$d_t = E(d) + \sum_{k=0}^{\infty} \delta_{t-k}d_t. \tag{6}$$

If we regard $E(d)$ as $E_{-\infty}(d_t)$, then this expression is just a tautology. It tells us, though, that $d_t t = 0, 1, 2, \ldots$ are just different linear combinations of the same innovations in dividends that enter into the linear combination in (5) which determine $\delta_t p_t t = 0, 1, 2, \ldots$. We can thus ask how large var(δp) might be for given var(d). Since innovations are serially uncorrelated, we know from (6) that the variance of the sum is the sum of the variances:

$$\text{var}(d) = \sum_{k=0}^{\infty} \text{var}(\delta d_k) = \sum_{k=0}^{\infty} \sigma_k^2. \tag{7}$$

Our assumption of stationarity for d_t implies that var$(\delta_{t-k}d_t) \equiv$ var$(\delta d_k) \equiv \sigma_k^2$ is independent of t.

In expression (5) we have no information that the variance of the sum is the sum of the variances since all the innovations are time t innovations, which may be correlated. In fact, for given $\sigma_0^2, \sigma_1^2, \ldots$, the maximum variance of the sum in (5) occurs when the elements in the sum are perfectly positively correlated. This means then that so long as var(δd) $\neq 0$, $\delta_t d_{t+k} = a_k \delta_t d_t$, where $a_k = \sigma_k/\sigma_0$. Substituting this into (6) implies

$$\hat{d}_t = \sum_{k=0}^{\infty} a_k \epsilon_{t-k} \tag{8}$$

where a hat denotes a variable minus its mean: $\hat{d}_t \equiv d_t - E(d)$ and $\epsilon_t \equiv \delta_t d_t$. Thus, if var$(\delta p)$ is to be maximized for given $\sigma_0^2, \sigma_1^2, \ldots$, the dividend process must be a moving average process in terms of its own innovations.[9] I have thus shown, rather than assumed, that if the variance of δp is to be maximized, the forecast of d_{t+k} will have the usual ARIMA form as in the forecast popularized by Box and Jenkins.

We can now find the maximum possible variance for δp for given variance of d. Since the innovations in (5) are perfectly positively correlated, $\text{var}(\delta p) = (\Sigma_{k=0}^{\infty} \bar{\gamma}^{k+1} \sigma_k)^2$. To maximize this subject to the constraint $\text{var}(d) = \Sigma_{k=0}^{\infty} \sigma_k^2$ with respect to $\sigma_0, \sigma_1, \ldots$, one may set up the Lagrangean:

$$L = \left(\sum_{k=0}^{\infty} \bar{\gamma}^{k+1} \sigma_k \right)^2 + \nu \left(\text{var}(d) - \sum_{k=0}^{\infty} \sigma_k^2 \right) \tag{9}$$

where ν is the Lagrangean multiplier. The first-order conditions for σ_j, $j = 0, \ldots \infty$ are

$$\frac{\partial L}{\partial \sigma_j} = 2 \left(\sum_{k=0}^{\infty} \bar{\gamma}^{k+1} \sigma_k \right) \bar{\gamma}^{j+1} - 2\nu\sigma_j = 0 \tag{10}$$

which in turn means that σ_j is proportional to $\bar{\gamma}^j$. The second-order conditions for a maximum are satisfied, and the maximum can be viewed as a tangency of an isoquant for $\text{var}(\delta p)$, which is a hyperplane in $\sigma_0, \sigma_1, \sigma_2, \ldots$ space, with the hypersphere represented by the constraint. At the maximum $\sigma_k^2 = (1 - \bar{\gamma}^2)\text{var}(d)\bar{\gamma}^{2k}$ and $\text{var}(\delta p) = \bar{\gamma}^2 \text{var}(d)/(1 - \bar{\gamma}^2)$ and so, converting to standard deviations for ease of interpretation, we have

$$\sigma(\delta p) \leq \sigma(d)/\sqrt{\bar{r}_2} \tag{11}$$

where

$$\bar{r}_2 = (1 + \bar{r})^2 - 1.$$

Here, $\bar{r}_2$ is the two-period interest rate, which is roughly twice the one-period rate. The maximum occurs, then, when d_t is a first-order autoregressive process, $\hat{d}_t = \bar{\gamma}\hat{d}_{t-1} + \epsilon_t$, and $E_t\hat{d}_{t+k} = \bar{\gamma}^k\hat{d}_t$, where $\hat{d} \equiv d - E(d)$ as before.

The variance of the innovation in price is thus maximized when information about dividends is revealed in a smooth fashion so that the stan-

---

9. Of course, all indeterministic stationary processes can be given linear moving average representations, as Hermann Wold showed. However, it does not follow that the process can be given a moving average representation in terms of its own innovations. The true process may be generated nonlinearly or other information besides its own lagged values may be used in forecasting. These will generally result in a less than perfect correlation of the terms in (5).

dard deviation of the new information at time t about a future dividend d_{t+k} is proportional to its weight in the present value formula in the model (5). In contrast, suppose all dividends somehow became known years before they were paid. Then the innovations in dividends would be so heavily discounted in (5) that they would contribute little to the standard deviation of the innovation in price. Alternatively, suppose nothing were known about dividends until the year they are paid. Here, although the innovation would not be heavily discounted in (5), the impact of the innovation would be confined to only one term in (5), and the standard deviation in the innovation in price would be limited to the standard deviation in the single dividend.

Other inequalities analogous to (11) can also be derived in the same way. For example, we can put an upper bound to the standard deviation of the change in price (rather than the innovation in price) for given standard deviation in dividend. The only difference induced in the above procedure is that Δp_t is a different linear combination of innovations in dividends. Using the fact that $\Delta p_t = \delta_t p_t + \bar{r} p_{t-1} - d_{t-1}$ we find

$$\Delta p_t = \sum_{k=0}^{\infty} \bar{\gamma}^{k+1} \delta_t d_{t+k} + \bar{r} \sum_{j=1}^{\infty} \delta_{t-j} \sum_{k=0}^{\infty} \bar{\gamma}^{k+1} d_{t+k-1} - \sum_{j=1}^{\infty} \delta_{t-j} d_{t-1}. \quad (12)$$

As above, the maximization of the variance of δp for given variance of d requires that the time t innovations in d be perfectly correlated (innovations at different times are necessarily uncorrelated) so that again the dividend process must be forecasted as an ARIMA process. However, the parameters of the ARIMA process for d which maximize the variance of Δp will be different. One finds, after maximizing the Lagrangean expression (analogous to (9)) an inequality slightly different from (11),

$$\sigma(\Delta p) \le \sigma(d)/\sqrt{2\bar{r}}. \quad (13)$$

The upper bound is attained if the optimal dividend forecast is first-order autoregressive, but with an autoregressive coefficient slightly different from that which induced the upper bound to (11). The upper bound to (13) is attained if $\hat{d}_t = (1 - \bar{r})\hat{d}_{t-1} + \epsilon_t$ and $E_t d_{t+k} = (1 - \bar{r})^k \hat{d}_t$, where, as before, $\hat{d}_t \equiv d_t - E(d)$.

2. High Kurtosis and Infrequent Important Breaks in Information

It has been repeatedly noted that stock price change distributions show high kurtosis or "fat tails." This means that, if one looks at a time-series of observations on δp or Δp, one sees long stretches of time when their (absolute) values are all rather small and then an occasional extremely large (absolute) value. This phenomenon is commonly attributed to a tendency for new information to come in big lumps infrequently. There seems to be a common presumption that this information lumping might cause stock price changes to have high or infinite variance, which would seem to contradict the conclusion in the preceding section that the variance of price is limited and is maximized if forecasts have a simple autoregressive structure.

High sample kurtosis does not indicate infinite variance if we do not assume, as did Fama (1965) and others, that price changes are drawn from the stable Paretian class of distributions.[10] The model does not suggest that price changes have a distribution in this class. The model instead suggests that the existence of moments for the price series is implied by the existence of moments for the dividends series.

As long as d is jointly stationary with information and has a finite variance, then p, p^*, δp, and Δp will be stationary and have a finite variance.[11] If d is normally distributed, however, it does not follow that the price variables will be normally distributed. In fact, they may yet show high kurtosis.

To see this possibility, suppose the dividends are serially independent and identically normally distributed. The kurtosis of the price series is defined by $K = E(\hat{p})^4/(E(\hat{p})^2)^2$, where $p \equiv \hat{p} - E(p)$. Suppose, as an example, that with a probability of $1/n$ the public is told d_t at the beginning of time t, but with probability $(n - 1)/n$ has no information about current or future dividends.[12] In time periods when they are told d_t, $\hat{p}_t$ equals $\bar{\gamma}\hat{d}_t$, otherwise $\hat{p}_t = 0$. Then $E(\hat{p}_t^4) = E((\bar{\gamma}\hat{d}_t)^4)/n$ and $E(\hat{p}_t^2) = E((\bar{\gamma}\hat{d}_t)^2)/n$ so that kurtosis equals $nE(\bar{\gamma}\hat{d}_t)^4/E((\bar{\gamma}\hat{d}_t)^2)$ which equals n times the kurtosis of the normal distribution. Hence, by choosing n high

10. The empirical fact about the unconditional distribution of stock price changes is not that they have infinite variance (which can never be demonstrated with any finite sample), but that they have high kurtosis in the sample.

11. With any stationary process X_t, the existence of a finite var(X_t) implies, by Schwartz's inequality, a finite value of cov(X_t, X_{t+k}) for any k, and hence the entire autocovariance function of X_t, and the spectrum, exists. Moreover, the variance of $E_t(X_t)$ must also be finite, since the variance of X equals the variance of $E_t(X_t)$ plus the variance of the forecast error. While we may regard real dividends as having finite variance, innovations in dividends may show high kurtosis. The residuals in a second-order autoregression for d_t have a studentized range of 6.29 for the Standard and Poor series and 5.37 for the Dow series. According to the David-Hartley-Pearson test, normality can be rejected at the 5 percent level (but not at the 1 percent level) with a one-tailed test for both data sets.

12. For simplicity, in this example, the assumption elsewhere in this article that d_t is always known at time t has been dropped. It follows that in this example $\delta_t p_t \neq \Delta p_t + d_{t-1} - rp_{t-1}$ but instead $\delta_t p_t = p_t$.

enough one can achieve an arbitrarily high kurtosis, and yet the variance of price will always exist. Moreover, the distribution of $\hat{p}_t$ conditional on the information that the dividend has been revealed is also normal, in spite of high kurtosis of the unconditional distribution.

If information is revealed in big lumps occasionally (so as to induce high kurtosis as suggested in the above example) $\text{var}(\delta p)$ or $\text{var}(\Delta p)$ are not especially large. The variance loses more from the long interval of time when information is not revealed than it gains from the infrequent events when it is. The highest possible variance for given variance of d indeed comes when information is revealed smoothly as noted in the previous section. In the above example, where information about dividends is revealed one time in n, $\sigma(\delta p) = \bar{\gamma} n^{1/2} \sigma(d)$ and $\sigma(\Delta p) = \bar{\gamma}(2/n)^{1/2} \sigma(d)$. The values of $\sigma(\delta p)$ and $\sigma(\Delta p)$ implied by this example are for all n strictly below the upper bounds of the inequalities (11) and (13).[13]

3. Dividends or Earnings?

It has been argued that the model (2) does not capture what is generally meant by efficient markets, and that the model should be replaced by a model which makes price the present value of expected earnings rather than dividends. In the model (2) earnings may be relevant to the pricing of shares but only insofar as earnings are indicators of future dividends. Earnings are thus no different from any other economic variable which may indicate future dividends. The model (2) is consistent with the usual notion in finance that individuals are concerned with returns, that is, capital gains plus dividends. The model implies that expected total returns are constant and that the capital gains component of returns is just a reflection of information about future dividends. Earnings, in contrast, are statistics conceived by accountants which are supposed to provide an indicator of how well a company is doing, and there is a great deal of latitude for the definition of earnings, as the recent literature on inflation accounting will attest.

There is no reason why price per share ought to be the present value of expected earnings per share if some earnings are retained. In fact, as Merton Miller and Franco Modigliani argued, such a present value formula would entail a fundamental sort of double counting. It is incorrect

---

13. For another illustrative example, consider $\hat{d}_t = \bar{\gamma} \hat{d}_{t-1} + \epsilon_t$ as with the upper bound for the inequality (11) but where the dividends are announced for the next n years every $1/n$ years. Here, even though $\hat{d}_t$ has the autoregressive structure, ϵ_t is not the innovation in d_t. As n goes to infinity, $\sigma(\delta p)$ approaches zero.

to include in the present value formula both earnings at time t and the later earnings that accrue when time t earnings are reinvested.[14] Miller and Modigliani showed a formula by which price might be regarded as the present value of earnings corrected for investments, but that formula can be shown, using an accounting identity to be identical to (2).

Some people seem to feel that one cannot claim price as present value of expected dividends since firms routinely pay out only a fraction of earnings and also attempt somewhat to stabilize dividends. They are right in the case where firms paid out *no* dividends, for then the price p_t would have to grow at the discount rate $\bar{r}$, and the model (2) would not be the solution to the difference equation implied by the condition $E_t(H_t) = r$. On the other hand, if firms pay out a fraction of dividends or smooth short-run fluctuations in dividends, then the price of the firm will grow at a rate less than the discount rate and (2) is the solution to the difference equation.[15] With our Standard and Poor data, the growth rate of real price is only about 1.5 percent, while the discount rate is about 4.8% + 1.5% = 6.3%. At these rates, the value of the firm a few decades hence is so heavily discounted relative to its size that it contributes very little to the value of the stock today; by far the most of the value comes from the intervening dividends. Hence (2) and the implied p^* ought to be useful characterizations of the value of the firm.

The crucial thing to recognize in this context is that once we know the terminal price and intervening dividends, we have specified all that investors care about. It would not make sense to define an *ex post* rational price from a terminal condition on price, using the same formula with earnings in place of dividends.

4. Time-Varying Real Discount Rates

If we modify the model (2) to allow real discount rates to vary without restriction through time, then the model becomes untestable. We do not observe real discount rates directly. Regardless of the behavior of P_t and D_t, there will always be a discount rate series which makes (2) hold

---

14. LeRoy and Porter do assume price as present value of earnings but employ a correction to the price and earnings series which is, under additional theoretical assumptions not employed by Miller and Modigliani, a correction for the double counting.

15. To understand this point, it helps to consider a traditional continuous time growth model, so instead of (2) we have $P_0 = \int_0^\infty D_t e^{-rt} dt$. In such a model, a firm has a constant earnings stream I. If it pays out all earnings, then $D = I$ and $P_0 = \int_0^\infty I e^{-rt} dt = I/r$. If it pays out only s of its earnings, then the firm grows at rate $(1 - s)$, $D_t = sIe^{(1-s)rt}$ which is less than I at $t = 0$, but higher than I later on. Then $P_0 = \int_0^\infty sIe^{(1-s)rt} e^{-rt} dt = \int_0^\infty sIe^{-srt} dt = sI/(rs)$. If $s \neq 0$ (so that we're not dividing by zero) $P_0 = I/r$.

identically. We might ask, though, whether the movements in the real discount rate that would be required aren't larger than we might have expected. Or is it possible that small movements in the current one-period discount rate coupled with new information about such movements in future discount rates could account for high stock price volatility?[16]

The natural extension of (2) to the case of time varying real discount rates is

$$P_t = E_t\left(\sum_{k=0}^{\infty} D_{t+k} \prod_{j=0}^{k} \frac{1}{1 + r_{t+j}}\right) \tag{14}$$

which has the property that $E_t((1 + H_t)/(1 + r_t)) = 1$. If we set $1 + r_t = (\partial U/\partial C_t)/(\partial U/\partial C_{t+1})$, i.e., to the marginal rate of substitution between present and future consumption where U is the additively separable utility of consumption, then this property is the first-order condition for a maximum of expected utility subject to a stock market budget constraint, and equation (14) is consistent with such expected utility maximization at all times. Note that while r_t is a sort of *ex post* real interest rate not necessarily known until time $t + 1$, only the conditional distribution at time t or earlier influences price in the formula (14).

As before, we can rewrite the model in terms of detrended series:

$$p_t = E_t(p_t^*) \tag{15}$$

where

$$p_t^* \equiv \sum_{k=0}^{\infty} d_{t+k} \prod_{j=0}^{k} \frac{1}{1 + \bar{r}_{t+j}}$$

$$1 + \bar{r}_{t+j} \equiv (1 + r_t)/\lambda.$$

This model then implies that $\sigma(p_t) \leq \sigma(p_t^*)$ as before. Since the model is nonlinear, however, it does not allow us to derive inequalities like (11) or (13). On the other hand, if movements in real interest rates are not too large, then we can use the linearization of p_t^* (i.e., Taylor expansion truncated after the linear term) around $d = E(d)$ and $\bar{r} = E(\bar{r})$; i.e.,

$$\hat{p}_t^* \cong \sum_{k=0}^{\infty} \bar{\gamma}^{k+1} \hat{d}_{t+k} - \frac{E(d)}{E(\bar{r})} \sum_{k=0}^{\infty} \bar{\gamma}^{k+1} \hat{\bar{r}}_{t+k} \tag{16}$$

---

16. James Pesando has discussed the analogous question: how large must the variance in liquidity premia be in order to justify the volatility of long-term interest rates?

where $\bar{\gamma} = 1/(1 + E(\bar{r}))$, and a hat over a variable denotes the variable minus its mean. The first term in the above expression is just the expression for p_t^* in (4) (demeaned). The second term represents the effect on p_t^* of movements in real discount rates. This second term is identical to the expression for p^* in (4) except that d_{t+k} is replaced by $\hat{r}_{t+k}$ and the expression is premultiplied by $-E(d)/E(\bar{r})$.

It is possible to offer a simple intuitive interpretation for this linearization. First note that the derivative of $1/(1 + \bar{r}_{t+k})$, with respect to $\bar{r}$ evaluated at $E(\bar{r})$ is $-\bar{\gamma}^2$. Thus, a one percentage point increase i $\bar{r}_{t+k}$ causes $1/(1 + \bar{r}_{t+k})$ to drop by $\bar{\gamma}^2$ times 1 percent, or slightly less than 1 percent. Note that all terms in (15) dated $t + k$ or higher are premultiplied by $1/(1 + \bar{r}_{t+k})$. Thus, if $\bar{r}_{t+k}$ is increased by one percentage point, all else constant, then all of these terms will be reduced by about $\bar{\gamma}^2$ times 1 percent. We can approximate the sum of all these terms as $\bar{\gamma}^{k-1}E(d)/E(\bar{r})$, where $E(d)/E(\bar{r})$ is the value at the beginning of time $t + k$ of a constant dividend stream $E(d)$ discounted by $E(\bar{r})$, and $\bar{\gamma}^{k-1}$ discounts it to the present. So, we see that a one percentage point increase in $\bar{r}_{t+k}$, all else constant, decreases p_t^* by about $\bar{\gamma}^{k+1}E(d)/E(\bar{r})$, which corresponds to the kth term in expression (16). There are two sources of inaccuracy with this linearization. First, the present value of all future dividends starting with time $t + k$ is not exactly $\bar{\gamma}^{k-1}E(d)/E(\bar{r})$. Second, increasing $\bar{r}_{t+k}$ by one percentage point does not cause $1/(1 + \bar{r}_{t+k})$ to fall by exactly $\bar{\gamma}^2$ times 1 percent. To some extent, however, these errors in the effects on p_t^* of $\bar{r}_t, \bar{r}_{t+1}, \bar{r}_{t+2}, \ldots$ should average out, and one can use (16) to get an idea of the effects of changes in discount rates.

To give an impression as to the accuracy of the linearization (16), I computed p_t^* for data set 2 in two ways: first using (15) and then using (16), with the same terminal condition p_{1979}^*. In place of the unobserved $\bar{r}_t$ series, I used the actual four–six-month prime commercial paper rate plus a constant to give it the mean $\bar{r}$ of Table 2. The commercial paper rate is a *nominal* interest rate, and thus one would expect its fluctuations represent changes in inflationary expectations as well as real interest rate movements. I chose it nonetheless, rather arbitrarily, as a series which shows much more fluctuation than one would normally expect to see in an expected *real* rate. The commercial paper rate ranges, in this sample, from 0.53 to 9.87 percent. It stayed below 1 percent for over a decade (1935–46) and, at the end of the sample, stayed generally well above 5 percent for over a decade. In spite of this erratic behavior, the correlation coefficient between p^* computed from (15) and p^* computed from (16) was .996, and $\sigma(p_t^*)$ was 250.5 and 268.0 by (15) and (16), respectively. Thus the linearization (16) can be quite accurate. Note also that while

Table 2   Sample Statistics for Price and Dividend Series

	Data Set 1: Standard and Poor's	Data Set 2: Modified Dow Industrial
Sample Period:	1871–1979	1928–1979
1) $E(p)$	145.5	982.6
$E(d)$	6.989	44.76
2) $\bar{r}$	.0480	0.456
$\bar{r}_2$	.0984	.0932
3) $b = \ln \lambda$	.0148	.0188
$\hat{\sigma}(b)$	(.0011)	(1.0035)
4) $\mathrm{cor}(p, p^*)$	.3918	.1626
$\sigma(d)$	1.481	9.828
Elements of Inequalities:		
Inequality (1)		
5) $\sigma(p)$	50.12	355.9
6) $\sigma(p^*)$	8.968	26.80
Inequality (11)		
7) $\sigma(\Delta p + d_{-1} - \bar{r}p_{-1})$	25.57	242.1
$\min(\sigma)$	23.01	209.0
8) $\sigma(d)/\sqrt{\bar{r}_2}$	4.721	32.20
Inequality (13)		
9) $\sigma(\Delta p)$	25.24	239.5
$\min(\sigma)$	22.71	206.4
10) $\sigma(d)/\sqrt{2\bar{r}}$	4.777	32.56

Note: In this table, E denotes sample mean, σ denotes standard deviation and $\hat{\sigma}$ denotes standard error. Min(σ) is the lower bound on σ computed as a one-sided χ^2 95 percent confidence interval. The symbols p, d, $\bar{r}$, $\bar{r}_2$, b, and p^* are defined in the text. Data sets are described in the Appendix. Inequality (1) in the text asserts that the standard deviation in row 5 should be less than or equal to that in row 6, inequality (11) that σ in row 7 should be less than or equal to that in row 8, and inequality (13) that σ in row 9 should be less than that in row 10.

these large movements in $\bar{r}_t$ cause p_t^* to move much more than was observed in Figure 2, $\sigma(p^*)$ is still less than half of $\sigma(p)$. This suggests that the variability $\bar{r}_t$ that is needed to save the efficient markets model is much larger yet, as we shall see.

To put a formal lower bound on $\sigma(\bar{r})$ given the variability of Δp, note that (16) makes $\hat{p}_t^*$ the present value of z_t, z_{t+1}, . . . where $z_t \equiv \hat{d}_t - \hat{r}E(d)/E(\bar{r})$. We thus know from (13) that $2E(\bar{r})\mathrm{var}(\Delta p) \leq \mathrm{var}(z)$. Moreover, from the definition of z we know that $\text{var}(z) \leq \text{var}(d) + 2\sigma(d)\sigma(\bar{r})E(d)/E(\bar{r}) + \text{var}(\bar{r})E(d)^2/E(\bar{r})^2$ where the equality holds if d_t and $\bar{r}_t$ are perfectly negatively correlated. Combining these two inequalities and solving for $\sigma(\bar{r})$ one finds

$$\sigma(\bar{r}) \geq (\sqrt{2E(\bar{r})}\,\sigma(\Delta p) - \sigma(d))E(\bar{r})/E(d). \tag{17}$$

This inequality puts a lower bound on $\sigma(\bar{r})$ proportional to the discrepancy between the left-hand side and right-hand side of the inequality (13).[17] It will be used to examine the data in the next section.

5. Empirical Evidence

The elements of the inequalities (1), (11), and (13) are displayed for the two data sets (described in the Appendix) in Table 2. In both data sets, the long-run exponential growth path was estimated by regressing $\ln(P_t)$ on a constant and time. Then λ in (3) was set equal to e^b where b is the coefficient of time (Table 2). The discount rate $\bar{r}$ used to compute p^* from (4) is estimated as the average d divided by the average p.[18] The terminal value of p^* is taken as average p.

With data set 1, the nominal price and dividend series are the real Standard and Poor's Composite Stock Price Index and the associated dividend series. The earlier observations for this series are due to Alfred Cowles who said that the index is

> intended to represent, ignoring the elements of brokerage charges and taxes, what would have happened to an investor's funds if he had bought, at the beginning of 1871, all stocks quoted on the New York Stock Exchange, allocating his purchases among the individual stocks in proportion to their total monetary value and each month up to 1937 had by the same criterion redistributed his holdings among all quoted stocks.   [p. 2]

In updating his series, Standard and Poor later restricted the sample to 500 stocks, but the series continues to be value weighted. The advantage to this series is its comprehensiveness. The disadvantage is that the dividends accruing to the portfolio at one point of time may not correspond to the dividends forecasted by holders of the Standard and Poor's portfolio

---

17. In deriving the inequality (13) it was assumed that d_t was known at time t, so by analogy this inequality would be based on the assumption that r_t is known at time t. However, without this assumption the same inequality could be derived anyway. The maximum contribution of $\bar{r}_t$ to the variance of ΔP occurs when $\bar{r}_t$ is known at time t.

18. This is not equivalent to the average dividend price ratio, which was slightly higher (.0514 for data set 1, .0484 for data set 2).

at an earlier time, due to the change in weighting of the stocks. There is no way to correct this disadvantage without losing comprehensiveness. The original portfolio of 1871 is bound to become a relatively smaller and smaller sample of U.S. common stocks as time goes on.

With data set 2, the nominal series are a modified Dow Jones Industrial Average and associated dividend series. With this data set, the advantages and disadvantages of data set 1 are reversed. My modifications in the Dow Jones Industrial Average assure that this series reflects the performance of a single unchanging portfolio. The disadvantage is that the performance of only 30 stocks is recorded.

Table 2 reveals that all inequalities are dramatically violated by the sample statistics for both data sets. The left-hand side of the inequality is always at least five times as great as the right-hand side, and as much as thirteen times as great.

The violation of the inequalities implies that "innovations" in price as we measure them can be forecasted. In fact, if we regress $\delta_{t+1}p_{t+1}$ onto (a constant and) p_t, we get significant results: a coefficient of p_t of $-.1521$ ($t = -3.218$, $R^2 = .0890$) for data set 1 and a coefficient of $-.2421$ ($t = -2.631$, $R^2 = .1238$) for data set 2. These results are not due to the representation of the data as a proportion of the long-run growth path. In fact, if the holding period return H_t is regressed on a constant and the dividend price ratio D_t/P_t, we get results that are only slightly less significant: a coefficient of 3.533 ($t = 2.672$, $R^2 = .0631$) for data set 1 and a coefficient of 4.491 ($t = 1.795$, $R^2 = .0617$) for data set 2.

These regression tests, while technically valid, may not be as generally useful for appraising the validity of the model as are the simple volatility comparisons. First, as noted above, the regression tests are not insensitive to data misalignment. Such low R^2 might be the result of dividend or commodity price index data errors. Second, although the model is rejected in these very long samples, the tests may not be powerful if we confined ourselves to shorter samples, for which the data are more accurate, as do most researchers in finance, while volatility comparisons may be much more revealing. To see this, consider a stylized world in which (for the sake of argument) the dividend series d_t is absolutely constant while the price series behaves as in our data set. Since the actual dividend series is fairly smooth, our stylized world is not too remote from our own. If dividends d_t are absolutely constant, however, it should be obvious to the most casual and unsophisticated observer by volatility arguments like those made here that the efficient markets model must be wrong. Price movements cannot reflect new information about dividends if dividends never change. Yet regressions like those run above will have limited power to reject the model. If the alternative hypothesis is, say, that $\hat{p}_t$

$= \rho \hat{p}_{t-1} + \epsilon_t$, where ρ is close to but less than one, then the power of the test in short samples will be very low. In this stylized world we are testing for the stationarity of the p_t series, for which, as we know, power is low in short samples.[19] For example, if post-war data from say, 1950–65 were chosen (a period often used in recent financial markets studies) when the stock market was drifting up, then clearly the regression tests will not reject. Even in periods showing a reversal of upward drift the rejection may not be significant.

Using inequality (17), we can compute how big the standard deviation of real discount rates would have to be to possibly account for the discrepancy $\sigma(\Delta p) - \sigma(d)/(2\bar{r})^{1/2}$ between Table 2 results (rows 9 and 10) and the inequality (13). Assuming Table 2 $\bar{r}$ (row 2) equals $E(\bar{r})$ and that sample variances equal population variances, we find that the standard deviation of $\bar{r}_t$ would have to be at least 4.36 percentage points for data set 1 and 7.36 percentage points for data set 2. These are very large numbers. If we take, as a normal range for $\bar{r}_t$ implied by these figures, a ± 2 standard deviation range around the real interest rate $\bar{r}$ given in Table 2, then the real interest rate $\bar{r}_t$ would have to range from -3.91 to 13.52 percent for data set 1 and -8.16 to 17.27 percent for data set 2! And these ranges reflect lowest possible standard deviations which are consistent with the model only if the real rate has the first-order autoregressive structure and perfect negative correlation with dividends!

These estimated standard deviations of *ex ante* real interest rates are roughly consistent with the results of the simple regressions noted above. In a regression of H_t on D_t/P_t and a constant, the standard deviation of the fitted value of H_t is 4.42 and 5.71 percent for data sets 1 and 2, respectively. These large standard deviations are consistent with the low R^2 because the standard deviation of H_t is so much higher (17.60 and 23.00 percent, respectively). The regressions of $\delta_t p_t$ on p_t suggest higher standard deviations of expected real interest rates. The standard deviation of the fitted value divided by the average detrended price is 5.24 and 8.67 percent for data sets 1 and 2, respectively.

6. Summary and Conclusions

We have seen that measures of stock price volatility over the past century appear to be far too high—five to thirteen times too high—to be attrib-

---

19. If dividends are constant (let us say $d_t = 0$) then a test of the model by a regression of $\delta_{t+1} p_{t+1}$ on p_t amounts to a regression of p_{t+1} on p_t with the null hypothesis that the coefficient of p_t is $(1 + \bar{r})$. This appears to be an explosive model for which t-statistics are not valid yet our true model, which in effect assumes $\sigma(d) \neq 0$, is nonexplosive.

uted to new information about future real dividends if uncertainty about future dividends is measured by the sample standard deviations of real dividends around their long-run exponential growth path. The lower bound of a 95 percent one-sided χ^2 confidence interval for the standard deviation of annual changes in real stock prices is over five times higher than the upper bound allowed by our measure of the observed variability of real dividends. The failure of the efficient markets model is thus so dramatic that it would seem impossible to attribute the failure to such things as data errors, price index problems, or changes in tax laws.

One way of saving the general notion of efficient markets would be to attribute the movements in stock prices to changes in expected real interest rates. Since expected real interest rates are not directly observed, such a theory cannot be evaluated statistically unless some other indicator of real rates is found. I have shown, however, that the movements in expected real interest rates that would justify the variability in stock prices are very large—much larger than the movements in nominal interest rates over the sample period.

Another way of saving the general notion of efficient markets is to say that our measure of the uncertainty regarding future dividends—the sample standard deviation of the movements of real dividends around their long-run exponential growth path—understates the true uncertainty about future dividends. Perhaps the market was rightfully fearful of much larger movements than actually materialized. One is led to doubt this, if after a century of observations nothing happened which could remotely justify the stock price movements. The movements in real dividends the market feared must have been many times larger than those observed in the Great Depression of the 1930s, as was noted above. Since the market did not know in advance with certainty the growth path and distribution of dividends that was ultimately observed, however, one cannot be sure that they were wrong to consider possible major events which did not occur. Such an explanation of the volatility of stock prices, however, is "academic," in that it relies fundamentally on unobservables and cannot be evaluated statistically.

Appendix

A.1. Data Set 1: Standard and Poor Series

Annual 1871–1979. The price series P_t is Standard and Poor's Monthly Composite Stock Price index for January divided by the Bureau of Labor Statistics wholesale price index (January *WPI* starting in 1900, annual average *WPI* before 1900 scaled to 1.00 in the base year 1979). Standard and Poor's Monthly Composite Stock Price index is a continuation of the Cowles Commission Common Stock index developed by Alfred Cowles and Associates and currently is based on 500 stocks.

The Dividend Series D_t is total dividends for the calendar year accruing to the portfolio represented by the stocks in the index divided by the average wholesale price index for the year (annual average *WPI* scaled to 1.00 in the base year 1979). Starting in 1926 these total dividends are the series "Dividends per share . . . 12 months moving total adjusted to index" from Standard and Poor's statistical service. For 1871 to 1925, total dividends are Cowles series Da-1 multiplied by .1264 to correct for change in base year.

A.2. Data Set 2: Modified Dow Jones Industrial Average

Annual 1928–1979. Here P_t and D_t refer to real price and dividends of the portfolio of 30 stocks comprising the sample for the Dow Jones Industrial Average when it was created in 1928. Dow Jones averages before 1928 exist, but the 30 industrials series was begun in that year. The published Dow Jones Industrial Average, however, is not ideal in that stocks are dropped and replaced and in that the weighting given an individual stock is affected by splits. Of the original 30 stocks, only 17 were still included in the Dow Jones Industrial Average at the end of our sample. The published Dow Jones Industrial Average is the simple sum of the price per share of the 30 companies divided by a divisor which changes through time. Thus, if a stock splits two for one, then Dow Jones continues to include only one share but changes the divisor to prevent a sudden drop in the Dow Jones average.

To produce the series used in this paper, the *Capital Changes Reporter* was used to trace changes in the companies from 1928 to 1979. Of the original 30 companies of the Dow Jones Industrial Average, at the end of our sample (1979), 9 had the identical names, 12 had changed only their names, and 9 had been acquired, merged or consolidated. For these latter 9, the price and dividend series are continued as the price and dividend of the shares exchanged by the acquiring corporation. In only one case was a cash payment, along with shares of the acquiring corporation, exchanged for the shares of the acquired corporation. In this case, the price and dividend series were continued as the price and dividend of the shares exchanged by the acquiring corporation. In four cases, preferred shares of the acquiring corporation were among shares exchanged. Common shares of equal value were substituted for these in our series. The number of shares of each firm included in the total is determined by the splits, and effective splits effected by stock dividends and merger. The price series is the value of all these shares on the last trading day of the preceding year, as shown on the Wharton School's Rodney White Center Common Stock tape. The dividend series is the total for the year of dividends and the cash value of other distributions for all these shares. The price and dividend series were deflated using the same wholesale price indexes as in data set 1.

$$\overline{\qquad\qquad\qquad}$$

I am grateful to Christine Amsler for research assistance, and to her as well as Benjamin Friedman, Irwin Friend, Sanford Grossman, Stephen LeRoy, Stephen Ross, and Jeremy Siegel for helpful comments. This research was supported by the National Bureau of Economic Research as part of the Research Project on the Changing Roles of Debt and Equity in Financing U.S. Capital Formation sponsored by the American Council of Life Insurance and by the National Science Foundation under grant SOC-7907561. The views expressed here are solely my own and do not necessarily represent the views of the supporting agencies.

References

AMSLER, C. "An American Consol: A Reexamination of the Expectations Theory of the Term Structure of Interest Rates." Unpublished manuscript, Michigan State Univ. 1980.

BASU, S. "The Investment Performance of Common Stocks in Relation to Their Price-Earnings Ratios: A Test of the Efficient Markets Hypothesis.' *J. Finance*, June 1977, *32*, 663–82.

BOX, G. E. P., and G. M. JENKINS. *Time Series Analysis for Forecasting and Control*, San Francisco: Holden-Day, 1970.

BRAINARD, W. C., J. B. SHOVEN, and L. WEISS. "The Financial Valuation of the Return to Capital." *Brookings Papers*, Washington, 1980, 2, 453–502.

COOTNER, PAUL H. *The Random Character of Stock Market Prices*. Cambridge: MIT Press, 1964.

COWLES, ALFRED, and Associates. *Common Stock Indexes, 1871–1937*. Cowles Commission for Research in Economics, Monograph No. 3, Bloomington: Principia Press, 1938.

FAMA, E. F. "Efficient Capital Markets: A Review of Theory and Empirical Work." *J. Finance*, May 1970, *25*, 383–420.

———. "The Behavior of Stock Market Prices." *J. Bus., Univ. Chicago*, Jan. 1965, *38*, 34–105.

GRANGER, C. W. J. "Some Consequences of the Valuation Model when Expectations are Taken to be Optimum Forecasts." *J. Finance*, Mar. 1975, *30*, 135–45.

JENSEN, M. C., et al. "Symposium on Some Anomalous Evidence Regarding Market Efficiency." *J. Financ. Econ.*, June/Sept. 1978, *6*, 93–330.

LeRoy, S., and R. Porter. "The Present Value Relation: Tests Based on Implied Variance Bounds." *Econometrica*, forthcoming.

Miller, M. H., and F. Modigliani. "Dividend Policy, Growth and the Valuation of Shares." *J. Bus., Univ. Chicago*, Oct. 1961, *34*, 411–33.

Modigliani, F., and R. Cohn. "Inflation, Rational Valuation and the Market." *Financ. Anal. J.*, Mar./Apr. 1979, *35*, 24–44.

Pesando, J. "Time Varying Term Premiums and the Volatility of Long-Term Interest Rates." Unpublished paper, Univ. Toronto, July 1979.

Samuelson, P. A. "Proof that Properly Discounted Present Values of Assets Vibrate Randomly." In Hiroaki Nagatani and Kate Crowley, eds. *Collected Scientific Papers of Paul A. Samuelson*, Vol. IV, Cambridge: MIT Press, 1977.

Shiller, R. J. "The Volatility of Long-Term Interest Rates and Expectations Models of the Term Structure." *J. Polit. Econ.*, Dec. 1979, *87*, 1190–219.

————, and J. J. Siegel. "The Gibson Paradox and Historical Movements in Real Interest Rates." *J. Polit. Econ.*, Oct. 1979, *85*, 891–907.

Wold, H. "On Prediction in Stationary Time Series." *Annals Math. Statist.* 1948, *19*, 558–67.

Commerce Clearing House. *Capital Changes Reporter*. New Jersey, 1977.

Dow Jones & Co. *The Dow Jones Averages 1855–1970*. New York: Dow Jones Books, 1972.

Standard and Poor's. *Security Price Index Record*. New York, 1978.

5

What Moves
Stock Prices?

*Moves in Stock Prices Reflect
Something Other Than News About
Fundamental Values*

DAVID M. CUTLER, JAMES M. POTERBA,
and LAWRENCE H. SUMMERS

Financial economics has been enormously successful in explaining the relative prices of different securities, a process facilitated by the powerful intuition of arbitrage. On the other hand, much less progress has been recorded in accounting for the absolute level of asset prices.

The standard approach holds that fluctuations in asset prices are attributable to changes in fundamental values. Voluminous evidence demonstrates that share prices react to announcements about corporate control, regulatory policy, and macroeconomic conditions that plausibly affect fundamentals. The stronger claim that *only* information affects asset values is much more difficult to substantiate, however.

The apparent absence of fundamental economic news coincident with the dramatic stock market movements of late 1987 is particularly difficult to reconcile with the standard view. This paper explores whether the 1987 market crash is exceptional in this regard, or whether a large fraction of significant market moves are difficult to explain on the basis of information.

Several recent studies of asset pricing have challenged the view that stock price movements are wholly attributable to the arrival of news. Roll (1988) shows that it is difficult to account for more than one-third of the

From: *The Journal of Portfolio Management*, pp. 4–12, Spring 1989. This copyrighted material is reprinted with permission from Institutional Investor, Inc.

monthly variation in individual stock returns on the basis of systematic economic influences. Shiller's (1981) claim that stock returns are too variable to be explained by shocks to future cash flows or plausible variations in future discount rates argues for other sources of movement in asset prices. French and Roll (1986) demonstrate that the variation in stock returns is larger when the stock market is open than when it is closed, even during periods of similar information release about market fundamentals.

The difficulty of explaining returns on the basis of information is not confined to equity markets. Frankel and Meese (1987) report similar findings in the foreign exchange market. Roll (1984) finds that news about weather conditions, the principal source of variation in the price of orange juice, explains only a small share of the movement in orange juice futures prices.

This paper estimates the fraction of the variation in aggregate stock returns that can be attributed to various types of economic news. The first section relates stock returns to the arrival of information about macroeconomic performance. We find that our news proxies can explain about one-third of the variance in stock returns.

To examine the possibility that the stock market moves in response to information that does not enter our definition of news, the next section analyzes stock market reactions to identifiable world news. While news regarding wars, the Presidency, or significant changes in financial policies affects stock prices, our results cast doubt on the view that "qualitative news" can account for all the return variation that cannot be traced to macroeconomic innovations. This finding is supported by the observation that many of the largest market movements in recent years have occurred on days when there were no major news events.

Our concluding section argues that further understanding of asset price movements requires two types of research. The first should attempt to model price movements as functions of evolving consensus opinions about the implications of given pieces of information. The second should develop and test "propagation mechanisms" that can explain why shocks with small effects on discount rates or cash flows may have large effects on prices.

1. The Importance of Macroeconomic News

Here we seek to determine whether unexpected macroeconomic developments can explain a significant fraction of share price movements. We analyze monthly stock returns for the 1926–1985 period, as well as annual returns for the longer 1871–1986 period.

For each data set, our analysis has two parts. First, we estimate regression models relating each macroeconomic variable to its own history and that of the other variables. We use these models (vector autoregressions) to identify the unexpected component of each time series and to consider the explanatory power of these news measures in explaining stock returns. Second, we adopt a less structured approach to the examination of macroeconomic news. After controlling for the influence of lagged economic factors on prices, we measure the incremental explanatory power of current and future values of our macroeconomic time series.

1.1 Structured Vector Autoregression Evidence

We begin by analyzing monthly stock returns for the 1926–1985 period, using seven measures of monthly macroeconomic activity, chosen to measure both real and financial conditions:[1]

1. The logarithm of real dividend payments on the value-weighted New York Stock Exchange portfolio, computed as nominal dividends from the Center for Research in Security Prices data base deflated by the monthly Consumer Price Index.
2. The logarithm of industrial production.
3. The logarithm of the real money supply (M1).
4. Thel nominal long-term interest rate, measured as Moody's AAA corporate bond yield.
5. The nominal short-term interest rate, measured as the yield on three-month Treasury bills.
6. The monthly CPI inflation rate.
7. The logarithm of stock market volatility, defined following French, Schwert, and Stambaugh (1987) as the average squared daily return on the Standard & Poor's Composite Index within the month.

To isolate the news component of these seven macroeconomic series, we fit vector autoregressions relating the current value of each to its own lagged values and those of the other six series. Each equation also includes a set of indicator variables for different months. We treat the

---

1. Most of the monthly data series were drawn from the Data Resources, Inc., data base. Money supply data prior to 1960 come from Friedman and Schwartz (1963). More recent data are from various *Federal Reserve Bulletins*. Moody's corporate bond yield is from the Board of Governors of the Federal Reserve System, *Banking and Monetary Statistics: 1914–1941 and 1941–70*, and various issues of the *Federal Reserve Bulletin*.

residuals from these equations (denoted $\hat{\zeta}_{it}$) as macroeconomic news and use them as explanatory variables for stock returns:

$$R_t = \alpha_0 + \alpha_1^* \hat{\zeta}_{1t} + \alpha_2^* \hat{\zeta}_{2t} + \alpha_3^* \hat{\zeta}_{3t} + \alpha_4^* \hat{\zeta}_{4t}$$
$$+ \alpha_5^* \hat{\zeta}_{5t} + \alpha_6^* \hat{\zeta}_{6t} + \alpha_7^* \hat{\zeta}_{7t} + \epsilon_t. \tag{1}$$

R_t is the real, dividend-inclusive return on the value-weighted NYSE index, and the seven variables on the right-hand side are the macroeconomic news variables. The $\bar{R}^2$ for Equation (1) measures the fraction of the return variation that can be explained by our right-hand side variables. In other words, it measures the importance of these types of macroeconomic news in explaining stock price movements.[2]

Table 1 reports estimates of Equation (1) using monthly data for both 1926–1985 and 1946–1985. Several conclusions emerge from this table. First, macroeconomic news as we have defined it explains only about one-fifth of the movement in stock prices. Increasing the number of lagged values included in the VARs does not substantially alter this finding. Second, most of the macroeconomic news variables affect returns with their predicted signs and statistically significant coefficients.[3] For the full sample period, an unexpected 1% increase in real dividends raises share prices by about one-tenth of 1%, while a 1% increase in industrial production increases share values by about four-tenths of 1%. Both inflation and market volatility have negative and statistically significant effects on market returns. An unanticipated 1% rise in volatility lowers share prices by slightly less than 0.025%, so a doubling of volatility would lower prices by about 2.5%. The other macroeconomic innovations appear to have a less significant effect on share prices.

We examine the robustness of our findings by performing similar tests for the 1871–1986 period. As monthly macroeconomic time series are unavailable for this extended period, we focus on annual returns. We measure R_t as the January-to-January return on the Cowles/Standard & Poor's stock price series. This series was developed by Robert Shiller and was used in Poterba and Summers (1988). Our macroeconomic variables include the logarithm of real dividend payments during the year, the

---

2. We report $\bar{R}^2$ because it is a measure of goodness of fit that corrects for the expected explanatory power of additional regressors. While adding irrelevant regressors to an equation will raise the equation's R^2, it will not affect the expected value of the $\bar{R}^2 = (T - 1)/(T - K)R^2 - (K - 1)/(T - K)$, where T is the total number of observations, and K the number of degrees of freedom used in estimation.

3. A related investigation by Chen, Roll, and Ross (1986) showed that various macroeconomic "factors" have positive prices. Their study is concerned with explaining the ex ante return on different securities, however, while ours considers the ex post movements in prices that result from macroeconomic innovations.

logarithm of real GNP from Romer (1988), the logarithm of real M1, the nominal long-term interest rate, the six-month commercial paper rate, and the inflation rate for the NNP deflator (all from Friedman and Schwartz, 1982), and the logarithm of stock market volatility, defined as the sum of squared monthly returns on the Cowles/S&P Index within the year.

The results for the longer sample period, presented in the bottom panel of Table 1, are similar to those for the post-1926 period. When two lagged values of the annual series are used in defining news components, the $\bar{R}^2$ in the returns equation is 0.064. Longer lags in the first stage reduce the extent to which the news can explain returns; with five lagged values, the $\bar{R}^2$ declines to 0.022. Using annual data for the post-1925 period, the $\bar{R}^2$ for the two-lag equation is -0.003, and that for the regression including five lags is -0.061. The estimated coefficients on the macroeconomic surprises for the 1871–1985 period resemble those for the post-1925 monthly return sample, adjusted for the annual rather than monthly span of the dependent variable, with one notable exception: the real dividend innovation has a negative coefficient for the long sample, although its large standard error also permits a wide range of positive values.

1.2 Unrestricted Regression Evidence

The foregoing method of defining macroeconomic news suffers from three potential problems. First, it does not capture new information about future macroeconomic conditions that is revealed in period t but not directly reflected in that period's variables. Second, if the models for measuring news are misspecified, our estimated residuals may not reflect new information accurately. If market participants operate with an information set larger than the one we have considered, our residuals may overstate the news content of contemporaneous series. Finally, there are timing issues associated with the release of macroeconomic information. The Consumer Price Index for month t, for example, is announced during month $t + 1$, but market participants may have some information about this variable during month t. These considerations motivate our less-structured approach to identifying the importance of macroeconomic news.

We implement such an approach by first regressing stock returns on the lagged values of our macroeconomic time series and then including current *and future* values of these time series in the regressions. The incremental $\bar{R}^2$ associated with these additional variables measures the importance of macroeconomic news in explaining stock returns.

This approach is not without shortcomings. It may understate the true

Table 1 Restricted VAR Evidence on Macroeconomic News and Stock Returns

| | Coefficients on Macroeconomic News Variables | | | | | | | |
| | | | | Interest Rates | | | | |
Lags in VAR	Real Dividends	Industrial Production	Real Money	Long	Short	Inflation	Volatility	$\bar{R}^2$
			1926–1986 Sample (Monthly Data)					
3	0.081	0.427	0.195	-2.64	-0.682	-0.079	-0.022	0.185
	(.011)	(.112)	(.152)	(1.57)	(.638)	(.071)	(.003)	
6	0.094	0.398	0.074	-2.18	-0.586	-0.123	-0.023	0.186
	(.012)	(.113)	(.158)	(1.62)	(.654)	(.073)	(.003)	
12	0.116	0.373	0.066	-1.91	-0.967	-0.111	-0.023	0.188
	(.014)	(.121)	(.165)	(1.73)	(.079)	(.079)	(.003)	
24	0.138	0.382	0.155	0.41	-1.340	-0.138	-0.025	0.187
	(.016)	(.133)	(.182)	(2.02)	(0.824)	(.088)	(.004)	

1946–1985 Sample (Monthly Data)

3	0.050	0.100	0.180	−2.15	−1.23	−0.075	−0.017	0.149
	(.012)	(.166)	(.355)	(1.24)	(.522)	(.059)	(.003)	
6	0.051	0.287	0.081	−2.15	−1.22	−0.110	−0.018	0.144
	(.013)	(.186)	(.206)	(1.31)	(.546)	(.062)	(.003)	
12	0.068	0.245	0.017	−1.92	−1.73	−0.114	−0.017	0.155
	(.016)	(.193)	(.482)	(1.42)	(.602)	(.072)	(.003)	
24	0.078	0.073	−0.304	0.352	−2.21	−0.148	−0.020	0.126
	(.020)	(.235)	(.567)	(1.83)	(.794)	(.095)	(.004)	

1871–1986 Sample (Annual Data)

2	−0.024	0.738*	0.150	−0.021	−4.91	−0.716	−0.006	0.064
	(.180)	(.483)	(.613)	(3.83)	(1.90)	(.532)	(.029)	
3	−0.074	0.875*	0.235	0.175	−5.23	−0.814	−0.004	0.063
	(.186)	(.450)	(.639)	(4.12)	(2.10)	(.591)	(.030)	
5	−0.066	0.810*	0.146	0.696	−6.04	−0.418	0.004	0.022
	(.220)	(.530)	(.729)	(5.07)	(2.36)	(.671)	(.034)	

The dependent variable is the real return on value-weighted NYSE. Estimates correspond to Equation (1), with standard errors in parentheses. The news variables are the logarithms of real dividends, industrial production, and real money supply, nominal long-term and short-term interest rates, inflation, and the logarithm of volatility. All VARs and the return equation include a time trend.

*Industrial Production is real NNP for the long-term sample period.

139

explanatory power of news, because we still omit changes in expectations about the distant future that are not reflected in macroeconomic variables in period t or the near future. Conversely, if stock market movements attributable to variables outside our information set affect future macroeconomic activity, our approach of including future macroeconomic realizations will overstate the role of expectational revisions.

Table 2 presents results using different numbers of lagged and led values of the macroeconomic variables for the 1926–1985 sample of monthly data. The findings are supportive of the results using the more structured VAR approach. Lagged values of the macroeconomic variables we consider can explain less than 5% of the variance of returns. Including the contemporaneous values of the seven macroeconomic time series

Table 2   Unrestricted VAR Evidence on Macro News and Stock Returns

Number of Lags in Specification	$\bar{R}^2$ for Equations Including:		
	Lagged	Lagged and Current	Lagged Current, and Led
1926–1985 Sample (Monthly Data)			
1	0.005	0.139	0.292
3	0.010	0.192	0.333
6	0.018	0.208	0.343
12	0.034	0.250	0.360
24	0.035	0.289	0.393
1946–1985 Sample (Monthly Data)			
1	0.060	0.194	0.318
3	0.087	0.254	0.332
6	0.080	0.259	0.327
12	0.065	0.267	0.327
24	0.136	0.355	0.396
1871–1986 Sample (Annual Data)			
1	0.078	0.210	0.515
2	0.122	0.149	0.509
3	0.113	0.162	0.511
5	0.124	0.102	0.534

Each entry reports the $\bar{R}^2$ from a regression of the real value-weighted NYSE return (Cowles return in annual data) on k lagged values, k lagged values and the current value, or k lagged, two led, and the current value, of the seven macroeconomic series noted in Table 1. Column 1 reports k. For the annual data, only one led value is included.

significantly raises the explanatory power of these equations. With only one lagged value of the series included, the $\bar{R}^2$ rises to 0.14, and with twenty-four lags of each variable the $\bar{R}^2$ is 0.29. Including the one- and two-period led values of the macro variables raises the $\bar{R}^2$ even more, to 0.29 when only one lagged value of the series is included and as high as 0.39 when the longer lags are included. Results for the postwar period, presented in the middle panel of Table 2, are consistent with those for the longer sample period. The lagged regressors have somewhat greater explanatory power in the more recent period.

We also applied our less structured approach to the 1871–1986 annual data sample. The explanatory power of the regressions with only lagged values of macroeconomic variables is greater for annual than for monthly data, ranging from 0.078 with one lag of each variable to a high of 0.124 with five lags. Adding the contemporaneous values of the macroeconomic series again raises the $\bar{R}^2$, with the largest gain an increase from 0.078 to 0.210 when only one lagged value is included. These results are similar to those obtained using monthly data.

Table 2 also reports the $\bar{R}^2$ for annual equations including lagged, contemporaneous, and one *led* value of the macroeconomic data series. The $\bar{R}^2$ exceeds 0.50, but this almost surely overstates the effect of macroeconomic news on share prices, because it also includes the effect of higher share prices on economic outcomes within the following year.[4] Fischer and Merton (1984) show that stock returns in year t can explain more than half of the variation in GNP growth in year $t + 1$, suggesting a strong correlation between returns and subsequent economic activity. While the same problem arises in our monthly analysis, the possibility of large feedback from the market to the economy is substantially greater with annual data.

Our results are broadly consistent with earlier studies, such as Fama (1981): a substantial fraction of return variation cannot be explained by macroeconomic news. The central question in interpreting this evidence is whether the unexplained return movements are due to omitted macroeconomic news variables and other information about future cash flows and discount rates, or to other factors that may not affect rational expectations of these variables. Below we present some evidence designed to distinguish these views.

---

4. The future dividend variable is the major source of the impressive fit when led values are included. The link between these series, however, is likely to be much stronger than would be the case if it reflected only information about $t + 1$ dividends that was released (and incorporated in prices) at t. In a model where dividends adjust to lagged share prices, as in Marsh and Merton (1987), future dividends are associated with current prices, but the principal causality is reversed.

2. Big News and Big Moves: Are They Related?

The foregoing analysis excludes a variety of important sources of information, besides macroeconomic developments, that could affect share prices. Political developments that affect future policy expectations and international events such as wars that affect risk premiums should also be important in asset pricing.

This section examines the importance of these other factors in two ways. First, we study the stock market reaction to major non-economic events such as elections and international conflicts. Neiderhoffer (1971) conducted a similar investigation for a wider sample of events during the 1960s. Second, we analyze the largest stock market movements of the last fifty years and review coincident news reports to identify, where possible, the proximate causes of these moves.

We begin by analyzing stock market reactions to non-economic events. We identified a sample of such events using the "Chronology of Important World Events" from the *World Almanac*. We first excluded events that we thought were unlikely to affect the stock market. We narrowed our set of events still further by considering only those events that the *New York Times* carried as the lead story, and that the *New York Times* Business Section reported as having affected stock market participants. Winnowing the events in this way biases our sample toward those news items that are likely to have had the largest impact on stock prices. This should bias our results toward finding a large stock market reaction to the forty-nine political, military, and economic policy events in our sample.

Table 3 lists these forty-nine events along with the associated percentage changes in the Standard & Poor's Composite Stock Index. Some of the events are clearly associated with substantial movements in the aggregate market. On the Monday after President Eisenhower's heart attack in September 1955, for example, the market declined by 6.62%. On the Monday after the Japanese attack on Pearl Habor, the market fell 4.37%. The orderly presidential transition after President Kennedy was assassinated coincided with a 3.98% market uptick, while the actual news of the assassination reduced share values by nearly 3%. On the two days in 1985 and 1986 when passage of the Tax Reform Act of 1986, the most significant tax legislation in three decades, became much more likely, aggregate market reactions were less than one-half of 1%.[5] For the set of events we analyze, the average absolute market move is 1.46% in contrast to 0.56% over the entire 1941–1987 period.

5. Cutler (1988) examines the events leading up to the Tax Reform Act in greater detail. The small aggregate market reaction on these days is matched by little abnormal cross-sectional variation in stock returns, despite the substantial differences in the law's likely impact across firms.

These findings suggest a surprisingly small effect of non-economic news, at least of the type we have identified, on share prices. The standard deviation (variance) of returns on the news days we have identified is 2.08% (4.33%), compared with the daily averge of 0.82% (0.67%) for the post-1941 period. This implies that the return on a typical event day in Table 3 is as variable as the cumulative return on 6.40 (4.33/0.67) "ordinary" days. If every day involved as much news as the forty-nine days in this sample, the standard deviation of annual returns would be 32% instead of the actual 13%. As most days do not witness information release as important as that on the days in Table 3, it may be difficult to explain the "missing variation" in stock returns with events of this kind.

An alternative strategy for identifying the importance of news is to examine large changes in share prices and related news developments. Table 4 lists the fifty largest one-day returns on the Standard & Poor's Composite Stock Index since 1946, along with the *New York Times* account of fundamental factors that affected prices.

It is difficult to link major market moves to release of economic or other information. On several of these days, the *New York Times* actually reported that there were no apparent explanations for the market's rise or decline. At the other extreme, some of the days clearly mark important information releases; the 1948 election outcome, President Eisenhower's heart attack, and the announcement of President Kennedy's success in rolling back the 1962 steel price increase are examples. On most of the sizable return days, however, the information that the press cites as the cause of the market move is not particularly important. Press reports on subsequent days also fail to reveal any convincing accounts of why future profits or discount rates might have changed. Our inability to identify the fundamental shocks that accounted for these significant market moves is difficult to reconcile with the view that such shocks account for most of the variation in stock returns.

3. Conclusions

Our results suggest the difficulty of explaining as much as half of the variance in aggregate stock prices on the basis of publicly available news bearing on fundamental values. The results parallel Roll's (1988) finding that most of the variation in returns for individual stocks cannot be explained using readily available measures of new information. Of course, it is possible that we have failed to consider some type of news that actually accounts for a significant fraction of asset price volatility. Although the hypothesis that stock prices move in response to news that is

Table 3   Major Events and Changes in the S&P Index, 1941–1987

Event	Date	Percent Change
Japanese bomb Pearl Harbor	Dec. 8, 1941	−4.37
US declares war against Japan	Dec. 9, 1941	−3.23
Roosevelt defeats Dewey	Nov. 8, 1944	−0.15
Roosevelt dies	Apr. 13, 1945	1.07
Atomic bombs dropped on Japan:		
Hiroshima bomb	Aug. 6, 1945	0.27
Nagasaki bomb; Russia declares war	Aug. 9, 1945	1.65
Japanese surrender	Aug. 17, 1945	−0.54
Truman defeats Dewey	Nov. 3, 1948	−4.61
North Korea invades South Korea	June 26, 1950	−5.38
Truman to send US troops	June 27, 1950	−1.10
Eisenhower defeats Stevenson	Nov. 5, 1952	0.28
Eisenhower suffers heart attack	Sep. 26, 1955	−6.62
Eisenhower defeats Stevenson	Nov. 7, 1956	−1.03
U-2 shot down; US admits spying	May 9, 1960	0.09
Kennedy defeats Nixon	Nov. 9, 1960	0.44
Bay of Pigs invasion announced;	Apr. 17, 1961	0.47
Details released over several days	Apr. 18, 1961	−0.72
	Apr. 19, 1961	−0.59
Cuban missile crisis begins:		
Kennedy announces Russian buildup	Oct. 23, 1962	−2.67
Soviet letter stresses peace	Oct. 24, 1962	3.22
Formula to end dispute reached	Oct. 29, 1962	2.16
Kennedy assassinated;	Nov. 22, 1963	−2.81
Orderly transfer of power to Johnson	Nov. 26, 1963	3.98
US fires on Vietnamese ship	Aug. 4, 1964	−1.25
Johnson defeats Goldwater	Nov. 4, 1964	−0.05
Johnson withdraws from race, halts Vietnamese raids, urges peace talks	Apr. 1, 1968	2.53
Robert Kennedy assassinated	June 5, 1968	−0.49
Nixon defeats Humphrey	Nov. 6, 1968	0.16
Nixon imposes price controls, requests Federal tax cut, strengthens dollar	Aug. 16, 1971	3.21
Nixon defeats McGovern	Nov. 8, 1972	0.55
Haldeman, Ehrlichman, and Dean resign	Apr. 30, 1973	−0.24
Dean tells Senate about Nixon cover-up	June 25, 1973	−1.40
Agnew resigns	Oct. 10, 1973	−0.83
Carter defeats Ford	Nov. 3, 1976	−1.14
Volcker appointed to Fed	July 25, 1979	1.09
Fed announces major policy changes	Oct. 6, 1979	−1.25
Soviet Union invades Afghanistan	Dec. 26, 1979	0.11

Table 3   *(Continued)*

Event	Date	Percent Change
Attempt to free Iranian hostages fails	Apr. 26, 1980	0.73
Reagan defeats Carter	Nov. 5, 1980	1.77
Reagan shot, NYSE closes early;	Mar. 30, 1981	−0.27
Reopens next day	Mar. 31, 1981	1.28
US Marines killed in Lebanon	Oct. 24, 1983	0.02
US invades Grenada	Oct. 25, 1983	0.29
Reagan defeats Mondale	Nov. 7, 1984	1.09
House votes for Tax Reform Act of 1986	Dec. 18, 1985	−0.40
Chernobyl nuclear reactor meltdown;	Apr. 29, 1986	−1.06
Details released over several days	Apr. 30, 1986	−2.07
Senate Committee votes for tax reform	May 8, 1986	−0.49
Greenspan named to replace Volcker	June 2, 1987	−0.47
Important Events		
Average Absolute Return		1.46
Standard Deviation of Returns		2.08
All Days Since 1941		
Average Absolute Return		0.56
Standard Deviation of Returns		0.82

Table 4   Fifty Largest Post-War Movements in S&P Index and Their "Causes"

	Date	Percent Change	New York Times Explanation*
1	Oct. 19, 1987	−20.47	Worry over dollar decline and trade deficit, fear of US not supporting dollar.
2	Oct. 21, 1987	9.10	Interest rates continue to fall; deficit talks in Washington; bargain hunting.
3	Oct. 26, 1987	−8.28	Fear of budget deficits; margin calls; reaction to falling foreign stocks.
4	Sep. 3, 1946	−6.73	"No basic reason for the assault on prices."
5	May 28, 1962	−6.68	Kennedy forces rollback of steel price hike.
6	Sep. 26, 1955	−6.62	Eisenhower suffers heart attack.
7	Jun. 26, 1950	−5.38	Outbreak of Korean War.
8	Oct. 20, 1987	5.33	Investors looking for "quality stocks."
9	Sep. 9, 1946	−5.24	Labor unrest in maritime and trucking industries.
10	Oct. 16, 1987	−5.16	Fear of trade deficit; fear of higher interest rates; tension with Iran.

Table 4   (*Continued*)

	Date	Percent Change	New York Times Explanation*
11	May 27, 1970	5.02	Rumors of change in economic policy. "The stock surge happened for no fundamental reason."
12	Sep. 11, 1986	−4.81	Foreign governments refuse to lower interest rates; crackdown on triple witching announced.
13	Aug. 17, 1982	4.76	Interest rates decline.
14	May 29, 1962	4.65	Optimistic brokerage letters; institutional and corporate buying; suggestions of tax cut.
15	Nov. 3, 1948	−4.61	Truman defeats Dewey.
16	Oct. 9, 1974	4.60	Ford to reduce inflation and interest rates.
17	Feb. 25, 1946	−4.57	Weakness in economic indicators over past week.
18	Oct. 23, 1957	4.49	Eisenhower urges confidence in economy.
19	Oct. 29, 1987	4.46	Deficit reduction talks begin; durable goods orders increase; rallies overseas.
20	Nov. 5, 1948	−4.40	Further reaction to Truman victory over Dewey.
21	Nov. 6, 1946	−4.31	Profit taking; Republican victories in elections presage deflation.
22	Oct. 7, 1974	4.19	Hopes that President Ford would announce strong anti-inflationary measures.
23	Nov. 30, 1987	−4.18	Fear of dollar fall.
24	Jul. 12, 1974	4.08	Reduction in new loan demands; lower inflation previous month.
25	Oct. 15, 1946	4.01	Meat prices decontrolled; prospects of other decontrols.
26	Oct. 25, 1982	−4.00	Disappointment over Federal Reserve's failure to cut discount rates.
27	Nov. 26, 1963	3.98	Confidence in Johnson after Kennedy assassination.
28	Nov. 1, 1978	3.97	Steps by Carter to strengthen dollar.
29	Oct. 22, 1987	−3.92	Iranian attack on Kuwaiti oil terminal; fall in markets overseas; analysts predict lower prices.
30	Oct. 29, 1974	3.91	Decline in short-term interest rates; ease in future monetary policy; lower oil prices.
31	Nov. 3, 1982	3.91	Relief over small Democratic victories in House.

Table 4 (*Continued*)

	Date	Percent Change	New York Times Explanation*
32	Feb. 19, 1946	−3.70	Fear of wage-price controls lowering corporate profits; labor unrest.
33	Jun. 19, 1950	−3.70	Korean War continues; fear of long war.
34	Nov. 18, 1974	−3.67	Increase in unemployment rate; delay in coal contract approval; fear of new mid-East war.
35	Apr. 22, 1980	3.64	Fall in short-term interest rates; analysts express optimism.
36	Oct. 31, 1946	3.63	Increase in commodity prices; prospects for price decontrol.
37	Jul. 6, 1955	3.57	Market optimism triggered by GM stock split.
38	Jun. 4, 1962	−3.55	Profit taking; continuation of previous week's decline.
39	Aug. 20, 1982	3.54	Congress passes Reagan tax bill; prime rate falls.
40	Dec. 3, 1987	−3.53	Computerized selling; November retail sales low.
41	Sep. 19, 1974	3.50	Treasury Secretary Simon predicts decline in short-term interest rates.
42	Dec. 9, 1946	3.44	Coal strike ends; railroad freight rates increase.
43	Jun. 29, 1962	3.44	"Stock prices advanced strongly chiefly because they had gone down so long and so far that a rally was due."
44	Sep. 5, 1946	3.43	"Replacement buying" after earlier fall.
45	Oct. 30, 1987	3.33	Dollar stabilizes; increase in prices abroad.
46	Jan. 27, 1975	3.27	IBM wins appeal of antitrust case; short-term interest rates decline.
47	Oct. 6, 1982	3.27	Interest rates fall; several large companies announce increase in profits.
48	Jul. 19, 1948	−3.26	Worry over Russian blockade of Berlin; possibility of more price controls.
49	Nov. 30, 1982	3.22	"Analysts were at a loss to explain why the Dow jumped so dramatically in the last two hours."
50	Oct. 24, 1962	3.22	Krushchev promises no rash decisions on Cuban Missile crisis; calls for US-Soviet summit.

* Per the financial section or front page.

observed by market participants but not by investigators studying the market is irrefutable, we are skeptical of this possibility. News important enough to account for large swings in the demand for corporate equities would almost surely leave traces in either official economic statistics or media reports about market movements.

The problem of accounting for price changes on the basis of fundamental values is not confined to the overall stock market. Studies of price behavior in settings where fundamental values can be measured directly have similar trouble in explaining prices. The classic example is closed-end mutual funds, discussed by Malkiel and Firstenberg (1978). These funds have traded at both discounts and premiums relative to their net asset value during the last twenty years. At any moment, the cross-sectional dispersion in discounts is substantial and difficult to link to fundamental factors. The widely documented patterns in stock returns over weekends, holidays, and different calendar periods, summarized in Thaler (1987a, 1987b), are also difficult to attribute to news about fundamentals, because fundamental values are not likely to move systematically over these periods.

The view that movements in stock prices reflect something other than news about fundamental values is consistent with evidence on the correlates of ex post returns. If prices were periodically driven away from fundamental values by something other than news but ultimately returned to fundamentals, one would expect a tendency for returns to be low when the market is high relative to some indicator of fundamental value, and high when the market is low relative to fundamental value. Such patterns emerge from studies of ex post returns that use the past level of prices, earnings, and dividends as indicators of fundamental value.[6]

Our results underscore the problem of accounting for the variation in asset prices. Throwing up one's hands and simply saying that there is a great deal of irrationality that gives rise to "fads" is not constructive. Two more concrete lines of attack strike us as potentially worthwhile. First, volatility may reflect changes that take place in average assessments of given sets of information regarding fundamental values as investors reexamine existing data or present new arguments. This view is suggested

---

6. Campbell and Shiller (1988), Cutler, Poterba, and Summers (1988), Fama and French (1988b), Poterba and Summers (1988), and Shiller (1984) find evidence consistent with this view. Models that explain the predictability of returns on the basis of trading by uninformed "noise traders" have been discussed by Black (1986) and DeLong, Shleifer, Summers, and Waldmann (1987).

by French and Roll's (1986) finding that return volatility is greater when the market is open than when it is closed.

Second, it may be fruitful in accounting for volatility to explore propagation mechanisms that could cause relatively small shocks to have large effects on market prices.[7] "Informational freeloading" on observed asset prices may have something to do with market volatility. In a world where most investors accept prices as indicators of fundamental value, small changes in the supply of or demand for securities can have large effects on prices.

Suppose, for example, that all investors desired to hold the market portfolio in order to achieve optimum diversification, except for one investor who wishes to concentrate holdings on a single security regardless of its price. The equilibrium price of this security would be infinite. This example, while extreme because speculators would intervene to sell an irrationally demanded stock well before its price approached infinity, makes an important point. If many investors accept market prices as indicators of value and so do not trade on the basis of their own assessment of values, market values will be more susceptible to those who trade on the basis of their own opinions.

The possibility that many investors do not formulate their own estimates of fundamental value is consistent with trading patterns surrounding the sharp stock market decline of October 1987.[8] Despite the market's dramatic drop, the vast majority of shares were not traded. This is only explicable if investors rely on market prices to gauge values, or if investors received information that led to significant downward revisions in fundamental values. It seems difficult to identify the information that would support the second explanation.

—————

The authors are grateful to Peter Bernstein, Eugene Fama, Kenneth French, and Andrei Shleifer for helpful comments, to the National Science Foundation for financial support, and to DRI for data assistance. This research is part of the NBER Programs in Economic Fluctuations and Financial Markets. A data appendix is available from the Interdisciplinary Consortium for Political and Social Research in Ann Arbor, MI.

7. Mandelbrot (1966) presents a rational model in which apparently small news releases can trigger large revaluations in expected future profits.

8. Frankel (1989) suggests a number of stylized facts regarding foreign exchange markets, such as the short-term focus of most traders, that are consistent with the absence of independent assessment of fundamentals by most investors.

References

BLACK, FISCHER. "Noise." *Journal of Finance* 41 (July 1986), pp. 529–542.

CAMPBELL, JOHN Y., and ROBERT SHILLER. "Stock Prices, Earnings, and Expected Dividends." *Journal of Finance* 43 (July 1988), pp. 661–676.

CHEN, NAI-FU, RICHARD ROLL, and STEPHEN ROSS. "Economic Forces and the Stock Market." *Journal of Business* 59 (July 1986), pp. 383–404.

CUTLER, DAVID M. "Tax Reform and the Stock Market: An Asset Price Approach." *American Economic Review* 78 (December 1988).

CUTLER, DAVID M., JAMES M. POTERBA, and LAWRENCE H. SUMMERS. "Why Do Dividend Yields Forecast Stock Returns?" Massachusetts Institute of Technology, 1988.

DELONG, J. BRADFORD, ANDREI SHLEIFER, LAWRENCE SUMMERS, and ROBERT WALDMAN. "The Economics of Noise Traders." Harvard University, 1987.

FAMA, EUGENE. "Stock Returns, Real Activity, Inflation, and Money." *American Economic Review* 71 (1981), pp. 545–565.

FAMA, EUGENE, and KENNETH FRENCH. "Dividend Yields and Expected Stock Returns." Forthcoming in *Journal of Financial Economics* 1988.

———. "Permanent and Transitory Components in Stock Prices." *Journal of Political Economy* 96 (April 1988), pp. 246–273.

FISCHER, STANLEY, and ROBERT MERTON. "Macroeconomics and Finance: The Role of the Stock Market." *Carnegie-Rochester Conference Series in Public Policy* 21 (1984), pp. 57–108.

FRANKEL, JEFFREY. "Fixed Exchange Rates: Experience Versus Theory." *Journal of Portfolio Management,* Winter 1989, pp. 45–54.

FRANKEL, JEFFREY, and RICHARD MEESE. "Are Exchange Rates Excessively Variable?" in S. Fischer, ed., NBER *Macroeconomics Annual 1987.* Cambridge; MIT Press, 1987, pp. 117–152.

FRENCH, KENENTH, and RICHARD ROLL. "Stock Return Variances: The Arrival of Information and the Reaction of Traders." *Journal of Financial Economics* 17 (September 1986), pp. 5–26.

FRENCH, KENENTH, G. WILLIAM SCHWERT, and ROBERT STAMBAUGH. "Expected Stock Returns and Stock Market Volatility." *Journal of Financial Economics* 19 (September 1987), pp. 330.

FRIEDMAN, MILTON, and ANNA SCHWARTZ. *A Monetary History of the United States, 1867–1960.* Princeton: Princeton University Press, 1963.

———. *Monetary Trends in the United States and the United Kingdom.* Cambridge: Cambridge University Press, 1982.

MALKIEL, BURTON G., and PAUL B. FIRSTENBERG. "A Winning Strategy for an Efficient Market." *Journal of Portfolio Management,* Summer 1978, pp. 20–25.

MANDELBROT, BENOIT. "Forecasts of Future Prices, Unbiased Markets, and Martingale Models." *Journal of Business,* 39 (Special Supplement, January 1966), pp. 242–255.

MARSH, TERRY, and ROBERT C. MERTON. "Dividend Behavior and the Aggregate Stock Market." *Journal of Business* 60 (January 1987), pp. 1–40.

NEIDERHOFFER, VICTOR. "The Analysis of World Events and Stock Prices." *Journal of Business* 44 (April 1971), pp. 193–219.

POTERBA, JAMES, and LAWRENCE SUMMERS. "Mean Reversion in Stock Prices: Evidence and Implications." Forthcoming in *Journal of Financial Economics*, 1988.

ROLL, RICHARD. "Orange Juice and Weather." *American Economic Review* 74 (December 1984), pp. 861–880.

———. "R^2." *Journal of Finance* 43 (July 1988), pp. 541–566.

ROMER, CHRISTINA. "The Prewar Business Cycle Reconsidered: New Estimates of Gross National Product, 1869–1908." Forthcoming in *Journal of Political Economy*.

SCHWERT, WILLIAM. "Why Does Stock Market Volatility Change Over Time?" Working Paper GPB-8711, William Simon Graduate School of Management, University of Rochester, 1987.

SHILLER, ROBERT. "Do Stock Prices Move Too Much to be Justified by Subsequent Dividends?" *American Economic Review* 71 (1981), pp.421–436.

———. "Stock Prices and Social Dynamics." *Brookings Papers in Economic Activity* 1984:2, pp. 457–498.

THALER, RICHARD. "Anomalies: The January Effect." *Journal of Economic Perspectives* 1 (Summer 1987), pp. 197–201.

———. "Anomalies: Weekend, Holiday, Turn of the Month, and Intraday Effects." *Journal of Economic Perspectives* 1 (Fall 1987), pp. 169–178.

6

Does the Stock Market Rationally Reflect Fundamental Values?

The proposition that securities markets are efficient forms the basis for most research in financial economics. A voluminous literature has developed supporting this hypothesis. Jensen (1978) calls it the best established empirical fact in economics.[1] Indeed, apparent anomalies such as the discounts on closed-end mutual funds and the success of trading rules based on earnings announcements are treated as indications of the failures of models specifying equilibrium returns, rather than as evidence against the hypothesis of market efficiency.[2] Recently the Efficient Markets Hypothesis and the notions connected with it have provided the basis for a great deal of research in macroeconomics. This research has typically assumed that asset prices are in some sense rationally related to economic realities.

Despite the widespread allegiance to the notion of market efficiency, a number of authors have suggested that certain asset prices are not rationally related to economic realities. Modigliani and Cohn (1979) suggest that the stock market is very substantially undervalued because of inflation illusion. A similar claim regarding bond prices is put forward in

---

1. Similar assertions are very common in the finance literature. While doubts along the lines of the discussion here, appear to be part of an oral tradition, the only reference I could find is Shiller (1981).

2. For examples, see the issue of the *Journal of Financial Economics* devoted to anomalies in the Efficient Market Hypothesis (1982).

From: *The Journal of Finance*, vol. XLI, no. 3, pp. 591–601, July 1986. Reprinted by permission of the American Finance Association.

Summers (1982). Brainard, Shoven and Weiss (1980) find that the currently low level of the stock market could not be rationally related to economic realities. Shiller (1979), (1981) concludes that both bond and stock prices are far more volatile than can be justified on the basis of real economic events. Arrow (1982) has suggested that psychological models of "irrational decision making" of the type suggested by Tversky and Kahneman (1981) can help to explain behavior in speculative markets. These types of claims are frequently dismissed because they are premised on inefficiencies and hence imply the presence of exploitable excess profit opportunities.

This paper argues that existing evidence does not establish that financial markets are efficient in the sense of rationally reflecting fundamentals. It demonstrates that the types of statistical tests which have been used to date have essentially no power against at least one interesting alternative hypothesis to market efficiency. Thus the inability of these tests to reject the hypothesis of market efficiency does not mean that they provide evidence in favor of its acceptance. In particular, the data in conjunction with current methods provide no evidence against the view that financial market prices deviate widely and frequently from rational valuations. The same considerations which make deviations from efficiency difficult to isolate statistically make it unlikely that they will be arbitraged away or eliminated by speculative trading. Thus the results here call into question the theoretical as well as empirical underpinnings of the Efficient Markets Hypothesis. The absence of compelling theoretical or empirical arguments in favor of the proposition that financial market valuations are efficient is significant in light of a number of types of evidence suggesting that large valuation errors are common in speculative markets.

The first section distinguishes alternative concepts of market efficiency and lays out the formulation used here. Tests of market efficiency in its weak and strong forms are considered in the second and third sections, along with other evidence often adduced to suggest that stock market valuations are rational. The implications of the results for our understanding of speculative markets are discussed in the fourth and final section.

1. Defining Market Efficiency

The notion of market efficiency has been defined in many ways. Fama (1976) presents a thorough discussion of both theoretical issues and empirical tests of this proposition. In the development below, I shall consider the evolution of the price of a single security. It can easily be taken to represent an entire portfolio. It is assumed that the required expected rate of return on the security is equal to a constant, r, which is known with certainty. As has frequently been observed, standard tests of market efficiency are really joint tests of efficiency and a model specifying expected returns. The assumption made here that the ex ante return is known and constant makes it possible to focus only on the test of market efficiency.[3]

Assume that the security in question yields a sequence of cash flows, D_t. These may be thought of as dividends if the security is a stock, or coupons if the security is a bond. If the security has a finite maturity, T, then D_T may be taken to represent its liquidation value, and all subsequent values of D_t may be taken to equal zero. One statement of the hypothesis of market efficiency holds that:

$$P_t = P_t^* = E\left[\left(\sum_{s=t}^{\infty} \frac{D_s}{(1 + r)^{s-t}}\right)\Big| \Omega_t\right] \tag{1}$$

where Ω_t represents the set of information available to market participants at time t. This is not the form in which the hypothesis is usually tested. Equation (1) is mathematically equivalent to the statement that, for all t:

$$P_t = E\left(\frac{P_{t+1}}{1 + r}\right) + E(D_t) \tag{2}$$

or the equivalent statement that

$$E(R_t) = E\left(\frac{P_{t+1}}{P_t} - 1 + \frac{(1 + r)_t}{P_t}\right) = r \tag{3}$$

where the information set in equations (2) and (3) is taken to be Ω_t. Note that once a transversality condition is imposed on the difference equation (3), it implies equation (1).[4]

Equation (3) also implies that:

$$R_t = r + e_t \tag{4}$$

---

3. Since the discussion here assumes that the model generating expected returns is known with certainty, it will overestimate the power of available statistical tests. Recent theoretical work suggests that the particular model of ex-ante returns considered here cannot be derived rigorously. This is immaterial for the points at issue here. What is crucial is that the discussion is carried on assuming full knowledge of the model characterizing ex-ante returns.

4. The transversality condition serves to rule out speculative bubbles.

where e_t is serially uncorrelated and orthogonal to any element of Ω_t. Market efficiency is normally tested by adding regressors drawn from Ω_t to (4) and testing the hypothesis that their coefficients equal zero, or by testing the hypothesis that e_t follows a white noise process.[5] The former represent tests of "semi-strong" efficiency while the latter are tests of "weak" efficiency. A vast literature, summarized in Fama (1976), has with few exceptions been unable to reject the hypothesis of market efficiency, at least for common stocks. The body of evidence supporting the hypothesis of market efficiency has been used to support two different conclusions. First, almost tautologously, failures to reject the hypothesis of market efficiency have been taken as evidence that portfolio managers cannot outperform the market to an important extent by trading using publicly available information. Second, evidence of market efficiency is often viewed as establishing that financial market prices represent rational assessments of fundamental values. The large event study literature rests on this premise.

2. Tests of Market Efficiency

The inability of a body of data to reject a scientific theory does not mean that the tests prove, demonstrate or even support its validity. As students of elementary statistics are constantly reminded, failure to reject a hypothesis is not equivalent to its acceptance. This principle applies to all scientific theories, not just those that are stated statistically. Experiments can falsify a theory by contradicting one of its implications. But the verification of one of its predictions cannot be taken to prove or establish a theory.[6]

How then do we evaluate the strength of the evidence supporting a hypothesis? Clearly we do not simply count the number of implications of a hypothesis which are validated. We give more weight to the verification of some implications than to the verification of others. For example, almost everyone would agree that findings that excess returns cannot be predicted using past data on sunspots provides less support for the hypothesis of market efficiency than do demonstrations that excess returns are not serially correlated. This is because we find it much easier

---

5. Abel and Mishkin (1983) and Jones and Roley (1978) show that other standard tests of efficiency are essentially equivalent to those described in this paragraph.

6. A discussion of what it means to establish evidence in favor of a scientific hypothesis may be found in Hempel (1965).

to imagine alternative models in which returns are serially correlated than we do alternative models in which sunspots can help predict returns. The usefulness of any test of a hypothesis depends on its ability to discriminate between it and other plausible formulations. Below I examine the usefulness of standard tests of market efficiency according to this criterion.

Evaluation of any test of a theory requires specification of an alternative hypothesis. A natural specification of an alternative hypothesis to market efficiency holds that:

$$P_t = P_t^* + u_t$$
$$u_t = \alpha u_{t-1} + v_t \tag{5}$$

where lower-case letters indicate logarithms and u_t and v_t represent random shocks. This hypothesis implies that market valuations differ from the rational expectation of the present value of future cash flows by a multiplicative factor approximately equal to $(1 + \mu_t)$. The deviations are assumed to follow a first-order autoregressive process. It seems reasonable to suppose that deviations tend to persist but not grow forever so that $0 \leq \alpha \leq 1$. The assumption that u_t follows an AR process is made for ease of exposition and does not affect any of the substantive points at issue. For simplicity, it is assumed that u_t and v_t are uncorrelated with e_t at all frequencies.

Many, though not all, of the plausible senses in which markets might fail to rationally reflect fundamental values are captured by this specification. It clearly captures Keynes's (1936) notion that markets are sometimes driven by animal spirits unrelated to economic realities. It also is consistent with the experimental evidence of Tversky and Kahneman (1981) that subjects overreact to new information in making probabilistic judgments. The formulation considered here captures Robert Shiller's (1979), (1981), (1981a) suggestion that financial markets display excess volatility and overreact to new information. One deviation from standard notions of market efficiency which does not take this form is Blanchard and Watson's (1982) suggestion of intermittent rational speculative bubbles.[7]

Adopting the approximation that $\log(1 + u_t) = u_t$, and that $\mathrm{Div}_t/P_t \simeq$

---

7. Olivier Blanchard has pointed out to me that if $\alpha = 1 + r$, equation (5) will characterize a speculative bubble. In this case however, market valuations will come to diverge arbitrarily far from fundamental valuations.

Div_t/P_t^* equations (3), (4) and (5) imply that excess returns $Z_t = (R_t - r)$ follow an ARMA $(1,1)$ process.[8] That is:[9]

$$Z_t = \alpha Z_{t-1} + e_t - \alpha e_{t-1} + v_t - v_{t-1}. \tag{6}$$

Granger and Newbold (1977) show that since Z_t can be expressed as the sum of an ARMA $(1,1)$ process and white noise, ARMA $(0,0)$, it can be represented as an ARMA $(1,1)$ process. Equation (6) can be used to calculate the variance and the autocorrelations of Z_t. These calculations yield:

$$\sigma_z^2 = 2(1 - \alpha)\sigma_u^2 + \sigma_e^2 \tag{7}$$

$$\rho_k = \frac{-\alpha^{k-1}(1 - \alpha)^2\sigma_u^2}{1(1 - \alpha)\sigma_u^2 + \sigma_e^2} \tag{8}$$

where ρ_k denotes the kth-order autocorrelation. Note that the model predicts that the Z_t should display negative serial correlation. When excess returns are positive, some part is on average spurious, due to a shock, v_t. As prices revert to fundamental values, negative excess returns result.

2.1 Weak Form Tests of Market Efficiency

At this point the power of "weak form tests" of market efficiency can be evaluated. These tests involve evaluating the hypothesis that the $\rho_k = 0$. Table 1 presents the theoretical first order autocorrelation for various parameter combinations. In all cases, the parameters are chosen to accord with the observed variance in stock market returns. Note that (8) implies that all subsequent autocorrelations are smaller in absolute value. In order to get a feeling for the magnitudes involved, it is useful to consider a concrete example. Suppose one is interested in testing market efficiency using aggregate data on monthly stock market returns over a 50-year period. With 600 observations, the estimated autocorrelations have a standard error of $1/\sqrt{597} \simeq .042$ on the null hypothesis of zero autocorrelation. This calculation leads to an overstatement of the power of tests because it counterfactually assumes a constant variance of excess returns and the normality of e_t. Suppose that $\sigma_u^2 = .08$ so that the standard

---

8. These approximations are necessary in order to obtain simple analytic expressions. Monte-Carlo results confirm that these approximations are innocuous. Shiller (1981a) presents an example similar to the one here in his defense of volatility tests.

9. This can be seen as follows. With the approximations assumed here, $R_t = Div_t/P_t^* + P_{t+1} - P_t = Div_t/P_t^* + P_{t+1}^* - P_t^* + u_{t+1} - u_t$, where the last equality is implied by equation (5). This can be written, using (3) and (4) as $R_t = r + e_t + u_{t+1} - u_t$. Combining this last equation with equation (5) yields equation (6).

Table 1 Theoretical Autocorrelation of Excess Return Assuming Market Inefficiency

$\dfrac{\sigma_e^2}{\sigma_u^2}$	α				
	.75	.90	.95	.99	.995
1.0	-0.042	-0.008	-0.003	0.000	0.000
0.5	-0.062	-0.014	-0.004	0.000	0.000
0.25	-0.083	-0.022	-0.007	0.000	0.000
0.1	-0.104	-0.033	-0.012	-0.001	0.000
0.05	-0.113	-0.040	-0.017	-0.001	0.000
0.01	-0.122	-0.048	-0.023	-0.003	-0.001

Note: Calculations are based on Equation (8).

deviation of the market's error in valuation is close to 30 percent, and that $\alpha = .98$. This implies that it takes about three years for the market to eliminate half of any valuation error, u_t. These assumptions, along with the observation that $\sigma_z^2 \simeq .004$, imply, using (7), that $\sigma_e^2 \simeq .001$.[10] Equation (8) implies that the theoretically expected value of ρ_1 is $-.008$. Thus, in this example, the data lack the power to reject the hypothesis of market efficiency even though market valuations frequently differ from the rational expectation of the present value of future cash flows by more than 30 percent.[11] In order to have a 50 percent chance of rejecting the null hypotl.esis it would be necessary to have data for just over 5000 years. Note also that in this example three-fourths of variance in excess returns is due to valuation errors, u_t, rather than genuine information, e_t. Even if $\sigma_u^2 = .10$, so that all the variance in market returns is spurious, and $\sigma_e^2 = 0$, the theoretical value of ρ_1 is only $-.01$, so that deviations from efficiency could not be detected. If, as is plausible, the serial correlation in valuation errors is greater, the power of standard tests is even lower.[12]

10. This estimate for σ_z^2 is consistent with the 20 percent annual standard deviation of market returns reported by Ibbotson and Sinquefield (1976/1979).

11. A more formal procedure would calculate the distribution of the test statistic (ρ_k/σ_k) under the alternative hypothesis. It should be obvious that carrying out this procedure would support the assertions in the text. Note that these calculations overstate the power of the tests actually performed by assuming that variances are constant and ignoring the special problem surrounding tests for unit roots.

12. Summers (1982) shows that using daily rather than monthly data or testing autocorrelations at many lags does not alter the conclusions reached here.

2.2 *Announcement-Based Tests*

These results have implications for tests of market efficiency which go beyond the examination of serial correlation and excess returns. One of the major pieces of evidence that is often adduced in favor of the hypothesis of market efficiency is the prompt response of stock prices to news. Countless studies have demonstrated that stock prices respond almost instantaneously to new information, and that no predictable excess returns can be earned by trading after information has been released. This finding has no power in distinguishing the traditional market efficiency hypothesis from the alternative considered here. Under the alternative hypothesis considered here, the market responds immediately to news about fundamentals, e_t. And no abnormal patterns in returns are generated subsequent to major news announcements. The "fads" hypothesis considered here and the market efficiency hypothesis make exactly the same prediction about true news and so announcement tests do not provide any basis for distinguishing between them.

3. Tests of Semi-Strong Efficiency

In closing the last section on weak-form tests we considered one type of test for semi-strong efficiency—examining the profitability of strategies of buying or selling following certain types of announcements. Here we consider a different type of test. Equation (5) implies that expected excess returns should be negative when $p_t > p_t^*$ and positive when $p_t < p_t^*$. This reflects the assumed tendency of market prices to return towards the rational expectation of the present value of future cash flows. The key question is whether these expected excess returns are large enough to be detectable.

In practice any effort used to test efficiency in this way runs into the problems that p_t^* is unobservable. This problem is assumed away so that the hypothetical tests considered here have far more power than any test which could actually be devised. Under the assumptions that have been made so far, it is easy to see that:

$$E(z_t) = -(1 - \alpha)u_{t-1} = (1 - \alpha)(p_t^* - p_t) \qquad (9)$$

In the example considered above with $\alpha = .98$, and $\sigma_u = .28$, (9) implies that when the market was undervalued by one standard deviation, the expected excess monthly return would be $(.02) \cdot (.28) = .0056$. This contrasts with a standard deviation of monthly returns of .06.

How much data would it take for these excess returns to be statistically discernible? Suppose that the regression equation

$$Z_t = a + b(p_t^* - p_t) + \eta_t \tag{10}$$

is estimated. Equation (9) implies that $E(\hat{b}) = (1 - \alpha)$. The standard error of $\hat{b}$ can be calculated from the expression:

$$\sigma_{\hat{b}}^2 = \frac{\sigma_\eta^2}{n\sigma_u^2} \tag{11}$$

In the example considered above, one can calculate that $\sigma_b \simeq .01$. This implies that the hypothesis of market efficiency would not be rejected at the five percent level, with probability of one-half.[13] If $\alpha = .99$, the probability of rejecting the null hypothesis is less than one-sixth. Of course this discussion vastly overstates the power of any test that could actually be performed. In addition to the problem of measuring p_t^*, there are the problems of non-normality in the residuals, and the problem of measuring expected returns. These factors combine to suggest that tests of semi-strong efficiency do not have much more power against the type of inefficiency considered here than do tests on serial correlation properties of excess returns.

As Merton (1985) stresses, a major piece of evidence in favor of the market efficiency hypothesis is the repeated finding that professional money managers do not consistently outperform the market. Professional managers do not outperform the market as a class, and convincing evidence that any individuals have the ability to outperform the market has yet to be presented. Merton argues that this finding indicates that no "hidden models" with market forecasting ability are in use. The power calculations reported above suggest that even if some individuals have the ability to identify periods of market over- and undervaluation, they would not be able to prove it during the relatively short horizons over which performance evaluations are usually undertaken.

4. Implications and Conclusions

The preceding analysis suggests that certain types of inefficiency in market valuations are not likely to be detected using standard methods. This means the evidence found in many studies that the hypothesis of efficiency cannot be rejected should not lead us to conclude that market

---

13. There is one-half chance that $\hat{b} < E(\hat{b}) = .02$. In these cases the null hypothesis of efficiency will be accepted.

prices represent rational assessments of fundamentals valuations. Rather, we must face the fact that most of our tests have relatively little power against certain types of market inefficiency. In particular, the hypothesis that market valuations include large persistent errors is as consistent with the available empirical evidence as is the hypothesis of market efficiency. These are exactly the sort of errors in valuation one would expect to see if market valuations involved inflation illusion or were moved by fads as some have suggested.

The weakness of the empirical evidence verifying the hypothesis that securities markets are efficient in assessing fundamental values would not be bothersome if the hypothesis rested on firm theoretical foundations, and if there were no contrary empirical evidence. Unfortunately, neither of these conditions is satisfied in practice.

4.1 Will Speculation Eliminate Valuation Errors?

The standard theoretical argument for market efficiency is that unless securities are priced efficiently, there will be opportunities to earn excess returns. Speculators will take advantage of these opportunities by arbitraging away any inefficiencies in the pricing of securities. This argument does not explain how speculators become aware of profit opportunities. The same problems of identification described here as confronting financial economists also plague "would be" speculators. If the large persistent valuations errors considered here leave no statistically discernible trace in the historical patterns of returns, it is hard to see how speculators could become aware of them. Moreover, cautious speculators may be persuaded by the same arguments used by economists to suggest that apparent inefficiencies are not present.[14]

There is another logically separate point to be made here as well. Even if inefficiencies of the type considered here could be conclusively identified, the excess returns to trying to exploit them would be small and uncertain. The same noise which confounds statistical tests for inefficiencies makes exploiting valuation errors risky. Risk-averse speculators will only be willing to take limited positions when they perceive valuation errors. Hence errors will not be eliminated unless they are widely noticed.

An example provided by Schaefer (1982) highlights one of the points being made here—that asset values can diverge significantly from fundamentals without leaving a statistically discernible trace in the pattern of

---

14. A more extensive discussion of the reasons why speculators are unlikely to eliminate miscalculations of fundamentals may be found in Summers (1982).

returns. The example is somewhat specialized because fundamentals cannot be valued directly in the case of most assets. But the inability to detect predictable excess returns here suggests that failure elsewhere should not be taken as conclusive evidence of rational valuation. Schaefer considers the case of British gilts. He shows that some gilts are priced in such a way that they were dominated securities for investors in all tax situations. Nonetheless, he concludes that (p. 155)

> In an economic sense the result for the Electricity 3% is 'highly significant': the bond is dominated over the period with probability one. On the other hand, the period to period returns on the bond and its dominating portfolio are imperfectly correlated, and thus we cannot achieve statistical significance when we analyze mean period by period returns.

Even where valuation errors are detectable, and the existence of excess returns can be documented, the errors may not be eliminated. An excellent example is provided by the case of stock market futures. When held to maturity, they yield a return which is perfectly correlated with the market portfolio. Yet they have frequently been priced so that the return from holding them exceeds the return from holding the underlying market portfolio by several percentage points. At one level this can be explained by pointing to the difficulty of achieving an arbitrage by shorting the whole market portfolio. But this does not resolve the issue. The fact remains that two assets are available for purchase with essentially perfectly correlated but unequal returns. The differences in expected returns are no larger than in the examples presented above where fads created valuation errors of thirty percent or more.

4.2 Are There Valuation Errors?

The analysis presented so far suggests that valuation errors, if present, will be difficult to detect by looking at observed returns. But this does not prove their existence. However, both theoretical and empirical considerations suggest the likelihood that market valuations differ frequently and substantially from fundamental values. Shleifer and Summers (1986) examine the likelihood that market forces will eventually eliminate irrational traders. We argue that this is unlikely. To the extent that risk is rewarded, irrational investors who plunge into particular securities may even come to dominate the market. And even a cursory examination suggests that there are many traders pursuing strategies not closely related to fundamental valuations. There are no grounds for assuming either that irrational traders will be eliminated, or that they will be unable to move market prices.

Indirect empirical evidence suggests the importance of valuation errors. Perhaps most striking is direct evidence of divergences between the market and fundamental valuations. A classic example is the discounts on closed end funds. Even though the underlying assets are easily valued, market values do not accurately reflect fundamentals. Schaefer (1982) suggests a similar pattern for British gilts. For most securities, fundamental values are hard to measure. But the large takeover premiums that are frequently paid even in cases where there are no obvious economic advantages to combination, suggests that valuation errors are being made in the market either ex ante or ex post.

The results of French and Roll (1984) can also be interpreted as suggesting market valuations diverge from fundamental values. They find that much of the volatility in the market is in some sense self-generating. Market prices move much more over intervals when the market is continuously open, than over otherwise similar intervals when the market is not continuously open. The "extra" movements in prices associated with the markets being open seem likely to lead to valuation errors. The evident difficulty economists have in explaining any significant amount of the variations in speculative prices on the basis of "news" about fundamentals also suggests that valuation errors are being made continuously.

4.3 Implications

The central message of the huge literature on market efficiency is the supreme difficulty of earning abnormal returns making use only of publicly available information. This paper has not disputed this conclusion. Rather it has taken issue with the corollary implication of the efficient market view that market prices represent rational assessments of fundamental values. While this does not call into question prescriptions about portfolio management derived from the efficient market hypothesis, it does suggest caution in treating stock prices or their changes as rational reflections of fundamental values. This point is important for both corporate financial policy and for event study research. It is even more important for macroeconomic theories such as the q investment theory which presume that asset prices can be used to reflect the present value of the rents an asset will generate.

This analysis suggests that a more catholic approach should be taken to explaining the behavior of speculative prices. It may be possible to model the process by which errors are incorporated into asset prices. The rich literature on individual choice under uncertainty may provide guidance here. Such an approach seems preferable to insisting on the basis of very weak available evidence that market valuations are always rational.

═══════════

I am grateful to Fischer Black, Zvi Griliches, Jim Pesando, Andrei Shleifer, and Jim Poterba for clarifying discussions, but remain responsible for any errors. This paper repeats and recasts much of the analysis in Summers.

References

ABEL, ANDREW and FREDERICK MISHKIN. "An Integrated View of Tests of Rationality Market Efficiency and the Short Run Neutrality of Monetary Policy." *Journal of Monetary Economics* 11 (January 1983), 3–24.

ARROW, KENNETH J. "Risk Perception in Psychology and Economics." *Economic Inquiry* 20 (January 1982), 1–9.

BLANCHARD, OLIVIER and MARK WATSON. "Bubbles, Rational Expectations and Financial Markets." NBER Working Paper No. 945, July 1982.

BRAINARD, WILLIAM C., JOHN B. SHOVEN and LAURENCE WEISS. "The Financial Valuation of the Return of Capital." *Brookings Papers on Economic Activity* 2 (1980), 453–502.

FAMA, EUGENE. *Foundations of Finance.* New York: Basic Books, 1976.

FRENCH, KENNETH R. and RICHARD ROLL. "Is Trading Self-Generating?" Center for Research in Securities Prices Working Paper No. 121, University of Chicago, February 1984.

GRANGER, CLIVE and PAUL NEWBOLD. *Forecasting Economic Time Series.* New York: Academic Press, 1977.

HEMPEL, CARL. *Aspects of Scientific Explanation.* New York: Free Press, 1965.

IBBOTSON, R. G. and R. A. SINQUEFIELD. "Stocks, Bonds, Bills and Inflation: Year-by-Year Historical Returns (1926–1974)." *Journal of Business* 49 (January 1976), 11–47 (and update, 1979).

JENSEN, M. C., et al. "Symposium on Some Anomalous Evidence Regarding Market Efficiency." *Journal of Financial Economics* 6 (June/September 1978), 93–330.

JONES, DAVID and V. VANCE ROLEY. "Rational Expectations, the Expectations Hypothesis, and Treasury Bill Yields: An Econometric Analysis." Unpublished manuscript, Federal Reserve Bank of Kansas City, 1982.

KEYNES, J. M. *The General Theory of Employment, Interest and Money.* New York: Harcourt, Brace and Co., 1936.

MERTON, ROBERT C. "On the Current State of the Stock Market Rationality

Hypothesis." Sloan School of Management Working Paper No. 1717-85, October 1985.

MODIGLIANI, FRANCO and RICHARD COHN. "Inflation, Rational Valuation and the Market." *Financial Analysis Journal* 35 (March/April 1979), 24–44.

SCHAEFER, STEVEN. "Tax Induced Clientele Effects in the Market for British Government Securities." *Journal of Financial Economics* 10 (July 1982), 121–159.

SHILLER, ROBERT. "The Volatility of Long-Term Interest Rates and Expectations Models of the Term Structure." *Journal of Political Economy* 87 (December 1979), 1190–1219.

SHILLER, ROBERT. "Do Stock Prices Move Too Much to be Justified by Subsequent Changes in Dividends?" *American Economic Review* 71 (June 1981), 421–436.

SHILLER, ROBERT. "The Use of Volatility Measures in Assessing Market Efficiency." *Journal of Finance* 36 (May 1981a), 291–304.

SCHLEIFER, ANDREI and LAWRENCE SUMMERS. "The Evolution of Irrationality in Financial Markets." Anticipated manuscript, Harvard University, 1986.

SUMMERS, LAWRENCE H. "Do We Really Know Financial Markets are Efficient?" NBER Working Paper No. 836, January 1982.

——. "The Non-Adjustment of Nominal Interest Rates: A Study of The Fisher Effect." In *Essays in Memory of Arthur Okun,* J. Tobin, ed. Washington, D.C.: Brookings Institute. 1983, 201–244.

TVERSKY, AMOS and D. KAHNEMAN. "The Framing of Decisions and the Psychology of Choice." *Science* 211 (January 1981), 453–458.

7

Stock Prices
and Social Dynamics

ROBERT J. SHILLER

Fashion is the great governor of this world; it presides not only in matters
of dress and amusement, but in law, physic, politics, religion, and all other
things of the gravest kind; indeed, the wisest of men would be puzzled to
give any better reason why particular forms in all these have been at certain
times universally received, and at others universally rejected, than that
they were in or out of fashion.

Henry Fielding[1]

Investing in speculative assets is a social activity. Investors spend a substantial part of their leisure time discussing investments, reading about
investments, or gossiping about others' successes or failures in investing.
It is thus plausible that investors' behavior (and hence prices of speculative assets) would be influenced by social movements. Attitudes or fashions seem to fluctuate in many other popular topics of conversation, such
as food, clothing, health, or politics. These fluctuations in attitude often
occur widely in the population and often appear without any apparent
logical reason. It is plausible that attitudes or fashions regarding investments would also change spontaneously or in arbitrary social reaction to
some widely noted events.

Most of those who buy and sell in speculative markets seem to take it
for granted that social movements significantly influence the behavior of
prices. Popular interpretations of the recurrent recessions that we ob-

1. Henry Fielding, *The True Patriot*, no. 1, 1745, in James P. Browne, ed., *The Works of
Henry Fielding, Esq.*, vol. 8 (London: Bickers and Son, 1903), p. 69.

From: *The Brookings Papers on Economic Activity*, vol. 2, pp. 457–510, 1984. Reprinted
by permission.

serve often include ideas that the shifts in, say, consumer confidence or optimism are also at work in other aspects of the business cycle, such as interest rates, inventories, and so on. Academic research on market psychology, however, appears to have more or less died out in the 1950s, at about the time the expected-utility revolution in economics was born. Those academics who write about financial markets today are usually very careful to dissociate themselves from any suggestion that market psychology might be important, as if notions of market psychology have been discredited as unscientific.[2] There is instead an enormous recent literature in finance that takes one of the various forms of the efficient markets hypothesis for motivation and a related literature in macroeconomics that is based on the assumption of rational expectations. In academic circles there has certainly been an interest in speculative bubbles, but pursued within the framework of rational expectations models with unchanging tastes.[3]

It is hard to find in the large literature on the efficient markets hypothesis any discussion of an alternative hypothesis involving social psychology in financial markets.[4] Yet the impression persists in the literature and in casual discussions that there are very powerful arguments against such social-psychological theories. Arguments confined to an oral tradition, tacitly accepted by all parties, and not discussed in the scholarly literature are particularly vulnerable to error. It is thus important to consider explicitly these arguments against a major role for mass psychology in financial markets.

Returns on speculative assets are nearly unforecastable; this fact is the basis of the most important argument in the oral tradition against a role for mass psychology in speculative markets. One form of this argument claims that because real returns are nearly unforecastable, the real price

2. The recent literature on behavioral economics associated with survey research has apparently not touched substantially on speculative markets. Some of their findings are relevant and will be cited below.

3. For example, David Cass and Karl Shell refer to market psychology in motivating their discussion of extraneous uncertainty, but they then assume economic agents are expected-utility maximizers with unchanging tastes. There is, however, a sense in which they and others are wrestling with some of the same issues that are of concern in this paper. See Cass and Shell, "Do Sunspots Matter?" *Journal of Political Economy,* vol. 91 (April 1983), pp. 193–227.

4. There are some casual arguments in the literature against such a role for mass psychology. The most-cited reference may be Eugene F. Fama, "The Behavior of Stock Market Prices," *Journal of Business,* vol. 38 (January 1965), pp. 34–105. The argument consists of no more than a few paragraphs pointing out that "sophisticated traders" might eliminate profit opportunities, thereby tending to make "actual prices closer to intrinsic values" (p. 38).

of stocks is close to the intrinsic value, that is, the present value with constant discount rate of optimally forecasted future real dividends. This argument for the efficient markets hypothesis represents one of the most remarkable errors in the history of economic thought. It is remarkable in the immediacy of its logical error and in the sweep and implications of its conclusion. I will discuss this and other arguments for the efficient markets hypothesis and claim that mass psychology may well be the dominant cause of movements in the price of the aggregate stock market.

I have divided my discussion into four major sections: arguments from a social-psychological standpoint for the importance of fashions in financial markets, a critique of the argument for the efficient markets hypothesis, a proposed alternative model based on social psychology, and some exploratory data analysis suggested by the alternative model.

The first section discusses what we know about changing fashions or attitudes in light of everyday experience, research in social psychology and sociology, and evidence from postwar stock market history. This will not be direct evidence that people violate the principle of expected-utility maximization, nor is the evidence of great value in judging how far we should carry the assumption of rationality in other areas of economics (although I think it is of value in understanding the business cycle). Rather, I will be motivated here by the relatively narrow question of why speculative asset prices fluctuate as much as they do.

The second section sets forth and evaluates the efficient markets model and the presumed evidence against a role for social psychology in determining prices. The fundamental issue is the power of statistical tests in distinguishing the efficient markets model from the important alternatives. If statistical tests have little power, then we ought to use the sort of qualitative evidence discussed in the first section to evaluate the efficient markets model.

The third section offers a simple though rather incomplete alternative model of stock prices that admits the importance of social-psychological factors. This model involves "smart-money investors" and "ordinary investors" and is intended to demonstrate how models of financial markets might better accommodate the econometric evidence on the near unforecastability of returns, evidence that is widely interpreted as favoring the efficient markets model.

The fourth section uses U.S. stock market data to explore some relations suggested by the alternative model. Using Standard and Poor's composite stock price index, I examine various forecasting equations for real returns. I consider whether stock price movements seem to follow simple patterns, as in an overreaction to dividends or earnings news, and whether this overreaction induces a sort of forecastability for returns. In doing this I present a time series model of the aggregate real dividend series associated with Standard and Poor's composite stock price index. I also propose a hypothetical scenario using the alternative model that shows for recent U.S. history what the smart-money investors may have been doing, the fraction of total trading volume that might have been accounted for by smart-money trades in and out of the market, and the extent to which ordinary investors may have influenced stock prices.

1. Evidence on Fashions and Financial Markets

1.1 Fashions in Everyday Life

Isn't it plausible that those who are so enlightened as to be readers of this journal might find themselves caught up in capricious fashion changes? Those of us involved in the current fashion of running for exercise may say that we do it because it is good for our health, but the health benefits of such exercise were known decades ago.[5] Talking with runners suggests that far more is at work in this movement than the logical reaction to a few papers in medical journals. Why wasn't the joy of running appreciated twenty years ago? Why are we thinking about running these days and not about once-popular leisure activities now in decline, such as leading Boy Scout troops or watching western movies?[6]

Fashions in one country may often move in one direction while those in another country are moving in a different direction. In politics, for instance, we have seen in the last decade a drift toward conservatism in some Western countries and a drift toward socialism in others. The objective evidence for or against socialism cannot have moved both ways. Something about the social environment, collective memories, or leadership is different and changing through time differently in these countries. Is there any reason to think that social movements affect investments any less strongly than they do these other activities? We know that attitudes toward investments are very different across cultures. In West Germany today investors are notably cautious; it is hard to raise venture capital,

---

5. A few minutes spent with an index to periodical literature will confirm that the idea that regular exercise helps prevent heart disease was part of the conventional wisdom by the mid-1950s.

6. There seems to be the same superabundance of theories to explain the decline of boy scouting since 1973 as for the decline in the stock market over the same period. See "Whatever Happened to . . . Boy Scouts: Trying to Make a Comeback," *U.S. News and World Report* (May 7, 1979), pp. 86–87. Those who think that people simply got tired of westerns will have to explain why it took a generation for them to do so.

and the stock market itself is very small. Isn't it plausible that attitudes that change across countries should also change within a country through time?

Some may argue that investing is less likely than other activities to be influenced by fashions because people make investment choices privately, based on their perception of the prospects for return, and usually not with any concern for what people will think. It is, however, plausible that these perceptions of return themselves represent changing fashions. The changing fashions in "physic" that Fielding noted are analogous. Sick people in Fielding's day asked physicians to bleed them because they thought they would get well as a result and not because they thought that they would impress other people by having it done. Therapeutic bleeding is an excellent example of a fashion because there has never been any scientific basis for it; the belief in its efficacy arose entirely from the social milieu.

1.2 Who Controls Equity Investments?

It is important first to clarify the identity of investors in corporate stock. It is widely and mistakenly believed that (1) institutional investors hold most stocks, (2) most wealthy individuals have delegated authority to manage their investments, and (3) smart money dominates the market. By suggesting that the market is more professionalized than it is, these misconceptions lend spurious plausibility to the notion that markets are very efficient.

It is true that the importance of institutional investors has been growing in the postwar period. Institutional holdings of New York Stock Exchange stocks as a percent of the total value of the stocks rose from 15.0 percent in 1955 to 35.4 percent in 1980.[7] Still, nearly 65 percent of all New York Stock Exchange stocks were held by individuals in 1980.

Most individually held corporate stock belongs to the wealthy. In 1971, the 1 percent of U.S. families (including single individuals) with the largest personal income accounted for 51 percent of the market value of stock owned by all families, while the 10 percent of families with

---

7. See New York Stock Exchange, *New York Stock Exchange Fact Book 1983* (NYSE, 1983), p. 52. This source says that institutional investors accounted for 65 percent of all public volume on the New York Stock Exchange in the fourth quarter of 1980 (p. 54). Thus, institutional investors trade much more frequently than do individual investors. Data that are probably more accurate on institutional holdings are in Irwin Friend and Marshall Blume, *The Changing Role of the Institutional Investor* (Wiley, 1978); they estimated that 24.9 percent of all stock was held by institutions and foreigners in 1971, up from 17.9 percent in 1960 (p. 32).

the largest income accounted for 74 percent of market value.[8] Wealthy individuals are of course part of the same society as the rest of us. They read the same newspapers and watch the same television programs. They are different, however, in one important way. For them, information costs are quite low relative to the income from their investments. One might be inclined to think that they would in practice delegate to experts the authority over their investments.

A 1964 Brookings study interviewed 1,051 individuals with 1961 incomes of more than $10,000 (or about $34,000 in 1984 prices) concerning their investment habits, among other things. The 1961 median income for the sample was about $40,000 (or about $135,000 in 1984 prices). "Only one-tenth reported delegating some or all authority over their investments, and this proportion reached one-fourth only for those with incomes over $300,000. Only 2 percent of the entire high-income group said they delegated 'all' authority."[9] Instead of delegating authority, most made their own investment decisions with some advice: "About three-fourths of the high income respondents who managed their own assets said that they got advice from others in making their investment decisions. One in three of those seeking advice said they 'always' sought advice when investing, while two out of three said they did 'occasionally.'"[10] Two-thirds of the investors said they tried to keep informed, and more than half said they made use of business magazines, but "only one-tenth of those trying to keep informed said that they read the financial statements and other reports issued by the corporations in which they were considering an investment."[11]

What is really important for one's view of financial markets is not directly the extent to which institutional investors or wealthy individuals dominate the market, but the extent to which smart money dominates the market. One commonly expressed view is that intelligent individuals can be assumed to take control of the market by accumulating wealth through profitable trading. This argument overlooks the fact that individuals consume their wealth and eventually also die. When they die they

8. See Marshall E. Blume, Jean Crockett, and Irwin Friend, "Stockownership in the United States: Characteristics and Trends," *Survey of Current Business*, vol. 54 (November 1974), pp. 16–40. In 1981, 7.2 percent of households had income above $50,000 (*Statistical Abstract of the United States, 1982–83*, p. 430).

9. Robin Barlow, Harvey E. Brazer, and James N. Morgan, *Economic Behavior of the Affluent* (Brookings, 1966), p. 26.

10. Ibid., p. 68.

11. Ibid., p. 71. These findings were also confirmed in other surveys. See George Katona, *Psychological Economics* (Elsevier, 1975), p. 269.

bequeath it to others who have perhaps only a small probability of being smart investors as well. In assessing this probability, one must bear in mind that the class of smart-money investors does not correspond closely to the intelligent segment of the population. What is at work behind smart money is not just intelligence but also interest in investments and timeliness. Presumably the probability is fairly low that heirs are smart investors.[12]

There are several factors that serve to mitigate the effects of higher returns on the average wealth of smart-money investors. One is that most people do not acquire most of their maximum wealth until fairly late in the life cycle and thus do not have as much time to accumulate. Another factor is that in a growing population, younger persons, whose portfolios have had less time to accumulate, will figure more prominently in the aggregate of wealth. Yet another factor is that saving early in the life cycle tends for institutional reasons to take the form of investing in a house rather than in speculative assets.

Roughly speaking, one can expect to live thirty years after receiving a bequest on the death of one's parents. A representative smart-money heir who earns and accumulates at a rate n greater than a representative ordinary investor in the middle of the thirty years will thus have on average, if original bequests were equal, roughly $(1 + n)^{15}$ times as much wealth. If n is 2 percent per year, this is 1.3; if 5 percent per year, this is 2.1. As long as the percentage of smart investors is small, returns that are higher by this order of magnitude will not cause the smart money to take over the market.

Of course, it is unlikely that smart-money investors are pure accumulators; because we lack data on their savings patterns versus the savings patterns of ordinary investors, it is impossible to say anything concrete about how much money smart investors accumulate. If the smart investors behave like good trustees of the family estate and consume at exactly the rate that would preserve the real value of the family wealth, then smart money will not accumulate at all, regardless of the return it earns.

1.3 The Ambiguity of Stock Value

Stock prices are likely to be among the prices that are relatively vulnerable to purely social movements because there is no accepted theory by which to understand the worth of stocks and no clearly predictable consequences to changing one's investments.

12. The median correlation (from 12 studies) between IQs of natural parents and of their children is 0.50. See H. J. Eysenck and Leon Kamin, *The Intelligence Controversy* (Wiley, 1980), p. 50.

Ordinary investors have no model or at best a very incomplete model of the behavior of prices, dividends, or earnings of speculative assets. Do projections of large future deficits in the federal budget imply that the price of long-term bonds will go up or down? Does the election of a conservative U.S. president imply that earnings of General Motors will go up or down? Does a rise in the price of oil cause the price of IBM stock to go up or down? Ordinary investors have no objective way of knowing.

Ordinary investors are faced with what Frank Knight in 1921 called "uncertainty" rather than "risk":

> The practical difference between the two categories, risk and uncertainty, is that in the former the distribution of the outcome in a group of instances is known (either from calculation *a priori* or from statistics of past experience), while in the case of uncertainty this is not true, the reason being in general that it is impossible to form a group of instances, because the situation dealt with is in a high degree unique. . . . It is this *true uncertainty* which by preventing the theoretically perfect outworking of the tendencies of competition gives the characteristic form of "enterprise" to economic organization as a whole and accounts for the peculiar income of the entrepreneur.[13]

Ordinary investors also cannot judge the competence of investment counselors in the way they can that of other professionals. It is very easy to learn whether a map company is producing correct maps; we can therefore take it for granted that others have done this and that any map that is sold will serve to guide us. It is much harder to evaluate investment advisers who counsel individual investors on the composition of their portfolios and who claim to help them make investments with high returns. Most investors lack data on past outcomes of a counselor's advice and on whether the current advice is based on the same approach that produced these outcomes. Moreover, most investors do not understand data analysis or risk correction, necessary knowledge for evaluating the data.

It is also much easier to change one's mind on one's investments than on one's consumption of commodities. The former has no apparent immediate effect on one's well being, whereas to change one's consumption of commodities, one must give up some habit or consume something one formerly did not enjoy.

---

13. Frank H. Knight, *Risk, Uncertainty and Profit* (Augustus M. Kelley, 1964), pp. 232–33.

1.4 Suggestibility and Group Pressure

Since investors lack any clear sense of objective evidence regarding prices of speculative assets, the process by which their opinions are derived may be especially social. There is an extensive literature in social psychology on individual suggestibility and group pressure. Much of this literature seeks to quantify, by well-chosen experiments, how individual opinions are influenced by the opinions of others. A good example of such experiments in Muzafer Sherif's classic work using the "autokinetic effect."[14] In this experiment, subjects were seated in a totally darkened room and asked to view at a distance of five meters a point of light seen through a small hole in a metal box. They were told that the point of light would begin to move and were asked to report to the experimenter the magnitude, in inches, of its movements. In fact, the point was not moving, and the viewer had no frame of reference, in the total darkness, to decide how it was moving. When placed in groups so that they could hear answers of others in the group, the individuals arrived, without any discussion, at consensuses (differing across groups) on the amount of movement. Subjects, interviewed afterward, showed little awareness of the influence of the group on their individual decision.

In another well-known experiment, Solomon Asch had individuals alone and in groups compare the lengths of line segments. The lengths were sufficiently different that, when responding alone, subjects gave very few wrong answers. Yet when placed in a group in which all other members were coached to give the same wrong answers, individual subjects also frequently gave wrong answers.[15] Through follow-up questions, Asch found that even though the subject was often aware of the correct answer, and the answer was completely inoffensive, the subject was afraid to contradict the group.

The research shows evidence of flagrant decision errors under social pressure but not of abandonment of rational individual judgment. It does help provide some understanding of possible origins of swings in public opinion. The Asch experiment suggests that group pressures do serve at the very least to cause individuals to remain silent when their own views appear to deviate from the group's, and their silence will prevent the dissemination of relevant information that might establish the dissenters' views more firmly.

14. See Muzafer Sherif, "An Experimental Approach to the Study of Attitudes," *Sociometry*, vol. 1 (1937), pp. 90–98.

15. See Solomon E. Asch, *Social Psychology* (Prentice Hall, 1952).

1.5 The Diffusion of Opinions

The dynamic process by which social movements take place is the subject of an extensive literature by social psychologists and sociologists, and the basic mechanisms are well known. The ideas that represent a movement may be latent in people's minds long before the movement begins. An idea may not become a matter of conviction or active thought until the individual hears the idea from several friends or from public authorities. This process takes time. The process may be helped along if some vivid news event causes people to talk about related matters or slowed if a news event distracts their attention.

Social movements can take place in a matter of hours after so vivid an event as the onset of a war. Or changes in attitudes can take decades to diffuse through the population, as evidenced by the fact that many fashion changes in dress seem to happen very slowly. The communications media may, if attention is given to some event, speed the rate of diffusion. However, the general finding of research on persuasion is that "any impact that the mass media have on opinion change is less than that produced by informal face-to-face communication of the person with his primary groups, his family, friends, coworkers, and neighbors."[16] This fact is recognized by television advertisers who, in promoting their products, often try to create with actors the illusion of such communication. Katona has used the term *social learning* to refer to the slow process of "mutual reinforcement through exchange of information among peer groups by word of mouth, a major condition for the emergence of a uniform response to new stimuli by very many people."[17] Thus, it is not surprising that in surveys in the 1950s and 1960s "the answers to the two questions 'Do you own any stocks' and 'Do you have any friends or colleagues who own any stocks' were practically identical."[18]

Such diffusion processes for news or rumor have been modeled more formally by mathematical sociologists drawing on the mathematical theory of epidemics.[19] For example, in what has been referred to as the "general epidemic model,"[20] it is assumed, first, that new carriers of news

16. William J. McGuire, "The Nature of Attitudes and Attitude Change," in Gardner Lindzey and Elliot Aronson, eds., *Handbook of Social Psychology* (Addison Wesley, 1969), p. 231.

17. See Katona, *Psychological Economics*, p. 203.

18. Ibid., p. 267.

19. See for example David J. Bartholomew, *Stochastic Models for Social Processes* (Wiley, 1967).

20. See Norman T. Bailey, *The Mathematical Theory of Epidemics* (London: C. Griffin, 1957).

(as of a disease) are created at a rate equal to an "infection rate" β times the number of carriers times the number of susceptibles and, second, that carriers cease being carriers at a "removal rate" τ. The first assumption is that of the familiar model which gives rise to the logistic curve, and the second assumption causes any epidemic or social movement eventually to come to an end. In this model a new infectious agent or an event interpreted as important news can have either of two basic consequences. If the infection rate is less than a threshold equal to the removal rate divided by the number of susceptibles, the number of carriers will decline monotonically. If the infection rate is above the threshold, the number of carriers will have a hump-shaped pattern, rising at first and then declining.

The removal rate and the infection rate may differ dramatically from one social movement to another depending on the characteristics of the sources, media, and receivers. One survey of the literature on removal rates after persuasive communications concluded that "the 'typical' persuasive communication has a half-life of six months" but that different experiments produced widely different half-lives.[21] Changes in the infection rate or removal rate may be what accounts for the sudden appearance of some social movements. A rise in the infection rate, for example, may cause an attitude long latent in people's minds to snowball into a movement.

We might expect then to see a variety of patterns in social movements: long-lasting "humps" that build slowly (low removal and infection rate) or that rise and fall quickly (high removal and infection rate); news events with a subsequent monotonic decline of infectives (zero infection rate) or followed by a monotonically increasing number of infectives (zero removal rate). Of course, such patterns may not be seen directly in prices of speculative assets, as the "alternative model" I present later in the paper will show.

1.6 Social Movements and the Postwar Stock Market

The real price of corporate stocks, as measured by a deflated Standard and Poor's composite stock price index (figure 1), shows what appears to be a pronounced uptrend between the late 1940s and the late 1960s and since then a downtrend (or, more accurately, a single major drop between

21. McGuire, "The Nature of Attitudes," pp. 253–54. A description of recent research in marketing journals on the removal rate is in Richard P. Bagozzi and Alvin J. Silk, "Recall, Recognition, and the Measurement of Memory for Print Advertisements," *Marketing Science*, vol. 2 (Spring 1983), pp. 95–134. See Bartholomew, *Stochastic Models*, for a discussion of empirical work on the infection rate.

Figure 1 Standard and Poor's Stock Price Data, 1926–84[a]

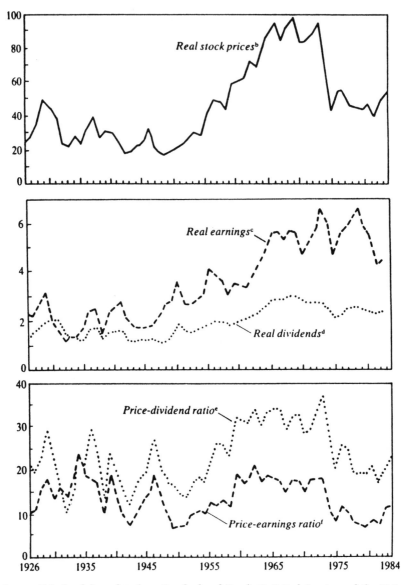

Source: Calculated from data from Standard and Poor's Statistical Service and the U.S. Bureau of Labor Statistics.

a. Annual data, fifty-nine observations from 1926 to 1984. The stock price index is Standard and Poor's composite stock price index.

1973 and 1975). The postwar uptrend period, the last great bull market, has often been characterized as one of contagious and increasingly excessive optimism. Is there any evidence of such a social movement then? Is there evidence that such a social movement came to an end after the late 1960s?

Such evidence will not take the form of proof that people should have known better than to price stocks as they did. The postwar period was one of rapidly growing real earnings and real dividends, and that the growth should be expected to continue was an idea backed by plausible reasons, such as:

> the constant speed-up in business research in order to cut costs and bring out ever newer and more competitive products; the extension of business expansion planning farther and farther into the future, which means that such plans are carried forward regardless of any jiggles in the trend of business; the improvement in business techniques that offset the effects of seasonal fluctuations; the advance in methods of monetary management by the Federal Reserve Board; and the similar advance in general understanding of the effects of the Government's tax and other economic policies.[22]

How was anyone to know whether these reasons were right or not?

The evidence for a social movement driving the bull market will come instead from other sources. The evidence will be the growing numbers of individuals who participated in, were interested in, or knew about the market; the changes in relations between investor and agent; and the changes in attitudes that might plausibly affect the valuation of stocks. The evidence is not intended to provide a tight theory of the movements of stock prices but to show that large social movements appear to have occurred that might plausibly have had a great impact on stock prices.

---

22. George Shea, *Wall Street Journal*, October 12, 1955, reprinted in *Forty Years on Wall Street* (Princeton, N.J.: Dow Jones, 1968), pp. 42–43.

---

b. Stock price index for January (1941–43 = 100) divided by the January producer price index, all items, times 100.

c. Four-quarter total for the fourth quarter of Standard and Poor's earnings per share adjusted to the stock price index, divided by the January producer price index, times 100.

d. Four-quarter total for the fourth quarter of Standard and Poor's dividends per share adjusted to the stock price index, divided by the January producer price index, times 100.

e. Computed by dividing the stock price series by the dividends series for the preceding year (in nominal terms).

f. Computed as for the price-dividend ratio, with earnings in place of dividends.

In fact, there is a superabundance of plausible reasons for the movements of the market.

Evidence for the growing numbers of individuals who participated in the market can of course be found most directly in the rising quantity of stocks held by institutional investors. The most important component of this increase was pension funds. The rise of employer pension funds in the postwar period might even be considered a social movement that probably caused an increased demand for shares. Individuals may, by saving less themselves, offset the saving done on their behalf by firms; but because most people do not hold any stocks, it is not possible for them (without short sales) to offset the institutional demand for stocks by holding fewer shares. Such changes in demand by institutions are likely to be important in determining asset prices but are not my main concern here. Others have studied such changes using flow-of-funds methodology.[23]

The period of rising stock prices also corresponds roughly with a period of a dramatic increase in the number of people who participated directly (not through institutions) in the stock market. The New York Stock Exchange shareownership surveys showed that the total number of individual shareowners as a percent of the U.S. population rose from 4 percent in 1952 to 7 percent in 1959 to a peak of 15 percent in 1970.[24] The corresponding numbers for 1975, 1980, and 1981 varied from 11 percent to 12 percent.[25]

The increase in individual stockownership appears to correspond to an increase in knowledge about and interest in the market. The 1954 New York Stock Exchange investor attitude survey, consisting of interviews of several thousand individuals, was motivated by the question, Why is it that "4 out of 5 doctors, lawyers, major and minor executives, engineers and salesmen *do not own* stock in publicly owned corporations?"[26] What came out of the survey was a sense of lack of information or interest in

23. For a recent example, see Benjamin M. Friedman, "Effects of Shifting Saving Patterns on Interest Rates and Economic Activity," *Journal of Finance*, vol. 37 (March 1982), pp. 37–62.

24. New York Stock Exchange, *Share-ownership 1952* through *1970* (NYSE, 1953 through 1971). The rise before 1970 of shareownership involved a trend toward somewhat more egalitarian distribution of stock. In 1958, 83.2 percent of stock value was owned by individuals with the top 10 percent of income. By 1970, this has fallen to 75.4 percent. See Friend, Blume, and Crockett, "Stockownership," p. 27.

25. New York Stock Exchange, *Share-ownership 1975, 1980,* and *1981* (NYSE, 1976, 1981, and 1982).

26. New York Stock Exchange, *The Public Speaks to the Exchange Community* (NYSE, 1955), p. 54.

the stock market and vague senses of prejudice against the stock market. Only 23 percent of the adult population knew enough to define corporate stock as "a share in profit," "bought and sold by public, anyone can buy," or "not preferred or a bond."

By 1959 there appeared a "much better understanding of the functions of the Stock Exchange as the nation's marketplace." The number of Americans who could "explain the functions of the Exchange" rose nearly 20 percent. The number who knew "that companies must meet certain standards before the Exchange will permit their stocks to be listed for trading" increased 36 percent in the same five-year period.[27]

The growth of numbers of people who knew about or were involved at all in the stock market is important evidence that something other than a reevaluation of optimal forecasts of the long-run path of future dividends was at work in producing the bull market. Any model that attributes the increase in stock prices to a Bayesian learning process will not stand up to the observation that most of the investors at the peak of the bull market were not involved or interested in the market at all at the beginning of the increase.

Evidence about changing relations between individual investors and their agents takes two forms: evidence regarding the rise of stockbrokers and of publicity campaigns from them and evidence regarding the investment club movement.

Between 1954 and 1959 stockbrokers were growing in reputation. In the 1954 New York Stock Exchange survey 30 percent of the adult population said they would turn first to a broker for investment advice; by 1959 this figure had risen to 38 percent. During this five-year period, stockbrokers replaced bankers as the first source of investment advice. An estimated 9 million adults said they were contacted by brokers in 1959, compared with fewer than 5 million in 1954.[28]

The New York Stock Exchange initiated an investors' education program as part of a broader shareownership program. Begun in 1954, the program by 1959 had a list of 2,500 lecturers in 85 cities. Lectures were held in local high schools as part of adult education programs by lecturers "bent on carrying the investing gospel . . . wherever there were ears to hear."[29]

By 1959 the program had conducted 4,500 lecture courses reaching 525,000 persons or about 4 percent of the total number of shareholders

27. See New York Stock Exchange, *The Investors of Tomorrow*, title page and p. 6 (NYSE, 1960).

28. New York Stock Exchange, *Investors of Tomorrow*, pp. 9, 14.

29. See *New York Times*, September 20, 1959.

in 1959. The investor education program used all the media, including advertisements in newspapers and magazines and on radio. As early as 1954, when the program was only six months old, 5 percent of the adult population in the United States could identify the New York Stock Exchange as the source of the slogan "Own Your Share of American Business."[30]

In contrast the 1970s was a period of low profits for the New York Stock Exchange and advertising in newspapers and magazines was suspended. In 1975 competitive commissions were established and amendments to the Securities Act threatened the viability of the New York Stock Exchange. Prices of seats on the exchange dropped. In response to the problems, the exchange in 1977 severely cut back the investors' education program and dropped the adult education program. Lack of public enthusiasm for the program was also offered as a reason for the cutback. The same factors that caused the New York Stock Exchange to suspend its investors' education program may have also had the effect of decreasing the efforts of individual brokers to promote corporate stocks. Such factors as competitive commissions, which reduce the profits in conventional brokerages, have "tended to shrink the numbers of people who are out there trying to encourage individual investors into this market place."[31]

Investment clubs are social clubs in which small groups of people pursue together a hobby of investing. Interest in such clubs might well give some indication of how much stocks were talked about and how much people enjoyed investing. The number of clubs in the National Association of Investment Clubs rose from 923 in 1954 to a peak of 14,102 in 1970 and then fell to 3,642 in 1980.[32] The total number of individuals directly involved in investment clubs and their aggregate wealth is of course small. However, the investment club movement is plausible evidence of a national movement that is not reflected in the membership rolls.

There is in the postwar period evidence of substantial changes in behavior big enough to have a major impact on the market. For example, the percentage of people who said that religion is "very important" in their lives fell from 75 percent in 1952 to 52 percent in 1978.[33] The birth rate hovered around 2.5 percent throughout the 1950s and then began a

30. New York Stock Exchange, *The Public Speaks*, p. 10.

31. Robert M. Gardiner, chairman of Reynolds Securities, Inc., as quoted in New York Stock Exchange, *Share-ownership 1975* (NYSE, 1976), p. 21.

32. Data from the National Association of Investment Clubs.

33. See "Religion in America," *The Gallup Report*, no. 222 (March 1984).

gradual decline to around 1.5 percent in the 1970s. These changes may reflect changing attitudes toward the importance of family, of heirs, or of individual responsibility for others.

Of all such changes, the one with perhaps the most striking importance for demand for shares in the postwar period is the pervasive decline in confidence in society's institutions after the bull market period. According to poll analyst Daniel Yankelovich:

> We have seen a steady rise of mistrust in our national institutions. . . . Trust in government declined dramatically from almost 80% in the late 1950s to about 33% in 1976. Confidence in business fell from approximately a 70% level in the late 60s to about 15% today. Confidence in other institutions—the press, the military, the professions—doctors and lawyers—sharply declined from the mid-60s to the mid-70s.[34]

To Yankelovich's list we may add stockbrokers. One of the findings of the New York Stock Exchange 1977–78 survey was that "a negative image of brokers and firms permeates all subgroups and even top quality clients have an unfavorable impression of the industry."[35] By their very pervasiveness, the negative attitudes toward institutions suggest a prejudice rather than an informed judgment.

2. The Efficient Markets Model

The observation that stock returns are not very forecastable is widely thought to mean that investor psychology could not be an important factor in financial markets. Why is it thought so? If investor fads influenced stock prices, the argument goes, then it would seem that these fads would cause stock price movements to be somewhat predictable. Moreover, because dividends themselves are somewhat forecastable (firms in fact announce changes in their dividends from time to time), and in spite of this we are unable to forecast well any change in returns, it must be true that stock prices in some sense are determined in anticipation of dividends paid. Thus, stock prices should be determined by optimal forecasts of dividends.

The above argument can be formalized by representing the unfore-

---

34. From a speech, April 1977, quoted in Seymour Martin Lipset and William Schneider, *The Confidence Gap: Business, Labor and Government in the Public Mind* (Free Press, 1983), p. 15. The Gallup Poll also documents a fairly steady decline in confidence in all major institutions over the years 1973–83. See *Gallup Report*, no. 217 (October 1983).

35. See New York Stock Exchange, *Public Attitudes Toward Investing: Marketing Implications* (NYSE, 1979), p. 5.

castability of returns by $E_t R_t = \delta$, where E_t denotes mathematical expectation conditional on all publicly available information at time t, R_t is the real (corrected for inflation) rate of return (including both dividends and capital gain) on a stock between time t and time $t + 1$, and δ is a constant. Here, R_t equals $(P_{t+1} - P_t + D_t)/P_t$ where P_t is the real price of the share at time t and D_t any real dividend which might be paid in the time period. This is a first-order rational expectations model of the kind familiar in the literature that can be solved, subject to a stability terminal condition, by recursive substitution.[36] Out of the negative result that we cannot seem to forecast returns we thus get the powerful efficient markets model:[37]

$$P_t = \sum_{k=0}^{\infty} \frac{E_t D_{t+k}}{(1 + \delta)^{k+1}}. \tag{1}$$

Equation (1) asserts the real price is the present discounted value of expected future dividends, and in this sense price anticipates optimally (that is, takes into account all publicly available information) the stream of dividends that the stock will pay in the future.

There is a fundamental error in this argument for the efficient markets model: it overlooks the fact that the statistical tests have not shown that returns are not forecastable; they have shown only that returns are not *very* forecastable. The word *very* is crucial here, since alternative models that have price determined primarily by fads (such as will be discussed below) also imply that returns are not very forecastable.

We can get some idea at this point of the power of the regression tests

---

36. One rearranges the equation to read $P_t = bE_t D_t + bE_t P_{t+1}$, where $b = 1/(1 + \delta)$, and then uses the fact that $E_t E_{t+k} = E_t$ if $k > 0$. One substitutes in the above rational expectations model for P_{t+1}, yielding $P_t = bE_t D_t + b^2 E_t D_{t+1} + b^2 E_t P_{t+2}$. One repeats this process, successively substituting for the price terms on the right hand side. The terminal condition assumption in the text is that the price term, $b^n E_t P_{t+n}$, goes to zero as n goes to infinity.

37. Paul Samuelson explains the relationship of this model to the random walk model in his "Proof that properly discounted present values of assets vibrate randomly," in Hiroaki Nagatani and Kate Crowley, eds., *The Collected Scientific Papers of Paul A. Samuelson*, vol. 4 (MIT Press, 1977), pp. 465–70. It should be emphasized of course that there is no agreement on the precise definition of the term "efficient markets model" or whether it corresponds to equation (1). For example, in his well-known survey, Eugene Fama says only that "a market in which prices always 'fully reflect' available information is called 'efficient.'" The empirical work he discusses, however, tests the hypothesis that price changes or returns are unforecastable. See Eugene F. Fama, "Efficient Capital Markets: A Review of Theory and Empirical Work," *Journal of Finance*, vol. 25 (May 1970), pp. 383–417.

of the efficient markets model against importantly different alternatives. Consider an alternative model in which the true (theoretical) R^2 in a regression of aggregate returns of corporate stocks on some set of information variables is 0.1. Given that the standard deviation of the real annual returns on the aggregate stock market is about 18 percent, such an R^2 implies that the standard deviation of the predictable component of returns is about 5.7 percent per year. Thus, under this alternative model we might well predict real returns of 14 percent in one year and 2 percent in another (these are one-standard-deviation departures from mean return). In an unusual year we might predict a real return of 19 percent or −3 percent (these are two-standard-deviation departures from the mean return). Yet if the alternative model is true with thirty observations (thirty years of data) and one forecasting variable, the probability of rejecting market efficiency in a conventional F-test at the 0.05 level is only 0.42. With two forecasting variables, the probability of rejecting is 0.32, and the probability becomes negligible as the number of explanatory variables is increased further.[38] As I have argued in a paper with Pierre Perron, increasing the number of observations by sampling more frequently while leaving the span in years of data unchanged may not increase the power of tests very much and may even reduce it.[39]

Someone may well wonder if there is not also some direct evidence that stock prices really do anticipate future dividends in the manner represented in equation (1). There is anecdotal evidence that the prices of some firms whose dividends can be forecasted to fall to zero (bankruptcy) or soar to new levels (breakthrough) do anticipate these movements. But these anecdotes do not show that there is not another component of the volatility of prices, a component that might dominate price movements in the stocks whose dividends are not so forecastable. For the aggregate stock market, there is no evidence at all that stock price movements have been followed by corresponding dividend movements.[40]

Some may argue that the constancy of discount rates in equation (1) may not be an appropriate feature for a general model of market efficiency. There are, of course, many variations on this model, such as the

---

38. These power computations are based on the usual assumption of normal residuals; as a result the conventional F-statistic is, under the alternative hypothesis, distributed as noncentral F, with $k - 1$ and $n - 1$ degrees of freedom and noncentrality parameter $(n/2)R^2/(1 - R^2)$, where R^2 is the theoretical coefficient of determination under the alternative hypothesis.

39. See Robert J. Shiller and Pierre Perron, "Testing the Random Walk Hypothesis: Power vs. Frequency of Observation" (Yale University, 1984).

40. See Robert J. Shiller, "Do Stock Prices Move Too Much to be Justified by Subsequent Changes in Dividends?" *American Economic Review*, vol. 71 (June 1981), pp. 421–36.

recent "consumption beta" models.[41] It is not possible to address all these alternatives here. Equation (1) is chosen as the most commonplace version of the efficient markets theory and a version that seems to have figured most prominently in the arguments against market psychology. Moreover, arguments about the power of tests of equation (1) may well extend to some of the other variants of the efficient markets hypothesis.

3. An Alternative Model

Let us postulate the existence of smart-money investors who, subject to their wealth limitations, respond quickly and appropriately to publicly available information. Consider a story that tells how they might alter the response of the market to the behavior of ordinary investors. This story is no doubt oversimplified and restrictive, but then so is the simple efficient markets model, with which it is to be compared.

Smart-money investors in this model respond to rationally expected returns but to an extent limited by their wealth. Suppose that their demand for stock is linear in the expected return on the market (or if the model is applied to an individual firm, the expected return on a share of that firm) over the next time period:

$$Q_t = \frac{(E_t R_t - \rho)}{\varphi}. \tag{2}$$

Here, Q_t is the demand for shares by smart money at time t expressed as a portion of the total shares outstanding, and $E_t R_t$ is the expected return starting at time t, defined as it is above. The symbols ρ and φ represent constants. Thus, ρ is the expected real return such that there is no demand for shares by the smart money. The real return at which $Q_t = 1$ is $\rho + \varphi$; that is, φ is the risk premium that would induce smart money to hold all the shares. The terms ρ and φ reflect the risk aversion of the smart money as well as the total real wealth of those smart-money investors who have evaluated the stock, the riskiness of the stock, and characteristics of alternative investments.

Ordinary investors include everyone who does not respond to expected returns optimally forecasted. Let us suppose that they overreact to news or are vulnerable to fads. We will not make assumptions about

41. My own discussion of these and their plausibility in light of data may be found in Robert J. Shiller, "Consumption, Asset Markets and Macroeconomic Fluctuations," in Karl Brunner and Allan H. Meltzer, eds., *Economic Policy in a World of Change*, Carnegie Rochester Conference Series in Public Policy, vol. 17 (Amsterdam: North-Holland, 1982), pp. 203–38.

their behavior at all, but merely define Y_t as the total value of stock demanded per share by these investors.[42] Equilibrium in this market requires that $Q_t + Y_t/P_t = 1$. Solving the resulting rational expectations model just as we did to derive equation (1) gives us the model

$$P_t = \sum_{k=0}^{\infty} \frac{E_t D_{t+k} + \varphi E_t Y_{t+k}}{(1 + \rho + \varphi)^{k+1}}, \tag{3}$$

so that real price is the present value, discounted at rate $\rho + \varphi$, of both the expected future dividend payments and φ times the expected future demand by ordinary investors. The limit of this expression as φ goes to zero (that is, as smart money becomes more and more influential) is the ordinary efficient markets model that makes price the present value of expected dividends. The limit of this expression as φ goes to infinity (as smart money becomes less and less influential) is the model $P_t = Y_t$, so that ordinary investors determine the price.

Equation (3) and the efficient markets model (equation [1]) could be equally consistent with the usual finding in the event-studies literature that announcements have their effect on returns as soon as the information becomes public and have little predictable effect thereafter. Equation (3) has, however, a very different interpretation for the jump in price that coincides with the announcement. The jump does not represent only what the smart money thinks the announcement means for future dividends. It also represents what the smart money thinks the announcement means for the demand for stock by ordinary investors. Equation (3) implies that the price effect of changes in the outlook for future dividends will be governed by equation (1) if Y_t is not also affected by these changes. However, if Y_t is always positive, the discount rate $\rho + \varphi$ in equation (3) is necessarily greater than or equal to the expected return on the market, which is the discount factor in equation (1). If $\rho + \varphi$ is high, then factors affecting expectations of distant dividends will have relatively little effect on price today.

The more persistent is the behavior of the variable Y_t through time (that is, the less we can expect changes in Y_t to be offset by subsequent changes in the opposite direction), the less the moving average in expression (3) will reduce its variance and the more, in general, will be its influence on P_t.

I argued above that models of the diffusion of opinions suggest a num-

---

42. That is, Y_t is the total shares demanded at current price times current price divided by number of shares outstanding. If we assume that demand elasticity by ordinary investors is unitary, we might regard Y_t as exogenous to this model.

ber of possible patterns of response, among them a hump-shaped pattern in which Y_t would rise for a while, level off, and then return to its normal level. The implication for real price P_t of such a hump-shaped response of Y_t to a piece of news depends on the time frame of the response relative to the discount rate $\rho + \varphi$. Suppose the hump can be predicted to build up very quickly and dissipate, say, in a matter of weeks. Then equation (3) implies that there will be very little impact on price. The relatively long moving average in equation (3) will smooth over the hump in Y_t so that it is observed, if at all, only in a very attenuated form. The demand for shares by ordinary investors will show the hump-shaped pattern as smart money sells shares to them at virtually unchanged prices only to buy the shares back after the ordinary investors have lost interest.

If the hump-shaped pattern takes longer to evolve, the effect on price will be bigger. Then as soon as the news that gives rise to the hump-shaped pattern becomes known to the smart money, the price of the stock will jump discontinuously. This jump will be instantaneous, taking effect as soon as the smart money realizes that the price will be higher in the future. After the initial jump, the effect of the news will be to cause the price of the stock to rise gradually as Y_t approaches its peak (not so fast as to cause higher than normal returns after the lower dividend-price ratio is taken into account); the price will peak somewhat before Y does and then decline. Returns, however, will tend to be low during the period of price rise.

A more explicit yet simple example along these lines will illustrate why tests of market efficiency may have low power even if the market is driven entirely by fashions or fads. Suppose that the dividend D_t is constant through time, so that by the efficient markets model (equation [1]) price would always be constant. Suppose also that $Y_t = U_{t-1} + U_{t-2} + \ldots + U_{t-n}$, where U_t is white noise, that is, U_t is uncorrelated with U_{t-k} for all k not equal to zero. Suppose current and lagged values for U are in the information set of the smart money. Here, Y responds to an unobserved shock in U with a rising, then falling (or square hump) pattern. Under these assumptions, $Y_{t+1} - Y_t$ is perfectly forecastable based on information at time t. However, $P_{t+1} - P_t$ will be hardly forecastable from information at time t. It follows from equation (3) that P_t will equal a constant plus a moving average of U with substantial weight on U_t. The theoretical R^2 in a regression of $P_{t+1} - P_t$ on P_t is only 0.015 for the case $n = 20$ years, $\rho = 0$, and $\varphi = 0.2$. If one included all information (the current and twenty lagged U values) in the regression, the theoretical R^2 would rise, but only to 0.151. If the U_t are for each t uniformly distributed from 0 to 1, and if the constant dividend is 0.5 (so that the mean dividend price ratio is 4 percent) then the theoretical R^2 (as estimated in a Monte Carlo experiment) in a regression of the return R_t on D_t/P_t is only 0.079.

Let us now consider three alternative extreme views of the behavior of Y_t: That it responds to exogenous fads whose origin is unrelated to relevant economic data, that it responds to lagged returns, and that it responds to dividends.

The first extreme view is that Y_t is independent of current and lagged dividends; it is exogenous noise caused by capricious fashions or fads. In this view, Y_t may respond systematically to vivid news events (say, the president suffering a heart attack) but not to any time-series data that we observe. It is reasonable also to suppose that Y_t is a stationary stochastic process in that it tends to return to a mean. Thus, if demand by ordinary investors is high relative to the mean of Y_t it can be expected eventually to decline. If dividends vary relatively little through time, an argument can then be made that would suggest that return is positively correlated with the dividend-price ratio D_t/P_t. In the next section this correlation will be examined with data.

The second extreme view is that Y_t responds to past returns, that is, Y_t is a function of R_{t-1}, R_{t-2}, and so on. Together with equation (2) this gives a simple rational expectations model whose only exogenous variable is the dividend D_t. If we were to specify the function relating Y_t to past returns and specify the stochastic properties of D_t, we would be left with the model that makes P_t driven exclusively by D_t. Depending on the nature of the function and the stochastic properties of D_t, price may overreact to dividends relative to equation (1).

The third extreme view is that Y_t responds directly to current and lagged dividends, that is, Y_t is directly a function of D_t, D_{t-1}, D_{t-2}, and so on. For example, dividend growth may engender expectations of future real dividend growth that are unwarranted given the actual stochastic properties of D_t. Such expectations might also cause price to overreact to dividends relative to equation (1). Such an overreaction (to dividends as well as to earnings) will be studied econometrically below.

My suggestions about the possible behavior of Y_t are perhaps too extreme and special to provide the basis for serious econometric modeling now. However, these possibilities and equation (3) provide the motivation for some exploratory data analysis.

4. An Exploratory Data Analysis

4.1 Stock Prices Appear to Overreact to Dividends

Aggregate real stock prices are fairly highly correlated over time with aggregate real dividends. The simple correlation coefficient between the annual (January) real Standard and Poor's composite stock price index P and the corresponding annual real dividend series D between 1926 and

1983 is 0.91 (figure 1).[43] This correlation is partly due to the common trend between the two series, but the trend is by no means the whole story. The correlation coefficient between the real stock price index P and a linear time trend over the same sample is only 0.60.[44] Thus, the price of the aggregate stock market is importantly linked to its dividends, and much of the movements of the stock market that we often regard as inexplicable can be traced to movements in dividends. One reason that most of us are not accustomed to thinking of the stock market in this way is that most of the data series cover a smaller time interval (years rather than the decades shown in the figure) and sample the data more frequently (monthly, say, rather than the annual rate shown in the figure). The correlation coefficient between real price and real dividends might be much lower with data from the smaller, more frequently sampled time interval or might appear to be more dominated by trend.

The correlation between real price P and the real earnings series E for 1926 to 1983 is 0.75. This number is closer to the correlation of P with a linear time trend. Although the correlation coefficient between P and D is fairly high, the real price is substantially more volatile than the real dividend. If P is regressed on D with a constant term in the 1926–83 sample period, the coefficient of D is 38.0 and the constant term is -0.28. The average price-dividend ratio P/D in this sample is 22.4. The real price moves proportionally more than the real dividend, and as a result P/D tends to move with real prices. The correlation in this sample of P/D with P (0.83) and with D (0.67) is strong enough that it can be seen in the figure. The volatility of stock prices relative to dividends is another reason why we tend not to view the stock market as driven so closely by dividends.

One would think that if the efficient markets model (equation [1]) is true, the price-dividend ratio should be low when real dividends are high (relative to trend or relative to the dividends' average value in recent history) and high when real dividends are low. One would also think that the real price, which represents according to equation (1) the long-run outlook for real dividends, would be sluggish relative to the real dividend. Therefore, short-run movements in the real dividend would correspond

---

43. The correlation of P with D for the years 1871–1925 was 0.84. In this paper, dividend and earnings series before 1926 are from the book which originated what is now called the Standard and Poor's composite stock price index: Alfred Cowles and Associates, *Common-Stock Indexes, 1871–1937* (Principia Press, 1938), series Da-1 and Ea-1. All series are deflated by the producer price index (January starting 1900, annual series before 1900), where 1967 = 100.

44. The correlation of P with time for 1871 to 1925 was 0.43.

to short-run movements in the opposite direction in the price-dividend ratio.

The observed perverse behavior of the price-dividend ratio might be described as an overreaction of stock prices to dividends, if it is correct to suppose that dividends tend to return to trend or return to the average of recent history. This behavior of stock prices may be consistent with some psychological models. Psychologists have shown in experiments that individuals may continually overreact to superficially plausible evidence even when there is no statistical basis for their reaction.[45] Such an overreaction hypothesis does not necessarily imply that the ultimate source of stock price movements should be thought of as dividends or the earnings of firms. Dividends are under the discretion of managers.[46] John Lintner, after a survey of dividend setting behavior of individual firms, concluded that firms have a target payout ratio from earnings but also feel that they should try to keep dividends fairly constant through time.[47] In doing this, managers, like the public, are forecasting earnings and may become overly optimistic or pessimistic. In reality, the dividends and stock prices may both be driven by the same social optimism or pessimism, and the "overreaction" may simply reflect a greater response to the fads in price than in dividends. The apparent response of price to earnings could also be attributed to the same sort of effect to the extent that reported earnings themselves are subject to the discretion of accountants. Fisher Black has claimed that the change in accounting practices through time might be described as striving to make earnings an indicator of the value of the firm rather than the cash flow.[48] An individual firm is substantially constrained in its accounting practices, but the accounting profession's concept of conventional accounting methods may be influenced by notions of what is the proper level of aggregate earnings, and these notions may be influenced by social optimism or pessimism.

45. See for example Amos Tversky and Daniel Kahneman, "Judgment under Uncertainty: Heuristics and Biases," *Science*, vol. 185 (September 1974), pp. 1124–31.

46. Marsh and Merton claimed that dividends are determined by management's optimal forecast of long-run earnings. See Terry A. Marsh and Robert C. Merton, "Aggregate Dividend Behavior and Its Implications for Tests of Stock Market Rationality," Working Paper 1475–83 (Massachusetts Institute of Technology, Alfred P. Sloan School of Management, September 1983).

47. See John Lintner, "Distribution of Incomes of Corporations among Dividends, Retained Earnings, and Taxes," *American Economic Review*, vol. 46 (May 1956, *Papers and Proceedings, 1955*), pp. 97–113.

48. See Fisher Black, "The Magic in Earnings: Economic Earnings versus Accounting Earnings," *Financial Analysts Journal* (November–December 1980), pp. 19–24.

The relation between real price and real dividend can be described perhaps more satisfactorily from a distributed lag regression of P on D, that is, a regression that predicts P as a weighted moving average of current and lagged D. One sees from rows one and two of table 1 that when the real price is regressed with a thirty-year distributed lag on current and lagged real dividends, the current real dividend has a coefficient greater than the average price-dividend ratio (22.6 for this sample), and the sum of the coefficients of the lagged real dividends is negative. The sum of all coefficients of real dividends, current and lagged, is about the average price-dividend ratio. Thus, this equation implies that the price tends to be unusually high when real dividends are high relative to a weighted average of real dividends over the past thirty years and low when dividends are low relative to this weighted average.

Rows 5 and 6 of table 1 show the same regression but with real earnings as the independent variable. The coefficient of current earnings is less than the average price-earnings ratio (13.0 for this sample). Compared with dividends, earnings show more short-run variability; therefore these results do not contradict a notion that prices overreact to earnings as well as to dividends. The lower $\bar{R}^2$ in this regression might be regarded as a reflection of the fact that dividends are not really well described by the Lintner model, which made dividends a simple distributed lag on earnings.[49] The $\bar{R}^2$ is high enough that some major movements in stock prices are explained by this regression. For example, the decline in earnings between 1929 and 1933 explains more or less the decline in P over that period (the regression had positive residuals in all these years). While the reasons for the market decline on particular days in 1929 may forever be a mystery, the overall market decline in the depression is explained fairly well as a reaction (or an overreaction) to earnings.

It is important to investigate whether the pattern of coefficients in rows 1 or 2 (or 5 or 6) of table 1 might be optimal given equation (1). The easiest test of equation (1) suggested by the pattern of reaction of real prices to real dividends documented here is to regress future returns on current and lagged dividends. The efficient markets model of equation (1) implies that returns are unforecastable and the overreaction alternative suggests that D can be used to forecast returns. Such a distributed lag appears in row 3 of table 1. The coefficient of the current dividend is negative and the sum of the coefficients of the remaining lagged dividends is positive. Indeed, as our overreaction story would suggest, when dividends are high relative to a weighted average of lagged dividends (so that stocks are by this interpretation overpriced) there is a tendency for

49. Ibid.

low subsequent returns. An F-test on all coefficients but the constant shows significance at the 5 percent level.[50] A similar pattern of coefficients found when E replaced D in the regression (row 7) suggests a similar overreaction for earnings, but the result is significant only at the 9 percent level.

By looking at the time-series properties of real dividends, one can better see why the pattern of reaction of prices to dividends causes returns to be forecastable. The class of models by Box and Jenkins that employ autoregressive integrated moving averages (ARIMA) has been very popular, and it would be instructive to see how the real dividend series could be represented by a model in this class.[51] Unfortunately, time-series modeling methods are partly judgmental and do not lead all researchers to the same model. In applying such methods one must decide whether to detrend the data prior to data analysis. In previous work I estimated a first order autoregressive model for the log of dividends around a deterministic linear trend. In this model, with the same annual real dividend series used here, the coefficient of lagged log dividends for 1872–1978 was 0.807, which implies that dividends always would be predicted to return half the way to the trend in about three years.[52] This result does not appear sensitive to the choice of price deflator used to deflate dividends. Taking account of the downward bias of the least squares estimate of the autoregressive coefficient, one can reject by a Dickey-Fuller test at the 5 percent level the null hypothesis of a random walk for log dividends in favor of the first order autoregressive model around a trend. Some, however, find models with a deterministic trend unappealing and prefer models that make dividends nonstationary. With a model of nonstationary dividends one can handle the apparent trend by first-differencing the data. The following model was estimated with the real annual 1926–83 Standard and Poor's dividend data.

$$\Delta D_t = 3.285 \times 10^{-3} + 0.850 \Delta D_{t-1} + u_t$$
$$(1.498) \qquad\qquad (11.753)$$

$$u_t = a_t - 0.981 a_{t-1},$$
$$(-69.434)$$

(4)

50. Tests for heteroskedasticity as proposed by Glejser were run using D, time, and a cubic polynomial in time as explanatory variables. Heteroskedasticity appeared remarkably absent in this regression. See H. Glejser, "A New Test for Heteroskedasticity," *Journal of the American Statistical Association*, vol. 64 (March 1969), pp. 316–23.

51. George E. P. Box and Gwylim M. Jenkins, *Time Series Analysis, Forecasting and Control* (Oakland, Calif.: Holden-Day, 1977).

52. See Robert J. Shiller, "The Use of Volatility Measures in Assessing Market Efficiency," *Journal of Finance*, vol. 36 (May 1981), pp. 291–304.

Table 1 Distributed Lag Regressions for Real Stock Prices or Returns on Real Dividends or Earnings, Selected Periods, 1900–83[a]

Sample Period	Dependent Variable[b]	Constant	Coefficient of Current Independent Variable	Sum of Coefficients of Lagged Independent Variable[c]	Coefficient of Lagged Error	F	Significance Level of F	$\bar{R}^2$	Durbin-Watson	Standard Error
				Independent variable is real dividends[d]						
1900–83	P	−0.08 (−2.95)	34.64 (14.16)	−11.79 (−4.34)	...	257.3	0.00	0.90	0.82	0.07
1900–83[e]	P	−0.07 (−1.20)	28.25 (9.13)	−5.37 (−1.14)	0.66 (7.89)	44.49	0.00	0.68	1.86	0.06
1900–82	$R(t+1)$	0.09 (1.21)	−6.57 (−1.03)	9.62 (1.40)	...	2.72	0.05	0.06	2.06	0.19
1926–82	$R(t+1)$	0.17 (1.33)	−7.62 (−0.94)	5.17 (0.57)	...	1.52	0.22	0.03	2.05	0.20

Independent variable is real earnings[f]

1900–83	P	0.10	11.73	−5.83	$\cdots$	57.59	0.00	0.67	0.27	0.13
		(2.61)	(5.61)	(−2.29)						
1900–83[e]	P	0.17	7.98	−2.58	0.90	10.74	0.00	0.32	1.61	0.06
		(1.07)	(6.52)	(−0.48)	(18.35)					
1900–82	$R(t+1)$	0.09	−5.77	7.45	$\cdots$	2.19	0.09	0.04	1.97	0.19
		(1.51)	(−1.90)	(1.91)						

a. Numbers in parentheses are t-statistics. Distributed lags based on second-degree thirty-year polynomial with far endpoint tied to zero were used throughout. The regression method is ordinary least squares except where noted otherwise. The stock price index throughout is the Standard and Poor's composite stock price index.

b. Dependent variable P is the stock price index for January divided by the January producer price index. Dependent variable $R(t+1)$ is the real return from January of the following year to January of two years hence (deflated by the producer price index) based on the stock price index and Standard and Poor's composite dividend series.

c. The sums are for the twenty-nine lagged values and do not include the coefficient of the current independent variable, which is shown separately.

d. Standard and Poor's dividends per share adjusted to the stock price index, total for four quarters, divided by the January producer price index.

e. Method is Cochrane-Orcutt serial correlation correction and sample statistics are for transformed regression.

f. Standard and Poor's earnings per share adjusted to the stock price index, total for four quarters, divided by the January producer price index.

where a_t is a serially uncorrelated zero mean random variable. This is what Box and Jenkins called an ARIMA $(1,1,1)$ model. It merely asserts that the change in real dividend is a linear function of its lagged value plus an error term, u_t, that is a moving average of a_t. The t-statistics, in parentheses, are misleading in that the likelihood function for this model has other modes with almost the same likelihood but very different parameter estimates. However, this model will suffice to tell how it might be plausible, given the past behavior of dividends, to forecast future dividends. This model cannot be rejected at usual significance levels with the usual Ljung-Box Q-test. It is noteworthy that when the same model was estimated with the sample period 1871–1925, almost the same parameter values emerged: the coefficient of ΔD_{t-1} was 0.840 and the coefficient of a_{t-1} was -0.973.

This estimated model is one that exhibits near parameter redundancy: the coefficient of a_{t-1} is so close to -1 that the moving average on a_t almost cancels against the first-difference operator. In other words, this model looks almost like a simple first order autoregressive model for dividends with coefficient on the lagged dividend of 0.850. It is more accurate to describe this model as a first order autoregressive model around a moving mean that is itself a moving average of past dividends. One can write the one-step-ahead optimal forecast of D_t implied by equation (4) in the following form:

$$E_t D_{t+1} = 0.869 D_t + 0.131 M_t + 0.173$$

$$\tag{5}$$

$$M_t \equiv (1 - 0.981) \sum_{k=0}^{\infty} (0.981)^k D_{t-k-1},$$

where M_t is a moving average of dividends with exponentially declining weights that sum to one. Since 0.981 is so close to 1.00, the moving average that defines M_t is extremely long (0.981 even to the twenty-fifth power is 0.619), and thus the term M_t does not vary much over this sample. Thus, for one-step-ahead forecasts this model is very similar to a first order autoregressive model on detrended dividends.

If real dividends are forecasted in accordance with equation (5), then equation (1) (with discount rate $\delta = 0.080$) would imply (using the chain principle of forecasting) that stock prices should be a moving average of dividends given by

$$P_t = 5.380 D_t + 7.120 M_t + 11.628. \tag{6}$$

Note that the distant past has relatively more weight in determining the price today (a weighted average of expected dividends into the infinite future) than it does in determining the dividend next period. This model thus accords with the intuitive notion that to forecast into the near future one need look only at the recent past, but to forecast into the distant future one need look into the distant past. Equation (6) implies that P_t, just as D_t, is an ARIMA $(1,1,1)$ process.[53] If I had modeled the real dividend series as a first-order autoregressive model around a trend, then P_t would be a weighted average of D_t (with about the same weight as in equation [6]) and a trend.

Equation (6) is very different from the estimated relation between P and D. The coefficient of D_t in equation (6) is 5.380, which is far below the estimated value in rows 1 or 2 of table 1. The coefficients of the lagged dividends sum to a positive number, not a negative number.

In summary, it appears that stock prices do not act, as they should, like a smoothed transformation of dividends over the past few decades. Instead dividends look like an amplification of the departure of dividends from such a transformation. It is as if the optimism of investors is too volatile, influenced by departures from trends rather than by the trends themselves.

4.2 Forecasting Regressions That Employ Dividend-Price and Earnings-Price Ratios

The most natural test of equation (1) is to regress return R_t on information available to the public at time t. Analogous tests of related models might regress excess returns on information at time t, or regress risk-corrected returns on information at time t. If the F-statistic for the regression (that is, for the null hypothesis that all coefficients save the constant term are zero) is significant, then we will have rejected the model. The simplest such tests use only price itself (scaled, say, by dividing it into earnings or dividends) as an explanatory variable and use the conventional t-statistic to test the model. If fads cause stocks to be at times overpriced, at times underpriced, and if these fads come to an end, then we would expect a high dividend-price or earnings-price ratio to predict high returns and a low dividend-price or earnings-price ratio to predict low returns. This would mean that the most naive investment strategy, buy when price is low relative to dividends or earnings and sell when it is high, pays off.

However, it is not easy to carry out such simple tests. One confronts a number of econometric problems: the independent variable is not "non-

---

53. For this result in a more general form, see John Y. Campbell, "Asset Duration and Time-Varying Risk Premia" (Ph.D. dissertation, Yale University, 1984).

stochastic," so that ordinary t-statistics are not strictly valid; the error term appears nonnormal or at least conditionally heteroskedastic; and risk correction, if it is employed, is not a simple matter. There is no agreed-upon way to deal with such problems, and I will not attempt here to deal rigorously with them. It is, however, worthwhile to note that high dividend-price or earnings-price ratios do seem to be correlated with high returns.

Whether stocks with a high earnings-price ratio will have a relatively high return has been the subject of much discussion in the literature. It was confirmed that there is a simple correlation across firms between such ratios and returns.[54] The question then arose, Can such a phenomenon be explained within the framework of the capital asset pricing model if there happens to be a positive correlation between the ratio and the beta of the stocks, or does firm size, which correlates with the ratio, affect expected returns? Recently, Sanjoy Basu concluded that risk-adjusted returns are positively correlated with the earnings-price ratio even after controlling for firm size.[55] As Basu notes, however, his tests depend on the risk measurement assumed.

It is apparently accepted today in the finance profession that expected returns fluctuate through time as well as across stocks. These results are interpreted as describing the time variation in the "risk premium."

The dividend/price ratio or earnings/price ratio has not figured prominently in this literature. Instead the variables chosen for forecasting were such things as the inflation rate,[56] the spread between low-grade and high-grade bonds,[57] or the spread between long-term and short-term bonds.[58]

Table 2 shows that a high dividend-price ratio (total Standard and Poor's dividends for the preceding year divided by the Standard and Poor's composite index for July of the preceding year) is indeed an indica-

---

54. See for example Francis Nicholson, "Price Ratios in Relation to Investment Results," *Financial Analysts Journal*, vol. 24 (January–February 1968), pp. 105–09.

55. See Sanjoy Basu, "The Relationship between Earnings' Yield, Market Value and Return for NYSE Common Stocks: Further Evidence," *Journal of Financial Economics*, vol. 12 (June 1983), pp. 129–56.

56. See Eugene F. Fama and G. William Schwert, "Asset Returns and Inflation," *Journal of Financial Economics*, vol. 5 (November 1977), pp. 115–46.

57. See Donald B. Keim and Robert F. Stambaugh, "Predicting Returns in the Stock and Bond Markets," University of Pennsylvania, 1984.

58. See John Y. Campbell, "Stock Returns and the Term Structure" (Princeton University, 1984).

Table 2   Forecasting Returns Based on the Dividend-Price Ratio, Selected Periods, 1872–1983[a]

Sample Period	Constant	Coefficient of Dividend-Price Ratio	$\bar{R}^2$	Sample Statistic Durbin-Watson	Standard Error
1872–1983[b]	−0.10	3.59	0.06	1.85	0.17
	(−1.52)	(2.85)			
1872–1908[b]	−0.02	2.26	0.00	2.05	0.14
	(−0.20)	(0.96)			
1909–45[b]	−0.14	3.89	0.03	1.46	0.21
	(−0.88)	(1.42)			
1946–83[b]	−0.16	5.23	0.14	1.80	0.17
	(−1.70)	(2.62)			
1889–1982[c]	−0.13	4.26	0.09	1.85	0.17
	(−1.94)	(3.15)			
1926–82[d]	−0.17	5.26	0.10	2.01	0.21
	(−1.73)	(2.71)			

a. Numbers in parentheses are t-statistics. The stock price index throughout is the Standard and Poor's composite stock price index. The dependent variable is the real return on the stock price index from January of the year to January of the following year (average for the month) except where otherwise noted. The return is the sum of the change in the stock price index plus Standard and Poor's four-quarter total of the composite dividends per share as adjusted to the stock price index, all divided by the stock price index. The independent variable is total dividends in the preceding year (which is Standard and Poor's four-quarter total of the composite dividends as adjusted to the stock price index) divided by the stock price index for July of the preceding year.

b. Price deflator is the producer price index.

c. Price deflator is the consumption deflator for nondurables and services.

d. Nominal returns were cumulated for the end of January until the end of January of the following year from monthly data in "Common Stocks Total Returns," Roger Ibbotson and Associates; the priced deflator is the January producer price index.

tor of high subsequent returns.[59] Thus, for example, the equation in row 1 asserts that when the dividend-price ratio (or "current yield") is one percentage point above its mean, the expected return on the stock is

59. There is evidence that the strategy of holding stocks with high dividend-price ratios has actually paid off for those investors who followed it. See Wilbur G. Lewellen, Ronald C. Lease, and Gary C. Schlarbaum, "Investment Performance and Investor Behavior," *Journal of Financial and Quantitative Analysis*, vol. 14 (March 1979), pp. 29–57.

Table 3 Forecasting Returns Based on the Earnings-Price Ratio, Selected Periods, 1872–1983[a]

Sample Period	Constant	Coefficient of Earnings-Price Ratio	$\bar{R}^2$	Sample Statistic	
				Durbin-Watson	Standard Error
1872–1983	0.01	0.85	0.01	1.90	0.18
	(0.24)	(1.41)			
1872–1908	0.00	1.28	−0.02	2.16	0.15
	(0.02)	(0.63)			
1909–45	0.08	0.03	−0.03	1.59	0.21
	(0.72)	(0.02)			
1946–83	−0.09	1.86	0.09	1.71	0.17
	(−1.09)	(2.13)			
1889–1982	0.01	0.78	0.01	1.96	0.18
	(0.19)	(1.24)			
1901–83[b]	−0.04	1.57[c]	0.05	1.81	0.19
	(−0.68)	(2.38)			

a. Numbers in parentheses are t-statistics. Dependent and independent variables and price deflators are as in table 2, with earnings in place of dividends.

b. Price deflator is the producer price index.

c. Earnings-price ratio is computed by forming the average real earnings for the previous thirty years (not counting the current year) and then dividing by the real stock price index for January of the current year.

3.588 percentage points above its mean. Thus, the high current yield is augmented by an expected capital gain that is two and a half times as dramatic as the high current yield. In contrast, equation (1) would predict that a high current yield should correspond to an expected capital loss to offset the current yield. The efficient markets hypothesis thus appears dramatically wrong from this regression: stock prices move in a direction opposite to that forecasted by the dividend-price ratio. This is true in every subperiod examined.[60]

In table 3, rows 1 through 5 show analogous regressions with the earnings-price ratio (total Standard and Poor's earnings for the preceding year divided by the Standard and Poor's composite index for July of the preceding year) in place of the dividend-price ratio. These forecasting

60. The same regressions were run using a different price deflator (row five of table 2) and a different measure of return (row six of table 2) with little change in results.

regressions work in the same direction (price low relative to earnings implies high returns) but are less significant.[61]

4.3 Excess Volatility of Stock Prices

Regression tests of the efficient markets model may not fully characterize the way in which the model fails. A simpler and perhaps more appealing way to see the failure of the model represented by equation (1) follows by observing that stock prices seem to show far too much volatility to be in accordance with the simple model.[62] The most important criticism of the excess volatility claim centers on the claim's assumption that stock prices are stationary around a trend of the dividend series.[63] Here I discuss the volatility tests in light of this criticism and present tests in a slightly different form that deals better with the issue of nonstationarity.

I showed that if the dividend D_t is a stationary stochastic process, then the efficient markets model (equation [1]) implies the variance inequality

$$\sigma(P - P_{-1}) \leq \frac{\sigma(D)}{(2\delta)^{0.5}}, \tag{7}$$

that is, that the standard deviation of the change in price $P - P_{-1}$ is less than or equal to the standard deviation of the dividend D divided by the square root of twice the discount factor.[64] If we know the standard deviation of D, then there is a limit to how much $P - P_{-1}$ can vary if equation (1) is to hold at all times. If the market is efficient, then price movements representing changes in forecasts of dividends cannot be very large unless dividends actually do move a lot. The discount factor δ is equal to the expected return $E(R_t)$, which can be estimated by taking the average return. Before we can use this inequality to test the efficient markets

---

61. The lower significance appears to be due to the relatively noisy behavior of the annual earnings series. If the earnings-price ratio is computed as the average annual Standard and Poor's earnings for the preceding thirty years divided by the Standard and Poor's composite index for January of the current year (row six of table 3), then the relation between returns and the earnings-price ratio looks more impressive.

62. The arguments for excess volatility in financial markets were put forth independently by Stephen F. LeRoy and Richard D. Porter, "The Present-Value Relation: Tests Based on Implied Variance Bounds," *Econometrica*, vol. 49 (March 1981), pp. 555–74, and by me in several papers beginning with "The Volatility of Long-Term Interest Rates and Expectations Models of the Term Structure," *Journal of Political Economy*, vol. 87 (December 1979), pp. 1190–1219, and in "Do Stock Prices Move Too Much."

63. In the case of LeRoy and Porter, the earnings series, instead of the dividend series, was assumed to be stationary.

64. Shiller, "Do Stock Prices Move Too Much."

model, we must somehow deal with the fact that dividends appear to have a trend; in an earlier paper, I handled the problem by multiplying prices and dividends by an exponential decay factor as a way to detrend them. This method of detrending has become a source of controversy. Indeed, as I noted in the original paper, the trend in dividends may be spurious, and dividends may have another sort of nonstationarity that is not removed by such detrending.[65] Thus, violating inequality (7) in these tests should not be regarded by itself as definitive evidence against equation (1). Most of the criticism of the variance-bounds inequality has centered on this point.[66] On the other hand, the violation of the variance inequality does show that dividend volatility must be potentially much greater than actually observed historically (around a trend or around the historical mean) if the efficient markets model is to hold; and this fact can be included among other factors in judging the plausibility of the efficient markets model.

Table 4 displays the elements of the above inequality but with the data detrended in a different and perhaps more satisfactory manner that depends only on past information. Let us define detrended price series $P5$, $P15$, and $P30$ and corresponding dividend series $D5$, $D15$, and $D30$ by

$$Pk_t = \frac{P_t}{Nk_t} \qquad k = 5, 15, 30 \tag{8}$$

and

$$Dk_t = \frac{D_t}{Nk_t} + P_{t-1}\left(\frac{1}{Nk_t} - \frac{1}{Nk_{t+1}}\right) \qquad k = 5, 15, 30, \tag{9}$$

where

$$Nk_t = \prod_{j=1}^{k} E_{t-j}^{1/k} \qquad k = 5, 15, 30. \tag{10}$$

---

65. Shiller, "The Volatility of Long-Term Interest Rates."

66. For example, see Marjorie A. Flavin, "Excess Volatility in the Financial Markets: A Reassessment of the Empirical Evidence," *Journal of Political Economy*, vol. 91 (December 1983), pp. 929–56; Allan W. Kleidon, "Variance Bounds Tests and Stock Price Valuation Models" (Stanford University, Graduate School of Business, 1983); and Terry A. Marsh and Robert C. Merton, "Dividend Variability and Variance Bounds Tests for the Rationality of Stock Market Prices," Working Paper 1584-84 (Massachusetts Institute of Technology, Alfred P. Sloan School of Management, August 1984).

Table 4   Sample Statistics for Detrended Price and Dividend Series, Selected Periods, 1871–1984[a]

Sample Period	Left-Hand Side of Inequality	Right-Hand Side of Inequality
1877–1984	$\sigma(P5 - P5_{-1}) = 2.83$	$\sigma(D5)/(2\delta)^{0.5} = 3.52$
1887–1984	$\sigma(P15 - P15_{-1}) = 2.93$	$\sigma(D15)/(2\delta)^{0.5} = 1.64$
1902–1984	$\sigma(P30 - P30_{-1}) = 3.39$	$\sigma(D30)/(2\delta)^{0.5} = 1.38$

Source: Equations (7)–(10).

a. The variables $P5$, $P15$, and $P30$ are the real stock price index detrended by dividing by the 5-year, 15-year, and 30-year geometric average of lagged real earnings respectively; σ denotes sample standard deviation. The variables $D5$, $D15$, and $D30$ are the corresponding dividend series as defined in the text. The constant δ equals 0.08, the average real return on the Standard and Poor's composite stock price index over the entire period 1871–1983.

The detrended price and dividend series have the following property: returns calculated with Pk and Dk in place of P and D in the formula for return R_t are the same as if P and D had been used. Thus, if equation (1) holds for P_t and D_t, then equation (1) holds where Pk_t and Dk_t replace P_t and D_t, and the same variance inequality 7 should hold for Pk and Dk. One can think of Pk and Dk as the price and dividend, respectively, of a share in a mutual fund that holds the same fixed portfolio (whose price is P_t and whose dividend is D_t) but buys back or sells its own shares so that it always has Nk_t shares outstanding. The variable Nk_t is a geometric moving average of lagged real earnings. This may cause the dividend of the mutual fund to be stationary even if the dividend D_t is not. A plot of $D30$, for example, shows no apparent trend and does not look unstationary. If, for example, the natural log of E is a Gaussian random walk and is thus nonstationary, and if $D_t = E_t$, then Pk_t will be a stationary lognormal process, and Dk_t will be the sum of stationary lognormal processes.[67] We see from table 4 that inequality (7) is not violated for $k = 5$ but is violated for $k = 15$ and $k = 30$. The detrending factor Nk_t gets smoother as k increases.

67. If $\log D_t - \log D_{t-1} = u_t$, where u is serially uncorrelated and normal with zero mean and variance s^2, then $E_t D_{t+k} = D_t h^k$, where $h = \exp(s^2/2)$. Calling $g = 1/(1 + \delta)$, then if $hg < 1$, it follows from equation (1) that $P_t = gD_t/(1 - hg)$. Substituting this into equation (8) and using equation (10) will provide the stationarity result for Pk and Dk noted in the text.

4.4 Implications of the Forecasting Equations in Connection with the Model

If we choose hypothetical values for ρ and φ in equation (2), we can use one of the equations forecasting R_t and produced in tables 1 through 3 to estimate the paths through time of Q_t and Y_t. Such an estimate will be admittedly quite arbitrary, and of course these forecasting regressions are not prima facie evidence that it would be "smart" to behave as will be supposed here. Considering such an estimate may nonetheless give some insights into the plausibility of the alternative model. We learn immediately in doing this that φ must be very large if swings in Q_t, the proportion of shares held by smart-money investors, are not to be extraordinarily large. This problem arises because stock prices are actually quite forecastable: the standard deviation of the expected return implied in many of the forecasting equations is so large that unless φ in equation (2) is large, Q_t will often move far out of the zero-to-one range.

Figure 2 shows a hypothetical example with estimated values of Y_t and Q_t implied by equation (2) and the forecasting equation based on the dividend-price ratio in row 1 of table 2 for $\rho = 0$ and $\varphi = 0.5$. Also shown is the real price P_t. For these values of ρ and φ, Q_t is always positive and thus Y_t is always less than P_t. The demand for shares by ordinary investors, Y_t, looks on the whole fairly similar to the price P_t itself. This arises because the forecasting equation is related to the dividend-price ratio and because dividends are fairly sluggish, so that Q_t itself resembles the reciprocal of P_t. However, Y_t is somewhat more volatile than P_t, showing a tendency to be lower proportionally at lows and higher proportionally at highs. The overreaction to dividends is more pronounced in Y_t than in P_t. The presence of smart money thus serves to mitigate the overreaction of ordinary investors. The year 1933 stands out for a very large proportion of smart-money investors and a low proportion of ordinary investors. This was the year when the dividend-price ratio reached an extreme high and when the highest returns were forecasted. The late 1950s and early 1960s were times of low demand by smart-money investors: the dividend-price ratio was low then and so they were "smart" ex ante to get out of the market, though of course ex post they would have liked to have stayed in the market. The demand by smart money is currently neither high nor low because the dividend-price ratio is not far from its historical average. The weighted average return $(\Sigma Q_t R_t / \Sigma Q_t)$ for 1926 to 1983 was 12.9 percent, in contrast to the average return (mean of R_t) for this period of 8.2 percent.

The volume of trade implied by the movements in and out of shares by smart money between t and $t + 1$ is $|Q_{t+1} - Q_t|$; the average value of this measure for the sample shown in figure 2 is 0.055. In this sample,

**Figure 2   Hypothetical Demand for Shares by Ordinary Investors
and Smart-Money Investors**

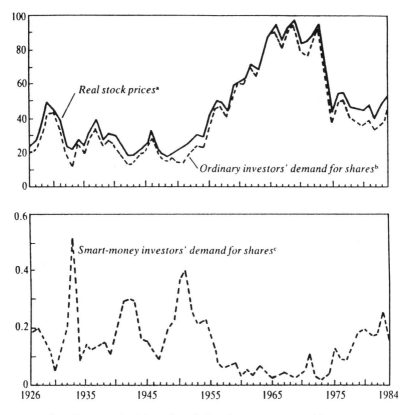

a. Real stock price index (P_t), as described in figure 1, notes a and b.

b. The hypothetical demand for shares by ordinary investors, equal to $P_t(1 - Q_t)$, where Q_t is the hypothetical demand for shares by smart-money investors.

c. The variable Q_t from equation (2) with $\rho = 0$ and $\varphi = 0.5$ and based on the forecasting equation for returns in row 1 of table 2.

the New York Stock Exchange turnover rate (reported annual share volume divided by average of shares listed) was between 9 percent (1942) and 42 percent (1982), except for the early depression years, when turnover was extremely high.[68] Thus, the story told in figure 2 is not one of an implausibly high volume of trade. Because corporate stock constitutes less than one-third of all wealth, we are also not talking about implausibly

68. New York Stock Exchange, *Fact Book 1983*, p. 68.

large wealth movements on the part of smart money.[69] Of course, not all household wealth is very liquid. The ratio of the market value of corporate equities to deposits and credit market instruments held by households ranged from 47.7 percent in 1948 to 136.2 percent in 1968.[70]

The results shown in figure 2 are not insensitive to the choice of forecasting equation, though as long as the forecasting equation is a simple regression on the dividend/price ratio (as in table 2), changing the equation has no more effect than changing ρ and φ. If an equation that forecasts with the earnings/price ratio (row six of table 3) is used to compute $E_t R_t$, the pattern through time of Q is somewhat different: Q is still high (though not as high in figure 2) in 1933 and low in the late 1950s and early 1960s. The weighted average return for smart money over this period would be 11.4 percent.

A discount rate $\rho + \varphi$ of 50 percent in equation (3) may or may not imply very forecastable returns, depending on the stochastic properties of Y_t. In the hypothetical example, the behavior of Y_t is sufficiently dominated by long (low-frequency) components that returns are not more forecastable than would be implied by the forecasting regression in table 2. A discount rate of 50 percent per year amounts to about 0.1 percent per day (compared to the standard deviation of daily return of about 1 percentage point), so that for event studies involving daily stock price data the discount rate is still very small. If equation (3) were to be applied to individual stocks, we might choose a smaller value of φ and hence a smaller discount rate.

5. Summary and Conclusion

Much of this paper relies on the reader's good judgment. A great deal of evidence is presented here that suggests that social movements, fashions, or fads are likely to be important or even the dominant cause of speculative asset price movements; but no single piece of evidence is unimpeachable.

The most important reason for expecting that stock prices are heavily influenced by social dynamics comes from observations of participants in the market and of human nature as presented in the literature on social

69. Between 1945 and 1980 corporate shares held by households and private financial institutions as a proportion of household net worth including tangibles and government debt ranged from 12.6 percent in 1948 to 31.8 percent in 1968. See Board of Governors of the Federal Reserve System, *Balance Sheets for U.S. Economy* (Washington, D.C., April 1981), table 700, "Consolidated Domestic Net Assets with Tangibles at Current Cost, 1945–1980."

70. Ibid.

psychology, sociology, and marketing. A study of the history of the U.S. stock market in the postwar period suggests that various social movements were under way during this period that might plausibly have major effects on the aggregate demand for shares. Must we rely on such evidence to make the case against market efficiency? Yes; there is no alternative to human judgment in understanding human behavior.

The reason that the random-walk behavior of stock prices holds up as well as it does may be two-fold. First, the aggregate demand of ordinary investors may itself not be entirely unlike a random walk. Fashions are perhaps inherently rather unpredictable, and ordinary investors may overreact to news of earnings or dividends, which behavior may also make their demand relatively unpredictable.

Second, and on the other hand, as shown by the model in equation (3) the ordinary investors' predictable patterns of behavior are prevented from causing big short-run profit opportunities by the limited amount of smart money in the economy, so that returns may be nearly unpredictable, and tests of market efficiency may have little power. However, in preventing large profit opportunities the smart money may not be preventing the ordinary investors from causing major swings in the market and even being the source of volatility in the market.

Data on stock prices show evidence of overreaction to dividends, and the forecasting equations for returns are consistent with such overreaction. However, an alternative interpretation for the correlation of prices to dividends might be that firms that set dividends are influenced by the same social dynamics that influence the rest of society. There are also other possible interpretations of this correlation; that is why I presented the data analysis as merely confirming that notions of overreaction suggested by qualitative evidence are consistent with the data.

It should also be emphasized that the model in equation (3) involves a present value of expected dividends and that it shares some properties of the efficient markets model. Despite all the inadequacies of the notion of market efficiency, modern theoretical finance does offer many insights into actual market behavior. The robustness of the models to variations like those here is a matter deserving more attention.

6. Comments and Discussion

Stanley Fischer: In an important and controversial series of papers published since 1979, Robert Shiller has brought sophisticated empirical evidence to support the view that the stock market fluctuates excessively. Shiller's contribution has been extraordinarily impressive: he has chosen a topic of central importance to both the economy and economics; he has formulated the hypothesis of excess volatility of stock prices in a testable fashion; and he has examined evidence on the volatility of interest rates, of stock prices, and on the co-movements of consumption and stock prices, all of which appear to support his viewpoint. He has understandably had the field of finance on the defensive ever since he first mounted his empirical challenge to the hypothesis of stock market efficiency, which many earlier studies in finance had appeared to support. Among these earlier studies were those of the responses of stock prices to dividend and earning changes, of the effects of changes in accounting measures of earnings on stock prices, and of the ability of individuals or institutions to outperform the market.

Before turning to the present paper, I will set the background by describing Shiller's early test of stock market efficiency and the related literature. The striking early Shiller finding of excess volatility of stock prices was based on a simple model of rational stock price determination in which the price is the present discounted value of expected future dividends.[71] Omitting some technical details, we can understand Shiller's finding that the market fluctuates excessively if we recognize that dividends fluctuate relatively little, and their present discounted value accordingly fluctuates even less, so that stock prices should be smoother than dividends. But they are not.

For some time, the Shiller result successfully withstood all attacks. During that period other evidence of excess volatility or apparent irrationality, including exchange rate behavior, consumption behavior, the covariation of consumption and stock returns, and interest rates, as well as the payment of dividends, seemed to reinforce his findings. Backing up that empirical evidence was the development, by Shiller among others, of the theory of speculative bubbles, providing a reason that prices could fluctuate excessively without smart investors being able to expect to profit from knowing they were living in a bubble.

Surprisingly, Shiller dismisses the speculative bubble literature, which is one explanation for excess volatility of the market and which has produced increasingly sophisticated empirical work. Apparently he objects both to the rational expectations assumptions in the speculative bubble approach and to the implication that there are no excess returns expected even when the bubble is full blown. Instead Shiller tries in this paper to make the case that excess variability is a result of fads in stock market investing. In a remarkable example of the perfect foresight of

---

71. Stephen F. LeRoy and Richard D. Porter, "The Present-Value Relation: Tests Based on Implied Variance Bounds," *Econometrica*, vol. 49 (May 1981), pp. 555–74, obtained similar results.

stock market investors, Shiller's explanation was anticipated by Bernard Baruch in his 1932 introduction to a reprint of the 1841 classic by Charles Mackay, *Extraordinary Popular Delusions and the Madness of Crowds.* Baruch says "I never see a brilliant economic thesis expounding, as though they were geometrical theorems, the mathematics of price movements, that I do not recall Shiller's dictum: 'Anyone taken as an individual, is tolerably sensible and reasonable—as a member of a crowd, he at once becomes a blockhead.'"[72]

Shiller claims and argues at some length that "mass psychology may well be the dominant cause of movements in the price of the aggregate stock market." That is, he argues the blockheads play a major role in the stock market. No one who has met more than a few stock market investors can fail to have some sympathy with this viewpoint. Nonetheless the paper does not bring much direct evidence to bear on the issue and leaves the links between social fads and excess volatility vague.

In the first section of the paper, Shiller takes us through some social psychology literature to persuade us of the importance of fashions. This is interesting material, some of it quite relevant to the stock market, but all it can do is soften us up for the more hard-boiled parts of the paper that follow. The difficulty with the first part of the paper is that I would be equally persuaded after reading it that the propensity to consume fluctuates wildly—which it does not—as that stock prices fluctuate wildly—which they do.

Shiller's dismissal of the efficient markets model is mild after his earlier characterization of the standard argument for the model—that stock returns are unforecastable—as "one of the most remarkable errors in the history of economic thought." The error actually is not that remarkable. Under the conditions Samuelson posited in his classic article, stock prices should fluctuate randomly.[73] This is a necessary condition—under Samuelson's assumptions—for stock market efficiency. It is not, however, sufficient, as the work on speculative bubbles tells us. But the failure to reject the random walk prediction in early tests was surely not evidence against stock market rationality. Of course Samuelson's assumptions were extremely strong, especially constancy of the discount rate. Stock market models imply that the discount rate should be a function of both the risk-free rate, which certainly varies, and the riskiness of stock returns,

---

72. Charles Mackay, *Extraordinary Popular Delusions and the Madness of Crowds* (Farrar, Straus and Giroux, 1932); foreword by Bernard M. Baruch, p. xiii.

73. Paul A. Samuelson, "Proof that Properly Anticipated Prices Fluctuate Randomly," *Industrial Management Review,* vol. 6 (Spring 1965), pp. 41–49.

which also varies. So it is entirely to be expected that the discount rate should vary.

For that reason the more convincing arguments against efficient stock pricing result from tests that allow the discount rate to vary, for instance those of Grossman and Shiller or Hansen and Singleton that implicitly or explicitly use consumption-based measures of rates of discount.[74] We should be clear, as Shiller is, that forecastability of stock returns is not inconsistent with efficient stock pricing, because there may be entirely predictable movements in the discount factor. Tests for efficiency can then be based on comparison of the behavior of rates of return on different assets. In this connection, Shiller's equation (1) is suspect, because it not infrequently predicts stock returns will be below Treasury bill returns. It would be far better to estimate stock and bill returns jointly, constraining the former to exceed the latter, for instance by estimating the premium for stocks over bills.

Shiller's model of pricing when some investors are irrational is an important positive contribution. Models of irrationality are not easy to create and test; perhaps the best-known earlier example is Modigliani and Cohn's hypothesis that stock market investors use nominal instead of real interest rates to discount expected earnings. In Shiller's model a group of blockheads owns a given value of shares in each period, which value is determined possibly irrationally, for instance being held constant. Another group, smart-money investors, worries about expected returns. The market equilibrium obtains when supply equals demand, with the smart-money investors looking ahead to try to predict both dividends and the value of shares the blockheads will be holding in the future. Changes in expectations of the holdings of blockheads, as well as changes in expected dividends, will change the price—which Shiller argues will therefore fluctuate excessively relative to a dividends-only pricing model if there are swings in fashion in holding stocks.

It is not quite clear what the appropriate benchmark for the Shiller model is. Suppose, to start with, that the blockheads own half the market and then become smart by acquiring exactly the same demand function as the smart money. The resultant equilibrium could show more variability of stock prices than in Shiller's "irrational" equilibrium. The irrational equilibrium could also produce excessively smooth stock prices, if, for

74. Stanford J. Grossman and Robert J. Shiller, "The Determinants of the Variability of Stock Market Prices," *American Economic Review*, vol. 71 (May 1981, *Papers and Proceedings, 1980*), pp. 222–27; Lars Peter Hansen and Kenneth J. Singleton, "Stochastic Consumption, Risk Aversion, and the Temporal Behavior of Asset Returns," *Journal of Political Economy*, vol. 91 (April 1983), pp. 249–65.

instance, the irrationality takes the form of slow adjustment of expectations of dividends to dividend innovations. Thus the model speaks more to the nonrationality of prices—because there is an extra Y term in the valuation formula—than to the volatility issue. But the model is sufficiently flexible that the irrational component of demand can vary enough for the market to fluctuate excessively relative to any benchmark.

At this stage Shiller has produced a model that could account for excess fluctuations in the stock market. This might seem to be a good place to stop, since his earlier work established that the market fluctuates excessively. Why go through the evidence again? There are three reasons. First, Shiller wants to show that dividends help predict stock returns: in particular, when the dividend-price ratio is high, expected returns are high—in other words, buy low and sell high is a good strategy. This contradicts the simple stock-pricing model of constant expected returns, but as Shiller himself notes, it does not contradict a version of the model in which the discount factor changes over time—as it surely does.

The second reason for re-examining the empirical evidence is that Shiller wants to address critics, for example Kleidon and Marsh and Merton, who have pointed to the fact that the excess variability test is crucially dependent on the assumption of stationarity of the dividend series.[75] Shiller's test is basically that stock prices should fluctuate less than dividends. Marsh and Merton point out that dividends are themselves chosen by managers, and that the micro evidence is that managers smooth dividends. If managers smooth dividends, then there is no necessity that stock prices, which are estimates of the present value of future dividends, be smoother than dividends. To understand the role of nonstationarity, consider the following example from my colleague Julio Rotenberg. Suppose managers smooth dividends by not paying them out at all, planning to do so only at some remote future date. Then in the sample of data, dividends will be entirely smooth but stock prices, the present value of what will eventually be paid out, fluctuate. Nonstationarity is critical because dividend behavior is not stationary when the managers plan to change their payout practices at some future date.

Shiller concedes this point to the critics and proposes an alternative method of detrending the data that he believes permits the excess variability tests to be applied to the detrended data—and which once again results in a rejection of efficiency.

75. Allan Kleidon, "Variance Bounds Tests and Stock Price Valuation Models" (Stanford University, Graduate School of Business, 1983), and Terry A. Marsh and Robert C. Merton, "Dividend Variability and Variance Bound Tests for the Rationality of Stock Market Prices," Working Paper 1584-84 (Massachusetts Institute of Technology, Alfred P. Sloan School of Management, 1984).

Since the issue is not the stationarity of the detrended data but rather of the underlying series, it is not obvious that the alternative procedure handles the nonstationarity problem. An alternative approach has been taken in very recent papers by Ken West, who has tests for the presence of speculative bubbles that are valid even if dividends do not follow a stationary process.[76] West's tests accept the presence of bubbles and accord them a major role in stock pricing, but he does not permit the discount rate to vary.

The third reason Shiller turns to the data is to examine, mainly in figure 2, implications of his particular model of irrationality. The volume of trading implied by the model is reasonable, but the risk aversion that has to be assumed for smart money and the very small holdings of stocks by the smart money from 1955 to 1969 are not. Thus the model has to be regarded as interesting but as yet in a preliminary stage.

Where does all this leave us? Much as the stock market fluctuates, the balance of the argument for excess variability is now weaker than it was a few years ago. The nonstationarity issue has for the moment deflected the early Shiller attack. The new detrending method in this paper and West's tests look like a new round in the econometric battle.

And despite Shiller's appeal for the use of qualitative evidence when statistical tests are weak, the outcome will turn on statistical tests. The reason is that there is no way of knowing how important are the fashions and fads described in the first section without quantitative evidence on the extent of departures from market efficiency. With the evidence of the last few years on varying real interest rates, the new tests will have to allow for changing discount rates on stocks. They will also in all likelihood be more closely related to the speculative bubble literature than to the fads literature—if indeed those approaches are ultimately different.

Benjamin M. Friedman: It is hardly unusual, in many fields of scientific inquiry, for a basic tenet of professional research to be the out-of-hand dismissal of a view popularly held by interested persons outside the field. In most such cases (one hopes), this rejection of popular belief rests on researchers' awareness of an overwhelming accumulation of evidence that is too technical, or somehow too inaccessible in other ways, to have made much impression on all but the best-informed laymen. In some cases,

---

76. Kenneth D. West, "Speculative Bubbles and Stock Price Volatility," and "A Specification Test for Speculative Bubbles" (Princeton University, Department of Economics, 1984). Similar tests were proposed in Olivier J. Blanchard and Mark W. Watson, "Bubbles, Rational Expectations, and Financial Markets," in Paul Wachtel, ed., *Crises in the Economic and Financial Structure* (Lexington, Mass.: Lexington Books, 1982), pp. 295–315.

however, professional researchers' near unanimous dismissal of a view held by most men and women of common sense rests on evidence that is either scant or weak or both. In such cases there is reason to believe that other factors, ranging from the social values typical of educated groups to various forms of outright self interest, play a large part in molding and maintaining the solidity of professional opinion.

Robert Shiller's paper does the economics profession a significant service by calling attention to the insubstantial evidence and even the weak logical structure underlying the almost unanimous rejection by economic researchers of a view of speculative investment markets held by large numbers of men and women who are apparently perfectly sensible in all ways except—or in this instance is it including?—that they are not economists. The typical investor of course believes that the willingness of investors to buy securities, and hence the price of securities set in the market, depends on perceptions of the objective values underlying those securities. But the investor also believes that fads, fashions, and changing societal attitudes affect those perceptions, and hence also affect securities prices, in ways that sometimes bear no relation to the underlying objective values in question. The unanimity—indeed, often the religiosity—with which professional researchers in economics and finance dismiss such a possibility is truly astounding; Shiller's frank analysis of the arguments on which it rests makes it all the more so.

Because Shiller's paper focuses somewhat narrowly on the arguments and evidence for the "efficient markets" credo, it is important to pause to remind ourselves of why the issue he addresses is such an important one. Reflecting on these matters is valuable for the usual reason of keeping in focus the ultimate objectives motivating any specific line of research, but it is also valuable in this case because asking why it matters whether these markets are "efficient" helps to understand the origins and merits of the key linchpin that Shiller rejects from the argument for market efficiency—in this context the identification of "efficiency" with nonforecastability.

Why, then, do we care if markets are efficient? There are at least two different senses in which securities markets may be efficient: one private and one public. From a private perspective, the central issue is the prospect for investors to earn above-average returns, systematically, over sustained periods of time. Here the connection between efficiency and nonforecastability is entirely appropriate. The presence of what Shiller calls fads in no way implies the prospect of making money in the market unless an investor has the ability to forecast whether today's fad is on the way in or out, and what will be tomorrow's. It is no coincidence that the research Shiller cites on the efficient markets theory, and especially on the identification of efficiency with nonforecastability, has emerged almost entirely from the nation's business schools. From the perspective of the private-interest orientation of these institutions, this identification is both understandable and appropriate.

From a public perspective, however, and indeed from the perspective in which economists have traditionally addressed questions of efficiency, the central question is whether the signals and incentives provided by prices set in securities markets are doing the best possible job of allocating the economy's scarce resources. At the level of analysis at which Shiller's paper deals, the issue is whether the equity market as a whole is correctly steering economywide outcomes for such financial matters as corporate retentions and such nonfinancial matters as investment in plant and equipment. (The nonfinancial corporate business sector typically accounts for some three-fourths of all nonresidential fixed investment in the United States.) The same issues also apply at less aggregate levels, of course. Are the signals and incentives provided by securities prices efficiently guiding the allocation of scarce resources among different industries and among competing firms within the same industry? Research analogous to Shiller's but focused on industry-specific stock price indexes or even on the prices of individual stocks would be straightforward to implement. Findings from such further, less aggregative research would be interesting in just the same way.

It is in this second, public sense of market efficiency that Shiller's objection to the identification of efficiency with nonforecastability is both apt and potentially of the utmost importance. As an example, just to make Shiller's point trivially obvious in this context, suppose that all New York Stock Exchange prices were secretly set not by market trading but by the daily run of a computer located in the basement of 11 Wall Street and programmed to generate random numbers. The resulting securities prices, and the returns to holding securities, would be completely nonforecastable. But no one would argue that these prices led to an efficient allocation of economic resources. Shiller's point is that equally nonforecastable elements, originating not from a hidden computer but from social interactions among real human beings, are significant determinants of actual securities prices. The immediate corollary to Shiller's point, given the important role of the capital markets in an economy like that of the United States, is that the resulting resource allocations are not efficient either.

What are the implications of these conclusions for public policy? Here substantial caution is necessary, and Shiller exercises the ultimate in caution by not even mentioning the possibility of such implications. From a policy perspective, the relevant question is not whether the economic allocations induced by the securities markets are efficient in the sense of freedom from distortions due to Shilleresque fads, but instead whether the corresponding allocations produced by any alternative process would be superior. In the absence of a clear statement of what such an alternative process would be, it is impossible even to begin to answer this question. Judging from the most prominently proposed alternatives, however, I am skeptical of the ability of governmental intervention to improve resource allocations except in cases of obvious externalities which securities markets are not expected to internalize anyway.

In sum, Shiller has given us a paper both persuasive in its content and potentially important in its implications. Before concluding these remarks, however, I want to challenge one aspect of Shiller's analysis that I find not persuasive. Interestingly enough, at least in this one respect Shiller's fault lies in attributing to the market too much efficiency rather than too little.

In particular, Shiller follows recent literature in assuming the existence of what he calls "smart-money investors," and informally identifies the smart money with institutional investors. This assumption and identification may be appropriate in some contexts, but not in Shiller's. It is certainly true, for reasons of differential costs of gathering and processing information, in addition simply to differing attitudes and inclinations, that some investors do a more thorough job than others of assessing the objective underpinnings of security values. It is also plausible in most cases to assume that institutional investors have advantages in this regard. Shiller's concern, however, is not whether these objective considerations play *any* role in setting securities prices—he shows that they do—but whether they play the *only* role. In the context of Shiller's argument, therefore, smart money ought to refer not to an advantage in assessing objective considerations but rather to the freedom, at least in comparison with other investors, from being subject to socially determined fads and fashions.

There is simply no reason to believe that institutional investors are less subject to such social influences on opinion than other investors, and there are substantial grounds for thinking that they may be even more so. To begin, apart from a few lonely Warren Buffetts, institutional investors exist in a community that is exceptionally closely knit by constant communication and mutural exposure. The familiar extent to which economists talk shop with one another, look at the same aspects of the world they study, read the same research, and congregate at meetings like this one, simply pales in comparison to the day-to-day activity of the typical institutional investor.

Second, competitive success or failure among institutional investors depends on relatives, not absolutes. Any investor who is delighted when his portfolio loses 30 percent of its value if the market is off by 32 percent and who bewails a gain of 40 percent if the market is up by 42 percent is not especially likely to be immune to socially formed opinions. Moreover, the standard that money managers seek to meet is in many cases not the performance of the market index but the index of performance of other managers.

Together with the well-known asymmetry of incentives to overperform versus disincentives to underperform, this orientation often enhances the "herd" aspect of institutional investors' opinions and decisions. Major project financings in the United States, for example, can often attract investments either from all of the major institutions or from none. In addition, when all of the major institutions do participate in a project financing, they often do so in rough proportion to their respective sizes. The reason is clear. If the project succeeds, no manager wants to stand out as having failed to participate. If the project fails, the loss to any one manager's portfolio is no greater than that to any other, and hence to the average of all.

Finally, as Shiller's own analysis implies, if fads and fashions do influence securities prices, is it really so smart not to pay attention? Not long ago a senior managing director of one of New York's leading securities firms confided that, within the not too distant future, he expected all major firms—including his own—to employ astrologers. He did not believe in astrology, to be sure, but he argued that some investors did. If they were to invest in large enough volume, then anything that influenced their actions could in principle affect securities prices. At that point, astrology too would enter the universe of factors that other, presumably more rational, investors would want to take into account. Who can yet say he will be wrong?

7. General Discussion

Christopher Sims pointed out more than one interpretation of Shiller's statistical rejection of the efficient market hypothesis. One interpretation is that people have mistaken expectations about the state of the economy and future returns so that stock price fluctuations contain little information about future returns. If true, private markets are likely to make bad decisions, and this might be a justification for countercyclical policy or for overruling market valuations in evaluating long-term structural projects. Another interpretation is that Shiller's fads represent real mass fluctuations in taste between present and future consumption and these are reflected in mass fluctuations in discount rates. Finally, it could be that the arbitrage implicit in relating current asset prices to expected future returns is simply not operative. Sims noted that Shiller does not attempt to distinguish among these three sources of failure of efficient markets, though they have importantly different implications.

Lawrence Summers suggested that the acceptance of the efficient markets hypothesis has itself represented a fad in the economics profession. He noted that empirical evidence against it was even stronger than Shiller suggested. In markets such as those for short-term financial instruments and foreign exchange, where futures prices must converge to actual prices within a relatively short time, tests are sharper and conclusively reject the efficient markets model. This adds to the plausibility that the model is not a good description of the stock market.

Summers added that the idea that fads can rationally influence stock decisions is consistent with a broad view of how information becomes available and is acted upon by agents. He also noted that the large volume of trading after takeover announcements is at odds with the efficient markets hypothesis. The theory would have predicted minimal trading: outsiders who know that they are at an information disadvantage would refuse to trade, and insiders could not trade with each other since they would all wish to hold the same position.

Martin Baily argued that the alternative hypothesis proposed by Shiller needed to be formulated more convincingly. As the paper does not define what a fad is, identification of fads is arbitrary. Although a fad will produce "swimming-with-the-tide" type of behavior, this may be the optimal investment strategy. Investors with limited information might be well advised to follow the smart money. Shiller's model does not explain how fads are formed and why they subsequently disappear, nor does it suggest any propagation mechanism that would explain why the stock market boom in the 1960s was a worldwide phenomenon.

Gardner Ackley endorsed Shiller's attempt to bring social factors into modeling markets. But if the stock market is a sociopsychological process, perhaps it needs to be studied using the concepts and methods of social psychology. Thomas Juster suggested that social processes are important in the stock market even for professional money managers. They are rewarded on the basis of relatively short-term results measured against the average performance of other professional managers, so there is a strong incentive to be near the crowd.

John Pound provided research assistance. This research was supported by the National Science Foundation under grant SES-8408565 and the Sloan Foundation.

8

Stock Return Variances

The Arrival of Information and the Reaction of Traders

KENNETH R. FRENCH
and RICHARD ROLL

1. Introduction

Equity returns are more volatile during exchange trading hours than during non-trading hours. For example, the variance of returns from the open to the close of trading on an average day is over six times larger than the variance of close-to-open returns over a weekend, even though the weekend is eleven times longer. On an hourly basis, the variance when the exchanges are open is between 13 and 100 times larger, depending on the non-trading period being considered.

The phenomenon has been pointed out by several authors including Fama (1965), Granger and Morgenstern (1970), Oldfield and Rogalski (1980), and Christie (1981), but it has not generated much attention. We believe it is important. It represents an empirical puzzle whose solution may provide a deeper understanding of information processing in financial markets.

We consider three possible explanations for the observed variance pattern. The first possibility is that more public information arrives during normal business hours. Under this hypothesis, most return volatility is caused by things like judicial decisions and tender offers and these announcements are clustered during the trading day. The second explanation assumes that most return volatility is caused by private information and that this information only affects prices through the trading of in-

From: *The Journal of Financial Economics*, vol. 17, pp. 5–26, 1986. Reprinted by permission of Elsevier Sequoia S.A.

formed investors. If the informed investors are more likely to trade when the exchanges are open, return variances will be high during this period.

The third possibility we consider is that the process of trading introduces noise into stock returns. For example, perhaps investors over-react to each other's trades. This trading noise would increase return variances when the exchanges are open.

To determine the relative importance of these three explanations, we examine the behavior of returns around business days when the New York and American Stock Exchanges were closed. If high trading-time variances are caused by the arrival of public information during the business day, return variances should not fall simply because the exchanges are closed. On the other hand, both the trading noise hypothesis and the private information hypothesis predict that return variances will be unusually low around exchange holidays. We find that the two-day return variance around exchange holidays is only slightly larger than the variance of a normal one-day return.

Our exchange holiday results are consistent with both the private information hypothesis and the trading noise hypothesis. To discriminate between these hypotheses we compare daily return variances with variances for longer holding periods. If daily returns are independent, the variance for a long holding period will equal the cumulated daily variances within the period. However, if daily returns are affected by trading noise, the longer holding period variance will be smaller than the cumulated daily variance.

These tests suggest that, on average, between 4% and 12% of the daily return variance is caused by mispricing. However, even if we assume that all of the mispricing occurs during the trading day, it has a small impact on the relation between trading and non-trading variances. It appears that the large difference between these variances is caused by differences in the arrival and incorporation of information during trading and non-trading periods.

2. Trading and Non-Trading Variances

If hourly stock return variances were constant across trading and non-trading periods, the variance of weekend returns (i.e., Friday close to Monday close) would be three times the variance of weekday returns (e.g., Tuesday close to Wednesday close). In this section we examine this proposition and we report on the relation between firm size and the trading/non-trading variance differential.

Our tests use the daily returns provided by the Center for Research in Security Prices for all common stocks listed on the New York and

American Stock Exchanges between 1963 and 1982. We break this twenty-year period into ten two-year subperiods. For each stock, we calculate return variances for weekdays, weekends, holidays, and holiday weekends during each subperiod. These estimates are used to compute multiple-to-single-day variance ratios for each stock in each subperiod.

The first column of table 1 reports grand averages of the estimated variance ratios. The grand averages are calculated by first averaging the variance ratios across the stocks within each subperiod and then averaging the ten subperiod averages. The grand averages are consistent with the evidence in earlier papers. The variance of the total return over a weekend or a holiday is only slightly higher than the variance of the total return over a normal weekday. For example, the variance for a three-day weekend return is only 10.7% higher than the variance for a normal one-day return.

Table 1 also reports standard errors of the grand averages. These standard errors, which are based on the distribution of the ten subperiod averages, range from 0.04 for weekends to 0.29 for holiday weekends. Under the assumption that the subperiod averages are independent and identically distributed, the grand averages are many standard errors below 2.0, 3.0, or 4.0.

One can imagine many factors that might affect the way investors acquire and react to information about particular firms. For example, perhaps firms in some industries are closely monitored by financial analysts, while little private information is collected about firms in other industries. In this study, we concentrate on firm size as a potential factor because it is easy to observe and because the rewards from acquiring and using firm-specific information are probably a function of this variable.

To examine whether the relation between trading and non-trading variances is a function of firm size, we sort firms into quintiles based on their equity values at the beginning of each subperiod. The averages of the subperiod averages for the quintiles are reported in columns 2 through 6 in table 1. There is no obvious relation between the estimated variance ratios and firm size. For example, the average two-day variance ratio for the smallest firms (column 2) is 1.30 with a standard error of 0.07 and the average ratio for the largest firms (column 6) is 1.28 with a standard error of 0.10.

To see what the estimated variance ratios imply about the difference between trading and non-trading variances, assume that

(a) returns are intertemporally uncorrelated,
(b) the exchange is open six hours per day (the present situation),

Table 1 Average ratios of multiple-day variances relative to single-day variances for all NYSE and AMEX stocks and for quintiles of stocks sorted by equity value.[a]

		All stocks	Smallest quintile[a]	2	3	4	Largest quintile
Two-day holidays	Average ratio[b]	1.247	1.301	1.199	1.239	1.217	1.281
	Standard error[c]	0.066	0.068	0.054	0.052	0.097	0.100
	Standard deviation[d]	1.354	1.446	1.270	1.371	1.149	1.351
	Number of firms[e]	1962.5	390.3	392.3	392.4	393.5	394.1
	Average sample size[f]	10.0	10.0	10.0	10.0	10.0	10.0
Weekends	Average ratio	1.107	1.122	1.108	1.119	1.105	1.082
	Standard error	0.012	0.010	0.016	0.014	0.014	0.017
	Standard deviation	0.385	0.412	0.379	0.435	0.337	0.286
	Number of firms	2055.3	411.2	410.8	410.6	411.2	411.5
	Average sample size	92.8	92.5	92.8	92.9	93.0	93.0
Holiday weekends	Average ratio	1.117	1.111	1.122	1.099	1.122	1.130
	Standard error	0.092	0.053	0.085	0.071	0.106	0.151
	Standard deviation	1.219	1.176	0.992	1.276	1.232	1.014
	Number of firms	2055.7	411.3	410.8	410.9	411.2	411.5
	Average sample size	11.1	11.0	11.1	11.1	11.1	11.1

a. Stocks are sorted into quintiles based on their equity values at the beginning of ten two-year subperiods between 1963–1982.

b. The average ratio comparing the variance of two-, three-, and four-calendar-day returns with the variance of one-day returns. This estimate is the average of the ten subperiod averages.

c. The standard error of the reported average ratio. This standard error is based on the distribution of the ten subperiod average ratios.

d. The average cross-sectional standard deviation. The ratios for individual firms are used to estimate the standard deviation for each subperiod. The reported standard deviation is the average of the ten subperiod standard deviations.

e. The average number of firms in each subperiod.

f. The average number of multiple-day returns for each stock in each subperiod.

(c) there are just two uniform regimes, trading and non-trading hours; returns are identically distributed within these regimes but have different variances between them.

(These assumptions are made at this point merely for temporary illustrative convenience. We relax them later.)

Let σ_T^2 be the variance of returns *per hour* during trading and let σ_N^2 be the variance per hour at other times. Since there are 66 non-trading hours over the weekend and 18 non-trading hours in a normal business day, the average weekend-to-weekday variance ratio for all firms implies

$$66\sigma_N^2 + 6\sigma_T^2 = 1.107(18\sigma_N^2 + 6\sigma_T^2). \tag{1}$$

Thus, based on the weekend variance ratio,

$$\sigma_T^2 = 71.8\sigma_N^2;$$

the hourly variance when the New York exchanges are open is roughly seventy times the hourly variance when they are closed. We can make similar transformations with the average variance ratios for two- and four-day holidays. Using the averages for all stocks in table 1 gives:

Non-trading interval	Hourly trading to non-trading variance ratio
Mid-week holidays	13.2
Weekends	71.8
Holiday Weekends	99.6

Trading hours are more volatile than non-trading hours. Among non-trading hours, weekends have lower volatility than normal holidays and holiday weekends have the lowest volatility of all.

3. Possible Explanations

There seem to be two general explanations for the empirical phenomenon that prices are more variable during exchange trading hours. The obvious possibility is that information arrives more frequently during the business day. The second possible explanation is that trading somehow induces volatility.

To examine the first possibility, it is useful to divide information into two categories: public information and private information. Public information is information that becomes known at the same time that it affects stock prices. Examples of this information include changes in the weather, Supreme Court decisions, and the outcome of the World Series. Information produced by firms, such as financial reports, or by the government, such as United States Department of Agriculture crop forecasts, is included in this category if no one trades on the information before it is released.

Private information is at the other end of the spectrum. While public information affects prices before anyone can trade on it, private information only affects prices through trading. Much of the information produced by investors and security analysts is in this category.

Obviously, most information falls in the continuum between public and private information. However, this artificial dichotomy is useful because it allows us to develop and test several hypotheses about the variance pattern we observe.

Our first hypothesis is that the higher trading-time volatility occurs because public information is more likely to appear during normal business hours. This explanation is plausible since most public information is probably a by-product of normal business activities.

The private information hypothesis is similar. Under this hypothesis, return variances are higher during trading hours because most private information is incorporated into prices during this period. There are two possible reasons for this. First, the production of private information may be more common when the exchanges are open. For example, security analysts are more likely to work at this time. Activities such as visiting corporate headquarters, examining company documents, and making recommendations to clients are all easier to do during the business day. In addition, the benefits of producing private information are larger when the exchanges are open and the information can be acted on quickly and conveniently.

Even if private information is produced at a constant rate during both trading and non-trading periods, trades based on this information could lead to high trading-time variances. Consider the effect of private information that is produced after the New York exchanges close. Since this information can only affect prices through the trading of informed investors, the price reaction is delayed until this trading occurs. If the informed investors trade on the New York exchanges, their information cannot affect prices until the exchanges open.

The fact that private information only affects prices when markets are open appears to offer a simple, yet general, explanation for high trading-time variances. However, this story will not explain the results in table 1 unless we assume that private information affects returns for more than one trading day. All of the estimates in table 1 are based on close-to-close returns, which include both a non-trading period and a trading period. If non-trading information is completely revealed in prices during the next trading day, it will affect the 'right' close-to-close return. For example, if private information produced during the weekend only affects Monday's return and information produced during a week-night only affects the next day's return, the weekend-to-weekday variance ratios in table 1 accurately reflect the private information produced during each period. Unless private information affects prices for more than one trading day, the hypothesis that informed investors only trade when the exchanges are open cannot explain the low variance ratios in table 1.

To summarize, the private information hypothesis says that the variance pattern we observe occurs either because most private information is produced during normal business hours or because informed investors usually trade when the exchanges are open and they trade on their information for more than one day.

The second general explanation for high trading-time variances is that the process of trading introduces noise into stock returns. Suppose each day's return can be broken into two components: an information component that reflects a rational assessment of the information arriving that day, and an independent or positively correlated error component.[1] If the daily pricing error occurs during the trading period, it will increase the trading-time variance. It is important to note that under this hypothesis at least some trading noise (the error component in the daily return) is not corrected during the trading day in which it occurs. If all trading noise were corrected quickly, the noise would increase intra-day return variances, but it would not affect our close-to-close returns.

In summary, the hypotheses to be examined are:

(H.1) High trading-time volatility is caused by public information which is more likely to be observed during normal business hours.

(H.2) High trading-time volatility is caused by private information which is more likely to affect prices when the exchanges are open.

(H.3) High trading-time volatility is caused by pricing errors that occur during trading.

---

1. In the discussion below, we add a third component that arises because of the bid/ask spread.

4. Tests of the Hypotheses

In this section we examine the predictions of the three hypotheses. It is important to recognize that the hypotheses are not mutually exclusive. In fact, the observed variance pattern might be caused by all three factors simultaneously. Our goal is to provide some sense of the empirical importance of each explanation.

4.1 Exchange Holidays

The New York and American Stock Exchanges were closed on Wednesdays during the second half of 1968 because of a paperwork backlog. The exchanges were also closed on many of the election days in our sample period. These exchange holidays give us an excellent opportunity to examine the relative importance of our three hypotheses.[2]

Under the public information hypothesis, the return variance for a business day should not depend on whether the exchanges are open or closed. Therefore, this hypothesis predicts that stock return variances will not be reduced by the exchange holidays in 1968. The prediction of the public information hypothesis for election holidays is less clearcut. One might expect unusually high variances on election days since election results are publicly observable information. However, perhaps the exchanges close on election days because less public information is available.

The private information hypothesis predicts that return variances will be reduced by both the election day closings and the exchange holidays in 1968. The size of this reduction depends on the interval used to compute returns. Since private information only affects prices when informed investors trade, the reduction in the variance should be large during the period that the exchanges are closed. For example, the variance of the return from the close of trading on Tuesday to the open on Thursday should be unusually low if the exchanges are closed on Wednesday.

Much of the reduction in the variance will be eliminated if the next day's trading is included in the return. The information that would have affected prices on Wednesday will affect prices during trading on Thursday instead. However, the variance for the two-day close-to-close return from Tuesday to Thursday should still be less than twice the variance of a normal one-day return. This difference may persist for two reasons. First, private information may affect prices for more than one trading

---

2. French (1980) also uses returns around the 1968 exchange holidays to make inferences about the exchange holidays.

day. The information that would have been revealed through trading on Wednesday and Thursday may not be fully incorporated in prices if trading is limited to Thursday. Second, less private information may be produced when the markets are closed. Exchange holidays reduce the value of private information. Informed investors either must delay acting on their information—and run the risk that someone else will discover it—or they must find a less convenient way to trade. Because of its reduced value, less private information will be produced when the exchanges are closed.

If we increase the holding period to one week, the private information hypothesis predicts that the effect of the exchange holiday on the total variance should be even smaller. Equivalently, the variance for the days following an exchange holiday should be larger than normal. Adding more trading days to the return interval allows more time for the private information to affect prices. Also, with less information produced on the exchange holiday, more will be produced on succeeding days. There are two reasons for this production effect. First, with more information available to produce, the cost of generating any particular amount should fall. Second, some of the information this is not produced privately because the exchanges are closed might become publicly observable after a few days.

Hypothesis H.3 makes a simpler prediction. If high trading-time variances are caused by trading noise, the variance should fall when the exchanges are closed and the variance that is lost should not be recovered.

Table 2 presents evidence to test these predictions. The first section of this table reports daily variance ratios comparing the two-day returns for exchange holidays in 1968 (from Tuesday close to Thursday close) with a normal one-day variance estimated between January 1963 and December 1982. The results are surprising. The average ratio across all stocks is 1.145. The averages for the size portfolios range from 1.043 for the second quintile to 1.274 for the fifth quintile. In other words, these point estimates indicate that, on average, the variance for the *two-day* exchange holiday returns is only 14.5% higher than the variance for normal one-day returns.

To get an idea about the reliability of these estimates, we construct similar ratios using the returns for Wednesday and Thursday during each half year from 1963 to 1982. For example, we compute a two-day variance for each stock using all of the Wednesday–Thursday returns observed during the first half of 1963. This variance is compared to the one-day variance estimated between July of 1963 and December of 1982. The ratio of these variances is averaged across stocks to get the average ratio

Table 2 Daily and weekly variance ratios for exchange holidays.

	All stocks	Smallest quintile[a]	2	3	4	Largest quintile
		Daily variance ratios				
Exchange holidays in 1968						
Average ratio[b]	1.145	1.077	1.043	1.180	1.239	1.274
Standard deviation[c]	0.882	0.857	0.647	0.979	0.944	1.001
Number of firms	2083	597	455	374	342	315
Average sample size[d]	22.7	22.8	22.7	22.6	22.7	22.85
Election holidays						
Average ratio[e]	1.165	1.131	1.073	1.186	1.159	1.332
Standard deviation	1.079	1.222	1.065	1.040	0.799	1.118
Number of firms	2026	572	426	367	347	314
Average sample size	8.5	8.2	8.2	8.1	8.7	9.5

Weekly variance ratios

Exchange holidays in 1968	Average ratio[f]	0.821	0.901	0.802	0.772	0.793	0.784
	Standard deviation	0.559	0.667	0.484	0.422	0.511	0.612
	Number of firms	2093	600	457	376	344	316
	Average sample size	20.6	20.7	20.6	20.5	20.7	20.8
Election holidays	Average ratio	0.839	0.876	0.776	0.889	0.779	0.868
	Standard deviation	0.614	0.707	0.627	0.678	0.501	0.527
	Number of firms	1188	278	221	192	229	268
	Average sample size	8.5	8.3	8.3	8.3	8.6	8.8

a. Firms are sorted into quintiles based on their relative equity values when they are first listed in the CRSP daily master file.

b. Average variance ratio comparing two-day exchange holiday returns with single-calendar-day returns between January 1963 and December 1982.

c. Cross-sectional standard deviation of the individual firm ratios.

d. Average number of exchange holidays for each firm.

e. Average variance ratio comparing two-day exchange holiday returns with single-calendar-day returns from 1962–1969, 1972, 1976, and 1980.

f. Average ratio comparing the return variance for weeks containing exchange holidays with the return variance for weeks containing five trading days.

for the first half of 1963. This process is repeated for each of the 39 half years in our sample. (The second half of 1968 is not included because it contains the Wednesday holidays.) The averages (which are not shown) range from 1.18 for the second half of 1964 to 4.32 for the second half of 1974, with a grand average of 2.00. It appears that the low 1968 variance ratio, 1.14, is not caused by chance, but by the exchange holiday.

The first section of table 2 also reports average daily variance ratios for election days. During our sample period, the exchanges closed for elections in 1962–1969, 1972, 1976, and 1980. Therefore, we compare the two-day election returns with one-day returns from those years. The average variance ratio for all stocks is 1.165. The portfolio averages range from 1.073 for the second quintile to 1.333 for the fifth quintile.

To check the reliability of the daily election ratios in table 2, we construct similar ratios using combined Tuesday–Wednesday returns for non-election weeks. Each replication involves one observation from each of the eight election years. For example, the first Tuesday–Wednesday pair of each election year is used in the first replication and the second pair is used in the second replication. This procedure generates a total of 45 replications, with average variance ratios ranging from 1.61 for the thirtieth Tuesday–Wednesday pair each year to 2.62 for the first pair. The grand average is 1.98. Again, it does not appear that the election holiday variance ratio of 1.17 is caused by chance. There appears to be a strong relation between the low variance ratios and the exchange holidays.

The daily variance ratios for election holidays and exchange holidays in 1968 are consistent with both the private information hypothesis and the trading noise hypothesis. However, these ratios provide little support for the public information hypothesis, which predicts that the two-day exchange holiday variance should be twice the one-day variance.

Weekly variance ratios in the second section of table 2 offer some evidence about the relative importance of private information and trading noise. Under the trading noise hypothesis, exchange holidays should cause a permanent reduction in the cumulated return variance. On the other hand, the private information hypothesis predicts that most of the lost variance will be recovered; when the holding period is increased there is more time to incorporate private information into prices and to discover information that was not produced on the exchange holiday.

To test these predictions, we compare the returns for weeks that include exchange holidays with the returns for normal five-trading-day weeks. For example, the weekly return for a Wednesday holiday in 1968 is measured from the close of trading on Tuesday to the close of trading on the following Tuesday. The five-trading-day variance is estimated using returns from Tuesday close to Tuesday close over all five-trading-day weeks in the full 1962–1982 sample period. The election week returns are measured from Monday close to Monday close and they are compared with weekly returns for 1962–1969, 1972, 1976, and 1980.

The weekly variance ratios in table 2 are consistent with the trading noise hypothesis. Across all stocks, the average weekly ratio for exchange holidays in 1968 is 0.82, and the average election week ratio is 0.84. However, neither of these estimates is very reliable. Simulated weekly variance ratios for the exchange holidays in 1968, which are constructed like the simulated daily ratios above, vary between 0.54 and 2.04. Simulated election week variances range from 0.76 to 1.53. The standard deviations of the simulated average ratios are 0.35 and 0.14, respectively. It is difficult to draw meaningful inferences from the weekly exchange holiday ratios.

4.2 Autocorrelations

The exchange holiday results support both the private information hypothesis and the trading noise hypothesis. We can obtain more information about the relative importance of these hypotheses by examining the autocorrelations of the daily returns. Neither public information nor private information will generate observable serial correlation. In principle, information may induce autocorrelation by changing the level of expected returns. However, the variance of expected returns is almost certainly so small that autocorrelation from this source is unobservable in realized returns for individual stocks.

Under the trading noise hypothesis, stock returns should be serially correlated. It is difficult to characterize short-run autocorrelations without a specific mispricing model. However, unless market prices are unrelated to the objective economic value of the stock, pricing errors must be corrected in the long run. These corrections would generate negative autocorrelations.

Two other factors may induce serial correlation under all three hypotheses. Close-to-close returns, such as those reported by CRSP, contain measurement error because each closing trade may be executed at any price within the bid/ask spread. If these measurement errors are independent from day to day, they will induce negative first-order autocorrelation. For example, suppose today's closing price is on the bid size of the market. Then today's observed return is negatively biased and tomorrow's observed return is positively biased. If today's price is on the ask side, the pattern is reversed but the observed returns are still negatively correlated.[3]

Systematic variation in expected returns can also induce serial correlation. For example, the day of the week effects documented by French (1980) induce positive autocorrelations at every fifth lag (5, 10, 15, etc.) and negative autocorrelations at all other lags. Day of the month effects documented by Ariel (1984) also imply non-zero autocorrelations. However, since the variance of daily realized returns is much larger than the variance of daily expected returns, autocorrelation from this source will have little effect on our results.[4]

Because the predictions of the trading noise hypothesis are not precise, we are not interested in a detailed study of the autocorrelation structure of daily returns. However, the general behavior of the autocorrelations can help us discriminate between the trading noise hypothesis and the information hypotheses. In summary, we expect that measurement error from the bid/ask spread will lead to negative first-order autocorrelation under all three hypotheses. Neither the public nor the private information hypothesis predicts any other serial correlation, while the trading noise hypothesis predicts that daily returns will be negatively correlated beyond lag one.

Table 3 shows average autocorrelations for lags between one and fifteen days. The general procedure used to compute these averages is similar to the procedure used in table 1. Autocorrelations are estimated for individual stocks during each two-year subperiod. The first column of table 3 reports grand averages that are calculated by averaging the autocorrelations across all of the stocks within each subperiod and then averaging the ten subperiod averages. Columns 2 through 6 report the average autocorrelations for firms that have been sorted into quintiles based on their equity values at the beginning of each subperiod. Table 3 also includes standard errors of the autocorrelation estimates. These standard errors are based on the distribution of the ten subperiod aver-

3. If daily bid/ask errors are not independent, they can induce negative autocorrelations beyond lag 1. The autocorrelations in table 3 use all of the prices in the CRSP daily master file. These prices include both trade prices and the mean of bid and ask prices when a stock did not trade during a day. To control for one potential source of dependence, we have also estimated the autocorrelations using just trade prices. Deleting returns involving bid/ask prices has only one noticeable effect—the first-order autocorrelations increase slightly. For example, the average first-order autocorrelation across all stocks increases from 0.003 to 0.009.

4. To examine this issue in more detail, we have recomputed the autocorrelations reported in table 3 below using returns which are adjusted for day-of-the-week effects. This adjustment does not alter any of our inferences.

Table 3 Average daily autocorrelations in percent for all NYSE and AMEX stocks and for quintiles of stocks sorted by equity value.[a]

Lag	All stocks	Smallest quintile	2	3	4	Largest quintile
1	0.33	− 6.42	− 1.66	1.17	2.49	5.44
	(0.87)	(1.55)	(1.07)	(0.83)	(0.84)	(1.01)
2	− 1.15	− 1.94	− 1.43	− 1.28	− 0.75	− 0.40
	(0.15)	(0.24)	(0.20)	(0.15)	(0.14)	(0.26)
3	− 1.15	− 1.35	− 1.39	− 1.26	− 1.00	− 0.81
	(0.15)	(0.16)	(0.23)	(0.19)	(0.21)	(0.22)
4	− 0.68	− 0.85	− 0.66	− 0.62	− 0.49	− 0.78
	(0.23)	(0.16)	(0.19)	(0.29)	(0.28)	(0.34)
5	− 0.28	− 0.44	− 0.15	− 0.05	− 0.15	− 0.59
	(0.23)	(0.17)	(0.28)	(0.22)	(0.27)	(0.39)
6	− 0.95	− 0.84	− 0.72	− 0.84	− 0.92	− 1.38
	(0.24)	(0.24)	(0.25)	(0.29)	(0.26)	(0.29)
7	− 0.64	− 0.53	− 0.53	− 0.50	− 0.63	− 0.98
	(0.25)	(0.19)	(0.30)	(0.27)	(0.26)	(0.32)
8	− 0.37	− 0.14	− 0.42	− 0.31	− 0.25	− 0.73
	(0.24)	(0.15)	(0.23)	(0.30)	(0.25)	(0.40)
9	− 0.45	− 0.34	− 0.47	− 0.27	− 0.57	− 0.60
	(0.19)	(0.13)	(0.16)	(0.17)	(0.20)	(0.40)
10	− 0.26	− 0.12	− 0.10	− 0.15	− 0.38	− 0.51
	(0.15)	(0.12)	(0.15)	(0.18)	(0.19)	(0.24)
11	− 0.52	− 0.27	− 0.54	− 0.58	− 0.57	− 0.65
	(0.18)	(0.10)	(0.13)	(0.21)	(0.23)	(0.32)
12	− 0.20	− 0.35	− 0.18	− 0.21	− 0.10	− 0.19
	(0.22)	(0.12)	(0.20)	(0.24)	(0.28)	(0.31)
13	− 0.15	− 0.11	0.02	− 0.03	− 0.14	− 0.47
	(0.20)	(0.12)	(0.18)	(0.20)	(0.28)	(0.35)
14	0.15	0.28	0.05	0.18	0.14	0.10
	(0.25)	(0.13)	(0.17)	(0.24)	(0.27)	(0.50)
15	0.42	0.28	0.38	0.49	0.43	0.52
	(0.15)	(0.12)	(0.17)	(0.17)	(0.21)	(0.28)

a. The autocorrelations and standard errors (in parentheses) are reported in percent. Autocorrelations are estimated for individual firms during each of ten two-year subperiods between 1963 and 1982. These autocorrelations are averaged to compute subperiod averages. Each reported autocorrelation is the average of ten subperiod averages. The standard error is based on the distribution of the ten subperiod averages. Approximately 500 returns are used to estimate the autocorrelations for each firm in each subperiod. On average, there are about 380 firms in each quintile during each subperiod.

ages, under the assumption that these averages are independent and identically distributed.[5]

The results in table 3 are generally consistent with the predictions of the trading noise hypothesis. All of the estimated autocorrelations from lag 2 to lag 12 are negative. Although the estimates are small in absolute magnitude, many are more than three standard errors from zero. The persistence of the negative autocorrelations suggests that trading noise is not completely corrected for at least two weeks.

The behavior of the first-order autocorrelations in table 3 is surprising. We expected measurement error within the bid/ask spread to induce negative first order dependence. While the estimates for the smallest two quintiles are consistent with this expectation, the estimates for quintiles three, four and five are not. In fact, the first-order autocorrelation for the largest quintile of stocks is 5.4%, with a standard error of 1.0%.

Although they are surprising, the positive autocorrelations also support the trading noise hypothesis. If we rule out the possibility that the reported prices contain positively correlated measurement errors, we are unable to imagine any sensible explanation of these results that does not involve trading noise. For example, suppose traders overreact to new information and this overreaction persists for more than one day. Then tomorrow's pricing error is positively correlated with both today's information component and today's pricing error. Alternatively, suppose the market does not incorporate all information as soon as it is released. Then today's pricing error is negatively correlated with today's information and tomorrow's error is positively correlated with today's information. The positive correlation between today's information and tomorrow's error could generate positively autocorrelated returns. Since negative first-order autocorrelation induced by the bid/ask spread is smaller for the larger firms, it dominates the error-induced positive autocorrelation only in the first and second quintiles.

The results in table 3 are consistent with the trading noise hypothesis. However, since the average autocorrelations are small in absolute magnitude, it is hard to gauge their economic significance. To estimate the importance of the trading noise hypothesis, we compare daily return variances with variances for longer holding period returns. If daily returns were independent, the variance for a long holding period would equal the cumulated daily variances within the period. On the other hand, if

---

5. Under the assumption that returns are serially independent, the expected value of the estimated autocorrelations for each firm is $-1/(T-1)$, where T is the number of observations used in the estimate. [See Moran (1948).] Therefore, we increase the individual autocorrelation estimates by $1/(T-1)$ before computing the subperiod and full period averages.

daily returns are temporarily affected by trading noise, the longer period variance will be smaller than the cumulated daily variances.

This comparison presumes that the relative importance of both pricing errors and bid/ask errors is reduced as the holding period is increased. For example, suppose mispricing is corrected within three weeks. Then pricing errors that occur during the first ten weeks of each three-month holding period have no effect on the three-month return and errors that occur during the last three weeks have a reduced effect. If pricing errors are corrected within three weeks and bid/ask errors are corrected over-night, most of the three-month return reflects a rational assessment of the information arriving during the three-month period. When the hold-ing period is extended to six months, this approximation becomes even more accurate. By comparing the variance of long holding period returns (which reflect information) with the variance implied by daily returns (which reflect information, pricing errors, and bid/ask errors), we can estimate the fraction of the daily variance that is caused by rational assess-ments of information.[6]

Table 4 reports average actual-to-implied variance ratios for holding periods of two trading days; one, two, and three weeks; and one, three, and six months. The general procedure used to compute these average ratios is similar to the procedure used in tables 1 and 3. We first compute actual-to-implied variance ratios for each stock in each two-year subpe-riod. This is done in four steps. For example, to estimate the weekly actual-to-implied variance ratio for a given stock in a particular two-year subperiod, we first calculate the average trading day return during the 104 weeks in that period. Next, we cumulate the daily squared deviations around this average. Then under the assumption that the daily returns are independent, we estimate the implied weekly variance by dividing this total by 104. Finally, we divide the actual weekly variance by the implied variance. The same procedure is used to estimate variance ratios for other holding periods.[7]

The first column of Table 4 reports grand averages that are calculated by averaging the estimated variance ratios across all the stocks within

6. This comparison was suggested to us by Eugene Fama. Perry (1982) uses a similar approach to examine the process generating stock returns.

7. These ratios may be affected by two sources of bias. Both the actual and implied variances are estimated with error. Since we are using the ratio of these estimates our measure is biased upward. However, simulations suggest that this bias is negligible. The second source of bias may be more important. We are assuming that the expected returns are constant over each estimation period. Violations of this assumption will have little effect on the implied variances since they are based on daily variance estimates. However, changing expected returns could positively bias the actual long-term variance estimates. To reduce this effect, we limit each estimation period to two years and we limit the holding periods to a maximum of six months.

Table 4 Actual-to-implied variance ratios for all NYSE and AMEX stocks and for quintiles of stocks sorted by equity value.

		All stocks	Smallest quintile[a]	2	3	4	Largest quintile
Two trading days	Average ratio[b]	0.999	0.933	0.979	1.007	1.021	1.048
	Standard error[c]	0.010	0.015	0.011	0.010	0.009	0.013
	Number of firms[d]	1900.2	362.6	374.6	373.9	386.8	402.3
	Average sample size[c]	250.5	249.0	250.3	250.8	251.0	251.0
One week	Average ratio	0.966	0.853	0.928	0.979	1.005	1.053
	Standard error	0.017	0.025	0.019	0.018	0.018	0.019
	Number of firms	1899.6	362.1	374.5	373.9	386.8	402.3
	Average sample size	103.6	102.7	103.6	103.9	104.0	104.1
Two weeks	Average ratio	0.943	0.803	0.900	0.959	0.995	1.045
	Standard error	0.024	0.026	0.025	0.025	0.027	0.025
	Number of firms	1899.5	362.0	374.5	373.9	386.8	402.3
	Average sample size	51.5	50.9	51.5	51.7	51.8	51.8
Three weeks	Average ratio	0.929	0.784	0.888	0.953	0.985	1.024
	Standard error	0.022	0.026	0.026	0.023	0.024	0.024
	Number of firms	1899.5	362.0	374.4	373.9	386.8	402.2
	Average sample size	34.0	33.5	34.0	34.1	34.2	34.2

One month	Average ratio	0.906	0.773	0.874	0.931	0.959	0.983
	Standard error	0.022	0.023	0.027	0.025	0.020	0.024
	Number of firms	1898.9	361.7	374.3	373.9	386.8	402.2
	Average sample size	23.6	23.0	23.6	23.8	23.8	23.9
Three months	Average ratio	0.894	0.752	0.876	0.949	0.942	0.941
	Standard error	0.045	0.032	0.043	0.051	0.055	0.066
	Number of firms	1895.3	359.8	373.6	373.5	386.6	401.8
	Average sample size	7.7	7.3	7.7	7.8	7.9	7.9
Six months	Average ratio	0.883	0.731	0.862	0.931	0.929	0.907
	Standard error	0.102	0.062	0.086	0.109	0.117	0.129
	Number of firms	1554.2	203.4	291.8	324.8	350.5	383.7
	Average sample size	4.0	4.0	4.0	4.0	4.0	4.0

a. Stocks are sorted in quintiles based on their equity value at the beginning of ten two-year subperiods between 1963–1982.

b. Average ratio comparing the actual holding period variance with the variance implied by single-trading-day returns under the assumption that the one-day returns are independent. The reported ratio is the average of ten subperiod averages.

c. The standard error of the reported average ratio. This standard error is based on the distribution of the ten subperiod average ratios.

d. The average number of firms in each subperiod.

e. The average number of multiple-day returns for each stock in each subperiod.

each subperiod and then averaging the ten subperiod averages. The averages for stocks that have been sorted into quintiles based on their equity values at the beginning of each subperiod are reported in columns 2 through 6. Table 4 also includes standard errors that are based on the distribution of the ten subperiod averages, under the assumption that the subperiod averages are independent and identically distributed.

The results in table 4 indicate that a significant fraction of the daily variance is caused by pricing and bid/ask errors. The six-month actual-to-implied variance ratio for all firms is 0.88. The six-month averages for the smallest and largest quintiles are 0.73 and 0.91, respectively. Based on these point estimates, 27% of the daily variance for the first quintile and 9% of the daily variance for the fifth quintile is eliminated in the long run. One would draw nearly identical inferences from the three-month variance ratios. This supports the assumption that bid/ask and pricing errors have relatively little effect on three- and six-month holding period returns.

Since both the pricing errors and the bid/ask errors are temporary, the six-month ratios in table 4 only allow us to make an estimate of their combined effect. However, by assuming that the variance of the bid/ask errors is zero, these ratios place an upper bound on the point estimate of the relative variance of the pricing errors. We can estimate a lower bound for this variance by combining the results in tables 3 and 4.

Suppose each day's return is made up of three independent components: a rational information component (X_t), a mispricing component (Y_t), and a bid/ask error (Z_t),

$$R_t = X_t + Y_t + Z_t. \tag{2}$$

Also, suppose that the daily information components are independent and identically distributed with variance $\text{var}(X_t)$. The bid/ask error in the daily return depends on the error in the current price (e_t), and the error in the previous day's price (e_{t-1}),

$$Z_t = e_t - e_{t-1}. \tag{3}$$

If the daily price errors (e_t) are independent and identically distributed, the variance and first-order autocovariance of the bid/ask errors equal

$$\text{var}(Z_t) = 2\,\text{var}(e_t) \tag{4}$$

and

$$\text{cov}(Z_t, Z_{t-1}) = -\text{var}(e_t) = -\text{var}(Z_t)/2. \tag{5}$$

Therefore, the first-order autocorrelation of the bid/ask errors is -0.5.[8]

---

8. This bid/ask spread phenomenon is examined in more detail by Cohen et al. (1983) and Roll (1984).

If pricing and bid/ask errors have a negligible effect on six-month returns, the six-month variance ratios in table 4 can be written as

$$V_6 = \text{var}(X_t)/\text{var}(R_t), \tag{6}$$

where $\text{var}(X_t)$ and $\text{var}(R_t)$ are the variances of the daily information component and the total daily return, respectively. Using eq. (5) and the assumption that the daily information components are serially independent, the first-order autocorrelation of the daily returns is

$$\rho_R = \text{cov}(R_t, R_{t-1})/\text{var}(R_t)$$
$$= [\text{cov}(Y_t, Y_{t-1}) + \text{cov}(Z_t, Z_{t-1})]/\text{var}(R_t)$$
$$= [\rho_{Y1}\text{var}(Y_t) - \text{var}(Z_t)/2]/\text{var}(R_t). \tag{7}$$

Eqs. (6) and (7) can be combined to obtain an expression for the relative variance of the pricing errors,

$$\text{var}(Y_t)/\text{var}(R_t) = (1 - V_6 + 2\rho_R)/(1 + 2\rho_{Y1}). \tag{8}$$

Unfortunately, we cannot observe ρ_{Y1}, the autocorrelation of the pricing errors. However, since this autocorrelation must be less than 1.0, eq. (8) gives a lower bound for the point estimate of the relative variance,

$$\text{var}(Y_t)/\text{var}(R_t) > (1 - V_6 + 2\rho_R)/3. \tag{9}$$

Using the average first-order autocorrelations in table 3 and the average six-month variance ratios in table 4, the upper and lower bounds on our point estimates of the relative pricing error variance for all stocks and for each quintile are:

	All stocks	Smallest quintile	2	3	4	Largest quintile
Upper bound	11.7%	26.9%	13.8%	6.9%	7.1%	9.3%
Lower bound	4.1%	4.7%	3.5%	3.1%	4.0%	6.7%

The lower bound is roughly constant across the five portfolios. This similarity is not limited to the lower bound. Differences in the relative pricing error variances will be small as long as the autocorrelation of these errors is approximately the same across portfolios.

4.3 Implications

The estimates in tables 3 and 4 suggest that a non-trivial fraction of the daily variance is caused by mispricing. However, pricing errors have a negligible effect on the weekend-to-weekday variance ratios in table 1. Suppose we adjust those ratios under a set of assumptions that magnifies the impact of mispricing. Specifically, assume that the variance of the weekday pricing errors and the variance of the weekday bid/ask errors are as large as the variance of weekend errors. Then the weekday and weekend returns (R_{1t} and R_{3t}, respectively) can be written as

$$R_{1t} = X_{1t} + Y_t + Z_t, \tag{10}$$

$$R_{3t} = X_{3t} + Y_t + Z_t. \tag{11}$$

Based on the average ratio for all firms in table 1, the variance of R_{3t} is 10.7% larger than the variance of R_{1t},

$$\text{var}(X_{3t} + Y_t + Z_t) = 1.107\text{var}(X_{1t} + Y_t + Z_t). \tag{12}$$

The average six-month variance ratio for all firms in table 4 is 0.88. To magnify the effect of mispricing further, assume that this ratio applies to the weekend variance,

$$\text{var}(X_{3t}) = 0.883\text{var}(X_{3t} + Y_t + Z_t). \tag{13}$$

Under the assumption that the information and mispricing components are independent, eqs. (12) and (13) can be combined to eliminate the bid/ask and pricing error variances,

$$\text{var}(X_{3t}) = 1.123\text{var}(X_{1t}). \tag{14}$$

Eliminating the effect of these errors increases the average weekend-to-weekday variance ratio for all firms by less than 2%. This effect varies from less than 1% for the largest quintile of stocks to less than 6% for the smallest quintile. Bid/ask and pricing errors also have a negligible effect on the two- and four-day variance ratios in table 1 and on the exchange holiday ratios in table 2.

It appears that the low daily variance ratios are caused by a reduction in the arrival of information when the exchanges are closed. Moreover, the exchange holiday variances suggest that private information causes most stock price changes.[9]

5. Summary and Conclusions

Asset returns display a puzzling difference in volatility between exchange trading hours and non-trading hours. For example, we estimate that the per hour return variance was about 70 times larger during a trading hour

---

9. In the appendix we develop some implications under the assumption that the information and error components are not independent.

than during a weekend non-trading hour, on average, over all stocks listed on the New York and American Exchanges from January 1963 through December 1982.[10]

We consider three factors that might explain the high trading-time variances. First, the arrival of public information may be more frequent during the business day. Second, private information may be much more likely to affect prices when the New York exchanges are open. Third, the process of trading may induce volatility.

Our results indicate that, on average, approximately 4 to 12% of the daily variance is caused by mispricing. However, even if we assume that pricing errors are generated only when the exchanges are open, these errors have a trivial effect on the difference between trading and non-trading variances. We conclude that this difference is caused by differences in the flow of information during trading and non-trading hours. Moreover, small return variances over exchange holidays suggest that most of this information is private.

Appendix

If we are willing to ignore sampling error (and just assume that sample estimates are population values), we can deduce additional information about the correlation between information and mispricing and about the quantity of information produced on a non-market business day (such as a Wednesday in 1968).

First, define $W_t = Y_t + Z_t$ as the sum of the mispricing component and the bid/ask error. Define X_t as the information-induced return for one day. The variance ratio for table 4 can be written as

$$a = \text{var}(X)/\text{var}(X + W). \tag{A.1}$$

Solving (A.1) with a = 0.883 (from table 4),

$$\sigma_X/\sigma_W = \frac{\rho_{XW} + \sqrt{\rho_{XW}^2 + 0.1325}}{0.1325}, \tag{A.2}$$

where ρ_{XW} is the contemporaneous correlation between X and W, and σ is the standard deviation. Thus, if there is *no* correlation between information and mispricing ($\rho_{XW} = 0$),

$$\sigma_X/\sigma_W = 2.75.$$

In principle, we could have a low information-to-mispricing variance ra-

---

10. This estimate is based on the variance ratio for weekends in table 1.

Table A.1 Exchange holiday information consistent with information variance exceeding mispricing variance (% of normal day).

Actual-to-implied variance ratio, a	Ratio of two-day exchange holiday return variance to normal day return variance, b					
	1.05	1.10	1.15	1.20	1.25	1.30
	Information produced on exchange holiday as a percentage of information produced, on a normal day, consistent with information variance exceeding mispricing variance[a]					
0.75	5.78 to 9.88	11.59 to 19.56	17.41 to 29.07	23.26 to 38.44	29.12 to 47.68	34.99 to 56.82
0.80	5.60 to 9.86	11.21 to 19.48	16.84 to 28.90	22.48 to 38.15	28.13 to 47.26	33.80 to 56.25
0.85	5.43 to 9.84	10.87 to 19.40	16.32 to 28.73	21.78 to 37.87	27.24 to 48.86	32.72 to 55.70
0.90	5.27 to 9.82	10.55 to 19.32	15.84 to 28.87	21.13 to 37.60	26.43 to 46.46	31.73 to 55.17
0.95	5.13 to 9.79	10.27 to 19.24	15.40 to 28.40	20.54 to 37.34	25.69 to 46.08	30.83 to 54.66

a. The lower and upper bounds are given by

$$K_L = 100\{(a-1) + [(a-1)^2 + 4ab]^{1/2}\}/2a \text{ and } K_U = 100\{(2a-1) + [(2a-1)^2 + 4a(b-a)]^{1/2}\}/2a.$$

tio. For example, if $\rho_{XW} = -1$, σ_X/σ_W is only 0.48. At the other extreme, if $\rho_{XW} = +1$, $\sigma_X/\sigma_W = 15.6$.

The variance ratios for business days which are not trading days can be written as

$$b = \text{var}(kX + W)/\text{var}(X + W), \tag{A.3}$$

where $k^2 - 1$ $(1 \le k \le \sqrt{2})$ is the information produced during a business-day-exchange holiday. For $b = 1.145$ (from table 2) and $\sigma_{XW} = 0$, (A.1) and (A.3) imply $K = 1.079$; i.e., only about 16 percent of a normal business day's information was produced on the 1968 Wednesday business days which were exchange holidays.

Going one step further, we can combine (A.1) and (A.3) to eliminate σ_{XW}. This provides an expression for the ratio of mispricing to information variance as a function of k.

$$q = \frac{\text{var}(W)}{\text{var}(X)} = \frac{ak^2 + (1 - a)k - b}{a(k - 1)} = k + \frac{1}{a} + \frac{1 - b}{a(k - 1)}. \tag{A.4}$$

We note that $\partial q/\partial k = 1 + ((b - 1)/a(k - 1)^2)$, which is positive because $b > 1$. The function q has a zero at $k_L = \{(a - 1) + [(a - 1)^2 + 4ab]^{1/2}\}/2a$. For values of k greater than $k_U = \{(2a - 1) + [(2a - 1)^2 + 4a(b - a)]^{1/2}\}/2a$, the mispricing variance exceeds the information variance, i.e., $q > 1$.

The information variance exceeds the mispricing variance only when k is between k_U and k_L. For our estimated parameters, $k_L = 1.074$ and $k_U = 1.130$. Under the assumption that the estimated values are population values, the information variance would exceed the mispricing variance if the information produced on a 1968 Wednesday was between 15.3 and 27.7 percent of that produced on a normal day. In fact, depending on the values of a and b, the range can be even narrower than $k_U - k_L$ because the implied correlation coefficient in (A.3) must lie between -1 and $+1$. From (A.1), the correlation between the information and mispricing components is obtained using the solution to (A.4),

$$\rho_{XW} = (1 - a - aq)/2a\sqrt{q}. \tag{A.5}$$

For instance, $q = 0$ is clearly ruled out by (A.5) unless $a = 1$. Thus, the lower bound on k must exceed k_L.

In general, the restriction on the correlation, $-1 \le \rho_{XW} \le 1$, implies from (A.5)

$$1 + \sqrt{1/a} > \sqrt{q} > \sqrt{1/a} - 1. \tag{A.6}$$

For our estimates $a = 0.883$, $b = 1.145$, $\sqrt{q}$ has a lower bound of 0.06419, implying a lower bound on k of 1.0745 (which is slightly higher than k_L).

There are sampling errors in the estimates of a and b. Thus, although the range of k where the information variance is larger than the mispricing variance is rather narrow for our point estimates, it could be much larger for other values of a and b. Table A.1 gives the range $100(k_U^2 - 1)$ to $100(k_L^2 - 1)$ for other values of a and b which could be conceivable given the sampling error.

As the other variance ratio b increases, the interval widens. But even for $b = 1.30$, the information variance is larger than the mispricing variance only if the amount of information produced on a 1968 Wednesday is *less* than about 56 percent of the information produced on a normal business day.

The results are rather insensitive to the variance ratio a. Also, for all the values in the table, the correlation between X and W is negative. It ranges from -0.33 for $a = 0.75$, $b = 1.05$, to -0.47 for $a = 0.95$, $b = 1.30$.

This paper has benefited from the comments of seminar participants at Boston College, the University of British Columbia, the University of Chicago, Dartmouth College, Harvard University, Northwestern University, Purdue University and Stanford University. We are also grateful to Craig Ansley, Merton Miller, Steven Ross, Robert Stambaugh, William Schwert, Jerold Warner (the referee), and especially, Douglas Diamond and Eugene Fama for comments on an earlier draft.

References

ARIEL, ROBERT A. 1986. A monthly effect in stock returns. *Journal of Financial Economics*, forthcoming.

CHRISTIE, ANDREW A. 1981. On efficient estimation and intra-week behavior of common stock variances. Unpublished working paper. April (University of Rochester, Rochester, NY).

COHEN, KALMAN J., GABRIEL A. HAWAWINI, STEVEN F. MAIER, ROBERT A. SCHWARTZ and DAVID K. WHITCOMB. 1983. Friction in the trading process and the estimation of systematic risk. *Journal of Financial Economics* 12, Aug., 263–278.

FAMA, EUGENE F. 1965. The behavior of stock market prices. *Journal of Business* 38, Jan., 34–105.

FRENCH, KENNETH R. 1980. Stock returns and the weekend effect. *Journal of Financial Economics* 8, March, 55–70.

GRANGER, CLIVE W.J. and OSKAR MORGENSTERN. 1970. Predictability of stock market prices (Heath-Lexington, Lexington, MA).

MORAN, P. A. P. 1948. Some theorems on time series. *Biometrika* 35, 255–260.

OLDFIELD, GEORGE S., JR. and RICHARD J. ROGALSKI. 1980. A theory of common stock returns over trading and non-trading periods. *Journal of Finance* 35, June, 729–751.

PERRY, PHILLIP R. 1982. The time-variance relationship of security returns: Implications for the return generating stochastic process. *Journal of Finance* 37, June, 857–870.

ROLL, RICHARD. 1984. A simple implicit measure of the bid/ask spread in an efficient market. *Journal of Finance* 39, Sept., 1127–1139.

PART

III

OVERREACTION

9

Does the Stock Market Overreact?

WERNER F. M. De BONDT
and RICHARD H. THALER

As economists interested in both market behavior and the psychology of individual decision making, we have been struck by the similarity of two sets of empirical findings. Both classes of behavior can be characterized as displaying *overreaction*. This study was undertaken to investigate the possibility that these phenomena are related by more than just appearance. We begin by describing briefly the individual and market behavior that piqued our interest.

The term overreaction carries with it an implicit comparison to some degree of reaction that is considered to be appropriate. What is an appropriate reaction? One class of tasks which have a well-established norm are probability revision problems for which Bayes' rule prescribes the correct reaction to new information. It has now been well-established that Bayes' rule is not an apt characterization of how individuals actually respond to new data (Kahneman et al. [1982]). In revising their beliefs, individuals tend to overweight recent information and underweight prior (or base rate) data. People seem to make predictions according to a simple matching rule: "The predicted value is selected so that the standing of the case in the distribution of outcomes matches its standing in the distribution of impressions" (Kahneman and Tversky [1982, p. 416]). This rule-of-thumb, an instance of what Kahneman and Tversky call the representativeness heuristic, violates the basic statistical principle that the extremeness of predictions must be moderated by considerations of predictability. Grether (1980) has replicated this finding under incentive

From: *The Journal of Finance*, vol. XL, no. 3, pp. 793–807, July 1986. Reprinted by permission of the American Finance Association.

compatible conditions. There is also considerable evidence that the actual expectations of professional security analysts and economic forecasters display the same overreaction bias (for a review, see De Bondt [1985]).

One of the earliest observations about overreaction in markets was made by J. M. Keynes: ". . . day-to-day fluctuations in the profits of existing investments, which are obviously of an ephemeral and nonsignificant character, tend to have an altogether excessive, and even an absurd, influence on the market" (1936, pp. 153–154). About the same time, Williams noted in this *Theory of Investment Value* that "prices have been based too much on current earning power and too little on long-term dividend paying power" (1938, p. 19). More recently, Arrow has concluded that the work of Kahneman and Tversky "typifies very precisely the excessive reaction to current information which seems to characterize all the securities and futures markets" (1982, p.5). Two specific examples of the research to which Arrow was referring are the excess volatility of security prices and the so-called price earnings ratio anomaly.

The excess volatility issue has been investigated most thoroughly by Shiller (1981). Shiller interprets the Miller-Modigliani view of stock prices as a constraint on the likelihood function of a price-dividend sample. Shiller concludes that, at least over the last century, dividends simply do not vary enough to rationally justify observed aggregate price movements. Combining the results with Kleidon's (1981) findings that stock price movements are strongly correlated with the following year's earnings changes suggests a clear pattern of overreaction. In spite of the observed trendiness of dividends, investors seem to attach disproportionate importance to short-run economic developments.[1]

The price earnings ratio (*P/E*) anomaly refers to the observation that stocks with extremely low *P/E* ratios (i.e., lowest decile) earn larger risk-adjusted returns than high *P/E* stocks (Basu [1977]). Most financial economists seem to regard the anomaly as a statistical artifact. Explanations are usually based on alleged misspecification of the capital asset pricing model (CAPM). Ball (1978) emphasizes the effects of omitted risk factors. The *P/E* ratio is presumed to be a proxy for some omitted factor which, if included in the "correct" equilibrium valuation model, would eliminate the anomaly. Of course, unless these omitted factors can be identified, the hypothesis is untestable. Reinganum (1981) has claimed that the small firm effect subsumes the *P/E* effect and that both are related to the same

---

1. Of course, the variability of stock prices may also reflect changes in real interest rates. If so, the price movements of other assets—such as land or housing—should match those of stocks. However, this is not actually observed. A third hypothesis, advocated by Marsh and Merton [1983], is that Shiller's findings are a result of his misspecification of the dividend process.

set of missing (and again unknown) factors. However, Basu (1983) found a significant *P/E* effect after controlling for firm size, and earlier Graham (1973) even found an effect within the thirty Dow Jones Industrials, hardly a group of small firms!

An alternative behavioral explanation for the anomaly based on investor overreaction is what Basu called the "price-ratio" hypothesis (e.g., Dreman [1982]). Companies with very low *P/E*'s are thought to be temporarily "undervalued" because investors become excessively pessimistic after a series of bad earnings reports or other bad news. Once future earnings turn out to be better than the unreasonably gloomy forecasts, the price adjusts. Similarly, the equity of companies with very high *P/E*'s is thought to be "overvalued," before (predictably) falling in price.

While the overreaction hypothesis has considerable a priori appeal, the obvious question to ask is: How does the anomaly survive the process of arbitrage? There is really a more general question here. What are the equilibria conditions for markets in which some agents are not rational in the sense that they fail to revise their expectations according to Bayes' rule? Russell and Thaler (1985) address this issue. They conclude that the existence of some rational agents is not sufficient to guarantee a rational expectations equilibrium in an economy with some of what they call quasi-rational agents. (The related question of market equilibria with agents having heterogeneous expectations is investigated by Jarrow [1983].) While we are highly sensitive to these issues, we do not have the space to address them here. Instead, we will concentrate on an empirical test of the overreaction hypothesis.

If stock prices systematically overshoot, then their reversal should be predictable from past return data alone, with no use of any accounting data such as earnings. Specifically, two hypotheses are suggested: (1) Extreme movements in stock prices will be followed by subsequent price movements in the opposite direction. (2) The more extreme the initial price movement, the greater will be the subsequent adjustment. Both hypotheses imply a violation of weak-form market efficiency.

To repeat, our goal is to test whether the overreaction hypothesis is *predictive*. In other words, whether it does more for us than merely to explain, ex post, the *P/E* effect or Shiller's results on asset price dispersion. The overreaction effect deserves attention because it represents a behavioral principle that may apply in many other contexts. For example, investor overreaction possibly explains Shiller's earlier (1979) findings that when long-term interest rates are high relative to short rates, they tend to move down later on. Ohlson and Penman (1983) have further suggested that the increased volatility of security returns following stock splits may also be linked to overreaction. The present empirical tests are to our knowledge the first attempt to use a behavioral principle to predict a new market anomaly.

The remainder of the paper is organized as follows. The next section describes the actual empirical tests we have performed. Section II describes the results. Consistent with the overreaction hypothesis, evidence of weak-form market inefficiency is found. We discuss the implications for other empirical work on asset pricing anomalies. The paper ends with a brief summary of conclusions.

1. The Overreaction Hypothesis: Empirical Tests

The empirical testing procedures are a variant on a design originally proposed by Beaver and Landsman (1981) in a different context. Typically, tests of semistrong form market efficiency start, at time $t = 0$, with the formation of portfolios on the basis of some event that affects all stocks in the portfolio, say, an earnings announcement. One then goes on to investigate whether later on $(t > 0)$ the estimated residual portfolio return $\hat{u}_{pt}$—measured relative to the single-period CAPM—equals zero. Statistically significant departures from zero are interpreted as evidence consistent with semistrong form market inefficiency, even though the results may also be due to misspecification of the CAPM, misestimation of the relevant alphas and/or betas, or simply market inefficiency of the weak form.

In contrast, the tests in this study assess the extent to which systematic nonzero residual return behavior in the period after portfolio formation $(t > 0)$ is associated with systematic residual returns in the preformation months $(t < 0)$. We will focus on stocks that have experienced either extreme capital gains or extreme losses over periods up to five years. In other words, "winner" (W) and "loser" portfolios (L) are formed *conditional upon past excess returns*, rather than some firm-generated informational variable such as earnings.

Following Fama (1976), the previous arguments can be formalized by writing the efficient market's condition,

$$E(\tilde{R}_{jt} - E_m(\tilde{R}_{jt}|F_{t-1}^m)|F_{t-1}) = E(\tilde{u}_{jt}|F_{t-1}) = 0$$

where F_{t-1} represents the complete set of information at time $t - 1$, $\tilde{R}_{jt}$ is the return on security t at t, and $E_m(\tilde{R}_{jt}|F_{t-1}^m)$ is the expectation of $\tilde{R}_{jt}$, assessed by the market on the basis of the information set F_{t-1}^m. The efficient market hypothesis implies that $E(\tilde{u}_{Wt}|F_{t-1}) = E(\tilde{u}_{Lt}|F_{t-1}) = 0$. As explained in the introduction, the overreaction hypothesis, on the other hand, suggests that $E(\tilde{u}_{Wt}|F_{t-1}) < 0$ and $E(\tilde{u}_{Lt}|F_{t-1}) > 0$.

In order to estimate the relevant residuals, an equilibrium model must be specified. A common procedure is to estimate the parameters of the market model (see e.g., Beaver and Landsman [5]). What will happen if the equilibrium model is misspecified? As long as the variation in $E_m(\tilde{R}_{jt}|F^m_{t-1})$ is small relative to the movements in $\tilde{u}_{jt}$, the exact specification of the equilibrium model makes little difference to tests of the efficient market hypothesis. For, even if we knew the "correct" model of $E_m(\tilde{R}_{jt}|F^m_{t-1})$, it would explain only a small part of the variation in $\tilde{R}_{jt}$.[2]

Since this study investigates the return behavior of specific portfolios over extended periods of time (indeed, as long as a decade), it cannot be merely *assumed* that model misspecification leaves the conclusions about market efficiency unchanged. Therefore, the empirical analysis is based on three types of return residuals: market-adjusted excess returns; market model residuals; and excess returns that are measured relative to the Sharpe-Lintner version of the CAPM. However, since all three methods are single-index models that follow from the CAPM, misspecification problems may still confound the results. De Bondt (1985) formally derives the econometric biases in the estimated market-adjusted and market model residuals if the "true" model is multifactor, e.g., $\tilde{R}_{jt} = A_j + B_j\tilde{R}_{mt} + C_j\tilde{X}_t + \tilde{e}_{jt}$. As a final precaution, he also characterizes the securities in the extreme portfolios in terms of a number of financial variables. If there were a persistent tendency for the portfolios to differ on dimensions that may proxy for "risk," then, again, we cannot be sure whether the empirical results support market efficiency or market overreaction.

It turns out that, whichever of the three types of residuals are used, the results of the empirical analysis are similar and that the choice does not affect our main conclusions. Therefore, we will only report the results based on market-adjusted excess returns. The residuals are estimated as $\hat{u}_{jt} = R_{jt} - R_{mt}$. There is no risk adjustment except for movements of the market as a whole and the adjustment is identical for all stocks. Since, for any period t, the same (constant) market return R_{mt} is subtracted from all R_{jt}'s, the results are interpretable in terms of raw (dollar) returns. As shown in De Bondt (1985), the use of market-adjusted excess returns has the further advantage that it is likely to bias the research design *against* the overreaction hypothesis.[3] Finally, De Bondt shows that winner and

---

2. Presumably, this same reasoning underlies the common practice of measuring abnormal security price performance by way of easily calculable mean-adjusted excess returns [where, by assumption, $E(\tilde{R}_j)$ equals a constant K_j], market-adjusted excess returns (where, by assumption, $\alpha_j = 0$ and $\beta_j = 1$ for all j), rather than more complicated market model residuals, let alone residuals relative to some multifactor model.

3. We will come back to this bias in Section II.

loser portfolios, formed on the basis of market-adjusted excess returns, do not systematically differ with respect to either market value of equity, dividend yield or financial leverage.

We will now describe the basic research design used to form the winner and loser portfolios and the statistical test procedures that determine which of the two competing hypotheses receives more support from the data.

1.1 Test Procedures: Details

Monthly return data for New York Stock Exchange (NYSE) common stocks, as compiled by the Center for Research in Security Prices (CRSP) of the University of Chicago, are used for the period between January 1926 and December 1982. An equally weighted arithmetic average rate of return on all CRSP listed securities serves as the market index.

1. For every stock j on the tape with at least 85 months of return data (months 1 through 85), without any missing values in between, and starting in January 1930 (month 49), the next 72 monthly residual returns u_{jt} (months 49 through 120) are estimated. If some or all of the raw return data beyond month 85 are missing, the residual returns are calculated up to that point. The procedure is repeated 16 times starting in January 1930, January 1933, . . . , up to January 1975. As time goes on and new securities appear on the tape, more and more stocks qualify for this step.

2. For every stock j, starting in December 1932 (month 84; the "portfolio formation date") $(t = 0)$, we compute the cumulative excess returns $CU_j = \Sigma_{t=-35}^{t=0} u_{jt}$ for the prior 36 months (the "portfolio formation" period, months 49 through 84). The step is repeated 16 times for all nonoverlapping three-year periods between January 1930 and December 1977. On each of the 16 relevant portfolio formation dates (December 1932, December 1935, . . . , December 1977), the CU_j's are ranked from low to high and portfolios are formed. Firms in the top 35 stocks (or the top 50 stocks, or the top decile) are assigned to the winner portfolio W; firms in the bottom 35 stocks (or the bottom 50 stocks, or the bottom decile) to the loser portolio L. Thus, the portfolios are formed conditional upon excess return behavior prior to $t = 0$, the portfolio formation date.

3. For both portfolios in each of 16 nonoverlapping three-year periods $(n = 1, \ldots, N; N = 16)$, starting in January 1933 (month 85, the

"starting month") and up to December 1980, we now compute the cumulative average residual returns of all securities in the portfolio, for the next 36 months (the "test period," months 85 through 120), i.e., from $t = 1$ through $t = 36$. We find $CAR_{W,n,t}$ and $CAR_{L,n,t}$. If a security's return is missing in a month subsequent to portfolio formation, then, from that moment on, the stock is permanently dropped from the portfolio and the CAR is an average of the available residual returns. Thus, whenever a stock drops out, the calculations involve an implicit rebalancing.[4]

4. Using the CAR's from all 16 test periods, *average* CAR's are calculated for both portfolios and each month between $t = 1$ and $t = 36$. They are denoted $ACAR_{W,t}$ and $ACAR_{L,t}$. The overreaction hypothesis predicts that, for $t > 0$, $ACAR_{W,t} < 0$ and $ACAR_{L,t} > 0$, so that, by implication, $[ACAR_{L,t} - ACAR_{W,t}] > 0$. In order to assess whether, at any time t, there is indeed a statistically significant difference in investment performance, we need a pooled estimate of the population variance in CAR_t,

$$S_t^2 = \left[\sum_{n=1}^{N} (CAR_{W,n,t} - ACAR_{W,t})^2 + \sum_{n=1}^{N} (CAR_{L,n,t} - ACAR_{L,t})^2 \right] / 2(N - 1).$$

With two samples of equal size N, the variance of the difference of sample means equals $2S_t^2/N$ and the t-statistic is therefore

$$T_t = [ACAR_{L,t} - ACAR_{W,t}] / \sqrt{2S_t^2/N}.$$

Relevant t-statistics can be found for each of the 36 postformation months but they do not represent independent evidence.

5. In order to judge whether, for any month t, the average residual return makes a contribution to either $ACAR_{W,t}$ or $ACAR_{L,t}$, we

---

4. Since this study concentrates on companies that experience extraordinary returns, either positive or negative, there may be some concern that their attrition rate sufficiently deviates from the "normal" rate so as to cause a survivorship bias. However, this concern is unjustified. When a security is delisted, suspended or halted, CRSP determines whether or not it is possible to trade at the last listed price. If no trade is possible, CRSP tries to find a subsequent quote and uses it to compute a return for the last period. If no such quote is available because the stockholders receive nothing for their shares, the return is entered as minus one. If trading continues, the last return ends with the last listed price.

can test whether it is significantly different from zero. The sample standard deviation of the winner portfolio is equal to

$$s_t = \sqrt{\sum_{n=1}^{N} (AR_{W,n,t} - AR_{W,t})^2 / N - 1}.$$

Since $s_t / \sqrt{N}$ represents the sample estimate of the standard error of $AR_{W,t}$, the t-statistic equals

$$T_t = AR_{W,t} / (s_t / \sqrt{N}).$$

Similar procedures apply for the residuals of the loser portfolio.

1.2 Discussion

Several aspects of the research design deserve some further comment. The choice of the data base, the CRSP Monthly Return File, is in part justified by our concern to avoid certain measurement problems that have received much attention in the literature. Most of the problems arise with the use of daily data, both with respect to the risk and return variables. They include, among others, the "bid-ask" effect and the consequences of infrequent trading.

The requirement that 85 subsequent returns are available before any firm is allowed in the sample biases the selection towards large, established firms. But, if the effect under study can be shown to apply to them, the results are, if anything, more interesting. In particular, it counters the predictable critique that the overreaction effect may be mostly a small-firm phenomenon. For the experiment described in Section A, between 347 and 1,089 NYSE stocks participate in the various replications.

The decision to study the CAR's for a period of 36 months after the portfolio formation date reflects a compromise between statistical and economic considerations, namely, an adequate number of independent replications versus a time period long enough to study issues relevant to asset pricing theory. In addition, the three-year period is also of interest in light of Benjamin Graham's contention that "the interval required for a substantial underevaluation to correct itself averages approximately 1½ to 2½ years" (1959, p. 37). However, for selected experiments, the portfolio formation (and testing) periods are one, two, and five years long. Clearly, the number of independent replications varies inversely with the length of the formation period.

Finally, the choice of December as the "portfolio formation month" (and, therefore, of January as the "starting month") is essentially arbitrary. In order to check whether the choice affects the results, some of the empirical tests use May as the portfolio formation month.

2. The Overreaction Hypothesis: Empirical Results

2.1 Main Findings

The results of the tests developed in Section I are found in Figure 1. They are consistent with the overreaction hypothesis. Over the last half-century, loser portfolios of 35 strocks outperform the market by, on average, 19.6%, thirty-six months after portfolio formation. Winner portfolios, on the other hand, earn about 5.0% less than the market, so that the difference in cumulative average residual between the extreme portfolios, $[ACAR_{L,36} - ACAR_{W,36}]$ equals 24.6% (t-statistic: 2.20). Figure 1 shows the movement of the ACAR's as we progress through the test period.

The findings have other notable aspects. First, the overreaction effect is asymmetric; it is much larger for losers than for winners. Secondly, consistent with previous work on the turn-of-the-year effect and seasonality, most of the excess returns are realized in January. In months $t = 1$, $t = 13$, and $t = 25$, the loser portfolio earns excess returns of, respectively, 8.1% (t-statistic: 3.21), 5.6% (3.07), and 4.0% (2.76). Finally, in surprising agreement with Benjamin Graham's claim, the overreaction

Figure 1   Cumulative Average Residuals for Winner and Loser Portfolios of 35 Stocks (1–36 months into the test period)

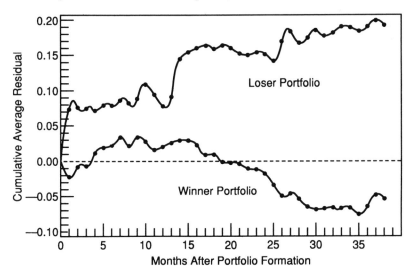

phenomenon mostly occurs during the second and third year of the test period. Twelve months into the test period, the difference in performance between the extreme portfolios is a mere 5.4% (t-statistic: 0.77).

While not reported here, the results using market model and Sharpe-Lintner residuals are similar. They are also insensitive to the choice of December as the month of portfolio formation (see De Bondt [1985]).

The overreaction hypothesis predicts that, as we focus on stocks that go through more (or less) extreme return experiences (during the formation period), the subsequent price reversals will be more (or less) pronounced. An easy way to generate more (less) extreme observation is to lengthen (shorten) the portfolio formation period; alternatively, for any given formation period (say, two years), we may compare the test period performance of less versus more extreme portfolios, e.g., decile portfolios (which contain an average 82 stocks) versus portfolios of 35 stocks. Table 1 confirms the prediction of the overreaction hypothesis. As the cumulative average residuals (during the formation period) for various sets of winner and loser portfolios grow larger, so do the subsequent price reversals, measured by $[ACAR_{L,t} - ACAR_{W,t}]$ and the accompanying t-statistics. For a formation period as short as one year, no reversal is observed at all.

Table 1 and Figure 2 further indicate that the overreaction phenomenon is qualitatively different from the January effect and, more generally, from seasonality in stock prices. Throughout the test period, the difference in ACAR for the experiment with a three-year formation period (the upper curve) exceeds the same statistic for the experiments based on two- and one-year formation periods (middle and lower curves). But all three experiments are clearly affected by the same underlying seasonal pattern.

In Section I, it was mentioned that the use of market-adjusted excess returns is likely to bias the research design against the overreaction hypothesis. The bias can be seen by comparing the CAPM-betas of the extreme portfolios. For all the experiments listed in Table I, the average betas of the securities in the winner portfolios are significantly larger than the betas of the loser portfolios.[5] For example, for the three-year experiment illustrated in Figure 1, the relevant numbers are respectively, 1.369 and 1.026 (t-statistic on the difference: 3.09). Thus, the loser portfolios not only outperform the winner portfolios; if the CAPM is correct, they are also significantly less risky. From a different viewpoint, therefore, the results in Table I are likely to *underestimate* both the

---

5. The CAPM-betas are found by estimating the market model over a period of 60 months prior to portfolio formation.

Table 1 Differences in Cumulative Average (Market-Adjusted) Residual Returns Between the Winner and Loser Portfolios at the End of the Formation Period, and 1, 12, 13, 18, 24, 25, 36, and 60 Months into the Test Period

Portfolio Selection Procedures: Length of the Formation Period and No. of Independent Replications	Average No. of Stocks	CAR at the End of the Formation Period		Difference in CAR (t-Statistics)							
		Winner Portfolio	Loser Portfolio	Months After Portfolio Formation							
				1	12	13	18	24	25	36	60
10 five-year periods	50	1.463	−1.194	0.070 (3.13)	0.156 (2.04)	0.248 (3.14)	0.256 (3.17)	0.196 (2.15)	0.228 (2.40)	0.230 (2.07)	0.319 (3.28)
16 three-year periods	35	1.375	−1.064	0.105 (3.29)	0.054 (0.77)	0.103 (1.18)	0.167 (1.51)	0.181 (1.71)	0.234 (2.19)	0.246 (2.20)	NA*
24 two-year periods[a]	35	1.130	−0.857	0.062 (2.91)	−0.006 (−0.16)	0.074 (1.53)	0.136 (2.02)	0.101 (1.41)	NA	NA	NA
25 two-year periods[b]	35	1.119	−0.866	0.089 (3.98)	0.011 (0.19)	0.092 (1.48)	0.107 (1.47)	0.115 (1.55)	NA	NA	NA
24 two-year periods[a] (deciles)	82	0.875	−0.711	0.051 (3.13)	0.006 (0.19)	0.066 (1.71)	0.105 (1.99)	0.083 (1.49)	NA	NA	NA
25 two-year periods[b] (deciles)	82	0.868	−0.714	0.068 (3.86)	0.008 (0.19)	0.071 (1.46)	0.078 (1.41)	0.072 (1.29)	NA	NA	NA
49 one-year periods	35	0.774	−0.585	0.042 (2.45)	−0.076 (−2.32)	−0.006 (−0.15)	0.007 (0.14)	−0.005 (−0.09)	NA	NA	NA

a. The formation month for these portfolios is the month of December in all uneven years between 1933 and 1979.

b. The formation month for these portfolios is the month of December in all even years between 1932 and 1980.

c. NA, not applicable.

259

Figure 2 Differences in Cumulative Average Residual Between Winner and Loser Portfolios of 35 Stocks (formed over the previous one, two, or three years; 1–24 months into the test period)

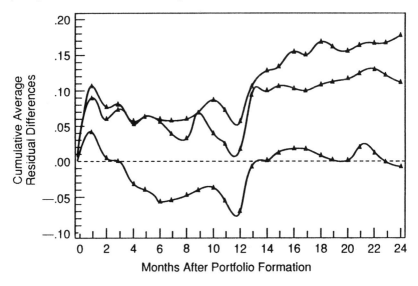

true magnitude and statistical significance of the overreaction effect. The problem is particularly severe with respect to the winner portfolio. Rather than 1.369, the residual return calculations assume the CAPM-beta of that portfolio to equal 1.00 only. This systematic bias may be responsible for the earlier observed asymmetry in the return behavior of the extreme portfolios.

To reiterate, the previous findings are broadly consistent with the predictions of the overreaction hypothesis. However, several aspects of the results remain without adequate explanation. Most importantly, the extraordinarily large positive excess returns earned by the loser portfolio in January.

One method that allows us to further accentuate the strength of the January effect is to increase the number of replications. Figure 3 shows the ACAR's for an experiment with a five-year-long test period. Every December between 1932 and 1977, winner and loser portfolios are formed on the basis of residual return behavior over the previous five years. Clearly, the successive 46 yearly selections are not independent. Therefore, no statistical tests are performed. The results in Figure 3 have some of the properties of a "trading rule." They represent the average

Figure 3 Cumulative Average Residuals for Winner and Loser Portfolios of 35 Stocks (1–60 months into the test period)

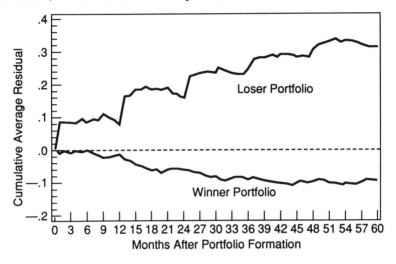

(cumulative) excess return (before transaction costs) that an investor, aware of the overreaction phenomenon, could expect to earn following any December in which he chose to try the strategy. The effect of multiplying the number of replications is to remove part of the random noise.

The outstanding feature of Figure 3 is, once again, the January returns on the loser portfolio. The effect is observed as late as five Januaries after portfolio formation! Careful examination of Figure 3 also reveals a tendency, on the part of the loser portfolio, to decline in value (relative to the market) between October and December. This observation is in agreement with the naive version of the tax-loss selling hypothesis as explained by, e.g., Schwert (1983). The winner portfolio, on the other hand, gains value at the end of the year and loses some in January (for more details, see De Bondt [1985]).

2.2 Implications for Other Empirical Work

The results of this study have interesting implications for previous work on the small firm effect, the January effect and the dividend yield and P/E effects. Blume and Stambaugh (1983), Keim (1982), and Reinganum (1981) have studied the interaction between the small firm and January effects. Their findings largely redefine the small firm effect as a "losing firm" effect around the turn-of-the-year.[6] Our own results lend further credence to this view. Persistently, losers earn exceptionally large January returns while winners do not. However, the companies in the extreme portfolios do not systematically differ with respect to market capitalization.

The January phenomenon is usually explained by tax-loss selling (see, e.g., Roll [1983]). Our own findings raise new questions with respect to this hypothesis. First, if in early January selling pressure disappears and prices "rebound" to equilibrium levels, why does the loser portfolio— even while it outperforms the market—"rebound" once again in the second January of the test period? And again, in the third and fourth Januaries? Secondly, if prices "rebound" in January, why is that effect so much larger in magnitude than the selling pressure that "caused" it during the final months of the previous year? Possible answers to these questions include the argument that investors may wait for years before realizing losses, and the observed seasonality of the market as a whole.

With respect to the P/E effect, our results support the price-ratio hypothesis discussed in the introduction, i.e., high P/E stocks are "overvalued" whereas low P/E stocks are "undervalued." However, this argument implies that the P/E effect is also, for the most part, a January phenomenon. At present, there is no evidence to support that claim, except for the persistent positive relationship between dividend yield (a variable that is correlated with the P/E ratio) and January excess returns (Keim [1982]).

3. Conclusions

Research in experimental psychology has suggested that, in violation of Bayes' rule, most people "overreact" to unexpected and dramatic news events. The question then arises whether such behavior matters at the market level.

Consistent with the predictions of the overreaction hypothesis, portfolios of prior "losers" are found to outperform prior "winners." Thirty-six months after portfolio formation, the losing stocks have earned about 25% more than the winners, even though the latter are significantly more risky.

---

6. Even after purging the data of tax-loss selling effects, Reinganum (1983) finds a (considerably smaller) January seasonal effect related to company size. This result may be due to his particular definition of the tax-loss selling measure. The measure is related to the securities' relative price movements over the last *six months* prior to portfolio formation only. Thus, if many investors choose to wait longer than six months before realizing losses, the portfolio of small firms may still contain many "losers."

Several aspects of the results remain without adequate explanation; most importantly, the large positive excess returns earned by the loser portfolio every January. Much to our surprise, the effect is observed as late as five years after portfolio information.

The financial support of the C.I.M. Doctoral Fellowship Program (Brussels, Belgium) and the Cornell Graduate School of Management is gratefully acknowledged. We received helpful comments from Seymour Smidt, Dale Morse, Peter Bernstein, Fischer Black, Robert Jarrow, Edwin Elton, and Ross Watts.

References

ARROW, K. J. "Risk Perception in Psychology and Economics." *Economic Inquiry* 20 (January 1982), 1–9.

BALL, R. "Anomalies in Relationships Between Securities' Yields and Yield-Surrogates." *Journal of Financial Economics* 6 (June–September 1978), 103–26.

BASU, S. "Investment Performance of Common Stocks in Relation to Their Price-Earnings Ratios: A Test of the Efficient Market Hypothesis." *Journal of Finance* 3 (June 1977), 663–82.

———. "The Relationship Between Earnings' Yield, Market Value and Return for NYSE Common Stocks: Further Evidence." *Journal of Financial Economics* 12 (June 1983), 129–56.

BEAVER, W. and W. R. LANDSMAN. "Note on the Behavior of Residual Security Returns for Winner and Loser Portfolios." *Journal of Accounting and Economics* 3 (December 1981), 233–41.

BLUME, M. and R. STAMBAUGH. "Biases in Computed Returns: An Application to the Size Effect." *Journal of Financial Economics* 12 (November 1983), 387–404.

DE BONDT, W. F. M. "Does the Stock Market Overreact to New Information?" Unpublished Ph.D. dissertation, Cornell University, 1985.

DREMAN, D. N. *The New Contrarian Investment Strategy.* New York: Random House, 1982.

FAMA, E. F. *Foundations of Finance.* New York: Basic Books, Inc., 1976.

GRAHAM, B. *The Intelligent Investor, A Book of Practical Counsel,* 3rd ed. New York: Harper & Brothers Publishers, 1959.

———. *The Intelligent Investor, A Book of Practical Counsel,* 4th rev. ed. New York: Harper & Brothers Publishers. 1973.

GRETHER, D. M. "Bayes Rule as a Descriptive Model: The Representativeness Heuristic." *Quarterly Journal of Economics* 95 (November 1980), 537–57.

JARROW, R. "Beliefs, Information, Martingales, and Arbitrage Pricing." Working Paper, Johnson Graduate School of Management, Cornell University, November 1983.

KAHNEMAN, D. and A. TVERSKY. "Intuitive Prediction: Biases and Corrective Procedures." In D. Kahneman, P. Slovic, and A. Tversky, (eds.), *Judgment Under Uncertainty: Heuristics and Biases*. London: Cambridge University Press, 1982.

KEIM, D. "Further Evidence on Size Effects and Yield Effects: The Implications of Stock Return Seasonality." Working Paper, Graduate School of Business, University of Chicago, April 1982.

———. "Size-Related Anomalies and Stock Return Seasonality: Further Empirical Evidence." *Journal of Financial Economics* 12 (June 1983), 13–32.

KEYNES, J. M. *The General Theory of Employment, Interest and Money*. London: Harcourt Brace Jovanovich. 1964 (reprint of the 1936 edition).

KLEIDON, A. W. "Stock Prices as Rational Forecasters of Future Cash Flows." Working Paper, Graduate School of Business, University of Chicago, November 1981.

MARSH, T. A. and R. C. MERTON. "Aggregate Dividend Behavior and Its Implications for Tests of Stock Market Rationality." Working Paper No. 1475–83, Sloan School of Management, MIT, September 1983.

OHLSON, J. A. and S. H. PENMAN. "Variance Increases Subsequent to Stock Splits: An Empirical Aberration." Working Paper, Graduate School of Business, Columbia University, September 1983.

REINGANUM, M. R. "Misspecification of Capital Asset Pricing: Empirical Anomalies. Based on Earnings' Yields and Market Values." *Journal of Financial Economics* 9 (March 1981), 19–46.

———. "The Anomalous Stock Market Behavior of Small Firms in January." *Journal of Financial Economics* 12 (June 1983), 89–104.

ROLL, R. "Vas ist das?" *Journal of Portfolio Management* 10 (Winter 1983), 18–28.

RUSSELL, T and R. THALER. "The Relevance of Quasi-Rationality in Competitive Markets." *American Economic Review* 75 (1985), forthcoming.

SCHWERT, G. W. "Size and Stock Returns, and Other Empirical Regularities." *Journal of Financial Economics* 12 (June 1983), 3–12.

SHILLER, R. J. "The Volatility of Long-Term Interest Rates and Expectations Models of the Term Structure." *Journal of Political Economy* 87 (December 1979), 1190–1219.

———. "Do Stock Prices Move Too Much to be Justified by Subsequent Changes in Dividends?" *American Economic Review* 71 (June 1981), 421–36.

WILLIAMS, J. B. *The Theory of Investment Value*. Amsterdam: North-Holland, 1956 (reprint of 1938 edition).

10

Measuring Abnormal Performance
Do Stocks Overreact?

NAVIN CHOPRA, JOSEF LAKONISHOK,
and JAY R. RITTER

1. Introduction

The predictability of stock returns is one of the most controversial topics in financial research. Various researchers have documented predictable returns over long and short horizons for both individual securities and indices.[1] While there is now a consensus that returns are predictable, there is widespread disagreement about the underlying reasons for this predictability. Fama (1991) observes that the interpretation of the evidence on return predictability runs 'head-on into the joint-hypothesis problem; that is, does return predictability reflect rational variation through time in expected returns, irrational deviations of price from fundamental value, or some combination of the two?'

One of the most influential, and controversial, papers in this line of research is by De Bondt and Thaler (1985), who present evidence of economically-important return reversals over long intervals. In particular, stocks that experience poor performance over the past three-to-five

---

1. Among the many recent studies documenting time-series return predictability for long and short horizons are Rosenberg, Reid, and Lanstein (1985), Keim and Stambaugh (1986), Fama and French (1988), Lo and MacKinlay (1988), Poterba and Summers (1988), Conrad and Kaul (1989), Jegadeesh (1990), Lehmann (1990), Jegadeesh and Titman (1991), and Brock, Lakonishok, and LeBaron (1992).

From: *Journal of Financial Economics*, vol. 31, pp. 235–268, 1992. Reprinted by permission of Elsevier Sequoia S.A.

years (losers) tend to substantially outperform prior-period winners during the subsequent three-to-five years. De Bondt and Thaler interpret their evidence as a manifestation of irrational behavior by investors, which they term 'overreaction'.

Various authors [e.g., Chan (1988) and Ball and Kothari (1989)], however, have argued that these return reversals are due primarily to systematic changes in equilibrium-required returns that are not captured by De Bondt and Thaler. One of the main arguments for why required returns on extreme winners and losers vary substantially follows from pronounced changes in leverage. Since the equity beta of a firm is a function of both asset risk and leverage, a series of negative abnormal returns will increase the equity beta of a firm, thus increasing the expected return on the stock (assuming that the asset beta is positive and does not decrease substantially, and that the firm does not change its debt to fully offset the decline in the value of its equity). Following the same logic, a decrease in the equity beta is expected for winners. Consistent with the prediction of the leverage hypothesis, Ball and Kothari report that the betas of extreme losers exceed the betas of extreme winners by a full 0.76 following the portfolio formation period. Such a large difference in betas, coupled with historical risk premiums, can account for substantial differences in realized returns.

Another reason that has been advanced for why losers outperform winners relates to the size effect. Zarowin (1990) and others have argued that the superior performance of losers relative to winners is not due to investor overreaction, but instead is a manifestation of the size and/or January effects, in that by the end of the ranking period, losers tend to be smaller-sized firms than winners.

In general, attempts to discriminate between market inefficiency and changing equilibrium-required returns are most difficult when long return intervals are used. This is because the measurement of abnormal performance over long horizons is very sensitive to the performance benchmark used, as emphasized by Dimson and Marsh (1986). In this paper, in addition to allowing time variation in betas, as recently applied in this context by Ball and Kothari (1989), we use three methodological innovations that enable us to perform a comprehensive evaluation of the overreaction hypothesis. Our methodology is applicable to any study measuring abnormal performance over long horizons.

First, we use the empirically-determined price of beta risk, rather than that assumed by a specific highly-structured model such as the Sharpe–Lintner capital asset pricing model (CAPM). Since the betas of extreme prior-period winners and losers differ dramatically, large differences in returns between winners and losers can be accounted for by the

Sharpe–Lintner CAPM, in which the compensation per unit of beta risk is $r_m - r_f$, where r_m is the return on the market and r_f is the risk-free rate. In the 1931–82 period, $r_m - r_f$ averages almost 15% per year using an equally-weighted index of NYSE stocks for r_m and Treasury bills for r_f. The Sharpe-Lintner CAPM assumption is innocuous in many other studies, where the portfolio betas typically do not differ much from 1.0. But in this study, the betas of winners are markedly different from the betas of losers. Numerous empirical studies, starting with Black, Jensen, and Scholes (1972), find a much flatter slope than that assumed by the Sharpe–Lintner CAPM.[2] Indeed, Fama and French (1992) question whether there is any relation at all between beta and realized returns.

Second, we calculate abnormal returns using a comprehensive adjustment for size. Numerous studies have found a relation between size and future returns. Portfolios of losers are typically comprised of smaller stocks than portfolios of winners. Thus, in order to ascertain whether there is an independent overreaction effect, a size adjustment is appropriate. However, because small-firm portfolios contain proportionately more losers, the common procedure of adjusting for size might overadjust and thus create a bias against finding an independent overreaction effect. To address this possibility, we purge stocks with extreme performance from our size-control portfolios.[3] Our methodology enables us to disentangle the effects of size and prior performance in calculating abnormal returns on winner and loser portfolios. In addition, we explore the generality of the effect in both January and non-January months.

Third, we examine abnormal returns over short periods of time. Abnormal returns calculated over long intervals are inherently sensitive to the benchmark used. Currently, there is no consensus on the 'best' benchmark, and research documenting abnormal returns calculated over long intervals is frequently treated with suspicion. Therefore, in one of our tests, we focus on short windows in which a relatively large amount of new information is disseminated, an approach analogous to that employed by Bernard and Thomas (1989, 1990) in their investigation of

2. Black, Jensen, and Scholes (1972), Miller and Scholes (1972), Fama and MacBeth (1973), Tinic and West (1984), Lakonishok and Shapiro (1986), Amihud and Mendelson (1989), and Ritter and Chopra (1989), among others, find flatter slopes than predicted by the Sharpe–Lintner CAPM.

3. Fama and French (1986) use a nearly identical procedure for controlling for size effects. For size deciles, they compare the average return on prior winners and losers with stocks in the same size decile that were in the middle 50% of returns during the portfolio formation period. They use continuously-compounded returns over three-year periods rather than the annual arithmetic returns over five-year periods that we use, but obtain somewhat similar results to those reported here.

abnormal returns following earnings announcements. We compute abnormal returns for winners and losers for the three-day period in which quarterly earnings announcements occur. Positive abnormal returns at subsequent earnings announcements for prior losers, and negative abnormal returns for prior winners, are consistent with the overreaction hypothesis. In drawing our inferences, we are careful in adjusting for size effects and the higher volatility that other researchers [e.g., Chari, Jagannathan, and Ofer (1988)] have documented at earnings announcement dates.

Our results indicate that there is an economically-significant overreaction effect present in the stock market. Moreover, it is unlikely that this effect can be attributed to risk measurement problems, since returns consistent with the overreaction hypothesis are also observed for short windows around quarterly earnings announcements. Depending upon the procedure employed, extreme losers outperform extreme winners by 5–10% per year in the years following the portfolio formation period. Interestingly, the overreaction effect is much stronger among smaller firms, which are predominantly held by individuals; there is at most only weak evidence of an overreaction effect among the largest firms, which are predominantly held by institutions. One interpretation of our findings might be that individuals overreact, but institutions do not.

There is a strong January seasonal in the return patterns, but long-term overreaction is not merely a manifestation of tax-loss selling effects, as captured by the prior year's performance. To examine this issue, we form portfolios based upon prior one-year returns, and examine the performance of these portfolios over the subsequent five years. One-year and five-year formation periods produce dramatically different patterns in returns during the subsequent five years. We find much smaller differences in returns between extreme portfolios when portfolios are formed based upon one-year returns rather than five-year returns. Much of this difference in behavior occurs in the first of the five post-ranking years: portfolios of winners and losers formed on the basis of one-year returns display momentum, rather than immediate return reversals.

The structure of the remainder of this paper is as follows. In section 2, we measure the extent of abnormal performance for portfolios formed on the basis of prior returns while alternately controlling for beta and size effects. In section 3, we present evidence on the abnormal returns for winners and losers while simultaneously controlling for beta and size effects. We also explore seasonal and cross-sectional patterns in the extent of overreaction. In section 4, we present evidence from the market's reaction to earnings announcements. Section 5 concludes the paper.

2. Beta and Size-Adjusted Abnormal Returns

2.1 Methodology

For comparability with prior studies [e.g., Ball and Kothari (1989)] we use the CRSP monthly tape of New York Stock Exchange issues from 1926 to 1986. All stocks that are continuously listed for the prior five calendar years are ranked each year on the basis of their five-year buy-and-hold returns and assigned to one of twenty portfolios. Thus, the first ranking period ends in December 1930, and the last one ends in December 1981, a total of 52 ranking periods. The post-ranking periods are overlapping five-year intervals starting with 1931–35 and ending with 1982–86. For each of the twenty portfolios, this procedure results in a time series of 52 portfolio returns for each of the ten event years -4 to $+5$, with the last year of the ranking period designated as year 0. These 52 observations are used to estimate betas and abnormal returns for the ten event years.

Annual portfolio returns for each firm are constructed from the monthly CRSP returns by compounding the monthly returns in a calendar year to create an annual buy-and-hold return. The annual returns of the firms assigned to a portfolio are then averaged to get the portfolio's annual return. If a firm is delisted within a calendar year, its annual return for that year is calculated by using the CRSP equally-weighted index return for the remainder of that year. In subsequent years, the firm is deleted from the portfolio.

To estimate the market model coefficients, we use Ibbotson's (1975) returns across time and securities (RATS) procedure. For each event year $\tau = -4, \ldots, 0, +1, \ldots, +5$ and portfolio p, we run the following regression using 52 observations:

$$r_{pt}(\tau) - r_{ft}(\tau) = \alpha_p(\tau) + \beta_p(\tau)[r_{mt} - r_{ft}] + e_{pt}(\tau), \tag{1}$$

where $r_{pt}(\tau)$ is the annual return on portfolio p in calendar year t and event year τ, r_{mt} is the equally-weighted market return on NYSE stocks meeting our sample selection criteria in calendar year t, and r_{ft} is the annual return on T-bills [from Ibbotson Associates (1988)]. The intercept in eq. (1) is known as Jensen's (1969) alpha, and is a measure of abnormal performance.

2.2 Beta-Adjusted Excess Returns

In columns (1)–(3) of table 1, we have formed portfolios by ranking firms according to their prior five-year returns. We report the annual returns,

Table 1 Average annual post-ranking-period percentage returns, alphas, and betas for twenty portfolios formed on the basis of either ranking-period returns or ranking-period betas. Average monthly post-ranking-period percentage returns, alphas, and betas are also reported for portfolios formed on the basis of five-year ranking-period returns.

Alphas and betas are estimated from time-series regressions with 52 observations, for ranking periods ending in 1930–81, for each of the five post-ranking years. The alphas and betas reported are the averages of these five post-ranking-period numbers. In columns (1)–(5) and (9)–(11), portfolio 1 is comprised of stocks with the lowest ranking-period returns, and portfolio 20 is comprised of the stocks with the highest ranking-period returns. In columns (6)–(8), portfolio 1 is comprised of stocks having the highest ranking-period betas, and portfolio 20 is comprised of stocks having the lowest ranking-period betas. EW and VW are, respectively, equally-weighted and value-weighted market indices of NYSE stocks. Columns (1)–(8) are based upon annual returns, whereas columns (9)–(11) are based upon monthly returns.

| | Portfolios Formed on the Basis of Ranking-Period Returns | | | | | Portfolios Formed on the Basis of Ranking-Period Betas | | | Portfolios Formed on the Basis of Ranking-Period Returns | | |
| | Average Annual Return (%) | Computed Using EW Index | | Computed Using VW Index | | Average Annual Return (%) | Computed Using EW Index | | Average Monthly Return (%) | Computed Using EW Index | |
Port-folio	(1)	Alpha (2)	Beta (3)	Alpha (4)	Beta (5)	(6)	Alpha (7)	Beta (8)	(9)	Alpha (10)	Beta (11)
1	27.3	−0.2	1.65	2.7	1.95	21.0	−3.0	1.42	2.36	0.26	1.52
2	23.0	0.5	1.31	2.5	1.62	19.4	−3.5	1.34	1.90	0.07	1.30

270

3	21.0	0.1	1.20	1.9	1.51	20.3	−1.2	1.25	1.80	0.05	1.23
4	21.2	0.9	1.16	2.9	1.45	20.4	−0.8	1.22	1.73	0.09	1.14
5	20.5	1.2	1.09	2.8	1.39	21.0	−0.6	1.24	1.65	0.09	1.07
6	19.9	0.7	1.08	2.2	1.40	20.2	0.0	1.15	1.59	0.06	1.05
7	19.4	0.0	1.09	1.6	1.40	20.2	0.1	1.14	1.52	0.01	1.03
8	18.5	1.5	0.94	2.9	1.24	19.8	0.1	1.12	1.48	0.06	0.95
9	17.6	0.2	0.95	1.7	1.26	18.5	−0.2	1.04	1.41	−0.03	0.98
10	17.8	0.7	0.94	2.1	1.24	18.3	−0.5	1.06	1.43	0.03	0.94
11	16.9	0.2	0.91	1.4	1.22	19.3	0.5	1.05	1.35	−0.04	0.93
12	16.6	0.1	0.89	1.2	1.22	17.3	0.0	0.95	1.34	−0.03	0.92
13	16.7	0.2	0.90	1.4	1.22	17.2	0.4	0.91	1.33	−0.00	0.88
14	16.1	−0.2	0.88	0.8	1.21	17.2	0.8	0.89	1.29	−0.06	0.90
15	15.5	−0.2	0.84	0.9	1.16	16.2	0.9	0.82	1.25	−0.07	0.87
16	15.3	−0.6	0.85	0.3	1.18	15.4	0.6	0.78	1.20	−0.07	0.83
17	14.6	0.1	0.76	1.0	1.08	15.2	1.4	0.72	1.16	−0.05	0.78
18	14.5	−1.3	0.85	−0.5	1.18	14.2	1.7	0.62	1.10	−0.12	0.79
19	14.3	−1.3	0.84	−0.7	1.19	14.4	1.1	0.67	1.11	−0.12	0.79
20	13.3	−2.7	0.86	−2.0	1.21	13.7	2.1	0.56	1.01	−0.24	0.81
Mean	18.0	0.0	1.00	1.35	1.32	18.0	0.0	1.00	1.45	−0.06	0.98
$r_1 - r_{20}$	14.0	2.5	0.79	4.7	0.74	7.3	−5.1	0.86	1.35	0.50	0.71

alphas, and betas averaged over the five years following the portfolio formation (ranking) period.[4] Our numbers are slightly different from those reported in Ball and Kothari's (1989) table 1 because of the different sample selection criteria employed. Ball and Kothari require that their firms remain listed on the NYSE for the entire five-year post-ranking period, whereas we do not impose such a requirement. Their sample selection criteria imposes a survivorship bias. In our sample, approximately 22% of the extreme loser portfolio's firms are delisted by the end of the post-ranking period, but only 8% of the extreme winner portfolio's firms are delisted. (In the 1930s, many of the delistings occurred due to bankruptcies, whereas by the 1970s, takeovers are the main reason for delistings. As might be expected, bankruptcies are rare among the extreme winners.)

The most striking result in table 1 is the inverse relation between the past and subsequent returns. Portfolio 1 (the prior-period losers) has a post-ranking-period average annual return of 27.3%, while portfolio 20 (the prior-period winners) has a post-ranking-period average annual return of 13.3%, a difference of 14.0% per year.[5] Over the five-year post-ranking period, even before compounding, this difference cumulates to 70%! The debate revolves around how much of this difference is attributable to equilibrium compensation for risk differences, and how much is an abnormal return. In fact, as demonstrated by Ball and Kothari, much

4. Two issues (at least) are raised by the procedure of averaging the returns, alphas, and betas over the five post-ranking years. First, since the last price of the ranking period is the first price of the post-ranking period, negative serial correlation might be induced by bid–ask spread effects. To examine the sensitivity of our results to this issue, in work not reported here, we have also calculated average returns, alphas, and betas using only event years +2 to +5. Our results are nearly identical to those found using event years +1 to +5. This raises the second issue: if the return reversals are due to overreaction, with firms whose market price has deviated from fundamental value eventually reverting, how long does this reversion take? One might expect a stronger reversion in event years +1 and +2 than in years +4 and +5. This is in fact the case: the per-year abnormal returns are slightly greater when a three-year post-ranking period is used rather than a five-year post-ranking period.

5. De Bondt and Thaler (1985) find a smaller difference in post-ranking-period returns between winners and losers than we (and Ball and Kothari) do. In their fig. 3, they find a difference of about 8% per year for their five-year post-ranking period, compared to our 14% per year. There are a number of reasons for this difference, most notably because the definition of extreme winners and losers is not the same. In most of their work, De Bondt and Thaler define their portfolios as the most extreme 35 firms in each year, whereas the number of firms in each of our portfolios increases from about 20 in the 1930s to about 50 in the 1970s, averaging about 43 firms. Further differences are that our last ranking period ends in 1981, whereas their last ranking period ends in 1978, and they use monthly return intervals versus our annual return intervals.

of this difference can be explained by the Sharpe–Lintner CAPM. According to column (3) of table 1, the difference in post-ranking betas between the extreme winner and loser portfolios is 0.79. Given a market risk premium $(r_m - r_f)$ in the 14–15% range using an equally-weighted portfolio of NYSE stocks, the CAPM predicts a difference in returns of approximately 11%, leaving only about 3% of the 14.0% difference unaccounted for. Indeed, using this approach, Ball and Kothari report a difference in alphas between extreme winner and loser portfolios of 3.9% per year, which they view as economically insignificant. Using our sample, we find an even smaller difference in alphas between extreme portfolios: only 2.5% per year.

Although not apparent from the numbers reported in table 1, the beta estimates for winners and losers are very different depending on whether the realized market risk premium $(r_m - r_f)$ is positive or negative. This raises a question, discussed in the appendix, about what beta really is measuring. Table 7 reports the beta estimates for up and down markets separately.

The conclusion that most of the difference in post-ranking returns between winners and losers can be accounted for as compensation for risk bearing is heavily dependent upon the Sharpe–Lintner CAPM's assumption that the return per unit of beta risk provided by the market is $r_m - r_f$. However, numerous empirical studies (see footnote 2) have invariably found a much flatter slope.

In order to estimate the empirical relation between risk and return, we form portfolios on the basis of ranking-period betas, using the same sample and the same methodology as in columns (1)–(3). The ranking-period beta of each firm has been calculated on the basis of a 60-observation regression using monthly returns during the ranking period. For each of the 52 ranking periods, firms are then ranked on the basis of these betas, and assigned to one of twenty portfolios. The post-ranking-period portfolio betas are then estimated using the RATS procedure during each of the five post-ranking years with annual returns. In columns (6)–(8), we report the average annual returns and the average alphas and betas computed using the RATS methodology for the five post-ranking years for portfolios formed on the basis of ranking-period betas. The dispersion in betas between the extreme portfolios reported in column (8) is 0.86, slightly greater than the 0.79 reported in column (3). This large difference in betas in column (8), however, is associated with a difference in returns between the two extreme portfolios of only 7.3%, dramatically less than the 14.0% reported when portfolios are formed on the basis of ranked prior returns. It should be noted that the only difference between columns (1)–(3) and (6)–(8) is in how the portfolios are formed: the universe of firms and the estimation methodology are identical.

Using the twenty post-ranking-period portfolio returns and betas reported in columns (6) and (8), respectively, we estimate the market compensation per unit of beta risk. The resulting regression has an intercept of 8.5% and a slope of 9.5%. These coefficients are consistent with those reported by other researchers (see footnote 2). Note that the 8.5% intercept is considerably higher than the average risk-free rate during the sample period of about 3.5%, and the slope coefficient of 9.5% is considerably lower than the 14–15% market risk premium. (In fact, the RATS procedure may overestimate the relation between realized returns and beta, because the betas are estimated contemporaneously with the post-ranking-period returns.) In other words, differences in betas do not generate differences in returns during the sample period as great as assumed by the Sharpe–Lintner CAPM.

In figs. 1a and 1b, we have plotted the regression equation estimated from the twenty portfolios formed on the basis of prior betas. The two extreme winner and loser portfolios are also plotted. In fig. 1a, we use annual data from columns (6) and (8) of table 1. In fig. 1b, we use monthly data (not reported in table 1). Using annual data, the extreme winner portfolio underperforms a portfolio with the same beta by 3.4%, while the extreme loser portfolio outperforms a portfolio with the same beta by 3.1%. Thus, the difference in abnormal returns is 6.5%, substantially higher than the 2.5% reported in column (2). The difference between these two numbers is attributable to different assumptions about the slope of the security market line (SML). Using the Sharpe–Lintner model's theoretical risk premium results in a lower estimate of the overreaction effect than when the empirical risk premium is used.

To examine the sensitivity of the results to the choice of a market index, columns (4) and (5) present results for annual measurement intervals using a value-weighted market index. The betas are all above 1.0, reflecting the fact that the equally-weighted index itself has a beta of 1.3 with respect to the value-weighted index. The difference in alphas between the extreme winners and losers widens from the 2.5% reported using an equally-weighted market index to 4.7% using a value-weighted index. Using the empirical security market line increases these spreads.

The discussion so far has focused on annual measurement intervals, even though monthly measurement intervals are much more commonly used in financial research. To examine the sensitivity of the results to the use of different measurement intervals, in columns (9)–(11) of table 1 we report monthly returns, alphas, and betas using an equally-weighted index. This procedure produces a slightly smaller spread in betas (0.71 vs 0.79 when annual measurement intervals are used) and a greater differ-

Figure 1a   Plot of the empirical security market line (SML) calculated using annual data from the realized post-ranking-period returns and betas for twenty portfolios formed on the basis of ranking-period betas, and the realized post-ranking-period return on extreme winner and loser portfolios.

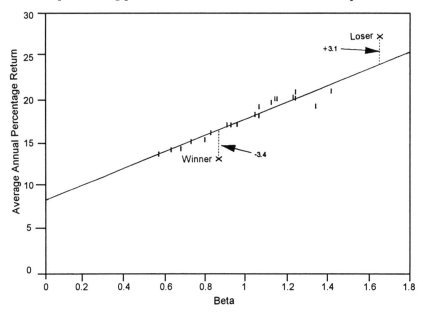

The empirical SML is estimated from the twenty portfolio returns and betas reported in columns (6) and (8) of table 1. The empirical SML has an intercept of 8.5% and a slope of 9.5%. Alphas are calculated as deviations from the empirical SML.

ence in abnormal returns (0.50% per month, or 6.0% per year) between extreme winner and loser portfolios. Using the empirical security market line calculated from monthly data with portfolios formed on the basis of ranked prior betas, extreme losers outperform extreme winners by 9.5% per year. With a value-weighted index and monthly data, the difference in alphas between extreme losers and winners is 12% per year using the Sharpe–Lintner model as the benchmark.[6] (These results are not reported here.) Applying a benchmark based upon the empirical security market line yields an even larger difference.

6. A caveat is in order, however, in regard to the use of monthly returns. As Conrad and Kaul (1991) discuss, monthly arithmetic returns on low-priced stocks are biased upwards in a manner that overestimates the magnitude of size and prior return effects. This is because small firms and losers are more frequently low-priced stocks. Our annual return measures, however, suffer from minimal bias.

Figure 1b   Similar to figure 1a, except that monthly returns are used, which are then annualized by multiplying by 12 before plotting.

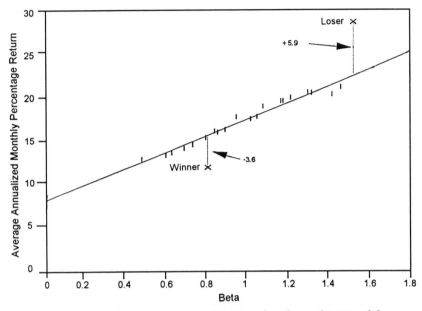

The empirical SML has an intercept of 8.2% and a slope of 9.3%. Alphas are calculated as deviations from the empirical SML. The mean annualized return is 17.5% rather than the 18.0% in figure 1a due to our procedure of multiplying the average monthly returns by 12, rather than compounding them.

2.3 Size-Adjusted Excess Returns

We have focused thus far on adjusting for differences in betas between winners and losers. However, winners and losers differ on another dimension as well. Prior research [e.g., Zarowin (1990)] has found that losers have lower market capitalizations than winners, on average, indicating that measurement of excess returns must be careful to control for size effects. The correlation of size and prior returns is apparent in fig. 2, which plots the percentage of each size quintile that falls into each prior return quintile. (We plot quintile results, rather than the twenty portfolios that we use in the empirical work, to minimize the clutter that would otherwise obscure the figure.) For example, fig. 2 shows that in the smallest size quintile, 40% of the firms are in the extreme loser quintile, while only 10% are in the extreme winner quintile. Because of this correlation between size and prior returns, a simple size adjustment may cause the extent of any overreaction effect to be underestimated.

Figure 2   The joint distribution of firms categorized by size and prior returns.

Percentage of
size quintile

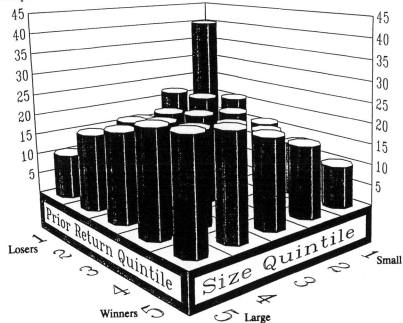

For each size quintile, the percentage of firms falling in each prior return quintile is plotted. Quintile portfolios are plotted rather than the twenty portfolios used in the empirical work because 400 portfolios (20 × 20) produces too cluttered a figure compared with the 25 portfolios plotted.

In fig. 3, we plot the joint distribution of annual raw percentage returns for the same quintile portfolios used in fig. 2. Inspection of this figure shows that, holding size constant, returns are higher the lower are prior returns, and holding prior returns constant, returns are higher the smaller is size. On average, holding size constant, the extreme loser quintile has a 5.4% higher average annual return than the extreme winner quintile. On average, holding prior returns constant, the smallest size quintile has an 8.2% higher average annual return than the largest size quintile.

In column (1) of table 2, we report the average annual returns on twenty portfolios [these numbers are the same as in column (1) of table 1]. In column (2), we report the returns on control portfolios formed by matching on size, which we refer to as size-control portfolios. To construct the size-control portfolios, we rank the population of firms at the

Figure 3   The joint distribution of average annual returns in the post-ranking period categorized by size and prior returns.

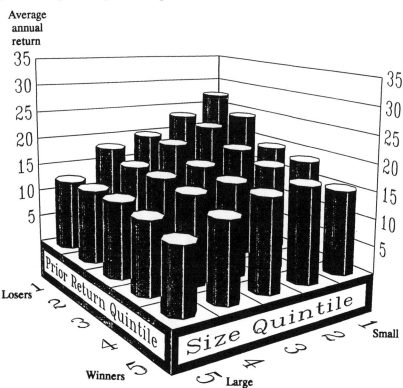

The average annual return on the smallest quintile of losers is 27.37%, while the average annual return on the largest quintile of winners is 11.59%.

end of each of the 52 portfolio formation periods on the basis of market capitalization, and then assign the firms to twenty portfolios formed on the basis of size. In computing the average annual returns on the twenty size portfolios, we follow the same procedure used in table 1 with the twenty prior-return portfolios. For each of the twenty prior-return portfolios, we form a size-control portfolio. This size-control portfolio is constructed to have the same size composition as its corresponding prior return portfolio, with the weights being determined by the proportion of the prior-return portfolio that falls in each size classification.

In column (3) of table 2, we report the average annual returns on size-control portfolios formed in a manner identical to that employed in column (2), with the exception that the population of firms from which the size portfolios are drawn has been purged of firms in prior return

Table 2   Average annual post-ranking-period percentage returns for twenty portfolios of firms ranked by their five-year ranking-period returns, size-control portfolios with and without losers and winners purged, and the associated size-adjusted returns.

The twenty size-control portfolios are constructed to have approximately the same market values as the twenty ranked portfolios. Excess returns are computed two different ways: (i) size-adjusted returns using all firms (unpurged) and (ii) size-adjusted returns after the portfolios have been purged of all firms in the top five and the bottom five portfolios of prior returns (purged).

Portfolio	Average Annual Return (%) in Years +1 to +5				Size-Adj. Returns (%) $e = r_p - r_s$	
		Control Firms				
	Ranked Firms (r_p) (1)	Unpurged (r_s) (2)	Purged (r_s) (3)	Difference (2)–(3) (4)	Unpurged (1)–(2) (5)	Purged (1)–(3) (6)
1	27.3	23.4	20.4	3.0	3.9	6.9
2	23.0	21.3	19.3	2.0	1.7	3.7
3	21.0	20.6	19.0	1.6	0.4	2.0
4	21.2	20.0	18.8	1.2	1.2	2.4
5	20.5	19.4	18.0	1.4	1.1	2.5
6	19.9	18.8	18.0	0.8	1.1	1.9
7	19.4	18.9	18.1	0.8	0.5	1.3
8	18.5	18.1	17.6	0.5	0.4	0.9
9	17.6	17.9	17.4	0.5	−0.3	0.2
10	17.8	17.5	17.2	0.3	0.3	0.6
11	16.9	17.3	16.9	0.4	−0.4	0.0
12	16.6	17.0	16.7	0.3	−0.4	−0.1
13	16.7	16.9	16.8	0.1	−0.2	−0.1
14	16.1	16.6	16.3	0.3	−0.5	−0.2
15	15.5	16.6	16.4	0.2	−1.1	−0.9
16	15.3	16.6	16.4	0.2	−1.3	−1.1
17	14.6	16.2	16.1	0.1	−1.6	−1.5
18	14.5	16.0	16.1	−0.1	−1.5	−1.6
19	14.3	16.0	15.9	0.1	−1.7	−1.6
20	13.3	16.0	16.1	−0.1	−2.7	−2.8
Mean	18.0	18.0	17.4	0.06	0.0	0.6
$r_1 - r_{20}$	14.0	7.4	4.3	3.1	6.6	9.7

portfolios 1–5 (losers) and 16–20 (winners). Because of the correlation of size and prior returns, more than 50% of the smallest (and largest) firms are purged, and slightly less than 50% of moderate-size firms are purged. The purpose of this purging is to minimize the confounding of any overreaction effects with size effects.

In column (5) of table 2, we report excess returns computed by subtracting the unpurged size-control returns. There is a nearly monotonic decrease in the excess returns as one goes from portfolio 1 (the losers) to portfolio 20 (the winners). The difference in excess returns between the extreme portfolios is 6.6% per year during the five post-ranking years.

In column (6), we report the excess returns computed using the purged size-control portfolios. The pattern in column (5) is accentuated, confirming our conjecture that controlling for size without taking the correlation of size and prior returns into account understates the overreaction effect. The difference between the extreme portfolio excess returns is 9.7% per year during the five post-ranking years. From these numbers, it appears that there is an economically-significant overreaction effect above and beyond any size effect.

2.4 Seasonal Patterns in Returns, Tax-Loss Selling, and Momentum

In table 3, we report the average post-ranking-period raw and size-adjusted (using purged size controls) returns using annual, January, and February–December returns. The February–December returns are 11-month returns, computed by compounding the monthly returns. In columns (1)–(6), the portfolios are formed on the basis of five-year prior returns; the annual numbers are identical to those reported in columns (1) and (6) of table 2. In columns (7)–(12), the portfolios are formed on the basis of one-year prior returns, although the post-ranking period remains five years. The population of returns used in columns (1)–(6) and (7)–(12) are identical; what is different is the ranking criteria to form the twenty portfolios.

Inspection of columns (1)–(6) discloses that the overreaction effect is disproportionately concentrated in January, consistent with the graphical evidence presented in De Bondt and Thaler's (1985) fig. 3. While the differences in average annual and January returns between portfolios 1 and 20 are reliably different from zero, the February–December difference is not significantly different from zero at conventional levels for either raw returns or size-adjusted returns. The January seasonal raises the question of whether there is an independent overreaction effect, above and beyond tax-loss selling effects.

To distinguish between these two effects, in columns (7)–(12) we report returns on portfolios formed on ranked one-year returns, which should produce a cleaner measure of the influence of tax-loss selling effects. The choice of one-year formation periods to examine tax-loss selling effects is consistent with prior work in this area. [Reinganum (1983), Chan (1986), and others form portfolios based upon return intervals that correspond to the short-term capital gains holding period, which has varied from six to twelve months at various times during our sample period, and Roll (1983) uses one-year returns.] In columns (7)–(12), there are much smaller return reversals than in columns (1)–(6), and they are much more concentrated in January. Using annual size-adjusted returns, the difference in returns between the extreme winners and losers is 9.7% per year using five-year ranking periods, but only 3.5% per year using one-year ranking periods. As in columns (1)–(6), only the annual and January return differences are reliably different from zero. Although the return differences $(r_1 - r_{20})$ are generally lower in columns (7)–(12) than in columns (1)–(6), the p-values tend to be similar because there is less time-series variability and less autocorrelation in the portfolio return series when one-year ranking periods are used than when five-year ranking periods are used.

In the last row of the table, we report the results of a test of the hypothesis that the return differences $(r_1 - r_{20})$ using five-year ranking periods are the same as those using one-year ranking periods. The p-values of 0.002 to 0.037 indicate that the higher return differences using five-year ranking periods are generally reliably so, even in February–December.

While the portfolios formed on the basis of five-year returns display greater return reversals during the subsequent five years than those formed on the basis of one-year returns, an interesting pattern is obscured. Specifically, the portfolios formed on the basis of one-year returns display return *momentum*, as shown in the row '$r_1 - r_{20}$ in year $+1$'. In this row, we report the average difference in returns on extreme portfolios during the first post-ranking year. Focusing on size-adjusted returns, in the first post-ranking year, prior five-year losers outperform winners by 11.0% in column (4), whereas prior one-year losers *underperform* winners by 8.6% in column (10). This underperformance is entirely in the February–December period, where column (12) reports that one-year losers underperform winners by 15.2%. In plain English, when winners and losers are chosen on the basis of one-year returns, losers continue to lose and winners continue to win during the next year. Similar momentum patterns are also reported by De Bondt and Thaler (1985, table 1), Ball and Kothari (1989, table 5), and Jegadeesh and Titman (1991). These momentum patterns may explain the Value Line anomaly

Table 3 Seasonal patterns in raw returns and size-adjusted returns for ranking periods of five years and one year.[a]

| | Five-Year Ranking Periods | | | | | | One-Year Ranking Periods | | | | | |
| | Av. Raw Returns (%) | | | Avg. Size-Adj. Returns[b] (%) | | | Avg. Raw Returns (%) | | | Avg. Size-Adj. Returns[b] (%) | | |
Portfolio	Annual (1)	Jan. (2)	Feb.–Dec. (3)	Annual (4)	Jan. (5)	Feb.–Dec. (6)	Annual (7)	Jan. (8)	Feb.–Dec. (9)	Annual (10)	Jan. (11)	Feb.–Dec. (12)
1	27.3	13.1	12.9	6.9	7.2	-0.8	23.5	11.2	11.3	2.6	4.7	-2.2
2	23.0	8.8	13.3	3.7	3.5	0.1	20.5	7.4	12.0	1.3	1.9	-1.0
3	21.0	7.4	12.9	2.0	2.5	-0.4	19.8	6.6	12.4	0.9	1.4	-0.5
4	21.2	6.6	13.8	2.4	1.7	0.7	18.4	5.9	11.9	0.1	0.8	-0.6
5	20.5	5.7	14.0	2.5	1.2	1.2	18.7	5.5	12.6	1.0	0.8	0.4
6	19.9	5.6	13.5	1.9	1.2	0.5	18.1	5.3	12.1	0.3	0.7	-0.4
7	19.4	5.1	13.6	1.3	0.9	0.5	17.5	5.0	12.0	-0.3	0.4	-0.5
8	18.5	4.7	13.2	0.9	0.5	0.5	18.2	4.6	12.8	0.7	0.2	0.3
9	17.6	4.5	12.4	0.2	0.4	-0.2	16.8	4.4	11.8	-0.4	0.1	-0.5
10	17.8	4.2	13.0	0.6	0.2	0.5	17.5	4.0	12.8	0.2	-0.2	0.4
11	16.9	4.1	12.3	0.0	0.1	0.1	16.9	4.3	12.3	-0.6	0.0	-0.2
12	16.6	3.9	12.2	-0.1	0.0	-0.1	17.6	4.0	12.8	0.3	-0.1	0.3
13	16.7	3.6	12.6	-0.1	-0.1	0.2	17.0	3.9	12.5	0.0	-0.3	0.3
14	16.1	3.3	12.3	-0.2	-0.3	0.3	16.7	3.8	12.3	-0.5	-0.4	0.0
15	15.5	3.3	11.8	-0.9	-0.3	-0.4	16.8	3.6	12.7	0.0	-0.4	0.5
16	15.3	3.2	11.4	-1.1	-0.4	-0.8	16.9	3.7	12.6	-0.1	-0.3	0.3
17	14.6	3.1	11.0	-1.5	-0.5	-0.9	16.9	3.5	12.7	0.1	-0.6	0.7
18	14.5	3.0	10.8	-1.6	-0.4	-1.2	16.3	3.6	12.2	-1.2	-0.7	-0.3

19	14.3	2.7	10.9	−1.6	−0.7	−1.0	17.5	3.7	13.1	−0.4	−0.8	0.5
20	13.3	2.6	10.0	−2.8	−0.7	−2.1	17.7	4.3	12.8	−0.9	−0.6	−0.1
$r_1 - r_{20}$[c]	14.0	10.5	2.9	9.7	7.9	1.3	5.8	6.9	−1.5	3.5	5.3	−2.1
p-values[c]	0.001	0.001	0.105	0.005	0.004	0.273	0.001	0.001	0.072	0.004	0.001	0.024
$r_1 - r_{20}$ in year +1[d]	15.3	15.1	−0.7	11.0	12.6	−2.6	−7.2	8.6	−15.1	−8.6	7.2	−15.2
p-values[e]	0.011	0.000	0.425	0.028	0.000	0.176	0.013	0.000	0.000	0.004	0.000	0.000

Tests of the hypothesis that $r_1 - r_{20}$ with five-year ranking periods = $r_1 - r_{20}$ in year +1' = $r_1 - r_{20}$ with one-year ranking periods:

| p-values[f] | 0.002 | 0.003 | 0.007 | 0.009 | 0.035 | 0.037 |

a. All numbers, except for the row labeled '$r_1 - r_{20}$ in year +1', are the equally-weighted averages of the five post-ranking years, for all 52 post-ranking periods beginning in 1931–1982. The January returns are monthly averages. The February–December returns are averages of eleven-month compounded returns.

b. The size-control portfolios have been purged of extreme winners and losers, using the procedures described in table 2. The purged firms for the one-year ranking periods are those in the bottom 25% and the top 25% of one-year returns.

c. The p-values test the hypothesis that the mean value of $r_1 - r_{20}$ is zero; p-values are computed adjusting for fourth-order autocorrelation as follows, and the standard deviation of the mean value of $r_1 - r_{20}$ is computed as

$$\text{s.d.} = \frac{\sigma}{T}\sqrt{T + 2(T-1)\rho_1 + 2(T-2)\rho_2 + 2(T-3)\rho_3 + 2(T-4)\rho_4},$$

with $T = 52$, where σ is the standard deviation of the portfolio returns and ρ_n is the estimated nth-order simple autocorrelation coefficient. (Four lags are used because of the five-year overlapping post-ranking periods.) The T observations are the time series of five-year average portfolio returns, expressed as annual numbers.

d. The numbers in this row represent the average value of $r_1 - r_{20}$ in the first year of the five post-ranking years.

e. The p-values test the hypothesis that the mean value of $r_1 - r_{20}$ is zero. A time series of 52 nonoverlapping year + 1 observations are used to calculate the standard deviation of the mean, adjusting for first-order autocorrelation. The autocorrelation coefficients are as high as 0.406 for the size-adjusted January returns in column (5). For February–December returns, the autocorrelations are insignificantly different from zero.

f. The p-values are calculated from a time-series of 52 values of $(r_1 - r_{20})_{5,t} - (r_1 - r_{20})_{1,t}$, adjusted for fourth-order autocorrelation, where $(r_1 - r_{20})_{i,t}$ is the average return difference over the five-year post-ranking period starting in year t with ranking period of length i.

[see Huberman and Kandel (1987)] and the post-earnings announcement drift anomaly [see Bernard and Thomas (1989, 1990)].

3. Multiple Regression Tests

In the previous section, we controlled for, respectively, beta and size in computing abnormal portfolio returns. In this section, we present multiple regression evidence that simultaneously incorporates the effects of beta, size, and prior returns on post-ranking period returns. This analysis uses 400 portfolios, each containing an unequal number of firms, formed on the basis of independent rankings of firm size and prior returns. For each of these portfolios, a beta is calculated from a pooled (across both post-ranking years and firms) regression, using $r_{it} - r_{ft}$ as the dependent variable and $r_{mt} - r_{ft}$ as the explanatory variable, where r_{it} is the return on firm i in year t. The portfolio excess return is also calculated as the pooled (across both firms and post-ranking years) average excess return.[7]

In table 8 of the appendix, we report results using two alternative procedures for calculating betas and returns for each of the 400 portfolios. In general, the results are qualitatively similar.

In panels A and B of table 4, we report the results of estimating eq. (2) using 400 portfolios constructed on the basis of independent rankings of prior returns and size:

$$r_p - r_f = a_0 + a_1 SIZE_p + a_2 RETURN_p + a_3 beta_p + e_p. \qquad (2)$$

The explanatory variables in panels A and B are relative market capitalization (SIZE), measured as the portfolio rank (1 small, 20 large), prior five-year returns (RETURN), measured as the portfolio rank (1 losers, 20 winners), and the portfolio beta.[8] In panel A, using annual returns, we find that all three explanatory variables are reliably different from zero

---

7. When annual returns are used, if a given portfolio, e.g., the largest extreme losers (size portfolio 20, return portfolio 1), has a total of 83 firms in it over the entire 52 formation periods (an average of 1.6 firms per formation period), there are up to 83×5 annual returns (if each of the 83 firms lasts for all five post-ranking years).

8. We have explored some alternatives to our use of portfolio rankings as measures of prior returns and size. For example, using the actual prior return rather than the portfolio rank produces a slightly better fit and a stronger measured overreaction effect. One reason for our preference for the use of portfolio rankings to measure size is that market capitalizations changed substantially over time during our 52-year sample period. This poses a problem for pooling observations over time. For a detailed discussion of some of the issues involved, see Chan, Hamao, and Lakonishok (1991). We have not attempted to conduct a comprehensive examination of alterative specifications, for this would then introduce data-snooping biases.

and the coefficients have the predicted signs. Furthermore, a large fraction of the variation in portfolio returns is explained (the R^2 is 0.68). The *RETURN* coefficient of -0.254 implies that after controlling for size and beta, extreme losers outperform extreme winners by 4.8% per year on average for the five post-ranking years. [Since *RETURN* (and *SIZE*) is measured as the portfolio rank, -0.254 multiplied by (1 minus 20) results in the 4.8% difference.] Also noteworthy is that in panel A, the coefficient on beta of 5.438% is lower than the 9.5% slope reported in fig. 1a. Apparently, estimates of the SML slope from single-variable regressions suffer from an omitted variable bias. Another aspect worth noting is that the magnitude of the overreaction effect is nearly as great as that of the size effect, as can be seen by comparing the two coefficients.

A straightforward approach to estimating the *t*-statistics for table 4 would be to use the standard errors from the pooled regressions with 400 observations. The resulting *t*-statistics, however, would be vastly overstated, because the pooled regression standard errors do not account for the time-series variability of the empirical relations. Consequently, the *t*-statistics that we report in panel A are based upon the time-series variability of the coefficients from 52 annual cross-sectional regressions. In general, these coefficients would be intertemporally dependent. Furthermore, our procedure of using overlapping post-ranking periods will induce strong autocorrelation in the parameter estimates. Thus, in computing the standard errors for the point estimates reported in panel A, we have adjusted for fourth-order autocorrelation using the formula reported in table 4. Without these adjustments, the *t*-statistics from the pooled cross-sectional regressions are approximately three times as large.

To examine the sensitivity of our conclusions to the use of annual returns rather than monthly returns (which are more commonly used in empirical studies), panel B reports results from monthly regressions. (In panels B and D, we use monthly returns to calculate betas, and we use the same procedure to calculate *t*-statistics as used in panel A.) These results, after multiplying the monthly coefficients by 12, are qualitatively similar to those in panel A. The overreaction effect is slightly stronger using monthly returns, with panel B reporting that extreme losers outperform extreme winners by 5.2% per year, ceteris paribus. The compensation per unit of beta is 4.4% per year using monthly data, a decrease from the 5.4% per year reported in panel A using annual returns.

In panels C and D, we permit the overreaction effect to vary by firm size by estimating three different slope coefficients, depending upon whether a portfolio is comprised of small, middle-size, or large firms. Panel C reveals that the overreaction effect is strongest among smaller firms. The *DS · RETURN* coefficient of -0.417 implies a 7.9% per year

Table 4   OLS regressions of average percentage excess returns for the first five post-ranking years for portfolios of NYSE firms formed on the basis of size and prior returns.

For each of the 52 ranking periods ending on December 31 of 1930 to 1981, firms are independently ranked on the basis of their December 31 market value and their five-year prior return, and assigned to one of 400 portfolios. Each portfolio beta is the pooled (over firms and post-ranking years) beta for the firms in the cell, calculated using annual returns and equally-weighted market returns. SIZE is measured as the portfolio ranking (1 to 20, with 1 being smallest), and RETURN is measured as the portfolio ranking (1 to 20, with 1 being the most extreme prior losers). In panels C and D, DS is a dummy variable equal to one if a portfolio is among the bottom 40% of SIZE vitiles, DM is a dummy variable equal to one if a portfolio is among SIZE portfolios 9 to 16 (the middle 40%), and DL is a dummy variable equal to one if a portfolio is among the largest 20% of SIZE portfolios. T-statistics are in parentheses. These are computed using a Fama–MacBeth (1973) procedure adjusted for fourth-order autocorrelation as follows: the t-statistic for coefficient a_i is computed as $a_i/\text{s.e.}$, where

$$\text{s.e.} = \frac{\sigma}{T}\sqrt{T + 2(T-1)\rho_1 + 2(T-2)\rho_2 + 2(T-3)\rho_3 + 2(T-4)\rho_4},$$

with $T = 52$, where σ is the time-series standard deviation of the coefficient estimates and ρ_t is the estimated nth-order simple autocorrelation coefficient. (Four lags are used because of the five-year overlapping post-ranking periods.) The T observations are the time series of cross-sectional regression coefficients. The first-order autocorrelations in panel A vary from 0.142 for the intercept to 0.649 for the coefficient on RETURN. The R^2 values are based upon the pooled regressions, and do not reflect the year-to-year variability in the regressions.

$$r_p - r_f = a_0 + a_1 SIZE_p + a_2 RETURN_p + a_3 Beta_p + e_p$$

Coefficient Estimates

Intercept	SIZE	RETURN	Beta	R^2_{adjusted}
Panel A: Annual Percentage Returns				
14.443	−0.364	−0.254	5.438	0.68
(10.517)	(−3.779)	(−2.996)	(1.707)	
Panel B: Monthly Percentage Returns, All Months				
1.236	−0.031	−0.023	0.369	0.68
(4.671)	(−2.926)	(−3.039)	(1.393)	

$$r_p - r_f = a_0 + a_1 SIZE_p + a_2 DS \cdot RETURN_p$$
$$+ a_3 DM \cdot RETURN_p + a_4 DL \cdot RETURN_p + a_5 Beta_p + e_p$$

Table 4   (*Continued*)

		Coefficient Estimates				
Intercept	*SIZE*	*DS · RETURN*	*DM · RETURN*	*DL · RETURN*	Beta	R^2_{adjusted}
		Panel C: Annual Percentage Returns				
18.113	−0.597	−0.417	−0.182	−0.136	4.364	0.72
(9.915)	(−5.440)	(−4.257)	(−2.009)	(−1.433)	(1.298)	
		Panel D: Monthly Percentage Returns, All Months				
1.631	−0.055	−0.039	−0.018	−0.010	0.238	0.73
(6.431)	(−5.675)	(−4.733)	(−2.235)	(−1.326)	(0.898)	

abnormal return difference between portfolios 1 and 20 for the smallest (bottom 40%) firms. For middle-size firms, this difference is 3.5%, while for the larger (upper 20%) firms, the difference is 2.6%. This relation between firm size and the extent of overreaction has not previously been emphasized.

To examine the robustness of our table 4 results, we have also run the regressions for the 1931–56 and 1957–82 subperiods. Our results (not reported here) indicate that there is a significant overreaction effect in both subperiods, although the effects are stronger in the second sub-period, in contrast to the evidence on index autocorrelations over three-to-five year periods reported by Fama and French (1988), who find weaker results for subperiods excluding the 1930s.

The evidence in panels C and D of table 4 demonstrates that the overreaction effect is stronger for smaller firms. This finding deserves further analysis. In table 5, we examine the extent of overreaction within each of ten size deciles by reporting regression results with *RETURN* and beta as explanatory variables. Each of the ten regressions uses the 40 portfolios out of the 400 formed for our table 4 analysis that correspond to the appropriate size grouping. In table 5, the coefficient on *RETURN* is generally closer to zero the larger is the size decile. The last column in the table reports the implied annual difference in returns between the extreme winner and loser portfolios, holding size and beta constant. These differences in returns are plotted in fig. 4. The numbers demonstrate that for the smaller firms an overreaction effect on the order of 10% per year (50% per five years, even before compounding) is present, while for the largest 20% of NYSE firms (roughly the S&P 500) no overreaction effect is apparent. Since individuals are the primary holders of the

Table 5   OLS regressions of annual average percentage excess returns on ranking-period returns and beta by size decile.

RETURN is measured 1 to 20 (1 = losers, 20 = winners), where prior returns are measured over the five years prior to the portfolio formation date. Firms are assigned to size deciles (1 = small, 10 = large) on the basis of their market capitalization at the end of the ranking period. The beta of each portfolio is calculated as the pooled (over firms and post-ranking years) beta. Each of the ten regressions uses forty observations (two ranks of size with twenty prior-return portfolios in each size rank). T-statistics, computed using the fourth-order autoregressive process described in table 4, are in parentheses.

$$r_p - r_f = a_0 + a_1 RETURN_p + a_2 Beta_p + e_p$$

Coefficient Estimates

Size Decile	Intercept	RETURN	Beta	$R^2_{adjusted}$	$-19 \times RETURN$ Coefficient[a]
1	9.888 (2.463)	−0.578 (−2.119)	9.980 (2.670)	0.76	10.98%
2	27.658 (4.379)	−0.729 (−6.436)	−2.784 (−0.426)	0.74	13.85%
3	21.218 (4.723)	−0.510 (−3.382)	0.402 (0.078)	0.65	9.69%
4	18.942 (6.730)	−0.350 (−3.811)	0.739 (0.242)	0.51	6.65%
5	16.356 (3.715)	−0.140 (−2.629)	−0.641 (−0.101)	0.10	2.66%
6	14.226 (1.982)	−0.293 (−2.242)	2.489 (0.288)	0.52	5.57%
7	9.149 (4.691)	−0.153 (−1.755)	4.838 (2.463)	0.51	2.91%
8	8.018 (3.012)	−0.113 (−0.764)	5.171 (1.000)	0.37	2.15%
9	6.101 (1.634)	−0.016 (−0.149)	4.524 (0.572)	0.01	0.30%
10	5.080 (1.932)	0.040 (0.327)	2.471 (0.466)	0.01	−0.76%

a. Multiplying the coefficients on RETURN by −19 gives the expected difference in annual returns for the five post-ranking years between prior-return portfolios 1 and 20, controlling for beta, for firms categorized by their size decile.

Figure 4   The difference in annual abnormal returns between extreme loser and winner portfolios by size decile.

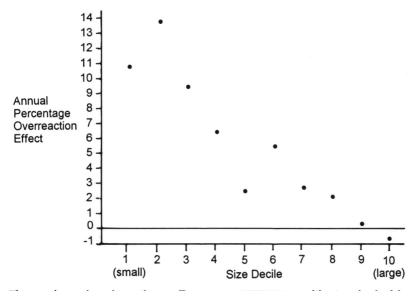

The numbers plotted are the coefficients on *RETURN* in table 5 multiplied by -19. This represents the expected difference in annual returns for the five post-ranking years between prior return portfolios 1 and 20, controlling for beta, for firms categorized by their size decile.

smaller firms, while institutions are the dominant holders of the larger firms, the results are consistent with the hypothesis that individuals over-react, while institutional investors do not.

Our finding that overreaction is concentrated among smaller firms is consistent with results reported in Fama and French (1988), where small-firm portfolios are found to have greater negative serial correlation than large-firm portfolios. Furthermore, Poterba and Summers (1988) provide evidence that there is greater long-term negative serial correlation in countries with less-developed capital markets than in countries such as the U.S. or Britain. Together, this evidence is consistent with the hypothesis that the further one moves away from large-capitalization stocks in well-developed capital markets, the more likely it is that stocks take prolonged swings away from their fundamental value.

Another noteworthy aspect of the table 5 regressions is that in contrast to the importance of the *RETURN* variable, which is statistically signifi-cant at the 0.05 level for the six smallest size deciles, the coefficient on beta is highly variable and statistically significant in only two of the ten regressions. For the largest two size deciles, which account for the majority of market capitalization, beta is far from statistically significant. For these two deciles, the compensation per unit of beta risk is substantially below the 5.4% reported in panel A of table 4 and the 9.4% reported in fig. 1a. Also noteworthy is that for these largest two deciles, the R^2s are essentially zero: neither prior returns nor beta are related to realized returns. In other words, a stock is a stock.

4. Evidence from Earnings Announcements

The evidence presented so far indicates that even after controlling for size and beta effects, there is an overreaction effect. However, because the magnitude of any effect measured over long intervals is sensitive to the benchmark employed, we also present evidence of overreaction around earnings announcements. Focusing on short windows such as the three-day period surrounding earnings announcements minimizes the sensitivity of results to misspecification of controls, which can provide further evidence on the existence of an overreaction effect. However, it cannot shed much light on the exact magnitude because there is no reason why the return towards fundamental value should occur on only a few discrete dates.

For the firms in the ranking periods ending in 1970–81, we searched the Compustat quarterly industrial, historical, and research files for their quarterly earnings announcements during the five years of the post-ranking periods.[9] Our search resulted in 227,522 earnings announcements. For each of the twenty portfolios formed by ranking firms on prior returns, we computed the average raw return for earnings announcements for a three-day window of $[-2, 0]$ relative to the Compustat-listed announcement date. This three-day window is commonly used in the earnings announcement literature [e.g., Bernard and Thomas (1990)].

In fig. 5, we plot the raw three-day earnings-announcement-period returns using the same size and prior-return quintiles as in figs. 2 and 3. The small losers have average returns of 0.958% per three days, while the large winners have average returns of 0.001% per three days.

Returning to the twenty portfolios, the average earnings-announce-

9. The quarterly industrial file contains only companies that are currently publicly-traded. The research file contains companies that were delisted. Combining these data files gives us a sample that covers almost all of the NYSE firms in our sample, but only for the most recent 48 quarters. Adding the historical data extends the sample back into the 1970s. Compustat's data on quarterly earnings announcement dates becomes progressively less comprehensive for earlier years, which is why we restrict our analysis to the 1970s and 1980s, rather than the full 52 years of data.

Figure 5 The joint distribution of three-day earnings announcement returns categorized by market capitalization and prior returns.

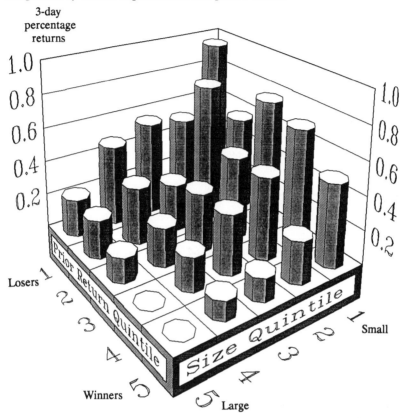

Firms are assigned to portfolios based upon independent rankings of size and prior returns. The average three-day raw return at subsequent earnings announcements is computed for Compustat-listed quarterly earnings announcement dates during the five-year post-ranking period. The average three-day raw return is 0.001% for the largest extreme winners and 0.958% for the smallest extreme losers.

ment-period return for firms in portfolio 1 (losers) is 0.63%. For firms in prior-return portfolio 20, the average earnings-announcement-period return is zero. Thus, the evidence from earnings announcements indicates that the market is systematically surprised at subsequent earnings announcements in a manner consistent with the overreaction hypothesis.

Recent research, however, finds anomalous returns at earnings announcement dates. [Much of the literature on earnings announcements is surveyed in Ball and Kothari (1991).] In particular, Chari, Jagannathan, and Ofer (1988) document that small firms tend to have higher earnings-announcement-period returns than large firms, and in our case, a disproportionate fraction of losers are small. Chari, Jagannathan, and Ofer hypothesize that because of the increased flow of information around earnings announcements, these periods are riskier than nonannouncement periods. Therefore, to examine whether past price changes affect returns around earnings announcements, we have to control for both size and risk, which we accomplish by using an approach similar to that employed in eq. (2). The analysis uses 400 portfolios formed on the basis of independent rankings of firm size and prior returns. For each of these 400 portfolios, we compute an average raw three-day holding period return. We also calculate a portfolio beta by running a pooled market model regression (over both firms and earnings announcements) using three-day announcement-period returns and three-day market returns.

In table 6 we report the results of a regression based on 394 observa-

Table 6   Regression of three-day earnings announcement portfolio returns on size, prior returns, and beta.

394 portfolios are used (400 portfolios based on independently ranking firms by size and prior return, with six portfolios deleted which had fewer than 100 earnings announcements). Size is measured with the smallest firms in portfolio 1, and the largest in portfolio 20. Prior returns (measured over the five prior years) are also ranked from 1 to 20, with 1 being the losers. Betas are calculated for each portfolio using all earnings announcement returns for all firms in the portfolio. The dependent variable is measured as the percentage return per three-day announcement period $[-2, 0]$, for earnings announcements made during the first five post-ranking years. Earnings announcement days are from Compustat's industrial, historical, and research tapes, for announcements during the five post-ranking years following the ranking periods ending in 1970–81. There are 227,522 earnings announcements. T-statistics, computed using the time-series variance of the cross-sectional regression coefficients, adjusted for first-order autocorrelation, are in parentheses.

$$R_p = a_0 + a_1 SIZE_p + a_2 RETURN_p + a_3 Beta_p + e_i$$

Coefficient Estimates

Intercept	SIZE	RETURN	Beta	R^2_{adjusted}
0.641	-0.027	-0.014	0.111	0.32
(3.230)	(-7.701)	(-2.548)	(2.018)	

tions (six portfolios with less than 100 earnings announcements are de-leted) where the portfolio three-day return is the dependent variable. Explanatory variables are *SIZE* (as measured by the size portfolio number), *RETURNS* (as measured by the prior returns portfolio number), and beta. The coefficients indicate that, holding beta and firm size constant, the earnings announcement returns are more positive for prior losers than winners. In particular, multiplying the coefficient of -0.0142 by (1 minus 20) is 0.27% per announcement. Since there are four quarterly earnings announcements per year, this is a difference of 1.08% during each calendar year for these 12 trading days alone, reinforcing our earlier results on the existence of an overreaction effect. Corroborating evidence is also found in Hand (1990), where differential earnings announcement effects are found depending upon the proportion of shares held by individuals.

5. Summary and Conclusions

One of the most controversial issues in financial economics in recent years is the question of whether stocks overreact. De Bondt and Thaler (1985) present evidence that stocks with poor performance (losers) over the past three-to-five years outperform prior-period winners during the subsequent three-to-five years. This work has received considerable attention because the authors find a very large difference in returns between winners and losers during the five-year post-ranking period (about 8% per year), and they interpret their findings as evidence that there are systematic valuation errors in the stock market caused by investor overreaction.

Subsequent papers suggest that De Bondt and Thaler's findings are subject to various methodological problems. In particular, Ball and Kothari (1989) show that when betas are estimated using annual returns, nearly all of the estimated abnormal returns disappear in the context of the Sharpe–Lintner CAPM. In another paper, Zarowin (1990) argues that the overreaction effect is merely a manifestation of the size effect. It is apparent that the quantitative magnitude of the overreaction effect is highly sensitive to the procedures used in computing abnormal returns, particularly in any study in which abnormal returns are being computed over multiple-year periods.

In this paper, we estimate event time-varying betas but do not use the restrictive assumptions of the Sharpe–Lintner CAPM in computing abnormal returns for winners and losers. The Sharpe–Lintner model assumes that the compensation per unit of beta risk is about 14–15% per year when an equally-weighted market portfolio is used. Given that the betas of extreme winners and losers differ by about 0.8 when annual returns are used, an adjustment for beta risk explains a large portion of the overreaction effect. We rely instead on the estimated market compensation per unit of beta risk, which is substantially smaller than that assumed by the Sharpe–Lintner model. We obtain results that are consistent with a substantial overreaction effect. Using annual return intervals, extreme losers out perform extreme winners by 6.5% per year. Using monthly return intervals, this spread increases to 9.5% per year. Furthermore, we show that the overreaction effect is not just a manifestation of the size effect. We demonstrate that the common procedure of adjusting for size underestimates the spread in abnormal returns between winners and losers, because part of the size effect is attributable to return reversals. After adjusting for size, but before adjusting for beta effects, we find that extreme losers outperform extreme winners by 9.7% per year after purging size-control portfolios of winners and losers.

In general, because size, prior returns, and betas are correlated, any study that relates realized returns to just one or two of these variables suffers from an omitted variable bias. In the context of a multiple regression using all three of these variables, we find an economically-significant overreaction effect of about 5% per year. This overreaction effect, however, has a pronounced January seasonal, consistent with the findings of other authors, which raises the question of whether there is an overreaction effect that is distinct from previously-documented tax-loss selling effects. To address this issue, we construct portfolios based upon prior one-year returns, a common measure of tax-loss selling intensity, and measure their performance over the subsequent five years. We find much smaller differences in returns between extreme portfolios than when portfolios are formed based upon five-year returns.

The overreaction effect, however, is not homogeneous across size groups. Instead, it is much stronger for smaller companies than for larger companies, with extreme losers outperforming extreme winners by about 10% per year among small firms. These smaller firms are held predominantly by individuals. In contrast, there is virtually no evidence of overreaction among the largest firms, where institutional investors are the dominant holders. This suggests that overreaction by individuals is more prevalent than overreaction by institutions.

In common with other studies that examine returns over long intervals, there is always the possibility that what we attribute to overreaction is instead equilibrium compensation for some omitted risk factor (or factors). However, we feel that our results cannot be explained by risk mismeasurement since returns consistent with overreaction are observed for the short windows surrounding quarterly earnings announcement days. We find that even after adjusting for the size effect and the higher risk that is present at earnings announcements, losers have significantly higher returns than winners.

If the return reversals documented here and elsewhere are not merely compensation for risk bearing, then why is it that the patterns do not disappear due to the actions of arbitrageurs? Shleifer and Vishny (1991) argue that 'smart money' investors are exposed to opportunity costs if there is no certainty that mispricing will be corrected in a timely manner. The periodic evaluation of money managers by their clients contributes to their unwillingness to undertake long-term arbitrage positions. For these reasons, 'smart money' will flock to short-term rather than long-term arbitrage opportunities, and resources devoted to long-term arbitrage will be quite limited. The trading strategies discussed in this paper require capital commitments over extended horizons in smaller firms, which may be why these opportunities can persist for so long.

In summary, we have documented an economically-important overreaction effect in the stock market, concentrated among smaller firms. While the underlying reasons for the valuation errors have not been uncovered, the fact that the effect is strongest for smaller stocks may indicate that a productive area for future research is understanding the difference in the investment patterns between individuals and institutions.

Appendix

A.1 Asymmetries in Beta Changes

Ibbotson's (1975) RATS procedure is ideally suited for estimating event time-varying betas in a situation where the sample firms are experiencing dramatic changes in their market capitalization over relatively short intervals. In the context of this study, substantial differences in betas between winners and losers are observed using this procedure.

One of the attractive features of the RATS procedure is that one can observe on a period-by-period basis how the betas are changing within the ranking or post-ranking periods. Ball and Kothari (1989) present evidence, in their tables 4 and 5 and fig. 1, that the betas of winner and loser portfolios change over time in the direction that would be predicted due to leverage changes. We replicate these patterns in columns (1) and (2) of our table 7. In this table, following De Bondt and Thaler (1985) and Ball and Kothari (1989), we have defined winners and losers to be the 50 stocks with the most extreme ranking-period returns. We have calculated betas for each year of a two-year pre-ranking period (years -6

Table 7   RATS betas on winner and loser portfolios for each event year from -6 to $+5$ for ranking periods in all markets, down markets ($r_{mt} - r_{ft} < 0$), and up markets ($r_{mt} - r_{ft} > 0$). Years -6 to -5 are the pre-ranking period, years -4 to 0 are the ranking period, and years $+1$ to $+5$ are the post-ranking period.[a]

$$r_{pt} - r_{ft} = a_p + \beta_p(r_{mt} - r_{ft}) + \epsilon_{pt}$$

Beta coefficient estimates

Year Relative to Ranking Year 0	All 52 Years		Years when $r_m - r_f < 0$ only		Years when $r_m - r_f > 0$ only	
	Winners	Losers	Winners	Losers	Winners	Losers
-6	1.15	1.19	1.20	1.03	1.01	1.10
-5	1.21	1.12	1.12	1.07	1.17	1.06
-4	1.58	0.78	1.11	0.96	2.02	0.52
-3	1.52	0.83	0.99	0.87	1.86	0.58
-2	1.47	0.95	0.99	0.75	1.78	0.83
-1	1.48	1.02	0.98	0.86	1.72	0.99
0	1.21	1.06	0.94	0.83	1.13	1.03
$+1$	0.85	1.54	0.94	0.97	0.63	1.73
$+2$	0.79	1.63	0.93	1.26	0.56	1.89
$+3$	0.86	1.54	0.80	1.22	0.74	1.71
$+4$	0.94	1.55	0.72	1.08	0.95	1.78
$+5$	0.88	1.61	0.77	0.95	0.88	1.88
Average, -6 to -5	1.18	1.15	1.16	1.05	1.09	1.08
Average, -4 to 0	1.45	0.93	1.00	0.85	1.70	0.79
Average, $+1$ to $+5$	0.86	1.57	0.83	1.10	0.75	1.80

a. Winner and loser portfolios consist of the stocks with the most extreme total returns over the five years -4 to 0. The 50 best and the 50 worst stocks in each ranking are assigned to the winner and loser portfolios. In the first two columns, α_p and β_p coefficients are estimated using a time serise of 52 annual portfolio returns, using Ibbotson's (1975) RATS methodology. For years -6 and -5, respectively, 50 and 51 annual returns are used because of the lack of CRSP data for 1924 and 1925. There are between 15 and 21 down-market years and 31 to 37 up-market years, for the years -6 to $+5$. Riskless annual returns are from Ibbotson Associates (1988). The market return is defined to be the equally-weighted market return on NYSE stocks with at least fives years of returns.

to −5), for the ranking period (years −4 to 0), and for the post-ranking period (years +1 to +5). The changes in the betas from the pre-ranking period to the ranking period, and from the ranking period to the post-ranking period, are striking. The ranking-period betas appear to suffer from severe biases. Apparently, the timing of the extreme returns on winners (and losers) is correlated with the market excess return. What is particularly noteworthy is that in the pre-ranking period, the firms that subsequently become the extreme winners and losers have betas that are practically indistinguishable from each other.[10] From year −5 to −4, the beta of the winner portfolio jumps from 1.21 to 1.58, whereas the beta of the loser portfolio falls from 1.12 to 0.78. These dramatic shifts are in the opposite direction to the changes predicted by the leverage hypothesis.

The leverage hypothesis predicts that, since year −4 is part of the ranking period, the beta of winners should fall and the beta of losers should rise. (In the ranking period, the winners have an average annual raw return of 55% for five years, while the losers have an average annual raw return of −9% for five years.) Throughout the ranking period, the betas of the winners remain high and the betas of the losers remain low. As soon as the ranking period ends, there is another huge change in betas. Between years 0 and +1, the winners' betas decrease by 0.36 and the losers' betas increase by 0.48, a combined swing of 0.84. One would expect a much smaller change, given that the market capitalizations change by a smaller amount between years 0 and +1 than between any two adjacent years during the ranking period. In contrast, the swing in betas during the entire five-year ranking period in which the relative market capitalizations changed dramatically is only 0.65 (0.27 for winners and 0.38 for losers).

These abrupt changes in betas cast doubt on the hypothesis that the changes are primarily due to movements in leverage. Thus, a fundamental question is raised about just what phenomenon is being captured by the betas of the winners and losers. The puzzle deepens when the patterns in betas for up and down markets are observed. [De Bondt and Thaler (1987) first documented these differences in betas between up and down markets.] During down markets, defined as years for which $r_m − r_f < 0$, the betas of winner and loser portfolios show little variation

---

10. The betas of both the subsequent winners and losers are above 1.0 during the pre-ranking period. Small firms tend to have high betas, and firms with a lot of unique risk are overrepresented among both extreme winners and extreme losers. Large firms are generally more diversified, and are thus less likely to become extreme winners or losers.

Table 8 OLS regressions of average annual percentage excess returns for the first five post-ranking years for portfolios of NYSE firms formed on the basis of size and prior returns.

For each of the 52 ranking periods ending on December 31 of 1930 to 1981, firms are independently ranked on the basis of their December 31 market value and their five-year prior return, and assigned to one of 400 portfolios. *SIZE* is measured as the size portfolio ranking (1 to 20, with 1 being smallest), and *RETURN* is measured as the prior-return portfolio ranking (1 to 20, with 1 being the most extreme prior losers). Annual returns and an equally-weighted market index are used in all three panels. *T*-statistics, computed using the autocorrelation-adjusted Fama–MacBeth procedure described in table 4, are in parentheses.

Panel A reports results using betas that are calculated by pooling observations across both firms and post-ranking event years. This is identical to panel A in table 4. Panels B and C report results using the two alternative procedures. In all three panels, *t*-statistics are based upon variation in the coefficients from a 52-observation times series of cross-sectional regressions, adjusted for fourth-order autocorrelation.

In panel B, the procedure is analogous to that used in table 1: for each of the 400 portfolios we run a time-series regression using (up to) 52 portfolio returns in each of the five post-ranking years, and then compute the portfolio beta as the average of these five numbers. A disadvantage of this procedure is that there are many portfolios that have missing observations in some of the 52 years.

In panel C, the procedure calculates separate betas for each of the five post-ranking years and then averages these five numbers to calculate the portfolio beta.

$$r_p - r_f = a_0 + a_1 SIZE_p + a_2 RETURN_p + a_3 Beta_p + e_p$$

Coefficient Estimates

Intercept	SIZE	RETURN	Beta	$R^2_{adjusted}$
Panel A: Betas Computed with Pooling over Both Firms and Event Years				
14.443	−0.364	−0.254	5.438	0.68
(10.517)	(−3.779)	(−2.996)	(1.707)	
Panel B: Betas Computed Using the RATS Procedure				
15.637	−0.290	−0.204	7.210	0.70
(4.949)	(−2.007)	(−2.259)	(2.062)	
Panel C: Betas Computed with Pooling Over Firms				
17.838	−0.314	−0.266	5.817	0.67
(6.381)	(−2.194)	(−3.022)	(1.646)	

between the ranking and post-ranking periods. Furthermore, in the post-ranking period the downmarket betas differ by only 0.27 (0.83 for winners, 1.10 for losers). In contrast, during up markets, defined as years for which $r_m - r_f > 0$, the betas of winners fall by roughly half from the ranking period to the post-ranking period, while the betas of losers approximately double. Furthermore, during the post-ranking period, the up-market betas of winners and losers differ by a full 1.05 (0.75 for winners, 1.80 for losers). Thus, the large difference in betas between winners and losers in the post-ranking period emphasized by Ball and Kothari is driven primarily by the extraordinarily high betas on losers during up markets. Thus, while the difference in betas during the post-ranking period between portfolios comprised of the 50 most extreme winners and losers is 0.70 (0.79 using extreme vitile portfolios in table 1), we have serious reservations whether the difference in risk that investors face is actually of this magnitude.

What is beta capturing? This is an open issue that requires further study. Work by Bhandari (1988) and Braun, Nelson, and Sunier (1990) finds only a weak association between changes in leverage and equity betas. Stroyny (1991) finds that heteroskedasticity in the returns distribution induces some of the biases, since percentage variances tend to be asymmetric between up and down markets.

A.2 Sensitivities to Alternative Measures of Beta Computation

In table 8, we report the results of alternative beta computation procedures for the table 4 regression using annual returns. As can be seen, the qualitative conclusions are not highly dependent on the procedure employed.

We gratefully acknowledge comments from seminar participants at Georgetown, Loyola of Chicago, Northwestern, Southern Methodist, and Temple Universities; the Universities of Chicago, Colorado, Florida, Illinois, Rochester, and Virginia; the Amsterdam Institute of Finance, the University of Wisconsin Johnson Symposium, the 1991 Tokyo Conference on Capital Markets, and the NBER/Behavioral Finance working group; and from Christopher Barry, Victor Bernard, William Bryan, Louis Chan, Eugene Fama, Kenneth French, Robert Harris, Thomas Lys, Prafulla Nabar, George Pennacchi, Gita Rao, Marc Reinganum (the referee), Andrei Shleifer, Thomas Stober, Seha Tinic, Paul Zarowin, Richard Zeckhauser, and G. William Schwert (the editor). We wish to thank Tim Loughran and especially Brian Bielinski for extensive research assistance.

References

AMIHUD, YAKOV and HAIM MENDELSON. 1989. The effects of beta, bid–ask spread, residual risk, and size on stock returns. *Journal of Finance* 44, 479–486.

BALL, RAY and S. P. KOTHARI. 1989. Nonstationary expected returns: Implications for tests of market efficiency and serial correlation in returns. *Journal of Financial Economics* 25, 51–74.

BALL, RAY and S. P. KOTHARI. 1991. Security returns around earnings announcements. *The Accounting Review* 66, 718–738.

BERNARD, VICTOR L. and JACOB K. THOMAS. 1989. Post-earnings-announcement drift: Delayed price response or risk premium?, *Journal of Accounting Research* 27, 1–36.

BERNARD, VICTOR L. and JACOB K. THOMAS. 1990. Evidence that stock prices do not fully reflect the implications of current earnings for future earnings, *Journal of Accounting and Economics* 13, 305–340.

BHANDARI, LAXMI. 1988. Debt/equity ratio and expected common stock returns: Empirical evidence. *Journal of Finance* 43, 507–528.

BLACK, FISCHER, MICHAEL C. JENSEN, and MYRON SCHOLES. 1972. The capital asset pricing model: Some empirical tests, in: MICHAEL C. JENSEN, ed., Studies in the theory of capital markets (Praeger Publishers, New York, NY).

BRAUN, PHILIP A., DANIEL B. NELSON, and ALAIN M. SUNIER. 1990. Good news, bad news, volatility, and betas, Working paper (University of Chicago, Chicago, IL).

BROCK, WILLIAM, JOSEF LAKONISHOK, and BLAKE LeBARON. 1992. Simple technical trading rules and the stochastic properties of stock returns. *Journal of Finance*, forthcoming.

CHAN, LOUIS, YASUSHI HAMAO, and JOSEF LAKONISHOK. 1991. Fundamentals and stock returns in Japan, *Journal of Finance* 46, 1739–1764.

CHAN, K. C. 1986. Can tax-loss selling explain the January seasonal in stock returns? *Journal of Finance* 41, 1115–1128.

CHAN, K. C. 1988. On the contrarian investment strategy, *Journal of Business* 61, 147–163.

CHARI, V. V., RAVI JAGANNATHAN, and AHARON R. OFER. 1988. Seasonalities in security returns: The case of earnings announcements. *Journal of Financial Economics* 21, 101–121.

CONRAD, JENNIFER and GAUTUM KAUL. 1989. Mean reversion in short-horizon expected returns. *Review of Financial Studies* 2, 225–240.

CONRAD, JENNIFER and GAUTUM KAUL. 1991. Long-term market overreaction or biases in computed returns?, Working paper (University of North Carolina, Chapel Hill, NC).

DE BONDT, WERNER F. M. and RICHARD H. THALER. 1985. Does the stock market overreact?, *Journal of Finance* 40, 793–805.

DE BONDT, WERNER F. M. and RICHARD H. THALER. 1987. Further evidence on investor overreaction and stock market seasonality, *Journal of Finance* 42, 557–581.

DIMSON, ELROY and PAUL MARSH. 1986. Event study methodologies and the size effect: The case of UK press recommendations, *Journal of Financial Economics* 17, 113–142.

FAMA, EUGENE F. 1991. Efficient capital markets: II, *Journal of Finance* 46, 1575–1617.

FAMA, EUGENE F. and KENNETH R. FRENCH. 1986. Common factors in the serial correlation of stock returns, Working paper (University of Chicago, Chicago, IL).

FAMA, EUGENE F. and KENNETH R. FRENCH. 1988. Permanent and temporary components of stock market prices, *Journal of Political Economy* 96, 246–273.

FAMA, EUGENE F. and KENNETH R. FRENCH. 1992. Cross-sectional variation in expected stock returns, *Journal of Finance* 47.

FAMA, EUGENE F. and JAMES D. MACBETH. 1973. Risk, return, and equilibrium: Empirical tests, *Journal of Political Economy* 71, 607–636.

HAND, JOHN R. 1990. A test of the extended functional fixation hypothesis. *The Accounting Review* 65, 740–763.

HUBERMAN, GUR and SHMUEL KANDEL. 1987. Value Line rank and firm size, *Journal of Business* 60, 577–589.

IBBOTSON ASSOCIATES. 1988. Stocks, bonds, bills and inflation 1988 yearbook (Ibbotson Associates, Inc., Chicago, IL).

IBBOTSON, ROGER G. 1975. Price performance of common stock new issues, *Journal of Financial Economics* 2, 235–272.

JEGADEESH, NARASIMHAN. 1990. Evidence of predictable behavior of security returns, *Journal of Finance* 45, 881–898.

JEGADEESH, NARASIMHAN and SHERIDAN TITMAN. 1991. Returns to buying winners and selling losers: Implications for stock market efficiency, Working paper (University of California, Los Angeles, CA).

JENSEN, MICHAEL C. 1969. Risk, the pricing of capital assets, and the evaluation of investment portfolios, *Journal of Business* 42, 167–247.

KEIM, DONALD B. and ROBERT F. STAMBAUGH. 1986. Predicting returns in the stock and bond markets, *Journal of Financial Economics* 17, 357–390.

LAKONISHOK, JOSEF and ALAN C. SHAPIRO. 1986. Systematic risk, total risk and size as determinants of stock market returns, *Journal of Banking and Finance* 10, 115–132.

LEHMANN, BRUCE N. 1990. Fads, martingales, and market efficiency. *Quarterly Journal of Economics* 105, 1–28.

LO, ANDREW W. and A. CRAIG MACKINLAY. 1988. Stock market prices do not follow random walks: Evidence from a simple specification test, *Review of Financial Studies* 1, 41–66.

MILLER, MERTON H. and MYRON SCHOLES. 1972. Rates of return in relation to risk: A re-examination of some recent findings, in: MICHAEL C. JENSEN, editor., *Studies in the theory of capital markets* (Praeger Publishers, New York, NY).

POTERBA, JAMES M. and LAWRENCE H. SUMMERS. 1988. Mean reversion in stock prices: Evidence and implications, *Journal of Financial Economics* 22, 27–59.

REINGANUM, MARC R. 1983. The anomalous stock market behavior of small firms in January: Empirical tests for tax-loss selling effects, *Journal of Financial Economics* 12, 89–104.

RITTER, JAY R. and NAVIN CHOPRA. 1989. Portfolio rebalancing and the turn-of-the-year effect, *Journal of Finance* 44, 149–166.

ROLL, RICHARD. 1983. Vas ist das? The turn-of-the-year effect and the return premia of small firms, *Journal of Portfolio Management* 9, 18–28.

ROSENBERG, BARR, K. REID, and R. LANSTEIN. 1985. Persuasive evidence of market inefficiency, *Journal of Portfolio Management* 11, 9–16.

SHLEIFER, ANDREI and ROBERT W. VISHNY. 1991. Equilibrium short horizons of investors and firms, *American Economic Review Papers and Proceedings* 80, 148–153.

STROYNY, ALVIN L. 1991. Heteroscedasticity and estimation of systematic risk, Ph.D. dissertation (University of Wisconsin, Madison, WI).

TINIC, SEHA M. and RICHARD R. WEST. 1984. Risk and return: January vs. the rest of the year, *Journal of Financial Economics* 13, 561–574.

ZAROWIN, PAUL. 1990. Size, seasonality, and stock market overreaction, *Journal of Financial and Quantitative Analysis* 25, 113–125.

11

Stock Price Reactions to Earnings Announcements

A Summary of Recent
Anomalous Evidence
and Possible Explanations

VICTOR L. BERNARD

1. Introduction

No firm-specific performance measure is more widely reported, followed, and analyzed than accounting earnings. Thus, although claims of incomplete initial stock price reactions to earnings announcements have existed in the finance and accounting literature for more than twenty years, they have often been greeted with skepticism (e.g., Ball [1978]). The skepticism stems not just from the economic logic underlying the efficient markets hypothesis, but also from direct concerns about potential research design weaknesses, including a failure to control fully for risk. Some of the recent evidence, however, makes it more difficult than ever to dismiss earnings-related anomalies as the product of research design flaws.

This paper reviews recent evidence on market efficiency with respect to accounting earnings. The survey includes evidence indicating that the average initial response to earnings announcements is an underreaction, as well as other evidence that has been interpreted to indicate extreme stock price movements may represent overreactions to earnings.

There are several categories of anomalous evidence consistent with an initial underreaction to earnings reports. First, there are more than twenty (nonindependent) studies of "post-earnings-announcement drift":

303

the phenomenon whereby estimated cumulative abnormal returns continue to drift upward (downward) after the announcement of earnings increases (decreases). A second well known anomaly, the so-called "Value Line enigma" (Copeland and Mayers [1982]), has recently been shown to be driven primarily by post-announcement drift (Affleck-Grabes and Mendenhall [1992]). If indeed stock prices underreact to earnings data, the phenomenon could also potentially explain at least a portion of a third anomaly, the "PE effect" (Basu [1977]).

Among the recent evidence on the possibility of an incomplete initial response to earnings announcements, the most puzzling appears in Bernard and Thomas (1989, 1990), Freeman and Tse (1989), Mendenhall (1991), and Wiggins (1991). Each of these studies entertains the possibility that post-announcement drift arises because stock prices fail to reflect fully what current earnings imply, on average, about earnings in subsequent quarters. As a result, when the subsequent quarters' earnings are announced, stock prices appear to reflect some surprise to earnings changes that should have been predictable in advance. Specifically, the short-term (three-day) reactions to the announcement of earnings for each of the next four quarters are partially predictable, based on the current quarter's earnings (Bernard and Thomas [1990] and Wiggins [1991]). Even more surprisingly, the signs and magnitudes of the predictable three-day reactions are related to the autocorrelation structure of earnings, as if stock prices failed to reflect the extent to which each firm's earnings series differs from a simple seasonal random walk. Several features of the evidence are difficult to explain as the product of a failure to control for risk or as transactions costs.

In seeming contrast to the above-mentioned studies, evidence in De Bondt and Thaler (1987) and Ou and Penman (1989a) *appears* consistent with stock prices overreacting to current changes in earnings. Specifically, both studies document positive (negative) estimated abnormal stock returns for portfolios that previously generated inferior (superior) stock price and earnings performance—as if the prior period stock price behavior constituted an overreaction to the earnings developments. However, Ou and Penman find no evidence of overreaction to earnings on the average, and conclude that their evidence is most appropriately characterized as an underreaction to financial statement data that in certain cases predicts current earnings changes are transitory.

Both DeBondt and Thaler (1987) and Ou and Penman (1989) have sparked continuing research. The interpretations of DeBondt and Thaler (1987) are challenged by Ball and Kothari (1989), Zarowin (1989), and Klein (1990), but are supported by DeBondt and Thaler (1990) and Chopra, Lakonishok, and Ritter (1992). The robustness or interpretation of the Ou-Penman results have been questioned by Greig (1992), Holthausen and Larcker (1992), and Stober (1992), but Holthausen and Larcker identify a closely related portfolio strategy that appears much more robust in its ability to predict abnormal returns. While it is too early to draw firm conclusions from a literature in such flux, the recent evidence in Chopra, Lakonishok, and Ritter (1992) appears to challenge conventional theories of market efficiency and asset pricing. Whether the evidence should be characterized as an overreaction to earnings is, however, uncertain.

The remainder of this paper is organized as follows. Section 2 is devoted to studies of apparent incomplete responses to earnings announcements. Within this section, all studies accumulated prior to 1990 can all be characterized as examinations of possible underreaction to earnings, but the most recent evidence cannot be categorized so neatly. For this reason, the title of this section refers to incomplete initial responses to earnings announcements, thus leaving open the possibility that subsequent corrections can go in a direction opposite to the initial response. In contrast, section 3 refers only to research focused on possible overreaction to earnings. I summarize some debates found in recent reexaminations of Ou and Penman (1989a) and De Bondt and Thaler (1987), and discuss how such evidence can be reconciled with the larger body of work on underreaction to earnings. Section 4 presents a brief summary of other recently studied earnings-related anomalies (Ball and Kothari (1991) and Hand (1990). Concluding remarks appear in section 5.

2. Evidence Suggesting an Incomplete Initial Response to Earnings Announcements

It has long been documented that there is much unusual stock price activity immediately surrounding earnings announcements. Beaver (1968) showed that unusual volatility and volume was largely concentrated within the week of the announcement. Patell and Wolfson (1984) showed that abnormal returns to knowledge of earnings were greatest within the 30 minutes of the announcement, with most of that return occurring within the first 5 to 10 minutes. The question left unanswered by this research, however, is whether this initial quick response is too large or too small. If the initial reaction represents an over- or underreaction that is corrected over a long period of time (perhaps as expectations about future earnings fail to materialize), the correction might not be apparent over short post-announcement intervals. Below, I review research consistent with the initial reaction being (on average) too small, and being completed over a period of at least six months.

2.1 Post-Earnings-Announcement Drift: Evidence Accumulated Prior to 1990

2.1.1 THE BASIC PHENOMENON. Ball and Brown (1968) were the first to document that, subsequent to the announcement of earnings, cumulative abnormal returns (CARs) continue to drift up for "good news" firms and down for "bad news" firms. (In this case, good (bad) news can be defined as an earnings increase (decrease).) The same basic phenomenon was also documented by Jones and Litzenberger (1970), Joy, Litzenberger, and McEnally (1977), Watts (1978), Givoly and Lakonishok (1979), Latane and Jones (1979), Rendleman, Jones, and Latane (1982), Foster, Olsen, and Shevlin (1984), and at least fifteen other studies

The early studies of post-earnings announcement drift suffered from a variety of limitations (in part due to data constraints) that could have biased the results. (See Ball [1978], Foster, Olsen, and Shevlin [1984], and Bernard and Thomas [1989] for discussions.) However, even after the known research design flaws were corrected, post-earnings announcement drift remained apparent. A graphical depiction of the drift from a recent study (Bernard and Thomas [1989]) appears in Figure 1. The figure is based on a sample of approximately 85,000 observations for NYSE and AMEX stocks over the 1974–1986 period.

In Figure 1, firms are assigned to one of ten portfolios on the basis of their standardized unexpected earnings, or SUE. The procedure for calculating SUEs involves producing a statistical forecast of earnings, based on the model proposed by Foster (1977).[1] The difference between actual earnings and the forecast is scaled by the historical standard deviation of the forecast errors to arrive at the SUE. For a given quarter, a firm's SUE is then compared to the distribution of all sample firms' SUEs from the prior quarter to place the firm in a decile portfolio. Abnormal (size-adjusted) returns for each portfolio are then cumulated beginning the day after the earnings announcement to estimate the postannouncement drift.

Figure 1 indicates that post-earnings-announcement abnormal returns increase monotonically across the ten SUE decile portfolios. Over the 60 trading days subsequent to the earnings announcement, firms with extreme good earnings news (SUE decile portfolio 10) experience a mean abnormal return of nearly 2 percent, while firms with extreme bad news (SUE decile portfolio 1) experience a negative abnormal return of approximately the same absolute magnitude. Thus, a movement of funds from the SUE 1 portfolio to the SUE 10 portfolio appears to generate a 60-day

---

1. The model is a univariate first-order autoregressive model in seasonal differences. A forecast based on a naive seasonal random walk model yields similar results.

Figure 1   Cumulative Abnormal Returns (CAR) for SUE Portfolios (84,792 earnings announcements, 1974–1986)

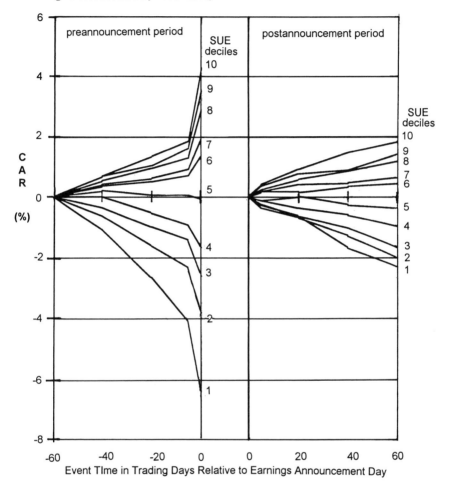

Earnings announcements are assigned to deciles based on the standing of standardized unexpected earnings (SUE) relative to prior quarter SUE distribution. SUE represents forecast errors from the Foster (1977) first-order autoregressive earnings expectation model (in seasonal differences) scaled by their estimation-period standard deviation. CARs are the sums over preannouncement and postannouncement holding periods (beginning day −59 and day 1, respectively) of the difference between daily returns and returns for NYSE-AMEX firms of the same size decile, based on January 1 market values of equity.

incremental abnormal return of 4.2 percent (before transactions costs), or about 18 percent on an annualized basis. (These amounts are based on summed returns that implicitly assume daily rebalancing, but are nearly identical when based on buy-and-hold portfolios.)

Larger abnormal returns are estimated when the research design is altered in particular ways. First, the absolute magnitude of the drift is larger for smaller firms (Foster, Olsen, and Shevlin [1984]). Second, the drift continues beyond the 60-trading-day interval displayed in Figure 1. Figure 2 (based on the same sample underlying Figure 1) shows that over a 180-trading-day post-announcement interval, a combined long position in SUE portfolio 10 and a short position in SUE portfolio 1 generates an abnormal return of approximately 10 percent, 9 percent, and 4.5 percent

Figure 2   Post-earnings-announcement Drift: By Firm Size, for 360 Trading Days beyond Announcement

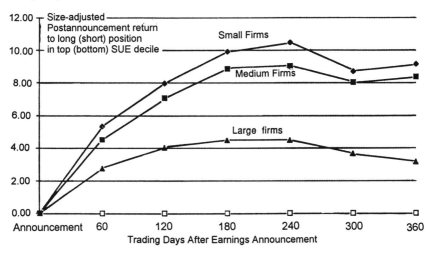

Source of data: Bernard and Thomas (1989, Table 1). Earnings announcements are assigned to deciles based on the standing of standardized unexpected earnings (SUE) relative to prior quarter SUE distribution. (84,792 announcements, 1974–1986.) SUE represents forecast errors from the Foster (1977) first-order autoregressive earnings expectation model (in seasonal differences) scaled by their estimation-period standard deviation. Size-adjusted returns are the sums over postannouncement holding periods of the difference between daily returns and returns for NYSE-AMEX firms of the same size decile, based on January 1 market values of equity. Small, medium, and large firms are in size deciles 1 to 4, 5, to 7, and 8 to 10, respectively, based on the January 1 market value of equity for all NYSE and AMEX firms.

for small, medium, and large firms, respectively. Third, the drift is about 50 percent larger when SUEs are measured relative to analysts' forecasts, rather than the statistical forecasts used in Figures 1 and 2 (Freeman and Tse [1989, Table 7]).

2.1.2 THE PLAUSIBILITY OF RISK AS AN EXPLANATION FOR POST-ANNOUNCEMENT DRIFT. While the evidence in Figures 1 and 2 is consistent with a market inefficiency—specifically, a delayed response to earnings announcements—it might also be explained by a failure to control fully for risk. That is, the good news firms may be riskier, and the bad news firms may be less risky, than the benchmark portfolios to which they are compared. Ball (1978) explains why such a difference in risk might be expected in this context. Ball, Kothari, and Watts (1990) set forth the economic logic that would predict temporary risk increases (decreases) for firms in the good news (bad news) category, and provide evidence that such risk shifts do occur.

The Bernard and Thomas (1989) study was largely devoted to assessing the plausibility that post-earnings-announcement drift can be explained by a failure to control fully for risk. There are several aspects of the evidence in that study that cast doubt on a risk-based explanation.

First, Bernard and Thomas tested the Ball-Kothari-Watts hypothesis that betas shift up (down) during years with good (bad) earnings news.[2] The premise of the hypothesis is that, for firms experiencing increases (decreases) in risk, a portion of the higher (lower) risk will be passed on to customers and/or suppliers in the form of price changes, thus translating into contemporaneous earnings increases (decreases). Using the Ball-Kothari-Watts methodology, Bernard and Thomas found evidence of beta shifts in the predicted direction, and noted that a portion of the shift persisted into the post-announcement period. However, the shifts were only about 8 percent to 13 percent as large as necessary to explain fully the magnitude of the drift.

Second, there was no evidence to indicate that long (short) post-announcement positions in extreme good (bad) news stocks were risky along any of five dimensions specified in the Chen, Roll, and Ross (1986) test of arbitrage pricing theory.

Third, there was little evidence that any risk to which the SUE portfolios were exposed had surfaced in the form of a loss. That is, estimated abnormal returns to a zero-investment portfolio with long (short) positions in extreme good (bad) news stocks were consistently positive, regardless

2. Bernard and Thomas's examination of risk was motivated in part by the first version of the Ball, Kothari, and Watts study, written in 1988.

of macroeconomic conditions. Over the 13 years from 1974 through 1986, the estimated abnormal returns were positive all 13 times. Over 50 quarters, the estimated abnormal returns were positive as many as 46 times, and the gains in these quarters exceeded the cumulative losses in the four remaining quarters by a factor of 35 to 1.

Fourth, mean raw (total) returns on extreme bad news stocks were so low as to raise doubts about whether declines in risk of *any* kind could plausibly explain their magnitude. Specifically, the raw returns were less than Treasury bill rates during the week after the earnings announcement, and were only slightly greater than Treasury bill rates during the first two months of the post-announcement period. While capital asset pricing theory does not rule out equilibrium expected returns on risky assets that are less than the risk-free rate, such low returns are permitted only under special conditions that many would find implausible in this context. Specifically, extreme bad news stocks would have to offer some hedge, the value of which exceeds the cost of any other risk to which the stocks are exposed.

Perhaps the most compelling result in the Bernard-Thomas (1989) study is the most simple: that the returns on zero-investment portfolios based on SUE are consistently positive. That result can be aligned with a claim that a SUE strategy is risky only if (1) the infrequency of losses in the 1974–1986 period is extremely unusual, relative to what would be observed over a longer period, or (2) the risk associated with the SUE strategy gives rise to infrequent but catastrophic losses, none of which was observed within this thirteen-year time span.

Figure 3 combines the evidence from three studies of post-announcement drift to examine whether the infrequency of losses noted above is unusual. The Latane, Jones, and Rieke (1974) study, the Rendleman, Jones, and Latane (1982) study, and the Bernard and Thomas (1989) study are used here because they disclose returns to SUE strategies on a period-by-period basis. The evidence must be used cautiously, because the methods vary across the three studies (e.g., in terms of how extreme the SUEs are that underly the test portfolios), and the earliest study might have contained biases not present in later work.[3] Notwithstanding these caveats, it is interesting to see that the combined studies indicate that long (short) positions in extreme high (low) SUE stocks generated positive estimated abnormal returns in each year from 1965 through 1986.

---

3. Latane et al assume that quarterly earnings were made public by two months after the fiscal-quarter end, which could induce some upward bias in abnormal returns. (On the other hand, since most firms announce earnings well before this date, the Latane et al study may have missed a significant portion of the drift.)

If the SUE strategy were risky along some dimension not fully controlled for in the studies, it is difficult to understand why these zero-investment portfolios did not generate a loss for twenty-two consecutive years.

Despite the above evidence, the Bernard-Thomas conclusion that risk shifts could at best explain a small portion of post-announcement drift is not unchallenged. Ball, Kothari, and Watts (1990) estimate that over the nine months following the presumed earnings announcement month, the difference in betas between top decile and bottom decile earnings performers is .29, or about twice as large as the average of the differences estimated by Bernard and Thomas for the first three post-announcement quarters. After controlling for beta, the Ball-Kothari-Watts estimate of the difference in abnormal returns between the extreme decile portfolios is only 2.98 percent over the nine months—certainly smaller than the drift estimated elsewhere. However, the issue of post-announcement drift is not the primary focus of Ball, Kothari, and Watts, and they "caution against making fine comparisons," due to the variety of differences in research design between their study and others. Perhaps most importantly, they form portfolios on the basis of changes in annual earnings, rather than quarterly earnings. Given that much of the change in annual earnings is old news by the time it is announced, this approach tends to reduce the power to capture the full magnitude of post-announcement drift. At the same time, so long as beta shifts have any degree of permanence, using annual data increases the power to identify firms with large beta shifts. Since the design magnifies the importance of beta risk premiums, relative to post-announcement drift, the study cannot provide clear indications about the extent to which the drift is explained by risk.

2.1.3 IMPLEMENTATION PROBLEMS AND TRANSACTIONS COSTS AS AN EXPLANATION FOR POST-ANNOUNCEMENT DRIFT. Bernard and Thomas (1989, section 3.2.4) find no implementation problems that would prevent traders from generating abnormal returns based on SUEs, at least before considering transactions costs and short-selling restrictions. They examine a stratgegy that (1) followed the approach of Holthausen (1983) to assure that SUE portfolio assignments were based entirely on information available prior to the assignment; (2) took positions in stocks only when both extreme good news and extreme bad news stocks were available, to ensure that the strategy requires zero initial investment;[4] (3) involved computing buy-and-hold (compounded) returns, as opposed to cumula-

---

4. On 86 percent of the trading days, both extreme good news and extreme bad news stocks were newly available, so positions could be taken immediately. In 97 percent of all cases, a match of good and bad news stocks could be made by waiting less than three days.

Figure 3   Returns to SUE Strategy by Year, 1965–1986: A Combination of Results Reported in Three Studies

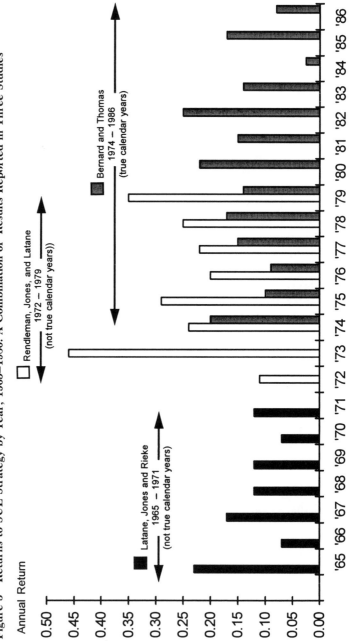

Latane, Jones, and Rieke (1974): Long (short) positions in stocks with SUE greater than (less than) 1.5 are assumed two months after the end of the fiscal quarter, and held for six months. Returns are not adjusted for risk. Estimated holding period betas are 1.14 for the long position and 1.09 for the short position. Returns shown above are calculated first by annualizing six-month returns taken after each of four quarters. The return for 1971 is based on the sum of only two six-month positions.

Rendleman, Jones, and Latane (1982): Long (short) positions are assumed in 20 stocks with highest (lowest) SUEs among a universe that grows from 170 to 972. The universe includes only stocks announcing earnings within one month of the fiscal quarter close; positions are taken at the beginning of the next month and held for three months. Portfolios are balanced to assure a pre-holding-period beta of zero, but no control for holding-period beta. Returns from four three-month holding periods are summed to arrive at the return.

Bernard and Thomas (1989): Long (short) positions are assumed in stocks among the top (bottom) quintile of SUE, relative to prior quarter distribution. Each $1 long position is always offset by a $1 short position in stock(s) of similar size (small, medium, or large). Balancing in this way sometimes requires waiting after earnings announcements until an offsetting match is available. Returns are not adjusted for risk, but controls for holding-period beta and five other risk factors have little impact on the returns. Returns are reported for calendar quarters and summed to arrive at the annual return. The return for 1986 is based on only nine months.

tive returns that implicitly assume daily rebalancing; and (4) avoided the use of control portfolios that would implicitly assume the feasibility of taking new positions in hundreds of stocks each day. The estimated abnormal returns to this strategy are similar to those already described above, in terms of magnitude, insensitivity to known risk factors, and consistency through time.

Whether transactions costs would offset gains to trading on SUEs is more difficult to assess, but it seems unlikely that they would. Transactions costs for the average transaction can be imputed by comparing the sum of economy-wide commission income, market-maker trading gains (including specialists' profit from the bid-ask spread), and underwriting profits with the aggregate trading volume on all stock exchanges. Using this approach, Stoll (1991) estimates mean round-trip transactions costs to be 1.2 percent. For institutions, the average round-trip costs would of course be lower—perhaps on the order of 0.75 percent. Even after doubling these average costs to account for positions involving both good news and bad news firms, they are still much lower than the abnormal returns presented in Figure 2 for the nine-month post-announcement interval: 4.5 percent, 8.9 percent, and 9.9 percent for large, medium, and small stocks, respectively.[5]

Although *mean* round-trip transactions costs fall far short of the amount necessary to offset gains from post-announcement drift, the costs could be much higher for those who trade aggressively and thus exert price pressure or bear a higher share of the bid-ask spread. However, given that post-announcement drift lasts for months, it is not clear why a trader would act on it aggressively. Moreover, insofar as the marginal returns to trading on SUEs are concerned, transactions costs are irrelevant for other traders already committed to buying or selling for reasons unrelated to earnings; it is not clear why their actions would not eliminate the drift.

There are more fundamental questions raised by this discussion, however. First, how could transactions costs of any magnitude explain post-announcement drift, given that trading occurs throughout the period of the drift? That is, given that traders have agreed to transact, why do they not transact at a price that appears to reflect all publicly available earnings information? Second, even if transactions costs could "explain" the drift, would we then label the stock market efficient with respect to earnings? Ball (1990) argues that a meaningful definition of efficiency should require

---

5. The costs and restrictions pertaining to short selling of bad news stocks are also relevant to those who do not already hold the bad news stocks. However, since bad news stocks could always be sold by those holding them without bearing these costs, it is not clear why short selling should play any role in explaining post-announcement drift.

that frictions such as transactions costs and trading restrictions do not influence price. (If instead, efficiency requires only the absence of trading profits net of transactions costs, even a market that is closed for trading would be considered efficient!)

2.2 Post-Earnings-Announcement Drift: Recent Evidence

2.2.1 EVIDENCE THAT STOCK PRICES REFLECT NAIVE EARNINGS EXPEC-TATIONS. Given that a long series of studies had failed to produce a satisfactory explanation for post-announcement drift based on research design flaws, incomplete controls for risk, or transactions costs, recent research turned to alternative possibilities involving market inefficiency. Following up on the suggestion of Rendleman, Jones, and Latane (1987) and initial evidence produced by Bernard and Thomas (1989) and Freeman and Tse (1989), two recent studies (Bernard and Thomas [1990] and Wiggins [1991]) investigated the possibility that post-announcement drift arises because stock prices fail to reflect the implications of current earnings for future earnings.

The essential hypothesis tested by Bernard and Thomas (1990) and Wiggins (1991) is that prices do not fully reflect the extent to which current changes in quarterly earnings (relative to the comparable quarter of the prior year) signal future changes in earnings. More specifically, stock prices appear to reflect, at least partially, a naive earnings expectation: one based on a seasonal random walk, where expected earnings are simply earnings for the corresponding quarter from the previous year. It is well known that earnings forecast errors based on such a naive model are correlated through time (e.g., Freeman and Tse [1989]). In contrast, in a market that fully impounds all prior earnings information, forecast errors should not be autocorrelated (by definition). What the recent studies examine is the possibility that market prices can be described partially as reflections of naive expectations, and that as a result, the reactions of prices to future earnings are predictable, just as the forecast errors of a naive expectation model are predictable.

For an investor who relies on a naive seasonal random walk forecast of earnings, forecast errors would be autocorrelated in a pattern that has remained consistent since at least 1946, the beginning of the first period for which the data have been studied (Watts [1975], Foster [1977], Bernard and Thomas [1990]). The cumulative evidence indicates that the pattern of autocorrelations can be viewed as including two components. First, there is a positive autocorrelation between seasonal differences (i.e., seasonal random walk forecast errors) that is strongest for adjacent quarters, but that remains positive over the first three lags. Thus, a change in earnings of quarter t (relative to the comparable quarter of the prior year) tends to be followed by progressively smaller changes of the same sign in quarters t + 1, t + 2, and t + 3. Second, there is a negative autocorrelation between seasonal differences that are four quarters apart. That is, a portion (about one-fourth, on average) of the change for quarter t is reversed in quarter t + 4; only the remaining portion of the initial change represents a permanent shock.

To offer a more specific description of the time series behavior of earnings, Table 1 presents summary statistics for the samples studied by Foster (1977), Hopwood and McKeown (1986), and Bernard and Thomas (1990). Together, the three samples span the 1946–86 period. In all three samples, the autocorrelations at the first three lags are positive but declining, and the autocorrelation at the fourth lag is negative. The general pattern shown in Table 1 is quite consistent across a variety of industries, and holds regardless of fiscal-quarter alignment (Bernard and Thomas [1990]).

Under the hypothesis that stock prices fail to reflect the extent to which the earnings process tends to deviate from a seasonal random walk, abnormal stock returns would depend on forecast errors that are autocorrelated and therefore predictable; the autocorrelations would mimic the same pattern observed in Table 1. For example, if an earnings increase over the prior year were announced in quarter t, the market would be surprised to learn that earnings tend to increase again, over the prior year, in quarters t + 1, t + 2, and t + 3, and thus would, on average, react positively to the earnings announcements for those quarters. The magnitude of this surprise would be declining over the three quarters, just as the corresponding autocorrelations decline. The hypothesis also predicts that the market would be surprised that a portion of the quarter t earnings increase tends to be reversed in quarter t + 4, and thus would, on average, react negatively to the announcement for that quarter. Note that the predictions of market reactions to announcements for quarters t + 1 through t + 4 are based solely on earnings information available as of quarter t. Note also that the prediction pertaining to quarters t + 1 through t + 3 is consistent with the view that stock prices initially underreact to quarter t earnings information, but the prediction for quarter t + 4 is more readily characterized in terms of a reversal of a prior overreaction.

The evidence in Bernard and Thomas (1990) and Wiggins (1991) is surprisingly consistent with the above predictions. In Bernard and Thomas (1990), a long (short) position in quarter t's extreme good news (bad news) firms yields a three-day abnormal return surrounding the next three earnings announcements that is positive and declining: 1.32

Table 1 Time Series Behavior of Quarterly Earnings

Panel A: Autocorrelations in seasonally differenced quarterly earnings, 1946–1974 (from Foster [1977], based on 69 firms):

Lag	1	2	3	4	5	6	7	8
Mean	.45	.24	.13	–.12	.01	.02	–.02	–.03

Panel B: Autocorrelations in seasonally differenced quarterly earnings, 1962–78 (from sample used by Hopwood and McKeown [1986], based on 267 firms[a]):

Lag	1	2	3	4	5	6	7	8
Mean (1962–1978)	.45	.21	.02	–.19	–.07	–.02	–.02	–.03
Mean (1962–1970II)	.36	.17	.05	–.18	–.07	–.05	–.07	–.07
Mean (1970III–1978)	.42	.17	–.03	–.22	–.11	–.05	–.06	–.06

Panel C: Autocorrelations in seasonally differenced quarterly earnings, 1974–1986 (from Bernard and Thomas [1989], based on 2,626 firms):

Lag	1	2	3	4	5	6	7	8
Mean	.34	.19	.06	–.24	–.08	–.07	–.07	–.06
25th percentile	.14	.05	–.10	–.46	–.26	–.24	–.24	–.25
Median	.36	.18	.06	–.29	–.09	–.08	–.06	–.06
75th percentile	.57	.35	.21	–.07	.08	.08	.09	.11

a. These statistics are not reported in Hopwood and McKeown (1986), but were furnished to me in personal correspondence with Jim McKeown.

percent, 0.70 percent, and 0.04 percent, respectively.[6] The same position yields a three-day abnormal return around the fourth subsequent announcement that is negative: −0.66 percent.

A graphical depiction of the main result in Bernard and Thomas (1990) appears in Figure 4. The figure describes the behavior of the combined long (short) positions in quarter t's good news (bad news) stocks throughout the four quarters subsequent to the announcement for quarter t. The data are aligned so that the announcement dates for each subsequent announcement coincide for all firms in the portfolio, leaving inter-announcement windows of varying lengths. The pattern of the three-day stock price movements—positive but declining reactions around the first three subsequent announcements, and a negative reaction at the fourth announcement—is consistent with the market being surprised that earnings deviate from a seasonal random walk. Abnormal returns measured over quarter-long intervals show the same pattern, but the concentration of abnormal returns around earnings announcements suggests that "corrections" of the earnings expectations embedded in stock prices tend to occur more frequently on those days.

The trading strategy suggested by the above would involve holding positions in the zero-investment portfolios in Figure 4 through the third subsequent announcement and then reversing the position during the fourth quarter. The indicated abnormal returns are approximately 11.5 percent, 10 percent, and 5 percent for small, medium, and large firms, respectively, for the four-quarter holding period. Bernard and Thomas (1990) describe another strategy that takes advantage of the concentration of drift around subsequent announcements; it involves taking positions 15 days prior to the expected date of a given subsequent earnings announcement (assumed equal to the announcement date of the prior year) and holding the position through the announcement. Long (short) positions are maintained in stocks that generated an extremely high (low) SUE within the last three quarters, or an extremely low (high) SUE four quarters prior. The indicated abnormal return is 4.2 percent for an average holding period of 15 days.

One might posit that the evidence is explainable as a function of the market's justifiable expectation of low levels of autocorrelation in seasonally-differenced earnings, and resulting justifiable surprise at the actual degree of autocorrelation. However, two features of the data cast doubt on this possibility. First, the estimates in Table 1 suggest that the degree of autocorrelation was if anything lower for the 1974–1986 period studied

---

6. Good news (bad news) is defined in Bernard and Thomas (1990) in terms of SUEs where the earnings expectation is based on a seasonal random walk with drift.

Figure 4   Cumulative Abnormal Returns for SUE Portfolios: Returns Aligned by Subsequent Earnings Announcements

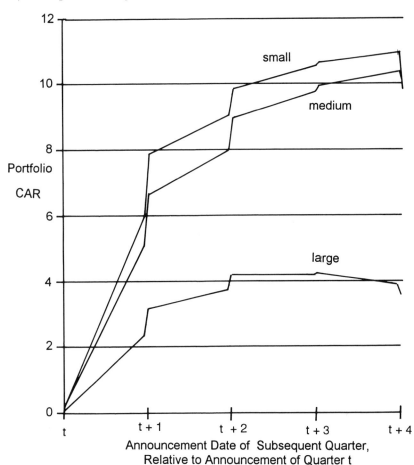

Portfolio CAR is the cumulative abnormal return over holding periods beginning after the earnings announcement day for quarter t, for a portfolio invested long (short) in the highest (lowest) decile of standardized unexpected earnings (SUE) at quarter t. SUE represents forecast error from the seasonal random walk (with trend) earnings expectation model scaled by its estimation-period standard deviation. Abnormal returns are the differences between daily returns for individual firms in a SUE decile portfolio, and returns for NYSE-AMEX firms of the same size decile, based on January 1 market values of equity. Small, medium, and large firms are in size deciles 1 to 4, 5 to 7, and 8 to 10, respectively. Holding periods are obtained by splitting the period between adjacent earnings announcement dates into a 3-day preannouncement window (day −2 to day 0) and an interannouncement window. While the actual interannouncement windows vary in length, the mean value of 60 days is used to illustrate the differential price responses occurring in the two windows.

by Bernard and Thomas (1990) than in the prior years, although noncomparability across samples renders this observation tentative. Second, the behavior of abnormal returns described above for the overall 1974–1986 period holds consistently for each of the 13 years studied.[7] Although the market might err in its expectations about the degree of autocorrelation in earnings, it is difficult to explain how it could justifiably err in the same direction year after year.

Overall, the evidence offers the following implications. First, it creates several added obstacles to contentions that the drift might ultimately be explained by errors in the methodology used to estimate expected returns. For example, an explanation based on failure to control for risk would now have to argue that good news firms experience delayed *increases* in risk over 3-day intervals that coincide with each of the next three earnings announcements, and then a *decrease* in risk over the 3-day interval coinciding with the fourth subsequent announcement. The converse would have to hold for bad news firms. At a minimum, any rationale for such behavior must have a more complex structure than explanations suggested to date. Ball, Kothari, and Watts (1990) conclude that "it is unlikely that risk changes can explain even a small proportion of the estimated abnormal returns that Bernard and Thomas [1989, 1990] attribute to specific days, such as 3 to 5 days immediately after the earnings announcement and those surrounding the following quarters' earnings announcements."[8] Ball (1992) also argues that the anomaly cannot be blamed on a failure to control for risk.

Second, by linking what appears to be the elimination of a discrepancy between prices and fundamentals to prespecified information events (i.e., earnings announcements), the evidence is perhaps the most direct indication to date that a market-efficiency anomaly is rooted in a failure of information to flow completely into price. Ball (1990) cautions reasonably that whether the results are consistent with efficiency or inefficiency is simply not knowable, at least today, but does note that the Bernard-

---

7. The predicted signs are obtained in every year, with the exception of the third subsequent announcement, for which the relation was not predicted to be strong.

8. The evidence also makes it more difficult than ever to argue that transactions costs are the sole cause of post-announcement drift. Even if transactions costs cause sluggishness in prices, it is hard to understand why the resulting mispricing would tend to be eliminated around subsequent earnings announcements according to a pattern that is related to the time series properties of earnings. It is particularly difficult to reconcile price sluggishness with the return reversal detected upon the announcement of earnings for quarter t + 4.

Thomas (1989, 1990) evidence "points to the delayed reaction hypothesis."

2.2.2 BUT WHY WOULD STOCK PRICES APPEAR TO REFLECT NAIVE EARNINGS EXPECTATIONS?

To suggest that stock prices reflect naive earnings expectations does not explain the anomaly with which we started; it simply raises another unanswered question. Under what kind of equilibrium could stock prices reflect naive earnings expectations?

Construction of an equilibrium explanation for the evidence would be difficult at best. However, it is less difficult to explain why, if stock prices are partially influenced by naive earnings expectations, at least some informed market participants would be unable to exploit the apparent profit opportunity. Specialists on the exchange can exploit what they believe to be mispricing only by exposing themselves to firm-specific risk (Bagehot [1971]), not to mention rendering themselves vulnerable to charges of a failure to maintain an orderly market. Even though transactions costs and other trading costs appear unlikely to offset the drift for all traders, they may preclude at least some speculators from fully exploiting SUE-based strategies.[9] The possibility that SUE strategies may involve *some* systematic risk would further limit their attractiveness.

Even if speculation based directly on SUEs cannot entirely eliminate any discrepancies between prices and fundamental values that are related to prior earnings, it remains to be explained how such discrepancies could arise in the first place. In other words, why wouldn't all available earnings information be taken into account even by traders who are not explicitly speculating on SUEs? Liquidity traders might be willing to trade at prices that fail to reflect all available information, but their seemingly random trades could not lead to a relation between mispricing and prior earnings with the systematic patterns described earlier. A full explanation requires a systematic tendency for some traders to maintain earnings expectations that are anchored too heavily on the comparable earnings of the prior year, in combination with the cost or risks mentioned above that might prevent speculators from fully exploiting this tendency.

Andreassen (1987, 1990) is among those who have hypothesized that

---

9. Indeed, most (not all) of the fund managers that trade on SUE-related signals and with whom I have spoken do not attempt to sell short on bad news, and trade only within a universe of the 500 or 1,000 largest stocks on the NYSE, where transactions costs are lower, and where large positions can be taken without much concern about price pressure.

systematic psychological forces could influence stock price behavior. Certainly, there is a large psychological literature documenting a tendency for individuals in certain prediction contexts to anchor on some value and place little weight on recent changes in a series.[10] Andreassen (1987) and Andreassen and Kraus (1990) note that this is particularly true unless, for those making the prediction, the recent changes are salient and can be attributed to a stable underlying cause.

Whether such basic psychological forces could survive among professionals in competitive markets is unanswered, and there are alternative reasons why market participants might update forecasts only gradually. In the case of one key group of players, financial analysts, such behavior might be encouraged by incentive structure. That is, there may be little to gain and much to lose by adjusting a forecast to a level far from the current consensus, if the analyst believes his or her forecast is already likely to be the most accurate.

Though the causes of partial and gradual adjustment to earnings news are not clear, there is evidence that analysts underreact to recent earnings changes in predicting future earnings. Mendenhall (1991) shows that Value Line quarterly earnings forecasts are revised insufficiently to account for the most recent Value Line forecast error (i.e., Value Line forecast errors are positively autocorrelated at the first lag). Abarbanell and Bernard (1992) confirm Mendenhall's result and document declining but positive autocorrelations over the first three lags, consistent with what would be expected if the forecasts were influenced in part by the seasonal random walk model underlying the tests in Bernard and Thomas (1990).

Abarbanell and Bernard also conduct tests to indicate that even though the Value Line analysts underreact to recent earnings, the expectations embedded in stock prices underreact to a much greater extent and more closely resemble naive (seasonal random walk) earnings expectations. Thus, postannouncement drift cannot be fully explained by inefficiencies in analysts' forecasts. A full explanation requires an understanding of not only why analysts' forecasts tend to underreact to earnings information but also why market prices underreact to analysts' forecasts

---

10. Another set of literature documents "recency effects" or "nonregressive predictions," where recent changes in a series receive heavy emphasis; this is the literature to which De Bondt and Thaler (1985) refer in their discussion of possible overreaction in the stock market. Andreassen (1987) and Andreassen and Kraus (1990) are among those who have attempted to discriminate between contexts where predictions are regressive or nonregressive.

2.3 Other Recent Evidence Consistent with an Incomplete Initial Response to Earnings

2.3.1 THE VALUE LINE ENIGMA.   It has long been recognized that investment strategies based on Value Line rankings of stocks appear to generate positive risk-adjusted abnormal returns (Black [1973]), Copeland and Mayers [1982]).[11] The evidence constitutes an anomaly, because Value Line purports to base its rankings solely on information that should be publicly available before the rankings are published.

Three of the indicators underlying the Value Line rankings are based on earnings information: quarterly earnings surprise, earnings momentum, and a function that relates earnings to prices. Thus, the apparent success of the Value Line strategy is consistent with stock prices failing to completely impound recent earnings information. This raises the question of whether the so-called Value Line enigma and post-earnings-announcement drift constitute the same basic anomaly. Indeed, Affleck-Graves and Mendenhall (1992) conclude that "the Value Line enigma is actually a manifestation of post-earnings-announcement drift."

There are indications that the funds created by Value Line to trade on their own rankings have generated performance that may fall considerably short of the paper portfolio profits studied in the academic literature (Bodie, Kane, and Marcus [1989, pp. 514–517]). The discrepancy raises questions about whether the costs of implementing such a trading strategy, at least on a stand-alone basis, are larger than they appear on the surface, and/or about how closely Value Line has followed their own rankings.

2.3.2 THE EP EFFECT.   If stock prices underreact to earnings information, or if prices reflect valuation errors that are unrelated to earnings and corrected over time, then earnings-price (EP) ratios should serve as positive predictors of abnormal returns. Indeed, one of the earliest documented anomalies was the "EP effect:" stocks with high earnings-price (EP) ratios generate higher returns than stocks with low EP ratios (Latane and Tuttle [1967], Latane, Tuttle and Jones [1969], Basu [1977]). While there has been considerable debate about whether the EP effect survives adjustments for the size effect (Reinganum [1981], Basu [1983], Cook and Rozeff [1984]) and various sources of hindsight bias (Banz and

---

11. Huberman and Kandel (1990) show that the apparent abnormal returns have a time series behavior consistent with an autoregressive risk premium, but do not attempt to identify the source of such risk.

Breen [1986]), the most comprehensive examination to date suggests the answer is yes (Jaffe, Keim, and Westerfield [1989]).

Although EP ratios are certainly correlated with SUEs (Kim [1987]), there are three related bits of evidence that suggest the EP effect is not driven by a delayed response to earnings information. First, Basu (1983) finds that the EP effect is just as strong when portfolios are formed six months after the presumed month of the earnings announcement, as it is when they are formed immediately after the presumed announcement date. Second, Jaffe, Keim, and Westerfield (1989) find a much larger EP effect in January, which is 10 or 11 months after the announcement of earnings on which the EP ratio is based. Third, Kim (1987) finds that most of the EP effect is independent of post-announcement drift, and vice versa.

What causes the EP effect is and probably will continue to be an open question. One possible driving force is mean reversion in the denominator—price—that could reflect the correction of prior valuation errors unrelated to earnings. If so, then the EP effect would be related to the literature to be summarized in the following section, which investigates long-term reversals of prior period stock price movements. Indeed, the relation of the EP effect to the January effect and the size effect (Jaffe, Keim, and Westerfield [1989]) is something it has in common with the long-term reversals studied by De Bondt and Thaler (1985).

Another distinct possibility is that the EP effect is largely explainable as a risk premium. Basu's (1983) evidence suggests that, after controlling for size, the remaining EP effect continues unabated for at least twelve months after the position is taken, as would be suggested by the risk-based explanation advanced by Ball (1978). Although the EP effect is not eliminated by controlling for systematic risk (Jaffe, Keim, and Westerfield [1989]), other risk factors could be at work. Unlike portfolios built to take advantage of post-announcement drift, zero-investment portfolios designed to exploit the EP effect do not produce estimated abnormal returns that are consistently positive over time (Kim [1987]). That makes a risk-based explanation at least plausible, if not likely.

3. Evidence Consistent with an Overreaction to Earnings Announcements

While most of the evidence discussed thus far is suggestive of an underreaction to earnings information, other evidence has been interpreted as indicating an overreaction. At least some of this research was motivated by a desire to identify the source of long-run mean reversion in stock prices documented by De Bondt and Thaler (1985) and others.[12] De Bondt and Thaler showed that firms with prior extreme negative stock price performance (the losers) seem to outperform those with prior extreme positive performance (the winners), as if a portion of the prior stock price movement constituted a deviation from fundamental values. If this is the appropriate interpretation of the evidence, it raises an interesting question: could the deviations be driven by an overreaction to prior years' earnings trends? For example, could market prices fail to reflect that extreme annual earnings changes tend to be reversed subsequently, as documented by Brooks and Buckmaster (1976) and Freeman, Ohlson, and Penman (1982)?

3.1 Evidence from De Bondt and Thaler and Ou and Penman

The first study to entertain the possibility of overreaction to earnings was De Bondt and Thaler (1987). Ou and Penman (1982a) also present evidence that has features consistent with overreaction, although, as discussed below, the authors have a different interpretation. In this section we review the evidence and discuss two questions. First, to what extent is the evidence consistent with overreaction, versus alternative explanations? Second, how can the evidence be reconciled with the previously described results suggesting underreaction to earnings?

Some central features of the De Bondt-Thaler (1987) and Ou-Penman (1989) evidence are summarized in Table 2. De Bondt and Thaler form winner and loser portfolios on the basis of market-adjusted stock returns over the prior four years; the overreaction hypothesis predicts a partial reversal of those returns during the subsequent test period. Table 2 Panel A shows that, consistent with this hypothesis, losers outperform winners by 37 percent over the four-year test period. In support of the possibility that the result could be driven by overreaction to earnings news, De Bondt and Thaler point to evidence (also summarized in Panel A) that indicates a pattern in earnings similar to that found in returns. That is, after losers (winners) experience earnings declines (increases) during the formation period, earnings move in the opposite direction in the subsequent test period. The evidence appears consistent with a failure of stock prices to reflect that annual earnings do not strictly follow a random walk, but show some mean reversion in the tails (Brooks and Buckmaster

---

12. Long-run mean reversion in stock prices was also documented by Fama and French (1988) and Poterba and Summers (1988), among others. However, the evidence most pertinent here is that pertaining to the firm-specific mean reversion documented by De Bondt and Thaler, as opposed to mean reversion at more aggregate levels.

Table 2 Summary of Evidence from De Bondt-Thaler [1987] and Ou and Penman [1989b]

Portfolio	Basis for construction	Median change in earnings-per-share				Market-adjusted returns	
		Portfolio formation period	Test period	Last year of formation period	First year of test period	Portfolio formation period	Test period
Panel A: De Bondt and Thaler (1987) (4-year test periods range from 1970–1973 to 1980–1983)							
Losers	CAR over prior four years in lowest quintile[a]	−49% over 3 yrs[b]	27% over 4 yrs	−12%	6%	−81% over 4 yrs	25% over 4 yrs
Winners	CAR over prior four years in highest quintile	20% over 3 yrs[b]	−5% over 4 yrs	8%	−3%	126% over 4 yrs	−12% over 4 yrs
Panel B: Ou and Penman (1989b) (2-year test periods range from 1973–1974 to 1983–1984)							
High Pr	Probability of earnings increase in highest decile[c]	−168% over 1 yr	not reported over 2 yrs	−168%	81%	−42% over 1 yr	6% over 2 yrs
Low Pr	Probability of earnings decrease in lowest decile[c]	66% over 1 yr	not reported over 2 yrs	66%	−11%	37% over 1 yr	−22% over 2 yrs

Sources: De Bondt and Thaler (1987, Tables V and VIII); Ou and Penman (1989, Tables 6 and 7).

a. CAR is a cumulative abnormal (market-adjusted) return, measured over a four-year period ending on the last trading day of a given year. The test period begins on the following trading day.

b. Although the portfolio formation period covers four years, data are reported only for the last three years.

c. Pr is an estimate of the probability of an annual earnings increase in the coming year, based on a function of financial statement variables identified and estimated using only historical data. The design assumes the financial data are available to calculate Pr within three months of the end of the fiscal year; the test period begins on the first day of the fourth month following the fiscal-year end.

[1976]). In that sense the evidence seems related to the previously discussed finding that stock prices appear to reflect only incompletely the mean reversion in quarterly earnings that surfaces in the form of a negative autocorrelation in seasonal differences at the fourth lag (Bernard and Thomas [1990]).

Table 2 Panel B shows that patterns of returns and earnings reported for Ou and Penman's portfolios have much in common with those of De Bondt and Thaler. Ou and Penman form portfolios on the basis of a Pr measure, which is essentially the outcome of a computerized fundamental analysis; Pr represents an estimate of the probability of an annual earnings increase in the coming year, based on a function of financial statement variables identified and estimated using only historical data. A key factor contributing to the success of Pr as a predictor of future earnings changes is mean reversion in earnings scaled by equity. Firms with recent earnings declines have high Prs and subsequently increasing earnings; the opposite earnings pattern holds for low Pr firms. In this sense, the high (low) Pr firms correspond to De Bondt and Thaler's losers (winners). Table 2 Panel B shows that the correspondence is apparent not only in earnings behavior, but also in returns behavior. That is, high Pr firms' stocks underperform low Pr firms during the portfolio formation period, just as DeBondt and Thaler's losers underperformed winners; the pattern is reversed in the test period.

3.1.1 ALTERNATIVE EXPLANATIONS FOR THE EVIDENCE: DE BONDT AND THALER. Whether the De Bondt-Thaler evidence should be interpreted as evidence of overreaction is a subject of continuing debate. De Bondt and Thaler discuss features of the data that would not follow directly from the overreaction hypothesis: in particular, the concentration of the return reversals in the month of January.[13] Ball and Kothari (1989) suggest that prior winners (losers) experience decreases (increases) in beta that are sufficiently large to explain nearly all of the estimated abnormal returns to the De Bondt-Thaler strategy.[14] Specifically, Ball and

13. Andreassen (1990) advances a behavioral explanation that could lead to a seasonal pattern in stock price overreactions.

14. De Bondt and Thaler (1987) and Chan (1988) also control for beta in a way that does not assume beta-stationarity across the formation and test periods. Ball and Kothari find larger beta shifts and smaller abnormal returns than De Bondt and Thaler; the source of the discrepancy is unexplained but may be in part related to Ball and Kothari's use of buy-and-hold returns, rather than the cumulated returns used by De Bondt and Thaler. (Chopra, Lakonishok, and Ritter [1992] replicate the De Bondt-Thaler methods but substitute buy-and-hold returns for cumulated returns, and obtain beta estimates very similar to those of Ball and Kothari.) The beta shifts estimated by Ball and Kothari are also greater

Kothari document that when one controls for beta shifts, the De Bondt-Thaler strategy generates an abnormal return that is never statistically significant in any of five post-ranking years.[15]

The recent work of Chopra, Lakonishok, and Ritter (1992) also examines the overreaction hypothesis while controlling for beta shifts. Chopra, Lakonishok, and Ritter argue that Ball and Kothari underestimate the abnormal returns by assuming that the compensation per unit of beta risk is equal to the excess return on the market portfolio. Although this is the amount implied by the Sharpe-Lintner capital asset pricing model (CAPM), several studies have documented empirical estimates of the risk premium that are substantially lower (e.g., Fama and MacBeth [1973] and Tinic and West [1984]). When Chopra, Lakonishok, and Ritter rely on empirical estimates of the market price of risk rather than assumed values, and while controlling for size, they find that prior extreme losers outperform prior extreme winners by nearly 5 percent per year (on averge across five years). The amount is 11 percent for firms in the smallest decile. The abnormal returns are more pronounced in January, but are also some evidence of positive abnormal returns in the February–December period. It is interesting that the size-adjusted abnormal returns are essentially zero for large firms, and are attributable primarily to small firms, as if overreaction occurs only outside the segment of the market dominated by institutions.

In addition to re-examining the Ball-Kothari (1989) tests, Chopra, Lakonishok, and Ritter present another analysis that points to overreaction. They show that during the five years following portfolio formation, and after controlling for beta and size, a disproportionate share (about 20 percent) of the apparent superior performance of losers over winners is concentrated within the three-day intervals surrounding earnings announcements. The evidence suggests that earnings expectations for losers (winners) are unduly pessimistic (optimistic), and thus the market is surprised by the subsequent earnings announcements. The magnitude of the mean three-day announcement period abnormal return—0.27 percent for extreme losers minus extreme winners—is small enough that,

---

than those estimated by Chan (1988), in large part because Ball and Kothari use annual data, rather than monthly data, to estimate betas, and allow betas to shift annually. (The advantages of using annual data in this context are discussed in Handa, Kothari, and Wasley [1989]).

15. The mean annual abnormal return over the five years is 3.1 percent, which Ball and Kothari indicate may be biased upward as the result of a survivorship bias that is not present in De Bondt and Thaler's sample. In contrast, De Bondt and Thaler (1987, Table III) report an average annual return of 9.2 percent before controlling for beta shifts, and 5.9 percent after instituting such controls.

given the evidence of other anomalous announcement-day return behavior (Ball and Kothari [1991]), some caution must be exercised in its interpretation.[16] Nevertheless, the evidence appears difficult to explain except as a correction of a prior overreaction.

Even if extreme stock price movements do constitute overreactions, and even if the overreactions tend to be corrected upon subsequent earnings announcement days, it remains to be shown that the genesis of the overreaction is a misinterpretation of past earnings numbers. Zarowin (1989) focuses directly on this possibility. He acknowledges that subsequent reversals of earnings among extreme prior period stock return performs are consistent with prior period overreactions to earnings. He suggests, however, that demonstration of overreaction to earnings requires predicting future period stock returns based on prior period earnings realizations. Zarowin thus forms portfolios of prior period extreme winners and losers defined in terms of changes in annual earnings. He hypothesizes that if stock prices overreact to earnings, there should be positive (negative) subsequent abnormal stock returns for prior losers (winners).

Although Zarowin finds evidence consistent with the overreaction hypothesis when he analyzes market-adjusted returns, he finds none after controlling for beta and the size effect.[17] Thus, the Zarowin evidence casts some doubt on the overreaction hypothesis—at least as a phenomenon occurring for the average extreme earnings winner or average extreme earnings loser. However, if overreaction is not widespread and varies across firms with similar earnings experience, Zarowin's approach of identifying winners and losers on the basis of prior period earnings changes would lack power, relative to the De Bondt-Thaler approach to identifying winners and losers in terms of prior period stock returns. In fact, when one moves to Zarowin's approach from De Bondt and Thaler's approach, the resulting mean annual test-period market-adjusted return declines to 5.3 percent from 9.1 percent—consistent with a substantial

16. Ball and Kothari (1991) show that mean abnormal returns are positive around earnings announcement days for small firms. The three-day abnormal return for the smallest quintile is about 1 percent. However, in zero-investment portfolios, this effect should cancel out, unless the long and short positions are mismatched on size. The Chopra-Lakonishok-Ritter result survives a size control, suggesting it is not explained by the general phenomenon documented by Ball and Kothari.

17. Chopra, Lakonishok, and Ritter (1992) argue that Zarowin's results may reflect a survivorship bias that would obscure an overreaction effect. However, Zarowin (p. 1387) discusses the issue and points to evidence that suggests the bias should not be serious.

loss of power.[18] Of course, the decline in market-adjusted returns might also reflect a reduction in exposure to uncontrolled risks.

Klein (1990) also examines the hypothesis that investors overreact to earnings numbers. She finds evidence more consistent with underreaction than overreaction. Specifically, she finds that analysts of loser firms (identified on the basis of prior years' stock returns) are unduly *optimistic* about future earnings prospects. (Analysts of winner firms have approximately unbiased expectations.) Klein's evidence may appear inconsistent with that of De Bondt and Thaler (1990), who show that analysts' forecasts of earnings changes tend to be too extreme and therefore "consistent with generalized overreaction." However, Abarbanell and Bernard (1992), who replicate the De Bondt-Thaler result, conclude that whatever is causing the overreaction, it could not be earnings. Abarbanell and Bernard (1992) explain that the key to reconciling the seemingly disparate results in Klein (1990) and De Bondt-Thaler (1990) is to recognize that the extreme forecasts driving the De Bondt-Thaler overreaction conclusion tend to be those where analysts expect a departure from the recent earnings trends—not the continuation that an overreaction to earnings would imply. With respect to earnings, the evidence is actually more consistent with an underreaction, as Klein (1990) would suggest.

Firm conclusions about the proper interpretation of the De Bondt-Thaler (1985, 1987) evidence are difficult to draw currently, given that the literature in this area is still in flux. On the one hand, when one allows for shifts in risks and imposes the standard restrictions implied by the Sharpe-Lintner CAPM, the evidence suggests no statistically significant overeaction (Ball and Kothari [1989]). On the other hand, one of the key restrictions of the CAPM is inconsistent with the data, and when it is relaxed, evidence of overreaction again surfaces, especially for small firms (Chopra, Lakonishok, and Ritter [1992]).

What is clearer is that even if overreaction exists, it appears too complicated to be characterized as a simple function of recent earnings changes. That is a topic to which we return later, in our reconciliation of the evidence on under- and overreaction to earnings.

---

18. Zarowin (p. 1391) reports a three-year market-adjusted return of 16.6 percent for long (short) positions in lowest (highest) quintile stocks based on prior earnings changes; this represents an average of 5.3 percent per year. De Bondt and Thaler (p. 572) report a four-year market-adjusted return of 24.6 percent (-11.7 percent) for positions in lowest (highest) quintile stocks, based on prior stock return changes; this represents an average of 9.1 percent for the combination of the two positions. The Zarowin test periods range from 1972 to 1984; De Bondt and Thaler's test periods range from 1970 to 1983.

3.1.2 ALTERNATIVE EXPLANATIONS FOR THE EVIDENCE: OU AND PEN-
MAN. Ou and Penman (1989a) note the similarity between their evidence and that of De Bondt and Thaler, but report some evidence to
suggest the two anomalies are distinct. (Most importantly, the Ou-
Penman abnormal returns are not concentrated in January.) Examination
of Table 2 also indicates that the Ou-Penman Pr portfolios are far more
extreme in terms of prior year earnings performance—suggesting that
the Pr portfolios must have different content than the De Bondt-Thaler
winner/loser portfolios.

Precisely how the Ou and Penman evidence should be explained,
as indicating market inefficiency or something else, is still undergoing
scrutiny. Consistent with market inefficiency, Stober (1992) finds that the
Pr factors work best as predictors of stock returns in those cases where
analysts' earnings forecasts appear to ignore some of the information in
Pr. On the other hand, the robustness of the Ou and Penman result is
questioned in preliminary work by Greig (1990). In addition, Stober
(1992) uses data not completely available at the time Ou and Penman
conducted their work to show that Pr predicts abnormal returns for at
least six years, with little or no sign of diminution. If the abnormal returns
do indeed last for many years, Pr would appear to be capturing a permanent risk shift rather than a discrepancy between prices and fundamentals
that should be corrected over time.[19]

Holthausen and Larcker (1992) present perhaps the most serious challenge to the Ou-Penman Pr strategy, by showing that it performs poorly
after 1983. The year 1983 was the last year of the Ou-Penman tests, and
even Ou and Penman noted that the strategy may not have been profitable in 1982 or 1983. However, when Holthausen and Larcker refine the
Ou-Penman strategy only slightly, so that the "computerized fundamental analysis" is focused directly on predictions of stock returns rather than
earnings changes, the resulting estimated abnormal returns are consistently positive. The authors "find it surprising that a statistical model,
derived without consideration of any economic foundations, can earn
excess returns of the magnitude (they) document," and have no explanation for the result.

---

19. One of the empirical issues that makes it difficult to interpret the Ou-Penman evidence,
as well as much of the previously described evidence on overreaction, concerns controlling
for size effects. Since small firms include a disproportionate share of prior losers and high
Pr firms, the size effect may be caused in part by the DeBondt-Thaler overreaction effect,
and/or the Ou-Penman Pr effect. If so, controlling for size through the introduction of size
control portfolios may "throw the baby out with the bath water." The Ou-Penman result is
much stronger when based on market-adjusted returns than on size-adjusted returns.

3.1.3 HOW CAN THE EVIDENCE CONSISTENT WITH OVERREACTION TO EARNINGS BE RECONCILED WITH THE PREVIOUSLY DESCRIBED RESULTS SUGGESTING UNDERREACTION TO EARNINGS?

Evidence in De Bondt and Thaler (1987) and Ou and Penman (1989a) may appear in conflict with the evidence in section 2 suggesting an underreaction to earnings. The two sets of results are, however, potentially reconcilable through several avenues.

One possibility is that, even if overreactions occur in the stock market, they cannot be characterized as an overreaction to earnings per se. A predictable reversal of prior period extreme price movements is consistent with a wide variety of market inefficiencies—including random deviations of prices from fundamental values—and need not be caused by any systematic misinterpretation of earnings information. Note that even where evidence of overreaction is found (De Bondt and Thaler [1985, 1987] and Chopra, Lakonishok, and Ritter [1992]), there is no direct linkage between the anomalous returns and an overemphasis on earnings. In the two studies that did test for such a linkage (Klein [1990] and Zarowin [1989]), there was no support for the overreaction hypothesis. In fact, Klein concludes the evidence is more consistent with underreaction. Beyond this, while Abarbanell and Bernard (1992) confirm the De Bondt-Thaler (1990) finding of overly extreme analyst forecasts, they show that the phenomenon could not be due to analyst overreaction to recent earnings; with respect to earnings, analysts tend to underreact.

A second possibility is that both underreactions and overreactions to earnings occur. Specifically, stock prices could underreact, on average, to earnings, while overreactions occur only under conditions too complex to be captured by a simple partition on prior period earnings changes. As noted earlier, this possibility could explain why research designs like that of Bernard and Thomas (1989), which partition on the basis of prior earnings changes, indicate underreaction, while the designs of De Bondt and Thaler (1987) and Chopra, Lakonishok, and Ritter (1992), which partition on the basis of prior returns, still suggest overreaction. Such evidence is, however, also consistent with the first possibility raised above; the second possibility could be distinguished from the first only by identifying some connection between any existing overreactions and the interpretation of prior earnings numbers. For example, there might be conditions under which stock prices would fail to reflect that current earnings trends are likely to be reversed. Indeed, Ou and Penman (1989b) characterize their own evidence as indicating an underreaction to non-earnings accounting data that suggest the current year's earnings change is transitory. Another way to say the same thing is that overreactions to earnings occur when such earnings are predictably transitory, even though they do not occur on average.

A third possibility is that the market's response to earnings announcements defies a simple characterization as underreaction or overreaction. If prices reflect earnings expectations that are naive in the sense described by Bernard and Thomas (1990)—that is, based on a simple seasonal random walk—then post-announcement abnormal returns would continue to move in the same direction as the earnings news only for three quarters. The drift to this point would appear like a completion of an initial underreaction. After that point, as prices reflect the tendency for earnings to gravitate to a level less extreme than the originally announced earnings, a reversal of some of the earlier abnormal returns would occur—thus taking on the appearance of a correction of an earlier overreaction. Such a pattern is evident in Figure 2, based on Bernard and Thomas [1989], and to some extent, in the year-by-year behavior of abnormal returns in Zarowin (1989, Table 3).

4. Other Recent Evidence on Earnings-Related Anomalies: the Resurrection of the Functional Fixation Hypothesis

Other recent anomalous results concerning stock price reactions to earnings cannot be classified neatly among the aforementioned studies. Hand (1990) resurrects and extends the functional fixation hypothesis in an examination of how stock prices reacted to earnings announcements for quarters in which firms had undertaken a debt-equity swap. Debt-equity swaps were common during 1981–1984, because they could be undertaken with no tax consequence. Swaps gave rise to accounting gains that averaged 21 percent of quarterly earnings excluding the swap gain. Hand's context provides an interesting test of functional fixation because one can argue that, upon the announcement of the earnings that include the gain, an efficient market should not react to the gain. First, the gain is artificial in the sense that it represents a previously unrealized economic gain that occurred prior to the swap, when interest rates rose. Second, the amount of the gain was either disclosed publicly or accurately calculable based on public information prior to the earnings announcement. Thus, the earnings announcement date simply constitutes the "reannouncement" of the swap gain. Unless stock prices are fixated mechanically on earnings numbers, there should be no reaction to the reannouncement of the swap gain at the earnings announcement date.

Hand reports a statistically significant positive response to the swap gain, consistent with the functional fixation hypothesis. He also finds the positive response is larger for firms that are small, and/or have less institutional following, which he interprets as consistent with the notion that the result is driven by "unsophisticated" traders. The magnitude of the positive response is small, on average—less than 0.5 percent—but the result is nevertheless puzzling.

Ball and Kothari (1991) investigate yet another earnings-related anomaly, and offer an alternative interpretation of Hand's evidence. Ball and Kothari show that, even after controlling for the possibility of beta shifts and some other potentially confounding factors, the estimated abnormal returns in the days surrounding earnings announcements are on average positive.[20] For large firms, the mean abnormal return is nearly zero, but for small firms it exceeds 0.5 percent on the announcement day, and exceeds 1 percent for the three days surrounding the announcement.

Ball and Kothari also reanalyze Hand's data, and interpret his evidence as a manifestation of the more general phenomenon of positive mean announcement-period returns for small firms, as opposed to functional fixation. This interpretation leaves unanswered the question of why Hand finds a significant result for his sample only during the swap quarter. Furthermore, in his response to Ball and Kothari, Hand (1991) discusses several additional features of the evidence that support the functional fixation hypothesis. Nevertheless, when Ball and Kothari combine their evidence with skepticism about several aspects of Hand's theory, they have "serious doubts" about Hand's attribution of his anomalous result to functional fixation.

There is at least some added support for functional fixation in other studies of reactions to earnings announcements. Dietrich (1984) finds an anomalous positive reaction to accounting gains resulting from bond-for-bond refinancing, even though those accounting gains may not correspond to "economic gains," and in any case should be known or accurately estimable from public information prior to the earnings release.

Givoly and Hayn (1992) find a statistically significant positive reaction to "paper gains" resulting from the change in deferred tax accounting required by Financial Accounting Standard No. 96. Consistent with Hand's theory, the positive reaction is driven by stocks for which institutional holding is relatively low and thus "unsophisticated" traders are

---

20. Chari, Jagannathan, and Ofer (1988) were the first to study this anomaly intensively, although they did not control for all the factors examined in Ball and Kothari. Evidence of positive mean announcement-period returns is also apparent in earlier papers, including Beaver (1968, Table 6).

presumably more prevalent. The result survives a control for size, suggesting the Ball-Kothari effect is not the underlying explanation. Nevertheless, Givoly and Hayn express some discomfort with the notion of functional fixation in competitive markets, and label their interpretation of the evidence "speculative."

5. Concluding Remarks

Nearly every major piece of evidence discussed in this review has been the subject of controversy, and several of the controversies remain the focus of ongoing research. Any conclusions can only be speculative, and must be drawn with the recognition that one can never overcome the ultimate quandary in testing market efficiency. That is, any conclusions about market efficiency cannot be divorced from some assumed model of market equilibrium—the correctness of which is not only unknown, but unknowable (Ball [1990]).

One can attempt, however, to categorize the evidence in terms of how much it challenges the imagination to reconcile it with standard theories of asset pricing in competitive markets. In this sense, much of the evidence reviewed here presents quite a challenge.

Whether an incomplete initial response to earnings is the true cause of post-earnings—announcement drift has long been debated. However, the recent evidence has thus far defied explanation in terms of potential research design flaws, including a failure to control fully for risk. The concentration of the abnormal returns around subsequent earnings announcements, in patterns that are predicted by a model in which stock prices reflect naive earnings expectations, is particularly difficult to explain. Brennan (1991) characterizes this evidence (along with that of Ou and Penman [1989]) as "perhaps the most severe challenge to financial theorists posed by the recent work on market reactions to earnings announcements." The ancillary evidence suggesting that even professional analysts at Value Line underreact to recent earnings news provides further support for the notion that stock prices may not be responding completely and immediately to earnings announcements.

The recent debate on the existence of overreaction in the stock market has been less one-sided, with several studies offering evidence both for and against the overreaction hypothesis. Ball and Kothari (1989) find no reliable indications of overreaction. On the other hand, when Chopra, Lakonishok, and Ritter (1992) relax an assumption within the Ball-Kothari analysis that is rejected by the data, they produce intriguing support for overreaction.

Evidence of underreactions to earnings and overreactions among extreme stock price movements is not necessarily inconsistent, as it may at first appear. After all, even though some evidence suggests overreactions do occur, no study to date has yet linked the overreaction directly to an overemphasis on recent earnings changes. A possibility consistent with all the data is mispricing due to a variety of unidentified causes, which is most likely to surface among stocks with extreme price changes and be labeled on overreaction, in combination with incomplete initial responses to fundamentals like earnings.

When viewed as a whole, the evidence summarized here presents a more serious challenge to the efficient markets hypothesis than could have been anticipated a few years ago. It is difficult to understand how the simple trading rules described here could apparently generate positive abnormal returns. Only time will tell whether attempts to resolve the anomalies within the existing paradigm will prove successful. In the meantime, we should remain open to unconventional approaches to understanding how prices might deviate from fundamental values in what appear to be extremely competitive markets.

I am grateful for useful comments and suggestions from Ray Ball, Werner De Bondt, John Hand, Gene Imhoff, Prem Jain, S. P. Kothari, Josef Lakonishok, Krishna Palepu, Stephen Penman, Jay Ritter, Terry Shevlin, Thomas Stober, Richard Thaler, Jacob Thomas, Jim Wahlen, and Paul Zarowin, and for unpublished evidence supplied by Jim McKeown and Hans Stoll.

References

ABARBANELL, J., and V. BERNARD. "Tests of Analysts Overreaction/Underreaction to Earnings Information as an Explanation for Anomalous Stock Price Behavior." *Journal of Finance* (July 1992), pp. 1181–1208.

AFFLECK-GRAVES, J., and R. MENDENHALL. "The Relation Between the Value Line Enigma and Post-Earnings Announcement Drift." *Journal of Financial Economics* (February 1992), pp. 75–96.

ANDREASSEN, P. "On the Social Psychology of the Stock Market: Aggregate Attributional Effects and the Regressiveness of Prediction." *Journal of Personality and Social Psychology* (Vol. 53, No. 3, 1987), pp. 490–496.

ANDREASSEN, P. "Judgmental Extrapolation and Market Overreaction: On the Use and Disuse of News." *Journal of Behavioral Decision Making* (Vol. 3, 1990), pp. 153–174.

ANDREASSEN, P., and S. J. KRAUS. "Judgmental Extrapolation and the Salience of Change." *Journal of Forecasting* (Vol. 9, 1990), pp. 347–372.

BAGEHOT, W. (J. TREYNOR) "The Only Game in Town." *Financial Analysts Journal* (March–April 1971), pp. 12–14, 22.

BALL, R. "Anomalies in Relationships Between Securities' Yields and Yield-Surrogates." *Journal of Financial Economics* (June–September 1978), pp. 103–126.

―――. "What Do We Know About Market Efficiency?" Working Paper, University of Rochester (1990).

BALL, R., and P. BROWN. "An Empirical Evaluation of Accounting Income Numbers." *Journal of Accounting Research* (Autumn 1968), pp. 159–178.

BALL R., and S. P. KOTHARI. "Nonstationary Expected Returns: Implications for Tests of Market Efficiency and Serial Correlation in Returns." *Journal of Financial Economics* (November, 1989), pp. 51–74.

―――. "Security Returns Around Earnings Announcements." *The Accounting Review* (forthcoming, 1991).

BALL, R., S. P. KOTHARI, and R. WATTS ."The Economics of the Relation Between Earnings Changes and Stock Returns." Working Paper, University of Rochester (December, 1990).

BANZ, R. W., and W. J. BREEN. "Sample Dependent Results Using Accounting and Market Data: Some Evidence." *Journal of Finance* (September 1986), pp. 779–794.

BASU, S. "Investment Performance of Common Stocks in Relation to Their Price-Earnings Ratios: A Test of the Efficient Markets Hypothesis." *Journal of Finance* (June 1977), pp. 663–682.

―――. "The Relationship Between Earnings' Yield, Market Value, and Return for NYSE Common Stocks: Further Evidence." *Journal of Financial Economics* (June 1983), pp. 129–156.

BEAVER, W. H. "The Information Content of Annual Earnings Announcements." *Journal of Accounting Research* (Supplement 1968), pp. 67–92.

BERNARD, V., and J. THOMAS. "Post-Earnings-Announcement Drift: Delayed Price Response or Risk Premium?" *Journal of Accounting Research* (Supplement 1989), pp. 1–36.

―――. "Evidence that Stock Prices Do Not Fully Reflect the Implications of Current Earnings for Future Earnings." *Journal of Accounting and Economics* (December, 1990), pp. 305–341.

BLACK, F. "Yes, Virginia, There Is Hope: Tests of the Value Line Ranking System." *Financial Analysts Journal* (Vol. 29, 1973), pp. 10–14.

BODIE, Z., A. KANE, and A. MARCUS. *Investments*. Irwin, Homewood, IL (1989).

BRENNAN, M. "A Perspective on Accounting and Stock Prices." *The Accounting Review* (January 1991), pp. 67–79.

BROOKS, L., and D. BUCKMASTER. "Further Evidence on the Times Series Properties of Accounting Income." *Journal of Finance* (December 1976), pp. 1359–1373.

CHAMBERS, A., and S. PENMAN. "Timeliness of Reporting and the Stock Price Reaction to Earnings Announcements." *Journal of Accounting Research* (Spring 1984), pp. 21–47.

CHAN, K. C. "On the Contrarian Investment Strategy."*Journal of Business* (Vol. 61, 1988), pp. 147–163.

CHARI, V., R. JAGANNATHAN and A. OFER. "Seasonalities in Security Returns: The Case of Earnings Announcements." *Journal of Financial Economics* (1988, Vol. 21, No. 1), pp. 101–121.

CHEN, N., R. ROLL, and S. ROSS. "Economic Forces and the Stock Market." *Journal of Business* (July 1986), pp. 383–404.

CHOPRA, N., J. LAKONISHOK, and J. RITTER. "Measuring Abnormal Performance: Do Stocks Overreact?" *Journal of Financial Economics* (April 1992), pp. 235–268.

COOK, T. J., and M. S. ROZEFF. "Size and Earnings/Price Ratio Anomalies: One Effect or Two?" *Journal of Financial and Quantitative Analysis* (December 1984), pp. 449–466.

COPELAND, T., and D. MAYERS. "The Value Line Enigma (1965–1978): A Case Study of Performance Evaluation Issues." *Journal of Financial Economics* (Vol. 10, 1982), pp. 289–321.

DE BONDT, W. F. M., and R. H. THALER. "Does the Stock Market Overreact?" *Journal of Finance* (July 1985), pp. 793–805.

———. "Further Evidence of Investor Overreaction and Stock Market Seasonality." *Journal of Finance* (July, 1987), pp. 557–582.

———. "Do Security Analysts Overreact?" *American Economic Review* (May 1990), pp. 52–57.

DIETRICH, J. RICHARD. "Effects of Early Bond Refundings: An Empirical Investigation of Security Returns." *Journal of Accounting and Economics* (April 1984), pp. 67–96.

FAMA, E., and K. FRENCH. "Permanent and Temporary Components of Stock Prices." *Journal of Political Economy* (Vol. 96, 1988), pp. 246–273.

FAMA, E., and J. D. MACBETH. "Risk, Return, and Equilibrium: Empirical Tests." *Journal of Political Economy* (Vol. 71, 1973), pp. 607–636.

FOSTER, G. "Quarterly Accounting Data: Time Series Properties and Predictive-Ability Results." *The Accounting Review* (January 1977), pp. 1–21.

FOSTER, G., C. OLSEN, and T. SHEVLIN. "Earnings Releases, Anomalies, and the Behavior of Security Returns." *The Accounting Review* (October 1984), pp. 574–603.

FREEMAN, R., J. OHLSON, and S. PENMAN. "Book Rate-of-Return and Prediction of Earnings Changes: An Empirical Investigation." *Journal of Accounting Research* (Autumn 1982), pp. 639–653.

FREEMAN, R., and S. TSE. "The Multi-period Information Content of Earnings Announcements: Rational Delayed Reactions to Earnings News." *Journal of Accounting Research* (Supplement 1989), pp. 49–79.

GIVOLY, D., and C. HAYN. "Investors Evaluation of Deferred Taxes: Is There Accounting Fixation?" Working paper, Northwestern University 1992.

GIVOLY, D., and J. LAKONISHOK. "The Information Content of Financial Analysts' Forecasts of Earnings: Some Evidence on Semi-Strong Form Inefficiency." *Journal of Accounting and Economics* (Vol. 1, 1979), pp. 165–185.

GREIG, A. C. "Fundamental Analysis and Subsequent Stock Returns." *Journal of Accounting and Economics* (June/September 1992), pp. 413–442.

HAND, J. R. "A Test of the Extended Functional Fixation Hypothesis." *The Accounting Review* (October, 1990).

———. "Extended Functional Fixation and Security Returns Around Earnings Announcements: A Reply to Ball and Kothari." *The Accounting Review* (forthcoming, 1991).

HANDA, P., S. P. KOTHARI, and C. WASLEY. "The Relation Between the Return Interval and Betas: Implications for the Size Effect." *Journal of Financial Economics* (Vol. 23, 1989), pp. 79–100.

HOLTHAUSEN, R. "Abnormal Returns Following Quarterly Earnings Announcements." *Proceedings of the Seminar on the Analysis of Security Prices* (University of Chicago, May 1983), pp. 37–59.

HOLTHAUSEN, R., and D. LARCKER. "The Prediction of Stock Returns Using Financial Statement Information." *Journal of Accounting and Economics* (June/September 1992), pp. 373–412.

HOPWOOD, W. S., and J. C. McKEOWN. "Univariate Time-Series Analysis of Quarterly Earnings: Some Unresolved Issues." *Studies in Accounting Research No. 25* (American Accounting Association, 1986).

HUBERMAN, G., and S. KANDEL. "Market Efficiency and Value Line's Record." *Journal of Business* (April, 1990), pp. 187–216.

JAFFE, J. J., D. B. KEIM, and R. WESTERFIELD. "Earnings Yields, Market Values and Stock Returns." *Journal of Finance* (March 1989), pp. 135–148.

JONES, C., and R. LITZENBERGER. "Quarterly Earnings Reports and Intermediate Stock Price Trends." *Journal of Finance* (March 1970), pp. 143–148.

JOY, O. M., R. LITZENBERGER, and R. McENALLY. "The Adjustment of Stock Prices to Announcements of Unanticipated Changes in Quarterly Earnings." *Journal of Accounting Research* (Autumn 1977), pp. 207–225.

KIM, J. "The EP Effect and the Earnings Forecast Error Effect: A Comparison of Two Stock Market Anomalies." Ph.D. Dissertation, University of California at Berkeley (1987).

KLEIN, A. "A Direct Test of the Cognitive Bias Theory of Share Price Reversals." *Journal of Accounting and Economics* (July 1990), pp. 155–166.

LATANE, H., C. JONES, and R. D. RIEKE. "Quarterly Earnings Reports and Subsequent Holding Period Returns." *Journal of Business Research* (April, 1974), pp. 119–132.

LATANE, H., and C. JONES. "Standardized Unexpected Earnings—1971–1977." *Journal of Finance* (June 1979), pp. 717–724.

LATANE, H., and D. L. TUTTLE. "An Analysis of Common Stock Price Ratios." *Southern Economic Journal* (January, 1967), pp. 343–353.

LATANE, H., D. L. TUTTLE, and C. JONES. "EP Ratios Versus Changes in Earnings in Forecasting Future Price Changes." *Financial Analysts Journal* (January–February 1969), pp. 117–123.

MENDENHALL, R. "Evidence of Possible Underweighting of Earnings-related Information." *Journal of Accounting Research* (forthcoming, 1991).

OU J., and S. PENMAN. "Financial Statement Analysis and the Prediction of Stock Returns." *Journal of Accounting and Economics* (November, 1989a), pp. 295–330.

————. "Accounting Measurement, Price-Earnings Ratios, and the Information Content of Security Prices." *Journal of Accounting Research* (Supplement 1989b), pp. 111–144.

PATELL, J., and M. WOLFSON. "The Intraday Speed of Adjustment of Stock Prices to Earnings and Dividend Announcements." *Journal of Financial Economics* (June 1984), pp. 223–252.

POTERBA, J., and L. H. SUMMERS. "Mean Reversion in Stock Prices: Evidence and Implications." *Journal of Financial Economics* (October, 1988), pp. 27–59.

REINGANUM, M. "Misspecification of Capital Asset Pricing: Empirical Anomalies Based on Earnings Yields and Market Values." *Journal of Financial Economics* 9 (1981), pp. 19–46.

RENDLEMAN, JR., R. J., C. P. JONES, and H. A. LATANE. "Empirical Anomalies Based on Unexpected Earnings and the Importance of Risk Adjustments." *Journal of Financial Economics* (1982), pp. 269–287.

————. "Further Insight into the Standardized Unexpected Earnings Anomaly: Size and Serial Correlation Effects." *The Financial Review* (February 1987), pp. 131–144.

STOBER, T. L. "Summary Financial Statement Measures and Analysts' Forecasts of Earnings." *Journal of Accounting and Economics* (June/September 1992), pp. 347–372.

STOLL, H. "Measuring Equity Trading Costs." Working Paper, Vanderbilt University (1991).

TINIC, S. M., and R. R. WEST. "Risk and Return: January vs. the Rest of the Year." *Journal of Financial Economics* (December 1984), pp. 561–574.

WATTS, R. L. "The Time Series Behavior of Quarterly Earnings." Working Paper, University of Newcastle, Newcastle, Newcastle-on-Tyne (1975).

————. "Systematic 'Abnormal' Returns after Quarterly Earnings Announcements." *Journal of Financial Economics* (June/September 1978), pp. 127–150.

WIGGINS, J. B. "Do Misperceptions about the Earnings Process Contribute to Post-Announcement Drift?" Working Paper, Cornell University (1991).

ZAROWIN, P. "Does the Stock Market Overreact to Corporate Earnings Information?" *Journal of Finance* (December 1989), pp. 1385–1400.

12

Overreactions in the Options Market

JEREMY STEIN

Are investors "rational"—do they behave like Bayesian statisticians—when it comes to incorporating new information into asset prices? Proponents of the efficient markets hypothesis would answer this question in the affirmative. Many others, however, believe that Bayesian rationality is a poor description of investor behavior and that, as a consequence, asset prices tend to be informationally inefficient.

One way in which inefficiencies might arise is through the overreactions of traders to the arrival of new information.[1] This possibility is raised by experimental and survey findings which indicate that people have a systematic tendency to overemphasize recent data at the expense of other information when making projections.[2]

The objective of this paper is to search for evidence of such overreactive behavior in a seemingly peculiar place: the options market. Options may appear to be unlikely candidates for overreaction because, unlike primary securities, their prices are closely tied down by arbitrage considerations. As Black and Scholes (1973) demonstrate, if stock price volatility is known, options prices are completely determined—any deviation from the prescribed value implies a riskless profit opportunity.

However, given that volatility is in fact unknown and changing, options do retain something of an independent nature, not wholly redundant with their underlying stocks. Options can be thought of as reflecting

---

1. Overreaction to new information is not the *only* way to generate inefficient prices, of course. Purely random noise unrelated to information will cause excess volatility also.

2. See, for example, Tversky and Kahneman (1974).

From: *The Journal of Finance*, pp. 1011–1022, 1989. Reprinted by permission of the American Finance Association.

a speculative market in volatility—the implied volatility on a given option (obtained by inverting a Black-Scholes-type formula) should equal the average volatility that is expected to prevail over the life of that option.[3]

This observation suggests that one can conduct "term structure" tests to check whether the temporal structure of options' implied volatilities is consistent with rational expectations. A simple example illustrates the idea behind the tests. Suppose that volatility averages fifteen percent, but that it fluctuates up and down quite rapidly, governed by a strongly mean-reverting process. If a one-month option currently has an implied volatility of twenty-five percent, a two-month option should have an implied volatility that is somewhat lower, with the exact level determined by the coefficient of mean reversion. Conversely, when a one-month option has an implied volatility of five percent, the two-month option should have a higher one.

The evidence presented here contradicts this rational expectations hypothesis for the term structure of implied volatility.[4] Although volatility shocks decay away very quickly, market participants do not take this fully into account when pricing options. Longer term options' implied volatilities move almost in lockstep with those on shorter term options, displaying less of the "smoothing" behavior than is warranted. In this sense, longer term options overreact relative to shorter term ones—they place too much emphasis on innovations in short-term options' implied volatility and too little emphasis on historical data that indicate that these innovations will not persist.

While statistically significant, the mispricings found in the options are small in magnitude compared to those that might conceivably arise with primary securities such as stocks or bonds. Nonetheless, there are a couple of reasons why these mispricings may still be construed as having strong implications. First, option pricing is unique in that it involves only one uncertain variable, namely volatility. In contrast, equity and bond prices contain risk premia. Thus, evidence that appears to suggest irrational excess variability in the stock and bond markets can also be interpreted as rational market responses to time-varying equilibrium rates of

---

3. This is somewhat loose. The statement will be literally true in a world of stochastic volatility only if two conditions are satisfied: 1) there is no risk premium for bearing volatility risk (or, equivalently, volatility stocks are uncorrelated with consumption) and 2) the options pricing formula is linear in volatility, so that there are no Jensen's inequality-type effects. While the latter condition does not hold generally, it does hold almost exactly for at-the-money options, which are the only kind used in the empirical work presented here. These issues are addressed in more detail in Section II.A.

4. More precisely, the evidence rejects the joint hypothesis that the pricing model used is the correct one and that agents form volatility expectations rationally.

return.[5] Since these required rates of return are not observable, it is often hard to come to a definitive conclusion.[6] This ambiguity does not arise in the context of options, where arbitrage considerations lead to prices that are independent of riskiness.[7]

A second reason why the mispricings found here are noteworthy is that they point to a specific cause of excess fluctuations, that of investor overreaction to new information. This is not the case with much of the "inefficient markets" literature. Furthermore, the inability of traders to behave in a proper Bayesian fashion when pricing longer term options is particularly striking because the problem they face is a relatively simple one: there is one clear source of information, the implied volatility on the short-term option. The only other required inputs are the parameters of the process driving volatility, which are easily objectively quantified in a parsimonious model. Comparing this to the mass of often subjective information that must be sorted through to correctly price stocks, one is tempted to conjecture that simplistic and perhaps overreactive rules of thumb must be of fundamental importance in the stock market.

The remainder of this paper is organized as follows. Section I derives the theoretical relationship between the implied volatilities on options of different maturities that should hold when volatility follows an AR1 process. Section II shows that an AR1 actually does provide a good description of the movements of volatility on S&P 100 options and goes on to test the theoretical relationship of Section I. Section III presents an alternative type of test, one that has the advantage of not requiring any particular specification for the process driving volatility. Section IV offers some conclusions.

1. The Term Structure of Implied Volatility

This section derives the restrictions on relative options prices that are implied by a given stochastic process for stock price volatility. Assume

---

5. One noteworthy example concerns the work of DeBondt and Thaler (1985), who find evidence of a "rebound" effect in the stock market—stocks that had once been extreme losers later tended to perform abnormally well. This can be reconciled with rationality as follows: a decline in stock prices leads to higher leverage, higher CAPM betas, and hence higher expected returns. See DeBondt and Thaler (1987) for a fuller discussion and references.

6. Time-varying rates of return have also been proposed as an explanation for the mean reversion in stock prices found by Fama and French (1988) and Poterba and Summers (1988).

7. Again, this assumes that volatility risk is idiosyncratic. Options prices will always be independent of the risk on the underlying assets.

that "instantaneous" volatility σ_t evolves according to the following continuous-time mean-reverting AR1 process:

$$d\sigma_t = -\alpha(\sigma_t - \bar{\sigma})dt + \beta\sigma_t dz. \tag{1}$$

At time t, the expectation of volatility as of time $t + j$ will be given by

$$E_t(\sigma_{t+j}) = \bar{\sigma} + \rho^j(\sigma_t - \bar{\sigma}), \tag{2}$$

where $\rho = e^{-\alpha} < 1$. That is, volatility is expected to decay geometrically back toward its long-run mean level of $\bar{\sigma}$.

Denote by $i_t(T)$ the implied volatility at time t on an option with T remaining until expiration. As noted earlier, this should equal the averaged expected instantaneous volatility over the time span $[t, t + T]$. Using (2), this implies

$$i_t(t) = \frac{1}{T}\int_{j=0}^{T} [\bar{\sigma} + \rho^j(\sigma_t - \bar{\sigma})]\, dj = \bar{\sigma} + \frac{\rho^T - 1}{T \ln \rho}[\sigma_t - \bar{\sigma}]. \tag{3}$$

Equation (3) provides the basis for the empirical tests that follow. It states that, when instantaneous volatility is above its mean level, the implied volatility on an option should be *decreasing* in the time to expiration. Conversely, when instantaneous volatility is below its mean, implied volatility should be increasing in the time to expiration.

Instantaneous volatility σ_t cannot be directly observed. However, this does not interfere with testing of the sort described above. Suppose there are two options: a "nearby," with time to expiration T and implied volatility $i_t^n(T)$, and a "distant," with time to expiration $K > T$ and implied volatility $i_t^d(K)$. Using equation (3), the following restriction can be derived:

$$(i_t^d - \bar{\sigma}) = \frac{T(\rho^K - 1)}{K(\rho^T - 1)}(i_t^n - \bar{\sigma}). \tag{4}$$

Equation (4) is directly testable because it does not involve the instantaneous volatility σ_t. It can be thought of as an elasticity relationship: given a movement in nearby implied volatility i_t^d, there should be a smaller movement in distant implied volatility i_t^d. The exact constant of proportionality depends on the mean reversion parameter ρ, as well as on the times to expiration of the two options.

2. An Empirical Test on S&P 100 Index Options

2.1 The Data

The data used in this section were generously provided by Mark Zurack of Goldman Sachs and Co. They consist of two daily time series on implied volatilities for S&P 100 index options for the period December 1983 to September 1987, a total of 964 observations for each series. The "nearby" series represents the options with the shortest time to expiration—between zero and one month, depending on the sampling date. The "distant" series represents the options with the next expiration date—between one and two months. Thus, the distant options always have one month longer to go than the nearby options.

For each series, implied volatility is calculated by averaging the implieds on the put and call option closest to being at the money. The options pricing model used to compute implied volatility is a Cox-Ross-Rubinstein (1979) binomial model that explicitly accounts for the dividend yield on the index and for the possibility of early exercise. The inputs are the daily closing prices of the options and the index.

There are several issues worth noting with regard to the quality of the data. First, a study by Evnine and Rudd (1985) found significant evidence of pricing errors in the S&P 100 options market over the period June–August 1984. They attribute some of this to data asynchronies (although they use real-time data) and some to difficulties in arbitraging an entire index. These types of mispricing, which should not lead to a bias in any particular direction, amount to random measurement errors in the implied volatilities being used here. It will be argued below that such measurement errors are not a serious problem for the tests to be performed below. Rather, they have the effect of making the tests *more conservative*—it will be more difficult to reject the null hypothesis of rationality in favor of an overreactions alternative.

A potentially more serious concern would be systematic biases in the implieds due to using an incorrect pricing model. In spite of this paper's premise of stochastic volatility, the pricing model employed in creating the data does not take it into account. Hull and White (1987) and Wiggins (1987) have found that stochastic volatility of the sort assumed here can have a significant impact on some options prices. Fortunately, however, problems are unlikely to arise here because the only data used come from at-the-money options. The prices of such options are almost exactly linear in σ at all maturities. Thus, the implieds derived from inverting a nonstochastic volatility formula should accurately reflect the average volatility that is expected to prevail over the life of these options—there will be no distortions due to using the simpler pricing model.

More fundamentally, it should be emphasized that pricing biases alone would not be enough to cause false acceptance of the overreactions hypothesis in the tests to be performed here. Such false acceptance will occur only if *changes* in the biases are correlated with volatility movements in a very peculiar way (for example, if a rise in volatility systematically increases the extent to which the pricing model overvalues two-month options relative to one-month options). Not only is there no a priori reason for expecting this to be the cause but, if biases are small, any daily changes in them are almost certainly of second order.

2.2 The Persistence of Volatility Stocks

The first step in the empirical analysis is to identify and estimate the stochastic process followed by volatility. Theoretically, we are interested in the serial correlation properties of the instantaneous volatility σ_t, which cannot be observed directly. However, it can be shown that the implied volatility on the nearby option has virtually the same serial correlation characteristics.

Equation (1) specifies the process for volatility as AR1 in levels. In a related study, French, Schwert, and Stambaugh (1987) examine the time-series properties of a measure of volatility constructed directly from stock price data. They find significant skewness in this series and conclude that the stochastic process should be specified in logs. A skewness test was performed here as well, with a different conclusion: there is no significant skewness in implied volatility. This should not be particularly surprising since implied volatilities are not forced to take on huge values after one or two extremely abrupt market moves in the same way as the constructed volatilities of French et al. (1987). In view of the lack of skewness, it seems appropriate to model the volatility process in levels.

The next step is to produce an autocorrelogram and a partial correlogram for i_t^n. Table I presents the results for both the raw i_t^n series and a detrended version. The detrended version is studied because of the presence of a significant ex post trend in volatility, which rises over the sample period. Such a trend can lead to spuriously high autocorrelations when the raw series is examined. In both cases, the autocorrelations have also been converted to an "implied weekly ρ" for ease of comparison. For example, the eight-week autocorrelation is converted to an implied weekly ρ by raising it to the one-eighth power.

The table indicates that an AR1 process provides a good description of the data. A smooth geometric decay in the autocorrelations leads to implied weekly ρ's that are similar at all lag lengths for both the raw and detrended series (although, as expected, using the detrended series leads to slightly lower estimated autocorrelations). The partial correlations are generally close to zero after the first lag, which is characteristic of an AR1 process. Another argument in favor of the AR1 specification is that adding additional lags does not improve the explanatory power of the regression. For example, with the raw series, the corrected R^2 is 0.82 when only a one-week lag is used, and it is the same when one- *through* eight-week lags are employed.

Table I Autocorrelograms and Partial Correlograms for i_t^n Series

i_t^n is the implied volatility on the nearby options, and the implied weekly ρ is the autocorrelation raised to the $1/n$ power, where n is the lag length in weeks.

Lag Length (Weeks)	Raw Series			Detrended Series		
	Autocorrelation*	Implied Weekly ρ	Partial Correlation*	Autocorrelation*	Implied Weekly ρ	Partial Correlation*
1	0.906 (0.014)	0.906	0.835 (0.033)	0.874 (0.016)	0.874	0.824 (0.033)
2	0.832 (0.018)	0.912	0.079 (0.043)	0.776 (0.020)	0.881	0.077 (0.043)
3	0.761 (0.028)	0.913	0.054 (0.043)	0.685 (0.024)	0.882	0.051 (0.043)
4	0.685 (0.023)	0.910	−0.089 (0.043)	0.587 (0.026)	0.875	−0.090 (0.043)
5	0.621 (0.025)	0.909	−0.086 (0.043)	0.505 (0.028)	0.872	−0.087 (0.043)
6	0.583 (0.026)	0.914	0.077 (0.043)	0.458 (0.029)	0.878	0.075 (0.043)
7	0.551 (0.026)	0.918	0.014 (0.043)	0.420 (0.030)	0.883	0.013 (0.043)
8	0.530 (0.028)	0.924	0.039 (0.043)	0.394 (0.030)	0.890	0.027 (0.033)

*Standard Errors in parentheses.

Table II Implied Weekly ρ's for Subsample Periods

The implied weekly ρ at a given lag length is the autocorrelation coefficient of nearby implied volatility at that lag, raised to the $1/n$ power, where n is the lag length in weeks.

Lag Length (Weeks)	Full Sample (Raw Series)	Full Sample (Detrended Series)	Annual Periods 1984	1985	(Raw Series) 1986	1987
1	0.906	0.874	0.656	0.874	0.757	0.779
2	0.912	0.881	0.727	0.893	0.737	0.764
3	0.913	0.882	0.748	0.900	0.703	0.731
4	0.910	0.875	0.781	0.898	0.569	0.661

These conclusions about the appropriateness of an AR1 specification are similar to those reached by Poterba and Summers (1986) in their study of a constructed volatility series. French et al., however, argue that a nonstationary model (specifically, an IMA (1, 3)) fits their data better. In order to check against such a nonstationary alternative, Dickey-Fuller (1981) tests were performed. Using a variety of specifications, the unit root hypothesis is rejected repeatedly, as it was in Poterba and Summers (1986).

Table II recalculates implied weekly ρ's for smaller subsample periods, with each calendar year being treated separately. This is done in order to check that the serial correlation properties of i_t^n are relatively stable. If this were not the case, it would be questionable to use the full sample ρ's as a basis for prediction at any given point in time. The table only displays the annual results for the raw i_t^n series. The detrended series leads to very similar results—the effect of the time trend is less important in shorter sample periods. While the table documents some variation in ρ over time, one conclusion emerges rather strongly: at no point in time is the weekly ρ ever greater than 0.90, and it is often substantially lower, perhaps as low as 0.75.[8]

Before proceeding, two potential problems should be touched on. The first is measurement error. To the extent that the i_t^n's are measured with

---

8. Diagnostic tests of the type described for the full sample were also run to see whether the AR1 specification was appropriate for the yearly subsamples. The results were generally similar to those documented in Table I for the full sample.

error, the estimates of ρ given above will be biased downward. However, as will be seen shortly, this bias will be offset in the testing procedure of the next subsection, with the net result being a test that errs on the side of conservatism.

A second possible cause for concern is that, while an AR1 model may be a good simple predictor of future volatility, it need not be the perfect one. Adding perfect further lags or changing the specification could conceivably improve predictive ability somewhat, and it also might be that market participants use information other than current and past volatility when forecasting future levels. In order to ensure that the results of the next subsection are not due to a misspecification of this sort, Section IV develops an alternative type of test, one that does not require any particular specification of how agents forecast future volatility.

2.3 A Test of Equation (4)

For the data used in this section, equation (4) can be rewritten as

$$(i_t^d - \bar{\sigma}) = \beta(\rho, T)(i_t^n - \bar{\sigma}). \tag{5}$$

That is, the elasticity β depends on both the decay parameter ρ and the time to expiration T of the nearby option. The time to expiration K of the distant option can be substituted out since this data set $K = T + 4$ (where time is measured in weeks).[9]

In principle, even for a fixed ρ, equation (5) is nonlinear since the β can be different for different values of T. However, for all practical purposes, this nonlinearity is negligible—over the range of parameters that will be of interest, variations in T have little impact.

Table III illustrates. It gives the values of β for different ρ's and for T's from one to four weeks. As the table shows, when ρ is close to one, β varies very little with changes in T. Indeed, β can be very closely approximated by the following simple function of ρ:

$$\beta \simeq \frac{(1 + \rho^4)}{2}. \tag{6}$$

This function represents a "linear endpoint approximation," with i_t^d given as the average of i_t^n today and the expected value of i_t^n one month hence. The approximation is exact when the nearby option has a maturity

---

9. This is not literally true—in actuality, K will equal either $T + 4$ or $T + 5$, depending on the number of Fridays in the month. However, using $T + 4$ everywhere amounts to a conservative testing procedure—it implies less mean reversion and, hence, will make it more difficult to find overreactions that violate the theoretically correct upper bounds for β.

Table III   Values of $\beta(\rho, T) = \dfrac{T(\rho^{T+4} - 1)}{(T + 4)(\rho^T - 1)}$

ρ is the autocorrelation coefficient of nearby implied volatility at a one-week lag, and T is the time to expiration of the nearby option. β then represents the theoretically correct elasticity of the distant option's implied volatility with respect to that of the nearby option.

T = No. of Weeks	$\rho = 0.9$	$\rho = 0.8$	$\rho = 0.7$
1	0.82	0.67	0.55
2	0.82	0.68	0.58
3	0.83	0.69	0.60
4	0.83	0.70	0.62
Linear Endpoint Approximation: $\beta = \dfrac{(1 + \rho^4)}{2}$	0.83	0.70	0.62

T of one month. Otherwise, it is inexact to the extent that volatility does not move linearly over the time period between T and one month.[10] Based on the estimates of ρ in Section II.B, the theoretical value of β is somewhere between 0.83 (corresponding to $\rho = 0.90$) and 0.66 (corresponding to $\rho = 0.75$). In other words, if the distant options are priced rationally relative to the nearby options, then, when the nearby implied volatility is one percent above its mean, the distant implied volatility should be *at most* about 0.83 percent above its mean.

One can test to see whether this holds empirically by regressing $(i_t^d - \bar{\sigma})$ against $(i_t^n - \bar{\sigma})$. Before turning to the regression results, the effects of measurement error in the i_t^n's should be discussed. Measurement error has two separate effects: 1) As noted earlier, it leads to a downward bias in ρ^4. Looking at equation (6), this by itself would tend to make us reject too easily the null of rationality in favor of an overreactions alternative—it lowers the "theoretically correct" β and, hence, lowers the empirical β that would have to be found to accept the overreactions hypothesis. 2) On the other hand, measurement error also biases downward the empirical β

10. To the extent that the approximation is incorrect, using it will only make the testing procedure more conservative since the approximation implies mean reversion that is too slow. See footnote 9.

Table IV   Regressions of i_t^d onto i_t^n

i_t^d is the implied volatility on the distant option series, and i_t^n is the implied volatility on the nearby option series.

Sample Period	Coefficient	Standard Error	R^2
Full Sample	0.929	(0.012)	0.96
1984	0.904	(0.042)	0.81
1985	0.940	(0.042)	0.92
1986	0.818	(0.028)	0.92
1987	0.819	(0.023)	0.94

that will be estimated when i_t^d is regressed against i_t^n. This will work in the opposite direction, making it harder to find overreactions.

Since the coefficient on ρ^4 in equation (6) is ½, the latter effect dominates—the downward bias in our estimated β will be twice the downward bias in the "theoretically correct" β (which is constructed using the biased ρ^4 estimate). Consequently, measurement error will make the test more conservative—it will be more difficult to find evidence of overreactions. This can be seen intuitively by considering the polar case of infinite measurement error. In this case, the estimated value of ρ^4 would be zero, and our "theoretically correct" β would be calculated as ½ from equation (6). However, a regression of i_t^d onto i_t^n would also produce a coefficient of zero, which would look like an *underreaction* relative to the "theoretically correct" regression coefficient of ½.

Table IV presents the results of the regression tests, both for the full sample and for each year run separately. All the regressions are OLS, and the standard errors have been corrected using the methodology of Hansen (1982) to deal with serial correlation in the residuals.[11] The coefficients for the full sample and for the first two years are significantly higher than the highest plausible theoretical β of 0.82. The coefficients for the last two years are somewhat lower. However, if one refers back to Table II and notes that there is no evidence of a ρ above 0.8 (which implies a theoretical β of 0.70) during these two years, they appear to be characterized by overreactions as well; while the elasticity of i_t^d with respect to i_t^n is lower, there is also a concurrent drop from the previous year in the persistence of volatility shocks.

---

11. The regressions use "raw" i_t^d and i_t^n data. However, using detrended data leads to virtually identical results. For example, the full sample coefficient using detrended data is 0.922, as opposed to the value of 0.929 reported here for the raw data.

It bears repeating that measurement error in the i_t^n's will tend to bias downward the regression coefficients and, on net, make the tests more conservative. Further downward bias might arise if the daily i_t^d and i_t^n data are not perfectly synchronized. To investigate this possibility, the regressions were rerun using weekly averages of the daily data. As it turned out, this had little effect on the results, suggesting that asynchronies of this type are not a problem.

3. An Alternative Test for Overreactions

The tests of the previous section relied on specifying a particular stochastic process for volatility. This section considers a more general test procedure which makes no such requirement. It is exactly analogous to the more recent tests of rational expectations in the term structure of interest rates, such as those performed by Campbell and Shiller (1984), among others. (See Froot (1989) for a survey of much of this literature.)

The linear endpoint approximation of equations (5) and (6) can be rewritten in more general form as

$$(i_t^d - \bar{\sigma}) = \tfrac{1}{2}[(i_t^n - \bar{\sigma}) + E_t(i_{t+4}^n - \bar{\sigma})]. \tag{7}$$

This in turn can be rearranged to yield

$$E_t[(i_{t+4}^n - i_t^n) - 2(i_t^d - i_t^n)] = 0. \tag{8}$$

The prediction error given within the expectations operator on the left-hand side of (8) should, according to rational expectations, be white noise. If, on the other hand, there are overreactions, this prediction error will be negatively correlated with i_t^n—when i_t^n is high, i_t^d is *too high*, leading to a negative prediction error.

Thus, one can test for overreactions simply by regressing the prediction error on i_t^n. Table V describes the results. Again, the regressions are OLS and the standard errors have been corrected to account for serial correlation of the residuals induced by the overlapping observations. The results generally bear out the overreactions hypothesis. The coefficients for the full sample and for each individual year are all negative. In all but one instance, the coefficients are either significantly different from zero at the five percent confidence level or very close to it.[12]

---

12. A couple of qualifying points should be made with respect to the results of Table V. First, not all months contain four weeks—some contain five. However, the same type of argument as in footnote 9 implies that using i_{t+4}^n instead of i_{t+5}^n only makes it more difficult to find evidence of overreactions. (This is supported by rerunning the regressions with i_{t+5}^n, which leads to stronger results.) Second, as discussed in the last section, the type of

Table V   Regressions of $[(i_{t+4}^n - i_t^n) - 2(i_t^d - i_t^n)]$ onto i_t^n

i^d is the implied volatility on the distant option series; i_t^n is the implied volatility on the nearby option series; and i_{t+4}^n is i_t^n led by four weeks.

Sample Period	Coefficient	Standard Error	t-Statistic
Full Sample	−0.166	(0.093)	−1.78
1984	−0.602	(0.150)	−4.01
1985	−0.346	(0.248)	−1.40
1986	−0.611	(0.206)	−2.97
1987	−0.461	(0.259)	−1.78

The point estimates in Table V are roughly consistent with the magnitudes seen in the previous section. Suppose that the theoretically correct β is 0.70 (corresponding to a weekly ρ of 0.80) but that the empirically measured elasticity is 0.90. Substitution into equation (8) yields a slope of −0.40 for the residual with respect to i_t^n, which is in the range seen in the annual regressions of Table V.

4. Conclusions

Two types of tests have been presented, both of which reject the joint hypothesis that the pricing model used to recover implied volatilities is correct and that volatility expectations are formed rationally. If one maintains the assumption that the pricing model is correct, the tests are evidence of consistent overreactive behavior in the term structure of options' implied volatilities. The first test used an AR1 model for volatility to derive theoretical upper bounds for the elasticity of distant implied volatility with respect to nearby implied volatility. It was then found that the empirical values of this elasticity exceeded the theoretical upper bounds.

The second test dispensed with the need for a specific stochastic model of volatility. Instead, it employed a more conventional rational expectations procedure, checking to see whether white noise residuals resulted when the $(i_t^d - i_t^n)$ spread was used to forecast future volatility changes.

---

linear endpoint approximation used in equation (7) is inexact when T is less than four weeks (although for reasonable parameter values, it is very accurate). Again, however, an argument similar to that in footnote 10 establishes that using the approximation simply amounts to a conservative testing procedure.

The negative coefficients obtained when the residuals were regressed on i_t^n reinforced the conclusions drawn from the first test.

In spite of their statistical significance, the overreactions found here are fairly small in economic magnitude. For example, if the theoretically correct elasticity is 0.85 but the actual is 0.95, then the distant options have an implied volatility that is typically one percent off the mark for every ten percent that volatility is away from its mean. Suppose that volatility averages fifteen percent, but that the implied on the nearby is currently at twenty-five percent. Then the implied on the distant "should" be at 23.5 percent $(23.5 = 15 + 0.85 (25 - 15))$ but will tend to be too high at around 24.5 percent. For a two-month European call option at the money, with an interest rate of ten percent and an initial stock price of 100, the "correct" volatility of 23.5 percent gives a price of 4.66. The "incorrect" volatility of 24.5 percent gives a price of 4.82—an overpricing of 3.4 percent. Even a very "aggressive" example leads to modest mispricings. If the theoretically correct elasticity is only 0.65, the correct volatility of 21.5 percent yields a price of 4.35, so that the incorrect price of 4.82 represents a 10.8 percent overpricing.

Of course, even the most naive rule of thumb cannot have all that large an impact if we are only comparing one- and two-month options. Suppose that investors ignored mean reversion in volatility altogether, so that one- and two-month options always had the same implied volatilities. The same reasoning as above shows that, once again, the deviations from theoretically correct prices would be small.

In order for such ignorance of mean reversion in volatility to translate into large pricing errors, the options involved would have to be quite long-lived. Thus, it would be very interesting to know whether investors in long-dated options also tend to overreact to changes in short-term implieds. If they do, the mispricings involved are likely to be much more economically significant.

Because of this potential interest, an attempt was made to construct tests analogous to those presented above, using data on warrants and short-term options for several individual companies that had both available. For example, American General has outstanding warrants that expire in 1989, as well as short-term options. The prices of these securities were used to create the data series i_t^d (the implied on the warrant) and i_t^n (the implied on the option) for American General. Regressions were then run to estimate the elasticity of the former with respect to the latter. Unfortunately, the data series were simply not of sufficient quality to generate any meaningful inferences. Unlike with the S&P 100 data, the implieds contain very large measurement errors due to infrequent trading and other problems. This was the case with all of the six companies studied.[13]

In spite of the lack of success in this endeavor, the methodology may yet prove useful in studying longer dated options. If, as is likely, markets for long-dated index options develop over the next few years, they may provide a high-quality source of data more suitable for the type of tests developed in this paper.

I am grateful to Mark Zurack of Goldman Sachs and Co. for providing me with the data on index options and to Bill Fairburn for stellar research assistance. Thanks also to Ken Froot for several helpful discussions and to Fischer Black, René Stulz, and an anonymous referee for their suggestions.

References

BLACK, FISCHER and MYRON SCHOLES. 1973. The pricing of options and corporate liabilities. *Journal of Political Economy* 81, 637–654.

CAMPBELL, JOHN and ROBERT SHILLER. 1984. A simpler account of the behavior of long-term interest rates. *American Economic Review Papers and Proceedings* 74, 44–48.

COX, JOHN, STEPHEN ROSS, and MARK RUBINSTEIN. 1979. Option pricing: A simplified approach. *Journal of Financial Economics* 7, 229–263.

DEBONDT, WERNER and RICHARD THALER. 1985. Does the stock market overreact? *Journal of Finance* 40, 793–805.

——— and RICHARD THALER. 1987. Further evidence on investor overreaction and stock market seasonality. *Journal of Finance* 42, 557–581.

DICKEY, DAVID and WAYNE FULLER. 1981. Likelihood ratio statistics for autoregressive time series with a unit root. *Econometrica* 49, 1057–1072.

EVNINE, JEREMY and ANDREW RUDD. 1985. Index options: The early evidence. *Journal of Finance* 40, 743–755.

FAMA, EUGENE and KENNETH FRENCH. 1988. Permanent and temporary components of stock prices. *Journal of Political Economy* 96, 246–273.

FRENCH, KENNETH, WILLIAM SCHWERT, and ROBERT STAMBAUGH. 1987. Expected stock returns and volatility. *Journal of Financial Economics* 19, 3–29.

13. In addition to American General, these companies were Asarco, Apache, FNMA, Lilly, and Southwest Air.

FROOT, KENNETH. 1989. New hope for the expectations hypothesis of the term structure of interest rates. *Journal of Finance* 44, 283–305.

HANSEN, LARS PETER. 1982. Large sample properties of generalized method of moments estimators. *Econometrica* 50, 1029–1054.

HULL, JOHN and ALAN WHITE. 1987. The pricing of options on assets with stochastic volatilities. *Journal of Finance* 42, 281–300.

POTERBA, JAMES and LAWRENCE SUMMERS. 1986. The persistence of volatility and stock market fluctuations. *American Economic Review* 76, 1142–1151.

———— and LAWRENCE SUMMERS. 1988. Mean reversion in stock prices: Evidence and implications. *Journal of Financial Economics* 22, 27–59.

TVERSKY, AMOS and DANIEL KAHNEMAN. 1974. Judgment under uncertainty: Heuristics and biases. *Science* 185, 1124–1131.

WIGGINS, JAMES. 1987. Options values under stochastic volatility. *Journal of Financial Economics* 19, 351–372.

PART
IV
INTERNATIONAL MARKETS

13

Forward Discount Bias

Is It an Exchange Risk Premium?

KENNETH A. FROOT
and JEFFREY A. FRANKEL

1. Introduction

There is by now a large literature testing whether the forward discount is an unbiased predictor of the future change in the spot exchange rate.[1] Most of the studies that test the unbiasedness hypothesis reject it, and they generally agree on the direction of bias. They tend to disagree, however, about whether the bias is evidence of a risk premium or of a violation of rational expectations. Some studies assume that investors are risk neutral, so that the systematic component of exchange rate changes in excess of the forward discount is interpreted as evidence of a failure of rational expectations. On the other hand, others attribute the same systematic component to a time-varying risk premium that separates the forward discount from expected depreciation.

Investigations by Fama (1984) and Hodrick and Srivastava (1986) have recently gone a step further, interpreting the bias not only as evidence of a nonzero risk premium, but also as evidence that the variance of the risk premium is greater than the variance of expected depreciation. Bilson (1985) expresses the extreme form of this view, which he calls a new "empirical paradigm:" expected depreciation is always zero, and changes

---

1. For a recent survey of the literature see Hodrick (1988).

From: *The Quarterly Journal of Economics*, February 1989. © 1989 by the President and Fellows of Harvard College and the Massachusetts Institute of Technology. Reprinted by permission.

in the forward discount instead reflect changes in the risk premium. Often cited in support of this view is the work of Meese and Rogoff (1983), who find that a random walk model consistently forecasts future spot rates better than alternative models, including the forward rate.

But one cannot address without additional information the basic issues of whether systematic expectational errors or the risk premium are responsible for the repeatedly biased forecasts of the forward discount, let alone whether the risk premium is more variable than expected depreciation. In this paper we use survey data on exchange rate expectations in an attempt to help resolve these issues. The data come from three surveys: one conducted by American Express Banking Corporation of London irregularly between 1976 and 1985; another conducted by the *Economist's Financial Report,* also from London, at regular six-week intervals since 1981; and a third conducted by Money Market Services (MMS) of Redwood City, California, every two weeks beginning in November 1982 and every week beginning in October 1984. Frankel and Froot (1985, 1987) discuss the data and estimate models of how investors form their expectations.[2] In this paper we use the surveys to divide the forward discount into its two components—expected depreciation and the risk premium—in order to shed new light on the large literature that finds bias in the predictions of the forward rate.

We want to be skeptical of the accuracy of the survey data, to allow for the possibility that they measure true investor expectations with error. Such measurement error could arise in a number of ways. We shall follow the existing literature in talking as if there exists a single expectation that is homogeneously held by investors, which we measure by the median survey response.[3] But, in fact, different survey respondents report different answers, suggesting that if there is a single true expectation, it is measured with error. Another possible source of measurement error in our expected depreciation series is that the expected future spot rate may not be recorded by the survey at precisely the same moment as the contemporaneous spot rate is recorded.[4]

---

2. Dominguez (1986) also uses some of the MMS surveys.

3. For an explicit consideration of heterogeneous expectations, see Frankel and Froot (1988).

4. To measure the contemporaneous spot rate, we experimented with different approximations to the precise survey and forecast dates of the AMEX survey, which was conducted by mail over a period of up to a month. We used the average of the 30 days during the survey and also the mid-point of the survey period to construct reference sets. Both gave very similar results, so that only results from the former sample were reported. In the case of the *Economist* and MMS surveys, which constitute most of our data set, this issue hardly arises to begin with, as they were conducted by telephone on a known day.

Our econometric tests allow for measurement error in the data, provided that the error is random. There is a formal analogy with the rational expectations approach which uses ex post exchange rate changes rather than survey data and assumes that the error in measuring true expected depreciation, usually attributed to "news," is random. One of our findings below is that the expectational errors made in predicting ex post sample exchange rate changes are correlated with the forward discount. This, of course, could be consistent with a failure of investor rationality, but it is also consistent with "peso problems," nonstationarities in the sample (such as a change in the process governing the spot rate), and learning on the part of investors. But there is an important respect for which the origin of these systematic expectational errors is immaterial: our results imply that widespread econometric practice—inferring from ex post data what investors must have expected—tends to give misleading answers.

The paper is organized as follows. In Section 2 we reproduce the standard regression test of forward discount bias. We then use the surveys to separate the bias into a component attributable to systematic expectational errors and a component attributable to the risk premium. Sections 3 and 4 in turn test the statistical significance of the component attributable to the risk premium and the component attributable to systematic expectational errors, respectively. Section 5 concludes.

2. The Regression of Forward Discount Bias

The most popular test of forward market unbiasedness is a regression of the future change in the spot rate on the forward discount:[5]

$$\Delta s_{t+k} = \alpha + \beta f d_t^k + \eta_{t+k}^k, \tag{1}$$

where Δs_{t+k} is the percentage depreciation of the currency (the change in the log of the spot price of foreign exchange) over k periods and $f d_t^k$ is the current k-period forward discount (the log of the forward rate minus the log of the spot rate). The null hypothesis is that $\beta = 1$. Some authors include $\alpha = 0$ in the null hypothesis as well. In other words, the realized spot rate is equal to the forward rate plus a purely random error term, η_{t+k}^k. A second but equivalent specification is a regression of the forward rate prediction error on the forward discount:

$$f d_t^k - \Delta s_{t+k} = \alpha_1 + \beta_1 f d_t^k + \eta_{t+k}^k, \tag{2}$$

where $\alpha_1 = -\alpha$ and $\beta_1 = 1 - \beta$. The null hypothesis is now that $\alpha_1 = \beta_1 = 0$: the prediction error is purely random.

5. References include Tryon (1979), Levich (1979), Bilson (1981), Longworth (1981), Hsieh (1984), Fama (1984), Huang (1984), Park (1984), and Hodrick and Srivastava (1984, 1986).

Most tests of (1) have rejected the null hypothesis, finding β to be significantly less than one. Often the estimate of β is close to zero or negative.[6] Authors disagree, however, on the reason for this finding of bias. Longworth (1981) and Bilson (1981), for example, assume that there is no risk premium, so that the forward discount accurately measures investors' expectations; they therefore interpret the bias as a rejection of the rational expectations hypothesis. Bilson describes the finding of β less than one as a finding of "excessive speculation," meaning that investors would do better to reduce the absolute magnitude of their expected exchange rate changes. In the special case of β = 0, the exchange rate follows a random walk, and investors would do better to choose $\Delta s_{t+k}^e = 0$. On the other hand, Hsieh (1984) and most others assume that investors did not make systematic prediction errors in the sample; they interpret the bias as evidence of a time-varying risk premium.

2.1 Standard Results Reproduced

We begin by reproducing the standard OLS regression results for (1) on sample periods that correspond precisely to those that we shall be using for the survey data.[7] We report these results, in part, to show that the results obtained when we use the survey data below cannot be attributed to small sample size, unless one is also prepared to attribute the usual finding of forward discount bias to small sample size.[8] Table 1 presents

---

6. The finding that forward rates are poor predictors of future spot rates is not limited to the foreign exchange market. In their study of the expectations hypothesis of the term structure, for example, Shiller, Campbell, and Schoenholtz (1983) conclude that changes in the spread between long-term and short-term rates are useless for predicting future changes in short-term interest rates. Froot (1987) uses survey data on interest rate expectations to test whether the premium's poor predictive power is evidence of a time-varying term premium.

7. DRI provided us with daily forward and spot exchange rates, computed as the average of the noontime bid and ask rates.

8. In these and subsequent regressions, we pool across currencies in order to maximize sample size. (The four currencies in the MMS survey are the pound, mark, Swiss franc, and yen, each against the dollar. The other two surveys include these four exchange rates and the French franc as well.) We must allow for contemporaneous correlation in the error terms across currencies, in addition to allowing for the moving average error process induced by overlapping observations (k > 1). We report standard errors that assume conditional homoskedasticity, because in this case they were consistently larger than the estimated standard errors that allow for conditional heteroskedasticity. We also at times pool across different forecast horizons to maximize the power of the tests, requiring correction for a third kind of correlation in the errors. We are not aware of this having been done before, even in the standard forward discount regression. Each of these econometric issues is discussed at greater length in the NBER working paper version of this paper.

Table 1 Tests of Forward Discount Unbiasedness

OLS Regressions of Δs_{t+k} on fd_t^k

Data Set	Dates	$\hat{\beta}$	$t: \hat{\beta} = 0$	$t: \hat{\beta} = 1$	R^2	DF	F Test $\hat{\alpha} = 0, \hat{\beta} = 1$	F Probability
Economist data	6/81–12/85	−0.5684 (1.0171)	−0.56	−1.54	0.16	509	2.12	0.007
Econ 3-month	6/81–12/85	−1.2090 (1.1596)	−1.04	−1.91*	0.01	184	1.29	0.262
Econ 6-month	6/81–12/85	−1.9819 (1.4445)	−1.37	−2.06**	0.07	174	1.47	0.191
Econ 12-month	6/81–12/85	0.2892 (1.2733)	0.23	−0.56	0.29	149	3.23	0.005
MMS 1-month	11/82–1/88	−1.7403 (0.9781)	−1.77	−2.80***	0.01	735	12.48	0.000
MMS 3-month	1/83–10/84	−6.2540 (2.1508)	−2.91***	−3.37***	0.50	183	12.01	0.000
AMEX data	1/76–7/85	−2.2107 (0.9623)	−2.30**	−3.34***	0.23	86	2.60	0.007
AMEX 6-month	1/76–7/85	−2.4181 (1.2608)	−1.92*	−2.71***	0.26	45	2.42	0.041
AMEX 12-month	1/76–7/85	−2.1377 (1.0549)	2.03**	−0.95***	0.21	40	1.66	0.157

Notes: Method of Moments standard errors are in parentheses. *Represents significance at the 10 percent level, ** and *** represent significance at the 5 percent and 1 percent levels, respectively. Regressions aggregate over all currencies. Constant terms were estimated for each currency, but are not reported to save space.

the standard forward discount unbiasedness regressions (equation [1]) for our sample periods.[9] All of the coefficients fall into the range reported by previous studies. There is ample evidence to reject unbiasedness: most of the coefficients are significantly less than one. More than half of the coefficients are even significantly less than zero, a finding of many other authors as well. The F-tests also indicate that the unbiasedness hypothesis fails in most of the data sets.

Are the commonly found results in Table 1 the consequence of a risk premium or systematic expectational errors?

2.2 Decomposition of the Forward Discount Bias Coefficient

The survey data allow us to answer the question directly. We can now allocate part of the deviation from the null hypothesis of $\beta = 1$ to each of the alternatives: systematic errors and the presence of a risk premium. The probability limit of the coefficient β in (1) is

$$\beta = \frac{\text{cov}(\eta^k_{t+k}, fd^k_t) + \text{cov}(\Delta s^e_{t+k}, fd^k_t)}{\text{var}(fd^k_t)}, \tag{3}$$

where η^k_{t+k} is market participants' expectational error, and Δs^e_{t+k} is the market expectation. We use the definition of the risk premium,

$$rp^k_t = fd^k_t - \Delta s^e_{t+k}, \tag{4}$$

and a little algebra to write β as equal to 1 (the null hypothesis) minus a term arising from any failure of rational expectations, minus another term arising from the risk premium:

$$\beta = 1 - b_{re} - b_{rp}, \tag{5}$$

where

$$b_{re} = \frac{-\text{cov}(\eta^k_{t+k}, fd^k_t)}{\text{var}(fd^k_t)}; \quad b_{rp} = \frac{\text{var}(rp^k_t) + \text{cov}(\Delta s^e_{t+k}, rp^k_t)}{\text{var}(fd^k_t)}.$$

9. Regressions were estimated with dummies for each currency, which we do not report to save space. For the regressions that pool over different forecast horizons (marked *Economist* data and AMEX data), each currency was allowed its own constant term for every forecast horizon. Note that in the *Economist* and AMEX data sets, in which forecasts' horizons were stacked, the standard errors fell in the aggregated regressions by 14 and 31 percent, respectively, in comparison with regressions that used the shorter-term predictions alone.

Table 2   Components of the Failure of the Unbiasedness Hypothesis

Data Set	Approximate Dates	N	Failure of Rational Expectations (1) b_{re}	Existence of Risk Premium (2) b_{rp}	Implied Regression Coefficient 1-(1)-(2) β
Economist data	6/81–12/85	525	1.49	0.08	−0.57
Econ 3-month	6/81–12/85	190	2.51	−0.30	−1.21
Econ 6-month	6/81–12/85	180	2.99	−0.00	−1.98
Econ 12-month	6/81–12/85	155	0.52	0.19	0.29
MMS 1-month	11/82–1/88	740	4.81	−2.07	−1.74
MMS 3-month	1/83–10/84	188	6.07	1.18	−6.25
AMEX data	1/76–7/85	97	3.25	−0.03	−2.21
AMEX 6-month	1/76–7/85	51	3.63	−0.22	−2.42
AMEX 12-month	1/76–7/84	46	3.11	0.03	−2.14

With the help of the survey data, both terms are observable. By inspection, $b_{re} = 0$ if there are no systematic prediction errors in the sample, and $b_{rp} = 0$ if there is no risk premium (or, somewhat more weakly, if the risk premium is uncorrelated with the forward discount).

The results of the decomposition are reported in Table 2. First, b_{re} is very large in size when compared with b_{rp}, often by more than an order of magnitude. In most of the regressions, the lion's share of the deviation from the null hypothesis consists of systematic expectational errors. For example, in the *Economist* data $b_{re} = 1.49$ and $b_{rp} = 0.08$. Second, while b_{re} is greater than zero in all cases, b_{rp} is sometimes negative, implying in (5) that the effect of the survey risk premium is to push the estimate of the standard coefficient β in the direction above one. Indeed, for the MMS 1-month data, our largest survey sample with 740 observations, $b_{re} = 4.81$, and $b_{rp} = −2.07$. In these cases, risk premiums do not explain a positive share of the forward discount's bias. The positive values for b_{re}, on the other hand, suggest the possibility that investors tend to overreact to other information, in the sense that respondents might have improved their forecasting by placing more weight on the contemporaneous spot rate and less weight on the forward rate. Third, to the extent that the surveys are from different sources and cover different periods of time, they provide independent information, rendering their agreement on the relative importance and sign of the expectational errors all the more forceful. In sum, the risk premium appears to have little economic importance for the bias of the forward discount.[10]

While the qualitative results above are of interest, we would like to know whether they are statistically significant, whether we can formally reject the two obvious polar hypotheses: (a) that the results in Table 2 are attributable to expectational errors, i.e., that the point estimates in column (1) are statistically significant; and (b) that they are attributable to the presence of the risk premium, i.e., that the point estimates in column (2) are statistically significant. We test these two (and several subsidiary) hypotheses in turn in Sections 3 and 4.

2.3 The Variance of Expected Depreciation Versus Variance of the Risk Premium

Notice that for most of the sample periods in Table 1, β is significantly less than $1/2$. It is precisely on the basis of such estimates that Fama (1984) and Hodrick and Srivastava (1986) have claimed that expected depreciation is less variable than the exchange risk premium. We state the Fama-Hodrick-Srivastava (FHS) interpretation of the results as

$$\text{var}(\Delta s^e_{t+k}) < \text{var}(rp^k_t). \tag{6}$$

To see how they arrive at this inequality, we use the definition of the risk premium in (4) to write the FHS proposition as

$$\text{var}(\Delta s^e_{t+k}) < \text{var}(rp^k_t) + \text{var}(fd^k_t) - 2\,\text{cov}(fd^k_t, \Delta s^e_{t+k}),$$

or

$$\frac{\text{cov}(fd^k_t, \Delta s^e_{t+k})}{\text{var}(fd^k_t)} < \frac{1}{2}. \tag{6'}$$

The regression coefficient β, as given by (3), is

$$\beta = \frac{\text{cov}(\Delta s_{t+k}, fd^k_t)}{\text{var}(fd^k_t)}. \tag{7}$$

Under the assumption that the prediction error, η^k_{t+k}, is uncorrelated with fd^k_t, the coefficient β becomes the same as the ratio in the inequality (6'). Thus, a finding of $\beta < 1/2$ satisfies the variance inequality in (6). Added intuition is offered by recalling the special case $\beta = 0$. This is the

---

10. The results in Table 2 are not a consequence of aggregation. In the NBER working paper version, we report some results by currency for each data set in Table 2. There is little diversity in the results across currencies.

case identified by Bilson (1985): the variation in fd_t^k consists entirely of variation in rp_t^k, and not at all variation in Δs_{t+k}^e.

We can use expectations as measured by the survey data to investigate the FHS claim directly, without having to assume that there is no systematic component to the prediction errors. Table 3 shows the variance of expected changes in the spot rate, as measured by the surveys, and the variance of the risk premiums, for each data set. The variance of expected depreciation (column 3) is of the same order of magnitude as the variance of the risk premium (column 4), but is nevertheless larger in each of the samples.[11] Thus, "random walk" expectations ($\Delta s_{t+k}^e = 0$) do not appear to be supported by the survey data. We test formally the FHS hypothesis that the variance of expected depreciation is less than the variance of the risk premium in Section 3.

3. Does the Risk Premium Explain Any of the Forward Discount's Bias?

In the previous section we offered point estimates of the bias in the forward discount, which suggested that more of the bias was due to systematic expectations errors than to a time-varying risk premium. In this section we formally test whether the risk premium is correlated with the forward discount. In the next section we shall formally test for systematic expectations errors.

Analogously to the standard regression equation, we regress our measure of expected depreciation against the forward discount:

$$\Delta \hat{s}_{t+k}^e = \alpha_2 + \beta_2 fd_t^k + \epsilon_t^k. \tag{8}$$

The null hypothesis that the correlation of the risk premium with the forward discount is zero implies that $\beta_2 = 1$. By inspection, $\beta_2 = 1 - b_{rp}$, so that a finding of $\beta_2 = 1$ would imply that the results in column 2 of Table 2 are not statistically different from zero.

Besides the hypothesis that there is no time-varying risk premium, (8) also allows us to test the hypothesis of a mean-zero risk premium: $\alpha_2 = 0$. The hypothesis that the risk premium is identically zero is given by $\Delta s_{t+k}^e = fd_t^k$. How then should we interpret the regression error ϵ_t^k? It is the random measurement error in the surveys. That is, $\Delta \hat{s}_{t+k}^e = \Delta s_{t+k}^e + \epsilon_t^k$, where Δs_{t+k}^e is the unobservable market expected change in the spot rate. Note also that in a test of (8) using the survey data, the properties of the error term, ϵ_t^k, will be invariant to any "peso problems,"

---

11. Although random measurement error in the survey data would tend to overstate each of these variances individually, it does not affect the estimate of their difference.

Table 3 Comparison of Variances of Expected Depreciation and the Risk Premium ($\times 10^2$ per annum)

Forecast Horizon	Source Survey	N	Dates	(1) Variance of Δs_{t+1}	(2) Variance of fd_t	(3) Variance of $\Delta \hat{s}^e_{t+1}$	(4) Variance of $\widehat{rp}_t$	(5) (3)–(4) (4)–(5)
1 week	MMS	247	10/84–2/86	2.756	NA	0.346	NA	NA
2 weeks	MMS	187	1/83–10/84	0.703	NA	0.113	NA	NA
1 month	MMS	740	11/82–11/88	0.831	0.008	0.249	0.222	0.027
3 months	MMS	187	1/83–10/84	0.610	0.014	0.067	0.062	0.005
	Economist	190	6/81–12/85	1.651	0.051	0.178	0.121	0.056
6 months	Economist	190	6/81–12/85	2.004	0.093	0.173	0.082	0.091
	AMEX	51	1/76–8/85	1.658	0.111	0.134	0.084	0.051
12 months	Economist	195	6/81–12/85	1.368	0.155	0.215	0.092	0.123
	AMEX	51	1/76–8/85	1.446	0.192	0.195	0.129	0.066

which affect, rather, the ex post distribution of actual spot rate changes.[12] Another way of stating the null hypothesis is the proposition that domestic and foreign assets are perfect substitutes in investors' portfolios.

Table 4 reports the OLS regressions of (8). In some respects the data provide evidence in favor of perfect substitutability of assets denominated in different currencies. Contrary to the hypothesis of a risk premium that is correlated with the forward discount, all but two of the estimates of β_2 are statistically indistinguishable from one. In the *Economist* and *AMEX* data sets which aggregate across time horizons, the estimates are 0.99 and 0.96, respectively.[13] Expectations seem to move very strongly with the forward rate. In addition, the coefficients are estimated with much greater precision than the corresponding estimates in Table 1.

In terms of our decomposition of the forward discount bias coefficient, Table 4 shows that the values of b_{rp} in column 2 of Table 2 are statistically far from one but are not significantly different from zero. Thus, the rejection of unbiasedness found in the previous section cannot be explained entirely by the risk premium, at any reasonable level of confidence. Indeed, we cannot reject the hypothesis that the risk premium explains no positive portion of the bias.

There is strong evidence of a constant term in the risk premium, however: α_2 is large and statistically greater than zero. Each of the F-tests reported in Table 4 rejects the parity relation at a level of significance that is less than 0.1 percent. Figures 1–4 make apparent the high average level of the risk premium (as well as its lack of correlation with the usual measure of the risk premium, the forward discount prediction errors).[14]

---

12. Assuming that covered interest parity holds, the forward discount fd_t^k is equal to the differential between domestic and foreign nominal interest rates $i_t^k - i_t^{*k}$. The null hypothesis then becomes a statement of uncovered interest parity: $\Delta s_{t+k}^e = i_t^k - i_t^{*k}$. In other words, investors are so responsive to differences in expected rates of return as to eliminate them. For tests of uncovered interest parity similar to the tests of conditional bias in the forward discount that we considered in Section 2, see Cumby and Obstfeld (1981).

13. For the *Economist* 6-month and 12-month and the AMEX 12-month data sets, the estimates of β_2 from (8) do not exactly correspond to $1 - b_{rp}$ in Table 2. This is because Table 4 includes a few survey observations for which actual future spot rates had not yet been realized, whereas these observations were left out of the decomposition in Table 2 for purposes of comparability. If we had used the smaller samples in Table 4, the regression coefficients would have been 0.92 and 1.03, for the *Economist* and AMEX data sets, respectively.

14. The degree to which the surveys qualitatively corroborate one another is striking. For example, the risk premium in the *Economist* data (Figure 1) is negative during the entire sample, except for a short period from late 1984 until mid-1985. The MMS 3-month sample (Figure 2) reports that the risk premium did not become positive until the last quarter of 1984, while MMS 1-month data (Figure 3) shows the risk premium then remained positive

Table 4 Tests of Perfect Substitutability

OLS Regressions of $\Delta\hat{s}_{t+k}^e$ on fd_t^k

Data Set	Dates	$\hat{\beta}_2$	$t: \hat{\beta}_2 = 0.5$	$t: \hat{\beta}_2 = 1$	R^2	DF	DW	F Test $\alpha_2 = 0, \hat{\beta}_2 = 1$	F Probability
Economist data	6/81–12/85	0.9880 (0.1465)	3.33***	−0.08	0.89	554	1.44	28.61	0.000
Econ 3-month	6/81–12/85	1.3037 (0.2557)	3.14***	1.19	0.70	184	1.56	16.55	0.000
Econ 6-month	6/81–12/85	1.0326 (0.1694)	3.14***	0.19	0.89	184	1.37	52.06	0.000
Econ 12-month	6/81–12/85	0.9286 (0.1499)	2.86***	−0.48***	0.91	184	1.44	65.82	0.000
MMS 1-month	11/82–1/88	3.0664 (0.4720)	5.44***	4.38	0.17	735	1.67	36.34	0.000
MMS 3-month	1/83–10/84	−0.1816 (0.4293)	−1.59	−2.75***	0.73	182	1.50	14.60	0.000
AMEX data	1/76–7/85	0.9605 (0.2495)	1.85*	−0.16	0.64	91	0.74	5.38	0.000
AMEX 6-month	1/76–7/85	1.2165 (0.2085)	3.44***	1.04	0.71	45	1.45	6.32	0.000
AMEX 12-month	1/76–7/85	0.8770 (0.2755)	1.37	−0.45	0.61	45	0.51	8.10	0.000

Notes: Method of Moments standard errors are in parentheses. *Represents significance at the 10 percent level, ** and *** represent significance at the 5 percent and 1 percent levels, respectively. Regressions aggregate over all currencies. Constant terms were estimated for each currency, but are not reported to save space.

Figure 1   Data Smoothed Forward Rate Errors and Risk Premium 3-Month Economist Survey

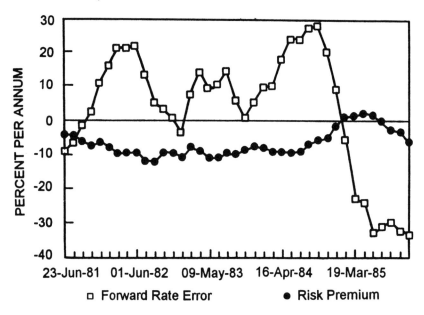

□ Forward Rate Error   ● Risk Premium

Thus, the qualitatively small values of b_{rp} reported in Table 2 should not be taken to imply that the survey responses include no information about investors' expectations beyond that contained in the forward rate.[15]

We can also use (8) to test formally the FHS hypothesis that the variance of the risk premium is greater than the variance of expected depreciation. This is the inequality (6), which we found to be violated by point estimates in Table 3. The probability limit of the coefficient β_2 is

$$\beta_2 = \frac{\text{cov}(\Delta \hat{s}^e_{t+k}, fd^k_t)}{\text{var}(fd^k_t)} = \frac{\text{cov}(\Delta s^e_{t+k}, fd^k_t)}{\text{var}(fd^k_t)}, \tag{9}$$

where we have used the assumption that the measurement error ϵ^k_t is uncorrelated with the forward discount fd^k_t. It follows from (9) that only

---

until mid-1985. That the surveys agree on the nature and timing of major swings in the risk premium is some evidence that the particularities of each group of respondents do not influence the results.

15. In Table 2 of the NBER working paper version of this study, we reported mean values of the risk premium as measured by the survey data. They were different from zero at the 99 percent level for almost all survey sources, currencies, and sample periods.

Figure 2   Data Smoothed Forward Rate Errors and Risk Premium 3-Month MMS Survey

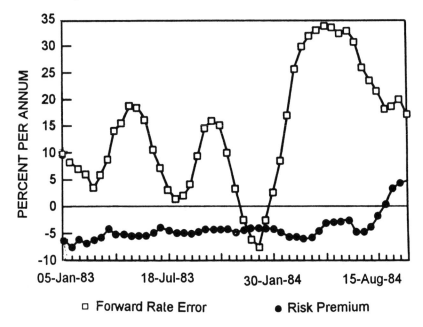

Figure 3   Data Smoothed Forward Rate Errors and Risk Premium 1-Month MMS Survey

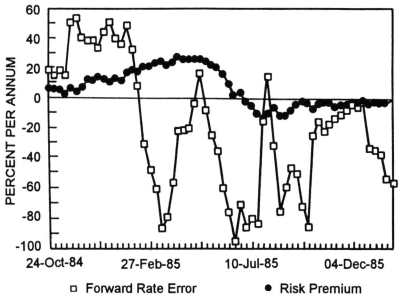

Figure 4   Forward Rate Errors and the Risk Premium

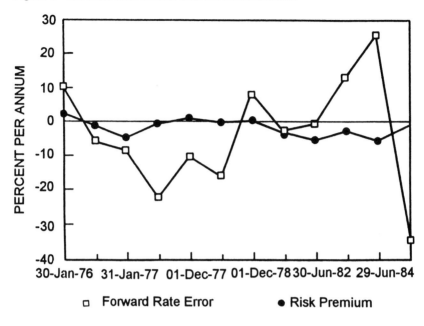

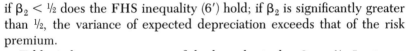

if $\beta_2 < \frac{1}{2}$ does the FHS inequality (6') hold; if β_2 is significantly greater than $\frac{1}{2}$, the variance of expected depreciation exceeds that of the risk premium.

Table 4 also reports a t-test of the hypothesis that $\beta_2 = \frac{1}{2}$. In six out of nine cases that data strongly reject the hypothesis that the variance of the true risk premium is greater than or equal to that of true expected depreciation; we have rather $\mathrm{var}(\Delta s^e_{t+k}) > \mathrm{var}(rp^k_t)$. Indeed, the finding that $\beta_2 = 1$ implies that the risk premium is uncorrelated with the forward discount:

$$\mathrm{var}(rp^k_t) + \mathrm{cov}(\Delta s^e_{t+k}, rp^k_t) = 0. \tag{10}$$

Thus, we cannot reject the hypothesis that the covariance of true expected depreciation and the true risk premium is negative (as Fama found), nor can we reject the extreme hypothesis that the variance of the true risk premium is zero.

Under the null hypothesis that there is no time-varying risk premium and the regression error ϵ^k_t in (8) is random measurement error, we can use the R^2s from the regressions to obtain an estimate of the relative importance of the measurement error component in the survey data. The R^2 statistics in Table 4 are relatively high, suggesting that measurement error is relatively small. For example, under this interpretation of the R^2s, measurement error accounts for about 10 percent of the variability in expected depreciation from the *Economist* data. For a standard of comparison, the R^2 for the sample period in Table 1, which uses ex post exchange rate changes as a noisy measure of expectations, implies that 84 percent of the variability in the measure is noise.[16] This suggests that the survey data are a better measure of investors' expectations than are the ex post exchange rate changes, for those contexts where it is desirable to have an accurate measure of investors' expectations (e.g., estimating asset demand equations).

4. Do Expectational Errors Explain Any of the Forward Discount's Bias?

In the previous section we formally tested the hypothesis that there exists no time-varying risk premium that could explain the findings of bias in the forward discount. In this section we formally test the hypothesis that there exist systematic expectational errors that can explain those findings.

4.1 A Test of Excessive Speculation

Perhaps the most powerful test of rational expectations is one that asks whether investors would do better if they placed more or less weight on the contemporaneous spot rate as opposed to all other variables in their information set.[17] This test is performed by a regression of the expectational prediction error on expected depreciation:

$$\Delta \hat{s}^e_{t+k} - \Delta s_{t+k} = a + d\Delta \hat{s}^e_{t+k} + v^k_{t+k}, \tag{11}$$

where the null hypothesis is $a = 0$, $d = 0$, and the error term is the measurement error in the surveys less the unexpected change in the spot rate, $v^k_{t+k} = \epsilon^k_t - \eta^k_{t+k}$. This is the equation that Bilson (1981) and others had in mind, which we already termed a test of "excessive" speculation (see equation [2]), with the difference that we are now measuring inves-

---

16. In Table 6 of the NBER working paper version, we correct for the potential serial correlation problem in the *Economist* and MMS data sets by employing a Three-Stage-Least-Squares estimator that allows for contemporaneous correlation (SUR) as well as first-order auto regressive disturbances. This procedure does not substantively change the conclusions.

17. Frankel and Froot (1985, 1987) test whether the survey expectations place too little weight on the contemporaneous spot rate and too much weight on specific pieces of information such as the lagged spot rate, the long-run equilibrium exchange rate, and the lagged expected spot rate. Dominguez (1986) also tests for bias in survey data.

tors' expected depreciation by the survey data instead of by the ambiguous forward discount.

Our tests are reported in Table 5. The findings consistently indicate that $d > 0$, so that investors could on average do better by giving more weight to the contemporaneous spot rate. In other words, the excessive speculation hypothesis is upheld. F-tests of the hypothesis that there are no systematic expectational errors, $a = d = 0$, reject at the 1 percent level for all of the survey data sets. The results in Table 5 would appear to constitute a resounding rejection of rationality in the survey expectations.

Up until this point, our test statistics have been robust to the presence of random measurement error in the survey data because the surveys have appeared only on the left-hand side of the equation. But now the surveys appear also on the right-hand side; as a result, under the null hypothesis, measurement error biases toward one our estimate of d in (11). In the limiting case in which the measurement error accounts for all of the variability of expected depreciation in the survey, the parameter estimate would be statistically indistinguishable from one. In Table 6, 12 of 15 estimates of d are greater than one; in five cases the difference is statistically significant. This result suggests that measurement error is not the source of our rejection of rational expectations. However, we shall now see that stronger evidence can be obtained.

4.2 Another Test of Excessive Speculation

Another test of rational expectations, which is free of the problem of measurement error, is to replace $\Delta \hat{s}^e_{t+k}$ on the right-hand side of (11) with the forward discount fd^k_t:

$$\Delta \hat{s}^e_{t+k} - \Delta s_{t+k} = \alpha_1 + \beta_1 fd^k_t + v^k_{t+k}. \tag{12}$$

There are several reasons for making the substitution in (12). We know from our results in Section 3 that expected depreciation is highly correlated with fd^k_t. Because fd^k_t is free of measurement error, it is a good candidate for an "instrumental variable." Indeed, if we as econometricians can look up the precise forward discount in the newspaper, we can also do so as prospective speculators. A finding of $\beta_1 > 0$ in either equation (9) or (13) suggests that a speculator could have made excess profits by betting against the market. But the strategy to "bet against the market" is far more practical if expressed as "bet against the (observable) forward discount" than as "do the opposite of whatever you would have otherwise done."

Equation (12) has additional relevance in the context of our decomposition of the forward rate unbiasedness regression in Section 2: the coeffi-

Table 5 Tests of Excessive Speculation

Regressions of $\Delta s^e_{t+k} - \Delta s_{t-k}$ on s^e_{t+k}

Data Set	Dates	d	$t: d = 0$	$t: d = 1$	R^2	DF	DW	F Test $\alpha = 0, d = 0$	F Probability
Economist data	6/81–12/85	1.0162 (0.4104)	2.48**	0.04	0.49	509		4.79	0.000
Econ 3-month	6/81–12/85	1.6141 (0.4664)	3.46***	1.32	0.26	184		2.91	0.010
Econ 6-month	6/81–12/85	2.5325 (0.6746)	3.73***	2.27**	0.41	174		3.54	0.002
Econ 12-month	6/81–12/85	−0.3005 (0.5241)	−0.57	−2.48**	0.67	149		6.32	0.000
MMS 1-week, 1-month	10/84–2/86	1.2561 (0.3544)	3.54***	0.72	0.24	414		6.07	0.000
MMS 1-week	10/84–2/86	1.1476 (0.2939)	3.90***	0.50	0.14	242	1.84	3.97	0.002
MMS 1-week, SUR	10/84–2/86	0.7858 (0.1109)	7.09***	−1.93*	0.18	239		12.42	0.000
MMS 1-month	11/82–1/88	0.9961 (0.1091)	9.12***	−0.04	0.23	735		38.11	0.000

MMS 2-week, 3-month	1/83–10/84	1.0494 (0.3159)	3.32***	0.16	0.59	365		7.87	0.000
MMS 2-week	1/83–10/84	1.0594 (0.2870)	3.69***	0.21	0.23	182	1.74	5.40	0.000
MMS 2-week, SUR	1/83–10/84	1.0469 (0.1813)	5.77***	0.26	0.16	179		9.42	0.000
MMS 3-month	1/83–10/84	1.0465 (0.3895)	2.69***	0.12	0.63	182		7.59	0.000
AMEX data	1/76–7/85	2.6082 (0.5123)	5.09***	3.14***	0.23	86		4.71	0.000
AMEX 6-month	1/76–7/85	2.5693 (0.7358)	3.49***	2.13**	0.37	45		4.22	0.002
AMEX 12-month	1/76–7/85	2.6382 (0.5812)	4.54***	2.82***	0.50	40		4.24	0.002

Notes: All regressions except those marked SUR are estimated using OLS, with Method of Moments standard errors (in parentheses), SUR regressions report asymptotic standard errors. Durbin-Watson statistics are reported for data sets in which the forecast horizon is equal to the sampling interval. *Represents significance at the 10 percent level, ** and *** represent significance at the 5 percent and 1 percent levels, respectively. Regressions aggregate over all currencies. Constant terms were estimated for each currency, but are not reported to save space.

Table 6 Tests of Rational Expectations

OLS Regressions of $\Delta \hat{s}^e_{t+1} - \Delta s_{t+1}$ on fd_t

Data Set	Dates	β_1	$t: \beta_1 = 0$	R^2	DF	F Test $\alpha_1 = 0, \beta_1 = 0$	F Probability
Economist data	6/81–12/85	1.4903 (1.0580)	1.41	0.48	509	4.75	0.000
Econ 3-month	6/81–12/85	2.5127 (1.2918)	1.95*	0.14	184	1.31	0.256
Econ 6-month	6/81–12/85	2.9866 (1.5974)	1.87*	0.28	174	1.46	0.194
Econ 12-month	6/81–12/85	0.5174 (1.2290)	0.42	0.67	149	6.01	0.000
MMS 1-month	11/82–1/88	4.8067 (1.2199)	3.94***	0.07	735	8.73	0.000
MMS 3-month	1/83–10/84	6.0725 (2.3392)	2.60**	0.66	182	11.93	0.000
AMEX data	1/76–7/85	3.2452 (1.1675)	2.78***	0.33	86	2.69	0.005
AMEX 6-month	1/76–7/85	3.6346 (1.3437)	2.70***	0.26	45	3.30	0.009
AMEX 12-month	1/76–7/85	3.1081 (1.2954)	2.40**	0.25	40	1.48	0.210

Notes: Method of Moments standard errors are in parentheses. *Represents significance at the 10 percent level, ** and *** represent significance at the 5 percent and 1 percent levels, respectively. Regressions aggregate over all currencies. Constant terms were estimated for each currency, but are not reported to save space.

378

cient β_1 is precisely equal to the deviation from unbiasedness due to systematic prediction errors, b_{re}. Thus, (12) can tell us whether the large positive values of b_{re} found in column 1 of Table 2 are statistically significant.

Table 6 reports OLS regressions of (12). We now see that the point estimates of b_{re} in Table 2 are measured with precision. The data continue to reject statistically the hypothesis of rational expectations, $\alpha_1 = 0$, $\beta_1 = 0$. They reject $\beta_1 = 0$ in favor of the alternative of excessive speculation. (Because the measurement error has been purged, the levels of significance are necessarily lower than those of Table 5.) The result that b_{re} is significantly greater than zero seems robust across different forecast horizons and different survey samples. In terms of the decomposition of the typical forward rate unbiasedness test in Table 2, we can now reject statistically the hypothesis that all of the bias is attributable to the survey risk premium. Also, we cannot reject the hypothesis that all of the bias is due to repeated expectational errors made by survey respondents. This finding need not mean that investors are irrational. If they are learning about a new exchange rate process, or if there is a "peso problem" with the distribution of the error term, then one could not expect them to foresee errors in the sample period, even though the errors appear to be systematic ex post.

5. Conclusions

Our general conclusion is that, contrary to what is assumed in conventional practice, the systematic portion of forward discount prediction errors does not capture a time-varying risk premium. This result was qualitatively clear from the point estimates in Section 2 or from the figures. But we can now make several statements that are more precise statistically.

1. We reject the hypothesis that all of the bias in the forward discount is due to the risk premium. This is the same thing as rejecting the hypothesis that none of the bias is due to the presence of systematic expectational errors.

2. We cannot reject the hypothesis that all of the bias is attributable to these systematic expectational errors, and none to a time-varying risk premium.

3. The implication of (1) and (2) is that changes in the forward discount reflect, one-for-one, changes in expected depreciation, as perfect substitutability among assets denominated in different currencies would imply.

4. We reject the claim that the variance of the risk premium is greater than the variance of expected depreciation. The reverse appears to be

the case: the variance of expected depreciation is large in comparison with the variance of the risk premium.

5. Because the survey risk premium appears to be uncorrelated with the forward discount, we cannot reject the hypothesis that the market risk premium we are trying to measure is constant. We do find a substantial *average* level of the risk premium. But, to repeat, the premium does not vary with the forward discount as conventionally thought.

═══════════

We would like to thank Alberto Giovannini, Robert Hodrick, and many other participants at various seminars for helpful comments; Barbara Bruer, John Calverley, Lu Cordova, Kathryn Dominguez, Laura Knoy, Stephen Marris, and Phil Young for help in obtaining data, Joe Mullally for expert research assistance, the National Science Foundation (under grant no. SES-8218300), the Institute for Business and Economic Research at U. C. Berkeley, and the Alfred P. Sloan Foundation for research support.

References

BILSON, JOHN. "The Speculative Efficiency Hypothesis." *Journal of Business*, LIV (1981), 435–51.

———. "Macroeconomic Stability and Flexible Exchange Rates." *American Economic Review*, LXXV (1985), 62–67.

CUMBY, ROBERT, and MAURICE OBSTFELD. "Exchange Rate Expectations and Nominal Interest Differentials: A Test of the Fisher Hypothesis." *Journal of Finance*, XXXVI (1981), 697–703.

DOMINGUEZ, KATHRYN. "Are Foreign Exchange Forecasts Rational?: New Evidence from Survey Data." *Economics Letters*, XXI (1986), 277–82.

FAMA, EUGENE. "Forward and Spot Exchange Rates." *Journal of Monetary Economics*, XIV (1984), 319–38.

FRANKEL, JEFFREY A., and KENNETH A. FROOT. "Using Survey Data to Test Some Standard Propositions Regarding Exchange Rate Expectations." NBER Working Paper No. 1672, 1985; revised as IBER Working Paper, No. 86-11, University of California, Berkeley, May 1986.

———. and ———. "Using Survey Data to Test Standard Propositions Regarding Exchange Rate Expectations." *American Economic Review*, LXXVII (1987), 133–53.

———, and ———. "Explaining the Demand for Dollars: International Rates of Return, and the Expectations of Chartists and Fundamentalists." In *Agriculture, Macroeconomics and the Exchange Rate*, by R. CHAMBERS and P. PAARLBERG, eds. (Boulder, CO: Westview Press, 1988).

FROOT, KENNETH A. "New Hope for the Expectations Hypothesis of the Term Structure of Interest Rates." NBER Working Paper no. 2363, 1987.

HODRICK, ROBERT. "The Empirical Evidence on the Efficiency of Forward and Futures Foreign Exchange Markets." In *Fundamentals of Pure and Applied Economics* (Chur, Switzerland: Harwood Academic Publishers, 1988).

———, and SANJAY SRIVASTAVA. "An Investigation of Risk and Return in Forward Foreign Exchange." *Journal of International Money and Finance*, III (1984), 5–30.

———, and ———. "The Covariation of Risk Premiums and Expected Future Spot Rates." *Journal of International Money and Finance*, V (1986), S5–S22.

HSIEH, DAVID. "Tests of Rational Expectations and No Risk Premium in Forward Exchange Markets." *Journal of International Economics*, XVII (1984), 173–84.

HUANG, ROGER. "Some Alternative Tests of Forward Exchange Rates as Predictors of Future Spot Rates." *Journal of International Money and Finance*, III (1984), 157–67.

LEVICH, RICHARD. "On the Efficiency of Markets of Foreign Exchange." In *International Economic Policy*, by R. DORNSBUSCH and J. FRENKEL, eds. (Baltimore, MD: Johns Hopkins University Press, 1979), pp. 246–266.

LONGWORTH, DAVID. "Testing the Efficiency of the Canadian-U.S. Exchange Market Under the Assumption of No Risk Premium." *Journal of Finance*, XXXVI (1981), 43–49.

MEESE, RICHARD, and KENNETH ROGOFF. "Empirical Exchange Rate Models of the Seventies: Do They Fit out of Sample?" *Journal of International Economics*, XIV (1983), 3–24.

SHILLER, R., J. CAMPBELL, and K. SCHOENHOLTZ. "Forward Rates and Future Policy: Interpreting the Term Structure of Interest Rates." *Brookings Papers on Economic Activity* (1983), 223–42.

TRYON, RALPH. "Testing for Rational Expectations in Foreign Exchange Markets." Federal Reserve Board International Finance Discussion Paper, No. 139, 1979.

14

Investor Diversification and International Equity Markets

KENNETH R. FRENCH
and JAMES M. POTERBA

Since the fortunes of different nations do not always move together, investors can diversify their portfolios by holding assets in several countries. The benefits of international diversification have been recognized for decades. In spite of this, most investors hold nearly all of their wealth in domestic assets. In this paper we use a simple model of investor preferences and behavior to show that current portfolio patterns imply that investors in each nation expect returns in their domestic equity market to be several hundred basis points higher than returns in other markets. The lack of diversification appears to be the result of investor choices, rather than institutional constraints.

1. International Asset Ownership Patterns

Most corporate equity is held by domestic investors. The domestic ownership shares of the world's five largest stock markets are: United States, 92.2 percent; Japan, 95.7 percent; United Kingdom, 92 percent; Germany, 79 percent; and France, 89.4 percent. This information, and other data on cross-border equity transactions, can be used to estimate the international equity holdings of investors in each country. Table 1 pre-

From: *American Economic Review*, vol. 81, No. 2, pp. 222–226, May 1991. Reprinted by permission of the American Economic Association.

Table 1   Equity Portfolio Weights: British, Japanese, U.S. Investors

	Portfolio Weight			Adj. Market Value
	U.S.	Japan	U.K.	
U.S.	.938	.0131	.059	$2941.3
Japan	.031	.9811	.048	1632.9
U.K.	.011	.0019	.820	849.8
France	.005	.0013	.032	265.4
Germany	.005	.0013	.035	235.8
Canada	.010	.0012	.006	233.5

Note: Estimates correspond to portfolio holdings in December, 1989. They are based on the authors' tabulations using data from the U.S. Treasury Bulletin and Michael Howell and Angela Cozzini (1990). Adjusted market values exclude intercorporate cross-holdings from total market value, and correspond to June 1990 values.

sents crude estimates of the equity portfolio allocation for investors in the United States, United Kingdom, and Japan.[1]

The estimates show little cross-border diversification for U.S. and Japanese investors. At the end of 1989, Japanese investors had only 1.9 percent of their equity in foreign stocks, while U.S. investors held 6.2 percent of their equity portfolio overseas. The British, by comparison, held 18 percent of their portfolio abroad, divided almost equally among the United States, continental Europe, and Japan.

Since the United Kingdom is a smaller share of the total world equity market than the United States or Japan, it is not surprising that its investors hold more equity outside their own borders. However, the diversification of U.K. portfolios is a recent phenomenon. At the end of 1979, U.K. pension funds, which today hold 21 percent of their assets in foreign equities, held only 6 percent of their portfolios abroad (Michael Howell and Angela Cozzini, 1990, p. 30). The growth of international equity investments followed Prime Minister Thatcher's relaxation of capital controls.

1. These estimates cumulate the net purchases of equity by investors in each country, with adjustments for both stock market and exchange rate movements. Ian Cooper and Costas Kaplanis (1986) also estimate cross-border equity holdings, but their calculations are largely imputations that do not rely on country-by-country equity flows.

2. Is Incomplete Diversification Costly?

The gains from diversification depend on the correlation of returns in different equity markets. We compute real returns from the perspective of a U.S. investor, assuming the investor uses three-month forward contracts to lock in an exchange rate for the amount of his initial investment each quarter. The average pairwise correlation between quarterly returns on the equity markets in the United States, Japan, the United Kingdom, France, Germany, and Canada for the 1975–89 period is .502. This suggests that nontrivial risk reduction is available from cross-border holdings. The correlations are similar if the returns are measured in yen or pounds, and whether or not the exchange rate risk is hedged.

To measure the costs of incomplete diversification, we assume that a representative investor in each country has a constant absolute-risk-aversion utility function defined over wealth, $U(W) = -e^{-\lambda W/W_0}$, and that he maximizes expected utility.[2] For a given set of portfolio weights w associated with a vector of mean returns μ and a covariance matrix Σ, this implies an expected utility of

$$E[U(w)] = -e^{-\lambda\{w\mu - \lambda w'\Sigma w/2\}}. \tag{1}$$

In this setting, optimal portfolio weights w^* satisfy

$$\mu = \lambda w^{*\prime}\Sigma. \tag{2}$$

With limited historical data on international equity returns, it is difficult to measure expected returns, μ, or to infer the optimal portfolio weights, w^*, with any precision. We can, however, make reasonable estimates of the covariance matrix, Σ. Under the assumption that investors put all their wealth in the equity of the six largest stock markets, we can ask what set of expected returns, $\mu^*(w,\Sigma)$, would explain the pattern of international portfolio holdings we observe. We use equation (2) to calculate the expected returns implied by the actual portfolio holdings of U.S., Japanese, and British investors. We also compute the expected returns implied by an international "value-weighted" portfolio strategy for investors in each nation. The last column of Table 1 shows the value weights, based on market capitalization data from Morgan Stanley Capital International but with corrections for intercorporate equity holdings as in our earlier article. The adjustment reduces the importance of the Japanese and German markets.

Panel A of Table 2 shows that substantial differences in expected re-

---

2. We set $\lambda = 3$; see our 1990 paper for more detail on calibration.

Table 2   Expected Real Returns Implied by Actual Portfolio Holdings

	U.S.	Japan	U.K.
A. Expected Returns Needed to Justify Observed Portfolio Weights			
U.S.	5.5	3.1	4.4
Japan	3.2	6.6	3.8
U.K.	4.5	3.8	9.6
France	4.3	3.4	5.3
Germany	3.6	3.0	4.8
Canada	4.7	3.0	4.0
B. Deviation Between Implied Returns for Actual and Value-Weighted Portfolios			
U.S.	0.9	−1.5	−0.2
Japan	−1.1	2.5	−0.3
U.K.	−0.7	−1.4	4.4
France	−0.3	−1.2	0.7
Germany	−0.2	−0.8	1.0
Canada	0.5	−1.2	−0.2

Note: See text for further description of calculations.

turns *across countries* for investors in a given nation are needed to rationalize observed portfolio holdings. In the most extreme case, British investors must expect annual returns in the U.K. market more than 500 basis points above those in the U.S. market to explain their 82 percent investment in domestic shares. This large implied differential reflects the substantially higher standard deviation of returns on the British market, relative to returns on the U.S. and Japanese markets. For U.S. investors, the annual expected return on U.S. stocks must be 250 basis points above the expected return on Japanese stocks. In contrast, for Japanese investors, the expected return on Japanese stocks must be 350 basis points above the expected return on U.S. stocks.

The difference in expectations for different investors judging the same market are also striking. Our estimates suggest that Japanese investors, for example, expect returns from Japanese stocks which are more than 300 basis points greater than the returns U.S. investors expect. There are similar differences in the expectations of foreign and domestic investors in both the U.S. and U.K. equity markets.

Although these differences in expected returns are striking, the implied alternative of equal expected returns across all markets may not be an appropriate benchmark. As another alternative, we estimate the expected returns that would induce investors in each country to hold an international value-weighted stock portfolio. The *difference* between the expected return vector implied by each country's actual investment pattern, and that implied by a value-weighted strategy, is shown in Panel B of Table 2. The results again suggest that investors expect domestic returns that are systematically higher than those implied by a diversified portfolio. The differences between the two sets of implied returns for U.S. and British investors, however, are rarely larger than 100 basis points. For example, U.S. investors' concentrated holdings of U.S. stocks can be explained by "optimistic" expectations of roughly 90 basis points. A similar "pessimism" of about 110 basis points is needed to justify U.S. investors' underweighting of the Japanese market. Explaining the behavior of both Japanese and British investors requires more "optimism" regarding their own markets: 250 basis points for the Japanese, and over 400 basis points in the United Kingdom.

3. Institutional and Behavioral Explanations for Underdiversification

What explains the apparent tendency for portfolio investors, particularly in the United Kingdom and Japan, to overweight their own equity market? There are two broad explanations. First, institutional factors may reduce returns from investing abroad or they may explicitly limit investors' ability to hold foreign stocks. It is difficult, however, to identify such constraints. Institutional barriers are unlikely to explain the low level of cross-border equity investment *today*, even though capital controls substantially restricted equity flows in the 1970's. Tax burdens that are higher on foreign than domestic equity income should lead investors toward holding domestic equity. There is little difference, however, between foreign and domestic tax burdens for most investors. Although all of the nations we examine impose a dividend withholding tax on payments to foreign shareholders, typically these payments can be credited against taxes in the investors' home country.[3]

Transaction costs also appear unable to explain limited international diversification. The cost of trading may be lower in more liquid markets such as New York than elsewhere, but this should incline all investors toward the most liquid market, not toward their own domestic market. Since all shares must be held by someone, differences in transaction costs

---

3. Tax-exempt investors may face a burden from such taxes, since they have no tax liability against which to claim the credit. Even for these investors, however, the tax would only reduce expected after-tax returns in foreign markets by about 50 basis points.

should be reflected in differences in expected returns. The large gross equity flows across borders also suggest that transaction costs cannot explain why investors specialize in their home markets. For the United States in 1989, gross foreign equity purchases were fifty times net purchases (see our earlier paper).

Explicit limits on cross-border investment could also affect portfolio holdings, although few of them appear to bind at present. In France, for example, a foreign investor may not hold more than 20 percent of any firm without authorization from the Ministry of Economy and Finance. In Japan, insurance companies cannot hold more than 30 percent of their assets in foreign securities. Many U.S. pension funds traditionally interpreted the "prudent man" rule as limiting their degree of international exposure.

The current level of international portfolio investment seems to be well below any institutional constraints. In the mid-1980's, for example, foreign investors were substantial net sellers of Japanese shares. Similarly, foreigners were net sellers of U.S. equities in 1988. Such reductions in international equity investments suggest that constraints on foreign holding are not binding, implying that incomplete diversification is the result of investor choices.

A second class of explanations for imperfect diversification focuses on investor behavior. One important possibility is that return expectations vary systematically across groups of investors. Robert Shiller et al. (1990) report direct evidence on this question. In early 1990, they surveyed portfolio managers in Japan and the United States. The U.S. investors expected an average return of −0.3 percent on the Dow Jones Industrial Average over the next twelve months, compared with an expected return of −9.1 percent on the Nikkei. In contrast, Japanese investors expected an average return of 12.6 percent on the Dow, and 10.8 percent on the Nikkei. While the Japanese investors were more optimistic than their U.S. counterparts with respect to both markets, they were relatively more optimistic about the Tokyo market.

The statistical uncertainties associated with estimating expected returns in equity markets makes it difficult for investors to learn that expected returns in domestic markets are not systematically higher than those abroad. The standard error of the estimated mean annual return on the U.S. stock market, based on 60 years of data, is 200 basis points. Thus, the 95 percent confidence interval for the mean return spans 800 basis points. Because it is difficult to estimate *ex ante* returns, investors may follow their own idiosyncratic investment rules with impunity.

Another important behavioral insight concerns the perception of risk in equity markets. Investors may not evaluate the risk of different investments based solely on the historical standard deviation of returns. They may impute extra "risk" to foreign investments because they know less about foreign markets, institutions, and firms.[4] Country-specific closed-end mutual funds, popular in the United States during the late 1980's, may overcome these fears (see Catherine Bosner-Neal et al. 1990, for a discussion).

Although the level of cross-border equity investment is low, it is growing and with time the international diversification puzzle may recede. Cross-border equity investment patterns may nevertheless provide important insights on how investors value risk and how they select portfolios. The evidence of incomplete diversification presented here is consistent with evidence from many other markets. Ronald Lease et al. (1974) show that in the late 1960's, many individuals held relatively few stocks. Both the mean and median in their sample of investors were close to eleven different securities. The rise of index mutual funds in the last two decades has improved the diversification of individual investors, but directly held equity still accounts for two and one-half times as much of household wealth as *all* mutual funds, of which index funds are only a small part.

Perhaps the most striking example of incomplete diversification is the tendency of most households to own residential real estate near where they work. The returns on their human and physical capital may consequently be highly correlated. This generates a much less diversified portfolio than holding, for example, a real estate investment trust with a national real estate portfolio.

We are grateful to the NSF, CRSP, the Alfred P. Sloan Foundation, and the John M. Olin Foundation for research support, to Michael Howell and Vincent Koen for data assistance, and to Cole Kendall, Richard Thaler, and Richard Zeckhauser for helpful comments. A data appendix for this project is available from the ICPSR in Ann Arbor, MI, or from the authors. This paper is part of the NBER program on Financial Markets and Monetary Economics.

References

BOSNER-NEAL, CATHERINE et al. "International Investment Restrictions and Closed-End Country Fund Prices," *Journal of Finance*, June 1990, *45*, 523–47.

---

4. Amos Tversky and Chip Heath (1991) present evidence that households behave as though unfamiliar gambles are riskier than familiar gambles, even when they assign identical probability distributions to the two gambles.

COOPER, IAN and KAPLANIS, COSTAS. "Costs to Crossborder Investment and International Equity Market Equilibrium," in J. EDWARDS et al., eds., *Recent Advances in Corporate Finance*, Cambridge: Cambridge University Press, 1986.

FRENCH, KENNETH R., and POTERBA, JAMES M. "Japanese and U.S. Crossborder Common Stock Investments," *Journal of the Japanese and the International Economics*, December 1990, *4*, 476–93.

——— and ———. "Were Japanese Stock Prices Too High?," *Journal of Financial Economics*, forthcoming, 1991.

HOWELL, MICHAEL and COZZINI, ANGELA. *International Equity Flows-1990 Edition*, London: Salomon Brothers European Equity Research, 1990.

LEASE, RONALD, LEWELLEN, WILBUR and SCHLARBAUM, GARY. "Individual Investor Attributes and Attitudes," *Journal of Finance*, May 1974, *29*, 413–33.

SHILLER, ROBERT J., FUMIKO KON-YA and YOSHIRO TSUTSUI. "Speculative Behavior in the Stock Markets: Evidence from the U.S. & Japan," mimeo., Yale University, 1990.

TVERSKY, AMOS and HEATH, CHIP. "Preferences and Beliefs: Ambiguity and Competence in Choice Under Uncertainty," *Journal of Risk and Uncertainty*, January 1991, *4*, 5–28.

PART
V

CORPORATE
FINANCE

15

Explaining Investor Preference for Cash Dividends

HERSH M. SHEFRIN
and MEIR STATMAN

1. Introduction

Why do so many individuals have a strong preference for cash dividends? This important question has intrigued financial theorists for years. The present paper is concerned with the way in which the preference for dividends is explained by two new theories of individual choice behavior: the theory of self-control by Thaler and Shefrin (1981) and the descriptive theory of choice under uncertainty by Kahneman and Tversky (1979).

It is generally accepted that dividends and capital gains should be perfect substitutes for each other if taxes and transaction costs are ignored. The reasoning is quite simple. Given a firm's investment plan, the payment of a one-dollar cash dividend results in a drop of exactly one dollar in the price of the firm's stock. Thus, an individual is indifferent between a one-dollar cash dividend and a one-dollar 'homemade' cash dividend created by selling one dollar's worth of stock.

Of course, the argument against generous cash dividend payout is the tax argument. Since the tax on cash dividends exceeds the tax on capital gains for most investors, investors should prefer to receive no dividends as long as the firm has investment opportunities with yields equal to or higher than the cost of capital. Yet the strong preference for cash dividends is difficult to refute. A well-known case reported by Loomis (1968) illustrates the point.

From: *Journal of Financial Economics*, vol. 13, pp. 253–282, 1984. North Holland. Reprinted by permission of Elsevier Science Publishers B.U.

Mr. Kuhns, president of General Public Utilities Corp. (G.P.U.) proposed to substitute stock dividends for cash dividends. He also offered to sell these stock dividends (with minimal brokerage costs) for any stockholder who wanted to realize the same cash income he had been receiving from dividends. The effect of substituting stock dividends for cash dividends would have resulted in a direct tax savings to the shareholders of at least $4 million annually. Direct savings to G.P.U. would have amounted to an additional $20 million annually. Yet most G.P.U. shareholders did not regard the proposal as reasonable. Reactions were strongly negative, if not outright hostile. The price of the company's stock dropped sharply, and a barrage of unfavorable mail arrived on Kuhn's desk. One stockholder called him a 'hypocritical ass'; another suggested that he seek psychiatric care. When both individual investors and institutions made it clear that implementation of the plan would lead them to sell their G.P.U. stock, it was abandoned.

Consider the major explanations which have been advanced to explain the strong preference for cash dividends. Black and Scholes (1974) argue that investors who concentrate their portfolios in stocks with any given yield will reduce the degree of diversification in their portfolios without a consistent offsetting benefit in terms of higher expected return (either before tax or after tax). Since Black and Scholes' empirical efforts did not uncover a statistically significant relationship between dividend yield and portfolio return, they suggest that investors simply ignore dividend yield in making portfolio decisions, and concentrate instead on diversification. However, this suggestion is not consistent with the available evidence. Using survey data, Pettit (1977) finds that investors in high marginal tax brackets concentrate their portfolios in stocks with low dividend yield. In addition, there is evidence from Rosenberg and Marathe (1979) and Litzenberger and Ramaswamy (1979, 1980, 1982) that high-dividend-yield stocks provide a higher before-tax return than low-dividend-yield stocks.

Not all authors accept the idea that cash dividends involve a tax disadvantage. Miller and Scholes (1978) present a rather complicated (and probably costly) arrangement to defer the tax on dividends indefinitely.[1] However, they do not explain why companies fail to choose the 'easier'

---

1. A provision of the Economic Recovery act of 1981 is that up to $1,500 (for a joint return) in dividends from public utilities are not taxed if reinvested in the firm. Capital gains tax must, of course, be paid on the shares bought with the dividends when these shares are sold (the cost basis for the shares is zero). Proponents of this provision actually tried to apply it to all stocks, not just utilities, and to make the dollar limit much higher ('Utilities get ready for a tax break', *Business Week*, November 16, 1981). Arrangements to defer taxes on dividends must be costly if efforts are expended on changes in the law that would make such deferments possible.

way: low or zero payout of dividends. Moreover, Feenberg (1981) finds that the special circumstances under which the Miller–Scholes arrangement can occur applies to recipients of only two-and-one-half percent of dividend income. Feenberg concludes that 'no dominant role may therefore be ascribed to their hypothesis in the determination of corporate dividend policy' (p. 265).

The only good argument supporting the preference for cash dividends is based on informational considerations. The basic idea is that raising and lowering of dividends provides information that is not otherwise available [see Miller and Modigliani (1961), Bhattacharya (1979), Hakansson (1982), and Asquith and Mullins (1983)]. It is worth mentioning that the motives for dividend preference that we discuss will often interact with the signalling function of dividends. At the same time our theory accounts for important features about the demand for dividends such as the clientele effect (see below) which signalling theory seems incapable of explaining. Therefore, while we are not arguing against the information-based explanation of cash dividends, we do agree with Brealey and Myers (1981, p. 345) that casual evidence, such as the G.P.U. dividend story, suggests the existence of alternative, plausible explanations. This paper considers alternative explanations based upon self-control theory and prospect theory which appear plausible on both theoretical and empirical grounds. The key point which emerges from the two theories is as follows: the perfect substitutes feature of capital gains and dividends (in the absence of taxes and transaction costs) which characterizes the standard approach is not always appropriate.

The paper is organized in two parts. First, we consider why capital and cash dividends need not be perfect substitutes, even in the absence of taxes and transaction costs. Section 2 discusses a self-control-based explanation of this phenomenon, while sections 3 and 4 develop two separate explanations which arise from the work of Kahneman and Tversky. The second part of the paper contains a discussion of some empirical implications of the theory. In particular, we focus on the clientele effect and draw on some important empirical studies concerning dividend clienteles (section 5). In section 6 we present an interesting and insightful case on dividend omission by Consolidated Edison. Section 7 presents further research directions, and section 8 contains some concluding remarks.

2. Self-Control and Dividends

Understanding what has come to be called the principle–agent conflict, together with its resolution, provides significant insights into many aspects of corporate behavior. In a pioneering paper, Jensen and Meckling

(1976) demonstrate how the principal–agent framework accounts for some apparent departures from the standard economic theory of the firm. Subsequent work such as Zimmerman's (1979) shows that the principal–agent framework can explain why firms persist in allocating overhead costs in spite of admonitions that such allocation is inherently arbitrary and serves no useful purpose. It appears that the allocation of overhead costs is a useful tool in the control of managers' actions.

Significantly, the descriptive power of the principal–agent framework is not confined to firms. Following the same line of inquiry in connection with individual behavior, Thaler and Shefrin (1981, 1983) demonstrate the use of the principal–agent framework in describing persistent departures in consumer choice from behavior predicted by the economic theory of the consumer.[2] The departures all involve the inability of individuals to delay gratification because of a lack of self-control.

There are numerous examples of self-control difficulties, as the prevalence of smoking clinics, credit counselors, diet clubs, and alcoholic assistance groups attests. In the Thaler–Shefrin framework such difficulties are regarded as signifying an internal conflict. The individual wishes to deny himself a present indulgence, yet simultaneously finds that he yields to the temptation. The representation of this conflict in terms of principal–agent theory is accomplished by identifying the individual's desire for self-denial with a principal, and the urge for immediate gratification with an agent. The principal is regarded as the individual's internal 'planner', who expresses consistent long-run preferences (through a utility function V). However, responsibility for carrying out the individual's date t action lies not with the planner but with an agent (the date t 'doer') who is also internalized. In order to identify the 'doer' with the urge for immediate gratification, the date t doer is assigned a utility function Z_t which overwhelmingly favors date t consumption.

Thaler and Shefrin assume that the planner has two kinds of self-control techniques which can be used to exert an influence over the doer's actions. The first technique is the exercise of 'will'. Specifically, increased will-power serves to induce greater 'self denial' on the part of the date t doer through the modification of that doer's incentives: this effect comes through $Z_t(\cdot)$. However, such self-denial is assumed to entail some utility cost to the planner; otherwise the exercise of will is simply not problematic. It is precisely because of this utility cost that the planner may wish to use the second technique, manipulation of the doers' opportunities. By imposing additional constraints upon a doer's opportunities,

---

2. This section presents a thumbnail sketch of the Thaler–Shefrin model. For further details, see the two papers by Thaler and Shefrin.

the planner may limit the amount of damage done when the individual is weak-willed (meaning the use of will-power is too costly). In addition, the restriction of a doer's opportunities reduces the temptation, and hence the amount of self-denial to be exercised. Both of these features play an important role in the analysis of dividends.

It appears that opportunity manipulation is widely used in self-control situations in everyday life. This technique seems to correspond with the generally accepted notion of a rule. For instance:

- jog at least two miles per day;
- do not consume more than 1,200 calories per day;
- bank the wife's salary and only spend from the husband's paycheck;
- save at least two percent of every paycheck for children's college education, and never withdraw from this fund;
- never touch a drop;

all provide examples of rules. Some may be enforced externally (e.g., 'fat farms', pension plans with automatic deductions), while others may be enforced internally (by habit). Thaler and Shefrin point out that such rules may also prevent the usual type of internal arbitrage that characterizes standard consumer choice theory. Individuals who simultaneously set aside funds for their children's college education at one interest rate, yet borrow to finance the purchase of durable goods at a higher interest rate, are not acting as standard utility maximizers. Yet the underlying rationale seems quite straightforward. By prohibiting withdrawals from the 'college fund', the possibility of not replenishing that fund because of a weak will is avoided. Alternatively, credit markets provide individuals with regimented loan repayments for which the default penalties are much more immediate than facing the prospect of a disappointed, disillusioned child in the distant future. In a similar vein, many people simultaneously borrow and yet take too few income tax exemptions in order to receive a large tax refund from the IRS.[3]

Observe that in the examples pertaining to college education and saving the wife's salary, money is not treated as a homogeneous item. It can be treated in a variety of ways depending on its source, or the use to

---

3. The degree to which any of the above self-control problems exist is something that varies across individuals. What one individual finds to be a severe self-control problem may be entirely absent in another. In addition, the subsequent discussion about dividend preference is part of a much broader picture dealing with pensions and the differential treatment of wealth and current income [Shefrin and Thaler (1984)].

which it will be put. Consequently, an individual who wishes to safeguard long-run wealth against a compulsion for immediate gratification might employ a rule that prohibits spending from capital. Such an individual may be better off by allowing current consumption to be determined by the dividend payout from his stock portfolio. In other words, this individual may wish to follow a *rule* stipulating that portfolio capital is not to be consumed, only dividends. What needs to be explained is why such a rule would be in the individual's interest since it imposes unnecessary constraints when viewed from standard financial theory. There may be times when disallowing the sale of capital for the purpose of increasing current consumption might be inconvenient, especially if one is short of liquid assets. However, the reason for actually employing such a rule is to stop the doer (meaning desire for immediate gratification) from gaining access to the capital. Moreover, with consumption financed by dividends instead of capital, the amount of will-power required by the planner decreases, along with the potential damage resulting from weakness of will. The exact same feature underscores why a parent may be reluctant to 'borrow' from the educational fund: a conscious worry about drawing the fund down too far, and experiencing difficulty in exercising the self-control necessary to replenish it.[4]

Of course, in standard theory the above discussion makes no sense. As Brealey and Myers (1981) argue, all the positions advanced to explain the favored treatment accorded firms which pay handsome dividends are poorly founded because the sale of stock serves as a perfect substitute for increased dividends. In a self-control framework the two are not perfect substitutes. Because of possible self-control difficulties, allowing oneself the discretion of selling stock for current consumption may cause the portfolio to be consumed more quickly than is consistent with one's long-term goals.

3. Prospect Theory and Dividends

Our first explanation of why investors prefer cash dividends deals with the distinction between 'issues of form' and 'issues of substance'. In standard financial theory it does not matter whether wealth is embodied in the form of a cash dividend or in the form of stock, because they are

---

4. There is a clear analogy with the Jensen–Meckling (1976) firm here. Jensen and Meckling were concerned about the 'overconsumption' of perquisites by manager/agents. Thaler and Shefrin are concerned with 'overly-early consumption' of wealth by the individual resulting from the desire for immediate gratification. In both cases improvements might be generated by adopting seemingly suboptimal rules that limit the agent's ability to exercise discretion.

perfect substitutes. Fischer Black (1976, p. 5) uses the following example to make this point succinctly:

> 'Suppose you are offered the following choice. You may have $2 today, and a 50–50 chance of $54 or $50 tomorrow. Or you may have nothing today, and a 50–50 chance of $56 or $52 tomorrow. Would you prefer one of these gambles to the other?'
>
> 'Probably you would not. Ignoring such factors as the cost of holding the $2 and one day's interest on $2, you would be indifferent between these two gambles.'

However, a substantial literature is now growing which indicates that 'form' matters. This literature is discussed by Arrow (1982) who provides a dramatic example from the work of McNeill, Pauker, Sox and Tversky (1981) to illustrate the importance of form. A group of physicians was presented with probabilistic data about the effectiveness of two alternative treatments (surgery and radiation therapy) for a particular form of cancer. Each physician was asked to choose between the two treatments. However, while some physicians were presented with the data in the form of 'survival probabilities', the remainder were given the *equivalent* information in the form of 'mortality probabilities'. The authors found that 84 percent of the physicians chose surgery over radiation when 'survival probabilities' were presented, but only 50 percent made that choice when 'mortality probabilities' were presented. Needless to say, the conversion of 'mortality probability' into 'survival probability' (and vice versa) is easily computed by subtraction from unity.

In standard theory it does not matter whether wealth is embodied in the form of dividends or in the form of capital, so long as they have the same value. However, the previous section made clear that the distinction between dividends and capital does matter in self-control theory. In the present section we discuss some additional reasons, quite apart from self-control, which cause the distinction in form to matter. These reasons concern the way individuals confront risk rather than the intertemporal considerations inherent in self-control.

Before taking up the uncertainty aspects of the dividend problem, we first outline the key features of the descriptive theory of choice under uncertainty due to Kahneman and Tversky (1979) and some related work by Thaler (1983). We then apply this theory to Black's preceding example, in order to discuss how the theory helps to explain dividend preference.

Kahneman and Tversky (1979, 1981) argue that decision-makers who face risky prospects consistently confuse issues of form and substance. In modelling such behavior these authors modify standard expected utility along the following lines. Let X be a (finite) set of certain outcomes with $x \in X$. Take p to be a probability distribution (or gamble) on X. Suppose that $u(x)$ is a von Neumann–Morgenstern utility function. Then the standard theory of choice under uncertainty has the space of gambles (or prospects) ranked according to the expected utility function

$$EU(p) = \sum_{x \in X} u(x)p(x).$$

Kahneman and Tversky modify this framework by replacing both u and p with transformations. The probability $p(x)$ is replaced by a term $\pi(p(x))$. While Kahneman and Tversky take $\pi(0)$ to be 0 and $\pi(1)$ to be 1, $\pi(p(x))$ is not equal to $p(x)$ for all intermediate values. For example, sufficiently small probabilities tend to get overweighted in the sense that $\pi(p(x)) > p(x)$. An important feature of $\pi(\cdot)$ which we discuss again later is the 'subcertainty' property: if a prospect p features some uncertainty in the sense that $0 < p(x') < 1$ for *some* outcome x', then

$$\sum_{x} \pi(p(x)) < 1.$$

For instance, this property would make a risk-averse individual willing to pay more for the *complete* elimination of uncertainty than his attitude to risk *alone* would suggest. [See Kahneman and Tversky (1979) for a full discussion.]

In Kahneman and Tversky's theory the utility function u is replaced by a 'value' function v which has as its argument the difference

$$x - \omega$$

between the certain outcome x and some standard reference point ω. Kahneman and Tversky argue that individuals tend to rank gambles according to gains or losses $(x - \omega)$ relative to some reference point ω, rather than according to the final consequence x.[5] Moreover, they postulate that individuals typically

(1) display risk-averse behavior over gambles which involve only gains;

(2) display risk-seeking behavior over gambles which involve only losses; and

---

5. It is important to understand that Kahneman and Tversky's model is not intended as a theory of rational behavior: their theory is positive, not normative.

(3) have losses loom larger than gains in those gambles which admit the possibility of either a gain or loss of equal magnitude.

Therefore, in the single-variable case, a standard Kahneman–Tversky value function is concave in gains and convex in losses with a somewhat non-symmetric shape to reflect the third property above. See figure 1.

Like Kahneman and Tversky, Friedman and Savage (1948) consider gambles which are defined in terms of gains and losses. However, Friedman and Savage use expected utility to rank gambles. Consequently, the associated preference relation satisfies the 'independence axiom' which says that an individual's preference relation over complex lotteries is determined by ranking simple lotteries. In addition, a Friedman–Savage individual exhibits preferences which are generally contingent upon initial wealth. By way of contrast, Kahneman–Tversky individuals have preferences which both violate the independence axiom, and are not contingent upon initial wealth. Kahneman and Tversky (1979) point out that it was Markowitz (1952) who first proposed that preferences be defined by gains and losses instead of on final-asset position. In discussing the differences between their approach and that of Markowitz, Kahneman and Tversky also indicate that Markowitz had both concave and convex regions in both regions of fig. 1. The Markowitz paper is also considered by Machina (1982) in his discussion of the independence axiom.

A germane issue raised by Kahneman and Tversky concerns the feature of 'coding'. They consider the way an individual would decide whether to pay a 'certain amount',[6] s, in order to purchase a lottery which promises amount x with probability $p(x)$, and amount y with probability $p(y) = 1 - p(x)$. The question is whether an individual will decide to purchase the lottery by noting that the net payoffs from the lottery are $x - s$ and $y - s$, respectively? Kahneman and Tversky refer to such netting as integration. If payoffs are integrated then the decision rule would be to purchase the lottery only if

$$\pi(p(x))v(x - s) + \pi(p(y))v(y - s) \geq v(0). \tag{1}$$

Yet Kahneman and Tversky postulate that the risky and riskless prospects will not be integrated in quite this way. Rather, they suggest that individuals typically evaluate lottery payoffs and lottery cost separately. Consequently, the individual will only purchase the lottery if the combined value is positive; that is, if

$$\pi(p(x))v(x) + \pi(p(y))v(y) + v(-s) \geq 0. \tag{2}$$

In this case the price s of the lottery is said to be segregated from the

---

6. Meaning a non-random amount with no uncertain component.

lottery payoffs. Kahneman and Tversky stress that (1) and (2) do not give rise to the same decision rule. Consequently, the issue of whether an individual makes his decision by integrating or segregating outcomes is germane. An obvious example involves the decision to buy stock: s represents the price of the stock at the time of purchase, while x and y signify possible future market value.

Thaler (1980) discusses the application of the Kahneman–Tversky framework to consumer choice theory. His (1983) paper employs the integration/segregation idea to study situations in which outcomes take the form (α, β) with total monetary payoff $\alpha + \beta$. Thaler argues that $v(x)$ may depend upon the decomposition of $\alpha + \beta$ into (α, β), and not just on the total. Significantly, he also represents the reference point ω in the decomposed form $(\omega_\alpha, \omega_\beta)$. Thaler than argues that the individual's decision about whether to segregate or to integrate depends on the magnitudes of both $(\alpha - \omega_\alpha)$ and $(\beta - \omega_\beta)$. His analysis establishes that the space $(\alpha - \omega_\alpha)$, $(\beta - \omega_\beta)$ will be partitioned into integration regions and segregation regions. Figure 2 portrays the regions with the dotted line demarcating the zone of net gain from the zone of net loss.

To understand what determines the regions in figure 2, consider a series of cases. In the first case (α, β) is such that $\alpha > \omega_\alpha$ and $\beta > \omega_\beta$. Then (α, β) can be regarded as an outcome involving two gains. In evaluating these gains, Thaler distinguishes between two distinct value functions $w(\cdot)$ and $v(\cdot)$: $w(\cdot)$ is a function of one variable, while $v(\cdot)$ is a function of two variables. Consider the act of integration. Assume that $w(\cdot)$ has the shape depicted in figure 1. Then integration means that the two gains $(\alpha - \omega_\alpha)$ and $(\beta - \omega_\beta)$ are netted together as $(\alpha - \omega_\alpha) + (\beta - \omega_\beta)$. It follows that the multi-variable value function $v(x) = v(\alpha - \omega_\alpha, \beta - \omega_\beta)$ would take the form

$$v(x) = w((\alpha - \omega_\alpha) + (\beta - \omega_\beta)). \tag{3}$$

Alternatively, segregation would represent the idea that the two gains α and β are 'savored' separately. Thaler (1983) describes this feature as wanting to have one's Christmas presents wrapped separately in order to experience the pleasure of opening each one individually. Formally, segregation means that the expression

$$v(x) = w(\alpha - \omega_\alpha) + w(\beta - \omega_\beta) \tag{4}$$

serves as a representation of $v(\cdot)$.

Given the same function $w(\cdot)$ in (3) and (4), it is clear that (4) yields a higher value for $v(x)$ than (3): this is because α and β both represent gains, and $w(\cdot)$ is concave in gains. Next, consider the plausible assumption that the Kahneman–Tversky value function $v(\cdot)$ serves as a utility indicator.

Figure 1   The Kahneman–Tversky value function representing an individual's preferences over gains and losses measured relative to some reference point in a gamble.

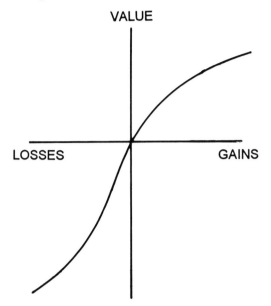

The figure shows that the individual is risk-averse in gains, risk-seeking in losses, with losses looming larger than gains.

Then it seems sensible to say that the decision about whether to segregate or to integrate will be determined according to the procedure which yields the higher value for $r(\cdot)$. That is, for $x = (\alpha - \omega_\alpha, \beta - \omega_\beta)$, $v(\cdot)$ is given by

$$v(x) = \max\{w((\alpha - \omega_\alpha) + (\beta - \omega_\beta)), w(\alpha - \omega_\alpha) + w(\beta - \omega_\beta)\}.$$

Carrying the above argument to its next step, suppose that both α and β signify losses. That is, suppose that

$$\alpha < \omega_\alpha \quad \text{and} \quad \beta < \omega_\beta.$$

Then it seems reasonable that the individual would want all losses reported in a lump sum rather than having to experience the psychological pain of considering them separately. The formal analogue of this last statement is that the integrated form (3) would be chosen over the segregated form (4). Indeed, notice that with $w(\cdot)$ being convex in losses, and both α and β signifying losses, the value of (3) will be higher than that of (4) [for fixed $w(\cdot)$].

In the mixed case, one component, say α, represents a gain, but the other, β, represents a loss. It is easy to see what happens in this situation by interpreting x within the context of a stock market problem. For the purpose of simplicity, consider a single stock. Let α correspond to the dividend, β to the current stock price, and ω_β to the price of the stock when it was originally purchased. For convenience, take the reference value for dividends ω_α to be zero. In order to clarify the main features of the integration/segregation decision in the mixed case, hold both the dividend α and the reference point stock price ω_β constant at strictly positive values. Observe that α is interpreted as a gain. Next consider how the decision changes as we vary the stock price, β. In figure 3, begin with the case of a capital-gain, meaning $\beta > \omega_\beta$. Then, as we discussed, the investor will wish to segregate. When $\beta = \omega_\beta$, and therefore $\beta - \omega_\beta = 0$, there is neither a capital gain nor loss: therefore, the investor will be indifferent between integration and segregation.

Next, consider the case in which $\beta < \omega_\beta$, so that a capital loss is incurred, but let this capital-loss be exactly offset by the dividend α. Notice that with integration the magnitude $v(x)$ is $w(0) = 0$ [from (3)], while with segregation we obtain

$$v(x) = w(\alpha) + w(\beta - \omega_\beta) = w(\alpha) + w(-\alpha) < 0.$$

This last inequality follows from (4) and figure 1 (since losses loom larger than gains). Consequently, integration is strictly preferred when $\beta - \omega_\beta = -\alpha$. Indeed, it is straightforward to verify that integration will be preferred to segregation for all β satisfying $-\alpha \leq \beta - v_\beta < 0$. Finally, consider the case in which the capital loss $\omega_\beta - \beta$ exceeds the dividend α. Notice from figure 1 that as $\beta - \omega_\beta$ becomes increasingly negative, the slope of $w(\cdot)$ grows smaller because of convexity. Consequently, there will be a sufficiently low stock price $\bar{\beta}$, for which segregation will be preferred to integration for all prices below this level. Figure 3 indicates the regions in which segregation or integration is preferred given a constant dividend α and varying capital gain $\beta - \omega_\beta$. Notice that figure 3 represents the points on a horizontal line drawn through the point $\alpha - \omega_\alpha > 0$ on the vertical axis of figure 2.

Figure 3 indicates that there are two distinct segregation regions which are relevant to dividends. To convey the intuition underlying these regions consider the following remarks from a manual for stockbrokers by Gross (1982, p. 177):

> 'By purchasing shares that pay good dividends, most investors persuade themselves of their prudence, based on the expected income. They feel the gain potential is a super added benefit. Should the stock fall in value

Figure 2   This figure portrays the integration and segregation regions for an individual who simultaneously incurs gains and/or losses in two distinct variables, α and β (measured relative to reference points ω_α and ω_β, respectively).

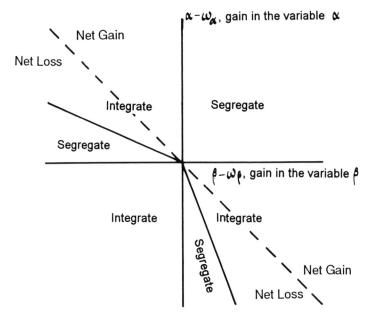

The figure indicates whether a given combination $((\alpha - \omega_\alpha), (\beta - \omega_\beta))$ leads the individual to segregate or to integrate. The net gain (or loss) associated with the final position is computed by adding $(\alpha - \omega_\alpha)$ to $(\beta - \omega_\beta)$.

from their purchase level, they console themselves that the dividend provides a return on their cost.'

Observe in figure 3 that the right-most segregation region is associated with a positive capital gain; therefore, the investor segregates in order to obtain 'super added benefit' from this gain. But in the left-most segregation region, where a sizeable capital loss is incurred, he segregates in order to treat the dividend as a silver lining with which he can 'console himself'. In the intermediate region of 'small' capital losses, he integrates in order to offset part or all of the capital loss by the dividend.

To see the contrast between our treatment of dividends and standard theory, recall the example from Black (1976) that illustrates the standard argument. Consider an interpretation of Black's two gambles in terms of

Figure 3 This figure portrays the integration and segregation regions associated with dividends and capital gains.

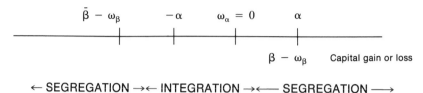

← SEGREGATION →←— INTEGRATION →←—— SEGREGATION ——→

The dividend per share is α, and the dividend reference point, ω_α, is zero. The original purchase price of the stock is ω_β, and the current stock price is β. The point $(\beta - \omega_\beta)$ signifies the critical capital loss for which the individual will be indifferent to segregating and integrating. The figure represents a horizontal cross-section of figure 2 at a fixed positive value of $(\alpha - \omega_\alpha)$. That is, it represents the points on a horizontal line which intersects the vertical axis at (a positive value of) $\alpha - \omega_\alpha$. In the right-most segregation region the capital gain serves as a 'super added benefit', while in the left-most region the dividend serves as a 'consolation' or 'silver lining'.

figure 3. Implicit in Black's argument is the assumption that the relative magnitude of capital gains (losses) to dividends plays no role. To underscore the importance of this feature in our treatment of dividends we extend Black's example to cover three special cases that differ only by the reference point the investor uses to define capital gains and losses. In each of these cases the dividend α is equal to 2, and β is either 50 or 54.

CASE 1. The investor purchased the stock for $40. Then the outcome of Black's first gamble consists of a $2 dividend together with a capital gain of either $10 or $14. In terms of figure 3 we have $\omega_\beta = 40$, with $\beta - \omega_\beta$ equal to either 10 or 14. Notice that this places the individual in the right-most segregation region in figure 3. Intuitively, the investor segregates the dividend from the capital gain in order to 'savor' the two separately, just as individually wrapped Christmas gifts are savored separately. Notice that the first gamble provides the investor with the flexibility to segregate or integrate as he wishes. That is, the investor can always perform the computation which transforms the first gamble into the second. However, he will not be able to transform the second (integrated) gamble into the first (segregated) gamble. Since the investor definitely prefers to segregate in this case, he will strictly prefer the first gamble to the second.[7]

---

7. We allow the decision about whether to segregate or integrate to be made after the realization of the gamble is revealed.

CASE 2.   Suppose the investor purchased the stock for $70. Therefore, a capital loss of either $16 or $20 will be incurred, although a $2 dividend will also be earned. Then $\omega_\beta = 70$, and $\beta - \omega_\beta$ is equal to either -16 or -20. For the purpose of this discussion, assume that the value of $\bar{\beta} - \omega_\beta$ in figure 3 is -5. Then the investor will find himself in the left-most segregation region of figure 3. Intuitively, the investor prefers to segregate because the dividend can be regarded as a 'silver lining'. That is, segregation enables the investor to stress the positive aspects of his (net) loss as much as possible.[8] Consequently, the first gamble will be preferred to the second just as in Case 1.

CASE 3.   Suppose the initial purchase price was $51. This case illustrates a situation where integration emerges. Observe that with a $2 dividend, there will be either a capital gain of $3 or a capital loss of $1. Then $\omega_\beta = 51$, and $\beta - \omega_\beta$ is either 3 or -1. Notice from figure 3 that this places the investor in the integration region. Intuitively, integration is preferred to segregation here because it eliminates any consideration of a loss. Therefore, the investor who faces gamble 1 would himself integrate, thereby transforming gamble 1 into gamble 2. Because the investor has this option available, the indifference suggested by Black will actually be achieved in this case.[9]

Observe that in Black's discussion the $2 dividend is treated as a certainty in gamble 1. This brings to mind Kahneman and Tversky's 'subcertainty' feature. Subcertainty suggests that for segregated gambles, the certain or 'bird in the hand' component (in this case $2) will provide an added attraction. To see how this would emerge, let the initial purchase price of the stock be $40 ($\omega_\alpha = 40$). Then from (2) Black's first gamble would be accorded a value of

$$w(2) + \pi(0.5)w(10) + \pi(0.5)w(14), \tag{5}$$

while from (1) his second gamble would be accorded a value of

$$\pi(0.5)w(12) + \pi(0.5)w(16). \tag{6}$$

8. The idea is also consistent with the principle of cognitive dissonance whose economic consequences have been discussed by Akerlof and Dickens (1982).

9. There is the possibility that the investor will be unable to carry out the integration from a psychological point of view. That is, the investor may not be able to forget about the segregated amounts. In this case he would strictly prefer gamble 2 to gamble 1. Thus, the investor would wish to segregate in some outcomes and integrate in others. Since the gamble involving the dividend might preclude integration (psychologically), he would need to compare the relative likelihoods of the outcomes before deciding whether to choose the dividend-paying stock. Given that the investor will generally choose a stock with a positive expected capital gain, and will wish to segregate if such a gain materializes, there is a strong tendency to select a dividend-paying stock.

Were $\pi(0.5) = 0.5$, then our earlier argument involving (3) and (4) would imply that (5) exceeds (6). This inequality will only be strengthened by the subcertainty feature $\pi(0.5) < 0.5$ [which must hold since $\pi(0.5) + \pi(0.5) < 1$].

We caution the reader that the subcertainty argument is by no means intended to portray the old 'bird in the hand' explanation of dividend preference as correct: Miller and Modigliani's (1961) analysis makes clear why it is flawed. However, our discussion points out that Kahneman–Tversky investors may find the certainty feature of dividends attractive because of the subcertainty property.[10]

Kahneman and Tversky's prospect theory also offers explanations for a variety of other curious features about dividends noted in the literature. We mention two particular issues. First, Kahneman and Tversky postulate that losses loom larger than gains and this appears to be consistent with the observation that announced dividend decreases have a much more pronounced effect on market value than do announced increases in dividends. See Charest (1978). Second, while the separation of dividends into 'regular' and 'extra' components can possibly convey information [see Brickley (1983)], prospect theory provides an additional independent explanation. Kahneman and Tversky emphasize the tendency of decision-makers to evaluate prospects in terms of gains and/or losses relative to a fixed reference point. Moreover, a reference point can change with time, for instance, as might happen when a dividend increase is announced. By segregating a dividend payment into 'regular' and 'extra' components, a firm may prevent an increase in total dividends per share from leading to a reference point shift on the part of the shareholder. Otherwise, a subsequent reversion of total dividend payout to its original level might be interpreted as a loss in view of a new (higher) reference point; and losses loom larger than gains. This explanation is consistent with Brickley's (1983) finding that dividend payouts in the year following dividend increases are significantly larger for regular dividend increases than for specially designated dividends.

4. Regret Aversion and Dividend Preference

Compare the following two cases:

(1) You take $600 received as dividends and use it to buy a television set.

(2) You sell $600 worth of stock and use it to buy a television set.

---

10. Attractive is not synonymous with rational. Recall that Kahneman and Tversky do not offer a theory of rational decision-making.

Subsequently, the price of the stock increases significantly. Would you feel more regret in case 1 or in case 2? If dividends and the receipts from the sale of stock are perfect substitutes, then it is clear that you should feel no more regret in case 2 than in case 1. However, evidence by Kahneman and Tversky (1982) indicates that for most people the sale of stock causes more regret.[11] What we argue here is that consumption from dividends may be preferred to consumption from capital for people who are averse to regret. Consequently, dividends and capital cannot be treated as perfect substitutes, even abstracting from tax and informational considerations.

The general idea of regret aversion and its effect on individual behavior is described well by Kahneman and Tversky (1982, pp. 172–173):

'Regret is a special form of frustration in which the event one would change is an action one has either taken or failed to take . . . Regret is felt if one can readily imagine having taken an action that would have led to a more desirable outcome. This interpretation explains the close link between the experience of regret and the availability of choice: actions taken under duress generate little regret. The reluctance to violate standard procedures and to act innovatively can also be an effective defense against subsequent regret because it is easy to imagine doing the conventional thing and more difficult to imagine doing the unconventional one.

A closely related hypothesis is that it is often easier to mentally delete an event from a chain of occurrences than it is to imagine the insertion of an event into the chain. Such a difference in imaginability could help to explain the observation that the regret associated with failures to act is often less intense than the regret associated with the failure of an action. Consider the following:

Paul owns shares in Company A. During the past year he considered switching to stock in Company B, but he decided against it. He now finds that he would have been better off by $1,200 if he had switched to the stock of Company B. George owned shares in Company B. During the past year he switched to stock in Company A. He now finds that he would have been better off by $1,200 if he had kept his stock in Company B. Who feels more regret?

Here again it is generally agreed that George is more upset than Paul, although their objective situations are now identical (both own the stock of Company A) and each reached his situation by deliberate decision.

11. We know an economist who refers to his $30,000 kitchen renovation. Actually, the renovation cost amounted to only $3,000, but it was paid for from the proceeds of the sale of stock. The economist added that he rarely sells stock to finance consumption. Subsequently, the price of the stock increased. Would he have felt the same regret if dividends were used to pay for the renovation?

Apparently it is easier for George to imagine not taking an action (and thereby retaining the more advantageous stock) than it would be for Paul to imagine taking the action. Furthermore, one would expect both men to anticipate the possibility of regret and to act accordingly. In general the anticipation of regret is likely to favor inaction over action and routine behavior over innovative behavior.'

Thaler (1980) discusses a related point. He considers why the possibility of regret discourages decisions in which the individual feels he must take 'responsibility' for the final outcome. This idea can be used to relate Kahneman and Tversky's treatment of regret to their formal analysis of prospect theory. Suppose that a favorable outcome enables the decision-maker to take pride in his action, while an unfavorable outcome involves regret. As Kahneman and Tversky argue, the reasons for regret and pride stem from the consideration of what would have occurred had another decision been made. If regret generates stronger emotions than pride, then decisions involving responsibility will tend to be avoided. One way of seeing how this feature relates to the previous section is to consider figure 4. This figure displays two value functions. The solid function is associated with a gamble in which the individual does not take responsibility, while the other function applies to the responsibility case. Notice that while pride increases the value of a gain, and regret increases the (absolute) value of a loss, the effect due to regret is the greater.

The implication of this discussion for dividend preference is not difficult to see. Consider the following case: Paul normally spends cash dividends. Therefore, when he receives a $1 cash dividend he spends it. George rarely sells stocks for consumption, but let him sell $1 worth of stock and spend it. Subsequently, the price of the stock increases. It is easier for George to imagine not selling the stock (i.e., not taking an action) than it is for Paul to imagine reinvesting the cash dividend in the stock (i.e., taking an action). George feels more regret because he feels 'responsible'. Paul, who can easily be in an identical net financial position, is able to avoid feeling regret because consuming dividends constitutes what Kahneman and Tversky call 'standard procedure'.[12] This point demonstrates that a rule (standard procedure) can perform functions other than self-control, like reducing regret. For instance, let Paul follow the

12. Figure 4 indicates how the value function is affected when responsibility for action is taken into account. This figure does not imply that a decision avoiding responsibility will always be chosen over a decision involving responsibility, since account must also be taken of the odds attached to the respective gambles. A similar point is made in Loomes and Sugden (1982, 1983). Interestingly, Loomes and Sugden as well as Bell (1982) use the idea of regret to explain the major features described by prospect theory.

Figure 4   This figure indicates how an individual's Kahneman–Tversky value function changes when he feels responsible for the outcome of a gamble.

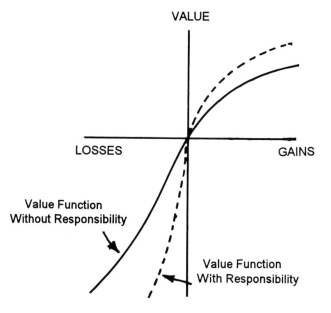

When the gamble results in a gain he receives extra value stemming from a sense of pride. When the gamble results in a loss he feels a sense of regret and receives less value. The figure is drawn so that the regret effect (measured by the vertical distance between the two functions in the third quadrant) is stronger than the pride effect (measured by the vertical distance between the two functions in the first quadrant). This feature tends to make individuals reluctant to choose gambles in which they feel responsible for the outcome.

rule of reinvesting his dividends, but suppose he deviated this one time. Then the theory holds that he will experience regret for breaking the rule and having it turn out badly. Thus, the argument that dividends and capital are perfect substitutes in the absence of taxes and transaction cost may not hold. Regret aversion can induce a preference for dividends through the use of a rule like 'finance consumption out of dividends, not capital'.

5. The Clientele Effect: Some Empirical Implications

Our interest is in providing plausible reasons why investors display a distinct preference for cash dividends. Of course, the strength of this preference need not be the same for all investors. Indeed, it could well be that investor clienteles with different characteristics favor dividends in varying degrees. To be more precise, there may be investors who favor high dividend yield stocks, investors who prefer low dividend yield stocks, and still others who are totally indifferent to dividend yield. In this section we discuss the implications of our theory for the clientele effect, suggest some testable hypotheses, and supply supporting evidence.

Our analysis of the clientele effect focuses upon the life cycle of a given investor who, because of self-control problems, might experience difficulty in accumulating savings for retirement. Thaler and Shefrin (1981) point out that saving for retirement may be especially problematic during the early phase of the life cycle when retirement seems such a long way off. Consequently, a young investor who appreciates this aspect of self-control may wish to adopt rules which both:

(i) encourage savings; and

(ii) discourage dissaving from already accumulated wealth.

We hypothesize that dividends play a significant role in rules which discourage dissaving; however, we see no compelling reason to expect that low (current) dividend payout acts to encourage (current) saving per se. Consider, therefore, a rule to limit dissaving which consists of the following two-pronged strategy:

(1) Do not consume out of investment capital.

(2) Choose a portfolio with a relatively low dividend yield.

Such a strategy clearly serves to discourage dissaving, since the low dividend yields prevent high consumption out of the portfolio.

Consider a somewhat older investor later in the life cycle who is still employed, owns most of the equity in his home, has no dependent children, and so on. Such an investor might now wish to begin dissaving from his portfolio on a regular basis, and possibly in significant amounts. Of course, the basic self-control conflict may still exist; that is, the individual might still have to worry about dissaving too rapidly. Thus, it is plausible to suggest that he will continue to employ the above consumption–dividend rule, but will adjust the overall dividend yield of the portfolio in order to facilitate greater dissaving.

Finally, in the retired stage of the life cycle labor income is sharply reduced, and the investor depends heavily on his portfolio to finance consumption. However, a self-control problem still remains because wealth must be allocated over the entire retirement phase. Since it is quite possible to deplete 'too great a portion' of wealth immediately after retirement, the same dividend–consumption rule might be retained, although the dividend yield of the portfolio would now need to be much higher.[13]

In summary, the self-control portion of our theory predicts that dividend yield will be positively correlated with the planned rate of dissaving for individual investors. Therefore, we would observe that whenever the rate of dissaving is positively correlated with age and negatively correlated with income, we should find that:

(a) portfolio dividend yield is positively correlated with age; and

(b) portfolio dividend yield is negatively correlated with income (from human wealth).

An additional implication emerges when the motives of self-control, segregation, and regret-aversion are considered jointly. Recall that an investor interested in self-control will design a portfolio in which consumption is financed out of dividends instead of the sale of stock. Observe that this practice will also serve to limit regret once it becomes what Kahneman and Tversky call 'standard procedure'. However, these motives may be in conflict with the desire to segregate, especially for an investor in the saving stage of the life cycle. This is because self-control theory suggests that such an investor will wish to hold a portfolio containing little or no dividend-paying stocks. However, the absence of dividends eliminates the ability to segregate. We would expect this investor to choose a portfolio which balances the conflicting motives. Consequently, the fraction of the portfolio devoted to dividend-paying stock will represent a compromise. There is no reason to expect a relationship between the strength of the motives for either segregation or regret-aversion and the stage of the life cycle. Therefore, our theory continues to imply that the proportion of the portfolio devoted to dividend-paying stock will increase when the investor moves from the saving stage of the life cycle to the dissaving stage.

In an important empirical study Lease, Lewellen and Schlarbaum (1976) use panel data collected at Purdue to analyze the demographic

---

13. Analyzing self-control during retirement is fairly complex as a general matter because there are a variety of factors to be taken into account. Space limitations do not permit a thorough analysis of the alternatives which a retired individual might choose. Instead, we focus on the implications which arise when 'don't dip into capital' is the rule being followed.

attributes and portfolio compositions of a wide variety of individual investors. These authors obtained comprehensive profile data on a large random sample of investors who had maintained an open account over the period 1964–1970 with a large national retail brokerage house.[14] The sample appears to be highly representative of the shareholding public. Lease, Lewellen, and Schlarbaum use cluster analysis in order to partition their sample into five relatively homogeneous groups:

1. young, unmarried professionals and managers;
2. highly educated young professional men;
3. older males still at work;
4. females, mostly retired;
5. retired males.

In their questionnaire Lease, Lewellen and Schlarbaum asked each respondent to rate, on a scale of one to four (where four denoted a 'very important' goal), short-term capital gains, long-term capital appreciation, and dividend income as portfolio objectives. It also asked investors to estimate the (perceived) proportionate representation in their portfolio of securities chosen primarily for their ability to generate dividend-income. Also, as a crude measure of diversification, the number of different companies' securities held was solicited. The responses are striking. We reproduce a portion of their table above.

The two groups of young investors devote 27 percent and 34 percent of their portfolios, respectively, to dividend-income-generating securities. This is consistent with the 2.04 and 2.30 rating accorded to dividends by these groups. For older working men, the proportion of the portfolio devoted to dividend-generation rises somewhat to 39 percent, and their rating of dividends rises to 2.46. Finally, the retired groups' proportions jump to 56 percent and 57 percent, respectively. These percentages, together with the two ratings, 3.36 and 3.39 on the scale of 1 to 4, show just how important dividends are to the retired groups.

These findings are consistent with the implications of our theory. Unfortunately, the Purdue data does not include direct information about the rate of dissaving by investors. Recall that the theoretical implication for dividend yield and age derive from the more fundamental relationship between dividend yield and the rate of dissaving, and similarly for the correlation between dividend yield and income. Using the Purdue data

---

14. The profiles describe age, sex, income, education, occupation, assets, marital status, portfolio composition, investment criteria, etc., of each investor.

further, Pettit (1977) regressed dividend yield (for a given investor's portfolio) on the investor's age, income, differential tax rate, and the beta of his portfolio. Consistent with our theory, his analysis indicates that the correlation between dividend yield and age is significantly positive, and the correlation between dividend yield and income is significantly negative. Interestingly, Pettit's analysis shows that age is negatively correlated (-0.15) with income. Of course, this is somewhat misleading in that age and income are almost certainly positively correlated for young investors. Nevertheless, it does point to the likely increase in dissaving as individuals get older and retire.

Consider next the implications which arise from the interaction of self-control, segregation, and regret-aversion. Notice from table 1 that young investors hold approximately one-third of their portfolios in dividend-paying stocks: this proportion can hardly be characterized as low. Second, observe that the proportion of dividend-paying stock in the portfolios of retired investors is considerably higher, exceeding 50 percent. Both features are consistent with the empirical implications outlined earlier.

Self-control can explain why people in the saving stage of the life cycle hold portfolios with lower dividend yields than those held by people

Table 1   **Importance of alternative investment goals to various demographic groups as measured by average rating (4 = very important goal, 1 = low priority goal) and percent of portfolio in income securities.**[a]

	(1) Young Unmarried Professionals & Managers	(2) Highly Educated Young Professional Men	(3) Older Males Still at Work	(4) Females, Mostly Retired	(5) Retired Males
Investment goal rating:					
Short-term capital gains	2.19	2.00	1.86	1.50	1.53
Long-term capital gains	3.61	3.54	3.63	3.46	3.45
Dividend income	2.04	2.30	2.46	3.36	3.39
Percent of portfolio in income securities	27%	34%	39%	57%	56%
Average number of securities in portfolio	9.4	10.4	11.6	12.1	12.1

[a]*Source:* Lease, Lewellen, and Schlarbaum (1976, table 3).

in the dissaving stage of the life cycle. Alternatively, transaction costs (brokerage commissions) make it more efficient for people who consume from their portfolios to consume from dividends rather than sell shares and pay brokerage commissions. Moreover, there is no conclusive evidence to suggest that the transaction cost explanation for dividend preference is false. Yet transaction cost undoubtedly plays some role in the preference for dividends, though it does not appear to provide a major (let alone complete) explanation of the phenomenon. For instance, when a corporation omits a dividend, shareholders do not seem to complain about the additional transaction costs incurred when they sell stock to obtain cash. Indeed, the next section deals with one dividend omission by Consolidated Edison in which shareholders argued that the corporation's action forced them to reduce consumption by the *full* amount of the omitted dividend. The question of transaction costs did not even arise during the course of the stockholders' meeting.

A second issue connected with dividend omission concerns the extent to which a capital gain from one stock in the portfolio can play the part of a silver lining for the capital loss in another stock. To some extent it certainly can; however, it needs to be understood that some investors may be interested in the magnitude of the silver lining just as they are interested in the magnitude of their general insurance coverage. In fact, the silver lining function of dividends is analogous to insurance against the disappointment of a capital loss. We suggest two reasons why dividends provide more effective 'coverage' than capital gains from other stocks in the portfolio.

1. The investors described in table 1 held portfolios consisting of no more than twelve securities on average. Suppose that none of the stocks in such a portfolio paid any dividends. In a down market it is quite likely that just one or two stocks might be up in price, and the capital gain may not be especially large. Thus, the silver lining may be smaller than the corresponding amount associated with a high dividend yield portfolio. Clearly, dividends are a more reliable source of consolation for capital losses in the portfolio.

2. Thaler (1980) argues that out-of-pocket gains are accorded greater weight than opportunity gains. This argument suggests that a dividend check-in-the-mail would be a more effective silver lining than a 'paper capital gain' on another stock. The argument also appears in a manual for stockbrokers by Gross (1982, p. 177):

'The regular dividend stream makes the losing investor a more patient holder and often a fairly eager willing purchaser of more shares with only the slightest encouragement from the salesperson.'

While the above analysis deals exclusively with individual investors, it is worth adding that similar arguments can be made for some institutional investors. Indeed, Thaler and Shefrin (1981) placed considerable emphasis on the fact that the types of rules followed by firms facing inter-person conflicts are very similar to the rules used by individuals with intra-person self-control problems. Thus Brealey and Myers (1981, p. 335) mention that 'most colleges and universities are legally free to spend capital gains from their endowments, but this is rarely done.' This suggests that institutions, as well as individuals, may use dividends as a control device. For instance, university trustees might use dividends as a way to control spending by deans, and the adoption of such a rule can also signal potential donors that the institution is financially prudent and likely to be around for a long time.[15]

6. Consolidated Edison: A Case of Dividend Omission

The case of Consolidated Edison Company of New York reinforces the previous discussion on clienteles and provides new insights into the basic problem. Con Ed income fell in 1973–74, largely because of the quadrupling of oil prices. Consequently, after 89 years of uninterrupted dividends, they omitted a dividend. Company representatives encountered an angry group of stockholders at the 1974 annual meeting.

In his opening remarks at the annual meeting, Charles F. Luce, the Chairman of the Board, described Con Ed's clientele (p. 3):

> 'Investors buy Con Edison stock for assured income. A typical stockholder lives in or near New York City, . . . , owns about 100 shares—of course, many own more but some own less—is retired or nearing retirement. Most of our stockholders are women, many are widowed . . . When the dividend check doesn't come, there is real hardship for many people.'

As for the main topic of discussion at the meeting, he stated (p. 3):

> 'I know, too, that your most immediate concern . . . is the dividend on your common stock. Why did we pass the June dividend, and when will we recommence paying dividends?'

Judging from shareholders' remarks, it appears that the Chairman's

---

15. Those institutions which do permit capital gains to be spent often adopt an iron-clad rule to limit the extent to which this is possible. For instance, the University of Rochester requires that annual expenditure not exceed five percent of the five-year moving average of its endowment portfolio value.

statements accurately reflected, indeed understated, the importance of dividends for this group. The following representative statements by stockholders at the meeting illustrate the point (p. 36):

> 'I recommend that you shall hold . . . a special meeting of the Board of Directors . . . ordering the restoration of the dividend, and to restore the good name of Con Edison that has been known for 89 years as a widow's stock, and no risk involved of ever eliminating the dividend.'

And (p. 109):

> 'What are we to do? You give us shorthand answers. You don't know when the dividend is coming back. Who is going to pay my rent? I had a husband. Now Con Ed has to be my husband.'

And (p. 65):

> 'A Lady came over to me a minute ago and she said to me, 'Please say a word for the senior citizens.' And she had tears in her eyes. And I really know what she means by that. She simply means that now she will get only one check a month, and that will be her Social Security, and she's not going to make it, because you have denied her that dividend.'

These angry comments make it clear that selling some Con Ed stock to create 'homemade' dividends (the standard device in financial theory), never occurred to the speakers. We believe that this is not without reason.[16] Indeed, it appears likely that most of these stockholders were following a rule which stipulates that consumption can only be financed out of dividends, but not out of capital. Some explicitly said that they viewed dividend receipts as pension benefits, having 'no other pensions except dividends' (p. 3). Moreover, several of the shareholders who protested quite vigorously about the omission of the cash dividend held several thousand shares of Con Ed stock apiece; so it is unlikely that the absence of the dividend would place them in 'real hardship', to use chairman Luce's phrase. What emerges from such remarks is that these invest-

---

16. Transaction costs might help to explain the disappointment of stockholders, but it seems unlikely to us that it could adequately account for the strength of the sentiments expressed. Specifically, on the date of the meeting, May 20, 1974, Con Ed stock was selling at $8.75. The sale of 100 shares valued at $875 would have entailed a brokerage fee of only $25.71. Moreover, shareholders did not complain that Con Ed's action would force them to incur unexpected brokerage fees when selling off stock to provide for consumption. Rather, they argued that Con Ed's action was forcing them to reduce consumption by the full amount of the dividend.

ors are very resistant to selling off stock already in their portfolios. Consequently, the shareholders' remarks are consistent with the implications of self-control theory. From the perspective of prospect theory there are two points to be made. First, if an investor breaks the rule and creates a 'homemade dividend' by selling off stock, then he or she will likely have to sell the stock at less than its original purchase price, given market conditions at that time.[17] In such a situation the Kahneman–Tversky reference point for the stock lies above the (current) price, and the investor will have to come to terms with a loss.[18] Second, the omission of the dividend also prevents the investor from segregating; and recall that in this case segregation would reduce the psychological effect of the decline in the value of Con Ed stock.

The declaration of a stock dividend could play a role with respect to each of the above aspects. In fact, one stockholder asked why such a dividend was not declared 'so at least the blow which was given to stockholders by the omission of the dividend would have been much less' (p. 28). The chairman gave the standard financial theory explanation of why stock dividends would not make most shareholders better off. However, our theory suggests a number of advantages to the declaration of a stock dividend, despite the G.P.U. experience described earlier. First, stock dividends are labeled as dividends. Consequently, the investor does not have to break his or her 'do not consume out of capital' rule by selling off and subsequently consuming the stock dividend. Second, the reference point for the stock acquired as a dividend will not generally be the same as stock already in the portfolio. The reference points of two blocks of the same stock typically varies according to the price paid for each block, so long as investors think in terms of gains and losses.[19] Consequently, selling the stock dividend entails no perceived loss on the sale. Finally, stock dividends provide some semblance of gain (a silver lining) which can be segregated out from the investor's portfolio.

17. The price of the stock had fallen from $23 to $8.75.

18. It is also likely that the foregone dividend is interpreted as a loss. That is, the investor will have to come to terms with a loss which is now 'out of pocket', not just on paper. Thaler (1980) argues that out-of-pocket costs are accorded much greater weight than opportunity costs.

19. Many stockholders at the Con Ed meeting viewed dividends in the same light as the salaries of Con Ed representatives. Consequently, they expressed a desire that the decrease in dividends be carried out with a parallel decrease in salary. This conforms with Brealey and Myers' (1981, p. 334) discussion concerning the call for dividend controls as part of an overall wage and price controls program. While Brealey and Myers argue that this last view is fallacious, our arguments suggest that some investors would indeed feel the effect of dividend controls.

7. Further Directions

Financial theory has tended to ignore the question of how individual investors actually behave, concentrating instead on how asset prices are determined. Indeed, the way individual investors behave does not seem to be especially important for the workings of financial models. In this regard it is usually argued that learning and arbitrage will serve to eliminate the effects of behavior not in conformity with standard normative precepts. However, a counterargument by Russell and Thaler (1982) has shown why the necessary arbitrage possibilities need not exist. Arrow (1982, p. 8) provides a second counterargument in which 'if everyone else is 'irrational', it by no means follows that one can make money by being rational . . . As Keynes argued long ago, the value of a security depends in good measure on other people's opinions.' There is also empirical support for these kinds of theoretical claims. Besides the dividend issue, standard models seem incapable of accounting for such features as the January anomaly and small firm anomaly.[20] This suggests the presence of a substantial gap in the finance literature, and the present paper can be viewed as a beginning towards filling this gap.

Our specific concern is with the question of why individual investors find cash dividends attractive. Consequently, our attention is confined to the demand side of the market. Extending the present analysis to a complete equilibrium is beyond the scope of this paper, although it is possible to offer a few tentative remarks about the direction of future research.

A first step would involve a formal analysis of the portfolio selection problem for an individual investor interested in self-control and segregation. This entails the development of a single model which captures the features discussed in both Shefrin and Thaler (1983) and Kahneman and Tversky (1979). Constructing such a model turns out to be relatively straightforward. This analysis will serve to make clear how an individual investor evaluates increases and decreases in the dividend yield of a given firm's stock. Because investors who use dividends as a self-control device select a dividend payout ratio which conforms with their desired consumption level, it is possible for a given firm's share price to fall if it increases its dividend payout ratio beyond a particular level, even if its shareholders belong to a single clientele. Dividend payouts which are 'too large' can induce the need for additional will-power. If a firm's shareholder constituency consists of members from several distinct groups, then the firm will have to choose its payout ratio to balance off the different demand responses of the various groups. In other words, when

---

20. See the June, 1983 symposium issue of the Journal of Financial Economics, especially the papers by Schwert and Reinganum.

the dividend yield is chosen to maximize the market value of the firm, then any further increase in this yield will cause a loss in demand by the members of some group(s) (say the group of young professionals) which is not offset by the others.

A similar feature can be found in Feldstein and Green's (1983) study of why companies pay dividends. In their model each firm sets a dividend yield to maximize the value of its shares by balancing off the demand of individual investors against that of tax-exempt institutions. However, in their model, individual investors choose to hold stock in companies that pay dividends only for diversification. Consequently, a Feldstein–Green firm pays dividends to attract institutions, not individual investors. This contrasts sharply with the treatment of investor preference for dividends in the present paper.

8. Conclusion

We present here a framework that explains why investors exhibit preference for dividends, based on the theory of self-control by Thaler and Shefrin and the theory of choice under uncertainty by Kahneman and Tversky. The essence of our argument is that dividends and capital cannot be treated as perfect substitutes. In the absence of taxes and transaction costs, the perfect substitutes feature forms the basis of dividend irrelevancy. Moreover, we argue that in our theory it can be reasonable for many investors to prefer specific dividend payouts, and we identify the demographic attributes of investors who prefer high and low dividend payout portfolios. Furthermore, available empirical evidence on this issue is consistent with the theory.

Our theory suggests that some investors would be willing to pay a premium for cash dividends because of self-control reasons, the desire to segregate, or the wish to avoid regret. John Long (1978) presents compelling evidence that 'there is a significant demand for cash dividends in spite of a generally lower after-tax total return to investors holding claims to these dividends.' Higher tax payments resulting from the preference for dividends may therefore be interpreted as a price paid for self-control, segregation, regret reduction, and possibly all three. Such tax payments are the intrapersonal analogue of what Jensen and Meckling call agency cost.

When discussing the possibility of finding alternatives to the standard explanations of the dividend phenomenon, Brealey and Myers (1980) indicate that investor behavior in these new explanations would be 'less rational'. However, interpreting rationality is an extremely delicate task in the theories advanced here. Clearly, an individual investor who incurs unnecessary 'agency costs' is acting irrationally. But what about an individual with a serious self-control problem such as impulse buying? Such an individual may be forced to choose from a group of alternatives, all of which involve agency cost. In this case the term 'irrational' is better applied to somebody who does not minimize agency cost, rather than somebody who incurs non-zero agency cost. In practice, however, great care must be taken in establishing that an individual investor is not minimizing agency cost. For instance, it can be argued that an individual investor could improve on the rule 'consume from dividends but don't dip into capital' by letting a financial manager assume partial control of his portfolio. Specifically, the fund manager could be instructed to sell off stock at regular intervals and send the investor an amount, part of which would represent capital gains. Such a strategy could conceivably lead to a higher after-tax return than the 'consuming from dividends' rule and also cope with the self-control problem. An alternative procedure to escape the double-tax bite associated with dividends is to purchase a portfolio consisting of both high yield bonds and stocks which pay no dividends. Consumption would then be financed out of bond coupons *alone*. Procedures such as these might make an investor better off, though an improvement is by no means guaranteed. For one thing, such changes represent alterations in 'form', and form seems to matter. In addition, a key feature of a successful internally enforced self-control technique is its habitual characteristic. Breaking old habits and creating new ones is rarely an intellectual decision alone. Consequently, the normative aspects associated with behavior like the dividend phenomenon should be approached with great care.

═══════

We would like to thank Richard Thaler, Amos Tversky, and Thomas Russell for their comments. We have also benefited from the suggested improvements by Fischer Black (the referee) and the editors, G. William Schwert and Michael C. Jensen. Responsibility for all errors rests with us.

References

AKERLOF, G. A. and T. DICKENS. 1982. The economic consequences of cognitive dissonance. *American Economic Review* 72, 307–319.

ARROW, K. J. 1982. Risk perception in psychology and economics, *Economic Inquiry* 20, 1–9.

ASQUITH, P. and D. MULLINS. The impact of initiating dividend payments on shareholders wealth, *Journal of Business* 56, 77–96.

BELL, D. 1982. Regret in decision making under uncertainty, *Operations Research* 30, 961–981.

BHATTACHARYA, S. 1979. Imperfect information, dividend policy, and the 'bird-in-the-hand' fallacy, *Bell Journal of Economics* 10, 259–270.

BLACK, F. and M. SCHOLES. 1974. The effects of dividend yield and dividend policy on common stock prices and returns, *Journal of Financial Economics* 1, 1–22.

BLACK, F. 1976. The dividend puzzle, *Journal of Portfolio Management* 2, 5–8.

BREALEY, R. and S. MYERS. 1981. Principles of corporate finance (McGraw-Hill, New York).

BRENNAN, M. 1970. Taxes, market valuation, and financial policy, *National Tax Journal* 23, 417–427.

BRICKLEY, J. 1983. Shareholder wealth, information signaling, and the specially designated dividend, *Journal of Financial Economics* 12, 187–209.

CHAREST, G. 1978. Dividend information, stock returns, and market efficiency, *Journal of Financial Economics* 6, 297–330.

Consolidated Edison Company of New York, Inc. 1974. Annual meeting of stockholders, May 20.

FEENBERG, D. 1981. Does the investment limitation explain the existence of dividends?, *Journal of Financial Economics* 9, 265–269.

FELDSTEIN, M. and J. GREEN. 1983. Why do companies pay dividends?, *American Economic Review* 73, 17–30.

FRIEDMAN, M. and L. J. SAVAGE. 1948. The utility analysis of choices involving risk, *Journal of Political Economy* 56, 279–304.

HAKANSSON, N. 1982. To pay or not to pay dividends, *Journal of Finance* 37, 415–428.

GROSS, L. 1982. The art of selling intangibles: How to make your million ($) by investing other people's money (New York Institute of Finance, New York).

JENSEN, M. and W. MECKLING. 1976. Theory of the firm: Managerial behavior, agency costs and ownership structure, *Journal of Financial Economics* 3, 305–360.

KAHNEMAN, D. and A. TVERSKY. 1979. Prospect theory: An analysis of decision under risk, *Econometrica* 47, 263–291.

KAHNEMAN, D. and A. TVERSKY. 1982. The psychology of preferences, *Scientific American* 246, 167–173.

LEASE, R., W. LEWELLEN and G. SCHLARBAUM. 1976. Market segmentation: Evidence on the individual investor, *Financial Analysts Journal* 32, 53–60.

LITZENBERGER, R. and K. RAMASWAMY. 1980. Dividends, short selling restrictions, tax-induced investor clienteles and market equilibrium, *Journal of Finance* 35, 469–482.

LITZENBERGER, R. and K. RAMASWAMY. 1979. The effect of personal taxes and dividends on capital asset prices: Theory and empirical evidence, *Journal of Financial Economics* 7, 163–195.

LITZENBERGER, R. and K. RAMASWAMY. 1982. The effect of dividends on common stock prices, tax effects or information effects, *Journal of Finance* 37, 429–443.

LONG, J. 1978. The market valuation of cash dividends, *Journal of Financial Economics* 6, 235–264.

LOOMES, G. and R. SUGDEN. 1982. Regret theory: An alternative theory of rationale choice under uncertainty, *Economic Journal* 92, 805–824.

LOOMES, G. and R. SUGDEN. 1983. A rationale for preference reversal, *American Economic Review* 73, 428–432.

LOOMIS, C. 1968. A case for dropping dividends, *Fortune Magazine*, June 15.

MCNEILL, B., S. J. PAUKER, H. C. SOX and A. TVERSKY. 1981. Patient preferences for alternative therapies, Unpublished.

MACHINA, M. 1982. Expected utility analysis without the independence axiom, *Econometrica* 50, 277–323.

MARKOWITZ, H. 1952. The utility of wealth, *Journal of Political Economy* 60, 151–158.

MILLER, M. and F. MODIGLIANI. 1961. Dividend policy and the valuation of shares, *Journal of Business* 34, 411–433.

MILLER, M. and M. SCHOLES. 1978. Dividends and taxes, *Journal of Financial Economics* 6, 333–364.

MILLER, M. and M. SCHOLES. 1982. Dividends and taxes: Some empirical evidence, *Journal of Political Economy* 90, 1118–1141.

PETTIT, R. 1977. Taxes, transactions costs and the clientele effect of dividends, *Journal of Financial Economics* 5, 419–436.

REINGANUM, M. 1983. The anomalous stock market behavior of small firms in January: Empirical tests for tax-loss selling effects, *Journal of Financial Economics* 12, 89–104.

ROSENBERG, B. and V. MARATHE. 1979. Tests of capital asset pricing hypotheses, in: Haim Levy, ed., *Research in finance* (JAI Press, Greenwich, CT).

RUSSELL, T. and R. THALER. 1982. The relevance of quasi-rationality in competitive markets, Working paper (Cornell University, Ithaca, NY).

SCHWERT, G. W. 1983. Size and stock returns, and other empirical irregularities, *Journal of Financial Economics* 12, 3–12.

SHEFRIN, H. M. and R. THALER. 1983. A self-control based theory of personal saving, Working paper 82-12 (Cornell University, Ithaca, NY).

SHEFRIN, H. M. and R. THALER. 1984. Life cycle vs. self-control theories of saving: A look at the evidence, Working paper 83-2 (Cornell University, Ithaca, NY).

SLOVIC, P. 1972. Psychological study of human judgment: Implications for investment decision making, *Journal of Finance* 27, 779–799.

THALER, R. 1980. Toward a positive theory of consumer choice, *Journal of Economic Behavior and Organization*, 1, 39–60.

THALER, R. 1983. Using mental accounting in a theory of consumer behavior, Working paper 83-02 (Cornell University, Ithaca, NY).

THALER, R. and H. SHEFRIN. 1981. An economic theory of self-control, *Journal of Political Economy* 89, 392–410.

TVERSKY, A. and D. KAHNEMAN. 1981. The framing of decisions and the psychology of choice, *Science* 211, 453–458.

WATTS, R. 1973. The information content of dividends, *Journal of Business* 46, 191–211.

ZIMMERMAN, J. 1979. The costs and benefits of cost allocations, *The Accounting Review* 54, 504–521.

16

Equilibrium
Short Horizons
of Investors and Firms

ANDREI SHLEIFER
and ROBERT W. VISHNY

This paper attempts to explain the often lamented pursuit by investors of short-term capital gains and the selection by firms of short-term investment projects. Our starting point is the observation that, in practice, arbitrage (trading based on knowledge that the price of an asset is different from its fundamental value) is cheaper for assets that cannot stay mispriced for long (short-term assets) than for assets that can (long-term assets). In equilibrium, the net expected return from arbitrage in each asset must be the same. Since arbitrage in long-term assets is more expensive than it is in short-term assets, the former must be more mispriced in equilibrium for net returns to be equal. Thus the rational behavior of arbitrageurs leads to greater mispricing of long-term assets in equilibrium.

Moreover, managers of firms are typically averse to severe underpricing of their equity because they risk getting fired or taken over. They should then avoid investments that raise the cost of arbitrage of their equity. Since mispricing of claims to long-term investment projects can take a long time to disappear, such projects will be avoided. In this way, short horizons of arbitrageurs lead to short horizons of corporate managers.

We stress the distinction between long (short) term investment projects and long (short) term assets. Long (short) term *investment projects*

From: *American Economic Review*, vol. 80, no. 2, pp. 148–153, May 1990. Reprinted by permission of the American Economic Association.

have distant (proximate) cash flows. However, an arbitrageur cares not when an investment project pays off, but rather when the mispricing of the claim to this project disappears, so that he can reap the rewards from his trade. A short-term *asset* is one where mispricing must disappear in the near future, whereas mispricing of a long-term *asset* can persist for a long time. The time to disappearance of mispricing depends on how fast fundamental uncertainty about an asset is resolved, how fast investor misperceptions are corrected, and how rapidly arbitrage drives the price to fundamental value. In general, mispricing of claims to long-term investment projects takes longer to disappear since it takes longer for fundamental uncertainty to be resolved. As a result, long-term assets are typically claims to long-term investment projects. Such association, however, is not automatic.

Examples of short-term assets are options, futures, and other instruments that have a fixed and relatively short expiration time. Examples of long-term assets are stocks and foreign exchange, where mispricing can take a long time to correct. Sometimes even stocks can be short-term assets. For example, an arbitrageur betting on the outcome of a takeover bid, or on an imminent earnings or other public announcement, can expect the mispricing that he is betting against to disappear quite fast. Such as arbitrageur can liquidate his position once the takeover bid fails even if he believes that the stock is still underpriced, and does not need to wait until *that* mispricing is corrected. What matters to the arbitrageur, then, is the horizon of the disappearance of mispricing.

In Section I we argue that arbitrage in short-term assets is much cheaper than arbitrage in long-term assets. Section II builds this observation into a model in which long-term assets must be more mispriced in equilibrium than short-term assets. Section III shows how short horizons of smart investors translate into short horizons of firm managers averse to underpricing of their equity (see also Jeremy Stein, 1988; 1989). Section IV shows how the flight of smart money to short-term arbitrage can be self-fulfilling.

1. The Relative Costs of Long- and Short-Term Arbitrage

By greater relative cost of long-term arbitrage, we mean that the expected carrying cost of a $1 investment held until the mispricing is eliminated is higher for the long-term arbitrage. This is not just a reflection of the time value of money. An arbitrageur with access to a perfect capital market does not care how long it takes a mispriced security to reach its fundamental price. Suppose that an asset with a fundamental value of $6 trades today for $5. Let the interest rate be 10 percent, which is also the rate of return on the fundamental value of the asset and the arbitrageur's cost of funds in a perfect capital market. In this case, the arbitrageur does not care when the price of the asset catches up with its equilibrium value. If it does so next period, the arbitrageur sells the asset for $6.60, repays $5.50 to his creditors, and gets $1.10 which has the present value of $1. If the price reaches fundamentals two periods from now, the arbitrageur sells the asset for $7.26, repays $6.05 to his creditors, and again ends up with $1 in present value. Moreover, if the price of the asset does not reach its fundamental value early, and the arbitrageur discovers another opportunity in the meantime, he can borrow more and pursue that one as well. There is no opportunity cost of tying up one's funds. The same irrelevance argument holds for short sales, and for the case of uncertainty where the arbitrageur can costlessly issue equity to sell off his risk.

Arbitrage, however, is often risky and risk cannot be completely sold off in the market. If, for example, an asset is underpriced relative to its fundamental value, and a smart investor buys it, he has to bear the risk that before mispricing is eliminated or reduced the fundamental value actually falls. In this case, his arbitrage trade results in a loss even though it was *ex ante* attractive. In addition to fundamental risk, the smart investor bears the risk that the mispricing gets worse before it is eliminated, called "noise trader risk" by Bradford De Long et al. (1990). If the smart investor has for some reason to liquidate his position when mispricing gets worse, his arbitrage trade results in a loss. Both fundamental and noise trader risk are more important for assets where the elimination of underpricing takes longer, since there is more time for bad news or a wave of pessimism to hit. These risks raise the cost of arbitraging long-term assets relative to short-term assets.

These risks can be perfectly shared in a perfect capital market that is well informed about the arbitrageur's true ability. But in practice, outside investors do not know whether an arbitrageur is smart, and worry that he might take risks with their money without earning an extra return. As a result, they restrict the supply of funds to the arbitrageur (Joseph Stiglitz and Andrew Weiss, 1981). First, his cost of funds exceeds the (risk-adjusted) interest rate at which he would be able to borrow if information was symmetric. Second, he faces a limit on the amount he can borrow. If in our earlier example the return on the fundamental value is 10 percent, but the cost of funds to the arbitrageur is 12 percent, he obviously prefers that mispricing be eliminated sooner.

Credit constraints impose an additional cost of long-term arbitrage relative to short-term arbitrage, namely the opportunity cost of having one's money tied up. When a smart investor dedicates the limited resources that he can get from others to an arbitrage position, he obviously cannot dedicate them to another position. The longer it takes for the price of a mispriced asset to return to its fundamental value, the longer is the period during which the arbitrageur's resources are tied up, and therefore the higher is the opportunity cost of this arbitrage trade.

Since the high cost of funds and the credit constraint reduce the arbitrageur's profits, he will try to convince his lenders that he is indeed smart and can earn abnormal returns, so that they lend him more and at more attractive rates. To do that, he will try to show good performance repeatedly and *fast*, presumably by making multiple short-term arbitrage trades rather than a single long-term trade. Demonstrating one's talents with long-term trades is expensive and risky by comparison. In this way, not only do the capital market imperfections raise an arbitrageur's cost of funds and so lead to a preference for short-term arbitrage, but the arbitrageur's efforts to reduce these problems and the cost of funds lead to a further bias for short terming.

As feared by Keynes, smart money does not flock to long-term arbitrage: it requires a lot of patience, and patience is costly.

2. A Simple Model

We assume there are three periods: 0, 1, and 2, and two types of investment projects: long and short term. Each firm undertakes a project of one of the two types. Both types of projects have a cash flow only in period 2. The expected period-2 payoff from a short-term project is V_s and the expected payoff from a long-term project is V_l. The true value of a short-term project becomes known in period 1, at which point its mispricing is eliminated. The same happens with a long-term project in period 2. This specification makes clear that arbitrageurs care not when the cash flow of a project is, but when mispricing disappears. All investors are risk neutral. We assume that the market interest rate is 0; the expected payoff from a project is then equal to its fair market value.

There are two types of investors in the model: noise traders and smart money. In period 0, noise traders are either pessimistic or optimistic about the value of each project i (whether long or short term). When noise traders are pessimistic, their combined period-0 demand schedule for the equity of firm i is given by

$$q(NOISE, i) = [V_i - S_i]/P_i, \tag{1}$$

where $S_i > 0$ is the pessimism shock and P_i is the price. When noise traders are optimistic, the demand curve is the same, except S_i is added rather than subtracted. Whether noise traders are bullish or bearish is known in period 0. We only consider the bearish case; the other case is symmetric. We assume that each stock i is in unit supply. Without a shock to their beliefs, noise traders would hold the whole supply at the fundamental price and there would be no need for arbitrage.

We assume that arbitrageurs have no money of their own, but each can borrow in period 0 up to the amount b at the gross interest rate $R > 1$. The cost of funds to the arbitrageurs in excess of the riskless rate of 0 and the credit constraint reflect the imperfections in the loan market, which we do not model explicitly. In this model, each arbitrageur actually wants to borrow all of b.[1] Since agents are risk neutral, they need not diversify, and we can assume that each arbitrageur invests all of b in the same asset i. If n_i arbitrageurs invest in asset i, their combined demand curve is

$$q(SMART, i) = n_i b / P_i. \tag{2}$$

Because of the borrowing constraint, arbitrageurs also have unit elastic demand. In period 0, demands for each asset must add up to the unit supply so,

$$P_i = V_i - S_i + n_i b. \tag{3}$$

We assume that the total number of arbitrageurs is not sufficient to bring prices of all assets to fundamentals in period 0: $n_i b < S_i$. In this model, the more arbitrageurs that trade in an asset, the closer its price is to the fundamental value and the less attractive it is for each of them to trade in that asset. As a result, arbitrageurs spread themselves out between assets and, in equilibrium, each asset is somewhat mispriced.

In period 1, payoff uncertainty is resolved for short-term assets and prices move to fundamental values. The same happens for long-term assets in period 2. When the price moves to the fundamental value, arbitrageurs settle their accounts and trading ends.

In equilibrium, returns from arbitrage in each security must be the same. In particular, the number of arbitrageurs investing in each security of a given type is the same, provided that S_i hitting each security of that type is the same. Denote the respective numbers of arbitrageurs by n_s and n_l.

Consider the return from investing in a short-term asset. In period 0, the arbitrageur buys $b/[V_s - S_s + n_s b]$ shares of that asset with borrowed b dollars, receives in expectation V_s for each share in period 1, and must

---

1. In our simple specification, the opportunity cost of tying up one's funds is not modeled. Introducing it strengthens the results.

in period 1 repay bR to his lenders. As of period 1, the value of this investment is equal to

$$b[V_s/[V_s - S_s + n_s b] - R].$$ (4)

If the arbitrageur invests in the long-term asset, he buys $b/[V_l - S_l + n_l b]$ shares of that asset in period 0. In period 1, he does nothing and in period 2, he gets the average of V_l per share and repays bR^2. As of period 1, the value of this investment is equal to

$$b[V_l/(R[V_l - S_l + n_l b]) - R].$$ (5)

The difference between (4) and (5) is that, in (5), capital gains are deferred and discounted at the rate R since the arbitrageur is at a borrowing constraint. As R rises, arbitrage in the long-term asset becomes less lucrative and eventually unattractive.

In equilibrium, the returns to arbitrage on the long- and the short-term assets must be equal. Setting (4) equal to (5) we get

$$\frac{V_l}{V_l - S_l + n_l b} \cdot \frac{1}{R} = \frac{V_s}{V_s - S_s + n_s b}.$$ (6)

The fraction on each side of (6) is the ratio of value to price of long- and short-term assets, respectively. Since $R > 1$, (6) says that, in equilibrium, the long-term asset is more underpriced in percentage terms (when the noise shock is negative) than the short-term asset. To induce the marginal arbitrageur to invest in the long-term asset, it must be more underpriced than the short-term asset. This result is independent of the values of noise shocks to the two types of assets, or of the relative attractiveness of long- and short-term projects. If we raise total arbitrage resources (raise the total number of arbitrageurs or b), more of them flow into each asset and the mispricing of each asset is reduced, but the greater relative mispricing of long-term assets continues.[2]

3. The Supply of Assets

The compensation of managers of firms with traded equity typically depends in part on short-term equity performance. Poor equity performance raises the likelihood of replacement, either by the board or through a hostile takeover (see our 1989 paper with Randall Morck). By comparison, increases in managers' incomes from good stock performance

---

2. Similar results obtain if arbitrageurs are risk averse and long-term arbitrage is more risky than short-term arbitrage.

are probably small. In this respect, temporary overpricing of the stock is much less of a benefit to managers than temporary underpricing is a cost.

This reasoning suggests that managers will choose short- over long-term investment projects, since picking the latter allows their equity to be more mispriced in equilibrium, *ceteris paribus*, and threatens their jobs. If the probability of replacement varies directly with the percentage underpricing, then all managers who are not also large, long-term shareholders would choose short-term investment projects on the margin. In this way, short terming by rational arbitrageurs leads to short terming by the firms. If $V_l > V_s$, managerial short terming is socially inefficient, since the economically more valuable long-term projects are priced less accurately in the stock market and therefore avoided.

If a manager does undertake a long-term project and his firm becomes underpriced, a hostile acquirer can profit by changing the firm's investment policy. A hostile acquirer *must* make a change to profit from his acquisition fast, for otherwise an acquisition is the same as long-term arbitrage and there is no reason to buy the whole firm at a premium. The changes that a hostile acquirer can make are of two sorts. He can remove the reason that some investors do not like the firm. For example, if the stock market does not like conglomerates, he can bust up the firm and sell off the pieces. More in the spirit of our model, the hostile acquirer can shift the firm's cash flow toward the present by cutting investment, raising dividends, and selling some of the divisions. Because these changes reduce uncertainty and the likely duration of mispricing, they attract more arbitrageurs and reduce underpricing, even if the underlying noise trader pessimism about the firm remains. After the acquirer makes these changes, he can sell the firm to the public at a higher price since underpricing caused by noise is now less significant.

Of course, this is precisely what some hostile acquirers as well as leveraged buyout specialists do. They first effectively reduce the duration of the firm's assets by cutting investment and selling off divisions, and then sell the firm to the public. Michael Jensen (1986) enthusiastically interprets such evidence as pointing to elimination of inefficient investment pursued by corporate managers dedicated to growth. Our model suggests, in contrast, that some of the investment cuts eliminate good long-term projects that have previously been responsible for greater stock market underpricing.

In this way, takeovers substitute for long-term arbitrage. With long-term arbitrage, the smart investor must wait until the elimination of mispricing to realize the returns on his trade. When a firm pursues a long-term investment project, the wait can be long. With a hostile takeover, in contrast, the smart investor can gain control and turn a long-term asset into a shorter-term asset that is less mispriced by the market. It is sometimes said that smart money, unless they are willing to wait a long time to profit from an investment, must be ready to take over the firm. Our model explains how this is so.

4.   Self-Fulfilling Short-Term Arbitrage

We have assumed throughout that participation of each arbitrageur brings the period-0 prices closer to their fundamental values, but has no effect on whether prices return to fundamentals in period 1 or period 2. As a result, participation by each arbitrageur reduces the returns from arbitrage to others. However, participation by each arbitrageur can also *raise* the attractiveness of arbitrage to others by bringing prices to fundamental values *faster*, and so reducing the time it takes others to profit from their own detection of mispricing. If the price returns to fundamentals not through a public news event but through the work of arbitrage, then each arbitrageur will trade more aggressively on a piece of information when he knows that other arbitrageurs will later detect the same mispricing and eliminate it more rapidly. Conversely, it does not pay to trade in an asset which no one else follows and which can therefore remain mispriced forever.

In addition, participation by more arbitrageurs reduces noise trader risk, since each smart trader knows that if noise traders become even more biased in the future, more smart traders will lean against them. Since price fluctuations in the asset are smaller when more traders participate, arbitrage is less risky for each of them. To be sure, it does not pay to be in a market with so many arbitrageurs that no mispricing occurs, but at the same time countering the mispricing of a security by oneself might be too risky.

These arguments provide a further reason why arbitrage will focus on short-term assets. When a lot of traders are arbitraging away price discrepancies in short-term assets, arbitrage in them becomes both faster and less risky. This presumably makes the attractiveness of arbitrage to each trader even greater. In contrast, because few traders arbitrage the mispricing in long-term assets, such mispricing might take even longer to correct as the forces bringing prices to fundamentals are weak. Moreover, the arbitrage in the long-term assets will be very risky, since so few traders will be countering future waves of noise trader sentiment. With positive externalities between arbitrageurs, the greater mispricing of long-term assets relative to short-term assets can be self-fulfilling. Almost all arbitrageurs will focus on the same assets and events, such as takeover or earnings announcements, and few will commit time and resources to long-term arbitrage.

5. Conclusion

Arbitrage generally serves the useful social function of bringing asset prices closer to fundamental values. Arbitrage itself, however, is guided by maximization of arbitrage profits. We have shown that the private costs and benefits of arbitrage lead to its clustering on the trading of short-term assets. This clustering in turn leads to systematically more accurate pricing of short-term assets than of long-term assets, even though efficient capital allocation and managerial evaluation might be better seved by the opposite bias.

References

DE LONG, J. BRADFORD et al. "Noise Trader Risk in Financial Markets." *Journal of Political Economy*, forthcoming 1990.

JENSEN, MICHAEL C. "The Agency Cost of Free Cash Flow, Corporate Finance and Takeovers." *American Economic Review Proceedings*, May 1986, 76, 323–29.

MORCK, RANDALL, ANDREI SHLEIFER, and ROBERT W. VISHY. "Alternative Mechanisms for Corporate Control." *American Economic Review*, September 1989, 79, 842–52.

STEIN, JEREMY. "Takover Threats and Managerial Myopia." *Journal of Political Economy*, February 1988, 96, 61–80.

———. "Efficient Stock Markets, Inefficient Firms: A Model of Myopic Corporate Behavior." *Quarterly Journal of Economics*, November 1989, 104, 655–70.

STIGLITZ, JOSEPH E. and ANDREW WEISS. "Credit Rationing in Markets with Imperfect Information." *American Economic Review*, June 1981, 71, 393–410.

17

The Hubris Hypothesis
of Corporate Takeovers

RICHARD ROLL

Finally, knowledge of the source of takeover gains still eludes us. [Jensen and Ruback 1983, p. 47]

1. Introduction

Despite many excellent research papers, we still do not fully understand the motives behind mergers and tender offers or whether they bring an increase in aggregate market value. In their comprehensive review article (from which the above quote is taken), Jensen and Ruback (1983) summarize the empirical work presented in over 40 papers. There are many important details in these papers, but Jensen and Ruback interpret them to show overall "that corporate takeovers generate positive gains, that target firm shareholders benefit, and that bidding firm shareholders do not lose" (p. 47).

My purpose here is to suggest a different and less conclusive interpretation of the empirical results. This interpretation may not turn out to be valid, but I hope to show that it has enough plausibility to be at least considered in further investigations. It will be argued here that takeover gains may have been overestimated if they exist at all. If there really are no aggregate gains associated with takeovers, or if they are small, it is not hard to understand why their sources are "elusive."

The mechanism by which takeover attempts are initiated and consummated suggests that at least part of the large price increases observed in

From: *Journal of Business*, 1986, vol. 59, no. 2, pt. 1, pp. 197–216. © 1986 by The University of Chicago. All rights reserved. 0021-9398/86/5902-0001$01.50. Reprinted by permission of The University of Chicago Press.

target firm shares might represent a simple transfer from the bidding firm, that is, that the observed takeover premium (tender offer or merger price less preannouncement market price of the target firm) overstates the increase in economic value of the corporate combination. To see why this could be the case, let us follow the steps undertaken in a takeover.

First, the bidding firm identifies a potential target firm.

Second, a "valuation" of the equity of the target is undertaken. In some cases this may include nonpublic information. The valuation definitely would include, of course, any estimated economies due to synergy and any assessments of weak management et cetera that might have caused a discount in the target's current market price.

Third, the "value" is compared to the current market price. If value is below price, the bid is abandoned. If value exceeds price, a bid is made and becomes part of the public record. The bid would not generally be the previously determined "value" since it should include provision for rival bids, for future bargaining with the target, and for valuation errors inter alia.

The key element in this series of events is the valuation of an asset (the stock) that already has an observable market price. The preexistence of an active market in the identical item being valued distinguishes takeover attempts from other types of bids, such as for oil-drilling rights and paintings. These other assets trade infrequently and no two of them are identical. This means that the seller must make his own independent valuation. There is a symmetry between the bidder and the seller in the necessity for valuation.

In takeover attempts, the target firm shareholder may still conduct a valuation, but it has a lower bound, the current market price. The bidder knows for certain that the shareholder will not sell below that; thus when the valuation turns out to be below the market price, no offer is made.

Consider what might happen if there are no potential synergies or other sources of takeover gains but when, nevertheless, some bidding firms believe that such gains exist. The valuation itself can then be considered a random variable whose mean is the target firm's current market price. When the random variable exceeds its mean, an offer is made; otherwise there is no offer. Offers are observed only when the valuation is too high; outcomes in the left tail of the distribution of valuations are never observed. The takeover premium in such a case is simply a random error, a mistake made by the bidding firm. Most important, the observed error is always in the same direction. Corresponding errors in the opposite direction are made in the valuation process, but they do not enter our empirical samples because they are not made public.

If there were no value at all in takeovers, why would firms make bids in the first place? They should realize that any bid above the market price represents an error. This latter logic is alluring because market prices do seem to reflect rational behavior. But we must keep in mind that prices are averages. There is no evidence to indicate that every individual behaves as if he were the rational economic human being whose behavior seems revealed by the behavior or market prices. We may argue that markets behave as if they were populated by rational beings. But a market actually populated by rational beings is observationally equivalent to a market characterized by grossly irrational individual behavior that cancels out in the aggregate, leaving the trace of the only systematic behavioral component, the small thread of rationality that all individuals have in common. Indeed, one possible definition of irrational or aberrant behavior is independence across individuals (and thus disappearance from view under aggregation).

Psychologists are constantly bombarding economists with empirical evidence that individuals do not always make rational decisions under uncertainty. For example, see Oskamp (1965), Tversky and Kahneman (1981), and Kahneman, Slovic, and Tversky (1982). Among psychologists, economists have a reputation for arrogance mainly because this evidence is ignored; but psychologists seem not to appreciate that economists disregard the evidence on individual decision making because it usually has little predictive content for market behavior. Corporate takeovers are, I believe, one area of research in which this usually valid reaction of economists should be abandoned; takeovers reflect individual decisions.

There is little reason to expect that a particular individual bidder will refrain from bidding because he has learned from his own past errors. Although some firms engage in many acquisitions, the average individual bidder/manager has the opportunity to make only a few takeover offers during his career. He may convince himself that the valuation is right and that the market does not reflect the full economic value of the combined firm. For this reason, the hypothesis being offered in this paper to explain the takeover phenomenon can be termed the "hubris hypothesis." If there actually are no aggregate gains in takeover, the phenomenon depends on the overbearing presumption of bidders that their valuations are correct.

Even if gains do exist for some corporate combinations, at least part of the average observed takeover premium could still be caused by valuation error and hubris. The left tail of the distribution of valuations is truncated by the current market price. To the extent that there are errors in valuation, fewer negative errors will be observed than positive errors. When gains exist, a smaller fraction of the distribution will be truncated than when there are no gains at all. Nonetheless, truncation will occur in every situation in which the gain is small enough to allow the distribution of valuations to have positive probability below the market price.

Rational bidders will realize that valuations are subject to error and that negative errors are truncated in repeated bids. They will take this into account when making a bid. Takeover attempts are thus analogous to the auctions discussed in bidding theory wherein the competing bidders make public offers. In the takeover situation, the initial bidder is the market, and the initial public offer is the current price. The second bidder is the acquiring firm who, conscious of the "winner's curse," biases his bid downward from his estimate of value. In fact, he frequently abandons the auction altogether, allowing the first bidder to win.

In a standard auction, we would observe all cases, including those in which the initial bid was victorious. Theory predicts that the winning bid is an accurate assessment of value. In takeovers, however, if the initial bid (by the market) wins the auction, we throw away the observation. If all bidders accounted properly for the "winner's curse," there would be no particular bias associated with discarding bids won by the market; but if bidders are infected by hubris, the standard bidding theory conclusion would not be valid. Empirical evidence from repeated sealed bid auctions (Capen, Clapp, and Campbell 1971; and Dougherty and Lohrenz 1976), indicates that bidders do not fully incorporate the winner's curse. Unless there is something curative about the public nature of corporate takeover auctions, we should at least consider the possibility that the same phenomenon exists in them.

The hubris hypothesis is consistent with strong-form market efficiency. Financial markets are assumed to be efficient in that asset prices reflect all information about individual firms. Product and labor markets are assumed efficient in the sense that (a) no industrial reorganization can bring gains in an aggregate output at the same cost or reductions in aggregate costs with the same output and (b) management talent is employed in its best alternative use.

Most other explanations of the takeover phenomenon rely on strong-form market inefficiency of at least a temporary duration. Either financial markets are ignorant of relevant information possessed by bidding firms, or product markets are inefficiently organized so that potential synergies, monopolies, or tax savings are being ineffectively exploited (at least temporarily), or labor markets are inefficient because gains could be obtained by replacement of inferior managers. Although perfect strong-form efficiency is unlikely, the concept should serve as a frictionless ideal, the benchmark of comparison by which other degrees of efficiency are measured. This is, I claim, the proper role for the hubris hypothesis of takeovers; it is the null against which other hypotheses of corporate takeovers should be compared.

Section 2 presents the principal empirical predictions of the hubris hypothesis and discusses supportive and disconfirming empirical results. Section 3 concludes the paper by summarizing the results and by discussing various objections to the hypothesis.

2. Evidence For and Against the Hubris Hypothesis

If there are absolutely no gains available to corporate takeovers, the hubris hypothesis implies that the average increase in the target firm's market value should then be more than offset by the average decrease in the value of the bidding firm. Takeover expenses would constitute the aggregate net loss. The market price of a target firm should increase when a previously unanticipated bid is announced, and it should decline to the original level or below if the first bid is unsuccessful and if no further bids are received.

Implications for the market price reaction of a bidding firm are somewhat less clear. If we could be sure that (a) the bid was unanticipated and (b) the bid conveys no information about the bidder other than that it is seeking a combination with a particular target, then the hubris hypothesis would predict the following market price movements in bidding firms:

1. a price decline on announcement of a bid;
2. a price increase on abandoning a bid or on losing a bid; and
3. a price decline on actually winning a bid.

It has been pointed out by several authors, most forcefully by Schipper and Thompson (1983), that condition *a* above is by no means assured in all cases. Bids are not always surprises. As Jensen and Ruback (1983, pp. 18–20) observe, this alone complicates the measurement of bidder firm returns.

The possibility that a bid conveys information about the bidding firm's own operations, that is, violation of condition *b*, is an equally serious problem (cf. Jensen and Ruback 1983, p. 19 and n. 14). For example, the market might well interpret a bid as signaling that the bidding firm's immediate past or expected future cash flows are higher than previously estimated, that this has actually prompted the bid, and that, although the takeover itself has a negative value, the combination of takeover and new information is on balance positive.

Similarly, abandoning a previous bid could convey negative information about the bidding firm's ability to pay for the proposed acquisition, perhaps because of negative events in its own operations. Losing a bid to rivals could signal limited resources. These problems of contaminating information make it difficult to interpret bidding firm price movements and to interpret the combined price movements of bidder and target.

2.1 The Evidence about Target Firms

Let us first examine, therefore, the more straightforward implications of the hubris hypothesis for target firms. Bradley, Desai, and Kim (1983b) present results for target firms in tender offers that are consistent with the implications. Target firms display increases in value on the announcement of a tender offer, and they fall back to about the original level if no combination occurs then or later.

A similar pattern is observed in Asquith's (1983) sample of target firms in unsuccessful mergers. These firms were targets in one or more merger bids that were later abandoned and for whom no additional merger bids occurred during the year after the last original bid was withdrawn. The original merger bid announcement was accompanied by a 7.0% average increase in target firm value that appears to be almost entirely reversed within 60 days (figure 1, p. 62). By the date when the last bid is abandoned, the target's price decline amounts to 8.1% (Table 9, p. 81), slightly more than offsetting the original increase.

The result may be partially compromised by the following problem. The "outcome date" of an unsuccessful bid is the withdrawal date of the final offer following which no additional bid is received for 1 year. Thus as of the outcome date the market could not have known for certain that other bids would not arrive. However, if the market had known that no other bids would arrive, the price decline would likely have been ever larger, so perhaps this partial use of hindsight was not material. In summary, target firm share behavior, as presented in Bradley et al. (1983b) for tender offers and in Asquith (1983) for mergers, is consistent with the hubris hypothesis.

2.2 The Evidence about Total Gains

The central prediction of the hubris hypothesis is that the total combined takeover gain to target and bidding firm shareholders is nonpositive.

None of the evidence using returns can unambiguously test this prediction for the simple reason that average returns of individual firms do not measure average dollar gains, especially in the typical takeover situation in which the bidding firm is much larger (cf. Jensen and Ruback 1983, p. 22). In some cases, the observed price increase in the target would correspond to such a trivial loss to the bidder that the loss is bound to be hidden in the bid/ask spread and in the noise of daily return volatility.

In an attempt to circumvent the problem that returns cannot measure takeover gains when bidder and target have different sizes, Asquith, Bruner, and Mullins (1983) take the unique approach of regressing the bidder announcement period return on the relative size of target to bidder. They reason that, if acquisitions benefit bidder firms, large acquisitions should show up as having larger return effects on bidder firm returns. They do find this positive relation for bidding firms. The same relation is not significant for target firms, although, as usual, target firms have much larger average returns. The positive relation for bidding firms is consistent with more than one explanation. It is consistent with the bidding firm losing on average, but losing less the larger the target. Perhaps a more accurate valuation is conducted when the stakes are large and this results in a smaller percentage loss to the bidder. Perhaps large targets are less closely held so that the takeover premium can be smaller relative to the preoffer price and still convince shareholders to deliver their shares. Perhaps bidders for larger targets have fewer rivals and can thus get away with a bidder-perceived "bargain."

The absence of any relation for target firms is puzzling under every hypothesis unless the entire gain accrues to the target firm shareholders (and Asquith et al. [1983] interpret their results to indicate that takeover gains are shared). If synergy is the source of gains, for example, target shareholder's returns would increase with the relative size of its bidder-partner.

Several studies have attempted to measure aggregate dollar gains directly. Halpern (1973) finds average market adjusted gains of $27.35 million in a sample of mergers between New York Stock Exchange–listed firms (p. 569); the gain was calculated over a period 7 months prior to the first public announcement of the merger through the merger consummation month. The standard error of this average gain, assuming cross-sectional independence, was $19.7 ($173.2/$\sqrt{77}$ [see table 3, p. 569]). In 53 cases out of 77, there was a dollar gain.

Bradley, Desai, and Kim (1982) present dollar returns for a sample of 162 successful tender offers from 20 days before the announcement until 5 days after completion. The average combined dollar increase in value of bidder plus target was $17 million, but this was not statistically significant. The $17 million gain was divided between a $34 million average gain by targets and a $17 million average loss to bidders. The authors note that the equally weighted average rate of return to bidders is positive, though the dollar change is a loss; they argue that this can be explained by skewness in the distribution of dollar changes.

In a revision of their 1982 paper, Bradley, Desai, and Kim (1983a) present slightly different results. The sample is expanded from 162 and 183 tender offer events, although the underlying data base appears to be the same (698 tender offers from October 1958 to December 1980). The only stated difference in the selection of samples is that the earlier paper excludes offers that are not "control oriented" (cf. Bradley et al. 1982, p. 13; and Bradley et al. 1983a, pp. 35–36). This sample change resulted in an average gain to targets of $28.1 million and to bidders to +$5.8 million (table 9). The authors say, however, that "the distributional properties of our dollar gain measures preclude any meaningful inferences about their significance" (p. 58).

Malatesta (1983) examines the combined change in target and bidder firms before, during, and after a merger. Jensen and Ruback summarize Malatesta's results as follows: "Malatesta examines a matched sample of targets and their bidders in 30 successful mergers and finds a significant average increase of $32.4 million ($t = 2.07$) in their combined equity value in the month before and the month of outcome announcement. . . . This evidence indicates that changes in corporate control increase the combined market value" (1983, p. 22).

Malatesta (1983) himself does not reach so definite a conclusion. In fact, his overall interpretation of the evidence is that "the immediate impact of merger per se is positive and highly significant for acquired firms but *larger in absolute value and negative* for acquiring firms" (p. 155; emphasis added). Jensen and Ruback were referring to smaller samples of matching pairs. Even for this sample, Malatesta says, the results "provide *weak* evidence that successful resolution of these mergers had a positive impact on combined shareholder wealth" (p. 170; emphasis added). In 2 months culminating in board approval of the merger, the combined gain was positive, but "over the entire interval −60 to 0 [months], the cumulative dollar return is a trival 0.29 million dollars" (p. 171). Of course, this could be due to selection bias; bidding or acquired firms or both may tend to be involved in mergers after a period of poor performance. According to Asquith's (1983) results, however, this is true only for targets. The opposite is true for bidders; they tend to display superior performance prior to the merger bid announcement. During the culminating merger months, the acquiring firms' gains in Malatesta's sample were not statistically significant (although the acquired firms' were).

Malatesta's month zero is when the board announced merger approval, not when the merger proposal first reached the public. Even if the merger per se has no aggregate value, the price reaction on approval could be positive because it signals that court battles, further bids to overcome rivals, and other costly events associated with hostile mergers will not take place in this case, although their possibility was signaled originally by the merger proposal. Malatesta does not present evidence about the dollar reactions of the combined firm on the first announcement of the merger proposal.

Firth (1980) presents the results of a study of takeovers in the United Kingdom. In his sample, target firms gain, and bidding firms lose, both statistically significantly. The average total change in market value of the two firms in a successful combination, from a month prior to the takeover bid through the month of acceptance of the offer, is £ − 36.6 million. No t-statistic is given for this number, but we can obtain a rough measure of significance by using the fact that 224 of 434 cases displayed aggregate losses. If these cases were independent, the t-statistic that the true proportion of losing takeovers is greater than 50% is about .67.

The relative division of losses was examined by Firth (1980) in an ingenious calculation that strongly suggests the presence of bidding errors. The premium paid to the target firm (in £) as a fraction of the size of the bidding firm was cross-sectionally related to the percentage loss in the bidding firm's shares around the takeover period. The regression coefficient was − .89 (t = − 5.94). Firth concludes (p. 254), "This supports the view that the stock market expects zero benefits from a takeover, that the gains to the acquired firm represent an 'overpayment' and that the acquiring company's shareholders suffer corresponding losses."

Using dollar-based matched pairs of firms, Varaiya (1985) finds that the aggregate abnormal dollar gain of targets is $189.4 million while the average abnormal dollar loss of bidders is $128.7 million for 121 days around the takeover announcement. The aggregate gain of $60.7 ($189.4 − 128.7) is not statistically significant, on the basis of a parametric test, though a nonparametric test does indicate significance. Varaiya also reports a cross-sectional regression that indicates that, the larger the target's dollar gain, the larger the bidder's dollar loss. The regression coefficient was − .81 (t = − 2.81).

To summarize, the evidence about total gains in takeovers must be judged inconclusive. Results based on returns are unreliable. Malatesta's dollar-based results show a small aggregate gain in the months just around merger approval in a small matched sample and an aggregate loss in a larger unmatched sample. The interpretation of Malatesta's results is rendered difficult by the possibility of losses or gains in prior months, after announcement of a merger possibility but before final approval is a certainty. Dollar-based results presented by Bradley et al. (1982, 1983*a*) show a small and insignificant aggregate gain. Firth's (1980) British results show an insignificant aggregate loss. Both Firth (1980) and Varaiva (1985) present persuasive evidence for the existence of overbidding. But, on balance, the existence of either gains or losses to the combined firms involved in corporate combinations remains in doubt.

This mixed and insignificant evidence is made even less conclusive (if that is possible) by potential measurement biases. There is a potential upward bias in the measured price reaction of bidding firms (and thus of the aggregate) caused by contaminating information. There is a potential downward bias due to prior anticipation of the takeover event, as explained by Schipper and Thompson (1983), and another potential downward bias in some studies due to an improper computation of abnormal returns (Chung and Weston 1985). These biases will be discussed in detail next, in connection with the empirical findings for bidding firms.

2.3 Evidence about Bidding Firms: The Announcement Effect

The hubris hypothesis predicts a decrease in the value of the bidding firm. As pointed out previously, this decrease may not be completely reflected in a market price decline because of contaminating information in a bid, because the bid has been (partly) anticipated, or simply because the economic loss is too small to be reliably reflected in prices.

The data contain several interesting patterns. Asquith (1983) finds that bidding firm shares show "no consistent pattern" around the announcement date, but, "in summary, bidding firms appear to have small but insignificant positive excess returns at the press day" (p. 66). Some of Asquith's other results are understandable under the hubris hypothesis. Before the first merger bid, for instance, firms who become successful bidders have much larger price increases than firms whose bids are unsuccessful. One would expect a higher level of hubris and thus more aggressive pursuit of a target in firms that had experienced recent good times.

Asquith's results are in conflict with those of Dodd (1980), who finds statistically significant negative returns at the bid announcement. Jensen and Ruback (1983) noted the difference in results, and they asked Dodd to check his data and computer program, which they report (Jensen and Ruback 1983, p. 17, n. 12) he did without finding an error.[1]

---

1. Recently, Chung and Weston (1985) suggested that part of the difference in results could be explained by an improper calculation of "abnormal" returns around the merger announcement. Chung and Weston point out that the premerger period generally displays statistically significant positive returns for bidding firms. If data from this period are used

Negative bidder returns were also found by Eger (1983) in her study of pure exchange (noncash) mergers. Bidding firm stock prices declined, on average by about 4%, from 5 days prior to merger bid announcement to 10 days afterward (Eger 1983, table 4, p. 563). The decline was statistically significant. Eger suggests that the difference between her results and Asquith's (1983) might be attributable to a difference between mergers involving cash and pure stock exchange mergers; and she notes that tender offers, which often involve cash, seem to display more positive bidder stock price reactions (see below).

In his study of United Kingdom takeovers, Firth (1980) reports statistically significant negative bidding firm returns in the month of the takeover announcement. Eighty percent of the bidders had negative abnormal returns during that month, and the t-statistic for the average return was about -5.0 (cf. Firth 1980, table 5, p. 248).

Varaiya (1985) also finds statistically significant negative returns for bidding firms on the announcement day. He reports also that the bidder's loss is significantly larger when there are rival bidders.

A recent paper by Ruback and Mikkelson (1984) documents announcement effects of corporate purchases of another corporation's shares according to the stated purpose of the acquisition (filed on form 13-D with the Securities and Exchange Commission). The 2-day announcement effect for acquiring firms was positive and statistically significant for the 370 firms whose stated purpose was not a takeover. In contrast, for 134 acquiring firms indicating an intention to effect a takeover, the announcement effect was negative and significant (table 4, p. 17).

Studies of individual cases have been mixed. For example, Ruback (1982) argues that DuPont's large stock price decline in announcing a bid to take over Conoco could be an indication that managers (of DuPont) "had an objective function different from that of shareholder wealth maximization" (p. 24). However, he rejects this explanation because of "the magnitude of Conoco's revaluation and the lack of evidence that DuPont's management benefitted from the acquisition" (p. 24). He also rejects every other explanation except inside information possessed by DuPont and not yet appreciated by the market; but even this hypothesis "cannot be confirmed since the nature of the information is unknown" (p. 25).

One interesting aspect of the DuPont/Conoco case is that DuPont's

---

to estimate abnormal returns at merger announcement, the measured announcement effect will be biased downward. The reported difference between, say, Dodd (1980) and Asquith (1983) would be reduced by a recalculation by Dodd excluding the preannouncement period. However, it probably would not be entirely eliminated; the bias appears to be only a small fraction of Dodd's observed announcement effect.

decline was more than offset by Conoco's gain; that is, the total gain was positive (although the bidding firm lost). This suggests that nonhubris factors were indeed present, bringing a total gain to the corporate combination, but that overbidding was present too, resulting in a loss to DuPont shareholders.

The other case study by Ruback (1983) finds only a small negative effect for Occidental Petroleum in its bid for Cities Service. Cities Service's stock price increased by a relatively small amount for a target firm, and the total effect was positive. Apparently, there was little significant hubris evidenced by Occidental (who offered only a small premium). An interesting sidelight was the performance of Gulf Oil, a rival bidder who withdrew. It suffered a loss far in excess of Cities Service's gain.

Schipper and Thompson (1983) find a positive price reaction around the announcement that a firm is embarking on a program of conglomerate acquisitions. Also they observe negative price reactions of such firms to antimerger regulatory events. The two findings are interpreted as at least consistent with the proposition that acquisitions are positive net present value projects for the bidding firm. However, the authors emphasize the tentative nature of their conclusion (pp. 109–11). For example, they note that the announcement of an acquisition program is sometimes accompanied by "announcements of related policy decisions, such as de-emphasis of old lines of business, changes in management, changes in capital structure or specific merger proposals" (p. 89). Even without such explicit contaminating information, announcement of the program could be interpreted as good news about the future profitability of the bidder's current assets rather than about the prospect of an undisclosed future target firm to be obtained at a bargain price.

The possibility of contaminating information is a central problem in interpreting the price movement of a bidding firm on the announcement date of an intended acquisition. Bidders are activists in the takeover situation, and their announcements may convey as much information about their own prospects as about the takeover. To mention one example of the measurement problem, mergers are usually leverage-increasing events. It is well documented from studies of other leverage-increasing events, such as exchange offers (Masulis 1980) and share repurchases (Vermaelen 1981), that positive price movements are to be expected. Thus to measure properly that part of the gain of a bidding firm in a merger that is attributable to the merger per se and not to an increase in leverage, we ought to deduct the price increase that would have been obtained by the same firm through independently increasing its leverage by the same amount.[2]

---

2. I am grateful to Sheridan Titman for pointing out this possibility.

The measurement problem induced by the disparate sizes of target and bidder is the subject of a paper by Jarrell (1983). Jarrell argues that, when a bidder is several times larger than a target, a gain to the bidder equal in size to the gain observed in the target can be hidden in the noise of the bidder's return variability; that is, the t-statistic for the bidder's effect is likely to be much smaller than for the target's effect. Jarrell suggests solving this problem by adjusting the bidder's t-statistic upward by a factor proportional to the relative sizes of bidder and target. When he makes the adjustment in his sample, bidding firms display significantly positive price movements from 30 days prior to 10 days after the takeover announcement. The mean abnormal return prior to adjustment is 2.3%; after adjustment it is 9.2%. Similarly, the combined bidder and target returns become more statistically significant.

The problem with the Jarrell adjustment is that it can be applied to any sample in order to render a sample mean of either sign statistically significant. For example, if Firth (1980) had adjusted his bidding firm returns downward according to the relative sizes of bidder and target, he could have concluded that British takeovers had significant aggregate negative effects on shareholders. This does not imply that Jarrell's conclusions are incorrect, but we are certainly entitled to remain skeptical. Several studies have reported positive bidder gains, and several others have reported losses. Applying the Jarrell technique indiscriminately to all of them could make the gains or losses more "significant," but this would simply create more confusion since the now "significant" results would disagree across studies.

2.4 Evidence about Bidding Firms: Resolution of Doubtful Success

There is some evidence available to help isolate the reevaluation of a bidding firm's own assets induced by the bid but not caused by the proposed corporate combination itself. Asquith's (1983) sample of bidding firms in mergers is separated into successful and unsuccessful bidders, and both samples are examined prior to bid announcement, between announcement and merger outcome, and after outcome. For the successful group, merger outcome is the actual date when the target firm is delisted; this is presumably the effective date of the merger. At the original bid announcement, the market cannot know for sure whether such firms actually will consummate the merger, that is, be in the "successful" group. There is only a probability of success. Between the bid announcement and the final outcome this probability goes to 1.0 for firms in the successful group. Thus if the combination itself has value for the bidder, these bidding firms should increase in value over this interim period. They do not. On average, successful bidding firms decline in value by .5% over the interim period (see Asquith 1983, fig. 4, p. 71; table 9, p. 81). The decrease in value is small and statistically insignificant, but the result has economic significance because the opposite sign must be observed if the corporate combination per se has value. If the combination has substantial value, one might have expected to observe a statistically significant upward price movement between bid announcement and outcome, provided, of course, that the upward revision in probability of success is large enough to show up.

Firms in Asquith's successful bidder group have very large prebid 20 days before the bid announcement. They have small positive returns (.2%) on the announcement date. The entire sequence of returns for successful bidding firms is consistent with the hubris hypothesis. In the prebid period, excellent performance endows management with both hubris and cash. A target is selected. The bid itself signals a small upward revision in the market's estimate of the bidding firm's current assets that is not completely offset by the prospect of paying too much for the target. Then there is a small downward revision in bidder firm value as it becomes more probable and then certain that the target will be acquired (at too high a price).

Eckbo (1983) reports a small and insignificant decline during the 3 days subsequent to the initial merger bid. But Eckbo's "successful" bidder is defined as one who is unchallenged on antitrust grounds; this may be a less relevant representation of actual success for our purposes here.

Eger (1983, p. 563) finds significant negative bidder firm returns averaging − 3.1% in the 20 days after the original announcement of a merger that is ultimately successful. Most of this decline occurs in the first 10 days after the merger announcement. The bonds of these firms also decline slightly in price over the same period. This is consistent with a price decline in the total value of the bidding firm as it becomes more certain that the merger will succeed.

The most significant price decline between merger proposal and outcome is reported by Dodd (1980). Successful bidding firms decline in value by 7.22% from 10 days before the bid is announced until 10 days after the merger outcome, where outcome is defined as target stockholder approval of merger bid. The price decline is statistically significant. In the 20 days prior to the outcome date, successful bidder firms in Dodd's sample fall in price by about 2% (p. 124).

Evidence from papers using monthly data is more difficult to interpret, but the patterns do seem consistent with a negative price movement between merger announcement and successful outcome. For example, Langetieg's (1978, p. 377) bidding firms show a significant price decline continuing in the combined firm after the merger outcome. Similarly,

Chung and Weston (1982, p. 334) report price declines between merger announcement month and merger completion in pure conglomerate mergers. However, the decline is not statistically significant.

Similar evidence is given in Malatesta (1983, table 4, p. 172). Acquiring firms in this sample have significant negative price performance in the period after the first announcement of a merger proposal. Since the data are monthly, the merger outcome date could be included somewhere in the sample period. This means that part of the puzzling post-outcome negative performance detected by Langetieg (1978) and Asquith (1983) might be included in Malatesta's table 4 results. In tables 5 and 6 Malatesta presents performance results for acquiring firms after the "first announcement of board/management approval of the merger" (p. 170). The returns are strongly negative in this period. This might not be such a puzzle if "board/management approval" still leaves open the possibility of withdrawal, for then the absolute certainty of merger (and the concomitant price drop expected under the hubris hypothesis) would occur sometime after this particular event date.

In summary, during the interim period between initial bid and successful outcome, the average price movement of successful merger bids is small, so it is not possible to draw strong implications. However, the pattern is generally consistent with the hubris hypothesis, which predicts the observed loss in value of bidding firm's shares. The loss is statistically insignificant in Asquith's sample but is significant in the samples of Dodd (1980) and Eger (1983) and in the monthly data samples of Langetieg (1978) and Malatesta (1983).

Evidence about the interim period from tender offer studies is mixed. One study seems to be clearly inconsistent with hubris alone; Bradley's (1980) sample of 88 successful bidding firms show a price rise after the announcement data and before the execution date. The number is not given, but the plot of the mean abnormal price index (p. 366) indicates that the gain is approximately 2%–3%.

The interim price movement of the successful acquiring firm is reported by Ruback and Mikkelson (1984) as -1.07% with a t-statistic of -2.34 (table 6). The sample is not dichotomized by merger vs. tender offers, however, and it probably contains some of both types of takeovers.

The results given by Kummer and Hoffmeister (1978) for a 17-firm matched sample of tender offers are more difficult to interpret because the data are monthly and, apparently because of the small size of the cross-sectional sample, the time series of prices relative to the event data appears to be more variable. Abnormal returns are positive and largest in the announcement month but are also positive in months $+1$ and $+2$. If the tender offer is revolved sometime during these 2 months, the results are basically the same as Bradley's (1980). Months +3 to +12 witness a decline of about 4%. If the success of the tender offer is not known until sometime during this period, an interpretation could be made similar to the one discussed above concerning Asquith's and Dodd's samples of successful merger bids.

An identical set of nonconclusive inferences can be drawn from the monthly data of Dodd and Ruback (1977). There appears to be a positive price movement by successful bidders just after the announcement month followed by a price decline later. The decline over the 12 months after a bid amounts to −1.32%, but it is not statistically significant.

Bradley's daily results probably represent the best available evidence against the hubris hypothesis. The detected movement is small, but, unlike the case of merger's, the bidding firm's price does increase on average in Bradley's sample. This is consistent with the proposition that tender offers increase aggregate value and that some of the increase accrues to tender offer bidders. Whether the evidence is sufficiently compelling, particularly when balanced against evidence of an opposite character, is up to further investigation to decide definitely.

One other piece of evidence from the interim period between announcement and outcome is worthy of contemplation. This is the price behavior of the first bidder's stock on the announcement of a rival bid. In their study of unsuccessful tender offers, Bradley et al. (1983b) report a significant price drop in the first bidder's stock. In contrast, Ruback and Mikkelson (1984) report a significant price increase (table 5); however, the latter sample consists not only of ultimately unsuccessful bidders in tender offers but of all corporate investors in other stock (including many who are not contemplating a takeover).

A price drop in the first takeover bidder's stock on the announcement of a rival bid is explainable by hubris. The rival bid may set off a bidding war that the market expects to result in a large loss for the winner. It would be extremely informative to observe the price reaction of the first bidder when it becomes evident that the rival bidder has won.

Finally, it should be noted that the price change after the resolution of a successful bid (either merger or tender offer) is almost uniformly negative (cf. Jensen and Ruback 1983, table 4, p. 21) and is relatively large in magnitude. This is a result that casts doubt on all estimates of bidding firm returns because it suggests the presence of substantial measurement problems.

3. Summary and Discussion

The purpose of this paper is to bring attention to a possible explanation of the takeover phenomenon of mergers and tender offers. This explanation, the hubris hypothesis, is very simple: decision makers in acquiring firms pay too much for their targets on average in the samples we observe. The samples, however, are not random. Potential bids are abandoned whenever the acquiring firm's valuation of the target turns up with a figure below the current market price. Bids are rendered when the valuation exceeds the price. If there really are no gains in takeovers, hubris is necessary to explain why managers do not abandon these bids also since reflection would suggest that such bids are likely to represent positive errors in valuation.

The hubris hypothesis can serve as the null hypothesis of corporate takeovers because it asserts that all markets are strong-form efficient. Financial markets are aware of all information. Product markets are efficiently organized. Labor markets are characterized by managers being employed in their best operational positions.

Hubris predicts that, around a takeover, (a) the combined value of the target and bidder firms should fall slightly, (b) the value of the bidding firm should decrease, and (c) the value of the target should increase. The available empirical results indicate that the measured combined value has increased in some studies and decreased in others. It has been statistically significant in none. Measured changes in the prices of bidding firms have been mixed in sign across studies and mostly of a very small order of magnitude. Several studies have reported them to be significantly negative, and other studies have reported the opposite. Target firm prices consistently display large increases, but only if the initial bid or a later bid is successful. There is no permanent increase in value for target firms that do not eventually enter a corporate combination.

The interpretation of bidding firm returns is complicated by several potential measurement problems. The bid can convey contaminating information, that is, information about the bidder rather than about the takeover itself. The bid can be partially anticipated and thus result in an announcement effect smaller in absolute value than the true economic effect. Since bidders are usually much larger than targets, the effect of the bid can be buried in the noise of the bidder's return volatility. There is weak evidence from the interim period between the announcement of a merger and the merger outcome that the merger itself results in a loss to the bidding firm's shareholders; but the interim period in tender offers shows some results that favor the opposite view. Both findings have minimal statistical reliability.

The final impression one is obliged to draw from the currently available result is that they provide no really convincing evidence against even the extreme (hubris) hypothesis that all markets are operating perfectly efficiently and that individual bidders occasionally make mistakes. Bidders may indicate by their actions a belief in the existence of takeover gains, but systematic studies have provided little to show that such beliefs are well founded.

Finally, I should mention several issues that have arisen as objections by others to the hubris idea. First, the hubris hypothesis might seem to imply that managers act consciously against shareholder interests. Several recent papers that have examined nontakeover corporate control devices have concluded that the evidence is consistent with conscious management actions against the best interests of shareholders.[3] But the hubris hypothesis does not rely on this result. It is sufficient that managers act, de facto, against shareholder interests by issuing bids founded on mistaken estimates of target firm value. Management intentions may be fully consistent with honorable stewardship of corporate assets, but actions need not always turn out to be right.

Second, it might seem that the hubris hypothesis implies systematic biases in market prices. One correspondent argued that stock prices would be systematically too high for reasons similar to those advanced in E. M. Miller's (1977) paper. This implication is not correct, however, for the simple reason that firms can be either targets or bidders. If bidders offer too much, their stock price will fall ex post while their target's price will rise. On average over all stocks, this cancels. Unless one can predict which firms will be targets and which will be bidders, there is no bias in any individual firm, and certainly no bias on average over all firms.

Third, an argument can be advanced that the hubris hypothesis implies an inefficiency in the market for corporate control. If all takeovers were prompted by hubris, shareholders could stop the practice by forbidding managers ever to make any bid. Since such prohibitions are not observed, hubris alone cannot explain the takeover phenomenon.

The validity of this argument depends on the size of deadweight takeover costs. If such costs are relatively small, stockholders would be indifferent to hubris-inspired bids because target firm shareholders would

---

3. See Bradley and Wakeman (1983), Dann and DeAngelo (1983), and DeAngelo and Rice (1983). Linn and McConnell (1983) disagree with the last paper. The possibility that managers do not act in the interest of stockholders has frequently been associated with the takeover phenomenon. For example, in a recent review, Lev (1983, p. 15) concludes by saying, "I think we are justified in doubting . . . the argument that mergers are done to maximize stockholder wealth." Foster (1983) seems to share this view or at least the view that bidders make big mistakes. Larcker (1983) presents interesting results that managers in large takeovers are more likely to have short-term, accounting-based compensation contracts. He finds that, the more accounting-based the compensation, the more negative is the market price reaction to a bid. Larcker also suggests that managers who own less stock in their own company are more likely to make bids.

gain what bidding firm shareholders lose. A well-diversified shareholder would receive the aggregate gain, which is close to zero.

Fourth, and finally, a frequent objection is that hubris itself is based on a market inefficiency defined in a particular way; in the words of one writer, "It seems to me that your hypothesis does not rest on strong form efficiency, because it presumes that one set of market bidders is systematically irrational" (private correspondence). This argument contends that a market is inefficient if some market participants make systematic mistakes. Perhaps one of the long-term benefits of studying takeovers is to clarify the notion of market efficiency. Does efficiency mean that every individual behaves like the rational, maximizing ideal? Or does it mean instead that market interactions generate prices and allocations indistinguishable from those that would have been generated by rational individuals?

═══

The earlier drafts of this paper elicited many comments. It is a pleasure to acknowledge the benefits derived from the generosity of so many colleagues. They corrected several conceptual and substantive errors in the previous draft, directed my attention to other results, and suggested other interpretations of the empirical phenomena. In general, they provided me with an invaluable tutorial on the subject of corporate takeovers. The present draft undoubtedly still contains errors and omissions, but this is due mainly to my inability to distill and convey the collective knowledge of the profession. Among those who helped were C. R. Alexander, Peter Bernstein, Thomas Copeland, Harry DeAngelo, Eugene Fama, Karen Farkas, Michael Firth, Mark Grinblatt, Gregg Jarrell, Bruce Lehmann, Paul Malatesta, Ronald Masulis, David Mayers, John McConnell, Merton Miller, Stephen Ross, Richard Ruback, Sheridan Titman, and, especially, Michael Jensen, Katherine Schipper, Walter A. Smith, Jr., and J. Fred Weston. I also benefited from the comments of the finance workshop participants at the University of Chicago, the University of Michigan, and Dartmouth College, and of the referees.

References

ASQUITH, P. 1983. Merger bids, uncertainty, and stockholder returns. *Journal of Financial Economics* 11 (April), 51–83.

ASQUITH, P., BRUNER, R. F., and MULLINS, D. W., JR. 1983. The gains to bidding firms from merger. *Journal of Financial Economics* 11 (April), 121–39.

BRADLEY, M. 1980. Interfirm tender offers and the market for corporate control. *Journal of Business* 53 (October), 345–76.

BRADLEY, M., DESAI, A., and KIM, E. H. 1982. Specialized resources and competition in the market for corporate control. Typescript. Ann Arbor: University of Michigan, Graduate School of Business.

BRADLEY, M., DESAI, A., and KIM, E. H. 1983a. Determinants of the wealth effects of corporate acquisition via tender offers: Theory and evidence. Typescript. Ann Arbor: University of Michigan, Graduate School of Business.

BRADLEY, M., DESAI, A., and KIM, E. H. 1983b. The rationale behind interfirm tenders offers: Information or synergy? *Journal of Financial Economics* 11 (April), 183–206.

BRADLEY, M., and WAKEMAN, L. MAC. 1983. The wealth effects of targeted share repurchases. *Journal of Financial Economics* 11 (April), 301–28.

CAPAN, E. C., CLAPP, R. V., and CAMPBELL, W. M. 1971. Competitive bidding in high risk situations. *Journal of Petroleum Technology* (June), pp. 641–53.

CHUNG, K. S., and WESTON, J. F. 1982. Diversification and mergers in a strategic long-range planning framework. In M. Keenan and L. I. White (eds.), *Mergers and Acquisitions.* Lexington, Mass.: D. C. Heath.

CHUNG, K. S., and WESTON, J. F. 1985. Model-created bias in residual analysis of mergers. Working paper. Los Angeles: University of California, Los Angeles, Graduate School of Management.

DANN, L. Y., and DEANGELO. H. 1983. Standstill agreements, privately negotiated stock repurchases, and the market for corporate control. *Journal of Financial Economics* 11 (April), 275–300.

DEANGELO, H., and RICE, E. M. 1983. Antitakeover charter amendments and stockholder wealth. *Journal of Financial Economics* 11 (April), 329–60.

DODD, P. 1980. Merger proposals, managerial discretion and stockholder wealth. *Journal of Financial Economics* 8 (June), 105–38.

DODD, P., and RUBACK, R. 1977. Tender offers and stockholder returns: An empirical analysis. *Journal of Financial Economics* 5 (December), 351–74.

DOUGHERTY, F. L., and LOHRENZ, J. 1976. Statistical analysis of bids for Federal offshore leases. *Journal of Petroleum Technology* (November), pp. 1377–90.

ECKBO, B. E. 1983. Horizontal mergers, collusion and stockholder wealth. *Journal of Financial Economics* 11 (April), 241–73.

EGER, C. E. 1983. An empirical test of the redistribution effect in pure exchange mergers. *Journal of Financial and Quantitative Analysis* 18 (December), 547–72.

FIRTH, M. 1980. Takeovers, shareholder returns and the theory of the firm. *Quarterly Journal of Economics* (March), 235–60.

FOSTER, G. 1983. Comments on M & A analysis and the role of investment bankers. *Midland Corporate Finance Journal* 1 (Winter), 36–38.

HALPERN, P. J. 1973. Empirical estimates of the amount and distribution of gains to companies in mergers. *Journal of Business* 46 (October), 554–75.

JARRELL, G. A. 1983. Do acquirers benefit from corporate acquisition? Typescript. Chicago: University of Chicago, Center for the Study of the Economy and the State.

JENSEN, M. C., and RUBACK, R. S. 1983. The market for corporate control. *Journal of Financial Economics* 11 (April), 5–50.

KAHNEMAN, D., SLOVIC, P., and TVERSKY, A. 1982. *Judgment under Uncertainty: Heuristics and Biases*. New York: Cambridge University Press.

KUMMER, D. R., and HOFFMEISTER, J. R. 1978. Valuation consequences of cash tender offers. *Journal of Finance* 33 (May), 505–16.

LANGETIEG, T. C. 1978. An application of a three-factor performance index to measure stockholder gains from merger. *Journal of Financial Economics* 6 (December), 365–83.

LARCKER, D. 1983. Managerial incentives in mergers and their effect on shareholder wealth. *Midland Corporate Finance Journal* 1 (Winter), 29–35.

LEV, B. 1983. Observations on the merger phenomenon and review of the evidence. *Midland Corporate Finance Journal* 1 (Winter), 6–16.

LINN, S. C., and MCCONNELL, J. J. 1983. An empirical investigation of the impact of "antitakeover" amendments on common stock prices. *Journal of Financial Economics* 11 (April), 361–99.

MALATESTA, P. H. 1983. The wealth effect of merger activity and the objective functions of merging firms. *Journal of Financial Economics* 11 (April), 155–81.

MASULIS, R. W. 1980. The effects of capital structure change on security prices: A study of exchange offers. *Journal of Financial Economics* 8 (June), 139–77.

MILLER, E. M. 1977. Risk, uncertainty and the divergence of opinion. *Journal of Finance* 32 (September), 1151–68.

OSKAMP, S. 1965. Overconfidence in case study judgments. *Journal of Consulting Psychology* 29 (June), 261–65.

RUBACK, R. S. 1982. The Conoco takeover and stockholder returns. *Sloan Management Review* 14 (Winter), 13–33.

RUBACK, R. S. 1983. The Cities Service takeover: A case study. *Journal of Finance* 38 (May), 319–30.

RUBACK, R. S., and MIKKELSON, W. H. 1984. Corporate investments in common stock. Working paper. Cambridge: Massachusetts Institute of Technology, Sloan School of Business.

SCHIPPER, K., and THOMPSON, R. 1983. Evidence on the capitalized value of merger activity for acquiring firms. *Journal of Financial Economics* 11 (April), 85–119.

TVERSKY, A., and KAHNEMAN, D. 1981. The framing of decisions and the psychology of choice. *Science* 211 (January 30), 453–58. Reprinted in Peter Diamond and Michael Rothschild. 1978. *Uncertainty in Economics*. New York: Academic Press.

VARAIYA, N. 1985. A test of Roll's Hubris Hypothesis of corporate takeovers. Working paper. Dallas, Tex.: Southern Methodist University, School of Business.

VERMAELEN, T. 1981. Common stock repurchase and marketing signaling: An empirical study. *Journal of Financial Economics* 9 (June), 139–84.

18

The Long-Run
Performance
of Initial Public Offerings

JAY R. RITTER

Numerous studies have documented two anomalies in the pricing of initial public offerings (IPOs) of common stock: (1) the (short-run) underpricing phenomenon, and (2) the "hot issue" market phenomenon. Measured from the offering price to the market price at the end of the first day of trading, IPOs produce an average initial return that has been estimated at 16.4%.[1] Furthermore, the extent of this underpricing is highly cyclical, with some periods, lasting many months at a time, in which the average initial return is much higher.[2] In this paper, I document a third anomaly: in the long-run, initial public offerings appear to be overpriced. Using a sample of 1,526 IPOs that went public in the U.S. in the 1975–84 period, I find that in the 3 years after going public these firms significantly underperformed a set of comparable firms matched by size and industry.

There are several reasons why the long-run performance of initial public offerings is of interest. First, from an investor's viewpoint, the existence of price patterns may present opportunities for active trading

---

1. A few of the many recent studies documenting positive initial returns include Carter and Manaster (1990), Miller and Reilly (1987), Ritter (1984, 1987), and Tinic (1988). Much of the recent work is discussed in Smith (1986) and Ibbotson, Sindelar, and Ritter (1988). The 16.4% average initial return figure is from Ibbotson, Sindelar, and Ritter, where the sample includes 8,668 IPOs going public in 1960–87.

2. The "hot issue market" phenomenon is documented in Ibbotson and Jaffe (1975), Ritter (1984), and Ibbotson, Sindelar, and Ritter (1988).

From: *The Journal of Finance*, vol. XLVI, No. 1, pp. 3–27, March 1991. Reprinted by permission of the American Finance Association.

strategies to produce superior returns. Second, a finding of nonzero aftermarket performance calls into question the informational efficiency of the IPO market. It provides evidence concerning Shiller's (1990) hypothesis that equity markets in general and the IPO market in particular are subject to fads that affect market prices. Third, the volume of IPOs displays large variations over time. If the high volume periods are associated with poor long-run performance, this would indicate that issuers are successfully timing new issues to take advantage of "windows of opportunity." Fourth, the cost of external equity capital for companies going public depends not only upon the transaction costs incurred in going public but also upon the returns that investors receive in the aftermarket. To the degree that low returns are earned in the aftermarket, the cost of external equity capital is lowered for these firms.

To summarize the empirical findings of this paper, the average holding period return for a sample of 1,526 IPOs of common stock in 1975–84 is 34.47% in the 3 years after going public, where this holding period return is measured from the closing market price on the first day of public trading to the market price on the 3-year anniversary. However, a control sample of 1,526 listed stocks, matched by industry and market value, produces an average total return of 61.86% over this same 3-year holding period. In other words, every dollar invested in a portfolio of IPOs purchased at the closing market price on the first day of trading results in a terminal wealth of $1.3447, while every dollar in the matching firms results in $1.6186, a ratio of only 0.831. In the long run, IPOs underperformed.

Possible explanations for this underperformance include (1) risk mismeasurement, (2) bad luck, or (3) fads and overoptimism. To ascertain whether risk mismeasurement could account for the poor long-run performance, alternative benchmark portfolios are used. To distinguish between the bad luck explanation and the fads and over optimism explanation, various cross-sectional and time-series patterns are documented. The pattern that emerges is that the underperformance is concentrated among relatively young growth companies, especially those going public in the high-volume years of the 1980s. While this pattern does not rule out bad luck being the cause of the underperformance, it is consistent with a scenario of firms going public when investors are irrationally over optimistic about the future potential of certain industries which, following Shiller (1990), I will refer to as the "fads" explanation.[3] Further support

---

3. Miller (1977) and Blazenko (1989) present models in which overoptimistic investors are the marginal investors in IPOs. Their models predict the long-run underperformance that is documented here.

for this interpretation is contained in Lee, Shleifer, and Thaler (1991) who find that the annual number of operating companies going public in the 1966–85 period is strongly negatively related to the discount on closed-end mutual funds, which they interpret as a measure of individual investor sentiment.

At least three published academic studies, plus a series of articles in *Forbes* magazine, have examined the long-run performance of IPOs. Stoll and Curley (1970), focusing on 205 small offers, found that, "in the short run, the stocks in the sample showed remarkable price appreciation. . . . In the long run, investors in small firms did not fare so well. . . ." (pp. 314–315).

Ibbotson (1975), using one offering per month for the 10-year period 1960–69, computed excess returns on IPOs with an offer price of at least $3.00 per share. He concludes that the "results generally confirm that there are no departures from market efficiency in the aftermarket" (p. 265). However, he does find evidence that there is "generally positive performance the first year, negative performance the next 3 years, and generally positive performance the last [fifth] year" (p. 252), although the standard errors of his estimates are high enough to make it difficult to reject market efficiency. In his Table 12 he reports initial public offerings underperforming by an average of approximately 1% per month in the second through fourth years of public trading, with positive excess returns in the first and fifth years.[4]

Buser and Chan (1987) evaluate the two-year performance of over 1,078 NASDAQ/National Market System (NMS)-eligible initial public offerings in 1981–1985.[5] Their sample has a positive average initial return of 6.2% and a mean 2-year market-adjusted return of 11.2% (exclusive of the initial return) where they use the NASDAQ Composite Index for their market adjustment.

The cover story of the December 2, 1985 *Forbes* magazine, entitled "Why New Issues Are Lousy Investments," reports the results of a study that finds, for the period from January 1975 through June 1985, that initial public offerings have underperformed the market in the long run. Stern and Bornstein (1985) find as reported on p. 152 that "from its date of going public to last month, the average new issue was down 22% relative to the broad Standard & Poor's 500 stock index." *Forbes* analyzed

---

4. In Ibbotson's (1975) Table 12 (p. 253), the months 43–48 alpha coefficient has a minus sign omitted, as can be seen from comparison with his Tables 11 and 13.

5. The primary qualification for National Market System (NMS) eligibility among the NASDAQ stocks is income of $300,000 or more in the most recent fiscal year prior to going public.

1,922 issues with an offering price of $1.00 or more. Unlike academic research, which typically uses event time, *Forbes* used calendar time, so their excess returns are computed over a period of anywhere from 10 years to a few months.

In summary, Stoll and Curley (1970), Ibbotson (1975), and Stern and Bornstein (1985) present evidence which suggests that at some point after going public the abnormal returns on initial public offerings may be negative. Ibbotson conducts the most satisfactory formal statistical tests, but his small sample size (120 issues) results in such large standard errors that he is unable to reject the hypothesis of market efficiency after a stock goes public. Only the Buser and Chan (1987) study does not find evidence of negative aftermarket performance after the initial return period.

The structure of this paper is as follows. Section 1 describes the data and methodology. Section 2 presents evidence regarding the aftermarket performance. Section 3 presents cross-sectional and time-series evidence on the aftermarket performance. Section 4 concludes the paper with a summary and interpretation of the findings.

1. Data and Methodology

The sample is comprised of 1,526 initial public offerings in 1975–1984 meeting the following criteria: (1) an offer price of $1.00 per share or more, (2) gross proceeds,[6] measured in terms of 1984 purchasing power, of $1,000,000 or more, (3) the offering involved common stock only (unit offers are excluded), (4) the company is listed on the CRSP daily Amex-NYSE or NASDAQ tapes within 6 months of the offer date,[7] and (5) an investment banker took the company public. These firms represent 85.1% of the aggregate gross proceeds of all firms going public in 1975–84.

Table 1 presents the distribution of the sample by year, both in terms of the number of offers and the gross proceeds. Inspection of Table 1 shows that the number and value of IPOs were not evenly distributed

6. The gross proceeds numbers are computed based upon the actual number of shares sold, including overallotment options, if exercised. Most firm commitment offers include overallotment options in which the underwriter has the option of selling additional shares (limited to a maximum of 10% prior to August 1983 and 15% thereafter) at the offer price within 30 days of the offering.

7. Of the 1,526 sample offers, 36 were initially traded on the American or New York stock exchanges, and the rest on NASDAQ. Of the 1,490 NASDAQ-listed issues, 128 changed to the American or New York stock exchanges within 3 years of going public. Of the 1,526 sample offers, 1,362 used a firm commitment contract, 157 used a best-efforts contract, and 7 used a combination firm commitment/best-efforts contract in going public. Only 13 of the 1,526 sample offers were not listed on the CRSP tapes within 1 month of the offer date. This sample of 1,526 firms is available from the author upon request.

Table 1   Distribution of Initial Public Offerings by Year, 1975–84

The number of total offers is based upon *Going Public: The IPO Reporter's* listings, after excluding closed-end mutual funds and real estate investment trusts. Gross proceeds calculations are based upon the amount sold in the United States, including the proceeds from overallotment options, if exercised. No price level adjustments have been made in this table.

Year	Total of 2,476 Offers		1,526 Offers in Sample		Total Included	
	No. of IPOs	Aggregate Gross Proceeds, $ millions	No. of IPOs	Aggregate Gross Proceeds, $ millions	No. of IPOs %	Aggregate Gross Proceeds %
1975	14	264.0	12	262.4	85.7	99.4
1976	33	237.3	28	213.9	84.8	90.1
1977	32	150.6	19	132.3	59.4	87.8
1978	48	247.3	31	218.4	64.6	88.3
1979	78	429.0	53	347.1	67.9	80.9
1980	234	1,408.3	129	1,097.9	55.1	78.0
1981	438	3,200.3	300	2,689.5	68.5	84.0
1982	199	1,335.0	93	1,104.2	46.7	82.7
1983	865	13,247.8	589	12,060.4	68.1	91.0
1984	535	4,237.1	272	2,940.8	50.8	69.4
Total	2,476	24,756.7	1,526	21,066.9	61.6	85.1

over the 1975–84 sample period. Only 143 of the 1,526 sample offers occurred during the first half of the period. Fifty-seven percent ($12,060.4 million of the $21,066.9 million total) of the aggregate gross proceeds in the sample was raised in 1983 alone.

To evaluate the long-run performance of initial public offerings, two measures are used: (1) cumulative average adjusted returns (CAR) calculated with monthly portfolio rebalancing, where the adjusted returns are computed using several different benchmarks, and (2) 3-year buy and hold returns for both the IPOs and a set of matching firms. The matching firms are represented by American and New York stock exchange-listed securities that are to some extent matched by industry and market capitalization with each IPO.[8]

8. Details of the matching procedure are provided in the appendix. Because the industry composition of Amex-NYSE firms differs so dramatically from that of the IPOs, only 36% of the matching firms are in the same three-digit SIC code industry as their IPO (57% at the

Returns are calculated for two intervals: the initial return period (normally 1 day), defined as the offering date to the first closing price listed on the CRSP daily return tapes (both NASDAQ and Amex-NYSE), and the aftermarket period, defined as the 3 years after the IPO exclusive of the initial return period. The initial return period is defined to be month 0, and the aftermarket period includes the following 36 months where months are defined as successive 21-trading-day periods relative to the IPO date. Thus, month 1 consists of event days 2–22, month 2 consists of event days 23–43, etc. For IPOs in which the initial return period is greater than 1 day, the month 1 period is truncated accordingly, e.g., if the initial return period is 6 days, month 1 consists of event days 7–22. For IPOs that are delisted before their 3-year anniversary, the aftermarket period is truncated, and the 3-year buy and hold return ends with CRSP's last listing. Firms which moved from NASDAQ to the American or New York stock exchanges during the 3 years after their offering date are not removed unless they are subsequently delisted from the Amex-NYSE tape. The CRSP NASDAQ daily returns file and the CRSP Amex-NYSE daily returns file are the source of the returns data.

Monthly benchmark-adjusted returns are calculated as the monthly raw return on a stock minus the monthly benchmark return for the corresponding 21-trading-day period. The benchmarks used are (1) the CRSP value-weighted NASDAQ index, (2) the CRSP value-weighted Amex-NYSE index, (3) listed firms matched by industry and size, and (4) an index of the smallest size decile of the New York Stock Exchange. The benchmark-adjusted return for stock i in event month t is defined as

$$ar_{it} = r_{it} - r_{mt}.$$

The average benchmark-adjusted return on a portfolio of n stocks for event month t is the equally-weighted arithmetic average of the benchmark-adjusted returns:

$$AR_t = \frac{1}{n} \sum_{i=1}^{n} ar_{it}.$$

The cumulative benchmark-adjusted aftermarket performance from event month q to event month s is the summation of the average bench-

---

two-digit level). Also, the matching firms have, on average, larger market capitalizations. Sensitivity tests (not reported here) done using subsets that are more closely matched by size and industry show qualitatively similar results to those reported in this paper. See footnote 16.

mark-adjusted returns:

$$CAR_{q,s} = \sum_{t=q}^{s} AR_t.$$

When a firm in portfolio p is delisted from the CRSP data, the portfolio return for the next month is an equally-weighted average of the remaining firms in the portfolio. The cumulative market-adjusted return for months 1 to 36, $CAR_{1,36}$, thus involves monthly rebalancing, with the proceeds of a delisted firm equally allocated among the surviving members of the portfolio p in each subsequent month. For the month in which an IPO is delisted, the return for both the IPO and the benchmark includes just the days from the start of the month until the delisting.

As an alternative to the use of cumulative average benchmark-adjusted returns, which implicitly assumes monthly portfolio rebalancing, I also compute 3-year holding period returns, defined as

$$R_i = \prod_{t=1}^{36} (1 + r_{it})$$

where r_{it} is the raw return on firm i in event month t. This measures the total return from a buy and hold strategy where a stock is purchased at the first closing market price after going public and held until the earlier of (i) its 3-year anniversary, or (ii) its delisting.[9] To interpret this 3-year total return, I compute wealth relatives as a performance measure, defined as

$$WR = \frac{1 + \text{average 3-year total return on IPOs}}{1 + \text{average 3-year total return on matching firms}}.$$

A *wealth relative* of greater than 1.00 can be interpreted as IPOs outperforming a portfolio of matching firms; a *wealth relative* of less than 1.00 indicates that IPOs underperformed.

In this paper, I have calculated performance measures without explicitly adjusting for betas. While I do not report them here, the betas of the IPO firms display the same time-series patterns documented in Ibbotson (1975), Chan and Lakonishok (1990), and Clarkson and Thompson (1990), i.e., the average beta is greater than 1.00, and the average betas decline

---

9. Unlike the Amex and NYSE in the 1975–1984 period, where mergers and takeovers are the predominant reasons for delisting, most NASDAQ delistings during this period are due to firms failing to meet the minimum capital requirements for continued listing. Because of early delistings, the average holding period is 34 months, rather than 36 months.

with the length of time since the IPO. This is true when betas are calculated using either the CRSP value-weighted NASDAQ or Amex-NYSE indices. The matching firms also have betas greater than 1.00. For post-issue months 1–12, 13–24, and 25–36, respectively, the average betas for IPOs are 1.39, 1.24, and 1.14 and the average betas for matching firms are 1.14, 1.13, and 1.04, using the CRSP value-weighted Amex-NYSE index.[10] Although the IPO betas are greater than 1.00 on average, the difference in betas between the IPOs and matching firms is too small to have economically significant effects on the conclusions. To the degree that the IPO betas are higher than the betas of control portfolios, computing adjusted returns without explicitly adjusting for beta differences results in conservative estimates of IPO underperformance when the market risk premium is positive, as it is for this paper's sample.[11]

2. Aftermarket Performance

Table 2 reports the average matching firm-adjusted returns (AR_t) and cumulative average matching firm-adjusted returns ($CAR_{1,t}$) for the 36 months after the offering date for 1,526 IPOs in 1975–84. Thirty-one of the 36 monthly average adjusted returns are negative, with 13 of them having t-statistics lower than -2.00. The negative average adjusted returns are reflected in a steady decline in the cumulative average adjusted returns, which, after a slight increase in the first 2 months of seasoning, falls to -29.13% by the end of month 36, exclusive of the initial return, with an associated t-statistic of -5.89. The underperformance of the IPOs is both economically and statistically significant.

In Figure 1, I have plotted the matching firm-adjusted CAR, where the initial return is also included. Also plotted are four other cumulative average returns with different adjustments. The five series plotted, in

---

10. For all of the beta calculations, I use Ibbotson's (1975) RATS procedure. As Chan and Lakonishok (1990) document, I also find that the initial return betas are much higher when the market return is positive rather than negative. Rao (1989) notes that one reason for the decline in average betas with the time since the IPO is that riskier firms are more likely to be delisted and so are less likely to be included in the averages the longer the time since the IPO.

11. The average total return, exclusive of the initial return, during the 3 years after going public is 34.47% for the IPOs in this sample, as reported in Table 3 of this paper. The average total return that an investor would have earned by rolling over T-bills for 3 years is approximately 28%. Thus, in spite of most of these IPOs going public before substantial market rises, the IPO investors outperformed T-bills by only about 2% per year. The betas of the IPOs would have to be implausibly low to reverse the conclusion that these IPOs underperformed in the 3 years after going public.

Table 2   Abnormal Returns for Initial Public Offerings in 1975–84

Average matching firm-adjusted returns (AR_t) and cumulative average returns ($CAR_{1,t}$), in percent, with associated t-statistics for the 36 months after going public, excluding the initial return. The number of firms trading begins at less than 1,526 because some firms have a delay of more than one month after going public before being listed. $AR_t = 1/n_t \Sigma_{i=1}^{n_t}(r_{ipo,it} - r_{match,it})$ where $r_{ipo,it}$ is the total return on initial public offering firm i in event month t, and $r_{match,it}$ is the total return on the corresponding matching firm. The t-statistic for the average adjusted return is computed for each month as $AR_t \cdot \sqrt{n_t}/sd_t$, where AR_t is the average matching firm-adjusted return for month t, n_t is the number of observations in month t, and sd_t is the cross-sectional standard deviation of the adjusted returns for month t. The cross-sectional standard deviations vary from a low of 19.02 percent in month 10 to a high of 25.24 percent in month 16. The t-statistic for the cumulative average adjusted return in month t, $CAR_{1,t}$, is computed as $CAR_{1,t} \cdot \sqrt{n_t}/csd_t$, where n_t is the number of firms trading in each month, and csd_t is computed as $csd_t = [t \cdot var + 2 \cdot (t - 1) \cdot cov]^{1/2}$, where t is the event month, var is the average (over 36 months) cross-sectional variance, and cov is the first-order autocovariance of the AR_t series. Var has a value of 0.04453 (21.10 percent squared) and cov has a value of 0.02097, representing an autocorrelation coefficient of 0.471.

Month of Seasoning	Number of Firms Trading	AR_t %	t-stat	$CAR_{1,t}$ %	t-stat
1	1,512	0.38	0.63	0.38	0.70
2	1,514	1.49	2.81	1.88	2.02
3	1,517	−0.12	−0.24	1.75	1.46
4	1,518	−1.07	−2.21	0.69	0.48
5	1,519	−0.81	−1.63	−0.12	−0.08
6	1,519	−0.55	−1.06	−0.67	−0.38
7	1,518	−1.59	−3.13	−2.27	−1.18
8	1,516	−1.10	−2.21	−3.37	−1.63
9	1,514	−1.73	−3.38	−5.10	−2.31
10	1,513	−1.63	−3.32	−6.72	−2.88
11	1,508	−1.59	−3.08	−8.32	−3.39
12	1,501	−1.91	−3.66	−10.23	−3.97
13	1,496	−0.32	−0.56	−10.55	−3.92
14	1,492	−0.82	−1.60	−11.37	−4.06
15	1,486	−1.19	−2.30	−12.56	−4.32
16	1,478	−1.26	−1.92	−13.82	−4.59
17	1,469	−0.47	−0.85	−14.29	−4.58
18	1,463	−0.49	−0.88	−14.78	−4.59
19	1,449	0.37	0.61	−14.42	−4.43
20	1,440	0.30	0.55	−14.11	−4.12

Table 2   (*Continued*)

Month of Seasoning	Number of Firms Trading	AR$_t$ %	t-stat	CAR$_{1,t}$ %	t-stat
21	1,429	− 0.94	− 1.66	− 15.05	− 4.27
22	1,416	− 0.20	− 0.33	− 15.25	− 4.21
23	1,403	− 0.56	− 0.92	− 15.80	− 4.24
24	1,397	− 1.09	− 1.97	− 16.89	− 4.43
25	1,388	0.30	0.50	− 16.59	− 4.25
26	1,372	− 0.26	− 0.44	− 16.85	− 4.20
27	1,354	− 1.66	− 2.87	− 18.51	− 4.50
28	1,347	− 1.02	− 1.72	− 19.54	− 4.65
29	1,339	− 0.97	− 1.84	− 20.51	− 4.78
30	1,324	− 1.51	− 2.74	− 22.01	− 5.01
31	1,309	− 1.02	− 1.57	− 23.03	− 5.13
32	1,296	− 0.63	− 1.00	− 23.66	− 5.16
33	1,283	− 1.31	− 2.16	− 24.96	− 5.33
34	1,270	− 1.39	− 2.39	− 26.35	− 5.52
35	1,260	− 1.10	− 1.89	− 27.45	− 5.64
36	1,254	− 1.67	− 2.80	− 29.13	− 5.89

order of their CAR$_{0,36}$, are, from top to bottom: (1) raw returns, (2) CRSP value-weighted NASDAQ-adjusted returns, (3) CRSP value-weighted Amex-NYSE-adjusted returns, (4) matching firm-adjusted returns, and (5) small firm-adjusted returns.

Focusing first on the raw returns, a positive initial return of 14.32% is followed by monthly average raw returns varying between negative 1.20% and positive 2.96%. The cumulative average raw return peaks at 42.49% in month 34. This rise can be at least partly attributed to the bull market prevailing from August 1982 to August 1987, a period comprising the three post-issue years for the vast majority of sample firms.

Figure 1 also plots cumulative average market-adjusted returns, formed by subtracting the market return each month, for two different market indices: (1) the CRSP value-weighted NASDAQ index, and (2) the CRSP value-weighted index of Amex-NYSE stocks. These indices are nearly identical to the NASDAQ Composite and S&P 500 index returns, respectively. The resulting CAR's display different patterns, which can be attributed to the different performance of the two indices, especially in 1984. During 1984, the total return on the CRSP value-weighted Amex-NYSE index was 5.02%, whereas the CRSP value-weighted NASDAQ index produced a total return of − 8.96%.

Figure 1   Cumulative average adjusted returns for an equally-weighted portfolio of 1,526 initial public offerings in 1975–84, with monthly rebalancing.

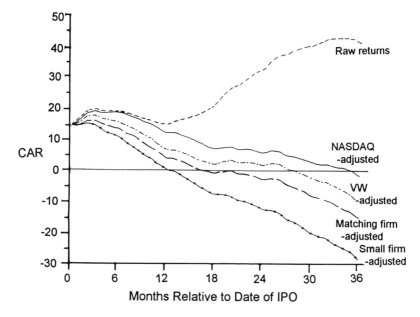

Five CAR series are plotted for the 36 months after the IPO date: 1) no adjustment (raw returns), 2) CRSP value-weighted NASDAQ index adjustment (NASDAQ-adjusted), 3) CRSP value-weighted Amex-NYSE index adjustment (VW-adjusted), 4) matching firm adjustment (matching firm-adjusted), and 5) lowest decile of NYSE market capitalization index adjustment (small firm-adjusted). Month 0 is the initial return interval.

The difference in the performance of the various indices sheds light on the discrepancy between Buser and Chan's (1987) findings of positive aftermarket performance and this study's findings of negative performance. Buser and Chan's use of the NASDAQ Composite index as their benchmark portfolio for a sample period in which this index substantially underperformed other indices accounts for part of the difference in findings. Furthermore, since much of the underperformance documented in Figure 1 occurs in the third post-issue year, their use of 2 years of aftermarket data, rather than the 3 years of this study, accounts for another part of the difference in findings. The rest of the difference in findings can largely be attributed to two differences in the sample selection criteria. Their restriction to NMS-qualifying issues removes many of the more speculative issues that this study includes, in which, as I will document in later tables, the poorest long-run performance occurs. Furthermore, a slight survivorship bias in their sample removes some of the issues that were subsequently delisted; these issues display a tendency to perform especially poorly, pulling down the average long-run performance.

In addition to the raw returns, market-adjusted returns, and matching firm-adjusted returns, Figure 1 also plots average small firm-adjusted returns, formed by subtracting a benchmark portfolio of the equally-weighted return on the smallest decile of NYSE stocks from the raw returns. Because many of the firms going public have low market capitalizations (measured in terms of 1984 purchasing power, the median gross proceeds are only $7.59 million, and the median post-issue market capitalization, valued at the closing market price on the first day of trading, is only $28.4 million), a small firm index may be appropriate to use as a benchmark portfolio. Using an equally-weighted index of small stock returns, as represented by the lowest decile of market capitalization stocks trading on the NYSE, the months 1–36 cumulative average small firm-adjusted return is −42.21%.

As Figure 1 shows, while all four adjustments display negative post-initial return performance, the quantitative measurement of the long-run performance of initial public offerings is very sensitive to the benchmark employed. This is not unusual in event studies using long windows, as indicated by Dimson and Marsh (1986). For evaluating the long-run performance of IPOs, it is not at all clear what constitutes the appropriate benchmark portfolio. Since the vast majority of the IPOs trade on NASDAQ, a natural candidate would be the NASDAQ index. This index has the advantage that the industry mix more closely matches that of the sample IPOs than does the Amex or NYSE. However, the reason that the NASDAQ index's industry mix so closely matches is because in the mid–1980s so many of the firms in the index had recently gone public. Hence, using the NASDAQ index as a benchmark would tend to bias the results in favor of finding no abnormal market-adjusted returns.

To have a quantitative measure of long-run performance, *some* benchmark must be used. Throughout the rest of the paper, I will focus on *wealth relatives*, defined as the average gross total return on IPOs divided by the average gross total return on the matching firms, where both of these are measured over the 3 years after the IPO, excluding the initial return, as the primary measure of IPO aftermarket performance.[12]

---

12. For IPOs that are delisted prior to their 3-year anniversary, the total return is computed up to the delisting date.

Table 3 reports the distribution of 3-year holding period returns for both the 1,526 IPOs and the matching firms. The median IPO 3-year return is -16.67% contrasted with 38.54% for the median matching firm. The distribution of IPO 3-year holding period returns is more skewed than that of the matching firms, but the mean IPO 3-year holding period return is only 34.47% compared to a mean of 61.86% for the matching firms.

The highest 3-year total return of 3964.43%, excluding the initial return of -3.23%, belongs to This Can't Be Yogurt, Inc. (now TCBY Enterprises), a March 28, 1984 IPO at $7.75 per share. After six 3 for 2 stock splits, its market price on NASDAQ was $27.50 on March 27, 1987, the equivalent of $313.25 on a pre-split basis. For 272 firms that were delisted before their 3-year anniversary, the mean 3-year holding period return, exclusive of their mean 17.02% initial return, is -13.34%, with a wealth relative value of 0.581. For the 1,254 firms that were not delisted, the mean 3-year holding period return, exclusive of their mean initial return of 13.42%, is 44.79%, with a wealth relative value of 0.880. As one might expect, delisted firms have lower mean gross proceeds than nondelisted firms: $10.9 million versus $16.0 million when measured in terms of 1984 purchasing power.

3. Cross-Sectional and Time-Series Patterns in the Aftermarket Performance of IPOs

3.1 Aftermarket Performance Categorized by Issue Size and Initial Returns

To investigate possible explanations for the long-run underperformance of IPOs, this section documents various cross-sectional and time-series patterns.

In Table 4, firms are segmented by the gross proceeds of the offer. This permits examination of the generality of the negative aftermarket performance of IPOs. Inspection of Table 4 discloses that there is a tendency for the smaller offers, which have the highest average matching firm-adjusted initial returns (henceforth, "adjusted initial returns"), to have the worst aftermarket performance. All gross proceeds categories display long-run underperformance.

In addition to reporting mean initial and aftermarket returns, Table 4 also reports median initial and aftermarket returns. For the initial returns, the median is a positive 4.61%, with only 368 of the 1,526 offers (22.2%) having negative adjusted initial returns.

DeBondt and Thaler (1985, 1987) have presented evidence that, at

Table 3   Distribution of Three-Year Holding Period Returns, Exclusive of the Initial Return, for 1,526 Initial Public Offerings and Matching Firms in 1975–84

Three-year holding period returns are calculated as $[\Pi_{t=1}^{756}(1 + r_{idt}) - 1] \times 100\%$ where r_{idt} is the daily return on stock i, with the CRSP daily NASDAQ returns tape and the daily Amex-NYSE returns tape being the source of the daily returns. For initial public offerings that were delisted before the 3-year anniversary, the total return is calculated until the delisting date. If the initial return period lasted for more than 1 day, the total return is calculated from the first CRSP-reported closing price until the 756th trading day after the IPO. The corresponding matching firm's total return is calculated over the same truncated return interval. If the matching firm is delisted early, a second (and possibly third) matching firm's return is spliced onto the first matching firm. For firms with no dividends and no stock splits the total return corresponds to $[(P_3/P_t) - 1] \times 100\%$ where P_3 is the price on the 3-year anniversary, and P_t is the first closing market price after the IPO.

	Three-Year Holding Period Total Return, in Percent	
Rank	Initial Public Offerings	Matching Firms
1 (lowest)	−99.02	−94.59
77	−92.27	−61.11
153	−85.80	−44.53
229	−79.16	−31.58
306	−72.98	−19.05
382 (25th percentile)	−66.25	−9.49
458	−57.98	0.00
535	−48.06	8.79
611	−38.28	18.75
687	−28.20	27.67
764 (median)	−16.67	38.54
840	−2.54	51.14
916	13.25	63.14
992	29.07	75.82
1,069	46.85	87.56
1,145 (75th percentile)	69.59	103.16
1,222	99.96	120.42
1,298	138.03	148.86
1,374	205.33	187.01
1,450	320.53	240.78
1,526 (highest)	3,964.43	1,268.56
Mean	34.47	61.86

Table 4   Mean Performance Measures for 1,526 IPOs in 1975–84 Categorized by Gross Proceeds

Gross proceeds are measured in dollars of 1984 purchasing power using the U.S. GNP deflator. Initial returns are computed as $r_{ipo} - r_{matching\ firm}$ over the initial return interval (one day for 1,203 of the 1,526 firms). The three-year holding period return is calculated excluding the initial return. For IPOs that are delisted prior to their three-year anniversary the matching firms' return is ended on the same date as the IPO. Total returns include both capital gains and dividends. The *wealth relative* is the ratio of one plus the mean IPO 3-year holding period return (not in percent) divided by one plus the mean matching firm 3-year holding period return (not in percent). For the smallest gross proceeds category, 1.1794/ 1.6754 = 0.704.

| | | Excluding Initial Returns | | | | |
| | Average Adjusted Initial Return % | Average 3-Year Holding Period Total Return | | | Sample Size | |
Gross Proceeds, $		IPOs %	Matching Firms %	*Wealth Relative*	Month 0	Month 36
1,000,000–2,999,999	27.45	17.94	67.54	0.704	221	146
3,000,000–4,999,999	18.00	20.89	58.72	0.762	296	238
5,000,000–9,999,999	11.28	40.06	69.87	0.825	379	316
10,000,000–14,999,999	7.51	46.25	55.99	0.938	211	183
15,000,000–24,999,999	10.09	43.97	50.56	0.956	200	179
25,000,000–353,950,260	9.96	39.81	62.50	0.860	219	193
All (mean)	14.06	34.47	61.86	0.831	1,526	1,254
All (median)	4.61	−16.67	38.54	0.601	1,526	1,254

least for low-capitalization stocks, there is a negative relation between past and subsequent abnormal returns on individual securities using holding periods of a year or more, which they interpret as evidence of market overreaction. Table 5 tests whether the IPO market is subject to overreaction by computing mean aftermarket returns for quintiles of adjusted initial returns for both small and large offers.[13] There is some tendency

13. Carter and Dark (1990) examine the correlation between initial returns and 18-month aftermarket returns for a sample of 911 firm commitment offers that went public between January 1, 1979 and November 11, 1984. They find that the abnormal 18-month aftermarket returns for firms having the highest initial returns tend to be slightly lower than for firms having the lowest initial returns which they interpret as evidence of valuation errors.

Table 5 Aftermarket Performance Categorized by Initial Return Quintiles, with Results for Small and Large Offerings, for 1,526 IPOs in 1975–84

Gross proceeds are measured in dollars of 1984 purchasing power. $7.59 million is the median gross proceeds for the 1,526 offerings. The *wealth relative* is the ratio of one plus the mean IPO 3-year holding period return (not in percent) divided by one plus the mean matching firm 3-year holding period return (not in percent), exclusive of the initial return.

| | All Offers | | | Segmented by Gross Proceeds | | | |
| Matching Firm-Adjusted Initial Return Quintile % | IPO Average 3-Year Total Return % | Matching Firm Average 3-Year Total Return % | Wealth Relative | Proceeds <$7.59 Million | | Proceeds >$7.59 Million | |
				Wealth Relative	Sample Size	*Wealth Relative*	Sample Size
23.70 < IR < 373.98	9.45	61.39	0.678	0.606	198	0.818	108
8.10 < IR < 23.70	27.94	65.52	0.773	0.702	157	0.848	148
2.37 < IR < 8.10	41.56	55.82	0.908	0.800	142	1.004	163
−0.84 < IR < 2.37	45.51	60.88	0.904	0.794	101	0.955	204
−92.38 < IR < −0.84	47.95	65.70	0.893	0.829	164	0.985	141

for firms with high adjusted initial returns to have the worst aftermarket performance. This tendency is stronger for smaller issues than larger issues. The evidence is mildly supportive of the overreaction hypothesis.

In some respects, the finding that there is a tendency for the offerings with the highest initial returns to do worst in the long run may be a manifestation of a desire by issuers to avoid future lawsuits (see Ibbotson [1975, p. 264] and Tinic [1988]), by not fully exploiting the market's overoptimism at the time of the offering. This may also shed light on the "partial adjustment" phenomenon which refers to a positive correlation between initial returns and changes in the offering price between the preliminary and final prospectuses (see Ibbotson, Sindelar, and Ritter [1988], Sternberg [1989], and Weiss [1990] for discussions).

3.2 Aftermarket Performance by Industry

Tables 6 and 7 segment firms by industry classifications based upon three-digit Standard Industrial Classification (SIC) codes.[14] Where two or more

14. The SIC codes are compiled from the CRSP NASDAQ database, the January 1987 *NASDAQ Company Directory*, and other sources. Where there are discrepancies between

SIC codes represent industries that are very similar, I have grouped them into a single industry. The 13 industries for which there were at least 25 IPOs in my sample are listed with the remaining 420 other firms grouped together. As inspection of Table 6 demonstrates, companies going public in 1975–84 were not evenly distributed over all industries. Oil and gas firms are heavily represented (with most of these offers conducted in 1980 and 1981) as are financial institutions. Following the deregulation of the airline industry in 1978, several dozen young airlines went public. High technology firms in the computer and biomedical fields also have high representation. On the other hand, very few auto and steel companies went public in 1975–84. The industry representation represents capital flowing into growing industries in a dynamic economy.[15]

Also reported in Table 6 are the mean and median gross proceeds and annual sales, expressed in terms of 1984 purchasing power, and the mean and median age of the issuing firm, categorized by industry. As can be seen, there are substantial industry differences. The overall median age at the time of issue is only 6 years. For oil and gas firms, however, the median age is only 2 years, while for financial institutions the median age is 49 years. Most of the financial institution IPOs involve mutual savings banks and mutual savings and loan associations converting to stock companies after a 1982 regulatory change. Masulis (1987) analyzes this process. Also noteworthy is the fact that the median oil and gas IPO raised 12 times its annual revenue when it went public.

Table 7 reports the long-run performance measures for IPOs, categorized by industry. As can be seen, the long-run performance of IPOs in different industries varies widely.[16] Financial institutions (almost all of

---

various sources (due, for example, to a company's having changed the nature of its business after going public), I have assigned an SIC code based upon *Going Public: The IPO Reporter's* description of its business at the time of the offer.

15. In the 1975–84 period, only 15 of the 1,526 companies going public represented "reverse LBOs," defined as a company going public that had been involved in a leveraged buyout. Among companies going public in 1986 and later, reverse LBOs have been more common. The industry representation of reverse LBOs is concentrated in mature industries, such as retailing and food companies. See Muscarella and Vetsuypens (1989a) for an analysis of these reverse LBOs.

16. Since only 57% of the matching firms are in the same two-digit industry as the IPOs, it is possible that the imperfect control for industry factors can account for the long-run underperformance. In tests not reported here, I restricted the long-run analysis to the IPOs for which I had a matching firm in the same two-digit industry (or the same industry as defined in Table 6). The wealth relative value for this subsample is 0.866 as contrasted with 0.831 for the entire sample. This indicates that IPOs tend to underperform relative to their industries, which in turn tend to underperform relative to the market in the 3 years after going public.

Table 6 Mean and Median Sales, Gross Proceeds, and Age of 1,526 Sample Offers Categorized by Industry

Both sales and gross proceeds are expressed in terms of dollars of 1984 purchasing power. Sales are measured as 12-month revenues for the most recent 12-month period prior to going public. Gross proceeds are measured including, for firm commitment offerings, the proceeds from overallotment options, if exercised. The age of the issuing firm is measured as the calendar year of going public minus the calendar year of founding. The year of founding is the same or earlier than the year of incorporation or reincorporation. The 39 firms with a founding date prior to 1901 have their age computed as the offer year minus 1901.

Industry	SIC Codes	Number of Offers	Annual Sales, $ Millions		Gross Proceeds, $ Millions		Age of Issuing Firm	
			Mean	Median	Mean	Median	Mean	Median
Computer manufacturing	357	144	18.78	14.36	21.40	13.46	6.20	5
Communications and electronic equipment	366, 367	138	14.16	8.26	11.25	6.21	9.28	7
Oil and gas	131, 138 291, 679	127	19.05	0.53	9.57	6.33	4.83	2

Industry	SIC	N						
Financial institutions (banks and S&L's)	602, 603 612, 671	125	120.20	49.43	27.41	12.00	43.13	49
Computer and data processing services	737	113	16.40	11.50	13.98	9.83	9.55	7
Optical, medical, and scientific instruments	381–384	111	10.89	2.23	9.29	4.66	8.08	5
Retailers	520–573 591–599	70	74.70	34.74	17.28	11.10	12.89	7
Wholesalers	501–519	63	56.58	13.41	12.32	4.72	9.65	6
Restaurant chains	581	54	34.54	10.98	10.34	5.55	7.33	4
Health care and HMOs	805–809	50	35.20	7.42	14.96	6.80	4.88	3
Drugs and genetic engineering	283	44	21.14	1.98	19.70	11.55	7.68	3
Miscellaneous business services	739	42	14.27	2.38	7.75	4.93	8.55	8
Airlines	451	25	20.65	14.33	11.68	6.00	7.84	4
All other firms	—	420	61.24	18.07	15.04	7.32	14.58	8
All firms	—	1,526	42.82	11.55	15.06	7.59	12.66	6

Table 7   Mean Performance Categorized by Industry

The *wealth relative* is the ratio of one plus the mean IPO 3-year holding period return (not in percent) divided by one plus the mean matching firm 3-year holding period return (not in percent).

| | | Excluding Initial Returns | | |
| | Average Matching Firm-Adjusted Initial Return | Average 3-Year Holding Period Total Return | | |
Industry	%	IPOs %	Matching Firms %	Wealth Relative
Computers	13.67	19.22	47.84	0.806
Electronic equipment	14.59	29.93	61.46	0.805
Oil and gas	30.92	−43.86	34.67	0.417
Financial institutions	3.69	128.21	59.23	1.433
Computer services	16.07	13.13	50.38	0.752
Scientific instruments	20.96	18.14	72.20	0.686
Retailers	7.60	54.05	113.63	0.721
Wholesalers	16.95	1.42	47.14	0.689
Restaurant chains	13.51	73.86	82.36	0.953
Health care	14.12	36.93	53.25	0.894
Drugs	14.63	121.69	91.96	1.155
Miscellaneous services	10.20	26.61	80.50	0.701
Airlines	6.26	61.62	42.93	1.131
All other firms	11.13	33.40	64.24	0.812
All firms	14.06	34.47	61.86	0.831

which went public in 1983 and 1984) had the best long-run performance, benefiting from the large drop in interest rates in 1985–86. Oil and gas firms (most of which went public in 1980 and 1981) substantially underperformed the market. As is well known, oil prices declined substantially during 1981–83, so the underperformance of oil and gas firms does not come as a surprise. However, the long-run underperformance of IPOs is present in all but three of the 14 industry groupings. The underperformance of the IPOs in so many industries relative to other firms in the same industries may be interpreted as evidence that is more consistent with a "fads" explanation than mere bad luck.

Table 8 Performance Categorized by Year of Issuance for Initial Public
Offerings in 1975–84

The average real gross proceeds, measured in dollars of 1984 purchasing power,
is computed as the product of the U.S. GNP Deflator index and the average
nominal gross proceeds. The *wealth relative* is the ratio of one plus the mean
IPO 3-year holding period return (not in percent) divided by one plus the mean
matching firm 3-year holding period return (not in percent), exclusive of the
initial return.

						Excluding Initial Returns		
					Average Matching Firm-Adjusted Initial Return	Average 3-Year Holding Period Total Return		
		Average Gross Proceeds, $ Millions					Matching	
Year	GNP Deflator	Nominal	Real	Number of Issues	Return %	IPOs %	Firms %	Wealth Relative
1975	1.76	21.87	38.49	12	−5.24	59.44	52.51	1.045
1976	1.67	7.64	12.76	28	6.38	122.58	124.11	0.993
1977	1.58	6.96	11.00	19	8.21	188.35	54.72	1.864
1978	1.47	7.05	10.36	31	31.78	134.60	97.37	1.189
1979	1.38	6.55	9.04	63	22.06	75.98	71.76	1.025
1980	1.26	8.51	10.72	129	38.27	46.28	68.56	0.868
1981	1.15	8.96	10.30	300	9.98	5.26	60.85	0.654
1982	1.08	11.87	12.82	93	15.18	26.07	119.92	0.573
1983	1.04	20.48	21.30	589	12.56	21.31	52.88	0.793
1984	1.00	10.81	10.81	272	8.40	52.03[a]	47.91	1.028[a]
All	—	13.81	15.06	1,526	14.06	34.47	61.86	0.831

[a] If one outlier (TCBY, Inc.) is removed, the average 3-year raw return falls to 37.59%
and the 3-year *wealth relative* falls to 0.930.

3.3 Aftermarket Performance by Year of Issuance

In Table 8, firms are categorized by their year of issuance. The results
in Table 8 show that the long-run underperformance is not as general a
phenomenon as the short-run underpricing that has been widely documented. The *wealth relatives* are less than one for only five of the ten
sample years. Because the volume of new issues was much heavier in
the early 1980s than in the late 1970s, however, the mean wealth relative
is only 0.831 when all issues are weighted equally.

The negative relation between annual volume and aftermarket performance that is evident in Table 8 is consistent with the following scenario: firms choose to go public when investors are willing to pay high multiples (price-earnings or market-to-book) reflecting optimistic assessments of the net present value of growth opportunities. The negative aftermarket performance that then typically results is due to disappointing realizations of the subsequent net cash flows. This is due to either (1) bad luck or (2) irrationally overoptimistic forecasts, or "fads." Tables 7 and 8 are consistent with both interpretations.

3.4 Aftermarket Performance by Age

In Table 9, firms are segmented on the basis of their age at the time of going public, computed as the year of the offer minus the year of founding. There is a strong monotone relation between age and aftermarket performance. For the initial return, there is a strong monotone pattern in the other direction, consistent with the notions that risky issues require higher average initial returns and that age is a proxy for this risk.[17] The initial return and aftermarket performance patterns are much clearer in Table 9, using age as a measure of both ex ante uncertainty and investor optimism, than are the patterns in Table 4, in which firms are segmented by gross proceeds. The patterns using gross proceeds are not as clear because of two confounding effects—larger issues are typically issued by more established firms, but a given firm will choose to float a larger issue when the market conditions are characterized by strong demand.

A po*_ial problem with interpreting Panel A of Table 9 is that many of the oldest firms are financial institutions, which had exceptionally good aftermarket performance during this period, and many of the youngest firms are oil and gas firms, which had exceptionally poor aftermarket performance, as documented in Table 7. Thus, the pattern of aftermarket performance documented in Table 9 is strengthened by these industry effects. To control for these effects, I report in Panel B of Table 9 the initial and aftermarket performance for firms categorized by their age at the time of issue, with the 125 financial institutions and the 127 oil and gas firms deleted. The patterns present in Panel A are still present in Panel B, demonstrating that the lack of underperformance by established companies is not merely a manifestation of strong aftermarket performance by financial institutions.[18] I interpret the poor long-run perfor-

17. Muscarella and Vetsuypens (1989b) also document a negative relation between initial returns and age.

18. In results not reported here I have prepared tables analogous to Panels A and B of Table 9 using sales and market-to-book ratios rather than age for categorizing firms with similar results.

Table 9   Aftermarket Performance Categorized by the Age
of the Issuing Firm

Panel A includes all 1,526 IPOs. Panel B includes the 1,274 IPOs remaining after excluding the two industries with the most extreme wealth relatives: oil and gas (primarily very young firms) which did poorly, and financial institutions (primarily very old firms) which did well. Oil and gas firms are defined as firms with SIC codes of 131, 138, 291, and 679, representing oil and gas exploration, production, servicing, refining, and holding companies. Financial institutions are defined as firms with SIC codes of 602, 603, 612, and 671, representing commercial banks, savings banks, savings and loans, and bank holding companies. The *wealth relative* is the ratio of one plus the mean IPO 3-year holding period return (not in percent) divided by one plus the mean matching firm 3-year holding period return (not in percent).

| | | | Excluding Initial Returns | | |
| | | | Average 3-Year Holding Period Total Return | | |
Age in Years	Sample Size	Average Matching Firm-Adjusted Initial Return %	IPOs %	Matching Firms %	Wealth Relative
		Panel A: All 1,526 firms			
0–1	252	29.42	5.34	68.98	0.623
2–4	381	14.51	15.69	48.69	0.778
5–9	328	13.15	28.47	62.33	0.791
10–19	312	9.05	40.74	66.70	0.844
20–up	253	5.42	91.81	68.03	1.142
		Panel B: Excluding oil and gas firms and financial institutions			
0–1	177	23.87	16.19	76.31	0.659
2–4	338	14.87	19.22	53.20	0.778
5–9	305	13.71	33.01	65.47	0.804
10–19	300	9.32	42.97	67.66	0.853
20–up	154	5.41	63.76	70.37	0.961

mance of the younger IPOs, which typically have higher market-to-book ratios than more established firms, as evidence consistent with the over-optimism and fads story.

3.5 Regression Results

The cross-sectional patterns documented in Tables 4 through 9 are not independent of each other. Among other correlations, the worst-performing industry in the long run (oil and gas) has the lowest median age and the highest average initial return, while the best-performing industry in the long run (financial institutions) has the highest median age and the lowest average initial return. To disentangle the effects, Table 10 reports the results of a multiple regression using the raw 3-year total return on IPOs as the dependent variable. The explanatory variables are the market-adjusted initial return, the 3-year total return on the market, the logarithm of one plus age, the volume of IPOs in the year of issuance, and dummy variables for the oil and financial institutions industries.[19]

The Table 10 results generally support the conclusions from earlier tables. The adjusted coefficient of determination is rather low at only 7%. Because the dependent variable (3-year total returns) is so skewed, the residuals are also highly nonnormal. Consequently, bootstrapped p-values are reported.[20] With the exception of the initial return, all of the coefficient estimates are statistically significant at conventional levels. The parameter estimates are also economically significant. The coefficient on annual IPO volume (divided by 100) of -0.109, for instance, indicates

19. Several additional variables were also included in other regressions (unreported) that were run, with no boost in the adjusted coefficient of determination. Among these other insignificant variables are the logarithm of sales and a dummy variable accounting for the use of a best-efforts contract.

20. The approximate randomization bootstrapping procedure described in Noreen (1989) creates a coefficient vector under the null hypothesis of no relation by randomly reordering the 1,526 dependent variable observations (sampling without replacement) and running an OLS regression. This is repeated 10,000 times, creating a distribution of least-squares coefficient vectors. The bootstrapped p-values are calculated by finding the location of the original coefficient vector in the ranked empirical distribution, variable by variable. The two-tailed p-values reported are calculated by doubling the percentile location. Intuitively, this simulation procedure answers the question "How likely is it to observe a value at least as large (in absolute value) as the original least squares coefficient estimate if there is no true relation, given the empirical distribution of the dependent variable?" The bootstrapped p-values that are reported are similar to the ordinary least squares values.

Table 10   Ordinary Least Squares Regression Results with the Three-year Total Return as the Dependent Variable, for 1,526 IPOs in 1975–84

$\text{Return}_i = b_0 + b_1 \text{IR}_i + b_2 \text{Log}(1 + \text{age}_i) + b_3 \text{Market}_i + b_4 \text{Vol}_i + b_5 \text{Oil}_i + b_6 \text{Bank}_i + e_i$. Return_i is the raw three-year return, measured from the first aftermarket closing price to the earlier of the three-year anniversary or its CRSP delisting date. IR_i is the market-adjusted initial return, calculated using the CRSP value-weighted index of Amex-NYSE stocks as the market index. $\text{Log}(1 + \text{age}_i)$ is the natural logarithm of one plus the difference between the year of going public and the year of founding, with firms founded before 1901 assumed to be founded in 1901. Market_i is the CRSP value-weighted market return for the same return interval as the dependent variable. Vol_i is the annual volume of IPOs in the year of issuance, divided by 100. The gross number of IPOs, given in Table 1, is used. Oil_i is a 0, 1 dummy variable taking on the value of 1 if the issuing firm has an SIC code of 131, 138, 291, or 679, representing oil and gas production, exploration, refining, and service companies, or oil and gas holding companies. Bank_i is a 0, 1 dummy variable taking on the value of 1 if the issuing firm has an SIC code of 602, 603, 612, or 671, representing banks, savings and loans, and associated holding companies. Bootstrapped p-values are in parentheses.

Panel A: Parameter estimates							
Intercept	IR	Log(1 + age)	Market	Vol	Oil	Bank	R^2_{adjusted}
0.238	−0.206	0.127	0.841	−0.109	−0.765	0.825	0.070
(0.186)	(0.143)	(0.010)	(0.001)	(0.001)	(0.001)	(0.001)	

Panel B: Summary statistics of variables			
Variable	Mean	Median	Standard Deviation
Return	0.345	−0.167	1.902
IR	0.141	0.040	0.309
Log(1 + age)	2.009	1.946	1.079
Market	0.566	0.580	0.246
Vol	5.520	5.350	2.831
Oil	0.083	0.000	0.276
Bank	0.082	0.000	0.274

that the difference in 3-year total returns for a firm going public in a low volume year such as 1976 (33 offerings) rather than in a high volume year such as 1983 (865 offerings) is 0.907 (90.7%), ceteris paribus. The coefficient on the market return of 0.841 is surprisingly low. I would have expected that the average beta would be slightly above 1.0, given the findings of Clarkson and Thompson (1990).

4. Summary and Conclusions

This paper has documented the time- and industry-dependence of the long-run performance of initial public offerings. A strategy of investing in IPOs at the end of the first day of public trading and holding them for 3 years would have left the investor with only 83 cents relative to each dollar from investing in a group of matching firms listed on the American and New York stock exchanges. Younger companies and companies going public in heavy volume years did even worse than average. I have attempted to shed some light on the reason for this underperformance. In particular, do the firms in this sample underperform merely due to bad luck, or does the market systematically overestimate the growth opportunities of IPOs? The evidence presented here is broadly consistent with the notion that many firms go public near the peak of industry-specific fads. It should be noted, however, that since the sample involves IPOs going public in only a 10-year period, alternative interpretations cannot be ruled out.

With 20–20 hindsight, investors in the 1,526 IPOs in this sample were overly optimistic about the firms' prospects. There are other securities markets in which investors in new issues have systematically lost money. Weiss (1989) and Peavy (1990) document that investors in new issues of closed-end funds in 1985–87 suffered substantial losses as the funds moved from premiums over net asset value at the time of issue to substantial discounts 6 months later. Elton, Gruber, and Rentzler (1989) document that publicly offered commodity funds going public in 1979–83 performed poorly, in spite of extremely high monthly returns reported in their offering prospectuses. Uhlir (1989) documents a pattern of returns of IPOs of common stock in West Germany that is almost identical to that presented here for the 12 months after going public.

The finding that initial public offerings underperform, on average, implies that the costs of raising external equity capital are not inordinately high for these firms. The high transaction costs of raising external equity capital in an IPO, documented in Ritter (1987) and Barry, Muscarella, and Vetsuypens (1990), are partly offset by the low realized long-run returns, at least for those firms going public at times when investor sentiment is optimistic. Consequently, the small growth companies that predominate among firms going public do not necessarily face a higher cost of equity capital than is true for more established firms.

For issuers, it appears that the concentrations in volume in certain years are associated with taking advantage of "windows of opportunity." Kim and Stulz (1988) present evidence that issuers take advantage of differences in borrowing costs that periodically arise between the domestic and Eurobond markets. Lee, Shleifer, and Thaler (1991) present evidence that closed-end funds are issued more frequently in periods when discounts are unusually small. Thus, evidence exists in several markets that issuers successfully time offers to lower their cost of capital.

Several issues have been left unresolved. In particular, I have analyzed the stock market returns in the 3 years after going public without finding any tendency for the underperformance to eventually end. My suspicion, however, is that the underperformance does not extend much beyond 3 years, based upon Ibbotson (1975) and Rao's (1989) findings. Ibbotson finds no underperformance in the fifth year after going public, the last year that he analyzes. Furthermore, Rao finds negative earnings in announcement effects in the first 3 years after going public, but not in years 4 through 6.

A second issue that is unresolved is the generality of my findings. Only by extending the sample period beyond the 10 years of this paper can additional evidence be gained regarding some of the patterns that have been documented. In this regard, Aggarwal and Rivoli (1990) report that IPOs issued in the high-volume years of 1985 and 1986 had negative market-adjusted returns, using a NASDAQ index as the market, during their first year of trading.

A third issue that is unresolved is the relation of the long-run underperformance to the short-run underpricing phenomenon. It has always been somewhat of a mystery why IPOs are priced in a manner that results in such large positive average initial returns. This paper's evidence indicates that the offering price is not too low, but that the first aftermarket price is too high. If issuers and their investment bankers set the offering price in a manner that reflects the firm's underlying fundamental value, however, it is even more of a mystery why some offerings have extremely high initial returns.

Appendix: Matching Firm Selection Procedure

To select matching firms for the 1,526 IPOs in 1975–84, the following procedure was employed: Among firms listed on the American and New York Stock Exchanges, their market values were computed on the dates December 31 of 1974, 1980, and 1983. Within each three-digit SIC code, these firms were ranked by market value. For firms going public in 1975–80 in a given three-digit industry, the listed firm with the closest (as of December 31, 1974) market value was chosen as the matching firm, with a matching firm used only once until 3 years had passed. If a matching firm in the same industry was not available, then a small firm in

Table A1 Distribution of Market Values for 1,526 IPOs and Matching Firms in 1975–84

Market values for IPOs are calculated using the post-offering number of shares multiplied by the CRSP-reported closing market price on the first day of trading. Market values for matching firms are calculated using the CRSP-reported number of shares for the prior December 31 multiplied by the market price on the date of the IPO. No price level adjustments have been made.

| | Market Values, $ | |
Percentile	IPOs	Matching Firms
1st	971,014	695,625
10th	7,024,060	9,892,187
20th	10,810,811	17,626,000
30th	14,033,019	28,428,000
40th	18,724,091	43,064,000
50th (median)	25,987,887	67,816,000
60th	35,654,362	106,260,736
70th	50,818,888	181,082,000
80th	76,545,169	314,312,192
90th	130,024,824	719,505,920
100th	1,694,854,118	35,028,414,500

another industry was chosen, with preference given to firms in similar industries. For companies going public in 1981–83, the market value of listed firms at the end of 1980 was used. For firms going public in 1984, the market value of listed firms at the end of 1983 was used. This procedure resulted in 1,526 matching firms, of which 543 (36%) were in the same three-digit industry. An additional 328 firms (21%) were matched by either two-digit SIC codes or by the industry groups as defined in Table 6, resulting in a total of 57% of IPOs matched with a firm in roughly the same industry. The low rate of matching industries is attributable to the large difference in the industry mix between the IPOs and the listed companies. Also, as shown in Table A1, in spite of the overrepresentation of small firms among the matching firms, the matching firms (with market values calculated at the time of the IPO, rather than merely at three discrete dates) tend to be larger than the IPOs.

For 277 out of the 1,526 IPOs, the original matching firm was delisted before the earlier of (1) the 3-year anniversary date, or (2) the delisting of the IPO. For these firms, a second matching company was chosen, using the same criteria as above, for the remainder of the aftermarket performance interval. For 61 companies, a third matching firm was needed for the remainder of the interval due to the delisting of the second matching company. A given matching company could be matched with several different IPOs that went public more than 3 years apart. This procedure allowed matching firms with low market capitalizations in certain industries to be used multiple times.

For all of the matching firm choices, care was taken to avoid "survivorship bias." This was accomplished by choosing a matching firm regardless of when it was delisted, with some matching firms being delisted as soon as a week after the offering date of its matched IPO. Almost all of the Amex-NYSE delistings occurring during this period are due to takeovers and management buyouts. For IPOs that were delisted before the 36-month aftermarket period ended, the last month of returns involves fewer than 21 days. The matching company's returns were matched up to end on exactly the same day as the IPO.

I wish to thank Clifford Ball, Chris Barry, Stephen Buser (the editor), Donald Keim, Josef Lakonishok, Gita Rao, Nejat Seyhun, René Stulz, Michael Vetsuypens, Ivo Welch, Joseph Williams, an anonymous referee, participants in workshops at Illinois, Iowa, Vanderbilt, and Wharton, and especially Harry DeAngelo for helpful suggestions. An earlier version of this paper was presented at the December 1988 AFA meetings, the September 1989 Garn Institute conference on The Capital Acquisition Process, the November 1989 CRSP Seminar on the Analysis of Security Prices, and the October 1990 Q Group meetings. Navin Chopra, Tim Loughran, and Tae Park provided extensive and very able research assistance. The research is partially supported by a grant from the Institute for Quantitative Research in Finance.

References

AGGARWAL, REENA and PIETRA RIVOLI. 1990. Fads in the initial public offering market? *Financial Management* 19 (Winter), 45–57.

BARRY, CHRISTOPHER B., CHRIS J. MUSCARELLA, and MICHAEL R. VETSUYPENS. 1990. Underwriter warrants, underwriter compensation, and the costs of going public. Unpublished working paper, SMU and TCU.

BLAZENKO, GEORGE W. 1989. Underpricing of unseasoned equity issues, aftermarket performance, and the winner's curse. Unpublished working paper, Simon Fraser University.

BUSER, STEPHEN A., and K. C. CHAN. 1987. NASDAQ/NMS qualification standards: Ohio registration experience and the price performance of initial public offerings. Columbus, Ohio Department of Commerce and National Association of Securities Dealers, Inc.

CARTER, RICHARD B., and FREDERICK H. DARK. 1990. Effects of differential information on the aftermarket valuation of initial public offerings. Unpublished working paper, Iowa State University.

—— and STEVEN MANASTER. 1990. Initial public offerings and underwriter reputation. *Journal of Finance* 45, 1045–1067.

CHAN, LOUIS and JOSEF LAKONISHOK. 1990. Robust measurement of beta risk. Unpublished working paper, University of Illinois.

CLARKSON, PETER M., and REX THOMPSON. 1990. Empirical estimates of beta when investors face estimation risk. *Journal of Finance* 45, 431–453.

DE BONDT, WERNER F. M., and RICHARD THALER. 1985. Does the stock market overreact? *Journal of Finance* 40, 793–805.

—— and RICHARD THALER. 1987. Further evidence of investor overreaction and stock market seasonality. *Journal of Finance* 42, 557–582.

DIMSON, ELROY, and PAUL MARSH. 1986. Event study methodologies and the size effect: The case of UK press recommendations. *Journal of Financial Economics* 17, 113–142.

ELTON, EDWIN J., MARTIN J. GRUBER, and JOEL RENTZLER. 1989. New public offerings, information, and investor rationality: The case of publicly offered commodity funds. *Journal of Business* 62, 1–15.

HOWARD & CO. 1975–84. *Going public: The IPO reporter* (Philadelphia).

IBBOTSON, ROGER G. 1975. Price performance of common stock new issues. *Journal of Financial Economics* 3, 235–272.

—— and JEFFREY F. JAFFE. 1975. 'Hot issue' markets. *Journal of Finance* 30, 1027–1042.

——, JODY L. SINDELAR, and JAY R. RITTER. 1988. Initial public offerings. *Journal of Applied Corporate Finance* 1, 37–45.

KIM, YONG CHEOL, and RENÉ M. STULZ. 1988. The Eurobond market and corporate financial policy: A test of the clientele hypothesis. *Journal of Financial Economics* 22, 189–205.

LEE, CHARLES, ANDREI SHLEIFER, and RICHARD THALER. 1991. Investor sentiment and the closed-end fund puzzle. *Journal of Finance* 46, 75–109.

MASULIS, RONALD W. 1987. Changes in ownership structure: Conversions of mutual savings and loans to stock charter. *Journal of Financial Economics* 18, 29–60.

MILLER, EDWARD M. 1977. Risk, uncertainty, and divergence of opinion. *Journal of Finance* 32, 1151–1168.

MILLER, ROBERT E., and FRANK K. REILLY. 1987. An examination of mispricing, returns, and uncertainty for initial public offerings. *Financial Management* 16, 33–38.

MUSCARELLA, CHRIS J., and MICHAEL VETSUYPENS. 1989a. The underpricing of 'second' initial public offerings. *Journal of Financial Research* 12, 183–192.

——— and MICHAEL VETSUYPENS. 1989*b*. Initial public offerings and information asymmetry. Unpublished working paper, Southern Methodist University.

NASDAQ COMPANY DIRECTORY. 1987. National Association of Securities Dealers, Inc. January number (Washington, DC).

NOREEN, E. W. 1989. *Computer Intensive Methods for Testing Hypotheses* (John Wiley and Sons, Somerset, NJ).

PEAVY, JOHN W. 1990. Returns on initial public offerings of closed-end funds. *Review of Financial Studies* 3, 695–708.

RAO, GITA. 1989. The relation between stock returns and earnings: A study of newly-public firms. Unpublished working paper, University of Illinois.

RITTER, JAY R. 1984. The 'hot issue' market of 1980. *Journal of Business* 32, 215–240.

———. 1987. The costs of going public. *Journal of Financial Economics* 19, 269–281.

SHILLER, ROBERT J. 1990. Speculative prices and popular models. *Journal of Economic Perspectives* 4, 55–65.

SMITH, CLIFFORD W., JR. 1986. Investment banking and the capital acquisition process. *Journal of Financial Economics* 15, 3–30.

STERN, RICHARD L., and PAUL BORNSTEIN. 1985. Why new issues are lousy investments. *Forbes* 136, 152–190.

STERNBERG, THEODORE D. 1989. Bilateral monopoly and the dynamic properties of initial public offerings. Unpublished working paper, Vanderbilt University.

STOLL, HANS R., and ANTHONY J. CURLEY. 1970. Small business and the new issues market for equities. *Journal of Financial and Quantitative Analysis* 5, 309–322.

TINIC, SEHA. 1988. Anatomy of initial public offerings of common stock. *Journal of Finance* 43, 789–822.

UHLIR, HELMUT. 1989. Going public in the F.R.G. In *A Reappraisal of the Efficiency of Financial Markets,* RUI M. C. GUIMARAES, B. KINGSMAN, and S. TAYLOR, eds. (Springer-Verlag, New York).

WEISS, KATHLEEN A. 1989. The post-offering price performance of closed-end funds. *Financial Management* 18, 57–67.

———. 1990. Investor demand for initial public offerings and the relationship of the offer price to the preliminary file range. Unpublished working paper, University of Michigan.

PART

VI

INDIVIDUAL
BEHAVIOR

19

Speculative Prices
and Popular Models

ROBERT J. SHILLER

The rational expectations revolution in economics was born of the recognition that the expectations people hold for future economic variables are fundamental to their behavior. Thus, our (economists') economic models require their (those who make up the economy) economic models, models which they use to generate their expectations. The key idea of rational expectations models is to collapse the two models into one: to assume that people know (or behave as if they know) the true model that describes the economy. This idea allows economists to construct simple and elegant models of the economy, models that are appealing theoretically and that can be studied without collecting any data about the models in the minds of economic actors.

The problem with the rational expectations models is that collapsing the two kinds of models into one is a gross oversimplification. Obviously, the popular models (the models that are used by the broad masses of economic actors to form their expectations) are not the same as those held by economists. Once one accepts the difference, economic modelling cannot proceed without collecting data on the popular models themselves.

This paper reports on such a data collection effort on popular models, using questionnaire survey methods, with the purpose of understanding speculative markets. I will report here on my research to understand the U.S. stock market crash of October 1987; research Fumiko Kon-ya, Yoshiro Tsutsui and I undertook to understand the Japanese stock market crash of October 1987; research Karl Case and I undertook to understand

From: *Journal of Economic Perspectives*, vol. 4, no. 2., pp. 55–65, Spring 1990. Reprinted by permission of the American Economic Association.

recent real estate booms; and research John Pound and I undertook to understand the periodic "hot" markets for initial public offerings (IPO's) of common stock.

Two basic questionnaire methods were used to study popular models. A response-coding method begins with road open-ended questions, to which respondents are asked to fill in their answers in their own words. The questions ask what they think is the cause of certain phenomena in the economy, or how they make decisions related to the phenomena. Respondents often interpret the open-ended questions in unpredictable ways and give answers that are short and impulsive, but the answers do give clues as to what people think. Their answers are coded into categories; the share of respondents who voluntarily mention certain themes (certainly downward-biased measures of the percents who *think* about such themes) are tabulated.

A trial-model method begins with the same questions posed in informal personal interviews. From this, the interviewer tries to infer what the popular models are, and then frames questionnaire items to ask a new set of respondents directly what they think about the presumed popular models.

The advantage of the response-coding method is that it gives a better quantitative indication of the importance of each popular model in popular thinking, since no ideas are put in respondents' minds. But the popular models respondents freely give are inevitably vaguely defined. The advantage of the trial-model method is that it enables the collection of sharper information about the popular models. By either method, popular models will be described by researchers in terms of the cognition and language of ordinary individuals, not the language of professional economists.

1. The Stock Market Crash of 1987

During the week of the stock market crash of October 19, 1987, I sent out 1000 questionnaires to institutional investors and 2000 questionnaires to individual investors, asking them to report "your own personal experiences" during the crash. Questionnaire responses were received from 284 institutional investors and 605 individual investors, Shiller (1986b). Four months later, Fumiko Kon-ya, Yoshiro Tsutsui and I (1989) sent out 114 similar questionnaires about the crash to Japanese institutional investors and received 52 responses.

Using the response-coding method, we asked the investors, "Can you remember any specific theory you had about the causes for the price declines of October 14–19, 1987?" The most common theme among U.S.

investors was that the market was overpriced. About a third of both individual and institutional investors wrote this. No consistent explanation was given what "overpriced" means or why the market was overpriced. The second most common theme was an institutional stop-loss theme, identified by key words: institutional selling, program trading, and stop-loss or computer trading. The third most common theme (offered by about a quarter of respondents) was an investor irrationality theme, that investors were crazy or that the fall was due to investor panic or capricious change in opinion.

After this, using the trial-model method, we asked investors to categorize the theory they had just written into "a theory about investor psychology" or "a theory about fundamentals such as profits or interest rates." Two-thirds of the U.S. investors, both individual and institutional, and three-quarters of the Japanese investors chose investor psychology. This perhaps gives an indication what people meant who wrote that the market was overpriced.

Investors were asked: "Did you think at any point on October 19, 1987, that you had a pretty good idea when a rebound was to occur?" In the United States, about a third of both individual and institutional investors said "yes," far more than the proportion who traded on October 19. The questionnaire then asked: "If yes, what made you think that you knew when a rebound would occur?" Again, respondents were given a space to write in their own answers. What struck me in reading the answers of U.S. respondents was the frequency with which people wrote "intuition," "gut feeling" or the like.

When respondents went beyond such vague statements the models expressed were usually extremely simple. The most frequently expressed theme among U.S. investors was a notion that large price drops should be followed shortly by a reversal; 37 percent of institutional investors and 14 percent of individual investors mentioned this. Less common was a notion that stock prices had reached such a low level that a price increase was to be expected; 14 percent of the institutional investors and 8 percent of the individual investors were coded as saying this. Reference to more established theories (like theories about portfolio insurance or technical indicators) were rare here.[1]

It is a striking fact that many investors think that they can forecast the market and some of these are eager to take action. The random walk theory of stock prices now has some currency as a popular model, but

---

1. The presence of a large amount of portfolio insurance also played a role in the crash. The popularity of portfolio insurance among institutional investors can be understood only as the response to a new fashion or peculiar popular model. See Shiller (1988).

other theories are still very much around. Why do some people think that they can forecast the market on a day of a record price drop? Sometimes comparisons with past experience, particularly 1929, were made. But people cannot have learned just from past experience what to expect on October 19, since the one-day drop was of unprecedented magnitude.

I asked U.S. respondents to rate (on a one to seven scale) the importance of various news stories "to you personally on October 19," with the admonition, "please tell how important *you* then felt these were, and not how others thought about them." I included on the list all of the stories over the past week that seemed to me to be possibly important in the transmission of the crash. I also included as news stories "the 200 point drop in the Dow on the morning of Monday, October 19" and the "drop in U.S. stock prices October 14–16, 1987." While all news stories were granted some importance, no picture emerged as to what "triggered" the crash. What stood out was the news stories about the price drops. The most popular news story among both individual and institutional investors was the 200 point drop that morning; the second most popular story was the price drops on October 14–16.[2]

We investigated the emotional environment at the time of the crash by asking respondents if they experienced "any unusual symptoms of anxiety (difficulty concentrating, sweaty palms, tightness in chest, irritability, or rapid pulse) regarding the stock market." On October 19, 23 percent of U.S. individual investors and 42 percent of U.S. institutional investors said yes. On October 20, 42 percent of Japanese investors answered yes. I find these percentages remarkably high, given that the samples were just random samples of all investors. But the anxiety does not necessarily mean that people were "panicking" or performing badly. It might mean that, in a sense, people were unusually alert and that other matters were brushed aside so that careful investment decisions could be made.

From this evidence, we begin to see how popular, intuitive, models of speculative prices informed investor behavior at the time of the crash. The suggestion we get of the causes of the crash is one of people reacting to each other with heightened attention and emotion, trying to fathom what other investors were likely to do, and falling back on intuitive mod-

---

2. Merton Miller has pointed out to me that similar conclusions were reached in a Securities and Exchange Commission study about the 6.1 percent one-day drop in stock prices of September 3, 1946. For each interviewee they coded the "major reason" for selling into one of 17 categories. The largest category, coded for 43 percent of interviewees, was "declining prices on September 3." The second largest category coded for 13 percent of respondents was another popular model, "Dow theory" (Securities and Exchange Commission, 1947).

els like models of price reversal or continuation. There appears to be no recognizable exogenous trigger for the crash. With such popular models, a feedback system is created with possibly complicated dynamics, and we do not need to refer to a trigger to explain a crash.

2. Recent Booms in Real Estate

Housing prices in California have recently boomed: prices increased around 20 percent between mid-1987 and mid-1988 in many California cities. Karl Case and I (1988) sent 1030 questionnaires to recent home buyers in two California cities, Anaheim (Orange County) and San Francisco. We also sent 500 questionnaires to home buyers in Boston, Massachusetts, where prices had fallen in the real estate market after a major boom a few years earlier, and 500 to Milwaukee, Wisconsin, where the real price of housing had remained nearly unchanged over the preceding five years. We received 886 responses.

The mailing lists were taken at random from public records of closings in May 1988. Since identical questionnaires were sent to the four cities (identical except for changes in the city names that appeared in the questionnaires) and since they were sent at the same time, the differences across cities in the results can be attributed only to local real estate conditions.

Using the response-coding method, the home buyers were asked for their theories of what explained recent changes in home prices in their city, and for any events that they thought might have changed the trends in housing prices. We coded the answers into 17 categories.

As with the stock market, we found no exogenous trigger that could be seen as precipitating the price surge. The most common theme in the answers in all four cities was interest rate changes. Since interest rates are virtually the same around the country, these could not explain the sharply different behavior of housing prices in the different cities.

Not a single person from among the 886 respondents cited any quantitative evidence about future trends in supply or demand, or professional forecasts of future supply or demand. There is a peculiar lack of interest in objective evidence about fundamentals. Instead, there is a resort to cliches or reference to evidence that one could see oneself while driving around the city (like traffic congestion or the racial composition of the population). The price movements are attributed to whatever seems to be the most plausible explanation. Thus, a quarter of Boston respondents referred to the stock market crash of October 1987 but less than 2 percent of respondents in the other cities did. Only in Boston was there a need to explain a sudden drop in real estate prices.

As with the stock market surveys, the home buyers were also asked to classify the theories they had just written. They were asked to specify whether the theory was "about the psychology of home buyers and sellers" or "a theory about economic or demographic conditions, such as population changes, changes in interest rates, or employment growth (decline)." In all four cities, less than a quarter picked the psychology. The popular model of housing prices tends not to emphasize the psychology of other investors, as does the popular model of the stock market crash.

Our survey revealed that speculative considerations were a prime motive for buying homes in boom cities. For example, 75 percent of our California respondents agreed with the statement: "Housing prices are booming. Unless I buy now, I won't be able to afford a home later," while only 28 percent of our Milwaukee respondents agreed.

It is peculiar, then, that there is so little apparent interest in quantitative evidence about fundamentals. There is instead a feeling in most cities that housing prices cannot decline. Respondents were asked to specify whether buying a home in their city involves "a great deal of risk," "some risk," or "little or no risk." The majority in the boom cities (63 percent in Anaheim and 56 percent in San Francisco) picked little or no risk. The theory that price movements are due to "economic or demographic conditions, such as population changes, changes in interest rates, or employment growth (decline)" would not itself seem to suggest that prices cannot decline. Anyone who reads newspapers carefully would know that home prices in Houston recently dropped 24 percent in two years. In Boston, where housing prices were reported to have declined in 1987, only 36 percent thought buying a home involves "little or no risk." The impression that housing prices cannot decline seems to be a local phenomenon, related to local rather than national experience.

There is evidence of emotional involvement in boom cities, much as we saw with the stock market crash. Of our California respondents, 55 percent agreed, "There has been a good deal of excitement surrounding recent real estate price changes. I sometimes think that I may have been influenced by it." Only 21.5 percent of our Milwaukee respondents agreed. In California, 51 percent of our respondents said that they talked about the housing market frequently with friends, while only 20 percent of the Milwaukee respondents said so.

One of the most common responses in California to our open-ended question asking for what explains recent changes in home prices was that the region is a good place to live. This was volunteered by 17 percent of our California respondents. But California has always been a good place to live. They are explaining changes in prices with an unchanging variable, which is suggestive of a "shortage illusion."

The shortage illusion in any market is that price changes will not tend to restore equilibrium in the market. Shortages (or surpluses) are seen as continuing indefinitely, and perhaps also price increases (or decreases) are seen as continuing indefinitely, so that observing excess demand may help to reinforce a boom. It seems that the popular model takes shortages or surpluses as reflecting absolute supply and demand, rather than supply and demand at a given price. Disequilibrium is not seen at all as a reflection of a barrier to price adjustment.

Respondents in our boom cities tended to think that the same sort of price increases seen in the last year would continue indefinitely. Anaheim respondents expected an increase of 15 percent in the succeeding year and 14 percent on average for each of the succeeding ten years. In San Francisco, the corresponding price increases were 13 percent and 15 percent. (The corresponding price increase expectations were in the 6 percent to 9 percent range in Boston and Milwaukee). We asked our respondents:

> In a "hot" real estate market, sellers often get more than one offer on the day they list their properties. Some are even over the asking price. There are also stories about people waiting in line to make offers. Which is the better explanation?
>
> —There is panic buying, and price becomes irrelevant.
>
> —Asking prices have adjusted slowly or sluggishly to increasing demand.

In the cities that had experienced recent housing price increases, the majority picked the first answer. In San Francisco, 71 percent of those answering picked the first, in Anaheim the figure was 73 percent, in Boston the figure was 61 percent. Now they really made an absurd choice; surely price is not "irrelevant." To an economist, the second choice is true almost as a tautology, given that prices have increased and that there is excess demand.

Only 35 percent of those answering picked the first answer in Milwaukee, where no major housing price increases have occurred recently. This striking difference across cities in answers to a question that is not specific to any city shows that the popular models are themselves influenced by recent experience, and indeed heavily influenced by the local market experience. This difference in perception across cities is useful to bear in mind in considering the possible reasons why speculative bubbles appear to be local phenomena, occurring in one city and not in another relatively nearby city. The difference also shows that part of the dynamics of speculative price changes may be changes in the popular models.

The misinterpretation by the public of excess demand is a factor in the transmission process of price increases. When prices increase, some proportion of sellers will make the mistake of failing to adjust up their asking price enough, and so some houses will sell for more than the asking price (8 percent of the houses in our California sample, while 59 percent went below asking). If the shortage illusion is operative, this phenomenon may serve to increase demand further. This is a possible link in the vicious circle of a speculative bubble; not only might price increases themselves serve to increase demand, but the appearance of excess demand might serve to increase demand, too.

3. Underpricing of Initial Public Offerings (IPO's)

In February 1987, John Pound and I sent out 1500 questionnaires to IPO investors and received 153 responses. In July 1989 I sent out 800 questionnaires to wealthy individuals and institutional investors and received 273 responses.

We undertook these surveys to try to understand why the IPO market shows very high initial returns and why the market goes in and out of "hot" periods. These phenomena in the IPO market have been just as puzzling as the stock market crash or the real estate bubbles discussed above. Prices of IPO's have shown a striking tendency to jump up dramatically as soon as the after–market trading begins. Roger Ibbotson, Jody Sindelar and Jay Ritter presented data that between 1977 and 1987 the average initial return—that is, percentage return from the offering price to the end-of-the-first-day bid price—was 20.25 percent. This is not an annualized rate; it is the actual average increase in value over, generally, no more than a few days. Moreover, periods of high initial returns tend to come and go. For example, they report that the years 1977 through 1980 were all years of above average, and gradually increasing, initial returns, culminating in an average initial return of 49.36 percent in the "hot" market of 1980. Other such "hot" markets, peaking in 1961 and in 1968, are also in evidence. Volume of new issues appears to lag initial returns by six to twelve months (Ibbotson, Sindelar and Ritter, 1988).

It should be borne in mind that investors as a whole cannot expect to claim these dramatic initial returns by buying all IPO's; one is prevented from doing so. One depends on a broker to allocate shares in an offering, and the broker's willingness to do so is likely to be related to the other business that one gives the broker. Still, it is puzzling why this underpricing that causes the high initial returns occurs at all, and why issuing firms will deal with underwriters who substantially underprice issues.

Using the response coding method, IPO investors were asked to explain the theory that led them to purchase a particular IPO. The most common answer was just some description of the product of the company or the "concept" of its strategic plan. They were asked to describe their theory as "a theory about the kinds of stocks that are becoming attractive to investors" or "a theory about fundamentals such as profits or dividends." The former was selected by 57 percent of respondents. As with the stock market crash respondents, investor psychology is very much on the minds of respondents. Whether or not "hot" markets are indeed fads, investors themselves think there are fads in these markets, contrary to the assumption of the rational expectations models in the literature.

Respondents were asked in 1989: "Can you remember a time in the past 10 years when you became substantially discouraged about investing in initial public offerings in general?" Among those in the sample who had ever bought IPO's, 40 percent of individual investors and 56 percent of institutional investors said yes, and 31 percent and 40 percent respectively said yes in answer to a question where "encouraged" was substituted for "discouraged." The followup questions were: Can you state what discouraged (encouraged) you, and what were your information sources? While answers were quite varied and difficult to classify, response coding revealed that about half of the respondents appeared to be referring to past price changes in stating their reasons: price drops caused them to be discouraged and price increases to be encouraged. Thus, waves of enthusiasm for IPO's appear to be related to interpretations of what other investors are thinking and to evidence on this from observed price movements.

But why are IPO's underpriced on average? Why don't underwriters price issues to clear markets? I have argued (1989a) that the underpricing reflects more than just the asymmetric information theory that the underpricing is compensation for the winner's curse for those who get allocations (Rock, 1986) or the litigation theory that underpricing reduces the probability that underwriters will be sued by investors (Tinic, 1988). Underpricing tends to occur on average for several other reasons. For one, there appears to be a common idea that IPO investors are serving underwriters by buying IPO's and not selling them for a while, providing a "home" and a stable price for the issue and thereby ultimately inducing other investors to reduce their fears about the issue. The high initial return is viewed by many as a payment from underwriters to investors for restricting their selling. For another, there appears to be an idea that underwriters should charge "fair" prices for issues, even when they could obtain a lot more, but underwriters can expect to be repaid for selling at below-market prices by subsequent business from those who obtained allocations in underpriced issues. The high initial return helps investors maintain appearances. I will emphasize here, however, a third theory for underpricing of issues, which I will call the impresario hypothesis.

Impresarios who manage musicians and other entertainers know that the public interprets empty seats in an auditorium as reflecting badly on the performer, and that a jam-packed auditorium is interpreted as evidence that the performer is very much in the public favor. (Again, this is the shortage illusion.) Thus, impresarios know that they should not always price tickets to an event so as to maximize profits on that single event. To do so runs the risk that the event will be undersubscribed. It is often better to create an excess demand for the tickets, creating scenes of people standing in long lines for tickets, or trading among themselves at higher prices. This impression will tend to produce greater demand for subsequent events. By the same token, underpricing IPO's will create the high initial returns that leave the impression that the stockbroker or underwriter is giving good investment advice. By this theory, "hot" markets appear when some salesmen for IPO's discover that some segment of the public is ripe for a "fad" for IPO's. Underwriters then let the high initial returns run for a while to generate publicity and good will for the IPO's.

A substantial fraction of both wealthy individuals and institutional investors openly admit that they interpret initial returns in accordance with the impresario theory. They were asked: "Imagine you buy shares in an initial public offering recommended you by a broker and the price jumps 15% on the first day making you a very nice profit for one day. Which statement best describes how this would change your opinion of this broker's (with his/her advisors) investment savvy or ability to pick investments whose market price would increase?" Forty-seven percent of individual investors and 28 percent of institutional investors chose either "strong evidence" or "positive evidence" of ability.

Our survey documented that while IPO investors tend to describe themselves as actively picking IPO's, they showed a strong concern with the reputation of the underwriter and stockbroker for helping them do this. Of the respondents, 57 percent said they would be more likely to buy an IPO that is underwritten by a particular investment bank or investment bank consortium. It is plausible that reputation of their advisors should matter, since IPO investors generally do not do careful research. Only 26 percent of the IPO investor sample said they had done any calculations of what true fundamental value of a share in the company was, and compared the price of a share with this value. IPO investors were generally repeat purchasers of IPO's and communicated extensively with others about IPO's, so that the reputation of the underwriter may well have an effect on subsequent underwriter profits.

Each issuing firm would rather that underwriters did not underprice its issue, but may find that it has no good alternative to dealing with firms that have a policy of underpricing; underwriters without this policy would have so much lower reputation that the price at which the issue could be sold would be even lower.

The impresario hypothesis does not imply that underwriters have any solid control over investor enthusiasm. Any given underwriter probably cannot expect to promote a fad, and certainly not repeatedly, but may find it profitable to follow a standard policy of underpricing. Each "hot" market for IPO's is somewhat concentrated in a certain class of industries and a certain group of underwriters (Ritter, 1984). The 1980 hot market was dominated by Denver area underwriters of natural resource stocks. The 1983 hot market was dominated by different underwriters and by "high tech" stocks. Popular models vary from time to time, and only in certain situations are investors ready to believe and act enthusiastically on IPO investing.

4. Conclusion

The research on popular models reported here offers glimpses of the thought processes that underlie speculative booms and crashes. I think that the picture that begins to be revealed is a complicated one—not like any of the simple stories that have been told of speculative bubbles. While the popular models are often unsophisticated, there is a lot to be described about them. By analogy, one might note that to describe a so-called "primitive" language one must define many thousands of words and an elaborate grammatical system, a system that cannot be described without recourse to a network of rules and exceptions. Like languages, systems of popular models are learned through years of common discourse. Investing is an activity that generates a great deal of popular conversation and popular media attention.

The three case studies of research on popular models discussed above—the stock market crash, real estate boom, and IPO underpricing cases—illustrate this complexity, in revealing how popular models differ across speculative markets and through time. At the same time, the case studies are also suggestive of some common tendencies among popular models.

For example, investors often thought that investor psychology was what was driving markets, although the incidence of this popular model was much lower in real estate markets. Apparently, certain market characteristics encourage the proliferation of this popular model.

As another example, the shortage illusion tends to arise in all real estate markets, but with substantially lower frequency in a market that has not undergone a boom in recent memory. Apparently the experience of a local real estate boom inclines people to a popular model that is responsible for the illusion.

Further research along these lines might accomplish a number of things. First, research can clarify and elaborate on the popular models already described here. All we have done here is tabulate responses to a few short questions. Different questions on the same topic may produce different answers. Wordings of questions may matter and circumstances may matter. Moreover, respondents may not mean what we think they mean and do not always answer truthfully. Economists can learn about what they really think by careful detective work using the same methods used here. As more data is collected along these lines, misinterpretations of their answers can be revealed by an apparent inconsistency in answers.

Second, further research can look at models at work in other situations, besides the very dramatic boom and bust situations studied here. People may have very different popular models in other times and markets.

Third, further research can look at how popular models change through time, how they diffuse through the population and how such changes are related with time series data on tangible economic variables.

References

CASE, KARL E., and ROBERT J. SHILLER. "The Behavior of Home Buyers in Boom and Post Boom Markets." *New England Economic Review*, November/December 1988, 29–46, reprinted in Robert Shiller, *Market Volatility*. Cambridge: M.I.T. Press, 1989, pp. 404–431.

CASE, KARL E., and ROBERT J. SHILLER. "The Efficiency of the Market for Single Family Homes." *American Economic Review*, March 1989, 79, 125–137.

IBBOTSON, ROGER G., JODY L. SINDELAR, and JAY R. RITTER. "Initial Public Offerings." *Journal of Applied Corporate Finance*, Summer 1988, 1, 37–45.

RITTER, JAY R. "The 'Hot Issue' Market of 1980." *Journal of Business*, April 1984, 57, 215–40.

ROCK, KEVIN. "Why New Issues Are Underpriced." *Journal of Financial Economics*, January/February 1986, 15, 187–212.

SECURITIES AND EXCHANGE COMMISSION, TRADING AND EXCHANGE DIVISION. *A Report on Stock Trading on the New York Stock Exchange on September 3, 1946*, reproduced, Securities and Exchange Commission, Washington, August 21, 1947.

SHILLER, ROBERT J. "Portfolio Insurance and Other Investor Fashions as Factors in the 1987 Stock Market Crash." In Fischer, Stanley, ed., *NBER Macroeconomics Annual 1988*. Cambridge: National Bureau of Economic Research, 1988.

SHILLER, ROBERT J., "Initial Public Offerings: Underpricing and Investor Behavior," unpublished paper, Yale Univeristy, 1989*a*.

SHILLER, ROBERT J. *Market Volatility*. Cambridge: M.I.T. Press, 1989*b*.

SHILLER, ROBERT J., FUMIKO KON-YA, and YOSHIRO TSUTSUI. "Investor Behavior in the October 1987 Stock Market Crash: The Case of Japan," Yale University, 1989, and forthcoming in *The Journal of Japanese and International Economics*.

TINIC, SEHA M. "Anatomy of Initial Public Offerings of Common Stock." *Journal of Finance*, September 1988, *43*, 789–822.

20

The Disposition to Sell Winners Too Early and Ride Losers Too Long

Theory and Evidence

HERSH M. SHEFRIN
and MEIR STATMAN

It has been well-known for over thirty years that individual decision makers do not behave in accordance with the axioms of expected utility theory. The famous Allais paradoxes (1953) have made this point abundantly clear. Recent work by Kahneman and Tversky (1979), Machina (1982), and others has sought to provide a theory which describes how decision makers actually behave when confronted with choice under uncertainty. One of the key findings by Kahneman and Tversky concerns decision makers whose recent gambling history reflects losses. They indicate that their

> analysis suggests that a person who has not made peace with his losses is likely to accept gambles that would be unacceptable to him otherwise (p. 287).

Kahneman and Tversky's finding was obtained in a controlled experimental situation. Economists tend to treat experimental evidence with some caution and are reluctant to conclude automatically that similar features will be exhibited in real-world market settings. Indeed, it is important to look at market behavior in order to ascertain whether such behavior patterns can be discerned in actual trading.

From: *The Journal of Finance,* vol. XL, no. 3, pp. 777–790. Reprinted by permission of the American Finance Association.

In this paper, we examine decisions to realize gains and losses in a market setting. Specifically, we focus attention on financial markets and seek to determine whether investors exhibit a reluctance to realize losses (disposition to "ride losers") even when the precepts of standard theory prescribe realization. In this respect, we draw on the work of Constantinides (1983), (1984), who has studied the character of a (normatively) optimal strategy for realizing gains and losses. This strategy is designed to exploit the fact that the U.S. tax code distinguishes between short-term gains (losses) which are taxed as ordinary income and long-term gains (losses) which are taxed at a lower rate. While the specific actions depend on the circumstances at hand, Constantinides' strategy generally requires immediate realization of any losses, whenever transaction costs are absent. When transaction costs exist, loss realization should follow a pattern in which the volume of realizations steadily increases, peaking in December, and then falling off drastically. Gains on medium and high variance stocks should be realized when they become long-term.

We will develop a positive theory of capital gain and loss realization in which investors tend to "sell winners too early and ride losers too long" relative to the prescriptions of Constantinides' normative theory. We shall refer to this as the "disposition effect."* The disposition effect is part of the general folklore about investing, yet does not arise within the standard neoclassical framework. Indeed, it does not even appear in the alternative positive theories of decision-making under uncertainty (Machina [1982], Chew [1983], and Chew and MacCrimmon [1979]).

The theoretical framework we employ is an extension of the behavioral model described in our earlier work on dividends (see Shefrin and Statman [1984]). That model has three major elements: prospect theory mental accounting; regret aversion; and self-control. This paper uses these same ideas to study the disposition effect. Each of these elements contributes something distinctive to the analysis. Prospect theory predicts a disposition to sell winners and ride losers when the proceeds realized are held, as opposed to being rolled over into another gamble. Its mental accounting component provides the structure under which the disposition effect holds when realization proceeds are reinvested in a "swap." Aversion to regret provides an important reason why investors may have difficulty realizing gains as well as losses. Finally, self-control is employed to explain the rationale for methods investors use to force themselves to realize losses. In addition, we introduce a fourth element,

---

* Schlarbaum, Lewellen, and Lease (1978) use the phrase "disposition to sell the winners and ride the losers."

the potential gain to be had from exploiting the Constantinides strategy, and consider its interaction with the other three. The theory that emerges should be understood as being descriptive (positive), as opposed to prescriptive (normative).

After presenting the elements of the theory in Section I, we introduce empirical evidence which casts some light on the prevalence of the disposition effect in practice. This is the subject of Section II. Section III contains some concluding remarks.

1. A Positive Theory of Selling Winners and Riding Losers

In this section, we proceed by setting out the main elements of the theory in sequence.

1.1 Prospect Theory

In a pioneering article, Kahneman and Tversky developed prospect theory as a descriptive theory of choice under uncertainty. Prospect theory suggests the hypothesis that investors display a disposition to sell winners and ride losers when standard theory suggests otherwise. This disposition emerges from a combination of several features. First, decision makers frame the choices before them in a particular way. Kahneman and Tversky refer to this as the "editing stage." Significantly, the editing phase frames all choices in terms of potential gains and/or losses relative to a fixed reference point. In the second stage (the "evaluation stage"), decision makers employ an S-shaped *valuation* function (meaning a utility function on the domain of gains and/or losses) which is concave in the gains region, and convex in the loss region. This reflects risk aversion in the domain of gains and risk seeking in the domain of losses.

To see how the disposition to sell winners and ride losers emerges in prospect theory, consider an investor who purchased a stock one month age for $50 and who finds that the stock is now selling at $40. The investor must now decide whether to realize the loss or hold the stock for one more period. To simplify the discussion, assume that there are no taxes or transaction costs. In addition, suppose that one of two equiprobable outcomes will emerge during the coming period: either the stock will increase in price by $10 or decrease in price by $10. According to prospect theory, our investor frames his choice as a choice between the following two lotteries:

A. Sell the stock now, thereby realizing what had been a $10 "paper loss".

B. Hold the stock for one more period, given 50–50 odds between losing an additional $10 or "breaking even."

Since the choice between these lotteries is associated with the convex portion of the S-shaped value function, prospect theory implies that B will be selected over A. That is, the investor will ride his losing stock.[1] An analogous argument demonstrates why prospect theory gives rise to a disposition to realize gains.

Given that the preference of B over A in the above discussion is strict, it follows that the investor would be willing to accept B even if the odds of breaking even were something less than 50–50. Of course were the odds in B to become sufficiently unfavorable, then the investor would prefer to realize the loss.[2]

1.2 Mental Accounting

While the preceding discussion of prospect theory explains the reluctance to sell a stock and realize a loss, it does not explain the reluctance to engage in a tax swap. To see why, consider an investor who believes that markets are efficient. Assume that this investor does not plan to dissave from his portfolio, and transaction costs are zero. Then this investor will only sell stocks to exploit the difference between short- and long-term tax rates. Suppose that this investor purchased a stock that experienced a price decline during the following month. Think about the following scenario. The IRS requires that thirty days pass before a stock can be repurchased, if the tax advantages stemming from it's sale are to be enjoyed. As is well known, wash sale regulations can be neturalized through a "swap" by replacing a stock sold for tax purposes (such as Chemical Bank) with a stock featuring an identical returns distribution (such as Citicorp). The crucial point here is that the swap reduces the investor's tax liability, and yet leaves him facing an equivalent gamble. Therefore, the tax swap offers an alternative which stochastically dominates the decision to continue holding Chemical Bank. It is this feature which underlies Constantinides' strategy.

Clearly, violations of dominance are suboptimal in standard theory. However, prospect theory does recognize that individuals may select

---

1. Commenting on this phenomenon, Kahneman and Tversky state: "The well known observation that the tendency to bet on long shots increases in the course of the betting day provides some support for the hypothesis that a failure to adapt to losses or to attain an expected gain induces risk seeking."

2. Prospect theory accords extra weight to trivial gambles which involve no risk. This feature is called *subcertainty* and reinforces the choice.

dominated lotteries. Kahneman and Tversky argue that the selection of dominated lotteries is not achieved knowingly, but is a consequence of a particular frame being employed which obscures the dominance property.

The discussion of prospect theory emphasizes the importance attached to the editing phase (framing) as well as to the location of the reference point. In order to provide a structure for the framing of gambles, consider the concept of *mental accounting*. The main idea underlying mental accounting is that decision makers tend to segregate the different types of gambles faced into separate accounts, and then apply prospect theoretic decision rules to each account by ignoring possible interaction.

Mental accounting also serves to explain why an investor is likely to refrain from readjusting his reference point for a stock. When the stock is purchased, a new mental account is opened. The natural reference point is the asset purchase price. A running score is then kept on this account indicating gains or losses relative to the purchase price. Recall the tax-motivated swap involving the stocks of Chemical Bank and Citibank. Consider how this swap might be framed. A normative frame (implicitly used in Constantinides) recognizes that there is no substantive difference between the returns distributions of the two stocks, only a difference in names (i.e., in form). However, a swap that involves selling the Chemical Bank stock at a loss, and using the proceeds to buy Citicorp, might be framed as *closing* the Chemical Bank mental account at a loss, and opening a Citicorp mental account. In a forthcoming study entitled "The Break Even Effect," Thaler and Johnson (1985) argue that decision makers encounter considerable difficulty in closing mental accounts at a loss.

In his manual for stock brokers, Gross (1982) describes many features which illustrate mental accounting. The following quotation illustrates his appreciation of the difficulty of loss realization.

Many clients, however, will not sell anything at a loss. They don't want to give up the hope of making money on a particular investment, or perhaps they want to get even before they get out. The "getevenitis" disease has probably wrought more destruction on investment portfolios than anything else. Rather than recovering to an original entry price, many investments plunge sickeningly to even deeper losses. Investors are also reluctant to accept and realize losses because the very act of doing so proves that their first judgment was wrong . . .

Investors who accept losses can no longer prattle to their loved ones, "Honey, it's only a paper loss. Just wait. It will come back." Investors who realize losses must admit their folly to the IRS, when they file that itemized tax return. For all those reasons and more, investors as a whole are reluctant to take losses, even when they felt that to do so is the right course of action . . .

When you suggest that the client close at a loss a transaction you originally recommended and invest the proceeds in another position you are currently recommending, *a real act of faith has to take place.* That act of faith can more easily be effected if you make use of some transitional words that I call "magic selling words."

The words that I consider to have magical power in the sense that they make for a more easy acceptance of a loss are these: *"Transfer your assets"* (p. 150; Emphasis added).

. . . The two separate transactions (moving out of the loss and moving into a new position) are made to flow together by the magic words "transfer your assets." The prospect thought he was making a single decision, switching one investment into another. He was not being asked to think in terms of selling XYZ and collecting the proceeds, then having to think of many different ways to reinvest the proceeds (pp. 150–152, emphasis added).

Gross' suggestion to "transfer your assets" seeks to overcome the major obstacle standing in the way of loss realization, namely, the need to close a mental account at a loss. A client who *transfers* his assets does not *close* his original mental account, and therefore does not have to come to terms with his loss. The "trick" of framing the transaction as a transfer (without a closure) is not an easy one, and Gross seems to suggest that it requires help (counselling) from an astute broker. This is why *an act of faith* has to take place, with the opening of a new mental account (Citicorp) without the closure of an old one (Chemical Bank) at a loss. In other words, the fundamental reluctance is not so much loss realization as the closure of a mental account at a loss. Note that the well-known practice of tax swaps serves to overcome the reluctance to close mental accounts at a loss.[3]

1.3 Seeking Pride and Avoiding Regret

In the above quotation, Gross suggests that investors may resist the realization of a loss because it stands as proof that their first judgment was wrong. Moreover, the regret at having erred may be exacerbated by

---

3. This discussion may also explain why investors insist on a swap during the year-end season, even though receiving the tax benefit only requires the sale of a losing stock. Peter Berstein indicated to us that in his experience, investors resist the suggestion to sell a losing stock and keep the proceeds in cash, rather than complete the swap, even when they agree that the market is likely to turn down.

having to admit the mistake to others (spouse, the IRS). This feature has been discussed by Thaler (1980), Kahneman and Tversky (1982), and Shefrin and Statman. Regret is an emotional feeling associated with the ex post knowledge that a different past decision would have fared better than the one chosen. The positive counterpart to regret is pride. While closing a stock account at a loss induces regret, closing at a gain induces pride.

The quest for pride and the avoidance of regret lead to a disposition to realize gains and defer losses. Yet as Kahneman, Tversky, and Thaler all argue, an asymmetry between the strength of pride and regret (regret is stronger) leads inaction to be favored over action. Consequently, investors who are prone to this bias may be reluctant to realize both gains and losses. For example, consider an investors who sells a particular stock, say GM, at a gain, but continues to monitor its progress. Should the price of GM continue to rise, then the initial feeling of pride will be tempered by the regret at having sold too quickly.

1.4 Self-Control

In a study of professional futures traders, Glick (1957) commented that the reluctance to realize losses constitutes a self-control problem. He states:

> [C]ontrary to the dictates of rationality, traders are very much prone to let their losses "ride" . . . At the same time traders frequently voice the view that when profits are involved they and their colleagues are more hasty to offset their position and to get out of the market with their profit. . . . "Small profits and large losses" is an expression often repeated by traders, emphasizing what they see as one aspect of their work problems . . . [I]t is the control of losses which constitutes the essential problem . . . It is likely that many of the ideas referred to in the above comments are best summarized by the notion of "self-control," and the feeling that losses become (and/or are) a problem to the degree that a trader is deficient in this personal quality. This notion, and the way in which it is considered an occupational problem, refers more to the *form* than to the *content* of decision making . . . (pp. 131–138).

In what respect is the disposition effect a self-control problem? To address this question, consider the Thaler-Shefrin (1981) framework which treats self-control as an intrapersonal (agency) conflict between a rational part (the planner or principal) and a more primitive, emotional, myopic part (the doer or agent). Because of the doer's strength in influencing individual action, the planner is seen as exhibiting willpower or employing precommitment devices. To adapt the planner-doer model to an analysis of the disposition effect, let doer utility be a function of the status of the various mental accounts. In our view, investors ride losers to postpone regret, and sell winners "too quickly" because they want to hasten the feeling of pride at having chosen correctly in the past. Thus, it is the doer which embodies the emotional reactions associated with regret and pride. For reasons discussed in Thaler and Shefrin, the (rational) planner may not be strong enough to prevent the (emotional) reactions of the doer from interfering with rational decision making. For example, the traders studied by Glick were clearly aware that riding losers was not rational. Their problem was to exhibit sufficient self-control to close accounts at a loss, thereby limiting losses!

Investors (or their planners) use a variety of precommitment techniques to control their doers' resistance to realizing losses. Here are some examples. Professional traders often adhere to iron-clad rules that mandate the realization of a loss, once it reaches a predetermined percentage (e.g., ten percent) of the original purchase price. The following excerpt from a professional trader (quoted in Kleinfield [1983]) illustrates the technique and its rationale.

> I have a hard and fast rule that I never let my losses on a trade exceed ten percent. Say I buy a ten-dollar stock. As soon as it goes to nine dollars, I must sell it and take a loss. Some guys have a five per cent rule. Some may have fifteen. I'm a ten man. The thing is, when you're right you're making eighths and quarters. So you can't take a loss of a point. The traders who get wiped out hope against hope. I've seen a good hundred come and go since I've been here in 1964. They're stubborn. They refuse to take losses . . . When you're breaking in a new trader, the hardest thing to learn is to admit that you're wrong. It's a hard pill to swallow. You have to be man enough to admit to your peers that you're wrong and get out. Then you're alive and playing the game the next day (pp. 17, 18, and 30).

Stop-loss orders provide another example. These are usually promoted as devices to limit risk, but their main advantages may be in allowing an investor to make loss realization at a predetermined point automatic.

There may also be particular times and circumstances in which investors find that less willpower is needed in order to realize a loss. For instance, realizing a loss in order to fund an emergency medical expenditure or a child's tuition payment may be easier than realizing a loss for tax purposes alone. In fact, while some emergencies are real, others may be contrived to render tax-loss selling less difficult. December 31 constitutes a case in point. Tax-motivated transactions at year-end have generated much interest in recent years. Most of the existing work focuses on the relationship between year-end selling and the seasonality in stock returns (see Branch [1977], Keim [1983], and Givoly and Ovadia [1983]). However, some work focuses specifically on the volume of trading in the month of December relative to the volume of trading year round. In particular, Dyl (1977) examined the volume of trading in the month of December relative to the volume of trading in other months. He has found that

> . . . there is significant abnormal trading volume in December in common stocks that have undergone a substantial price change during the preceding year. The data reveal abnormally low volume for stocks that have appreciated during the year, presumably reflecting the year-end capital gains tax lock-in effect, and abnormally high volume for stocks that have declined in price during the year, presumably reflecting year-end tax loss selling" (p. 174).

Constantinides has argued that concentrated tax-loss selling will occur in December when transaction costs exist, and this is consistent with Dyl's evidence. However, we shall argue that standard theory provides no basis for this finding. Rather, we postulate that concentrated December tax-loss selling reflects a self-control strategy. The argument is as follows:

In the presence of transaction costs, Constantinides' results predict heavy December tax-loss selling for stocks purchased during the preceding July. However, what about stocks purchased after that, such as in November? Given that the short-term period for such a stock extends beyond the following December 31, it is not at all clear that Constantinides' theory predicts December tax-loss selling for this stock. In fact, it seems that, if anything, his theory predicts that any such selling would largely occur during the subsequent April because the six-month period for November purchases expires in May. According to this reasoning, Constantinides' theory would explain December tax-loss selling only if stock purchases were concentrated in July.

Since a regular concentration of purchases in July seems unlikely, we are led to ask: What is the rationale for a heavier volume of loss realizations in December than in other months? Indeed, empirical evidence suggests that the volume of loss realization is higher in December. Constantinides (as well as Branch, Givoly and Ovadia, Dyl, and Keim, all cited earlier) seem to believe that this feature is consistent with rational behavior, presumably because it is better for an investor to take a loss "this year" rather than "next year" because of the additional (year's) interest involved.

However, we believe that December has no special role in models based upon rational behavior. Consider the following. A rational individual wage earner (or a self-employed individual) can be expected to forecast his income and deductions at the beginning of the year, and set the number of exemptions (or estimated tax payments) accordingly.[4] A rational individual would consider the realization of losses expected during the year, and increase his exemptions. This way, the tax benefits of these realizations would accrue *early* in the year, because less tax would be withheld, rather than after the following April 15. Loss realizations would be concentrated close to the six-month deadline in accordance with Constantinides' analysis. As December comes along the rational individual may find that he has underpaid his taxes because he has realized fewer losses than his earlier forecast, possibly because the stock market went up unexpectedly during the year. He may wish to realize losses on stocks bought in October or November before the end of the year to bring his tax liability in line with his tax withholdings. However, why would a rational individual be expected to overestimate *consistently* the opportunities for loss realization available during the year? Does learning not take place? Moreover, this individual can change, with only a little trouble, the number of exemptions during the year. Therefore, the tax rebate that accompanies low realization arrives almost immediately in the form of lower tax withholding.[5]

Consider the contrast between the rational individual in Constantinides' theory and the individual in our behavioral framework. Like the rational individual, the individual in our framework is aware of the tax consequences of gain and loss realization. The desire of our individual to take advantage of these tax laws is no less than that of the rational individual. However, our individual is affected by elements of mental accounting, regret aversion, and self-control that do not affect a rational individual. Because of its *perceived* deadline characteristic, our individual regards December as significant for tax planning. For instance, financial service firms frequently remind investors about the importance of not leaving tax planning decisions until December. We conjecture that tax planning in general, and loss realization in particular, is disagreeable and requires self-control. Should this be the case, then it is reasonable to

---

4. This remark needs to be qualified by taking account of IRS requirements on minimum withholding rates as a function of the previous year's income.

5. This argument is reinforced by the strong tendency of individuals to overwithhold on their income tax (see Thaler and Shefrin [1981]). After all, why is it so important to claim the loss on *this* year's return, when too much is being deducted for tax purposes (and interest is being foregone) anyway?

expect that self-motivation is easier in December than other months because of its perceived deadline characteristic. Thus, a concentration of loss realizations in December is consistent with our behavioral framework, but inconsistent with Constantinides' rational individual.

In the next section, we shall consider empirical evidence concerning the above issues. Our specific concern is to test whether available data conform with Constantinides' original predictions, or suggest that his predictions should be modified to reflect a disposition to sell winners and ride losers.

2. Empirical Evidence

In this section, we consider empirical evidence pertaining to our theory. This evidence concerns the time that passes between the point when an investor buys a stock and the point when he sells it. Our major interest is in ascertaining whether investors time the realization of their losses differently from their realization of gains, and if so what the nature of the difference is. In this respect, observe that tax considerations suggest that losses should be realized while they are short-term, while gains should be realized only when they are long-term. However, the disposition to sell winners too early and ride losers too long operates in the opposite direction. Consequently, the major questions concern the strength of the two effects, taken both separately and together. To address these questions, we shall make use of data drawn from two sources. The first source is a study by Schlarbaum et al. (1978) dealing with the stock trading history of individual investors, where transaction costs exist. The second source is aggregate data on mutual fund trades, where transaction costs are negligible.

In analyzing the empirical evidence, we take note of the fact that the investors studied are likely to be composed of heterogeneous clienteles. For example, some investors may realize losses soon after they occur throughout the year, and encounter no difficulty in doing so. Others may be aware of the tax benefits from realizing losses quickly, but be unable to exploit them because of the disposition effect. These investors sell winners too early and ride losers too long. Still a third group may find it difficult to sell securities, be it for gain or loss. In this last respect, Feldstein and Yitzhaki (1978, p. 25) point out that more than half of all stockholders in their sample did not sell any stock in their study period of 1963–1964. This same feature has been found by Blume and Friend (1978, p. 67), who note that fully half of all stockholding families that had ever bought or sold mutual fund shares did not engage in such transactions over the period 1973–1975.

We begin with Schlarbaum et al. who provide panel information about individual trades by selected investors between 1964 and 1970. Their article describes the data set in detail and uses this set to analyze realized returns on common stock investments. A *round trip duration* denotes the length of time that an investor holds a stock before selling it. Consider a partition of the trades in the authors' data set according to round trip duration. In particular consider these categories: one month or less; one month to six months; and six months to one year. Significantly, the authors found that no matter which value for round trip duration they selected, approximately forty percent of all realizations corresponded to losses. What inferences does this finding suggest about the hypothesis that realizations are predominantly tax-motivated as opposed to an alternative hypothesis in which realizations are tempered by the disposition effect?

Suppose that investors trade primarily to take advantage of the tax option discussed by Constantinides and are not subject to the disposition effect. Then, we should find that few gains are realized when they are short-term. This is because of two reasons. First, the tax rate on such gains is high, and second, transaction costs involved in frequent trading serve to discourage realization. Thus, the number of transactions where a gain is realized should be very low for round trip durations of six months or less. However, gains on high and medium variance stocks should be realized as soon as they become long-term. So, the number of realizations of gains during the seven- to twelve-month duration category should be high. See column 1 of Table 1. Realization of a loss within the first month is advantageous from the tax perspective, but transaction costs will serve to deter it, so the number of such realizations would be "average." However, as the short-term deadline nears, we should find that losses are realized lest they become long-term. So, the number of loss realizations for the two-to-six-month round trip duration category should be high. Few losses should be left to realize in the seven-to-twelve-month category. See column 2 of Table 1. This implies that the ratio of the number of transactions where a gain is realized to all transactions should display a pattern where it is low for the less-than-one-month category, very low for the two-to-six-month category, and high for the seven-to-twelve month category. See column 3 of Table 1. Is this what the Schlarbaum et al. data show? The answer is no. Schlarbaum et al. found no significant differences in the ratios associated with the three duration categories. Roughly speaking, forty percent of the realizations in every category correspond to losses (see column 4 of Table 1).

What are we to conclude from this? One possible inference is that tax-induced trades form a minor portion of all trades. (It might well

Table 1 Expected Capital Gain and Loss Realizations Under the Assumption that Trades are Primarily Motivated by the Tax Option in Contrast with Actual Realizations Data

	Expected Capital Gain and Loss Realizations Under the Assumption that Trades are Primarily Motivated by the Tax Option			Actual Capital Gain and Loss Realizations in the Schlarbaum et al. Sample
Round-Trip Duration (Months)	(1) No. of Transactions where a Gain is Realized	(2) No. of Transactions where a Loss is Realized	(3) Ratio of the No. of Transactions where a Gain is realized to All Realizations	(4) Ratio of the No. of Transactions where a Gain is Realized to All Realizations
0–1	Very low	Average	Low	0.58
2–6	Very low	High	Very low	0.57
7–12	High	Low	High	0.59

be that most trades are motivated by considerations of liquidity and/or information.) Another possible inference is that the significant contribution of investors who engage in tax-motivated trades is offset by those who typify the disposition effect. However, it cannot be argued that investors are ignorant of the tax option, since we know from Dyl and others that investors are generally aware of this tax option.

We turn next to the analysis of evidence on the realizations of gains and losses in mutual funds. Mutual funds provide a very useful vehicle for analysis because the realization of gains and losses is possible with negligible transaction costs. Data on purchases and redemptions of mutual fund shares were provided to us by the Investment Company Institute (1983), the trade organization of mutual funds. The institute classifies funds into three categories by the method of distribution, or sale, of the fund shares; Broker/Dealer, Direct Sellers, and No-Load funds.[6]

The Investment Company Institute publishes an annual Statistical Workbook that contains data on monthly purchases and redemptions of mutual fund shares separated according to the three fund classifications discussed earlier. We have used monthly data from January 1961 through December 1981, a total of 252 months. We have used only data from January 1961 through December 1973 for No-Load funds.[7]

The data we have are aggregate monthly purchases and redemptions

---

6. Broker/Dealer funds, such as the family of funds by Massachusetts Financial Services (e.g., Massachusetts Investors Trust, Massachusetts Investors Growth Stock, Massachusetts Income Development funds, etc.) act as wholesalers sponsored by brokers and dealers who act as retailers, selling the fund shares to investors. Brokers and dealers receive a commission, or load charge, of up to 8.5 percent of the amount invested in the fund. Direct Seller funds (such as the family of funds by John Hancock advisers (e.g., John Hancock Bond Fund, John Hancock Cash Management Trust, John Hancock Growth Fund, etc.) combine the functions of wholesaler and retailer. They employ their own sales force and charge commissions similar to those of Broker/Dealer funds. No-Load funds, such as the family of funds by Vanguard Group Inc. (e.g., Vanguard Index Trust, Vanguard Municipal Bond, Wellington Funds, etc.) do not charge any sales commission. They are sold directly to investors who contact the fund. Purchases and redemption of No-Load funds do not involve commissions. Broker/Dealer and Direct Seller funds actually offer possibilities that are similar to those of No-Load funds for the purpose of switching from fund to fund. Generally, the sales commission has to be paid only with the initial purchase into a particular family of funds. Subsequent switching to another fund of the same family can be made either at no cost or at a minimal fee (typically $5). Thus, all three types of funds offer the possibility of free (or practically free) switching from fund to fund.

7. Post-1973 data includes money market funds, and these have characteristics that make them more similar to an interest-bearing checking account than to other mutual funds. Specifically, the accounting methods used for most money market funds are such that a loss (due to an increase in interest rates) is impossible because they use an accrual method rather than a mark-to-market method.

for each of the three fund categories. We do not have data for transactions by individual investors (as in the Schlarbaum et al. study) or even fund by fund data in purchases and redemptions. However, we believe that significant inferences can still be drawn from aggregate data.

We also need data on monthly capital gains and losses. We have used the figures for capital appreciation of common stock from Ibbottson and Sinquefield (1982, Exhibit B-3). The assumption used is that, in aggregate, the capital appreciation of mutual funds will closely follow the appreciation of the market as a whole.

Consider the ratio of redemptions (dollar amounts) of a fund in month t, say February, to purchases (dollar amounts) of the fund in the preceding month. If trades are primarily motivated by the tax option, we should find that losses in January and February would induce the January purchasers to redeem in February. Similarly, gains in January and February would deter January purchasers from redeeming in February. Therefore, we would expect a high level of the ratio when losses occur, and a low level when gains occur. We begin our analysis with No-Load funds. We have selected sixty observations, thirty corresponding to the highest gains, and thirty corresponding to the highest losses. Our rationale for focusing on these two groups is as follows. Gains (losses) were calculated in three ways: (1) gain in month t only; (2) gain in month $t - 1$ only; and (3) gain in months $t - 1$ through t. These three ways were used because we do not know the exact time during the month when a purchase or redemption was made. We note that the mean one-month gain and loss in our groups is greater than five percent, a significant amount. What do the data show? The mean ratio of redemptions to purchases associated with gains is higher than the mean ratio associated with losses in two of the three cases, although the differences between the means are not statistically significant. Similar comments apply to the Broker/Dealer funds and the Direct Sellers funds (see Table 2). These results are virtually the same as the findings on stock trading discussed above, and the same conclusions therefore apply.

3. Conclusions

One of the most significant and unique features in Kahneman and Tversky's approach to choice under uncertainty is aversion to loss realization. This paper is concerned with two aspects of this feature. First, we place this behavior pattern into a wider theoretical framework concerning a general disposition to sell winners too early and hold losers too long. This framework includes other elements, namely regret aversion, self-control, and tax considerations. Significantly, we argue that the tendency to con-

Table 2 Mutual Funds Redemption Ratios Associated with Capital Gains and Capital Losses

	Mean Ratios of Redemptions (Dollar Amounts) in Month t to Purchases (Dollar Amounts) in Month $t - 1$ in the Capital Gains Group, $\bar{X}_G$, and in the Capital Losses Group $\bar{X}_L$*		t-Statistic of the Difference between $\bar{X}_G$ and $\bar{X}_L$**	Mean of Capital Gains (Percent) in the Capital Gains Group and Mean Capital Losses (Percent) in the Capital Losses Group.	
	Capital Gains	Capital Losses		Capital Gains	Capital Losses
No-load, Funds (January 1961–December 1973)					
Capital gains or losses in month $t - 1$ only	0.53 (0.18)	0.53 (0.23)	−0.09	5.2	−5.3
Capital gains or losses in month t only	0.61 (0.25)	0.53 (0.19)	1.32	5.1	−5.3
Capital gains or losses in months t and $t - 1$	0.62 (0.25)	0.59 (0.21)	0.42	7.8	−7.4
Broker-Dealer Funds (January 1961–December 1981)					
Capital gains or losses in month $t - 1$ only	0.93 (0.50)	0.74 (0.34)	1.69***	7.0	−6.9
Capital gains or losses in month t only	0.90 (0.47)	0.86 (0.42)	0.39	7.0	−6.8
Capital gains or losses in months t and $t - 1$	0.92 (0.49)	0.91 (0.43)	0.04	9.9	−9.9
Direct-Seller Funds (January 1961–December 1981)					
Capital gains or losses in month $t - 1$ only	0.92 (0.55)	0.66 (0.43)	1.62	7.0	−6.9
Capital gains or losses in month t only	0.86 (0.49)	0.79 (0.44)	0.43	7.0	−6.8
Capital gains or losses in months t and $t - 1$	0.90 (0.50)	0.84 (0.46)	0.47	9.9	−9.9

*The thirty ratio observations with the highest capital gains are in the capital gains group. The thirty ratio observations with the highest capital losses are in the capital losses group. Standard deviations are in parentheses.

**The hypothesis tested is H_0: $\bar{X}_G = \bar{H}_L$ H_1: $\bar{X}_G > \bar{X}_L$. The t-statistic was calculated as

$$t = \frac{\bar{X}_G - \bar{X}_L}{\sqrt{\dfrac{N_G S_G^2 + N_L S_L^2}{N_G + N_L - 2}}} \sqrt{\frac{N_G N_L}{N_G + N_L}}$$

where $N_G = N_L = 30$, and S_G and S_L are the standard deviations of the ratios of redemptions in the capital gains and capital losses groups, respectively.

***Denotes statistically significant at the 0.05 level.

centrate loss realizations in December is not normatively based; however, it is consistent with our descriptive theory. Second, we discuss evidence which suggests that this disposition shows up in real-world financial markets, not just in contrived laboratory experiments. In particular, we find that tax considerations alone cannot explain the observed patterns of loss and gain realization, and that the patterns are consistent with a combined effect of tax considerations and a disposition to sell winners and ride losers. Our conclusion can be taken only as tentative. There is a clear need to analyze more detailed data on loss and gain realization. Such data may be available from the IRS and from the Purdue observations on individual investor behavior. In addition, it will also be important to look at other reasons for realization: examples include consumption and trading on information (public or private).

While this paper has focused upon stocks and mutual funds, the general tendency to treat sunk costs as relevant has much wider application. For example, both corporate managers and shareholders are well aware of a tendency "to throw good money after bad" by continuing to operate losing ventures in the hope that a recovery will somehow take place. The case of Lockheed's decision to terminate (finally!) its well-known L-1011 white elephant was greeted with joy by the investment community. The price of Lockheed stock jumped 18 percent in the day following the formal announcement of cancellation. Other examples abound.

We would like to acknowledge the helpful remarks made on earlier versions by Peter Bernstein, Fischer Black, Ben Branch, Ivan Brick, Werner De Bondt, Edward Dyl, Avner Kalay, Seymour Smidt, and Richard Thaler. Special thanks go to George Constantinides whose incisive discussion led to major improvements that are reflected in this version of the paper. We retain full responsibility for all errors.

References

ALLAIS, M. "Le Comprtement de l'Homme Rationnel devant le Risque, Critique des Postulats et Axiomes de l'Ecole Americaine." *Econometrica* 21 (October 1953), 503–46.

BLUME, MARSHALL E. and IRWIN FRIEND. *The Changing Role of the Individual Investor.* New York: John Wiley & Sons, 1978.

BRANCH, BEN. "A Tax Loss Trading Rule." *Journal of Business* 50 (April 1977), 198–207.

CHEW, SOO HONG. "A Generalization of the Quasilinear Mean with Applications to the Measurement of Income Inequality and Decision Theory Resolving the Allais Paradox." *Econometrica* 51 (July 1983), 1065–92.

CHEW, S. H. and K. R. MacCRIMMON. "Alpha-Nu Choice Theory: A Generalization of Expected Utility Theory." University of British Columbia Faculty of Commerce and Business Administration Working Paper No. 669, 1979.

CONSTANTINIDES, GEORGE M. "Capital Market Equilibrium with Personal Tax." *Econometrica* 51 (May 1983), 611–36.

———. "Optimal Stock Trading with Personal Taxes: Implications for Prices and the Abnormal January Returns." *Journal of Financial Economics* 13 (March 1984), 65–89.

DYL, EDWARD A. "Capital Gains Taxation and Year-End Stock Market Behavior." *Journal of Finance* 32 (March 1977), 165–75.

FELDSTEIN, MARTIN and SHLOMO YITZHAKI. "The Effects of the Capital Gains Tax on the Selling and Switching of Common Stock." *Journal of Public Economics* 9 (February 1978), 17–36.

GIVOLY, DAN and ARIE OVADIA. "Year-End Tax-Induced Sales and Stock Market Seasonality." *Journal of Finance* (March 1983), 171–85.

GLICK, IRA. "A Social Psychological Study of Futures Trading." Ph.D. Dissertation, University of Chicago, 1957.

GROSS, LEROY. 'The Art of Selling Intangibles: How to Make your Million($) by Investing Other People's Money." New York Institute of Finance, New York, 1982.

IBBOTTSON, ROGER G. and REX A. SINQUEFIELD. "Stocks, Bonds, Bills and Inflation: The Past and the Future." The Financial Analysis Research Foundation, Charlottesville, Virginia, 1982.

Investment Company Institute. *1983 Statistical Workbook.* Washington, D.C., 1983.

KAHNEMAN, D. and A. TVERSKY. "Prospect Theory: An Analysis of Decision Under Risk." *Econometrica* 47 (March 1979), 263–91.

———. "The Psychology of Preferences." *Scientific American* 246 (February 1982), 167–73.

KEIM, DONALD B. "Size-Related Anomalies and Stock Return Seasonality: Further Empirical Evidence." *Journal of Financial Economics* 12 (June 1983), 13–32.

KLEINFIELD, SONNY. *The Traders.* New York: Holt, Rinehart and Winston, 1983.

MACHINA, MARK. "Expected Utility Analysis Without the Independence Axiom." *Econometrica* 50 (March 1982), 277–323.

SCHLARBAUM, GARY G., WILBUR G. LEWELLEN, and RONALD C. LEASE. "Realized Returns on Common Stock Investments: The Experience of Individual Investors." *Journal of Business* (April 1978), 299–325.

SHEFRIN, HERSH M. and MEIR STATMAN. "Explaining Investor Preference for Cash Dividends." *Journal of Financial Economics* 13 (June 1984), 253–82.

THALER, R. "Toward a Positive Theory of Consumer Choice." *Journal of Economic Behavior and Organization* 1 (March 1980), 39–60.

THALER, R. "Using Mental Accounting in a Theory of Consumer Behavior." Working Paper, Cornell University, 1984.

THALER, R. and H. SHEFRIN. "An Economic Theory of Self-Control." *Journal of Political Economy* 89 (April 1981), 392–410.

THALER, RICHARD and ERIC JOHNSON. "The Break Even Effect." Forthcoming working paper, 1985.

21

The Failure
of Competition in the
Credit Card Market

LAWRENCE M. AUSUBEL

This article presents and discusses a collection of data which is paradoxical within the paradigm of perfect competition. The market studied, the bank credit card industry in the United States, contains literally 4,000 firms who sell a relatively homogeneous good to 75 million consumers. The ten largest firms account for only about two-fifths of market share. Firms have historically operated without regulatory barriers to conducting business across state lines—and at least 20 firms aggressively solicit business on a national scale. Firms have also operated in the virtual absence of price regulations for most of a decade. There do not appear to be any particularly constrained inputs, significant sunk costs, or significant barriers to entry. Finally, there is no evidence of any explicit collusion on price or quantity.

Given such a favorable market description, or one not even half so optimistic, many economists would prefer to presume that the market must behave as a competitive spot market in continuous equilibrium. It is the purpose of this article to argue that this presumption is empirically unjustified in the market for bank credit cards in the 1980's. Section 1 outlines the market structure of the bank credit card industry. Section 2 offers empirical evidence of extreme price stickiness in credit card interest rates. Section 3 provides direct profit data on the industry, arguing that the 50 largest credit card issuers have earned from three to five times the ordinary rate of return for the banking industry during the

From: *American Economic Review*, vol. 81, No. 1, pp. 50–81, March 1991. Reprinted by permission of the American Economic Association.

period 1983–1988. Section 4 examines profits over a larger sample of banks and a longer time period. Section 5 presents additional data on resales of credit card portfolios between banks, suggesting that the extraordinary profits exist *ex ante* as well as *ex post* (and that bankers expect the profitability to persist). Section 6 explores some theoretical explanations for price stickiness and supra-normal profits. Section 7 calculates what would be "competitive" interest rates. Section 8 briefly discusses the extent of welfare loss in the market and the merits of regulation to correct market failure. Conclusions are presented in Section 9.

1. The Bank Credit Card Market: Is 4,000 Enough for Competition?

Credit cards are the currency of late 20th-century America. The aggregate charge volume on plastic in the United States was estimated at $375 billion in 1987.[1] Almost half of this total—$165 billion in volume—was charged on MasterCard and Visa credit cards (the primary focus of this article), and volume was growing at well over 10 percent per year.[2] The remaining volume arose largely from similar credit cards (e.g., the Discover and Optima cards), "travel and entertainment" cards (e.g., the American Express card), and retail cards (e.g., department store and oil company cards).

Borrowing via credit cards (and all consumer borrowing) is also significant and has been even more of a growth industry. Outstanding U.S. balances on revolving credit accounts equaled $203 billion at year-end 1989, up from only $70 billion in 1982.[3] More than $130 billion of this total consisted of MasterCard and Visa balances, more than a threefold increase from 1982, and bank card balances were still increasing at more than a 15-percent annual rate.[4] Overall outstanding consumer installment credit balances in the United States reached $717 billion, up from $356

---

1. Moreover, Americans were estimated to have made 9.1 billion credit card transactions in 1987 (*The Nilson Report*, Number 428, May 1988, p. 5).

2. U.S. volume in 1987 consisted of $138 billion in sales slips (i.e., charged goods and services) and $27 billion in cash advances. Visa accounted for 59 percent of this value and MasterCard accounted for the remaining 41 percent. (*The Nilson Report*, Number 422, February 1988, p. 6, and Number 423, March 1988, pp. 4–5).

3. Federal Reserve Board's series of Consumer Installment Credit, as published in *Federal Reserve Bulletin*, April 1990, table 1.55, line 15 (and previous issues).

4. *Federal Reserve Bulletin*, April 1990, table 1.55, lines 16, 19, and 21. Revolving credit held by commercial banks, savings institutions, and pools of securitized assets consists almost entirely of MasterCard and Visa balances.

billion in 1982;[5] it is worth observing that many of the considerations explicitly discussed here in connection with the credit card industry apply also to other forms of consumer borrowing (especially other unsecured credit).

If Visa and MasterCard were the relevant levels of business to examine, then two firms would control a substantial part of the credit card market. However, most relevant business decisions are made at the level of the issuing bank. Individual banks own their cardholders' accounts and determine the interest rate, annual fee, grace period, credit limit, and other terms of the accounts. (Only charges such as the "interchange fee" from the merchant's bank to the cardholder's bank are standardized, and the cardholder's bank appears only to break even on such charges. Moreover, there is absolutely no indication that the MasterCard and Visa organizations serve to facilitate collusion on other prices.[6]) In essence, MasterCard International and Visa U.S.A. are organizations largely irrelevant to this discussion; "firms" will henceforth refer to the issuing banks.

The market for MasterCard and Visa cards, thus, is relatively unconcentrated. The top ten firms control only about two-fifths of the market, and the next ten firms control only one-tenth of the market (see Table 1). Moreover, the market is exceptionally broad. A bank that ranked number 100 in 1987 still had approximately 160,000 active accounts, $125 million in outstanding balances, and $250 million in annual charge volume.[7]

Unlike most aspects of American banking, the credit card business has historically operated free of interstate banking and branch banking restrictions. Indeed, the largest issuers today conduct truly national businesses. For example, Maryland Bank (ranked number seven in Table 1) conducts business in all 50 states and has only five percent of its accounts in its home state.[8] The only states where more than five percent of its

---

5. *Federal Reserve Bulletin*, April 1990, table 1.55, line 1 (and previous issues).

6. Moreover, the observed interest rate behavior does not seem to fit the conventional view of collusive pricing. Around 1985, three major issuers (Chase Manhattan, Manufacturers Hanover, and Maryland Bank) reduced their interest rates on standard cards to the 17.5–17.9-percent range. Far from this triggering an industry price war, other major issuers (e.g., Citibank and First Chicago) steadfastly maintained 19.8-percent rates on most accounts, without apparent detriment to their customer bases. Finally, in the spring of 1989, the three price-cutters announced rate increases, apparently finding *without facing retaliation* that the earlier cuts had been unprofitable (*The New York Times*, April 27, 1989, p. 32; *Wall Street Journal*, March 22, 1989, p. B1).

7. *The Nilson Report*, Number 406 (June 1987), p. 7.

8. "Prospectus for Maryland Bank, N.A., Credit Card Trust 1987-A," December 9, 1987, pp. 17–18.

Table 1 Top Ten Issuers of MasterCard and Visa Cards, 1987

Bank	Number of Accounts	Percentage Market Share (by number of accounts)	Outstanding Balances ($ billion)	Percentage Market Share (by outstanding balances)
Citibank	10,000,000	8.4	$15.3B	16.3
Chase Manhattan Bank	5,000,000	4.2	$5.4B	5.8
Bank of America	4,800,000	4.0	$5.2B	5.5
First Chicago	4,500,000	3.8	$4.6B	4.9
Manufacturers Hanover	3,300,000	2.8	$2.0B	2.1
Wells Fargo Bank	1,800,000	1.5	$2.8B	3.0
Maryland Bank	1,800,000	1.5	$1.7B	1.8
Marine Midland Bank	1,700,000	1.4	$1.4B	1.5
Chemical Bank	1,500,000	1.3	$1.3B	1.4
Associates National Bank	1,200,000	1.0	$1.0B	1.1
Top ten	35,600,000	30.0	$40.7B	43.4
Second ten	11,500,000	9.7	$9.0B	9.6
Total	118,900,000	100.0	$93.9B	100.0

Sources: Individual banks' numbers of accounts surveyed by *American Banker,* (March 1, 1988, pp. 1–2) and *Credit Card News* (August 15, 1988, pp. 4–16); total number of accounts from *Nilson Report* (Number 406 [June 1987], p. 4). Individual banks' outstanding balances based on *American Banker* (September 21, 1987, p. 43 [call report data]) and *Nilson Report* (Number 406 [June 1987], pp. 4–5); total outstanding balances from *Federal Reserve Bulletin* (December 1988, table 1.55; revolving credit outstanding at commercial banks and savings institutions, minus loans outstanding at Greenwood Trust Co. [Discover card] and American Express Centurion Bank). Data reported for December 31, 1986, adjusted for acquisitions effective in 1987. Conflicts between sources were resolved using best available information.

business is concentrated are California (10.7 percent), Texas (6.7 percent), Pennsylvania (6.0 percent), and New Jersey (5.8 percent).

In the past, credit card issuers were constrained by state usury laws. However, the U.S. Supreme Court's December 1978 *Marquette* decision paved the way for the practical elimination of price regulations.[9] The Court held that only the usury ceiling of the state in which the bank is located, and not that of the state in which the consumer is located, restricts the interest rate the bank may charge. This gave banks the option of shifting their credit card operations to wholly owned subsidiaries situated in states without usury laws. By 1982, amid *Marquette*-created bank pressure and historically high market interest rates, most leading banking states had relaxed or repealed their interest rate ceilings. Meanwhile, South Dakota and Delaware had established themselves as attractive homes-away-from-home for credit card issuers. While a number of states maintain binding usury laws at this writing (most notably, Arkansas, with a ceiling of five percentage points above the Federal Reserve discount rate), essentially all major issuers can pursue business in those states free of restriction. It is fair to say that the bank credit card market in the United States was functionally deregulated in 1982.

2. Credit Card Interest Rate Behavior

2.1 Sticky Interest Rates

The cost of funds is obviously the primary determinant of the marginal cost of lending via credit cards, and it is usually the only component of marginal cost that varies widely from quarter to quarter. Thus, a model of continuous spot market equilibrium would predict a substantial degree of connection between the interest rate charged on credit cards and the banks' cost of funds. However, Figure 1, which compares credit card interest rates with the cost of funds, displays stark empirical rejection of this prediction. Credit card interest rates were highly sticky during the period 1982–1989 and, in fact, were virtually constant.[10]

---

9. *Marquette National Bank* v. *First of Omaha Service Corporation*, 439 U.S. 299 (1978). The *Marquette* decision applies to credit cards issued by nationally chartered banks, but not to retail cards (e.g., oil company credit cards). The decision explicitly permits banks to "export" their interest rates; banks have interpreted this also to permit the "export" of annual fees and other customer fees. At this writing, at the behest of the Iowa Attorney General, courts are considering whether this rule does indeed apply to fees.

10. Indeed, the highest value reported in the *Federal Reserve Bulletin* series in the period 1982–1989 is 18.85 percent (first quarter, 1985) and the lowest value reported is 17.77 percent (fourth quarter, 1988).

Figure 1 Sticky Credit Card Interest Rates, 1982–1989

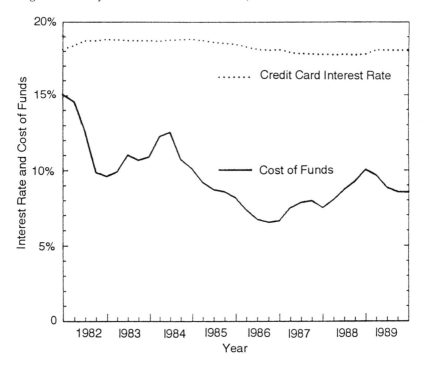

Notes: Credit card interest rate is the quarterly Federal Reserve System series; cost of funds is the quarterly one-year Treasury bill yield plus 0.75 percent.

In this section, credit card interest rates are captured by two distinct sets of data: one aggregated and one disaggregated. The first set of data is the *Federal Reserve Bulletin* series for credit card interest rates, based on the Federal Reserve Board's quarterly survey of banks. Reported are arithmetic averages of each bank's "most common" rate charged during the first week of each mid-quarter month.[11] This series is plotted in Figure 1. The second set of data (and much of the empirical discussion of this and the next section) is derived from the author's own bank credit card survey (BCCS) of 58 of the largest bank issuers of credit cards. The first mailing (21 responses) asked primarily for pricing and cost data; it generated a quarterly interest rate series for 17 credit card issuers and an annual loan-loss series for 10 issuers. The follow-up mailing (11 responses)

11. Federal Reserve Board's G.19 statistical release, April 5, 1990; *Federal Reserve Bulletin*, April 1990, table 1.56, line 4 (and previous issues).

included a request for direct profit calculations, which were provided by seven banks. Appendix A provides details of the construction of the BCCS. Table 2 includes the size distribution of banks that reported data. Respondents were promised anonymity.

The most aesthetically pleasing way for an economist to determine the cost of funds is to "let the market decide it." In the case of credit cards, this is feasible because of the phenomenon of credit card securitization. Consistently, during 1987–1989, credit-card-backed securities offered yields in the vicinity of 0.75 percent above those of Treasury securities with comparable maturities.[12] Meanwhile, the Visa systemwide average cardholder payment rate (i.e., cardholder payments as a percentage of outstanding balances) ranged from 13 to 17 percent per month during the years 1983–1987, implying an average maturity for credit card receivables of 6–8 months.[13] To be conservative, I will define the cost of funds to equal the one-year Treasury bill yield[14] plus 0.75 percent, averaged over each quarter. This series is also plotted in Figure 1.

The proposition that interest rates are sticky can be formally supported by regressing credit card interest rates on the cost of funds. First, using the Federal Reserve series, an aggregate credit card interest rate is regressed on its own lagged value, the lagged cost of funds, and a constant. Second, a more thorough regression can be run using the author's BCCS series for the 17 individual banks: each bank's credit card interest rate is regressed on its own lagged value, the lagged cost of funds, and a dummy variable for that bank. The results of these linear regressions are reported in Table 3. Note that, in the second regression, every coefficient has a *t* statistic of at least 6, while inclusion of additional variables with other lags tended to cause some coefficients to become insignificant. To aid in comparing the results of the two regressions, the Fed series is used

---

12. See, for example, "Credit Card Bonds are Hot, but Maybe Stingy on Yield," *Wall Street Journal*, April 16, 1990, p. C1; *Credit Card News*, Volume 1, Number 3 (June 15, 1988), p. 2, and Volume 1, Number 14 (November 15, 1988), p. 7; *Credit Card Management*, May/June 1988, p. 34.

13. The source of the systemwide cardholder payment rate is Standard & Poor's *Asset-Backed Securitization CreditReview*, March 16, 1987, p. 19. Individual banks' prospectuses have reported cardholder payment rates of 9–23 percent per month, never implying an average maturity of more than one year (see list of prospectuses in Appendix B). This impression was substantiated by a trade-publication report quoting the chairman of FCC National Bank (First Chicago's Delaware credit card subsidiary, listed fourth in Table 1) as saying that his bank finances its credit card portfolio with a variety of financial instruments with combined maturities equivalent to a 145-day duration (*Credit Card News*, March 15, 1989, p. 2).

14. *Federal Reserve Bulletin*, April 1990, table 1.35, line 21 (and previous issues).

Table 2 Size of Bank Credit Card Issuers for Which Data Are Reported

1987 Ranking by Number of Active Accounts (1 = largest)	Number of Banks with BCCS Reports Enabling Computation of Profits	Number of Banks with Call Reports Enabling Computation of Profits	Number of Banks with Prospectuses Enabling Estimation of Profits	Number of Banks with BCCS Reports of Interest Rate Series
1–10	1	3	4	2
11–20	2	3	0	5
21–30	2	1	1	3
31–40	1	1	2	1
41–50	1	1	1	4
51+	0	0	0	2
Total:	7	9	8	17

Sources: Author's bank credit card survey (BCCS), consolidated reports of condition and income (call reports), and prospectuses and registration statements. Ranks according to *The Nilson Report*, Number 406 (June 1987), pp. 6–7.

534

only for the period 1982–1987; using 1982–1989 data yields the same conclusions.[15]

The coefficient on the cost of funds, while statistically significant in each of the two regressions, is economically insignificant. Whereas a competitive-spot-market model would predict a coefficient near 1, the regressions using aggregated and disaggregated data yielded coefficients of only 0.042 and 0.054, respectively. It takes many years for the price to adjust to changes in marginal cost when the rate of adjustment is only on the order of 5 percent per quarter.

2.2 Nonprice Competition

The credit card industry has defended its high interest rates in the mid-to-late 1980's, in part, by asserting that the increased spread between the credit card interest rate and the cost of funds had been caused by an increase in the industry's rate of bad loans. The loan-loss data from the author's BCCS indicate that, in the period 1982–1987, the charge-off rate actually did increase roughly coincident with the increase in the interest rate spread (see Table 4). However, higher loan losses are an explanation for the higher interest rate spreads only if one believes that the latter are solely determined by costs. If credit card interest rates are determined otherwise, then *the causation may run in the reverse direction*: an increased interest rate spread may cause an increase in charge-offs.

Suppose, for example, that a bank can select both its interest rate and the default risk of its marginal customer. By choosing a higher marginal default rate, the bank increases its total number of loans but also its charge-off rate (the average default rate). Suppose that the bank first selects its interest rate and then its marginal default rate. Profit maximization requires the bank to set its marginal default rate equal to the difference between the interest rate it charges and the marginal cost (net of defaults) of lending funds. (The net marginal cost should equal the cost of funds plus a constant that is fairly stable in the short run.) Thus, the prediction is that an optimizing bank should set its marginal default rate equal to the interest rate spread plus a constant.

Suppose now that there is an independent reason why credit card interest rates fail to fall when general market interest rates decline (for example, see Section 6, below). The logic of the previous paragraph dictates that loan losses will subsequently increase. If firms do not compete and drive price down toward marginal cost, they are likely instead

---

15. With the 1982–1989 *Federal Reserve Bulletin* series, one obtains a coefficient of 0.0439 on COST OF FUNDS$_{-1}$, a coefficient of 0.864 on CREDIT CARD INTEREST RATE$_{-1}$, and a constant of 2.06.

Table 3   Ordinary Least-Squares Regression of Credit Card Interest Rate on Cost of Funds and Lagged Credit Card Interest Rate (Quarterly, 1982–1987)

Variable	Federal Reserve Board Survey Data	Bank Credit Card Survey Data
COST OF FUNDS$_{-1}$	0.0422	0.0540
	(0.00584)	(0.00896)
CREDIT CARD	0.895	0.685
INTEREST RATE$_{-1}$	(0.0444)	(0.0326)
Constant	1.51	
	(0.807)	
Bank-1 dummy		5.75
		(0.659)
Bank-2 dummy		5.11
		(0.594)
Bank-3 dummy		6.38
		(0.719)
Bank-4 dummy		5.79
		(0.657)
Bank-5 dummy		5.70
		(0.651)
Bank-6 dummy		4.18
		(0.500)
Bank-7 dummy		5.69
		(0.645)
Bank-8 dummy		5.12
		(0.595)
Bank-9 dummy		5.61
		(0.644)
Bank-10 dummy		5.44
		(0.634)
Bank-11 dummy		5.00
		(0.589)
Bank-12 dummy		5.12
		(0.595)
Bank-13 dummy		4.99
		(0.586)
Bank-14 dummy		4.88
		(0.577)
Bank-15 dummy		5.50
		(0.636)
Bank-16 dummy		5.22
		(0.593)

Table 3   (*Continued*)

Variable	Federal Reserve Board Survey Data	Bank Credit Card Survey Data
Bank-17 dummy		6.17
		(0.707)
Number of observations:	24	408
R^2:	0.96	0.937
Durbin h:	-0.69	0.10

Notes: CREDIT CARD INTEREST RATE is the dependent variable in each regression. COST OF FUNDS is defined as the yield on one-year Treasury bills plus 0.75 percent. Observe that there is no cross-firm variation in this variable, so that year dummy variables cannot be included in the second regression equation. Banks included in the author's bank credit card survey were assured anonymity. Numbers in parentheses are standard errors.

Table 4   **Loan Losses on Credit Cards of Ten Survey Banks during 1976–1987 (Fewer than Nine During 1976–1978 and 1986–1987) and the Spread Between Credit Card Interest Rates and the Cost of Funds**

Year	Average Charge-Off Rate (percentage)	Interest Rate Spread (percentage)
1976	1.15	10.57
1977	0.99	10.36
1978	1.27	8.11
1979	1.44	5.78
1980	2.04	5.08
1981	1.48	2.94
1982	1.67	6.42
1983	1.32	8.79
1984	1.36	7.69
1985	1.94	9.82
1986	3.01	11.55
1987	2.60	10.43

Source: Author's bank credit card survey (Appendix A, Table A1, questions 7 and 1).

to compete and drive marginal cost up toward price,[16] in the form of issuing cards to less credit-worthy customers.

3. The *Ex Post* Profitability of the Credit Card Market

As seen in Section 1., the credit card market of the 1980's possessed most of the usual prerequisites for invoking the model of perfect competition. A perfectly competitive model would at least predict zero long-run economic profits for "marginal" firms. Moreover, since free entry into the industry is possible and no input appears to be in scarce supply,[17] there is no credible source of rents to distinguish "inframarginal" firms from "marginal" firms. Thus, the competitive model would predict that all credit card issuers earn zero long-run economic profits. Many models of imperfect competition which preserve the free-entry assumption would also yield the zero-profit prediction.

By way of contrast, the interest rate stickiness documented in the previous section suggests that credit cards must become extraordinarily profitable whenever the cost of funds drops. Indeed, in this section, I will present a rather paradoxical set of data which indicates that returns from the credit card business were several times greater than the ordinary rate of return in banking during the years 1983–1988.

At the same time, this profitability data will help to assure that the above evidence of interest rate stickiness has been correctly interpreted. One might have thought to argue that price rigidity is consistent with competitive spot markets, if unobservable increases in quality exactly offset reductions in factor costs. The profitability data enable one to dis-

---

16. A related argument was made in the context of airline regulation. George W. Douglas and James C. Miller (1974) argued that the Civil Aeronautics Board's price regulations, at a time when the introduction of jet engines reduced the fundamental cost of air transportation, led airlines to compete and drive their costs up to price by placing fewer passengers on a given airplane. The arguments differ in two important ways. First, in the airline industry, price rigidity may have been caused by price regulation, whereas with credit cards, there is price stickiness despite a deregulated environment. Second, under regulation, the airlines apparently competed away their profits.

17. Free entry is a reasonable depiction of a credit card market in which 4,087 banks (and other deposit institutions) already issued their own Visa cards and a similar (largely overlapping) number issued their own MasterCards in September 1987. All of these institutions could legally offer accounts to customers anywhere in the United States. Nonmember institutions could join the Visa system by paying a fairly trivial entry fee: six dollars per million dollars in assets, plus one thousand dollars, according to a Visa official. (Only the assets of the subsidiary that issues the cards, and not the assets of the holding company, are figured into this formula.) Furthermore, it would seem strained to argue either that adjustment to the "long run" requires many years or that some input is in scarce supply, given the deluge of credit card solicitations made by banks in recent years.

miss this possibility: profits, in fact, dramatically rose at the time that the cost of funds dropped.

It is possible to object to the following analysis on several grounds. First, the data reported, by their very nature, represent *ex post* profits. Perhaps (especially since the sample period is during a cyclical boom) the observed profits are merely a very favorable realization of a random variable whose *ex ante* returns were quite ordinary. Second, it might be thought that, while the credit card market was extremely profitable in the years 1983–1988, the market has now equilibrated and henceforth normal returns will be observed. Third, the profitability figures might be derived from accounting data that either are being misinterpreted or are systematically misstating true economic profits.

I consider each of these concerns elsewhere in the paper. In Section 4, I briefly discuss an additional source of evidence (the Federal Reserve System's functional cost analysis), which, while significantly less reliable than the other data (in this author's opinion), gives profits over a longer period that includes the previous cyclical downturn. In Section 5, I introduce another independent set of data which examines resale prices of credit card portfolios between banks and finds that they trade at large premia. The latter data indicate that *ex ante* returns from credit cards are quite large and, since they are based on market valuations, should help allay any fears that the accounting data are being misinterpreted. Finally, it should be recalled from Table 4 that the interest rate spread was quite healthy except for a brief period around 1981 and that this brief spell of unprofitability can be attributed to banks not having yet established credit card subsidiaries exploiting the Supreme Court's *Marquette* decision. This episode does not seem likely to be repeated.

The *ex post* profit data reported and discussed in this section originate from three independent sources and were assembled by the author.

Bank credit card survey: The author's follow-up survey yielded profit calculations performed directly by executives of seven of the 50 largest bank issuers of credit cards.

Call reports: Profitability data for another nine of these issuers were extracted from call reports filed by the banks with the FDIC.

Prospectuses: Partial data on profitability for an additional eight large banks were obtained from filings with the SEC in connection with the sale of credit-card-backed securities.

Respondents to the author's survey were promised anonymity (but details of the construction are provided in Appendix A). The call reports and prospectuses are part of the public record. Table 2 reports the size distribution of banks included in each of the survey, call report, and prospectus samples.

3.1 An Illustrative Profit Calculation

As will be detailed in the next two subsections, earnings in the banking industry are usefully expressed as a percentage of assets: returns on assets are linked with returns on equity by the banking system's capital requirements. Before reporting summary profit figures for 15 and estimates for eight of the 50 largest issuers, I will examine in detail the components of revenues and costs for one individual credit card issuer. I consider here Maryland Bank, N.A. (MBNA), the Delaware-based credit card arm of MNC Financial, which is ranked seventh in Table 1.[18] This institution was selected because more public information exists on its credit card operations than on any other bank's: MBNA, which is required to file its own call report, has credit card loans exceeding 92 percent of its assets, and it has also made several credit-card-backed securities offerings.

MBNA's credit card operations (and their profitability) are fairly typical of major issuers, with the exception that the bank has stressed the concept of "affinity credit cards," whereby cards are marketed to members of professional organizations, fraternal orders, and cause-related groups (with the organizations' endorsements). As a consequence, its interest rates are somewhat lower and its customers are somewhat more creditworthy than average. Indeed, it may interest readers that, during the period when this article was undergoing the journal's review process, MBNA's marketing agent proposed to establish an official American Economic Association Visa card. This card would have carried a $20 annual fee ($40 for a gold card) and an 18.9-percent annual fee; the AEA would have received $1 for each account opened, $3 for each account renewed, and $0.25 per retail transaction. MBNA's agent estimated that 1,000 cards would be issued, generating $13 in revenue per card per year for the AEA. However, the AEA's executive committee, concerned that the AEA "would be viewed as endorsing a specific credit card by entering into such a contract," voted against establishing the affinity card program.[19]

---

18. MNC Financial is the 39th largest U.S. bank holding company and the corporate parent of Maryland National Bank, the largest commercial bank in Maryland. MBNA was founded in Newark, Delaware, in 1982, apparently to avoid Maryland's usury law. See also the text near footnote 9.

19. Draft minutes of the March 23, 1990, meeting of the AEA Executive Committee; Report of the Secretary to the Executive Committee. I thank Orley Ashenfelter and C. Elton Hinshaw for providing this information.

An item-by-item profit calculation for MBNA is displayed in Table 5. As is typical for credit card issuers, the single largest component of revenue is the finance charge (which, for MBNA, derives from annual percentage rates of 14.5–18.9 percent, depending on the account). Despite the fact that the bank provides a 25-day grace period during which no finance charge is assessed if the account balance is paid in full, more than 80 percent of the bank's credit card outstanding balances do accrue interest.[20] The drop in finance-charge revenues displayed in Table 5 is largely attributable to the bank's decision to reduce the interest rates on some of its accounts during 1985–1987.

MBNA also derives direct customer revenues from the annual fee and other customer charges (e.g., $15 late payment, over-limit, and returned-check charges). Indirect revenues are derived from the interchange fee, the portion of the merchant discount that is paid to the customer's bank. It is worth reemphasizing that the price schedules that determine direct customer revenues are set entirely at the bank level; only the interchange fee is set systemwide by the MasterCard and Visa organizations.

Costs can be divided among interest expenses, operating expenses, and loan losses. Interest expense is determined by market interest rates and thus is relatively uniform across banks, as a percentage of outstanding balances. Noninterest expenses, which include employee salaries, occupancy, equipment, and data processing, are also available from the banks' direct reports and call reports. These noninterest expenses typically equal 4–6 percent of outstanding balances for large issuers and are mostly (but not entirely) a proper component of total cost. The exception is that the expense of generating a new account (mostly advertising and marketing costs) should properly be considered an investment and thus should be amortized over a longer period. Nevertheless, I have no systematic way to separate out these new-account expenses from banks' profits; consequently, I use the entire "noninterest expense" in my computations. Observe that this will tend to overstate costs and understate the returns on assets and equity. Loan losses are best measured by the bank's "net credit losses" or "net charge-offs," which represent the outstanding balances that the bank newly treats as uncollectable.[21] (Typically, a bank

20. A good rule of thumb mentioned in credit card trade publications is that 90 percent of an issuer's overall outstanding balances accrue interest. See the discussion in Section 6.3.

21. The follow-up bank credit card survey specifically asked for the bank's "net credit losses" (see Appendix A). The item used from call reports is the "net charge-offs." An alternative measure of losses that could have been used from the call reports is the bank's "provision for loan losses," which is often higher and which may include an allowance for loans that the bank (statistically) expects to charge off in the future. There are two reasons not to use the figure for provision. First, credit card accounts incur most of their charge-offs

Table 5   Components of Profits for Maryland Bank, N.A.

Components	1985	1986	1987
Finance charges	16.66%	14.92%	13.21%
Annual fees	1.40%	1.58%	1.29%
Other customer charges	1.10%	1.42%	1.17%
Interchange fees	3.06%	3.00%	2.92%
Total revenue:	22.22%	20.92%	18.60%
Interest expenses	9.57%	7.80%	7.13%
Noninterest expenses	4.47%	4.71%	4.87%
Net charge-offs	1.09%	1.77%	1.80%
Total cost:	15.13%	14.28%	13.80%
Return on assets (pretax profits expressed as a percentage of outstanding balances)	7.09%	6.63%	4.80%

Sources: Consolidated reports of condition and income (call reports), prospectuses, and registration statements for Maryland Bank, N.A.

charges off a balance six months after the cardholder ceases payment on an account.) MBNA's charge-off rate is 1–2 percent lower than that of many large credit card issuers.

As seen in Table 5, MBNA's *pretax* return on assets (ROA) in credit cards equaled 7.09 percent in 1985, 6.63 percent in 1986, and 4.80 percent in 1987. The 1987 figure, for example, interacts with a 42-percent tax rate to yield an *after-tax* return on assets of 2.78 percent. For evidence of the accuracy of this computation, one need look no further than MNC Financial's 1987 annual report:

> Our credit card operations had another outstanding year. Maryland Bank, N.A. (MBNA) is by no means typical of the industry, which often is the target for criticism and concern. Over the past five years, MBNA has been

---

in the initial two years of the life of the account. Hence, the difference between "provision" and "net charge-offs" (and, in fact, some of "net charge-offs" itself) typically represents an expense of generating new accounts and, as in the case of marketing expenses, should properly be treated as an investment which is amortized over a longer period. Using "net charge-offs" mitigates this effect and gives a better measure of cost. Second, "provision" is a quantity that is easily manipulated by the bank: one can use a large loss provision to defer income taxes or a small loss provision to report high current earnings. "Net charge-offs" is less manipulable. The Federal Reserve System's functional cost analysis also uses "net credit losses" in earnings computations.

one of our fastest growing businesses. With $2 billion in outstandings, it continues to be a low cost, high-volume producer with chargeoffs of about 2%—about half of the industry average. We think most investors will find it hard not to be impressed with a business that earns more than 2.5% (after-tax, 1987) on assets.[22]

By way of comparison, the bank holding company as a whole earned a 1.36-percent ROA before taxes and a 1.00-percent ROA after taxes in 1987.[23] The holding company, minus its credit card business, earned less than a 0.80-percent ROA after taxes in 1987.

3.2 The Ordinary Rate of Return in the Banking Industry

The pretax return on assets for all U.S. commercial banks during the sample years equaled 0.85 percent in 1983, 0.83 percent in 1984, 0.90 percent in 1985, 0.80 percent in 1986, 0.28 percent in 1987, and 1.14 percent in 1988.[24] Taking into account that some areas of banking were effectively taxed at a lower rate than the credit card businesses (which were taxed at close to the statutory tax rates of 34–46 percent during this period), it is probably correct to think of 1.20 percent as the ordinary (pretax) return on assets in the banking industry at large.

The relationship between the ordinary rate of return on assets and the ordinary rate of return on equity in the banking industry depends on the capital requirements of banks. For the period 1983–1988, the capital requirement equaled about 6 percent of assets. First, in 1984–1985, U.S. banking regulators promulgated capital standards for all commercial bank activities equaling 6 percent of assets for total capital (and 5.5 percent of assets for primary capital).[25] Second, *actual* total equity capital for all insured U.S. commercial banks equaled 5.96 percent of assets in 1983, 6.01 percent in 1984, 6.17 percent in 1985, 6.21 percent in 1986, 6.06 percent in 1987, and 6.10 percent in 1988 (with substantially smaller

---

22. MNC Financial, 1987 Annual Report (dated March 1988), p. 4.

23. MNC Financial, 1987 Annual Report (dated March 1988), p. 1.

24. *Federal Reserve Bulletin,* July 1989, p. 462 (table 1), and July 1988, p. 404 (table 1). The substantially lower earnings for 1987 reflect the decision of large banks to set aside large sums to cover troubled loans to developing countries. Excluding international operations, the banks' rates of earnings in 1987 appear to have very slightly exceeded those of 1986.

25. At this writing, bank capital standards are scheduled to rise, by international agreement, to 8 percent of total risk assets in 1992. At the same time, the new and rapidly expanding practice of securitizing credit card assets has the effect of removing the credit card accounts from banks' balance sheets, thus reducing the effective capital requirement.

percentages for the larger banks).[26] Dividing an ordinary (pretax) return on assets of 1.20 percent by a capital requirement of 6 percent would imply an ordinary (pretax) return on equity of 20 percent per year.

3.3 Computations of Ex Post Profitability for 15 Large Issuers

Several different summary measures of (*ex post*) profitability are presented in Tables 6 and 7. The first measure of return on assets, ROA (reported), is precisely the calculation we illustrated above for MBNA. One potential flaw in this calculation is that it relies on the bank's own reported cost of funds. The problem here is that some banks may not have been allocating the true opportunity cost of their low-cost core deposits (e.g., passbook accounts and non-interest-bearing checking accounts) to their credit card businesses; in that event, some of the profits allocated to the credit card operations would in fact be attributable to the branch banking business.

This difficulty is easily remedied by replacing each bank's reported interest expense with the standardized index of the cost of funds defined and defended in Section 2. My second measure of return on assets, ROA (adjusted), is computed by using an interest expense of COST OF FUNDS applied to the nonequity portion of assets; thus, interest expense as a percentage of assets equals 94 percent of COST OF FUNDS.[27] If anything, my adjustment tends to reduce systematically the reported returns; observe in Table 7 that ROA (reported) exceeds ROA (adjusted) in four out of six years.

The return on equity is computed in two different ways in Table 7. The first and most obvious measure, ROE (actual cap), merely divides (pretax) profits by the actual capital residing in the credit card bank at the previous year's end. (Since each bank in Table 7 is a legally distinct entity, its capital is a well-defined quantity.[28]) However, ROE (actual cap) is not an entirely appealing measure of return on equity. Observe

---

26. *Federal Reserve Bulletin*, July 1989, pp. 474–83 (table A.1), and July 1988, p. 405 (table 2). For money-center banks, equity capital equaled 4.30, 4.56, 4.69, 4.78, 4.33, and 4.42 percent of assets in the respective years. For other banks with $5 billion or more in assets, equity capital equaled 4.76, 5.08, 5.42, 5.50, 5.29, and 5.29 percent of assets in the respective years.

27. ROA (adjusted), as computed from the call report data, also contains a second, minor adjustment: to the extent that a bank has purchased credit card portfolios from other banks at a premium (see Section V) and subtracted a portion of the premium from its profits, ROA (adjusted) adds it back in.

28. Data on credit card capitalization for the firms reported in Table 6 do not exist. In fact, six of the seven firms operate their credit card businesses within the same bank as their other lines of businesses, so there does not exist capital separately allocated to the credit card business; "actual capital," then, is not a well-defined quantity.

Table 6   Return on Assets and Return on Equity (Pretax) Based on Direct Reports of Credit Card Issuers

Bank	Rank	Measure	Percentage Returns				
			1984	1985	1986	1987	1988
A	1–10	ROA (reported)	5.98	4.36	5.59	6.91	N.A.
		ROA (adjusted)	6.09	6.06	6.64	6.53	N.A.
		ROE (adjusted)	101.5	101.1	110.7	108.8	N.A.
B	11–20	ROA (reported)	8.09	7.78	3.74	4.21	N.A.
		ROA (adjusted)	8.00	7.22	7.15	5.04	N.A.
		ROE (adjusted)	133.3	120.3	119.1	84.0	N.A.
C	11–20	ROA (reported)	5.01	5.70	3.82	4.55	4.30
		ROA (adjusted)	5.00	6.21	6.49	5.33	4.23
		ROE (adjusted)	83.3	103.5	108.2	88.8	70.5
D	21–30	ROA (reported)	7.20	7.86	7.81	7.93	8.05
		ROA (adjusted)	3.28	6.39	7.33	6.39	5.84
		ROE (adjusted)	54.7	106.5	122.2	106.5	97.4
E	21–30	ROA (reported)	8.48	8.92	8.74	9.96	9.69
		ROA (adjusted)	7.48	9.20	10.02	8.09	7.31
		ROE (adjusted)	124.6	153.3	166.9	134.8	121.8
F	31–40	ROA (reported)	7.27	7.54	6.41	8.39	5.87
		ROA (adjusted)	5.75	6.62	5.91	6.98	4.95
		ROE (adjusted)	95.9	110.3	98.5	116.4	82.5
G	41–50	ROA (reported)	2.24	6.37	6.26	6.15	2.75
		ROA (adjusted)	1.67	6.54	6.41	5.81	2.74
		ROE (adjusted)	27.8	109.0	106.8	96.9	45.6
Direct report averages:							
		ROA (reported)	6.32	6.93	6.05	6.87	6.13
		ROA (adjusted)	5.32	6.89	7.14	6.31	5.01
		ROE (adjusted)	88.7	114.9	118.9	105.2	83.6

Source: Author's bank credit card survey (Appendix A, follow-up survey, Table A2, question 4).

that, for example, the quantity of capital that resides in Citibank South Dakota (as opposed to the principal New York bank or the parent holding company) is relatively discretionary and arbitrary. Indeed, one finds that the credit card subsidiary of a bank is often relatively undercapitalized in some years and relatively overcapitalized in other years. While ROE (actual cap) is reported in Table 7, this datum should probably be interpreted skeptically.

A preferred measure to consult is ROE (adjusted), which is computed simply by dividing ROA (adjusted) by 6 percent. The logic behind this

Table 7   Return on Assets and Return on Equity (Pretax) Based on Call Reports Filed with the FDIC

Bank	Rank	Measure	Percentage Returns					
			1983	1984	1985	1986	1987	1988
Citibank (South Dakota), N.A.	1	ROA (reported)	7.44	7.05	6.02	6.24	5.31	4.26
		ROE (actual cap)	81.4	80.3	75.5	75.1	77.7	48.6
		ROA (adjusted)	5.40	5.24	5.56	6.62	5.61	3.92
		ROE (adjusted)	90.1	87.4	92.7	110.3	93.5	65.4
Chase Manhattan Bank (U.S.A.)	2	ROA (reported)	4.73	5.63	5.29	6.03	4.50	3.84
		ROE (actual cap)	56.4	71.2	109.1	146.5	75.2	53.9
		ROA (adjusted)	3.32	3.62	4.28	5.46	3.24	2.68
		ROE (adjusted)	55.3	60.4	71.3	91.1	54.0	44.7
Maryland Bank, N.A.	7	ROA (reported)	8.14	7.35	7.09	6.63	4.80	N.A.
		ROE (actual cap)	74.8	142.0	121.6	128.8	86.8	N.A.
		ROA (adjusted)	7.72	6.76	8.04	7.67	4.86	N.A.
		ROE (adjusted)	128.6	112.7	134.0	127.8	81.0	N.A.
Beneficial National Bank (U.S.A.)	15[a]	ROA (reported)	4.23	5.10	3.20	1.61	N.A.	N.A.
		ROE (actual cap)	34.3	77.7	39.6	22.0	N.A.	N.A.
		ROA (adjusted)	1.31	4.01	4.27	3.70	N.A.	N.A.
		ROE (adjusted)	21.9	66.9	71.1	61.7	N.A.	N.A.
Lomas Bank U.S.A.	18	ROA (reported)	N.A.	N.A.	N.A.	3.59	4.74	4.35
		ROE (actual cap)	N.A.	N.A.	N.A.	60.6	80.7	39.9
		ROA (adjusted)	N.A.	N.A.	N.A.	4.47	5.20	4.71
		ROE (adjusted)	N.A.	N.A.	N.A.	74.5	86.6	78.5
CoreStates Bank of Delaware	20	ROA (reported)	2.86	4.21	5.09	6.46	5.03	4.10
		ROE (actual cap)	63.9	61.9	100.1	131.8	95.1	70.1
		ROA (adjusted)	2.71	4.65	6.14	7.55	5.91	4.57
		ROE (adjusted)	45.1	77.6	102.3	125.9	98.6	76.2
First City Bank—Sioux Falls	21	ROA (reported)	N.A.	N.A.	6.88	4.15	5.34	6.85
		ROE (actual cap)	N.A.	N.A.	74.0	41.6	43.4	48.5
		ROA (adjusted)	N.A.	N.A.	5.82	4.56	5.59	6.58
		ROE (adjusted)	N.A.	N.A.	97.1	75.9	93.2	109.6
First Omni Bank, N.A.	33	ROA (reported)	8.68	5.98	8.07	6.77	5.69	5.01
		ROE (actual cap)	29.8	32.2	58.0	99.8	93.2	72.4
		ROA (adjusted)	6.19	3.36	6.51	6.85	5.51	4.38
		ROE (adjusted)	103.2	56.0	108.5	114.2	91.8	73.0
Avco National Bank	44[a]	ROA (reported)	N.A.	4.82	3.72	1.19	N.A.	N.A.
		ROE (actual cap)	N.A.	344.6	103.6	27.9	N.A.	N.A.
		ROA (adjusted)	N.A.	4.23	4.66	5.06	N.A.	N.A.
		ROE (adjusted)	N.A.	70.5	77.7	84.3	N.A.	N.A.
Call-report averages:		ROA (reported)	6.01	5.73	5.67	4.74	5.06	4.74
		ROE (actual cap)	56.8	115.7	85.2	81.6	78.9	55.6
		ROA (adjusted)	4.44	4.55	5.66	5.77	5.13	4.47
		ROE (adjusted)	74.0	75.9	94.3	96.2	85.5	74.6

Source: Consolidated reports of condition and income (call reports).

a. Bank's credit card portfolio was acquired in 1986–1987; see Table 9.

measure is that, as argued above, the capital requirement during the sample period has in practice equaled about 6 percent of assets, uniformly across banking activities. Thus, it seems more sensible to impute the 6-percent capital standard to all credit card assets than to rely on a capriciously chosen bank number. ROE (adjusted), which is the last measure provided in Tables 6 and 7, is probably the most informative to examine and discuss.

By the standards of the previous subsection, the rates of return reported in Tables 6 and 7 are extraordinary. All seven banks that provided direct reports of profit data for 1985 and six out of seven that provided direct reports for 1986 attained (pretax) returns on equity exceeding 100 percent per year! The sample average for these banks also exceeded 100 percent in 1987 and exceeded 80 percent in 1984 and 1988. The profit figures drawn from call reports are not quite as large but still are generous. Sample averages for return on equity exceeded 90 percent in 1985 and 1986 and exceeded 70 percent in all remaining years. It is unclear why the direct reports provided returns on equity systematically 10–20 percentage points higher than the call reports. Part of the reason is undoubtedly that firms that established separate credit card banks sustained higher rates of growth in assets, concealing a greater investment in new accounts in the cost data.[29]

3.4 Estimates of Ex Post Profitability for an Additional Eight Issuers

The computations of the preceding subsection were performed for 15 credit card issuers for whom all components of profits were known. If the data set is expanded to include banks for whom most, but not all, components are known, it is possible to make statements about an even larger proportion of the 50 largest firms.

Eight additional banks, including Bank of America (ranked third largest), First Chicago (ranked fourth), and Manufacturers Hanover (ranked fifth), have disclosed significant information in connection with the issuance of credit-card-backed securities.[30] All items in Table 5 except

---

29. An anonymous referee correctly observed that the return on assets derived from direct reports uses credit card balances in place of total assets as denominator. However, the call report data show that this does not appreciably overstate the true return on assets. Premises and fixed assets typically equaled no more than 0.3–2.0 percent of a credit card bank's total assets, while credit card loans generally exceeded 97 percent of total assets.

30. See Appendix B for a listing of the relevant registration statements. While information in connection with credit-card-backed securities is also available for Citibank, Maryland National, and Lomas Bank U.S.A., these banks are already represented in Table 7 and so are excluded from the current discussion.

noninterest expenses (i.e., non-credit-related operating expenses) and interchange fees are thus known for these issuers; moreover, these two missing items (unlike customer revenue and net charge-offs) do not vary widely among comparable banks. I approximate their rates of profit by assuming that the additional eight issuers' operating expenses and interchange fees are equal (as a percentage of assets) to those for which I have direct knowledge. Making the same normalizations for these banks as before, I obtain conservative[31] average pretax returns on equity (adjusted) of 65 percent in 1984 (three banks), 87 percent in 1985 (five banks), 92 percent in 1986 (all eight banks), 76 percent in 1987 (seven banks), and 62 percent in 1988 (six banks). It is worth noting that all of these numbers are quite close to the adjusted ROE's of Table 7, and all exceed 60 percent per year.

The sample from which a conclusion about profitability can be based is rather large. Exact computations or good estimates are available for as many as 23 of the 50 largest issuers of bank credit cards, with approximately 50 percent of industry market share (by outstanding balances). Included in the sample are all of the five largest firms.

The conclusion drawn from Table 6, Table 7, and the numbers stated two paragraphs above is quite straightforward. As argued above, the ordinary (pretax) return on equity in banking is on the order of 20 percent per year. Credit card businesses earned annual returns of 60–100 percent or more during the years 1983–1988. Plastic earned strongly positive economic profits: the credit card business earned 3–5 times the ordinary rate of return in the banking industry.

4. Additional Evidence from the Functional Cost Analysis

The previous discussion has focused on the profitability of the 50 largest issuers of credit cards during the period 1983–1988. It is interesting to consider briefly whether the conclusions change when the sample of banks and the time period examined are extended.

This exercise should help address two potential questions.[32] First, suppose it were the case that the smaller players in the market earned only the ordinary rate of return on capital. Then, the reader may be troubled by the possibility that the larger firms may possess some unobservable

---

31. Some prospectuses report gross rather than net charge-offs, reducing the reported level of profits. Furthermore, the figures I used for noninterest expense (generally 5.40 percent of outstanding balances) seem to be on the high side.

32. These are questions that were raised by two anonymous referees. I am grateful to them for raising these issues.

attributes which are not reproducible (e.g., "business acumen") that earn positive rents. (However, there would still remain the question of why 50 larger firms is not enough for competition.) On the other hand, if literally hundreds of firms, including small regional banks, all earn supranormal profits, it becomes much more convincing that none of these firms possesses anything special (except for a base of customers). Second, the reader may be concerned that the article has focused on a period of time that coincides with a cyclical boom in the national economy. Part of this selection of time is unavoidable: as observed in Section 1., the credit card market did not become functionally deregulated until about 1982; much of the earlier experience can be dismissed as the result of state usury ceilings. In addition, my reliable sources of data only extend back to this time. Nevertheless, it may be helpful to present some (albeit imperfect) data which provide a better sense of the extent to which profitability is cyclical.

Both of these points can be discussed by introducing an additional source of data: the Federal Reserve System's functional cost analysis (FCA). In this author's opinion, the FCA data are considerably less reliable than the other profitability data utilized in this article, and so they should be interpreted cautiously. There has been little effort to track the same banks from year to year; in particular, the sample size has dropped approximately 60 percent from 1976 to 1988. One also obtains the sense that the accounting data provided by the smaller banks in the Fed's sample do not do as good a job as the other sources of properly allocating costs between credit cards and the banks' other lines of business. Nevertheless, it is the only available source of profitability figures for the smaller banks and for earlier years.

The average charge-off rate and the average return on assets from the functional cost analysis for the years 1976–1988 are displayed in Table 8. The typical credit card issuer represented in the FCA sample is ranked approximately between number 300 and 400, nationally, by outstanding balances. The first observation to make is that the charge-off experience of the smaller banks is broadly consistent with what has already been seen in Table 4. As before, loan losses remained tightly in the 1–3 percent per year range.

Since bank credit card operating expenses are believed to exhibit increasing returns to scale over a range (Christine Pavel and Paula Binkley, 1987), one would expect that the return on assets would be somewhat lower than that reported above for the largest issuers. Indeed, during the period 1983–1988 (for which numbers are available for both the smaller issuers and the larger issuers), the smaller banks earned only about 60 percent of the returns of the larger banks and only about 50

Table 8 Return on Assets for Smaller Credit Card Issuers, 1976–1987, from the Federal Reserve System's Functional Cost Analysis (FCA)

Year	Number of Banks in Sample	Average Charge-Off Rate (percentage)	Average Return on Assets (percentage)
1976	236	1.48	2.72
1977	224	1.41	3.07
1978	181	1.66	2.44
1979	184	1.92	1.60
1980	139	2.54	−1.52
1981	128	2.25	0.97
1982	138	1.93	2.40
1983	102	1.58	2.37
1984	98	1.24	3.45
1985	85	1.81	3.97
1986	76	2.33	3.28
1987	93	1.65	3.94
1988	89	2.51	2.72

Notes: Data are taken from the Board of Governors of the Federal Reserve System's *Functional Cost Analysis, National Average Report, Commercial Banks*, Credit Card Function (Card Banks), 1976–1988. The third column represents "net credit losses + net fraud losses"; the fourth column represents "net earnings after cost of money." Both columns are expressed as percentages of average outstanding balances on credit cards and are weighted averages based on individual banks' average outstanding balances. Earnings are before taxes. In Section 3.2, it is argued that the ordinary return on assets is approximately 1.20 percent.

percent of the "excess" returns of the larger banks. Nevertheless, the returns do remain substantially above the ordinary rate of return in banking; over the longer period that includes the cyclical downturn, the smaller issuers still appear to have earned roughly twice the ordinary rate of return in banking.

These numbers may significantly understate the profitability of credit cards over the entire business cycle. First, banks have the ability (with some lags) to increase their lendings at cyclical peaks and to cut their lendings at cyclical troughs. (This is not merely conjectural: their ability to act in this way is fairly apparent from data on banks' levels of outstanding balances.) Thus, greater weight should be placed on the returns in boom years. Second, as emphasized above, banks took some time to learn how to exploit the December 1978 *Marquette* decision and so were hindered in their ability to react to climbing costs of funds during 1979–

1981. The learning has now been done, and so the 1979–1981 earnings experience is unlikely to be repeated.

5. The *Ex Ante* Profitability of the Credit Card Market

As was emphasized in the fourth paragraph of Section 3, there is good reason to be a bit skeptical of *ex post* profitability data. In this section, I will seek (as directly as possible) to examine *ex ante* returns of the credit card market.

Suppose that bank I has issued credit cards to consumers and has $X in balances outstanding on these accounts. The question one may ask is how much bank II will pay bank I to acquire these accounts, as a function of X. If the credit card accounts were expected, *ex ante*, to pay the ordinary rate of return on capital (or the risky equivalent), then the transaction would presumably occur at about *par* (i.e., bank II would pay bank I the same $X to assume the accounts). If there existed a substantial probability that consumers would default on the loans and if the contractual interest payments and fees did not adequately compensate for this eventuality, then bank II could presumably acquire these loans at a *discount*.[33] Finally, only if the owner of the credit card accounts could be expected to earn above the ordinary rate of return on capital would the accounts sell at a *premium* above $X; then, the future stream of positive economic profits would be capitalized in the transaction price. If bank II pays bank I $120 million for accounts on which only $100 million is owed, I will refer to this as a 20-percent premium.

The model of perfect competition predicts that resales of credit card accounts will occur at par, in the long run.[34] During the equilibrating process toward the long run, the theory would tolerate discrepancies from par but firmly predicts that resale prices will monotonically converge toward par. However, a systematic failure of competition in the credit card market (as suggested by the profit figures in the previous

---

33. For a good example of discounted loans, consider the resale among banks of loans to developing countries; in the late 1980's, such transactions frequently occurred at prices well below 50 percent of face value.

34. One may argue that there should exist a premium representing the cost of establishing an ongoing business. An important point to observe is that, typically, when a bank acquires another bank's credit card portfolio, it transfers the acquired portfolio over to its own preexisting offices and processing facilities. That is to say, basically the only portion of the "ongoing business" that the acquirer desires is the customer base. In the model of perfect competition, customers inexorably gravitate to the low-priced firm; the phenomenon of "captive" or "loyal" customers does not exist. Thus, an existing base of customers, by itself, should draw no premium.

sections) would require, to the contrary, that interbank transactions persistently occur at substantial premia. Fortunately, there exist real data against which to test these two divergent predictions.

The premia paid by banks in credit card deals during the years between 1984 and early 1990 are compiled in Table 9. All 27 such interbank transactions for which I could find a public disclosure of the premium are reported. The average premium in Table 9 equals 20 percent; all transactions occurred at premia between 3 percent and 27 percent. There is no tendency for the premia to vanish monotonically; if anything, the largest premia are associated with the most recent transactions.

The resale data clearly suggest that, at this writing in 1990, and throughout the period of 1984–1988, the *ex ante* expected economic profits (adjusted for risk) on existing credit card accounts were substantially positive. The premium that is theoretically justified for credit card accounts depends on a number of parameters for which I possess no data. However, Table 10 presents the premia that are justified for a number of sets of assumptions. The expected "lifetime" of an account represents the number of years that a bank anticipates that the consumer will continue to maintain his credit card account, under the same borrowing patterns and the same rate of profitability. The growth rate represents the rate at which a bank believes that the outstanding balances on the acquired credit card accounts will increase during their lifetime; meanwhile, I assume that the bank discounts using a 10-percent interest rate. The ordinary rate of return in banking is taken, as above, to be a 1.20-percent annual pretax return on assets. The calculations in Table 10 implicitly assume that the seller of credit card accounts receives all of the gains from trade; if (as one may reasonably expect) the buyer also obtains some gains, then the indicated premia require still higher rates of return from credit cards. Thus, these should only be taken as lower bounds on implied profitability.

As Table 10 indicates, it is difficult to justify the recent flurry of premia in the range of 23–27 percent unless returns equaling at least three times the ordinary rate of return in banking are expected to persist. Even with the optimistic[35] assumptions that the typical account will be maintained for six years after the acquisition and that the outstanding balances will grow at an overly fast 40 percent per year during that period, profits at three times the ordinary rate of return lead to a premium of only 28.60

---

35. For example, at the date of the First RepublicBank transaction, First Republic's average outstanding balance per active account equaled about $1,000, roughly the national average. A 40-percent growth rate for five years would increase the average outstanding balance by more than a factor of five, justifying the adjective "optimistic."

percent. The more typical premium of 20 percent, in conjunction with reasonable projections of lifetime and growth, still requires profitability of three or more times the ordinary rate of return in banking. Finally, it should be observed that one of the lowest reported premia (Colonial National Bank, at 11 percent) involved credit cards with a mean outstanding balance per active account equaling $2,000, or about twice the national average. It would be rather unrealistic to project growth of more than 10 percent per year on these balances, which still suggests profitability about three times the ordinary rate.

I will make three final notes on *ex ante* profitability. First, the reader may still worry that, since credit card debts are unsecured, charge-off rates will jump and profitability will plummet in the next recession. Some historical data should allay these concerns. In Tables 4 and 8, one may trace back net charge-offs through the last recession. One finds, for these samples, that charge-offs in the early 1980's increased only fractionally above prior years and peaked at only about 2.5 percent of outstandings. Independently, Visa system-wide data traces back credit losses through the last two recessions, and finds (annualized) quarterly charge-off rates peaking at 3 percent in 1974 and again in 1980.[36] Solicitation of new accounts, and not cyclical phenomena, are the important contributors to credit card charge-offs (see also Section 2.2, above).

Second, the reader may have noted that substantial premia (although not as large as for credit card accounts) have also been reported in sales of regional banks. If anything, this makes the credit card premia even more surprising. The premia for regional banks represent "goodwill," which economists should interpret as economic rents derived from local monopolies in banking. By way of contrast, the national market for credit cards has no local monopolies, so the competitive model predicts that "goodwill" should equal zero.[37] Third, the magnitude of resale premia may be taken as clear evidence that players within the industry itself attach little credence to the possibility that the credit card market will begin to behave competitively in the years immediately following 1990. (If, for example, it were believed that competition would drive economic profits to zero in two years, this would be the same as using an expected "lifetime" in Table 10 of two years.) Data in the previous section showed that the zero-profit prediction failed in the years 1983–1988. If bankers

36. The source of system-wide net charge-offs is Standard & Poor's *Asset-Backed Securitization CreditReview*, March 16, 1987, p. 19.

37. In addition, a regional bank may own appreciated real estate whose book value equals historic cost, also contributing to reported premia over book value. The credit card transactions typically do not involve any real assets that have appreciated in value.

Table 9   Premia in Resales of Credit Card Accounts

Date	Seller	Buyer
April 1984	Continental Bank	Chemical Bank
December 1986	Texas American Bancshares	Republic Bank
December 1986	Beneficial National Bank	First Chicago
February 1987	National Bancshares Texas	Lomas & Nettleton
April 1987	Louisiana Bancshares	Lomas & Nettleton
May 1987	Avco National Bank	Household Bank
July 1987	Bank of Mid-America	Lomas & Nettleton
July 1987	Colonial National Bank	Household Bank
September 1988	First RepublicBank Delaware	Citicorp
November 1988	Equibank	CoreStates Bank
February 1989	Meritor Financial Group	Chase Manhattan
March 1989	Society for Savings Bancorp	First Chicago
May 1989	Michigan National Bank	Chase Manhattan
May 1989	Empire of America	Citicorp
June 1989	Colonial National Bank	Household Bank
July 1989	Leader Federal Savings	Chase Manhattan
August 1989	California Federal Bank	Household Bank
September 1989	Chevy Chase Savings	CoreStates Bank
September 1989	Imperial Savings & Loan	Wells Fargo Bank
September 1989	Dreyfus Corp.	Bank of New York
October 1989	First City Bancorporation	Bank of New York
December 1989	Bank South	Society National
December 1989	Bank of Boston	Chase Manhattan
December 1989	Investors Savings Bank	Chase Manhattan
January 1990	Bank of New England	Citicorp
February 1990	Colonial National Bank	Household Bank
April 1990	Fleet/Norstar	Norwest

Sources: WS = *Wall Street Journal;* NY = *The New York Times;* AB = *The American Banker;* KP = Kidder Peabody (Anderson and Deans, 1989).

Table 9 (*Continued*)

Outstanding Balances	Premium Reported (percentage)	Primary Source
$824 million	21	WS April 2, 1984
$50 million	14	WS January 2, 1987
$1,100 million	13	AB January 2, 1987
$41 million	14	WS February 23, 1987
$157 million	16	WS April 16, 1987
$322 million	19	WS April 29, 1987
$120 million	19	WS July 23, 1987
$317 million	11	WS July 23, 1987
$623 million	25	NY September 12, 1988
$100 million	25	KP
$85 million	24	AB February 2, 1989
$230 million	18	NY April 13, 1989
$1,100 million	21	WS July 19, 1989
$650 million	3	AB June 2, 1989
$98 million	25	AB June 23, 1989
$36 million	20	KP
$125 million	18	AB September 18, 1989
$200 million	23	AB September 18, 1989
$280 million	22	WS January 11, 1990
$790 million	21	AB September 20, 1989
$552 million	24	AB October 19, 1989
$41 million	24	AB December 27, 1989
$625 million	23	AB January 5, 1990
$24 million	25	AB January 5, 1990
$652 million	27	NY January 30, 1990
$50 million	20	AB March 7, 1990
$200 million	20	AB April 3, 1990

Table 10 Premia in Resale of Credit Card Accounts Justified by Various Expected Lifetimes of Accounts, Annual Growth Rates of Outstandings per Account, and Credit Card Profitability (as a Multiple of Ordinary Rate of Return)

Expected Lifetime (years)	Multiple of Ordinary Rate of Return	Premia (percentage)			
		10-Percent Growth	20-Percent Growth	30-Percent Growth	40-Percent Growth
2	1	0.00	0.00	0.00	0.00
	2	2.40	2.51	2.62	2.73
	3	4.80	5.02	5.24	5.45
	4	7.20	7.53	7.85	8.18
	5	9.60	10.04	10.47	10.91
4	1	0.00	0.00	0.00	0.00
	2	4.80	5.50	6.27	7.15
	3	9.60	10.99	12.55	14.29
	4	14.40	16.49	18.82	21.44
	5	19.20	21.98	25.10	28.58
6	1	0.00	0.00	0.00	0.00
	2	7.20	9.05	11.38	14.30
	3	14.40	18.10	22.76	28.60
	4	21.60	27.15	34.15	42.90
	5	28.80	36.19	45.53	57.20

Calculations: For N = expected lifetime of credit card accounts, g = annual growth rate of outstandings per account (during lifetime of account), r = 0.10 = interest rate used by bank in discounting, ROA_{cc} = return on assets from credit cards, ROA_{ord} = 0.012 = ordinary return on assets in banking, and Φ = premium in resale of credit card accounts (as proportion of outstanding balances at time of sale),

$$\Phi = (ROA_{cc} - ROA_{ord}) \sum_{K=0}^{N-1} \left(\frac{1+g}{1+r} \right)^K.$$

have had rational expectations in their acquisitions of accounts, then supranormal profits should persist for at least the period 1990–1993. Credit
card profits will then have equaled three times the ordinary rate of return
for more than an entire decade, certainly an extended adjustment period
to the long run!

6. Theoretical Explanations for the Failure of Competition

In this section, I briefly outline some theoretical models that lead to
predictions of price stickiness and positive economic profits. I also discuss
some empirical evidence related to these theories. Formal modeling details are available in Appendix C, taken from the working-paper precursor
of the AER article.

6.1 Search/Switch Cost Theories

One of the common explanations offered for high credit card interest
rates is that consumers find it difficult to locate banks offering favorable
terms. Indeed, the U.S. Congress enacted legislation in October 1988
that requires all issuers to disclose their interest rates, fees, and grace
periods on solicitations and applications; supporters of the bill articulated
the rationale of enabling consumers to shop around for the least expensive
card, (i.e., of reducing consumer search costs).

Models with search costs may plausibly lead to sticky interest rates
and positive profits. While other explanations also exist for price stickiness (e.g., menu costs; see e.g., Julio J. Rotemberg and Garth Saloner,
1987), there is good reason to focus on search/switch costs in the credit
card market. Banks have recently begun to use marketing techniques
that are consistent with this type of story. Issuers frequently waive the
annual fee for a fixed period of time and, in a few cases, offer "to pay
you up to $100 when you transfer your other credit card balances" to
their MasterCard or Visa accounts.[38] The focus of federal regulation on
disclosure provides additional support for the search-cost explanation.

In models that are thematically related to that of Peter Diamond (1971)
and subsequent papers, there may exist a continuum of symmetric equilibrium prices that are consistent with any given marginal cost.[39] There-

---

38. The quotation is taken from a direct-mailed solicitation, dated April 1989, from Imperial
Savings (approximately the fifth-largest S&L issuer of credit cards).

39. Mitchell Berlin and Loretta J. Mester (1988) tested and rejected a (very different)
model, in which consumer search costs were used to try to explain price dispersion in credit
card interest rates.

fore, the historical price may continue to be an equilibrium even after a change in marginal cost. That is, price stickiness may be consistent with equilibrium. (Detailed analysis of a straightforward model that yields this conclusion is provided in Appendix C. It should also be noted that a formal model of switch costs [see e.g., Ausubel, 1984; Joseph Farrell and Carl Shapiro, 1987; Paul Klemperer, 1987] can result in conclusions similar to those from search-cost models.)

Such models also provide a reason why supranormal profits may not be competed away. If prices remain sticky when costs drop, firms begin to earn supranormal profits. Profits continue at high levels until prices unstick, costs rise again, or the customer base is sufficiently eroded. The logic is that, if consumers face search costs in locating (or face switch costs in moving to) lower-priced firms, then higher-priced firms can hold onto many of their (captive) customers despite their high prices. As suggested above, competitors may try to defeat this inertia by offering sign-up bonuses to new customers, but to the extent that such devices are limited in their effectiveness and practicality, firms may derive supranormal profits from their existing customer base. Finally, observe that this story enables a firm with a base of "loyal customers" to earn supranormal profits despite competition both from other existing firms (who want to increase their own customer bases) and from new entrants (who want to establish customer bases).

The credit card industry is a business where both search costs and switch costs are likely to be especially prevalent. They include: (a) the information cost of discovering which banks are offering lower interest rates; (b) the cost in time, effort, and emotional energy in filling out an application for a new card (and possibly getting rejected); (c) the fact that the card fee is usually billed on an annual basis, so that if one switches banks at the wrong time, one forgoes some money; (d) the perception that one acquires a better credit rating or a higher credit limit by holding the same bank's card for a long time; and (e) the time lag between applying for a card and receiving one.

While credit card consumers undoubtedly face some positive level of search costs and switch costs (and this gives entirely rational justification for the observed market behavior), there remains an empirical question as to whether the actual search/switch costs are of sufficient magnitude to justify what is observed. A typical credit card account in the late 1980's had an outstanding balance slightly over $1,000 (see Section 6.3 and Table 11, below). The prevailing premium on resales of these accounts (see Section 5 and Table 9) then translates to almost $250 per account. In a search/switch cost equilibrium, one would expect the resale premium to equal the search or switch cost; yet it is hard to imagine that the costs

Table 11 Percentage of Customers Who Avoid Finance Charges and Average Outstanding Balances Per Active Account

Year	Percentage of Customers Who Avoid Finance Charges	Number of Banks Reporting Percentage of Customers	Average Outstanding Balance of Active Account	Number of Banks Reporting Outstanding Balance
1979	31.8	6	$523	7
1980	28.7	6	$590	8
1981	21.9	6	$660	8
1982	21.0	6	$726	9
1983	22.8	8	$711	10
1984	21.9	10	$852	10
1985	21.4	12	$1,014	12
1986	24.6	14	$1,018	17
1987	27.6	9	$1,038	10

Source: Author's bank credit card survey (Appendix A, Table A1, question 8).

enumerated in the previous paragraph are the monetary equivalent of $250! Given this caveat, it is not at all clear that search or switch costs could provide a full explanation of observed market behavior; it would be valuable for future empirical work (using data at the customer level) to examine this question.

6.2 A New Adverse-Selection Theory

I now propose an adverse-selection theory that relies on a very specific form of irrationality (which will be given some indirect empirical support in the following subsection). Since a credit card is really quite an expensive medium on which to borrow, I posit a class of consumers who do not intend to borrow on their accounts but find themselves doing so anyway.[40] Consumers in this first class are precisely the best customers from a (rational) bank's viewpoint: they borrow at high interest rates, yet they eventually (in most cases) repay their loans. At the same time, these consumers are unlikely to be responsive to any interest rate cut by a bank, as they do not intend to borrow at the outset.

I also assume that there is a second class of consumers who fully intend to borrow on their credit card accounts. These are the consumers who are bad credit risks and thus lack less expensive alternatives; bank cards are their best sources of credit. Consumers in the second class are less than ideal from a bank's perspective: they borrow large sums but often default. Insidiously, these customers are more likely to comparison shop on interest rates than the better credit risks, as they actually plan to be paying substantial finance charges. (There is also a third class of consumers, the "convenience" users, whom I can neglect in this discussion. They never borrow on their credit cards and, thus [rationally], are completely unresponsive to interest rate differentials.)

Given this environment of consumers, banks will be hesitant to compete in the interest-rate dimension, as a lower price on credit would disproportionately draw the class of consumers who plan to utilize their credit lines. If consumer behavior along these lines is superimposed on a search-cost model, the tendency toward interest-rate stickiness that was described in the preceding subsection becomes magnified (see Appendix C, taken from the working-paper precursor of the AER article, for a formalization of this story).

Such reasoning additionally provides an explanation for the apparent cross-subsidy from the transaction function to the credit function of the

---

40. It may be possible to rationalize these consumers' behavior by assuming that they face a commitment problem: consumers cannot commit their future selves not to borrow.

bank card.[41] Banks only face adverse selection when they compete on the credit-sensitive portions of prices; they do not face adverse selection when they unilaterally improve the terms facing customers who charge purchases on their credit cards but do not borrow beyond the due date on their bills. This would seem to be a powerful explanation why essentially all large issuers offer a substantial grace period on new purchases (provided that the previous balance was paid in full). It also suggests why issuers hardly ever impose transaction charges, often ask for rather small (and, sometimes, zero) annual fees, and occasionally offer transaction subsidies (for example, rebates on purchases or frequent-flyer miles). At the same time, issuers may install punitive prices for bad credit risks: for example, disproportionately high fees for missing a minimum required payment. Since such large proportions of revenues are derived from finance charges, while the adverse-selection argument implies that the interest rate should not be used as an instrument for competition, it becomes much more difficult for credit card issuers to compete away profits. Thus, adverse selection helps to explain the observed extraordinary profits.

Finally, the present adverse-selection theory may be compared with that of Joseph E. Stiglitz and Andrew Weiss (1981). Stiglitz and Weiss argue that, if all banks are charging the same interest rate, no one bank will unilaterally deviate and charge a higher interest rate. The explanation is that the only consumer who would borrow at such a high interest rate is one who probably will not repay the debt (i.e., he is undertaking a very risky project). In contrast, if all banks are earning positive economic profits, the Stiglitz-Weiss effect would quicken the banks' tendencies to cut prices. A lower interest rate draws not only more customers but also better customers. Thus, Stiglitz and Weiss predict that interest rates are "upward-sticky" when costs rise and, if anything, interest rates are "downward-quick" in their model.

This is hardly a good description of real-world credit markets. Empirically, interest rates on loans have an asymmetric response to the cost of funds: they are quicker to move upward in response to increases in the cost of funds than to move downward in response to decreases in the cost of funds. (Marcelle Arak et al. [1983] detected an asymmetric response in movements of the prime rate, and in work in progress, I have found an asymmetric response in many consumer credit markets.)

My adverse-selection theory is a *reverse* Stiglitz-Weiss effect: it creates

---

41. Credit card issuers appear, at best, to break even on their "convenience" users and, perhaps, lose money on them. Meanwhile, issuers earn supranormal profits on consumers who borrow on their cards.

reluctance to cut interest rates. Thus, it is a completely different and new adverse-selection theory, which may also be useful in explaining other credit markets.

6.3 Evidence of Consumer Irrationality

The adverse-selection theory of the previous section crucially relies on the assumption that there are consumers who do not intend to borrow but continuously do so. (Many other forms of irrationality would also render consumers insensitive to credit card interest rates.[42]) In this subsection, I indicate some formal and anecdotal evidence of this and other forms of consumer irrationality in this market.

First, in the author's bank credit card survey, banks were asked for the percentage of their customers who pay off their full outstanding balances (and so are not subject to finance charges) and for the average outstanding balance (see question 8 in Table A1 for the exact text). The responses, summarized in Table 11, reveal that significant finance charges are being paid on the majority of credit card accounts. Despite interest rates exceeding 18 percent per year, typically *three-quarters* of active credit card accounts at major banks are incurring these high finance charges (on balances averaging over $1,000) at any moment in time.[43] The proclivity of consumers to borrow at these high rates suggests a substantial breakdown in optimizing behavior among credit card holders.[44] Moreover, the percentages in Table 11 are based on reliable bank data yet contradict the authoritative University of Michigan consumer survey. According to Glenn B. Canner and James T. Fergus (1987 table 3), the 1983 Michigan survey found that 47 percent of all families that use bank or retail cards "nearly always pay in full," 26 percent "sometimes pay in full," and only 27 percent "hardly ever pay in full." Unless this is evidence of a bad consumer survey, it suggests that a sizeable proportion of consumers who borrow on credit cards are unaware of how frequently they do it or, more likely, deny (to themselves and others) that they do

42. For example, many consumers may not understand how interest rates work and underestimate the consequences of borrowing.

43. The three-quarters figure should not come as a complete surprise. It would certainly have to be in this range, in order for typically 90 percent of a credit card issuer's outstanding balances to be accruing interest. See also footnote 20.

44. One would expect that optimizing behavior would lead many consumers to (a) shop around for lower-priced credit cards, (b) shift into different modes of borrowing (e.g., home equity loans), or (c) rearrange their intertemporal stream of consumption (i.e., not borrow).

it.[45] In this sense, the data provide indirect empirical confirmation of the presence of consumers who act as though they do not intend to borrow but who continuously do so.

Second, the experience of credit card marketers is that consumers are much more sensitive to increases in the annual fee than to commensurate increases in the interest rate, despite the fact that the majority of cardholders pay significant finance charges. This is behavior that is difficult to rationalize and is again consistent with the presence of consumers who do not intend to borrow but do so anyway.

Third, if advertising campaigns predicated on price are ineffective, it may be wondered what does attract new customers. One notable recent success has been the "Elvis card," which despite a 17.88-percent interest rate (about average) and $36 annual fee (extremely high for a standard bank card) generated three times the response rate normally experienced by direct mail.[46]

Fourth, anecdotal evidence suggests that credit card consumers behave significantly different from the ideal of *Homo economicus*. This author's favorite story (heard twice, independently) involves consumers who immerse their credit cards in trays of water and place them in the freezer. The purpose of entombing the card in ice is to precommit to not making impulsive purchases.

Finally, these observations are not specifically confined to the credit card market and, in fact, are consistent with earlier work that has been done in other areas of consumer credit. One of the most surprising such articles is a study by James J. White and Frank W. Munger (1971) which found that recipients of new car loans were extremely insensitive to interest rates. It would be reasonable to expect that consumers are relatively more price sensitive in seeking out automobile loans than credit cards, as the large dollar amount would justify greater search or switch behavior. Nevertheless, White and Munger report that roughly half of the borrowers from the high-cost providers of auto loans in the Michigan locality they studied would have qualified for loans from low-cost providers. Many consumers who apparently could have borrowed at appreciably lower interest rates failed to do so. Moreover, 29 percent of the borrowers from the high-cost providers were specifically aware of at least one nearby lender who charged a lower interest rate, leading White and Munger to

---

45. It is possible that consumers who borrow also hold more charge accounts than those who do not borrow; but multiple accounts cannot nearly fully explain the statistical discrepancy.

46. *Credit Card News*, October 1, 1988.

conclude that lack of knowledge of lower interest rates was not the principal deterrent to obtaining cheaper loans.

7. Calculation of a "Competitive" Interest Rate

This article has thus far focused on the discrepancy between the predictions of the competitive model and actual observed behavior in the bank credit card market, while Section 8 will discuss the relative merits of regulating this market. As a bridge between these two strands of thought, this section will briefly inquire as to "competitive" interest rates: what level of interest rates would have been consistent with ordinary returns in the credit card market in the late 1980's?[47]

Suppose an explicit calculation is to be done for the year 1987. Above, I have reported the average adjusted return on assets to be 6.31 percent in the BCCS data (seven banks) and 5.13 percent in the call-report data (seven banks, with one overlap). For the following calculation, I will take 5.72 percent (the arithmetic average for the two samples) to be the actual pretax return on assets. Recall that 1.20 percent has been taken to be the ordinary pretax return on assets in the banking industry. Subtracting and taking "assets" to be equivalent to "outstanding balances," one could conclude that the excess revenues in 1987 were 4.52 percent of outstanding balances. Also recall that, typically, about 90 percent of an issuer's outstanding balances actually accrue interest. This suggests that, if interest rates had been approximately five percentage points lower (i.e., 4.52/0.9) in 1987, the top 50 credit card issuers would have still earned the ordinary rate of return in banking. Given that the average annual percentage interest rate for banks in this sample equaled 18.67 percent in 1987, this would imply a "competitive" interest rate of just 13.65 percent. Given that the average one-year Treasury bill yield equaled 7.52 percent in 1987, this also suggests an approximate rule of thumb that, at 1987 levels of annual fees and credit losses and with current usage patterns, the break-even point is roughly approximated by the one-year Treasury bill yield plus slightly more than six percentage points.

Analogous calculations for the period 1983–1988 are displayed in Table

---

47. Obviously, this is precisely the same question that would have to be asked if the government were to choose to regulate the bank credit card market. Please note that the calculation provided here is meant only to be illustrative and would not be suitable for inclusion in any future statute without further refinement. Note that the calculation assumes, for simplicity, that credit card borrowing is perfectly inelastic in the interest rate (although this may not be a bad approximation of reality). Also note that the calculation assumes a continuous 20-percent return on equity; in fact, one would expect some degree of variation over the business cycle.

12. Obviously, these calculations are sensitive to the estimate of credit card profitability. However, even using the much more conservative FCA profitability data (see Table 8), one would still find that credit card interest rates in 1987 were three percentage points above the break-even level.

8. Implications for Regulation

While this article has argued that the bank credit card market does not mirror the predictions of the model of perfect competition, neither does it necessarily lead to the conclusion that usury ceilings on credit card interest rates should be reestablished. As experience in many industries (e.g., airlines, trucking, railroads, and banking itself) has demonstrated, it is often difficult to formulate a regulatory rule that unambiguously improves industrial performance. In the industry in question, the particular hazard associated with price controls is the possibility that they would impair the ability of some individuals to obtain credit cards, which are virtual necessities in certain aspects of modern life (such as renting an automobile or ordering by telephone). This section discusses the trade-offs between regulated and unregulated interest rates.

Even if this article does not criticize the recent outcome of the legislative process (i.e., rejecting the reimposition of credit card interest rate ceilings), it does at least argue that the terms of debate have been

Table 12   Implied Differential Between "Competitive" Credit Card Interest Rate and Actual Rate

Year	Number of Banks in Sample	Adjusted Return on Assets (percentage)	Implied Actual Minus "Competitive" Interest Rate (percentage)
1983	6	4.44	3.60
1984	13	4.94	4.16
1985	14	6.23	5.59
1986	15	6.37	5.74
1987	13	5.72	5.02
1988	10	4.72	3.91
Average:	—	5.59	4.88

Notes: Adjusted return on assets is calculated by pooling the banks in Tables 6 and 7 for each year and calculating the arithmetic average of ROA (adjusted). The number of banks in the sample reflects one overlap in the years 1984–1988.

flawed.[48] Underpinning the antiregulation argument has been the market description of the credit card business (as presented in the first paragraph of this paper) and the implication that such an industrial structure inexorably leads to the perfectly competitive outcome (with all its desirable efficiency properties). For example, Martha R. Seger, a Governor of the Federal Reserve System, concluded her recent Congressional testimony on the subject by stating:

> I would like to reemphasize the Board's conviction that financial markets distribute credit most efficiently and productively when interest rates are determined without artificial restraints, insofar as possible. In the credit card business, the balance of the evidence suggests that reasonably competitive conditions exist, notwithstanding the lack of variation in finance rates. Furthermore, recent developments have reflected some tendency for credit card rates to decline.[49]

A similar strand of thought is reflected in a recent *Wall Street Journal* editorial: "Credit-card interest almost certainly will come down. It will come down without rate ceilings. Nothing does it like competition."[50]

Such arguments are insufficient. One cannot implicitly rely on the model of perfect competition as the principal defense for laissez-faire, given that the data cast severe doubt on the predictions of zero economic profits and cost-based pricing in this industry.

In order to make a cogent argument against regulation, one must proceed in a much more sophisticated fashion. First, it must be recognized that the behavior of the unregulated credit card market of the 1980's deviates in systematic ways from competitive predictions. The price of credit far exceeds its fundamental marginal cost, and the industry expects this situation to persist for some time. While nonprice competi-

48. Possible reregulation of credit card interest rates has been the subject of controversy in recent years. In the 1987 Congressional session, no fewer than five bills dealing with credit cards were introduced: Senate Bill S.241 (mandating certain disclosures), S.242 (setting a national ceiling of four percent above the Internal Revenue Service's interest rate), S.616 (disclosure), S.674 (a ceiling of six percent above the Federal Reserve's discount rate), and House Bill H.R. 515 (a ceiling eight percent above the one-year Treasury bill rate). In 1987–1988, Congress rejected all proposed bills and amendments setting credit card interest rate ceilings but enacted a mandatory disclosure bill.

49. "Credit Card Interest Rates," Hearing before the Subcommittee on Consumer Affairs and Coinage of the Committee on Banking, Finance, and Urban Affairs, House of Representatives, Ninety-Ninth Congress, First Session, on H.R. 1197 and H.R. 3408 (October 29, 1985), Serial No. 99-44, U.S. Government Printing Office, Washington, 1986, page 39; also see *Federal Reserve Bulletin*, March 1986, p. 184.

50. *Wall Street Journal*, March 16, 1987, editorial page.

tion has so far failed to impair firms' profits seriously, it appears to be steadily escalating, meaning that one can envision a day in the not-too-distant future when economic profits from new customers would be completely competed away via nonprice means. (Banks might still earn significant economic rents from their existing "captive" customers.)

Second, it should equally be recognized that regulation has only a limited potential to improve the outcome. The principal difficulty is that consumers occupy a spectrum of levels of credit-worthiness. Let ρ_n denote the bank's best estimate of the nth consumer's probability of default and let c denote the marginal cost of lending funds to a consumer (exclusive of default risk). Then, the social optimum has every consumer paying his own, individualized interest rates: consumer n holds a credit card bearing a finance charge of $(\rho_n + c)$.[51] Since conventional usury laws do not set interest rates according to the individual's default risk, ρ_n, they necessarily lead to outcomes that fall short of the optimum. The regulation is typically written: no bank is permitted to charge an interest rate greater than r^*. Under such a regulatory regime, no consumer whose default risk (to an external observer) exceeds $(r^* - c)$ will be serviced. Thus, if r^* is sufficiently low to ameliorate excess profits, it will also generally create deadweight loss by depriving individuals of the opportunity to hold credit cards. Moreover, it has been widely observed that, in an environment with price ceilings, there is a tendency for all firms to charge *exactly* the price ceiling. Hence, one could expect further deviation from the ideal, individualized interest rates: all consumers with default risks less than $(r^* - c)$ may end up paying interest rates equaling r^*.

A decision regarding the advisability of regulation thus involves a comparison of two less-than-ideal alternatives. The case for laissez-faire is strongest when one is only interested in efficiency and when non-interest-rate competition exclusively takes the form of recycling revenues to consumers. It has already been observed that credit card borrowers are highly interest-rate inelastic. Thus, high interest rates may not appreciably reduce the quantity borrowed, and so there may be little efficiency loss arising directly from excessive interest rates. The primary avenue for social loss is then the nonprice competition. However, to the extent that competition takes the form of frequent-flyer miles, cash rebates, or other relatively efficient means of recycling revenues to consumers, there is still no appreciable social loss.

---

51. Either some banks could offer a spectrum of interest rates to different consumers, or banks could each offer just a single interest rate but specialize in consumers of different qualities of credit-worthiness.

The case for regulation is strongest when one is upset by redistribution away from consumers or when nonprice competition expends substantial resources. I have already observed that high interest rates may be essentially neutral from an efficiency point of view. However, they presumably have a strongly undesirable redistributive effect from the comparatively poor (consumers who borrow on credit cards) to the comparatively rich (owners of bank stock). Moreover, there is a true (and potentially large) deadweight loss when nonprice competition takes the form of advertising.[52] Some banks' reported noninterest expenses increased significantly from 1983 to 1988 even as the intrinsic cost of servicing accounts declined (e.g., Citibank, which advertises on national television); much of the additional expense probably represents marketing, and some fraction of this constitutes social loss.

9. Conclusion

Despite the presence of 4,000 competitors, the bank credit card market of the 1980's behaved widely at variance with the predictions of a competitive model in continuous spot-market equilibrium. Interest rates approximated constancy, at levels around 18 percent per year, in the face of wide changes in banks' marginal costs. Profits persistently equaled three or more times the ordinary return on banking equity, with no sign of abatement. A breakdown of the optimizing consumer behavior so basic to the model of perfect competition may be an important element in the story.

The facts of the market are roughly consistent with a model of adverse selection in which many consumers are insensitive to interest-rate differentials because they believe they will pay within the grace period (although they repeatedly fail to do so). This hypothesis is lent some empirical support by the finding that, assurances to the contrary, three-quarters of consumers pay finance charges on their outstanding credit card balances. Given the presence of such consumers, any bank that unilaterally reduced its credit card interest rate would disproportionately draw customers who actually do intend to borrow (i.e., the worst credit risks). Thus, the finance charges remain at high levels and become the main contributors to supranormal profits.

The facts of the market appear to be inconsistent with the predomi-

---

52. The direct-mail credit card solicitations which I received at the rate of one per week while writing the article inspired this observation. One important, additional aspect of this problem is that the large interest-rate spread (see Section 2.2) encourages banks to market cards in an aggressive way that makes them susceptible to fraud losses.

nance of well-informed consumers who are attempting to minimize their borrowing costs. There is no evidence that consumers are generally offered competitive interest rates on bank card balances, nor that most consumers respond to lower interest rates when they are offered.

The empirical findings of this article suggest a broader question: is it that the bank credit card market of the 1980's was uniquely pathological, or can one identify other markets whose structures seem equally conducive to the competitive model but whose empirical outcomes are similarly noncompetitive? This would seem to be a ripe area for further research.

Appendix A: The Bank Credit Card Survey

In May 1986, a pilot survey was mailed to 32 banks which were believed to be among the 50 largest bank issuers of credit cards. Five responses were received. The bank credit card survey (BCCS) was formed by using these responses to refine the questions asked. The BCCS was mailed in November 1986 to each of the 50 largest bank issuers of credit cards, as ranked in the *Nilson Report* (Number 371, January 1986), plus five banks ranked numbers 51–60. (The BCCS was not sent to the five banks that had responded to the pilot survey.) Following reminder letters in December 1986 and March 1987, as well as reminder telephone calls, 16 responses to the BCCS were received. Thus, the pilot survey and BCCS together elicited a total of 21 responses from a sample consisting of the following 58 banks:

Associates National Bank

Avco National Bank

BancOhio

Bank of America

Bank of New York

Bank One

Barnett Bank

Beneficial National Bank

Chase Manhattan Bank

Chemical Bank

Citibank

Citizens & Southern National Bank

Comerica Bank

Commerce Bank

Connecticut Bank and Trust Co.

CoreStates Bank of Delaware

Crocker National Bank

European American Bank

First City Bank

First Interstate Bank

First National Bank of Atlanta

First National Bank of Boston

First National Bank of Chicago

First National Bank of Omaha

First Omni Bank

First Tennessee Bank

First Wisconsin National Bank

Harris Trust and Savings Bank

Indiana National Bank

InterFirst Bank

Manufacturers Hanover Trust Co.

Marine Midland Bank

Maryland Bank

MBank

Mellon Bank

Mercantile Trust Co.

Michigan National Bank

National Bank of Detroit

National Westminster Bank

NCNB

Norwest Bank

PNC National Bank

Rainier National Bank

RepublicBank Dallas

Rocky Mountain Bankcard System

Seattle First National Bank

Security Bank and Trust Co.

Security Pacific National Bank

Signet Bank

Southeast Bank

Sovran Bank

State Street Bank and Trust Co.

Sun Bank

United Bank of Denver

United States National Bank

United Virginia Bank

Valley National Bank

Wells Fargo Bank

Several of the listed banks had ceased to exist as credit card issuers by the relevant time period, due to merger of the banks or acquisition of their portfolios. Seventeen responses included full interest rate series for the years 1982–1986 (see Table 2 for sizes), extended through 1987 by contemporaneous telephone calls. Respondents were promised anonymity.

The follow-up bank credit card survey was mailed to the 21 initial respondents in January 1988, requesting both 1987 updates of data that the original survey had elicited and direct reports of credit card profits. Follow-up survey II was mailed to the 21 respondents in February and July 1989, requesting both 1988 updates of data that the original survey had elicited and direct reports of credit card profits. Following reminder letters, 11 responses were received, seven of which contained data on profits for 1984–1987 (see Table 2 for sizes) and five also for 1988. The profit reports of Bank F and all 1988 profit reports were completed by banks after the working-paper precursor of this article was made available to the banks. Respondents were again promised anonymity. The BCCS and follow-up BCCS are reprinted in Tables A1 and A2 in condensed form.

Table A1 Bank Credit Card Survey

1. Please indicate the interest rate, beginning in 1976 and through the present, on your most widely issued bank credit card:

Name of Card: _____

Year	February	May	August	November
1976	_____	_____	_____	_____
. . .	. . .	. . .	. . .	. . .
1986	_____	_____	_____	_____

Any additional information (for example, a different rate on premium cards, a floating-rate formula which you currently use, etc.):

2. Same as 1, for annual fee.

3. Please briefly describe the method your bank uses to compute bank card finance charges (include grace periods, etc.):

4. Please list charges other than annual fees (e.g., transaction charges, late fees, minimum finance charges, etc.) which your bank has charged between 1976 and the present. Please indicate relevant dollar amounts and dates:

5. Please list all major state and federal regulations (e.g., interest rate ceilings, laws prohibiting annual fees, etc.) which have hampered your operations between January 1976 and the present, indicating effective dates:

6. If your bank has any statement or position paper on credit card regulation, please enclose it with the completed survey.

7. Please indicate your number of total accounts, number of active accounts, total outstanding balances (at June 30 of each year, or another standardized date), annual charge volume, and charge-off rate:

Year	Number of total accounts	Number of active accounts	Outstanding balances	Annual charge volume	Charge-off rate
1976	_____	_____	_____	_____	_____
. . .	. . .	. . .	. . .	. . .	. . .
1986	_____	_____	_____	_____	_____

8. Please provide the following information about your cardholders, indicating for each column which of two possible pieces of information you are providing. [If both are available, please provide (A).]

Table A1   (*Continued*)

Column 1:

_____ (A) In an average month, what percent of your active accounts pay off their full outstanding balances (and so are not subject to a finance charge on those balances)?

_____ (B) What percent of your active accounts pay off their full outstanding balances at least 11 months per year (and so are only subject to a finance charge on their balances at most one month per year)?

Column 2:

_____ (A) Of your active accounts with outstanding balances, what is the average outstanding balance?

_____ (B) Of all active accounts, what is the average outstanding balance?

Year	Percent who pay in full	Average outstanding balance
1976	_____	_____
. . .	. . .	. . .
1986	_____	_____

9. Please enclose a copy of the credit card application/solicitation(s) your bank uses most.

10. Please indicate which, if any, of the following factors you emphasize in the marketing of your cards.

_____ Our high credit limit
_____ New customers can transfer their existing credit card balances onto our account
_____ New customers are waived our first year's annual fee
_____ Our interest rate is lower than our competitors'
_____ Our annual fee is lower than our competitors'
_____ Our card gives "bonus dollars" with each dollar charged, for discounts on merchandise
_____ Pre-approved credit card applications
_____ Free airline insurance
_____ Other freebies—list them:
_____ Other factors—list them:

11. Feel free to include any additional comments, either below or on separate sheets of paper.

Table A2   Follow-Up Bank Credit Card Survey (and Follow-Up Survey II)

1. 1987 (1988) updates of Questions 1 and 2 from Bank Credit Card Survey.

2. 1987 (1988) updates of Question 7 from Bank Credit Card Survey.

3. 1987 (1988) updates of Question 8 from Bank Credit Card Survey.

4. Please enter all available dollar figures for your bank's *credit card business only.* [Question 4 was patterned after the Federal Reserve System's *Functional Cost Analysis.* A xerox copy of p. 38 of the 1986 report was enclosed.]

	1984	. . .	1987 (1988)
1. Average total outstanding balances:	$ _____	. . .	$ _____
Income:			
2. Finance charge interest and customer fees (including annual fee):	$ _____	. . .	$ _____
3. Merchant discount, interchange fees, and other income:	$ _____	. . .	$ _____
4. Total income (2 + 3):	$ _____	. . .	$ _____
Operating expenses:			
5. Marketing and advertising:	$ _____	. . .	$ _____
6. Enhancements and affinity program expenses:	$ _____	. . .	$ _____
7. All other expenses (including salaries, fringe benefits, data services, processing, franchise fees; excluding items below):	$ _____	. . .	$ _____
8. Total operating expenses (5 + 6 + 7):	$ _____	. . .	$ _____
Earnings:			
9. Net earnings before losses (4 − 8):	$ _____	. . .	$ _____
10. Net credit losses:	$ _____	. . .	$ _____
11. Net fraud losses:	$ _____	. . .	$ _____
12. Net earnings (9 − 10 − 11):	$ _____	. . .	$ _____
Memoranda:			
13. Cost of funds:	$ _____	. . .	$ _____
14. Net earnings (pretax) after cost of funds (12 − 13):	$ _____	. . .	$ _____

Appendix B: Profitability Calculations

B.1 Bank Credit Card Survey Data

COST OF FUNDS is defined by taking the one-year Treasury-bill yield plus 0.75 percent, averaged over the calendar year, and multiplying by 0.94. The Treasury-bill yield is taken from the *Federal Reserve Bulletin*, April 1990, table 1.35, line 21 (and previous issues). The number 0.75 represents the spread between yields on Treasury securities and yields on credit-card-backed securities. The number 0.94 represents 1 minus the banking system's capital requirement of 6 percent.

The numbers reported in Table 6 were constructed as follows (see also Table A2):

$$\text{ROA (reported)} = \text{BCCS Line 14/BCCS Line 1}$$

$$\text{ROA (adjusted)} = (\text{BCCS Line 14} + \text{BCCS Line 13}$$
$$- \text{COST OF FUNDS}$$
$$\times \text{BCCS Line 1})/\text{BCCS Line 1}$$

$$\text{ROE (adjusted)} = \text{ROA (adjusted)}/0.06.$$

B.2 Call Report Data for Credit Card Banks

The calculations reported in Table 7 are based on the quarterly consolidated reports of condition and income ("call reports") which "credit card banks" filed with the FDIC. Included in the sample were all commercial banks that met both of the following criteria:

1. credit card balances constituted at least 75 percent of the bank's total assets (so that the bank's profits are a good proxy for profits attributable to the credit card business);
2. the bank's balance sheet was not seriously marred by credit card securitizations or portfolio acquisitions.

For example, Maryland Bank was excluded from the sample in 1988, because that bank's credit card balances averaged $3.1 billion in that year, while only $1.7 billion appeared on the bank's Report of Condition (the remainder having been securitized). Typically, for banks in Table 7, credit card balances constituted 97 percent or more of total assets.

In the description immediately below, the December 31, 1987 call report for Citibank (South Dakota), N.A., is used to standardize line numbers. The following data were extracted from credit card banks' call reports:

AVERAGE TOTAL ASSETS = Schedule RC-K, line 9 [Total Assets] − Schedule RC, line 10 [Intangible Assets] (this calculation is performed for each of the March 31, June 30, September 30, and December 31 reports; I work with the arithmetic average of the four numbers);

TOTAL EQUITY PREVIOUS YEAR = Schedule RI-A, line 3 [Amended Balance End of Previous Calendar Year];

INCOME BEFORE TAXES = Schedule RI, line 8 [Income Before Income Taxes and Extraordinary Items];

PROVISION FOR LOAN LOSS = Schedule RI, line 4A [Provision for Loan and Lease Losses];

NET CHARGEOFFS = Schedule RI-B, Line 9, column A [Total Charge-Offs] − Schedule RI-B, line 9, column B [Total Recoveries];

INTEREST EXPENSE = Schedule RI, line 2F [Total Interest Expense];

COST OF FUNDS = as in first paragraph of this appendix;

AMORTIZATION EXPENSE OF PREMIA = Schedule RI-E, line 2A [Amortization Expense of Intangible Assets].

The numbers reported in Table 7 were then constructed as follows:

ROA (reported) = (INCOME BEFORE TAXES + PROVISION FOR LOAN LOSS − NET CHARGEOFFS)/AVERAGE TOTAL ASSETS;

ROE (actual cap) = (INCOME BEFORE TAXES + PROVISION FOR LOAN LOSS − NET CHARGEOFFS)/TOTAL EQUITY PREVIOUS YEAR;

ROA (adjusted) = (INCOME BEFORE TAXES + PROVISION FOR LOAN LOSS − NET CHARGEOFFS + INTEREST EXPENSE − COST OF FUNDS × AVERAGE TOTAL ASSETS + AMORTIZATION EXPENSE OF PREMIA)/AVERAGE TOTAL ASSETS;

ROE (adjusted) = ROA (adjusted)/0.06.

B.3 Prospectus Data

The calculations reported in Section 3.4 are based on information contained in prospectuses and registration statements filed with the SEC in connection with all public credit card securitizations by commercial banks from 1987 to early 1990. The following is a complete list of the banks and the prospectuses used.

1. BancOhio (National City Corporation): National City Credit Card Trust 1990-A, registration statement dated January 2, 1990, pp. 17, 23;

2. Bank of America: California Credit Card Trust 1987-A, prospectus dated February 25, 1987, pp. 10, 14; California Credit Card Trust 1987-B, prospectus dated June 19, 1987, pp. 11, 14;

3. Chemical Bank: Chemical Bank Credit Card Trust 1988-A, prospectus dated August 16, 1988, pp. 14, 15; Chemical Bank Credit Card Trust 1989-A, prospectus dated October 30, 1989, pp. 16, 19;

4. Citibank (South Dakota)/Citibank (Nevada): Money Market Credit Card Trust 1989-1, prospectus dated January 25, 1990, pp. 21, 23;

5. Colonial National Bank U.S.A.: Colonial Credit Card Trust 1988-A, preliminary prospectus dated March 23, 1988, pp. 18, 23;

6. First National Bank of Chicago/FCC National Bank: First Chicago CARDS Trust 1987-1, prospectus dated September 29, 1987, pp. 13, 15; First Chicago Master Trust, registration statement dated November 16, 1989, pp. 16, 17;

7. Lomas Bank U.S.A.: Lomas Credit Card Trust 1989-A, registration statement dated July 3, 1989, pp. 17, 24;

8. Manufacturers Hanover Trust Company: MHARCCS Trust 1988-1, prospectus dated June 21, 1988, pp. 17, 18 (1988 only through March 31);

9. Maryland Bank, N.A.: MBNA Credit Card Trust 1988-B, prospectus dated September 9, 1988, pp. 16, 21; MBNA Credit Card Trust 1989-B, registration statement dated November 8, 1989, pp. 16, 20;

10. RepublicBank Delaware: securitization of January 16, 1987, as summarized in Standard & Poor's *Asset-Backed Securitization CreditReview*, March 16, 1987, pp. 21, 22;

11. Southeast Bank: Southeast Bank Credit Card Trust 1990-A, registration statement dated January 29, 1990, pp. 17, 22.

B.4 *Premia Paid for Credit Card Portfolios*

Table 9, the list of premia paid for credit card portfolios, reflects manual and computerized searches of national newspaper indexes over the period

January 1984–April 1990. In order to be included, a transaction was required to meet all of the following criteria:

1. the transaction was reported in the *Wall Street Journal, The New York Times, The American Banker,* or the Kidder, Peabody & Co. report (Kristina E. Andersson and Alison A. Deans, 1989);
2. the exact premium, the parties to the transaction, the approximate date of the transaction, and the approximate size of the portfolio were reported;
3. the transaction was essentially an unbundled sale of credit card accounts and nothing else.

In the event of conflicting reports, the conflict was resolved using the best available information.

Appendix C

C.1 A Model with Search Costs

Consider a market containing n firms, $n \geq 3$, offering a homogeneous product, and a continuum of consumers. Each consumer knows the distribution of prices being offered by the firms, but not which firm is charging which price. Consumers select firms to investigate by *sampling with replacement,* with equal probabilities of drawing each firm. Hence, if a consumer is initially situated at one firm, the expected number of searches needed to find another firm equals $n/(n - 1)$ and to find one particular firm equals n. The first visit to a firm is free. The expected cost of one additional search is s, where s varies according to the consumer, and $F(\cdot)$ is the distribution function of search costs over all consumers. We assume "increasing marginal frustration of search": the cost of an expected $n/(n - 1)$ additional searches is given by $[n/(n - 1)]s$, but the cost of an expected n additional searches is given by αs, where $\alpha > n$. For simplicity, we let $F(s) = s$, for $s \in [0,1]$. Each consumer purchases either zero or one unit of the good and places a value of v on the good; if a consumer pays p for the good, he obtains utility (which he seeks to maximize) of (v − p − search costs). V is assumed to be sufficiently large that consumers purchase. Meanwhile, firms face a common, constant marginal cost of c, and seek to maximize profits.

We seek symmetric Nash equilibria (in pure, price strategies) in the game where firms simultaneously name prices $(p_1, \ldots, p_n)$. Suppose $p_1 > p_2 = p_3 \ldots = p_n \equiv p$. A consumer, initially assigned to firm 1, searches for a cheaper firm if and only if his expected search cost, $[n/(n-1)]s$, is less than $(p_1 - p)$; this has probability $F([(n-1)/n][p_1 - p]) = [(n-1)/n][p_1 - p]$. Thus, it is easy to see that the profits to firm 1, when $p \equiv p_2 = p_3 = \ldots = p_n$ and $p_1 > p$, are given by:

$$(C.1) \qquad \pi_1^{upper}(p_1, p) = \frac{1}{n}[p_1 - c][1 - \left(\frac{n-1}{n}\right)(p_1 - p)],$$

where we have normalized the aggregate quantity of consumers to equal one.

Suppose $p_1 < p_2 = p_3 \ldots = p_n \equiv p$. A consumer initially assigned to any of firms $2, 3, \ldots, n$ searches for firm 1 if and only if his expected search cost, αs, is less than $(p - p_1)$; this has probability $F([p - p_1]/\alpha)$. Thus, the profits to firm 1, when $p \equiv p_2 = p_3 = \ldots = p_n$ and $p_1 < p$, is given by:

$$(C.2) \qquad \pi_1^{lower}(p_1, p) = \frac{1}{n}[p_1 - c][1 + \left(\frac{n-1}{\alpha}\right)(p - p_1)],$$

implying that $p_1 = p_2 = \ldots = p_n \equiv p$ is a Nash equilibrium if and only if:

$$(C.3) \qquad \frac{\partial \pi_1^{upper}}{\partial p_1}\bigg|_{p1=p} \leq 0 \text{ and } \frac{\partial \pi_1^{lower}}{\partial p_1}\bigg|_{p1=p} \geq 0.$$

Observe that (C.3) is satisfied if and only if:

$$(C.4) \qquad c + \frac{n}{n-1} \leq p \leq c + \frac{\alpha}{n-1}.$$

Since $\alpha > n$, (C.4) is nonvacuous and, in fact, contains an interval of possible solutions.

First, observe that this permits the possibility of price stickiness. Suppose cost is initially c. One possible symmetric equilibrium is given by $p = c + n/(n-1)$. Now suppose cost drops to c' satisfying: $c - (\alpha - n)/(n-1) \leq c' < c$. Then $p = c + n/(n-1)$ remains an equilibrium; price may remain constant despite a drop in cost. Second, observe that firms earn positive profits, since $p > c$. The intuition for this result is that, even though the cost of funds is less than price, firms will hesitate to cut their prices. Each firm has its own "captive" customers—those with high search costs randomly assigned to the firm. Furthermore, search costs reduce the likelihood of drawing customers away from a competing firm via price cuts. Price cutting has the penalty of reducing profits from the captive customers to the firm, so the incentive for competition is reduced.

C.2 Adding Adverse Selection to the Model

Assume essentially the same search cost model as above. However, there will now be two classes of customers of equal size and with the same distribution of intrinsic search cost. Consumers of type a *intend* to purchase only quantity q_a of the good. In fact, they purchase quantity $q_{a'}$ of the good ($q_{a'} > q_a$). Meanwhile, consumers of type b intend to purchase quantity q_b and do purchase quantity q_b. For simplicity, let $q_{a'} = q_b = 1$ and write $q_a \equiv a < 1$. The n firms cannot distinguish between types a and b; the marginal cost of serving type a (b) is c_a (c_b), where $c_a < c_b$. Similar to before, suppose $p_1 > p_2 = p_3 = \ldots = p_n \equiv p$. A consumer of type b, initially assigned to firm 1, searches for a cheaper firm if and only if his expected search cost is less than $(p_1 - p)$; this has probability $F([(n - 1)/n][p_1 - p])$. However, a consumer of type a expects to save only $a(p_1 - p)$ on price, so he searches only if his expected search cost is less than $a(p_1 - p)$. Thus:

$$(C.5) \qquad \pi_1^{\text{upper}}(p_1, p) = \frac{1}{n}\left\{\frac{1}{2}[p_1 - c_a]\left[1 - a\left(\frac{n-1}{n}\right)(p_1 - p)\right]\right.$$

$$\left. + \frac{1}{2}[p_1 - c_b]\left[1 - \left(\frac{n-1}{n}\right)(p_1 - p)\right]\right\}.$$

analogous to (C.1). Following the development of (C.2), we have:

$$(C.6) \qquad \pi_1^{\text{lower}}(p_1, p) = \frac{1}{n}\left\{\frac{1}{2}[p_1 - c_a]\left[1 + a\left(\frac{n-1}{\alpha}\right)(p - p_1)\right]\right.$$

$$\left. + \frac{1}{2}[p_1 - c_b]\left[1 + \left(\frac{n-1}{\alpha}\right)(p - p_1)\right]\right\}.$$

Again, $p_1 = p_2 = \ldots = p_n \equiv p$ is a Nash equilibrium if and only if (C.3) is satisfied. This has the solution:

$$(C.7) \quad a\gamma c_a + \gamma c_b + 2\gamma\left(\frac{n}{n-1}\right) \leq p \leq a\gamma c_a + \gamma c_b + 2\gamma\left(\frac{\alpha}{n-1}\right),$$

where $\gamma \equiv 1/(1 + a)$.

The comparison between (C.7) and (C.4) is instructive. First, observe that the length of the interval in (C.7) equals $2\gamma(\alpha - n)/(n - 1)$. Hence, as a is reduced from 1, the length of the interval—and, hence, the degree of possible price stickiness—is increased. Second, the minimum symmetric equilibrium price equals $a\gamma c_a + \gamma c_b + 2\gamma n/(n - 1)$. If c_a equaled c_b, the minimum price would be $c_{\text{average}} + 2\gamma n/(n - 1)$. However, since

$c_a < c_b$ and a larger weight is placed on c_b, we actually have that the minimum price *exceeds* $c_{average} + 2\gamma n/(n - 1)$. The adverse selection described above exacerbates price stickiness and augments potential bank profits.

═══════════

The author acknowledges the support of the Kellogg School's Banking Research Center, The Lynde and Harry Bradley Foundation, and the C. V. Starr Center at New York University and appreciates the diligent research work of Gail Eynon and Paul Palmer. I thank Alan Blinder, Charles Calomiris, Raymond Deneckere, Peter Diamond, Stuart Greenbaum, Robert Johnson, Charles Khan, Robert Porter, and three anonymous referees for helpful comments. I also thank seminar participants at the American Economic Association Meetings, the Econometric Society Meetings, the NBER Economic Fluctuations Conference, the Northwestern University Summer Industrial Organization Conference, the Federal Reserve Bank of Chicago, New York University, Princeton University, and the University of Delaware. Special thanks are also due to the officers of 21 major banks who cooperatively responded to my requests for data.

References

ANDERSSON, KRISTINA E. and ALISON A. DEANS. *Credit Cards: How to Pick a Winner in a Consolidating Industry,* industry report, New York: Kidder, Peabody & Co., September 1989.

ARAK, MARCELLE, A. STEPHEN ENGLANDER, and ERIC M. P. TANG. "Credit Cycles and the Pricing of the Prime Rate," *Federal Reserve Bank of New York Quarterly Review,* Summer 1983, 8, 12–18.

AUSUBEL, LAWRENCE M. "Oligopoly When Market Share Matters," mimeo, Stanford University, May 1984.

———. "The Failure of Competition in the Credit Card Market," Banking Research Center Working Paper No. 153, Northwestern University, October 1988.

BERLIN, MITCHELL and LORETTA J. MESTER. "Credit Card Rates and Consumer Search," mimeo, Federal Reserve Bank of Philadelphia, February 1988.

CANNER, GLENN B. and JAMES T. FERGUS. "The Economic Effects of Proposed Ceilings on Credit Card Interest Rates." *Federal Reserve Bulletin,* January 1987, 73, 1–13.

DIAMOND, PETER. "A Model of Price Adjustment." *Journal of Economic Theory,* 1971, 3, 156–68.

DOUGLAS, GEORGE W. and JAMES C. MILLER. *Economic Regulation of Domestic Air Transport: Theory and Policy,* Washington, DC: Brookings Institution, 1974.

FARRELL, JOSEPH and CARL SHAPIRO. "Dynamic Competition with Lock-In," Department of Economics Working Paper No. 8727, University of California, Berkeley, January 1987.

KLEMPERER, PAUL. "Markets with Consumer Switching Costs." *Quarterly Journal of Economics*, May 1987, *102*, 375–94.

PAVEL, CHRISTINE and PAULA BINKLEY. "Cost and Competition in Bank Credit Cards." *Economic Perspectives* (Federal Reserve Bank of Chicago), March/April 1987, *11*, 3–13.

ROTEMBERG, JULIO J. and GARTH SALONER. "The Relative Rigidity of Monopoly Pricing." *American Economic Review*, December 1987, *77*, 917–26.

STIGLITZ, JOSEPH E. and ANDREW WEISS. "Credit Rationing in Markets with Imperfect Information." *American Economic Review*, June 1981, *71*, 393–410.

WHITE, JAMES J. and FRANK W. MUNGER. "Consumer Sensitivity to Interest Rates: An Empirical Study of New-Car Buyers and Auto Loans." *Michigan Law Review*, June 1971, *69*, 1207–58.

ASSET-BACKED SECURITIZATION CREDITREVIEW. Supplement to *CreditWeek*, New York: Standard & Poor's, March 16, 1987.

CONSOLIDATED REPORTS OF CONDITION AND INCOME. Washington, DC: Federal Deposit Insurance Corporation, quarterly, 1983–1988.

CREDIT CARD INTEREST RATES. House of Representatives Subcommittee Hearing, Washington, DC: U.S. Government Printing Office, Serial No. 99-44, 1986.

CREDIT CARD MANAGEMENT. New York: Faulkner & Gray, monthly, 1988–1989.

CREDIT CARD NEWS. New York: Faulkner & Gray, biweekly, 1988–1989.

FEDERAL RESERVE BULLETIN. Washington, DC: Board of Governors of the Federal Reserve System, monthly, 1982–1990.

FUNCTIONAL COST ANALYSIS, NATIONAL AVERAGE REPORTS, COMMERCIAL BANKS. Washington, DC: Board of Governors of the Federal Reserve System, annual, 1976–1988.

NILSON REPORT. Los Angeles: HSN Consultants, biweekly, 1986–1989.

PROSPECTUSES AND REGISTRATION STATEMENTS. Washington, DC: Securities and Exchange Commission, irregular, 1987–1990.

INDEX

Page numbers in **boldface** refer to figures and tables.

A

Abarbanell, J., 322, 330, 332
Abel, Andrew, 156n
abnormal returns: for IPOs, **467–468**; measuring, 265–299; *see also* excess returns
Ackley, Gardner, 217
Admati, Anat R., 5n
adverse-selection theory, 560–562, 568
Affleck-Grabes, J., 304, 323
agency costs theory, 59, 62–63, 95, 421–422
Aggarwal, Reena, 485
Aizenman, Joshua, 18n
Akerlof, G. A., 407n
Allais paradoxes, 507
Alpert, Marc, 26
American Express Banking Corporation of London (AMEX survey), 360, 364n, 369, 369n
American South African (ASA) fund, 73, 75, 75n, 84n
Amihud, Yakov, 9n, 267n
Amsler, Christine, 111n
Anderson, Seth C., 61–62
Andreassen, P., 321–322, 322n, 327n
announcement effect: bid or takeover, 446–449, 453–454, 485; earnings, 153, 268, 290–293, **291**, **292**, 294–295, 303–336, **326**
Arak, Marcell, 561
arbitrage, 216–217; and closed-end funds, 68–69, 70; and individual behavior, 420; internal, and self control, 397; long vs. short-term, 427–435; and options market, 341, 343; and overreaction

hypothesis, 251, 295; pricing theory, 309; riskless, 31, 52, 101
arbitrageurs, 24, 25, 26, 29, 37, 47, 48, 51, 54, 55
Arrow, Kenneth J., 6n, 154, 250, 399
Asch, Solomon, 175
Ashenfelter, Orley, 540n
Asquith, P., 395, 442, 443, 444, 446, 447, 447n, 449, 450, 451, 452
asset market behavior, and noise trading, 44–54
asset prices, 305; and fundamental values, 50–51, 162–163; and new information, 133–149; and noise trader risk, 23, 25; *see also* capital asset pricing model
assets, long vs. short-term, 427–435
Ausubel, Lawrence M., 527–578

B

Bagehot, W. 321
Bagozzi, Richard P., 177n
Bailey, Martin, 217
Bailey, Norman T., 176n
Ball, Ray, 250, 266, 269, 272, 273, 281, 292, 293, 295, 303, 304, 305, 306, 309, 311, 314–315, 320, 324, 327, 327n, 328, 328n, 329, 329n, 330, 334, 335
bank credit card survey (BCCS), 532, 533, 539, 564, 569–571, **572–574**
banking industry: capital requirements, 543, 543n; credit card issuer size, **534**; ordinary rate of return, 543–544, 564
Banz, R. W., 323–324
Barlow, Robin, 172n

of, 471–474, **474**; long-run performance,
459–487; and overoptimistic investors,
460, 460n, 484; underperformance of,
460, 484–485, 500–503; underpricing,
and popular models, 500–503; and year
of issuance, 479–480
institutional investors, 95, 98, 171, 180,
215–216, 496; and clientele effect, 417;
and overreaction, 268; and popular
models of price rebounds, 495; and
underdiversification in international
equity markets, 387–388
integration/segregation idea, 402–408,
405, 413, 415, 420; and capital gains,
405–408, **406**, 407n
interest rates, 12, 208, 250n; and arbitrage, 429; calculation of "competitive",
564–565, **565**; expected real, and stock
price volatility, 129; long- vs. short-
term, 251; price stickiness in credit
card, 527, 528, 531–536, **532**, **536–537**,
538, 558, 561; regulation of credit card,
566n; term structures, 93–94, 111, 352,
362n
international economy, 3; equilibrium, and
noise, 17–18
international equity markets, investor
diversification and, 383–389; ownership
patterns, 383–384
investment: clubs, 182; counselors, 174;
diversification, and international equity
markets, 383–389; long and short term,
427–428; vs. speculation, 51–52
investor: portfolio objectives, and age,
414–416, **415**; preference for cash dividends, 393–421; psychology, popular
model, 495, 503–504; sentiment, 461;
sentiment, and closed-end fund puzzle,
59–60, 65–101
investors, 169, 170, 174, 186–187, 188,
204, **205**, 207, 210
irrational equilibrium, 210–211
irrationality: and arbitrageurs, 68n; in
financial markets, 55–56

J

Jaffe, Jeffrey F., 4n, 324
Jagannathan, Ravi, 268, 292, 334n

January effect, 331, 420; of closed-end
funds, 85, 86; and excess returns, 257,
258, 260–262, 262n, 266, 267; and over-
reaction effect, 268, 280–281, 327
Japan, 383–384, **384**, 385, 386, 387, 388;
stock market crash of 1987, 493, 494–
497; stocks, 47
Japan Fund, 73, 75
Jarrell, G. A., 449
Jarrow, R., 251
Jegadeesh, Narasimhan, 265n, 281
Jenkins, Gwylim M., 118, 193, 196
Jensen, Michael C., 23, 53, 111n, 153,
267, 267n, 269, 342, 395–396, 398n,
421, 433, 437, 441, 443, 444, 446,
452
Johnson, Eric, 511
Jones, C., 306, 310, **312–313**, 315, 323
Jones, C. P., 306
Jones, David, 156n
Joy, O. M., 306
Juster, Thomas, 217

K

Kahneman, Daniel, 9n, 10n, 154, 157,
191n, 249, 250, 341n, 393, 395,
399–402, **403**, 407–411, 419, 420, 439,
507, 509, 510n, 511, 513, 521
Kalay, Avner, 10n, 13n
Kamin, Leon, 173n
Kan, Raymond, 82n
Kandel, Shmuel, 284, 323n
Kaplanis, Costas, 384n
Katona, George, 172n, 176
Kaul, Gautum, 265n, 275n
Keim, Donald B., 198n, 261, 262, 265n,
324, 515
Kennedy, John F., 142, 143
Keynes, J. M., 157, 250, 420, 430
Kim, E. H., 442, 443, 444
Kim, J., 324
Kim, Yong Cheol, 484
Kleidon, Allan W., 44, 202n, 211, 250
Klein, A., 304, 330, 332
Kleinfield, Sonny, 514
Klemperer, Paul, 558
Knight, Frank H., 174
Kon-ya, Fumiko, 493, 494